BROADCAST AND INTERNET INDECENCY

Indecency – arguably among the most provocative and incendiary issues in today's media – is speech at the edge of social tolerance. This timely volume examines broadcast and Internet indecency from legal and social perspectives, utilizing current cases and well-publicized examples. In exploring the issues associated with this highly controversial area, author Jeremy Harris Lipschultz makes headway toward an understanding of how indecency, as communication on the fringes of social norms, functions in defining free expression through specific types of speech. He contrasts conceptualizations of indecency and obscenity, synthesizes case law and social research, and develops theoretical generalizations for future research and study. His work provides a comprehensive examination of broadcast and Internet indecency issues and cases that serve to test generalizations about freedom of expression and one's ability to define free speech.

The book is appropriate for undergraduate and graduate courses in communication law, telecommunication regulation, First Amendment issues, and free expression theory. Additionally, the book may be used as a supplemental text in mass communication theory, mass communication and society, sociology, and political science courses.

Author **Jeremy Harris Lipschultz** (PhD, Southern Illinois University) is the Robert Reilly Diamond Professor and School of Communication Director at The University of Nebraska at Omaha. Lipschultz has authored and coauthored numerous books, articles, and chapters on topics ranging from free expression, broadcast news, and indecency, to new technologies and the use of media by aging Americans. He currently serves as co-editor of SIMILE, an online journal published by the University of Toronto Press.

LEA'S COMMUNICATION SERIES
Jennings Bryant/Dolf Zillmann, General Editors

Selected Titles in the Communication Series include:

Butler • *Television: Critical Methods and Applications*, Second Edition

Eastman • *Research in Media Promotion*

Keirstead • *Computers in Broadcast and Cable Newsrooms: Using Technology in Television News Production*

MacFarland • *Future Radio Programming Strategies: Cultivating Listenership in the Digital Age*, Second Edition

Metallinos • *Television Aesthetics: Perceptual, Cognitive, and Compositional Bases*

Orlik • *Electronic Media Criticism: Applied Perspectives*, Second Edition

Plum • *Underwriting 101: Selling College Radio*

Silcock/Heider/Rogus • *Managing Television News: A Handbook for Ethical and Effective Producing*

Sterling/Kittross • *Stay Tuned: A Concise History of American Broadcasting*, Third Edition

Webster/Phalen/Lichty • *Ratings Analysis: The Theory and Practice of Audience Research*, Third Edition

BROADCAST AND INTERNET INDECENCY

Defining Free Speech

Jeremy Harris Lipschultz

Routledge
Taylor & Francis Group

NEW YORK AND LONDON

First published 2008
by Routledge
270 Madison Ave, New York, NY 10016

Simultaneously published in the UK
by Routledge
2 Park Square, Milton Park, Abingdon, Oxon OX14 4RN

Routledge is an imprint of the Taylor & Francis Group, an informa business

Typeset in by Prepress Projects Ltd, Perth, Scotland

Printed and bound in the United States of America on acid-free paper by
Sheridan Books, Inc.

Library of Congress Cataloging in Publication Data

Lipschultz, Jeremy Harris, 1958–

Broadcast and internet indecency : defining free
speech/by Jeremy Harris Lipschultz.

p. cm. – (Lea's communication series)

Includes bibliographical references and index.

Freedom of speech – Un'ited States. 2. Broadcasting – Law and legislation
– United States – Criminal provisions. 3. Internet –Law and legislation–
United States – Criminal provisions. 4. Obscenity (Law)–United States.
5. Mass media – Social aspects. I. Title.

KF4772.L575 2008
342.7308′53–dc22
2007025231
ISBN 10: 0-8058-5909-8 (hbk)
ISBN 10: 0-8058-5910-1 (pbk)
ISBN 10: 0-203-92712-5 (ebk)
ISBN13: 978-0-8058-5909-6 (hbk)
ISBN 13: 978-0-8058-5910-2 (pbk)
ISBN 13: 978-0-203-92712-0 (ebk)

CONTENTS

Figures		vii
Boxes		ix
Preface		x
About the author		xii
1	Introduction	1
2	History of American broadcasting	17
3	Theory and research in broadcast and Internet indecency	48
4	Adult entertainment	62
5	The legacy of *Pacifica* and the *Action for Children's Television* cases	76
6	Cable television, new technologies, and new definitions	95
7	New media issues	117
8	The fight over indecent content	130
9	Political and religious issues	145
10	Trends	159
	Appendices	185
	Bibliography	388
	Index	401

FIGURES

1.1	Janet Jackson and Justin Timberlake at the 2004 Super Bowl	1
1.2	The opening war scenes of *Saving Private Ryan*	3
1.3	Howard Stern shown on the Sirius web site as he helps define the early days of satellite radio	4
1.4	Non-traditional family shown here in PBS kids show that features a cartoon rabbit named Buster	6
1.5	Nicole Richie used the F-word on live television	15
3.1	Justice William O. Douglas	50
3.2	William Blackstone	52
4.1	*Girls Gone Wild* pornography issue	63
5.1	Comic George Carlin had popular albums during the Vietnam War era	77
5.2	George Carlin: "The original seven words were, shit, piss, fuck, cunt, cocksucker, mother-fucker, and tits"	77
6.1	The industry urges parents to monitor viewing by their children	115
7.1	Mancow Muller was a leader among a new generation of shock jocks	120
7.2	Mancow's webpage	120
7.3	YouTube sexual videos are hard to regulate	121
7.4	YouTube content changes quickly and offers images from around the globe	122
7.5	Fox Sports may have inadvertently used this crowd shot, which displayed the words "FUCK DA EAGLES"	123
8.1	A search of "explicit" on iTunes reveals content labeled as such	142
8.2	An ABC News podcast featured an interview with an Air Force training instructor who posed for pictures in Playboy magazine	143
9.1	NBC network show *Las Vegas* raises eyebrows	152
9.2	American Family Association urges computerized complaints	153
9.3	Faith in a Box Study finds negative depictions	155
10.1	A *Survivor Vanuatu* contestant uttered the word "bullshitter" in an early morning news show interview	159

10.2 FCC lawyer challenged by Second Circuit Court of Appeals panel   168
10.3 Oral arguments in the Second Circuit Court of Appeals   169
10.4 Cher uses the F-word on live television   169
10.5 Appeals Court Judge Peter Hall asks questions   170
10.6 FCC Attorney Eric Miller is grilled by judges during
      oral arguments   170
10.7 Judge Rosemary Pooler   171
10.8 "It's my dick in a box." Justin Timberlake's "parody of two
      boy-band singers" featured the unusual Christmas present   177

BOXES

1.1 Stern helps define the issues   4
1.2 *Postcards from Buster*   5
1.3 To regulate or not   10
1.4 A link between indecency and media ownership concentration?   12
2.1 *National Broadcasting Co., Inc.,* et al. v. *United States* et al. 19
2.2 Newton Minow calls television in 1961 a "vast wasteland"   27
2.3 TV Watch study finds opposition to current FCC regulation   46
3.1 Douglas's near-absolutist view   49
3.2 Carlin monologue as transcribed by *Pacifica* court   54
4.1 *Girls Gone Wild* video producer guilty of exploiting children   62
6.1 Appendix to the opinion of the court   100
7.1 Mancow thrives in post-indecency complaint career   120
7.2 Fox shows F-word during playoff game   123
9.1 Kansas Republic Sam Brownback sees media decency
     as a reform issue   149
9.2 Congressman Fred Upton seeks to have broadcasters think twice   150
9.3 NBC show *Las Vegas* draws AFA complaints   152
9.4 Faith in a box study   155
10.1 FCC tells the public about indecency regulation   160
10.2 FCC lawyer challenged by Second Circuit Court of Appeals panel   168
10.3 *Saturday Night Live* censored skit plays on YouTube   176

PREFACE

Following Janet Jackson's clothing malfunctions during the live halftime show of the 2004 Super Bowl, federal regulators and lawmakers vowed to clean up the nation's airwaves. Congressional hearings were held. Legislation was passed. Federal Communications Commission enforcement of statutes was tightened. The failure of decency definitions again became obvious. At the same time, the United States Supreme Court debated for the second time in less than a decade legislation restricting Internet indecency. The emphasis in this book will be on the social context of this form of regulation.

Broadcast and Internet indecency are fringe speech at the edge of social tolerance, and this is why we can understand free expression values through the social conflicts that routinely emerged. The purpose of this book is to examine broadcast and Internet indecency from legal, historical, and social perspectives. The book will contrast conceptualizations of indecency and obscenity. Case law and social research will be synthesized, and the book will develop theoretical generalizations useful in future research and study. A comprehensive examination of broadcast and Internet indecency issues and cases will be used to test generalizations about freedom of expression and our ability to define free speech.

The book may be used in undergraduate and graduate courses in communication law, telecommunication regulation, First Amendment issues, and free expression theory. Additionally, the book may be used as a supplemental text in mass communication theory, sociology, and political science courses.

This book could not have happened without the excellent questions and comments from students and faculty members during eighteen years at the University of Nebraska at Omaha. Further, the administrative support for this and previous projects on indecency and free expression was essential to the successful development of a research program on indecency and free expression. My time in the College of Arts and Sciences, now the College of Communication, Fine Arts and Media, has been productive because of great people at the University of Nebraska at Omaha who help make projects happen.

I also wish to acknowledge that support and assistance of my family, which encouraged me to write this book and helped keep me focused in completing it. Sandy's love for twenty-five years has defined a rich and rewarding life. Our children, Jeff and Elizabeth, help place priorities in the correct order, and their grandmother Faye's interest in media always provides enlightening insights.

Jeremy Harris Lipschultz
Omaha, Nebraska
January, 2007

ABOUT THE AUTHOR

Jeremy Harris Lipschultz (PhD, Southern Illinois University, 1990) is the Robert Reilly Diamond Professor and School of Communication Director, University of Nebraska at Omaha. Lipschultz is the author of *Broadcast Indecency: F.C.C. Regulation and the First Amendment* (Boston, MA: Focal Press, 1997) and *Free Expression in the Age of the Internet: Social and Legal Boundaries* (Boulder, CO: Westview Press, 2000). He has written the New Communications Technology chapter for Wat Hopkins' textbook *Communication and the Law* (Northport, AL: Vision Press, 2007). He is also co-author of *Crime and Local TV News: Dramatic, Breaking and Live from the Scene* (Mahwah, NJ: Lawrence Erlbaum, 2002) and *Mass Media, an Aging Population and the Baby Boomers* (Mahwah, NJ: Lawrence Erlbaum, 2005).

Lipschultz has written numerous scholarly articles in refereed publications such as *Journalism Quarterly, Journalism & Mass Communication Educator, Journal of Broadcasting & Electronic Media, Educational Gerontology, Journal of Social Behavior and Personality, Journal of Radio Studies, Newspaper Research Journal, Studies in Media & Information Literacy Education* (*SIMILE*), and *Communications and the Law*. He currently serves as co-editor of *SIMILE*, an online journal published by the University of Toronto Press.

1

INTRODUCTION

The Janet Jackson "wardrobe malfunction" during the 2004 Super Bowl halftime show (Figure 1.1) sparked numerous calls for media decency in the United States. Jackson appeared to be wearing a "Nipple Shield" – a metal jewelry accessory that made her nipple appear like a sun. The scene lasted only a few frames before she covered herself, and CBS went to a break. A modern regulatory firestorm followed.

Attempts to purify communication and art can be found throughout the centuries – sexual content exists across recorded history, but the most aggressive attempts to stop it have been documented in the past few hundred years. Thomas Bowdler, for example, sanitized literature such as the *Family Shakespeare* in 1818, according to Merriam-Webster's explanation of the origins of the word "bowdlerize." Likewise, Anthony Comstock crusaded in the 1870s, as he found New York to be a "carnal showcase of the Western world" (Blanchard and Semonche, 2006: 321).

By the mid-twentieth century, radio and television had taken center stage, with social satirists, shock jocks, and steamy drama pushing the envelope. So, by the time of the now famous Janet Jackson breast shot, the heightened media attention that followed fueled congressional and public

Figure 1.1 Janet Jackson and Justin Timberlake at the 2004 Super Bowl, as Jackson's right breast is revealed for a second before the network cuts to a break. Source: Digital television screen shot, SunFyre (http://www.sunfyre.com/janetjackson. htm).

debate over media norms. This book is about how broadcast and Internet indecency complaints, and media coverage help define the limits to free expression in a free society. To a lesser extent, cable and other new media issues are addressed, however there has been recent pressure to adopt regulation that would restrict cable and new media content.

Broadcast and Internet indecency have been subjects of intense discussion and action by federal regulators, the United States Congress, and the courts for more than thirty years, yet the controversy over what government may or may not do in the name of protecting children remains as heated as ever. The various social and legal battles pit those attempting to shield children from adult media or assist parents in protecting their kids against proponents of a robust, if not near-absolute, First Amendment right of free expression. This book will explore the legal and social issues and begin to understand how indecency, as communication on the fringes of social norms, helps us to define free expression through certain types of speech. When the Federal Communications Commission (FCC) responds to viewer and listener complaints with notices to broadcasters of apparent liability (Appendix A), or reviews a specific broadcast, such as a controversial teen sex scene in CBS's *Without a Trace* (Appendix B), it may create a chilling effect that influences future production decisions.

You might easily come to the incorrect conclusion that the issues surrounding indecency were resolved by the FCC's action against CBS following the Jackson flap (Appendix C). To the contrary, it has led to a set of interesting questions.

The engaging questions

Fans of Howard Stern, the most famous of all "shock jocks" on the radio, might reasonably wonder why the once over-the-air broadcasts were moved in 2006 to subscription satellite radio. His seventy-seven uses of the F word on the first satellite show, unthinkable over the broadcast airwaves, offer some explanation. Likewise, teenagers and pre-teens might be curious about parental attempts to use the V-chip technology to prevent them from viewing adult cable television content. The V-chip, a relatively unsuccessful if crude mechanism for filtering adult content, helps us to see that, as a social problem, indecency will not be solved by mere technology. Adults might reasonably wonder why many ABC Television affiliates refused to air the movie *Saving Private Ryan* (Figure 1.2) which had been scheduled for a special Veterans' Day broadcast in 2005, while others aired the show without complaint. To answer these questions, we must examine specific examples from the case law in order to evaluate and interpret what is happening. Additionally, FCC data help describe changes, such as the dramatic rise in complaint numbers since 2000, as well as the subsequent ongoing focus on indecency through 2006 and beyond (Appendix D).

Figure 1.2 The opening war scenes of *Saving Private Ryan* feature ambient sound
that includes soldiers in combat – complete with their profanities in the
background.

The FCC, with delegated congressional authority to license broadcasters
and set standards, examines each case and its public complaints through
a *contextual* analysis. Further, there is an established process for review
of all complaints (Appendix E). Once identified by audience complaints,
the FCC may make an example of a specific broadcast. For example, in
April of 2004, the FCC set fines against Clear Channel Communications,
the largest radio chain of stations in the nation, at $495,000 for remarks
about oral and anal sex on the Howard Stern Show, which aired on six
stations a year earlier. Clear Channel received maximum fines at the time
of $27,500 for each of three references ($82,500 per station). As licensee,
Clear Channel was held responsible for what its managers allowed to be
placed on the public airwaves. Clear Channel had appeared to persist in
testing the FCC, despite being singled out in examples published by the
commission in 2001 in an effort to offer guidance on what was or was
not indecent (Appendix F). The landscape, however, changed dramatically
after a top Clear Channel official was called to testify on Capitol Hill.
In response, the company began for the first time to attempt to hold its
announcers responsible via contracts that could allow the corporate giant
to pass along fines. The company seemed to be looking for political cover.

Similarly, the FCC appeared to be bowing to political pressures from
the Congress and lobbyists to "clean up" the public's airwaves. As such, for
the first time the agency chose to fine a licensee for each indecent reference rather than to count a show as one violation of the law. While the
original complaint had been filed against only one of the stations, the FCC
fined all stations in the group airing the show. Because the show originated
through Infinity Broadcasting Corporation, which had not been the target
of complaints for the broadcast, the FCC decided to launch an investigation against it, as well.

The subsequent ongoing investigations and fines no doubt played a role
in the decision to later move Stern's show to Sirius Satellite Radio. Stern
concluded that the shift to subscription radio would free him from the
FCC, which he had been battling for two decades over the right to say
whatever came to his mind on the radio.

Box 1.1 Stern helps define the issues

Radio "shock jock" Howard Stern (Figure 1.3) in many ways brought the issue of broadcast indecency regulation to the forefront by challenging the FCC on and off the air. Stern first burst on to the scene in the 1980s as the most celebrated example of a genre of radio designed to attract public attention to a struggling industry. By January 2006, Stern had left New York City airwaves for the brave new world of subscription Sirius Satellite Radio. Within a year, many business analysts were asking whether the new model would survive in the economic marketplace. An emerging model developed that would bring satellite broadcasters back to the broadcast airwaves, perhaps in a sanitized form.

Figure 1.3 Howard Stern shown on the Sirius web site as he helps define the early days of satellite radio. Source: Press photograph, Sirius 2005 (www. sirius.com).

Social and legal issues

Broadcast and Internet indecency raise a complex combination of social and legal issues. Social norms in a pluralistic society compete for dominance. In the case of indecency, not all adults agree about what is fit for children to see or hear. In the public opinion arena, activist groups often purport to represent parents, the industry, or consumers. Yet, it may be the case that the vast majority of Americans are simply not as concerned as those who make political hay over the issues. In this way, broadcast and Internet indecency may be utilized as a test of the validity of previous generalizations about free expression in an Internet age (Lipschultz, 2000: 286–7):

> 1) Free expression is not the product of an idealistic search for "truth" or objective reality, but rather it is subjective by its very nature. Individuals interpret (encode and decode) speech, which must be studied in a social context; 2) Free expression is not only understood in terms of presumed psychological value to individuals, but also it is a component in a social, political and economic system; 3) That which passes for "free expression" in no way

resembles what might be at the fringes because all speech is limited by a variety of social constraints, both real and imagined; and 4) Popular concepts such as "social responsibility" and "marketplace of ideas" hold no utility in learning about free expression, except to the extent individuals adopt and use these notions as political tools of power.

These generalizations will be addressed in the final chapter of this book as a set of heuristic questions, which help to focus free expression discussion.

Box 1.2 *Postcards from Buster*

The Public Broadcasting Service (PBS) in 2005, under government pressure, pulled an episode of the children's cartoon *Postcards From Buster* (Figure 1.4), following complaints that two lesbian mothers were portrayed. Education Secretary Margaret Spellings criticized the show in a letter and asked the network to consider returning $160,000 in federal funds used to produce it: "Many parents would not want their young children exposed to the lifestyles portrayed in this episode." PBS reportedly pulled the show the day the letter arrived. Buster, a talking cartoon rabbit, visited Vermont, where he learned about maple sugar and met some real-life children. At dinner the animated rabbit was introduced to their "mom and Gillian."

[Warning! The following dialogue may contain sophisticated themes for mature audiences.]

Buster:	So Gillian's your mom, too?
Emma:	She's my stepmom.
Buster:	Boy, that's a lot of moms!
Emma:	Yup. [Showing framed family photo.] This is mom and Gillian right here.
Buster:	That's a nice picture.
Emma:	This is one of my favorite pictures.
Buster:	How come?
Emma:	Because it has my mom and Gillian, people I love a lot, and they read a lot to me.

The mom, Pike, and lesbian partner Gillian Pieper had taken part in a civil union in 2001. PBS executives acknowledged in interviews with various media representatives that their response was in part a function of the political climate and in part an understanding that

---

some parents would not want unsupervised children watching the WGBH, Boston show. PBS added: "The presence of a couple headed by two mothers would not be appropriate curricular purpose that PBS should provide." Vermont Public Television and more than ninety (covering 53 percent of households) of the other 349 PBS member stations, according to the *The Washington Post*, later decided to air the episode, but it amazingly remained deleted from the official PBS Buster web site listing of "Places I've been . . ."

Figure 1.4 Non-traditional family shown here in PBS kids show that features a cartoon rabbit named Buster.

Sources

Montgomery, David, "What has floppy ears and a subversive tale?," *Washington Post*, March 6, 2005, p. D01.

PBS Censors Postcards from Buster, Fair, Fairness & Accuracy In Reporting (http://www.fair.org/index.php?page=2040).

PBS Kids Buster web site blog (http://pbskids.org/buster/blog/; http://farkleberries.blogspot.com/2005_01_01_farkleberries_archive.html).

Ryan, Suzzanne C., and Shanahan, Mark, "Fallout from 'Postcards' decision: Family angry over PBS move to shelve show featuring lesbians," *Boston Globe*, January 27, 2005 (http://Boston.cm).

While self-censorship by broadcasters is an ongoing social issue, the legal concerns focus upon the illegality of obscenity and the inconsistent standards for defining acceptable versus unacceptable indecency.

Federal statutes and case law govern broadcast and Internet indecency in the United States. One must understand the proposition that anything deemed *obscene* does not reside under an umbrella of First Amendment protection. The guiding case in obscenity law is more than thirty years old, and *Miller* v. *California* (1973) offered a three-part test, which judges and juries could apply to media content and make determinations.

Miller v. California

In 1973, the United States Supreme Court came to grips with the concern over obscenity and attempted to define it. The issue was important because it had long been held that obscene speech was not protected speech under the First Amendment. Therefore, any speech deemed as obscene could be prosecuted under state obscenity laws. The same was not the case for the seemingly lesser class of indecent speech. The test asks three questions:

1 Whether the average person, applying contemporary community standards, would find that the work, taken as a whole, appeals to prurient interest.

In the case of broadcast and Internet indecency, two separate approaches emerged on this first prong. Obscenity cases prosecuted locally (typically adult book store content and club performances) tend to seek to settle on community standards within a particular community. The FCC judges indecency, which is content that falls short of obscene. It uses a national average-person standard. Obscenity law, therefore, varies from state to state, as explained in the second prong of the Miller test:

2 Whether the work depicts or describes, in a patently offensive way, sexual conduct specifically defined by applicable state law.

Patent offensiveness is used in both obscenity and indecency cases. However, while obscenity is always about sexual conduct, indecency cases may be about media content that dwells on sexual or excretory matters.

The third part of the Miller test offered courts and juries the opportunity to offer First Amendment protection, if there were serious value.

3 Whether the work, taken as a whole, lacks serious literary, artistic, political, or scientific value.

As we will see, in the case of broadcast indecency, the contextual analysis has much the same outcome by considering similar types of speech – protecting that which has a serious political or educational context.

In the case of the online communication, state obscenity law applies under Miller, as it does with any form of media. However, as we will see, the Supreme Court has refused to regulate Internet indecency, as it has allowed in broadcasting. Therefore, while one may be indecent but not obscene on the Internet, the courts have allowed indecent broadcast speech only at times when children are not likely to be present in the audience. Thus, the FCC and courts have utilized a balancing approach between the First Amendment rights of adults and government regulation that assists parents to protect children from indecency.

Broadcasting, cable, and the Internet

For a variety of historical reasons, broadcasting, cable, and the Internet are regulated under different sets of rules. As recently as its Broadcast Indecency Policy Statement (2001), the FCC reminded broadcasters that it is a violation of federal law to broadcast obscene or indecent programming. Specifically, Title 18 of the United States Code (USC), section 1464 (18 USC §1464), prohibits the utterance of "any obscene, indecent, or profane language by means of radio communication." The FCC's three-part test begins with asking about:

1 Explicitness or graphic nature of the depiction of sexual or excretory organs or activities.

So, while a passing sexual reference might not be considered actionable by regulators, explicit scenes or comments and duration matter in the second prong:

2 Whether the materials dwell on or repeat at length such sexual depictions.

Even if media content does dwell on sexuality, it would not be found indecent by the FCC if the context were considered of some value other than mere shock value:

3 The context and whether the depiction appears to pander or titillate, or is presented for shock value.

Congress has delegated the responsibility for administratively enforcing 18 USC §1464 to the FCC. In doing so, the FCC may revoke a station license, impose a monetary forfeiture, or issue a warning for the broadcast of indecent material. Although section 1464 is a criminal statute, the FCC has the authority to impose civil penalties for the broadcast of indecent material without regard to the criminal nature of the statute (*FCC* v. *Pacifica Foundation*, 438 US 726, 739, n. 13, 1978).

While obscene speech has no First Amendment protection, indecent speech has some. The courts have struggled on the question of where to draw the line:

> ... the Supreme Court has determined that obscene speech is not entitled to First Amendment protection, obscene speech cannot be broadcast at any time. In contrast, indecent speech is protected by the First Amendment, and thus, the government must both identify a compelling interest for any regulation it may impose on

indecent speech and choose the least restrictive means to further that interest. Even under this restrictive standard, the courts have consistently upheld the Commission's authority to regulate indecent speech, albeit with certain limitations.

(FCC, 2001)

A central question in the regulation of broadcast indecency has been over the definition of content: The definition, "language or material that, in context, depicts or describes, in terms patently offensive as measured by contemporary community standards for the broadcast medium, sexual or excretory activities or organs," has remained substantially unchanged since the time of the *Pacifica* decision.

Safe harbor issues

In 1995, the United States Court of Appeals, District of Columbia Circuit, *en banc,* held in *ACT III* that the less restrictive 10:00 p.m. to 6:00 a.m. "safe harbor" had been justified as a properly tailored means of vindicating the government's compelling interest in the welfare of children.

1 The material alleged to be indecent must fall within the indecency definition – that is, the material must describe or depict sexual or excretory organs or activities.
2 The broadcast must be *patently offensive* as measured by contemporary community standards for the broadcast medium.
3 In determining whether material is patently offensive, the *full context* in which the material appeared is critically important.

Thus, while obscenity law focused on unique local community standards, broadcast indecency regulation revolves around a national standard targeted at an "average viewer."

The determination as to whether certain programming is patently offensive is not a local one and does not encompass any particular geographic area. Rather, the standard is that of an "average viewer" or listener and not the sensibilities of any individual complainant.

Former FCC Commissioner Susan Ness went so far as to issue a separate statement from the commission majority in its 2001 order:

Despite an onslaught of on-air smut, the Commission necessarily walks a delicate line when addressing content issues, and must be careful not to tread on the First Amendment – the constitutional bulwark of our free society. Even words that might be construed as indecent are subject to some constitutional protection against government regulation.

Likewise, former FCC Commissioner Gloria Tristani reasoned:

> There is simply no proof that broadcast licensees are in need of this Policy Statement. No factual basis exists for concluding that confusion about the standards or overreaching enforcement by the FCC requires this Statement.

Box 1.3 To regulate or not

Broadcast indecency has risen to level of being an issue of international interest, as evidenced by global interest in the subject. The US Department of State, which is responsible for promoting US policy to other nations, considered the issue of media regulation in a 2006 web chat entitled "Indecency on the airwaves: to regulate or not to regulate" (February 17, 2006). Heritage Foundation Senior Fellow James Gattuso suggested that market solutions offer a reasonable alternative to extensive government regulation. The Heritage Foundation is a nonprofit policy research institute that seeks to advance free-market and conservative principles.

Q [Dennis]: What is your take on the FCC trying to increase fines for indecency and to regulate indecency on cable and satellite? As a pay service, shouldn't cable and satellite be exempt from regulation?

A: Yes. Cable TV has an additional difference – it doesn't use airwaves licensed by the government at all, it uses, as the name implies, cables that are privately owned and operated. There have been efforts to extend broadcast indecency limits to cable, but the feeling generally (even among proponents) is that they would be overturned by the Supreme Court. That is why most of the debate over indecency on cable has recently turned to "pro-choice" solutions, i.e., letting consumers have more power to control and filter what's shown on their TVs, rather than central limits on speech.

Q [Musa]: When does indecency regulation turn into censorship?

A: In a narrow sense, it is not censorship, since there is no prior restraint. In other words, the government cannot go to any broadcaster and prohibit them in advance from saying or showing anything. They can only impose fines afterward. That's a technical distinction

---

in my mind, however. If you can be fined millions of dollars for speech, then you are restrained. Whether it's technically censorship or not, the effect is the same.

Q [Marek]: In some countries it is common for nudity on TV. In the US it seems to be a big problem . . . but killing and violence are common on US TV. What is "offensive"?

A: What is "offensive" really is different based on the individual. If you look at the public complaints to the Federal Communications Commission, there are all sorts of things that people claim to be offensive. Many people complained about the nude statues at the Athens Olympics. Some complained about the movie *Saving Private Ryan*. A big part of the problem is that it is an impossible thing to define.

The FCC has a definition of what is indecent, which is limited to "sexual" or "excretory" language or depictions. But there is no reason why that is singled out and violence isn't. I'd be concerned, though, with EXPANDING the scope of these rules – since you very quickly get into definitions of "offensive" that include political or religious beliefs, where it is even more dangerous for the government to interfere. That's why I think a consumer choice approach is much better than any government rules.

Source
Heritage Foundation expert addresses broadcast media regulation, The Washington File, Bureau of International Information Programs, US Department of State, USINFO web chat transcript (http://usinfo.state.gov), February 17, 2006.

Indecency and obscenity

A common mistake on the part of the government and the public it represents is to blur the line between indecency and obscenity laws. While obscenity has no legal protection under the First Amendment, communication that is short of obscene, as defined under the *Miller* test, i.e., indecent speech, must be treated differently. The crux of the problem is that, particularly since the 2004 Janet Jackson Super Bowl halftime show's wardrobe malfunction, there has been a tendency to back-pedal on the right of broadcasters to be edgy.

The safe harbor rules allow broadcasters to be indecent after 10 p.m., but these are overnight hours when relatively few listeners and viewers are in the audience. Nevertheless, broadcasters during safe harbor hours appear to have an absolute right to be indecent but not obscene. Cable, satellite, and Internet media have a right, just as print media have a right, to be indecent but not obscene at *any* hour.

So, many of the controversies over broadcast indecency have arisen because of the singling out of broadcasters in a multimedia era when all other media have broader rights to be indecent. Especially during the morning prime-time radio hours and evening prime-time television hours, broadcasters face competitive market pressures to attract and maintain the audiences they deliver to advertisers, and this produces the revenue to pay bills and even be profitable.

An ongoing challenge of broadcast indecency regulation is the time zone problem. In the Midwest, dramatic programs air at 9 p.m. while these same shows air at 10 p.m. in the East because of differing regional norms of when profitable local television news shows should be broadcast. Thus, the 10 p.m. rule disadvantages some parts of the nation. When the safe harbor was being debated during the early 1990s, various approaches were considered – from starting the safe harbor period at 8 p.m. at one end of the spectrum to midnight at the other. None of these efforts to regulate broadcasting provided a workable solution because broadcasters are not isolated in the media landscape. In many markets, more than two-thirds of broadcast audiences receive the signal through cable lines. So, it seems unreasonable to continue to operate under a regulatory structure that pre-dates this important technological change.

Box 1.4 A link between indecency and media ownership concentration?

The following is a reproduction of a press release from the Center for Creative Voices in Media.

FOR IMMEDIATE RELEASE

OCTOBER 23, 2006

2:05 PM

CONTACT: Center for Creative Voices in Media

Jonathan Rintels, Center for Creative Voices in Media, (202) 747–1712

FCC media ownership policies make television's "vast wasteland" even vaster, Creative Voices tells Commission

WASHINGTON – October 23 – Misguided FCC media ownership policies harm competition, diversity of viewpoints, and localism – the Commission's key policy goals in regulating media ownership – and prevent the American public from receiving better broadcast television, the Center for Creative Voices in Media told the Commission in comments filed today.

"Former FCC Chairman Newton Minow once famously referred to television as a 'vast wasteland,'" says Jonathan Rintels, Executive Director of Creative Voices. "By harming competition, diversity of viewpoints, and localism, recent ill-considered FCC media ownership policies have had the unintended consequence of making that 'wasteland' vaster. In its current media ownership proceeding, the Commission must reverse these policies and remedy these consequences, so that the public gets what all would agree is truly in the public interest – better television", Rintels said.

"At the FCC's recent public hearing in Los Angeles, the Commissioners heard for themselves from every corner of the creative community, from writers to directors to actors to producers, as well as from their audience, the American public. The opinions were unanimous: action to reverse the consolidation trend in television is pro-creative, and creativity is in the public interest. Network broadcasters have used their control over the public's airwaves to put their competitors – independent producers – out of business. And that is not in the public interest," Rintels said.

"General Electric's recent announcement that it would reduce or eliminate scripted programming on its NBC network in the 8–9 p.m. hour of primetime is particularly illustrative of the unintended harmful consequences of FCC policy changes that have had the practical effect of eliminating independently-produced programming from the public's airwaves. Just two years ago, NBC's 8 p.m. hour block was home to *Friends*, a hugely popular hit produced by strong independent producers – one of the few shows still running from the days when FCC policies properly protected the right of independents to access the network airwaves. Prior to that, NBC's 8 p.m. hour block was home to *The Cosby Show*, *Family Ties*, *3rd Rock From the Sun*, *Golden Girls*, *Diff'rent Strokes* – the list could go on and on – all family-friendly shows, all produced by strong independent producers," Rintels said.

But with GE/NBC taking advantage of FCC rule changes to eliminate independent producers and take over for itself the production of programming, NBC's own in-house studio has developed and produced few successful 8 p.m. scripted shows. Now, admitting failure, NBC will forgo scripted programming in the 8 p.m. hour, and replace it with game shows and so-called "reality" programming – some of the very programming that Newton Minow cited when he described television as a "vast wasteland." At the same time, NBC also announced that it would rely even more heavily on programming produced by its own "in-house" studio – the very studio that has been so markedly unsuccessful in producing scripted programming for the 8 p.m. hour block. Could anything more starkly illustrate how solidly shut the network's doors are to programming from independent sources? And how this is clearly not in the public interest?

Rintels added "NBC received the right to use the publicly-owned airwaves at no cost from the American public in exchange for its promise to serve the public interest. The public – and the Commission – must now ask whether GE/NBC is now using its free ride on those public airwaves to simply serve GE's narrow corporate interest, at the expense of the public interest?"

"Tim Winter, Executive Director of the Parents' Television Council, correctly observed at the Los Angeles FCC hearing that families and children benefit as much as anyone from a diverse media environment. Groups like the PTC are not often on the same page as the creators they sometimes criticize. But it has become clear that family-friendly programming has a better chance of reaching audiences in a creative environment where competition, diversity of viewpoints, and localism exist, while crass, lowest common denominator programming is much more likely to proliferate in a consolidated media environment.

Ownership Concentration and Indecency in Broadcasting: Is There a Link?, a Creative Voices research report submitted to the FCC with our comments, demonstrates with empirical data that localism, diversity, and competition are good for families and children, as well as for creators and adult audiences," Rintels said.

The Center for Creative Voices in Media (CCVM) is a nonprofit 501(c)(3) organization dedicated to preserving in America's media the original, independent, and diverse creative voices that enrich our nation's culture and safeguard its democracy. Peggy Charren and Steven Bochco are members of Creative Voices' Board of Advisors, which includes numerous winners of Oscars, Emmys, Tonys, and other awards for creative excellence.

As 2007 began, two major court challenges were under way that could force the United States Supreme Court to address the broadcast indecency issue in a direct way for the first time since the *Pacifica* (1978) decision, which upheld the FCC's right to regulate indecent content. In the Second Circuit Court of Appeals in New York, a three-judge panel considered the issue of "fleeting expletives," such as those that had repeatedly aired on awards programs (Figure 1.5). The panel sided with the networks, ruling that the FCC had not explained its change in policy or provided adequate evidence on the dangers of fleeting expletives (Appendix G).

Meantime, the Third Circuit Court of Appeals considered the CBS appeal of the $550,000 Super Bowl case, which also focused on an unscripted and fleeting event – pop star Justin Timberlake tearing off one of Janet Jackson's breast coverings. The FCC made a defense of its fines in court filings: "The FCC reasonably concluded that, although brief, this display of nudity violated longstanding federal prohibitions on the broadcast of indecent material" finding 'willful' intent on the part of CBS (Pelofsky, 2006: para. 3).

Figure 1.5 Nicole Richie used the F-word on live television. The Simple Life reality TV star quipped: "It was hardly all that simple – does anyone know how fucking hard it is to get cow shit out of a Prada purse?"

The FCC brief read:

> By continuing to argue that it is okay to say the f-word and the s-word on television whenever it wants . . . Hollywood is demonstrating once again how out of touch it is with the American people. We believe there should be some limits on what can be shown on television when children are likely to be watching.
>
> (Eggerton, 2006, November 27: 10)

CBS Network attorneys, in their legal briefs, argued for "a return to the FCC's previous time-honored practice of more-measured indecency enforcement" (ibid.).

CBS, in the *Without a Trace* case, had also challenged the indecency definition when it comes to sexually charged scenes that are not pornographic. In that case, CBS had aired a graphic scene of a teen sex party. While there was no actual full nudity, the dimly lit living room scene shows a group of young people engaging in sexual behavior while dressed only in their underwear. In late 2007, the US Department of Justice, on behalf of the FCC, asked the Supreme Court to overturn one lower-court ruling that offered First Amendment protection to fleeting expletives, at the same time as FCC fines against CBS were under review by another court.

Even if one sets aside the challenges that a wide-open Internet – complete with explicit and global podcasts – brings to the current regulatory framework, age-old questions remain about the viability of media sanitation campaigns. As Blanchard and Semonche (2006: 366) concluded:

> Today's battles over topics of sexual expression are directly tied to the campaigns conducted with such vigor by Anthony Comstock. Many of the issues that were raised in his campaigns are present into today's controversies over sexually explicit speech. Worry continues about the exposure of children to nudity and details about sex. Discussions over the kind of sexually oriented material may be made available over the Internet often include arguments over whether the Internet should be made safe for children.

Thus, the social conflict over broadcast and Internet indecency can be seen within the broader context of moral crusades, political utility, and genuine concern. The value of free expression and the push for absolute free speech rights is inconsistent with the desire to purify or sanitize media content.

Chapter summary

Broadcast indecency has received intense political, media, and public scrutiny. While government officials seek to protect children from adult-oriented messages, creative radio personalities and television producers seek to extend boundaries and explore new subject matter.

One solution has been to move questionable programs to pay services, such as satellite radio, cable television, and the Internet. However, there is a substantial question about the nature of the public airwaves. While broadcasters have historically been licensed to serve the public interest, we have never been able to utilize this vague legal standard to clarify the rights of adults to have access to programming beyond that which is fit for children to see and hear.

Even in children's programming, such as the *Postcards From Buster* example, personal values tend to guide thinking about what is appropriate or not. Portrayal of nontraditional family units are applauded by some and derided by others.

Review questions

1 Why might it make a difference that the FCC indecency regulation attempts to define a national average viewer rather than utilize local community standards?
2 How did the 2001 FCC order define broadcast indecency, and what impact did it have on the industry?
3 What concerns were raised by dissenting FCC commissioners in 2001? Were they right? Why or why not?
4 Do you think that satellite radio is the appropriate location for Howard Stern's show? Why or why not?
5 Was PBS correct to drop the *Buster* episode that depicted lesbian mothers? Why or why not?

2

HISTORY OF AMERICAN BROADCASTING

The history of American broadcasting has had a significant impact upon our understanding of the nature of indecency, particularly as it relates to profanity. As the medium developed, laws and regulation emerged that required government judgments to be made about content.

Broadcasters may make the mistake in believing that the United States Supreme Court is where the law of broadcast indecency is found. In fact, the *Pacifica* decision, which divided on a 5–4 vote and failed to settle the matter, left much to the United States Court of Appeals, District of Columbia Circuit, to deal with in the 1980s and 1990s.

The "politics" of broadcast regulation – namely, the influence of various political players – can be seen clearly in the case of broadcast indecency policy (Krasnow, Longley & Terry, 1982). While the FCC, Congress, the White House, the United States Supreme Court, citizens' groups, and industry lobbyists have played a part in the unfolding drama, this chapter reminds us that the United States Court of Appeals for the District of Columbia Circuit (DC Circuit) has been most active in the evolution of broadcast indecency policy.

Historical context of broadcast regulation

Mass media historian Louise Benjamin (1990) found that, even before the Radio Act of 1927, American courts were influential in defining broadcast regulatory principles. When a state court protected the signal of WGN, Chicago from interference, the decision was "hailed as a means of clearing up the ether" (Rivera-Sanchez, 1995: 1). Prior to 1927,

> Congress had passed only two laws dealing with radio: the Wireless Ship Act of 1910 and the Radio Act of 1912. However, because the laws were not aimed at mass audience broadcasting, Secretary of Commerce Herbert Hoover found that *self-regulation* of frequency usage was not working. However, before the Second Radio Conference of 1923, the courts stepped in stating: "[s]hortly

before the conference, Hoover's attempts to regulate were seriously undermined when the US Court of Appeals for the District of Columbia Circuit ruled that the secretary of commerce lacked legal discretion to withhold licenses from broadcast stations."

(Krasnow et al., 1982: 11)

It is clear, therefore, that before there ever was a Federal Radio Commission or an FCC, the political struggle over who would control the airwaves, as well as how they would be regulated, was under way. It can be said that many of the defining moments in broadcast regulation policy came through judicial decision-making rather than from Congress or the FCC.

In *National Broadcasting Company* v. *United States* (1943), for example, the United States Supreme Court dealt with the "public interest" standard and the right of the FCC to manage the public airwaves beyond technical standards.

Ship-to-shore communications and interference chaos

The earliest radio communication in the first part of the twentieth century involved the use of the technology to aid distressed ships by enabling them to communicate with other ships and people on shore. In the wake of many disasters that led to loss of life, radio communication was seen as a way to protect civilians. It may have been that sailors have a tendency to use profanity, which moved the earliest regulatory landscape toward checking speech over the airwaves.

As radio went commercial in the 1920s, it became so popular that the industry and government were forced to collaborate on ways to improve broadcast signal quality. With so many stations surging onto the airwaves so quickly, interference between competing signals was inevitable. The problem was that broadcasters with enough money could move anywhere on the spectrum and freely raise signal power to effectively drown out others. Worse, when two signals collided, neither could be heard. So, the solution was to license operators to serve the "public interest, convenience and necessity." While this seems like a vague standard, the story goes that it came from earlier railroad regulation.

NBC v. *FCC* (1943)

The public interest standard was severely tested, as network radio came of age. Licensees, in order to offer high-quality programming, were forced to sign restrictive network contracts. The FCC reasoned, however, that local broadcasters could not sign away their public interest obligations. The stage was set for the first major broadcast regulation case.

Box 2.1 *National Broadcasting Co., Inc.,*
et al. v. United States et al.

In the *NBC* judgment below, the Supreme Court agreed that the FCC has the power to regulate broadcasting. In this decision, the Supreme Court utilized data from a report on chain broadcasting issues and subsequent regulation.

319 US 190

Argued February 10, 11, 1943

Decided May 10, 1943

Mr Justice FRANKFURTER delivered the opinion of the Court. . . . These suits were brought on October 30, 1941, to enjoin the enforcement of the Chain Broadcasting Regulations promulgated by the Federal Communications Commission on May 2, 1941, and amended on October 11, 1941 . . .

᳁ ᳁

On March 18, 1938, the Commission undertook a comprehensive investigation to determine whether special regulations applicable to radio stations engaged in chain [194] broadcasting [note 1] were required in the "public interest, convenience, or necessity." The Commission's order directed that inquiry be made, *inter alia*, in the following specific matters: the number of stations licensed to or affiliated with networks, and the amount of station time used or controlled by networks; the contractual rights and obligations of stations under their agreements with networks; the scope of network agreements containing exclusive affiliation provisions and restricting the network from affiliating with other stations in the same area; the rights and obligations of stations with respect to network advertisers; the nature of the program service rendered by stations licensed to networks; the policies of networks with respect to character of programs, diversification, and accommodation to the particular requirements of the areas served by the affiliated stations; the extent to which affiliated stations exercise control over programs, advertising contracts, and related matters; the nature and extent of network program duplication by stations serving the same area; the extent to which particular networks have exclusive coverage in some areas; the competitive practices of stations engaged in chain broadcasting; the effect of chain broadcasting upon stations not licensed to or affiliated with networks; practices or agreements in restraint of trade, or in furtherance of monopoly, in connection with chain broadcasting; and the scope of concentration of control over stations, locally, regionally, or nationally, through contracts, common ownership, or other means.

❧ ❧

The Commission found that at the end of 1938 there were 660 commercial stations in the United States, and that 341 of these were affiliated with national networks. One hundred and thirty-five stations were affiliated exclusively with the National Broadcasting Company, Inc., known in the industry as NBC, which operated two national networks, the 'Red' and the 'Blue'. NBC was also the licensee of ten stations, including seven thatoperated on so-called clear channels with the maximum power available, 50 kilowatts; in addition, NBC operated five other stations, four of which had power of 50 kilowatts, under management contracts with their licensees. One hundred and two stations were affiliated exclusively with the Columbia Broadcasting System, Inc., which was also the licensee of eight stations, seven of which were clear-channel stations operating with power of 50 kilowatts. Seventy-four stations were under exclusive affiliation with the Mutual Broadcasting System, Inc. In addition, twenty-five stations were affiliated with both NBC and Mutual, and five with both CBS and Mutual. These figures, the Commission noted, did not accurately reflect the relative prominence of the three companies, since the stations affiliated with Mutual were, generally speaking, less desirable in frequency, power, and coverage. It pointed out that the stations affiliated with the national networks utilized more than 97 percent of the total night-time broadcasting power of all the [198] stations in the country. NBC and CBS together controlled more than 85 percent of the total night-time wattage, and the broadcast business of the three national network companies amounted to almost half of the total business of all stations in the United States.

The Commission recognized that network broadcasting had played, and was continuing to play, an important part in the development of radio. "The growth and development of chain broadcasting," it stated,

> found its impetus in the desire to give widespread coverage to programs which otherwise would not be heard beyond the reception area of a single station. Chain broadcasting makes possible a wider reception for expensive entertainment and cultural programs and also for programs of national or regional significance which would otherwise have coverage only in the locality of origin. Furthermore, the access to greatly enlarged audiences made possible by chain broadcasting has been a strong incentive to advertisers to finance the production of expensive programs . . . But the fact that the chain broadcasting method brings benefits and advantages to both the listening public and to broadcast station licensees does not mean that the prevailing practices and policies of the networks and their outlets are sound in all respects, or that they should not be

altered. The Commission's duty under the Communications Act of 1934, 47 USCA. 151 et seq., is not only to see that the public receives the advantages and benefits of chain broadcasting, but also, so far as its powers enable it, to see that practices which adversely affect the ability of licensees to operate in the public interest are eliminated.

(Report: 4)

֍ ֎

It is the station, not the network, which is licensed to serve the public interest. The licensee has the duty of determining what programs shall be broadcast over his station's facilities, and cannot lawfully delegate this duty or transfer the control of his station directly to the network or indirectly to an advertising agency. He cannot lawfully bind himself to accept programs in every case [206] where he cannot sustain the burden of proof that he has a better program. The licensee is obliged to reserve to himself the final decision as to what programs will best serve the public interest. We conclude that a licensee is not fulfilling his obligations to operate in the public interest, and is not operating in accordance with the express requirements of the Communications Act, if he agrees to accept programs on any basis other than his own reasonable decision that the programs are satisfactory.'

(Report: 39, 66)

֍ ֎

The Commission stated that if the question had arisen as an original matter, it might well have concluded that the public interest required severance of the business of station ownership from that of network operation. But since substantial business interests had been formed on the basis of the Commission's continued tolerance of the situation, it was found inadvisable to take such a drastic step. The Commission concluded, however, that "the licensing of two stations in the same area to a single network organization is basically unsound and contrary to the public interest," and that it was also against the "public interest" for network organizations to own stations in areas where the available facilities were so few or of such unequal coverage that competition would thereby be substantially restricted. Recognizing that these considerations called for flexibility in their application to particular situations, the Commission provided that "networks will be given full opportunity, on proper application for new facilities or renewal of existing licenses, to call to our attention any reasons why the principle should be modified or held inapplicable" (Report: 68) [208] . . .

᳆ ᳆

Section 1 of the Communications Act states its "purpose of regulating interstate and foreign commerce in communication by wire and radio so as to make available, so far as possible, to all the people of the United States a rapid, efficient, nationwide, and world-wide wire and radio communication service with adequate facilities at reasonable charges." Section 301 particularizes this general purpose with respect to radio:

> It is the purpose of this Act, among other things, to maintain the control of the United States over all the channels of interstate and foreign radio transmission; and to provide for the use of such channels, but not the ownership thereof, by persons for limited periods of time, under licenses granted by Federal authority, and no such license shall be construed to create any right, beyond the terms, conditions, and periods of the license.

To that end, a Commission composed of seven members was created, with broad licensing and regulatory powers.

Section 303 provides:

> Except as otherwise provided in this Act, the Commission from time to time, as public convenience, interest, or necessity requires, shall- (a) Classify radio stations; [215] (b) Prescribe the nature of the service to be rendered by each class of licensed stations and each station within any class; (f) Make such regulations not inconsistent with law as it may deem necessary to prevent interference between stations and to carry out the provisions of this Act . . . ; (g) Study new uses for radio, provide for experimental uses of frequencies, and generally encourage the larger and more effective use of radio in the public interest.

᳆ ᳆

The Act itself establishes that the Commission's powers are not limited to the engineering and technical aspects of regulation of radio communication. *Yet we are asked to regard the Commission as a kind of traffic officer, policing the wave lengths to prevent stations from interfering with each other. But the Act does not restrict the Commission [216] merely to supervision of the traffic. It puts upon the Commission the burden of determining the composition of that traffic* [emphasis added]. The facilities of radio are not large enough to accommodate all who wish to use them. Methods must be devised for choosing from among the many who apply. And since Congress itself could not do this, it committed the task to the Commission.

⁊ ⁊

The avowed aim of the Communications Act of 1934 was to secure the maximum benefits of radio to all the people of the United States. To that end Congress endowed the Communications Commission with comprehensive powers to promote and realize the vast potentialities of radio. Section 303(g) provides that the Commission shall "generally encourage the larger and more effective use of radio in the public interest"; subsection (i) gives the Commission specific "authority to make special regulations applicable to radio stations engaged in chain broadcasting"; and subsection (r) empowers it to adopt "such rules and regulations and prescribe such restrictions and conditions, not inconsistent with law, as may be necessary to carry out the provisions of this Act."

⁊ ⁊

Generalities unrelated to the living problems of radio communication of course cannot justify exercises of power by the Commission. Equally so, generalities empty of all concrete considerations of the actual bearing of regulations promulgated by the Commission to the subject-matter entrusted to it, cannot strike down exercises of power by the Commission. While Congress did not give the Commission unfettered discretion to regulate all phases of the radio industry, it did not frustrate the purposes for which the Communications Act of 1934 was brought into being by attempting an itemized catalogue of the specific manifestations of the general problems for the solution of which it was establishing a regulatory agency. That would have stereotyped the powers of the Commission to specific details in regulating a field of enterprise the dominant characteristic of which was the rapid pace of its unfolding. And so Congress did what experience had taught it in similar attempts at regulation, even in fields where the subject-matter of regulation was far less fluid and dynamic than radio. The essence of that [220] experience was to define broad areas for regulation and to establish standards for judgment adequately related in their application to the problems to be solved.

For the cramping construction of the Act pressed upon us, support cannot be found in its legislative history. The principal argument is that 303(i), empowering the Commission "to make special regulations applicable to radio stations engaged in chain broadcasting," intended to restrict the scope of the Commission's powers to the technical and engineering aspects of chain broadcasting. This provision comes from

4(h) of the Radio Act of 1927. It was introduced into the legislation as a Senate committee amendment to the House bill (HR 9971, 69th Cong., 1st Sess.) This amendment originally read as follows:

(C) The commission, from time to time, as public convenience, interest, or necessity requires, shall –

〜 〜

We conclude, therefore, that the Communications Act of 1934 authorized the Commission to promulgate regulations designed to correct the abuses disclosed by its investigation of chain broadcasting. There remains for consideration the claim that the Commission's exercise of such authority was unlawful.

The Regulations are assailed as "arbitrary and capricious." If this contention means that the Regulations are unwise, that they are not likely to succeed in accomplishing what the Commission intended, we can say only that the appellants have selected the wrong forum for such a plea. What was said in *Board of Trade* v. *United States*, 314 US 534, 548, 62 SCt 366, 372, is relevant here: "We certainly have neither technical competence nor legal authority to pronounce upon the wisdom of the course taken by the Commission." Our duty is at an end when we find that the action of the Commission was based upon findings supported by evidence, and was made pursuant to authority granted by Congress. It is not for us to say that the "public interest" will be furthered or retarded by the Chain Broadcasting Regulations. The responsibility belongs to the Congress for the grant of valid legislative authority and to the Commission for its exercise. [225] It would be sheer dogmatism to say that the Commission made out no case for its allowable discretion in formulating these Regulations. Its long investigation disclosed the existences of practices which it regarded as contrary to the "public interest". . .

〜 〜

We come, finally, to an appeal to the First Amendment. The Regulations, even if valid in all other respects, must fall because they abridge, say the appellants, their right of free speech. If that be so, it would follow that every person whose application for a license to operate a station is denied by the Commission is thereby denied his constitutional right of free speech. Freedom of utterance is abridged to many who wish to use the limited facilities of radio. Unlike other modes of expression, radio inherently is not available to all. That is its unique characteristic, and that is why, unlike other modes of expression, it is subject to governmental regulation. Because it cannot be used by all, some who wish to use it must be denied. But Congress did not authorize the Commission to choose among applicants upon the basis of their political, economic or social views, or upon any other capricious basis. If it did, or if the Commission by these Regulations proposed a choice among applicants upon some such basis, the issue before us would be wholly different [emphasis added]. The question here is simply whether the Commission, by announcing that it will refuse licenses to persons who engage in specified network practices (a basis for choice which we hold is comprehended within the statutory criterion of [227] "public interest"), is thereby denying such persons the constitutional right of free speech. The right of free speech does not include, however, the right to use the facilities of radio without a license. The licensing system established by Congress in the Communications Act of 1934 was a proper exercise of its power over commerce. The standard it provided for the licensing of stations was the "public interest, convenience, or necessity." Denial of a station license on that ground, if valid under the Act, is not a denial of free speech.

∾ ⌣

AFFIRMED.

Mr Justice BLACK and Mr Justice RUTLEDGE took no part in the consideration or decision of these cases.

Mr Justice MURPHY, dissenting.

I do not question the objectives of the proposed regulations, and it is not my desire by narrow statutory interpretation to weaken the authority of government agencies to deal efficiently with matters committed to their jurisdiction by the Congress. Statutes of this kind should be construed so that the agency concerned may be able to cope effectively with problems which the Congress intended to correct, or may otherwise perform the functions given to it. But we exceed our competence when we gratuitously bestow upon an agency power which the [228] Congress has not granted. Since that is what the Court in substance does today, I dissent.

In the present case we are dealing with a subject of extreme importance in the life of the nation. Although radio broadcasting, like the press, is generally conducted on a commercial basis, it is not an ordinary business activity, like the selling of securities or the marketing of electrical power. In the dissemination of information and opinion radio has assumed a position of commanding importance, rivalling the press and the pulpit. Owing to its physical characteristics radio, unlike the other methods of conveying information, must be regulated and rationed by the government. Otherwise there would be chaos, and radio's usefulness would be largely destroyed. But because of its vast potentialities as a medium of communication, discussion and propaganda, the character and extent of control that should be exercised over it by the government is a matter of deep and vital concern. Events in Europe show that radio may readily be a weapon of authority and misrepresentation, instead of a means of entertainment and enlightenment. It may even be an instrument of oppression. In pointing out these possibilities I do not mean to intimate in the slightest that they are imminent or probable in this country, but they do suggest that the construction of the instant statute should be approached with more than ordinary restraint and caution, to avoid an interpretation that is not clearly justified by the conditions that brought about its enactment, or that would give the Commission greater powers than the Congress intended to confer.

Red Lion (1969)

Another interesting regulatory challenge surfaced during the 1964 presidential election and the question of whether the FCC's fairness doctrine rules were constitutional. The case was not decided for five years, but it finally established an important precedent that remains in place today – because of spectrum scarcity and the public interest standard, broadcasters were obligated to be fair not only during campaign period covered by statutory rules, but also at other times when public affairs programming was being presented. The fairness doctrine had two prongs:

1 Broadcasters were required to air controversial issues of public importance.
2 In doing so, broadcasters were required to offer important contrasting viewpoints.

Eventually, in the late 1980s, a series of cases established that the 1949 FCC fairness doctrine had never been codified into the statutes governing broadcasting. Therefore, if the FCC had come to believe that the marketplace was a better mechanism for ensuring fairness, then it had the power to rescind its own rules. It did so.

The standard was set forth in the Communications Act of 1934, as a criterion for the exercise of power by the FCC. The Court stated that the licensing of stations, required because not everyone wanting a station could have one, meant that the First Amendment could not prevent the FCC from its concern for not only radio traffic, but also the composition of that traffic. In *Red Lion Broadcasting Company* v. *FCC* (1969: 389–90), it was argued that the rights of viewers and listeners were *more* important than the rights of broadcasters:

This is not to say that the First Amendment is irrelevant to public broadcasting. On the contrary, it has a major role to play as the Congress itself recognized in 326, which forbids FCC interference with "the right of free speech by means of radio communication." Because of the scarcity of radio frequencies, the Government is permitted to put restraints on licensees in favor of others whose views should be expressed on this unique medium. But the people as a whole retain their interest in free speech by radio and their collective right to have the medium function consistently with the ends and purposes of the First Amendment. It is the right of the viewers and listeners, not the right of the broadcasters, which is paramount.

In the area of broadcast indecency, a sharply divided Supreme Court in *FCC* v. *Pacifica Foundation* upheld FCC attempts to consider the content of broadcast speech on a case-by-case basis. But lack of clarity in that opinion, coupled with FCC ambiguity, led to a nearly thirty-year period of regulatory confusion. In such a climate, it should not be surprising that the courts, and specifically the DC Circuit, became major participants in the political process.

Public interest, convenience, and necessity

The public interest standard effectively accomplished several results. First, it guaranteed that broadcasters would be treated in a manner that placed high value on their content. The FCC was to be more than an agency that licensed spectrum allocation, allotment, and assignment.

If the FCC could judge content against a public interest standard, then it meant that profanity could be restricted using Section 1464 as a basis for regulation. Also, it meant that broadcasters could be forced to serve *local* interests. Because not everyone wanting a broadcast license could have one, licensees had a *fiduciary responsibility* to serve the public interest, convenience, and necessity – whatever that came to mean.

Box 2.2 Newton Minow calls television in 1961 a "vast wasteland"

On May 9, 1961, FCC Chairman Newton Minow, appointed by President John F. Kennedy, shocked broadcast managers attending the National Association of Broadcasters meeting in Washington by refusing to be an industry cheerleader and instead challenging broadcasters to do better.

Thank you for this opportunity to meet with you today. This is my first public address since I took over my new job. It may also come as a surprise to some of you, but I want you to know that you have my admiration and respect. Yours is a most honorable profession. Anyone who is in the broadcasting business has a tough row to hoe. You earn your bread by using public property. When you work in broadcasting, you volunteer for public service, public pressure, and public regulation. You must compete with other attractions and other investments, and the only way you can do it is to prove to us every three years that you should have been in business in the first place.

I can think of easier ways to make a living.

But I cannot think of more satisfying ways.

I admire your courage – but that doesn't mean I would make life any easier for you. Your license lets you use the public's airwaves as trustees for 180 million Americans. The public is your beneficiary. If you want to stay on as trustees, you must deliver a decent return to the public – not only to your stockholders. So, as a representative of the public, your health and your product are among my chief concerns.

I have confidence in your health.

But not in your product.

It is with this and much more in mind that I come before you today.

∂∘ ∘⑀

It would not surprise me if some of you had expected me to come here today and say in effect, "Clean up your own house, or the government will do it for you."

Well, in a limited sense, you would be right – I've just said it.

But I want to say to you earnestly that it is not in that spirit that I come before you today, nor is it in that spirit that I intend to serve the FCC.

I am in Washington to help broadcasting, not to harm it; to strengthen it, not to weaken it; to reward it, not to punish it; to encourage it, not threaten it; to stimulate it, not censor it.

Above all, I am here to uphold and protect the public interest.

What do we mean by "the public interest"? Some say the public interest is merely what interests the public.

I disagree.

So does your distinguished president, Governor Collins. In a recent speech he said, "Broadcasting, to serve the public interest, must have a soul and a conscience, a burning desire to excel, as well as to sell; the urge to build the character, citizenship, and intellectual stature of people, as well as to expand the gross national product . . . By no means do I imply that broadcasters disregard the public interest . . . But a much better job can be done and should be done."

I could not agree more.

❧ ❧

. . . When television is good, nothing – not the theater, not the magazines or newspapers – nothing is better.

But *when television is bad, nothing is worse. I invite you to sit down in front of your television set when your station goes on the air and stay there without a book, magazine, newspaper, profit-and-loss sheet, or rating book to distract you – and keep your eyes glued to that set until the station signs off. I can assure you that you will observe a vast wasteland* [emphasis added].

You will see a procession of game shows, violence, audience participation shows, formula comedies about totally unbelievable families, blood and thunder, mayhem, violence, sadism, murder, western bad men, western good men, private eyes, gangsters, more violence and cartoons. And, endlessly, commercials – many screaming, cajoling, and offending. And, most of all, boredom. True, you will see a few things you will enjoy. But they will be very, very few. And if you think I exaggerate, try it.

Is there one person in this room who claims that broadcasting can't do better?

Well, a glance at next season's proposed programming can give us little heart. Of seventy-three and a half hours of prime evening time, the networks have tentatively scheduled 59 hours to categories of "action-adventure," situation comedy, variety, quiz, and movies.

Is there one network president in this room who claims he can't do better?

Well, is there at least one network president who believes that the other networks can't do better?

Gentlemen, your trust accounting with your beneficiaries is overdue.

Never have so few owed so much to so many.

Why is so much of television so bad? I have heard many answers: demands of your advertisers; competition for ever higher ratings; the need always to attract a mass audience; the high cost of television programs; the insatiable appetite for programming material – these are some of them. Unquestionably these are tough problems not susceptible to easy answers.

❧ ❧

Certainly I hope you will agree that ratings should have little influence where children are concerned. The best estimates indicate that during the hours of 5 to 6 p.m., 60 percent of your audience is composed of children under twelve. And most young children today, believe it or not, spend as much time watching television as they do in the schoolroom. I repeat – let that sink in – most young children today spend as much time watching television as they do in the schoolroom. It used to be said that there were three great influences on a child: home, school, and church. Today there is a fourth great influence, and you ladies and gentlemen control it.

If parents, teachers, and ministers conducted their responsibilities by following the ratings, children would have a steady diet of ice cream, school holidays, and no Sunday school. What about your responsibilities? Is there no room on television to teach, to inform, to uplift, to stretch, to enlarge the capacities of our children? Is there no room for programs deepening their understanding of children in other lands? Is there no room for a children's news show explaining something about the world to them at their level of understanding? Is there no room for reading the great literature of the past, teaching them the great traditions of freedom? There are some fine children's shows, but they are drowned out in the massive doses of cartoons, violence, and more violence. Must these be your trademarks? Search your consciences and see if you cannot offer more to your young beneficiaries whose future you guide so many hours each and every day.

∿ ∿

Let me make clear that what I am talking about is balance. I believe that the public interest is made up of many interests. There are many people in this great country, and you must serve all of us. You will get no argument from me if you say that, given a choice between a Western and a symphony, more people will watch the Western. I like Westerns and private eyes too – but a steady diet for the whole country is obviously not in the public interest. We all know that people would more often prefer to be entertained than stimulated or informed. But your obligations are not satisfied if you look only to popularity as a test of what to broadcast. You are not only in show business; you are free to communicate ideas as well as relaxation. You must provide a wider range of choices, more diversity, more alternatives. It is not enough to cater to the nation's whims – you must also serve the nation's needs.

∿ ∿

Some of you may say, "Yes, but I still do not know where the line is between a grant of a renewal and the hearing you just spoke of." My answer is, Why should you want to know how close you can come to the edge of the cliff? What the Commission asks of you is to make a conscientious good-faith effort to serve the public interest. Every one of you serves a community in which the people would benefit by educational religious instructive or other public service programming. Every one of you serves an area which has local needs – as to local elections, controversial issues, local news, local talent. Make a serious, genuine effort to put on that programming. When you do, you will not be playing brinkmanship with the public interest . . .

☞ ☜

I hope that we at the FCC will not allow ourselves to become so bogged down in the mountain of papers, hearings, memoranda, orders, and the daily routine that we close our eyes to the wider view of the public interest. And I hope that you broadcasters will not permit yourselves to become so absorbed in the case for ratings, sales, and profits that you lose this wider view. Now more than ever before in broadcasting's history, the times demand the best of all of us.

We need imagination in programming, not sterility; creativity, not imitation; experimentation, not conformity; excellence, not mediocrity. Television is filled with creative, imaginative people. You must strive to set them free.

☞ ☜

What you gentlemen broadcast through the people's air affects the people's taste, their knowledge, their opinions, their understanding of themselves and of their world. And their future.

The power of instantaneous sight and sound is without precedent in mankind's history. This is an awesome power. It has limitless capabilities for good – and for evil. And it carries with it awesome responsibilities – responsibilities which you and I cannot escape.

☞ ☜

I urge you to put the people's airwaves to the service of the people and the cause of freedom. You must help prepare a generation for great decisions. You must help a great nation fulfill its future.

Do this, and I pledge you our help.

The high point of regulation

Thus, the high point of 1960s and 1970s broadcast regulation began to recede. In actuality, long before the FCC action on fairness doctrine rules, the stage had been set for dramatic change. Beginning with the Carter presidency, but ramping up during the Reagan presidency a "less government" approach to all forms of regulation took hold. Ronald Reagan had appointed as chair of the FCC Mark Fowler, who said simply that broadcasters were "marketplace participants." Fowler used deregulation philosophy to establish a national policy utilizing market forces in radio and television to encourage First Amendment rights of licensees. Fowler and Brenner (1982) proposed a trustee model of broadcast regulation that favored a "deregulated marketplace approach" under the thesis that "the perception of broadcasters as community trustees should be replaced by a view of broadcasters as marketplace participants" (p. 207). The second term of the Reagan administration was marked by the view that marketplace forces work better than government regulation. Dennis Patrick continued to move the FCC in the direction of deregulation in key areas.

This trend continued in the Bush Sr, Clinton, and Bush Jr presidencies that followed. However, there was an exception: broadcast indecency. Despite the philosophy that less government produced better outcomes for the public than more, there were repeated public and media outcries over profanity on the radio, explicit sex and violence on television, exploitation in children's programming, and advertisements and fears over the presumed effects from music lyrics and video games.

Deregulation, FCC policy statements, and congressional responses

While the FCC lessened general restrictions on licensees, the Telecommunications Act of 1996 did nothing to change the status quo with respect to broadcast indecency regulations.

The FCC set out to address criticism that its rules were vague by issuing a series of statements that attempted to provide case-by-case examples of actionable and nonactionable content, as well as offer a coherent rationale and system. In doing so, the agency attempted to create a predictable environment in which broadcasters would be able to operate without fear of indecency fines.

Congress responded first by raising the amount of fines, second by applying guidance that allowed the FCC to fine each individual instance of indecency, and third by passing legislation that raised fines from $32,500 per incident all the way to $325,000. By increasing these fines tenfold, as well as encouraging multiple fines within a broadcast, Congress and the President elevated a chilling environment.

Data and processes

While the number of complaints has increased dramatically in the years since 2000, the number of cases involving possible fines has always remained relatively small. In 2000, the FCC received 111 complaints against 111 programs (eighty-five radio, twenty-five television, and one cable). The result was seven notices of apparent liability (NALs) for $48,000 in fines. By 2004, a high-water mark in the data, there were a whopping 1,405,419 complaints against 314 programs (145 radio, 140 television, and twenty-nine cable). The effect of interest group-driven Internet complaints could be clearly seen. Nevertheless, the result was a mere twelve NALs against nine radio and three television broadcasts. What was dramatic, however, was the total amount of the proposed fines – $7,928,080. Of those proposed fines, some were later cancelled (see Appendix D).

The FCC uses a linear flow process to resolve indecency complaints against broadcasters. The FCC does not monitor content. Instead, the regulatory agency responds to complaints. This leads to the first step of the process.

1 Complaints may be filed via mail, fax, email and even toll free telephone calls.
2 The complaint is logged and tracked by the FCC.
3 An initial analysis of the complaint is made. The FCC seeks evidence of the offense. For example, previous complaints have been strengthened by the existence of audiotape or videotape. The FCC may at this point:
   a request additional information from the "consumer";
   b request additional information from the company (letter of inquiry).
4 The FCC conducts a review of information:
   a An NAL may be issued for "forfeiture," which includes a possible fine: Any company response is reviewed by the FCC to determine if the complaint is "actionable." If so, a forfeiture order is granted.
   b If the FCC determines that the complaint is "not actionable," then an order denying the complaint is issued: A complainant may appeal the decision by filing a petition for review by the Bureau of Enforcement or the full commission (see Appendix E).

It is against this regulatory backdrop that the present broadcast indecency conflict plays out.

In April of 2001, the FCC, struggling to define indecency in the broadcast regulation context, issued a clarifying order titled, *In the Matter of Industry Guidance on the Commission's Case Law Interpreting 18 USC §1464 and Enforcement Policies Regarding Broadcast Indecency* (2001). In it, the FCC said the policy statement was developed as "guidance" to broadcasters (p. 1). They were reminded that,

> It is a violation of federal law to broadcast obscene or indecent programming . . . Title 18 of the United States Code, Section 1464 (18 USC §1464), prohibits the utterance of "any obscene, indecent, or profane language by means of radio communication". . . Congress has given the Federal Communications

Commission the responsibility for administratively enforcing 18 USC §1464. In doing so, the Commission may revoke a station license, impose a monetary forfeiture, or issue a warning for the broadcast of indecent material.

(p. 1)

Under the regulatory scheme outlined in the 2001 guidance, the FCC must make two determinations:

> . . . the material alleged to be indecent must fall within the subject matter scope of our indecency definition – that is, the material must describe or depict sexual or excretory organs or activities.
>
> (p. 4)

> . . . the broadcast must be *patently offensive* as measured by contemporary community standards for the broadcast medium.
>
> (p. 4)

The FCC does *not* use a local community standard, but rather, "the standard is that of an average broadcast viewer or listener and not the sensibilities of any individual complainant" (p. 4). The FCC judges each case in its context:

> a) In determining whether material is patently offensive, the *full context* in which the material appeared is critically important . . . It is not sufficient, for example, to know that explicit sexual terms or descriptions were used, just as it is not sufficient to know only that no such terms or descriptions were used. Explicit language in the context of a *bona fide* newscast might not be patently offensive, . . . while sexual innuendo that persists and is sufficiently clear to make the sexual meaning inescapable might be. . . Moreover, contextual determinations are necessarily highly fact-specific, making it difficult to catalog comprehensively all of the possible contextual factors that might exacerbate or mitigate the patent offensiveness of particular material. . . . An analysis of Commission case law reveals that various factors have been consistently considered relevant in indecency determinations. By comparing cases with analogous analytical structures, but different outcomes, we hope to highlight how these factors are applied in varying circumstances and the impact of these variables on a finding of patent offensiveness.
>
> (pp. 4–5)

The FCC used extensive examples to demonstrate the differences between actionable and nonactionable content (pp. 6–16). A few of the examples are reproduced here below (see Appendix F for complete listing).

WYSP(FM), Philadelphia, PA: *Howard Stern Show*

God, my testicles are like down to the floor . . . you could really have a party with these . . . Use them like Bocci balls.

I mean to go around porking other girls with vibrating rubber products . . . [As part of a discussion of lesbians]

Have you ever had sex with an animal? Well, don't knock it. I was sodomized by Lambchop.

Indecent – warning issued
Infinity Broadcasting Corporation of Pennsylvania (WYSP(FM)), 2 FCC Rcd 2705 (1987), aff'd 3 FCC Rcd 930 (1987), aff'd in part, vacated in part on other grounds, remanded sub nom. Act I, 852 F.2d 1332 (DC Cir. 1988) (subsequent history omitted). Excerpted material (only some of which is cited above) consisted of "vulgar and lewd references to the male genitals and to masturbation and sodomy broadcast in the context of . . . 'explicit references to masturbation, ejaculation, breast size, penis size, sexual intercourse, nudity, urination, oral-genital contact, erections, sodomy, bestiality, menstruation and testicles.'"

3 FCC Rcd at 932

WSUC-FM, Cortland, NY: "I'm Not Your Puppet" (rap song)

The only thing that was on my mind, was just shoving my dick up this bitch's behind. I looked at the girl and said, babe, your ass ain't nothing but a base hit. I'm going to have to get rid of your ass, yeah, 'cause you're on my dick, dick, ding-a-ling. Popped my dick in her mouth, and we rocked it back and forth. Now that she sucked my dick and Tony fuck you in the ass. I pulled out my dick, popped it in her mouth, and she sucked it.

Indecent – NAL issued
State University of New York (WSUC-FM), 8 FCC Rcd 456 (1993), *forfeiture reduced* 13 FCC Rcd 23810 (1998) (forfeiture paid). The Commission concluded that the language used in this broadcast

"describes sexual activities in patently offensive terms and is therefore indecent."

8 FCC Rcd at 456

WXTB(FM), Clearwater, FL: "Bubba, The Love Sponge"

Most women don't like swallowing, but I do. The trick is you need to swallow at the right time. Do it when you're deep throating. . . . I like pleasure giving, I like a pleasure giving woman who really, really likes to enjoy giving oral . . . . She does more than just go up and down, she's creative by licking, nibbling and using overall different techniques. . . . The sexy turn on for me is when I . . . expel into my partner's mouth . . . . I don't mind giving BJs . . . if a man doesn't get off, that means he wasn't quite excited by my techniques.

Indecent – NAL issued
   Citicasters Co. (WXTB(FM)), 13 FCC Rcd 22004 (1998), aff'd FCC 00-230, released June 27, 2000 (forfeiture paid).

b) Less explicit material and material that relies principally on innuendo to convey a sexual or excretory meaning have also been cited by the Commission as actionably indecent where the sexual or excretory meaning was unmistakable.

KLOL(FM), Houston, TX: *Stevens and Pruett Show*

The doctor was talking about size. The man complained earlier that he was so large that it was ruining his marriages. Big is good if the guy knows how to use it. She is so big she could handle anything. Some of these guys, a very few of them, a hand full are like . . . two hands full. Twelve inches, about the size of a beer can in diameter. So, now could you handle something like that? It's actually ruined marriages. A big organ for a big cathedral. Somebody big is just going to have to find somebody that's big.

Indecent – NAL issued
   The Rusk Corporation (KLOL(FM)), 8 FCC Rcd 3228 (1993) (forfeiture paid). As to the use of innuendo in the cited passages, the Commission said: "[W]hile [the licensee] may have substituted innuendo and double entendre for more directly explicit sexual references and descriptions in some instances, unmistakable sexual references remain that render the sexual meaning of the innuendo inescapable.

8 FCC Rcd at 3228

c) Compare the following case in which the material aired was deemed not to be actionably indecent.

WFBQ(FM)/WNDE(AM), Indianapolis, IN: "Elvis" and "Power, Power, Power"

As you know, you gotta stop the King, but you can't kill him . . . So you talk to Dick Nixon, man you get him on the phone and Dick suggests maybe getting like a mega-Dick to help out, but you know, you remember the time the King ate mega-Dick under the table at a 095 picnic . . . you think about getting mega-Hodgie, but that's no good because you know, the King was a karate dude . . .

Power! Power! Power! Thrust! Thrust! Thrust! First it was Big Foot, the monster car crunching 4x4 pickup truck. Well, move over, Big Foot! Here comes the most massive power-packed monster ever! It's Big Peter! (Laughter) Big Peter with 40,000 Peterbilt horsepower under the hood. It's massive! Big Peter! Formerly the Big Dick's Dog Wiener Mobile. Big Peter features a 75-foot jacked up monster body. See Big Peter crush and enter a Volvo. (Laughter) . . . strapped himself in the cockpit and put Big Peter through its paces. So look out Big Foot! Big Peter is coming! Oh my God! It's coming! Big Peter! (Laughter)

Not indecent

Great American Television and Radio Company, Inc. (WFBQ(FM)/ WNDE(AM)), 6 FCC Rcd 3692 (MMB 1990). The licensee provided a fuller transcript of the cited "Elvis" excerpt and explained the context in which it was aired, arguing that no sexual meaning was intended and that no such meaning would be reasonably understood from the material taken as a whole. The licensee also explained the regional humor of the Power, Power, Power excerpt and the context in which it was broadcast. The Mass Media Bureau held that the material was not indecent because the "surrounding contexts do not appear to provide a background against which a sexual import is inescapable.

6 FCC Rcd at 3693

d) In assessing explicitness, the Commission also looks to the audibility of the material as aired. If the material is difficult or impossible to understand, it may not be actionably indecent. However, difficulty in understanding part of the material or an attempt to obscure objectionable material will not preclude a finding of indecency where at least some of the material is recognizable or understandable.

KGB-FM, San Diego, CA: "Sit on My Face" Song

Sit on my face and tell me that you love me. I'll sit on your face and tell you I love you, too. I love to hear you moralize when I'm between your thighs. You blow me away. Sit on my face and let me embrace you. I'll sit on your face and then I'll love you (?) truly. Life can be fine, if we both sixty-nine. If we sit on faces (?) the ultimate place to play (?). We'll be blown away.

Indecent – NAL issued
KGB, Inc. (KGB-FM), 7 FCC Rcd 3207 (MMB 1992), forfeiture reduced 13 FCC Rcd 16396 (1998) (forfeiture paid). The song was found to be actionably indecent despite English accent and "ambient noise" because the lyrics were sufficiently understandable.

7 FCC Rcd at 3207

Dwelling/repetition versus fleeting reference

Repetition of and persistent focus on sexual or excretory material have been cited consistently as factors that exacerbate the potential offensiveness of broadcasts. In contrast, where sexual or excretory references have been made once or have been passing or fleeting in nature, this characteristic has tended to weigh against a finding of indecency.

WXTB(FM), Clearwater, FL: "Bubba, The Love Sponge"

Could you take the phone and rub it on you Chia Pet? Oh, let me make sure nobody is around. Okay, hang on a second (Rubbing noise). Okay I did it. . . . Now that really your little beaver? That was mine. Your what? That was my little beaver? Oh I love when a girl says beaver. Will you say it again for me honey please? It was my little beaver. . . . Will you say, Bubba come get my beaver? Bubba, would come get my little beaver? . . . tell me that doesn't do something for you. That is pretty sexy. . . . bring the beaver. It will be with me. We got beaver chow. I can't wait, will you say it for me one more time? Say what? My little beaver or Bubba come get my little beaver? Okay, Bubba come get my beaver. Will you say, Bubba come hit my beaver? Will you say it? Bubba, come hit my beaver. That is pretty sexy, absolutely. Oh, my God, beaver.

Indecent – NAL issued
Citicasters Co. (WXTB(FM)), 13 FCC Rcd 15381 (MMB 1998) (forfeiture paid).

Compare the following cases where material was found not indecent because it was fleeting and isolated.

WYBB(FM), Folly Beach, SC: The Morning Show"

The hell I did, I drove mother-fucker, oh. Oh.

Not indecent
> *L.M. Communications of South Carolina, Inc. (WYBB(FM))*, 7 FCC Rcd 1595 (MMB 1992). The "broadcast contained only a fleeting and isolated utterance which, within the context of live and spontaneous programming, does not warrant a Commission sanction.
>
> 7 FCC Rcd at 1595

KPRL(AM)/KDDB(FM), Paso Robles, CA: news announcer comment

Oops, fucked that one up.

Not Indecent
> *Lincoln Dellar, Renewal of License for Stations KPRL(AM) and KDDB(FM)*, 8 FCC Rcd 2582, 2585 (ASD, MMB 1993). The "news announcer's use of single expletive" does not "warrant further Commission consideration in light of the isolated and accidental nature of the broadcast."

In contrast, even relatively fleeting references may be found indecent where other factors contribute to a finding of patent offensiveness. Examples of such factors illustrated by the following cases include broadcasting references to sexual activities with children and airing material that, although fleeting, is graphic or explicit.

KUPD-FM, Tempe, AZ: announcer joke

What is the best part of screwing an eight-year-old? Hearing the pelvis crack.

Indecent – NAL issued
> *Tempe Radio, Inc. (KUPD-FM)*, 12 FCC Rcd 21828 (MMB 1997) (forfeiture paid). Although fleeting, the language clearly refers to sexual activity with a child and was found to be patently offensive.

WEZB-FM, New Orleans, LA: announcer joke

What's the worst part of having sex with your brother? . . . You got to fix the crib after it breaks and then you got to clean the blood off the diaper.

Indecent – NAL issued
EZ New Orleans, Inc. (WEZB(FM)), 12 FCC Rcd 4147 (MMB 1997) (forfeiture paid).

KLBJ(FM), Austin, TX: DJ comments

Suck my dick you fucking cunt.

Indecent – NAL issued
LBJS Broadcasting Company, L.P. (KLBJ(FM)), 13 FCC Rcd 20956 (MMB 1998) (forfeiture paid). Although fleeting, the material is explicit and was found to be indecent.

Presented in a pandering or titillating manner or for shock value

The apparent purpose for which material is presented can substantially affect whether it is deemed to be patently offensive as aired. In adverse indecency findings, the Commission has often cited the pandering or titillating character of the material broadcast as an exacerbating factor. Presentation for the shock value of the language used has also been cited. As Justice Powell stated in his opinion in the Supreme Court's decision affirming the Commission's determination that the broadcast of a comedy routine was indecent,

> [T]he language employed is, to most people, vulgar and offensive. It was chosen specifically for this quality, and it was repeated over and over as a sort of verbal shock treatment.
> *FCC* v. *Pacifica Foundation,* 438 US 726, 757 (1978)
> (Powell, J., concurring in part and concurring in the judgment)

On the other hand, the manner and purpose of a presentation may well preclude an indecency determination even though other factors, such as explicitness, might weigh in favor of an indecency finding. In the following cases, the decisions looked to the manner of presentation as a factor supporting a finding of indecency.

WEBN(FM), Cincinnati, OH: "Bubba, The Love Sponge"

All I can say is, if you were listening to the program last night you heard Amy and Stacy . . . come in here, little lesbians that they are. Little University of Cincinnati ho's and basically that we could come over and watch them. We got over to the house . . . They start making out a little bit. They go to bed. They get, they start, they're starting like a mutual 69 on the bed. Guido all of a sudden whips it out . . . Rather than take care of each other . . . Guido is like knee deep with the butch bitch and all of a sudden here is the fem bitch looking at me. Hot. I get crazy. I hook up a little bit. Then Guido says, hey, I done got mine, how about we switching? So I went into the private bedroom with the butch bitch and then got another one.

Indecent – NAL issued
   Jacor Broadcasting Corporation (WEBN(FM)), 13 FCC Rcd 4152 (MMB 1997), *aff'd* 13 FCC Rcd 5825 (MMB 1997) (forfeiture paid).

In determining whether broadcasts are presented in a pandering or titillating manner, the context of the broadcast is particularly critical. Thus, even where language is explicit, the matter is graphic, or where there is intense repetition of vulgar terms, the presentation may not be pandering or titillating, and the broadcast may not be found actionably indecent.

KING-TV, Seattle, WA: "Teen Sex: What About the Kids?"

Broadcast of portions of a sex education class in a local high school that included the use of very realistic sex organ models and simulated demonstrations of various methods of birth control as well as frank discussions of sexual topics.

Not Indecent
   King Broadcasting Co. (KING-TV), 5 FCC Rcd 2971 (1990). The Commission held that although the program dealt explicitly with sexual issues and included the use of very graphic sex organ models, "the material presented was clinical or instructional in nature and not presented in a pandering, titillating or vulgar manner."
                                                            5 FCC Rcd at 2971

WABC-TV, New York, NY: *Oprah Winfrey Show* ("How to Make Romantic Relations with Your Mate Better")

Okay, for all you viewers out there with children watching, we're doing a show today on how to make romantic relations with your mate better. Otherwise known as s-e-x . . . I'm very aware there are a number of children who are watching and so, we're going to do our best to keep this show rated "G" but just in case, you may want to send your kids to a different room. And we'll pause for a moment while you do that . . . According to experts and recent sex surveys the biggest complaints married women have about sex are . . . their lovemaking is boring . . . American wives all across the country have confessed to using erotic aids to spice up their sex life and . . . thousands of women say they fantasize while having sex with their husbands. . . . And most women say they are faking it in the bedroom.

[Quiz:] I like the way my partner looks in clothing . . . I like the way my partner looks naked . . . I like the way my partner's skin feels . . . . I like the way my partner tastes . . .

[Psychologist and panelists:] Do you know that you can experience orgasm, have you experienced that by yourself? No, I have not . . . Okay, one of the things that, well, you all know what I'm talking about . . . You need to at least know how to make your body get satisfied by yourself. Because if you don't know how to do it, how is he going to figure it out? He doesn't have your body parts, he doesn't know.

Not indecent
Letter from Chief, Complaints and Investigations Branch, Enforcement Division, Mass Media Bureau, to Chris Giglio (July 20, 1994). Subject matter alone does not render material indecent. Thus, while material may be offensive to some people, in context, it might not be actionably indecent.

KTVI-TV, St. Louis, MO: *Geraldo Rivera Show* ("Unlocking the Great Mysteries of Sex")

We have seen such a slew of sex books . . . *Your G-spot, How to Have Triple Orgasms.* One of the biggest myths . . . either we go all the way or we do nothing . . . He just missed an opportunity to make love, not all the way . . . but to share a moment of passion and a moment of closeness . . . It's important that a man learn to use the penis the way an artist uses a paintbrush . . . and if a woman is also willing to learn how to move her vagina . . . With good control of PC muscles, a man can separate orgasm from ejaculation and have more than one orgasm . . . Really great sex is always based on feeling safe enough with your partner to open up. Passion is just the expression of a tremendous sense of connection you feel. If you think sex is pleasurable, try making love and having sex at the same time for turning pleasure into ecstasy.

Not indecent
Letter from Chief, Complaints and Investigations Branch, Enforcement Division, Mass Media Bureau, to Gerald P. McAtee (October 26, 1989). While offensive to some, the material was not found to be indecent.

WSMC-FM, Collegedale, TN: "All Things Considered" (National Public Radio)

Mike Schuster has a report and a warning. The following story contains some very rough language. [Excerpt from wiretap of telephone conversation in which organized crime figure John Gotti uses "fuck" or "fucking" ten times in seven sentences (110 words).]

Not indecent
Peter Branton, 6 FCC Rcd 610 (1991) (subsequent history omitted). Explicit language was integral part of a bona fide news story concerning organized crime; the material aired was part of a wiretap recording used as evidence in Gotti's widely reported trial. The Commission explained that it did "not find the use of such [coarse] words in a legitimate news report to have been gratuitous, pandering, titillating or otherwise "patently offensive" as that term is used in our indecency definition.

6 FCC Rcd at 610

Compare the following cases where licensees unsuccessfully claimed that, because of the context of the broadcasts (i.e., alleged news stories), the broadcasts were not pandering.

KNON(FM), Dallas, TX: "I Want to Be a Homosexual" song

But if you really want to give me a blowjob, I guess I'll let you as long as you respect me in the morning. Suck it baby. Oh yeah, suck it real good . . . Are you sure this is your first rim job? . . . Stick it up your punk rock ass. You rub your little thing, when you see phony dikes in *Penthouse* magazine . . . Call me a faggot, call me a butt-loving fudge-packing queer . . . You rub your puny thing, when you see something (?) pass you on the street.

Indecent – NAL issued
Agape Broadcasting Foundation, Inc. (KNON(FM)), 9 FCC Rcd 1679 (MMB 1994), *forfeiture reduced* 13 FCC Rcd 9262 (MMB 1998) (forfeiture paid). Licensee claimed that "'the words and the song constitute political speech' aired in a good faith attempt to present meaningful public affairs programming . . . to challenge those who would use such language to stigmatize . . . members of the gay community."

13 FCC Rcd at 9263

The Mass Media Bureau responded that the licensee has "considerable discretion as to the times of the day . . . when it may broadcast indecent material . . . Consequently, we find unavailing Agape's argument that, in essence, its duty to air public affairs programming required a mid-afternoon presentation of lyrics containing repeated, explicit, and vulgar descriptions of sexual activities and organs."

Ibid.

The absence of a pandering or titillating nature, however, will not necessarily prevent an indecency determination, as illustrated by the following case.

WIOD(AM), Miami, FL: "Penis Envy" song

If I had a penis, . . . I'd stretch it and stroke it and shove it at smarties . . . I'd stuff it in turkeys on Thanksgiving day . . . If I had a penis, I'd run to my mother, Comb out the hair and compare it to brother. I'd lance her, I'd knight her, my hands would indulge. Pants would seem tighter and buckle and bulge. (Refrain) A penis to plunder, a penis to push, 'cause one in the hand is worth one in the bush. A penis to love me, a penis to share, To pick up and play with when nobody's there . . . If I had a penis, . . . I'd force it on females, I'd pee like a fountain. If I had a penis, I'd still be a girl, but I'd make much more money and conquer the world.

Indecent – NAL issued
WIOD, Inc. (WIOD(AM)), 6 FCC Rcd 3704 (MMB 1989) (forfeiture paid). The Mass Media Bureau found the material to be patently offensive. In response to the licensee's assertion that this song was not pandering or titillating and therefore should not be considered indecent, the

Bureau stated: "We believe . . . that it is not necessary to find that the material is pandering or titillating in order to find that its references to sexual activities and organs are patently offensive. (Citations omitted.) Moreover, humor is no more an absolute defense to indecency . . . than is music or any other one component of communication."

6 FCC Rcd at 3704

Parental control or government control

Kuhl (2006) reported data that go to the issue of how media content should be treated:

- By 2010, 30 million US households will have a connected entertainment network.
- Time Warner cable's new interface features a content advisory control and ratings guide.
- TVWatch Executive Director Jim Dyke concluded: "All TV isn't for kids, that's why informed parents are so important and must make informed decisions for each child. We all need to do a better job with parental controls" (p. 2B).
- Cox Community Relations Director Mallard Holliday said: "The biggest challenge has been getting parents to show interest in parental control. The parents are the best parental control feature there is, and we've attacked the issue from that perspective, and not just about TV control, but the Internet and phone as well" (p. 2B).

The special report summarized findings by consultant Russell Research into consumer awareness of TV ratings, blocking technologies, and other tools:

- Ninety-one percent of parents claim to take steps to manage TV viewing by their children. The same percentage say parental involvement is the best method to keep kids from seeing programs they want them to avoid.
- Eighty-five percent of parents said they find TV ratings are useful. The same percentage believe people should exercise personal choice over TV watching.
- Sixty-four percent of parents said they allow their children to have a television set in their bedroom.
- Parents say they limit their children's viewing by watching with them (63 percent), restricting viewing to certain shows (61 percent), limiting the duration of viewing (55 percent), employing the TV ratings system (52 percent), and using cable controls (17 percent) or satellite TV controls (12 percent). Only five percent said they used V-chip technology (p. 2B).

45

Box 2.3 TV Watch study finds opposition to current FCC regulation

The Russell Research TV Watch Study (2006) produced support for the view that a majority of Americans prefer choice over government regulation.

Item	Strongly agree (%)	Somewhat agree (%)	Somewhat disagree (%)	Strongly disagree (%)
Some people will always be able to find something on television or radio that offends them. But the sensistivities of a few should not dictate the choices for everyone else	57	29	7	7
It's futile for the government to fine network programs when the same or similar programming is available any time on cable, satellite, and the Internet	26	38	19	17
The federal government should not spend its time investigating and fining a local broadcaster when only one complaint is made and yet thousands of people watched and did not complain	44	29	14	14

Source: Russell Research (2006) *TV Watch Study*, available at Center for Creative Voices in Media (March 31, 2006). "Survey: Americans don't want government to censor TV."

Chapter summary

Broadcast regulation in the United States is based upon a scarcity rationale – namely that not everyone who wants one can own a station because of spectrum scarcity. Therefore, those using the spectrum are licensed to serve the public interest, convenience, and necessity. This is a vague standard that has afforded broadcasters wide latitude in making programming decisions. Nevertheless, the rights of viewers and listeners may be paramount to those of broadcasters. In the area of indecency, the government has recognized a substantial interest in assisting parents in their protection of children. The FCC has attempted to offer examples of acceptable and unacceptable content during the hours when children are likely to be in the audience. In the end, the public appears to prefer exercising their judgment rather than having the government restrict adult media content.

Review questions

1 How would you define the public interest, convenience, and necessity?
2 Should the broadcast licensee have a fiduciary responsibility to represent those who cannot have a license? Why or why not?
3 Should broadcasters do more to raise their own standards? Do you agree or disagree that the marketplace is the best determinant of public interest?
4 Should the FCC and the Congress be more responsive to the majority of Americans, who favor freedom of choice in media content? Why or why not?
5 Was the FCC correct in finding that the broadcasts excerpted in this chapter were indecent? How should the FCC balance the need to follow federal regulations with the interest in protecting free speech for broadcasters?

3

THEORY AND RESEARCH IN
BROADCAST AND INTERNET
INDECENCY

Our understanding of the nature of broadcast and Internet indecency has been influenced by legal philosophy, court decisions, political positions, and public opinion. In this chapter, we examine the role that social research plays in illuminating our understanding of the social and legal contexts of indecency.

Normative First Amendment theories

One needs to consider the social basis for protecting free expression under the First Amendment. In fact, many theorists have developed reasoning that has found its way into Supreme Court decisions.

The first significant example of this, the marketplace of ideas philosophy, is found in John Milton's book *Areopagitica* (1644):

> Though all the winds of doctrine were let loose to play upon the earth, so Truth be in the field, we do injuriously by licensing and prohibiting to misdoubt her strength. Let her and Falsehood grapple; who ever knew Truth put to the worse in a free and open encounter?

In the *Abrams* v. *United States* (1919) anti-war leaflet case, Justice Oliver Wendell Holmes offered this dissenting opinion on the prosecution and conviction of those expressing opinions on the streets of New York City:

> Persecution for the expression of opinions seems to me perfectly logical. If you have no doubt of your premises or your power and want a certain result with all your heart you naturally express your wishes in law and sweep away all opposition. To allow opposition by speech seems to indicate that you think the speech impotent, as when a man says that he has squared the circle, or that you do not care whole-heartedly for the result, or that you doubt either your power or your premises. But when men have realized that time

has upset many fighting faiths, they may come to believe even more than they believe the very foundations of their own conduct that the ultimate good desired is better reached by free trade in ideas – that the best test of truth is the power of the thought to get itself accepted in the competition of the market, and that truth is the only ground upon which their wishes safely can be carried out. That at any rate is the theory of our Constitution. It is an experiment, as all life is an experiment.

(p. 630)

The marketplace of ideas philosophy remained a minority view on the court throught the first half of the twentieth century.

Box 3.1 Douglas's near-absolutist view

Justice William O. Douglas (Figure 3.1), who served more than thirty-six years on the US Supreme Court, the longest term of any justice, applied a literalist interpretation to a near-absolutist view of the meaning of the First Amendment.

Justice Douglas wrote: "Unless and until extreme and necessitous circumstances are shown, our aim should be to keep speech unfettered and to allow the processes of law to be invoked only when the provocateurs among us move from speech to action" (*Dennis* v. *US*, 341 US 494, 1951: 590–1).

Justice Douglas was born in 1898, nearly died at age three from polio, and vaulted into the national limelight after receiving top academic honors at Columbia Law School. According to the Yakima Valley Museum, located where Douglas graduated Phi Beta Kappa from high school, he practiced law only briefly, in Yakima in 1926. He returned to Columbia a year later and then accepted a teaching position at Yale. He left academe a decade later for a life of politics and the Supreme Court:

- In 1937, Douglas was appointed chair of the Securities and Exchange Commission, interestingly replacing Joseph Kennedy – the father of President John Kennedy.
- In 1939 he was appointed to the Supreme Court by President Franklin D. Roosevelt to replace Justice Louis D. Brandeis.
- In 1940 and 1944 he was considered a possible vice presidential nominee by President Franklin Roosevelt, and again in 1948 by President Harry Truman. He also declined to run for president in 1952.

- In 1970, Representative and future President Gerald Ford led an attempted impeachment effort against Justice Douglas.
- Douglas suffered a stroke in 1974, and he retired the next year after serving thirty-six years on the Court. He died in 1980.

Figure 3.1 Justice William O. Douglas. Source: www.ocpd.state.ct.us

Source
"The Life of William O. Douglas," The Yakima Valley Museum (http://yakimavalleymuseum.org/identity/douglas.html).

Strict scrutiny

First Amendment analyses in individual cases may be guided by any number of legal tests. An early approach was restrict any speech that had a "bad tendency," such as the fears that anti-war leaflets would incite public disturbances. Thus, the answer was to jail those attempting to challenge the government. Broadcast indecency cases often rest on such assumptions that, although we have no evidence, we fear that the content would be harmful to some children. About the same time as the bad tendency approach, the Supreme Court offered what amounted to a "clear and present danger" test – one that suggested restricting only that speech that presented a serious and immediate danger. Clearly, broadcast indecency typically would not present such a danger. The Court also has attempted a "balancing" approach to, for example, balance the rights of adults to access media against the need to protect children. The problem with this model for broadcast indecency cases is that it is very unpredictable in terms of how the FCC or a court will decide a particular case based on some set of facts.

For those wishing to truly protect our First Amendment rights, a strict scrutiny approach – one in which the burden falls to the government to show a compelling reason for the regulation – works best. Under such a test, "narrowly tailored" restrictions may be upheld.

The scrutiny approach has been operationalized in what has been labeled intermediate scrutiny in the *O'Brien* (1967) case. Scrutiny would require a court to ask four pivotal questions about any broadcast indecency case:

1 Is the government regulation within constitutional power? In other words, does the government truly have a right to treat broadcasting differently from other media with respect to the First Amendment? This is a tricky question, because clearly the record of cases such as *NBC, Red Lion* and *Pacifica* adds to the spectrum scarcity rationale. However, the *Red Lion* court did suggest that at some future time technology might render an end to scarcity. Many have argued that cable, satellite, and Internet media now offer so many alternatives that scarcity is withering. However, it remains the case that it is extremely difficult to become a broadcast licensee. The barriers to entry – economic, technical, and legal qualifications – remain extremely high. Further, media concentration by huge corporations continues to accelerate. For the purposes of this analysis, let us assume that the government does have the power through the Interstate Commerce Clause of the US Constitution and that Congress has legally delegated that authority to the FCC. This moves us to the second key question.

2 Does the regulation further an important or substantial interest? There is no question that the raising of our children is important and the government has a substantial interest in the nation's future. However, as we will examine later in this text, there is virtually *no* evidence that broadcast indecency harms children. If anything, the evidence raises concerns about the effects of violence – an area that has not been targeted by the FCC. Even if one could draw a linkage between indecency and potential harm, scrutiny requires that a court address a third question.

3 Is the interest unrelated to the suppression of free expression? For the most part, broadcast indecency regulation is not about the suppression of important political ideas – political communication is at the core of protection under the First Amendment. However, the George Carlin monologue, which went to the Supreme Court in *Pacifica*, was political satire that challenged the Vietnam War. Additionally, it is unfair to conclude that the speech of Howard Stern and other shock jocks does not have political significance in terms of the culture of the USA. One could easily argue from a perspective of liberty that all speech has some value. Even if a court were to overcome all three parts reviewed here, there is a fourth remaining question:

4 Is the incidental restriction of free expression no greater than is essential to the furtherance of the stated government interest? Courts have attempted to address this in broadcast indecency cases by arguing that the creation of a "safe harbor" – a time when children are not likely

to be in the audience (10 p.m. to 6 a.m.) – that the FCC regulation is narrowly tailored and no greater than needed. Here, it is easy to argue that the broad safe harbor effectively restricts broadcast indecency to times when few people are in the audience. Broadcast ratings show how audience size explodes outside the safe harbor during the waking hours. Therefore, even if one could provide evidence for the need to regulate broadcast indecency, one would need to broaden the safe harbor to include more hours when there is a legitimate audience.

Theories of FCC and FTC regulation

Regulatory theories abound, which offer justification for the Congress to delegate some of its power to the agency that functions under the rules of administrative law. Our common law tradition from Europe was interpreted by the text of William Blackstone (Figure 3.2) in his *Commentaries on the Laws of England* (1769).

> Every freeman has an undoubted right to lay what sentiments he pleases before the public . . . but if he publishes what is improper, mischievous, or illegal, he must take the consequences for his own temerity.

The legal theory of restricting prior restraint in favor of a doctrine of subsequent punishment was imported into American law.

Thomas Emerson, a Yale Law School professor and First Amendment scholar, has offered the strongest arguments for defending a robust set of First Amendment rights. Emerson (1970) contended that free speech allows for discovery of truth needed to make reasonable decisions in a democracy. In this way, free speech enables self-government because the mass media serve as a check on excessive government power. Quite interestingly, Emerson suggested that free speech increases political stability by offering a safety valve to relieve pressure that builds. Like the pressure relief valve atop a water heater, which expels excess pressure to avoid an explosion, free speech serves as a mechanism in society, the theory goes, to promote slower and less traumatic social change. One can even debate

Figure 3.2 William Blackstone.

whether free media promote social change or reinforce the status quo. In any event, Emerson's theory concludes that free speech allows for the fulfillment of individual enrichment. Without free speech, it is difficult to see how repression encourages the human spirit to dream of a life yet done. It is through communication that we learn about each other and ourselves. For those who close their eyes and ears to likes of Howard Stern and "Bubba, the Love Sponge," preferring to avoid that which is different, perhaps what is lost is a greater understanding of what defines our own identities.

Legal analyses

The law may produce consistent or inconsistent results, as judges balance various interests. The law thrives on the value of legal precedent and the need to "find the law" in the case law. However, such legal reasoning may fall short by accepting on faith presumptions of government or others. In broadcast indecency, for example, various courts have accepted as fact the link between exposure to indecent content and possible negative effects on minors. For example, even in the dissenting opinion of Justices Brennan and Marshall in the key *FCC* v. *Pacifica Foundation* (1978) case dealing with George Carlin's monologue on the words you cannot say on television, it is written that: "Most parents will undoubtedly find understandable as well as commendable the Court's sympathy with the FCC's desire to prevent offensive broadcasts from reaching the ears of unsupervised children" (p. 767). Rather than attacking the assumption of harm, the justices were concerned with weakening the legal and constitutional distinction between illegal obscenity under *Miller* and legal indecency: "Because the Carlin monologue is obviously not an erotic appeal to the prurient interests of children, the Court, for the first time, allows the government to prevent minors from gaining access to materials that are not obscene, and are therefore protected, as to them" (p. 767). At the same time, however, there is acknowledgment that at least some parents might welcome exposing their children to profanity:

> In concluding that the presence of children in the listening audi-
> ence provides an adequate basis for the FCC to impose sanctions
> for Pacifica's broadcast of the Carlin monologue, the opinions [in
> this case] . . . stress the time-honored right of a parent to raise
> his child as he sees fit – a right this Court has consistently been
> vigilant to protect . . . Yet this principle supports a . . . result
> directly contrary to that reached by the Court. [Previous cases
> concluded] . . . that parents, not the government, have the right to
> make certain decisions regarding the upbringing of their children.
> As surprising as it may be to individual Members of this Court,

some parents may actually find Mr. Carlin's unabashed attitude towards the seven "dirty words" healthy, and deem it desirable to expose their children to the manner in which Mr. Carlin defuses the taboo surrounding the words. Such parents may constitute a minority of the American public, but the absence of great numbers willing to exercise the right to raise their children in this fashion does not alter the right's nature or its existence. Only the Court's regrettable decision does that.

(pp. 769–70)

Interestingly, the Supreme Court in *Pacifica* focused on the dispute over social value of the language used by Carlin and, therefore, its need for First Amendment protection, rather than the lack of social psychological evidence on any negative effects from the use of such language.

Box 3.2 Carlin monologue as transcribed by *Pacifica* court

Appendix to opinion of the court
The following is a verbatim transcript of "Filthy Words" prepared by the FCC:

Aruba-du, ruba-tu, ruba-tu. I was thinking about the curse words and the swear words, the cuss words and the words that you can't say, that you're not supposed to say all the time, [']cause words or people into words want to hear your words. Some guys like to record your words and sell them back to you if they can, (laughter) listen in on the telephone, write down what words you say. A guy who used to be in Washington knew that his phone was tapped, used to answer, Fuck Hoover, yes, go ahead. (laughter) Okay, I was thinking one night about the words you couldn't say on the public, ah, airwaves, um, the ones you definitely wouldn't say, ever, [']cause I heard a lady say bitch one night on television, and it was cool like she was talking about, you know, ah, well, the bitch is the first o'ne to notice that in the litter Johnie right (murmur) Right. And, uh, bastard you can say, and hell and damn so I have to figure out which ones you couldn't and ever and it came down to seven but the list is open to amendment, and in fact, has been changed, uh, by now, ha, a lot of people pointed things out to me, and I noticed some myself. *The original seven words were, shit, piss, fuck, cunt, cocksucker, motherfucker, and tits* [emphasis added]. Those are the ones that will curve your spine, grow hair on your hands and (laughter) maybe, even bring us, God help us, peace without honor (laughter) um, and a bourbon. (laughter) And now the first thing that we noticed was that word fuck was really repeated in there because the word motherfucker is a compound word and it's another form of the word fuck. (laughter) You want to be a purist it [438 US 726, 752] doesn't really – it can't be on the list of basic words. Also, cocksucker is a compound word and neither half of that is really dirty. The word – the half sucker that's merely suggestive (laughter) and the word cock is a half-way dirty word, 50 percent dirty – dirty half the time, depending on what you mean by it. (laughter) Uh, remember when you first heard it, like in 6th grade, you used to giggle. And the cock crowed three times, heh (laughter) the cock – three times. It's in the Bible, cock in the Bible. (laughter) And the first time you heard about a cock-fight, remember – What? Huh? naw. It ain't that, are you stupid? man. (laughter, clapping) It's chickens, you know, (laughter) Then you have the four letter words from the old Anglo-Saxon fame. Uh, shit and fuck. The word shit, uh, is an interesting kind of word in that the middle class has never really accepted it and approved it. They use it like, crazy but it's not really okay. It's still a rude, dirty, old kind of gushy word. (laughter) They don't like that, but they say it, like, they say it like, a lady now in a middle-class home, you'll hear most of the time she says it as an expletive, you know, it's out of her mouth before she knows. She says, Oh shit oh shit, (laughter) oh shit. If she drops something, Oh, the shit hurt the broccoli. Shit. Thank you. (footsteps fading away) (papers ruffling)

Read it! (from audience)

Shit! (laughter) I won the Grammy, man, for the comedy album. Isn't that groovy? (clapping, whistling) (murmur) That's true. Thank you. Thank you man. Yeah. (murmur) (continuous clapping) Thank you man. Thank you. Thank you very much, man. Thank, no, (end of continuous clapping) for that and for the Grammy, man, [']cause (laughter) that's based on people liking it man, yeh, that's ah, that's okay man. (laughter) Let's let that go, man. I got my Grammy. I can let my hair hang down now, shit. (laughter) Ha! So! Now the word shit is okay for the man. At work you can say it like crazy. Mostly figuratively, Get that shit out of here, [438 US 726, 753] will ya? I don't want to see that shit anymore. I can't cut that shit, buddy. I've had that shit up to here. I think you're full of shit myself. (laughter) He don't know shit from Shinola. (laughter) you know that? (laughter) Always wondered how the Shinola people felt about that (laughter) Hi, I'm the new man from Shinola. (laughter) Hi, how are ya? Nice to see ya. (laughter) How are ya? (laughter) Boy, I don't know whether to shit or wind my watch. (laughter) Guess, I'll shit on my watch. (laughter) Oh, the shit is going to hit de fan. (laughter) Built like a brick shit-house. (laughter) Up, he's up shit's creek. (laughter) He's had it. (laughter) He hit me, I'm sorry. (laughter) Hot shit, holy shit, tough shit, eat shit, (laughter) shit-eating grin. Uh, whoever thought of that was ill. (murmur laughter) He had a shit-eating grin! He had a what? (laughter) Shit on a stick. (laughter) Shit in a handbag. I always like that. He ain't worth shit in a handbag. (laughter) Shitty. He acted real shitty. (laughter) You know what I mean? (laughter) I got the money back, but a real shitty attitude. Heh, he had a shit-fit. (laughter) Wow! Shit-fit. Whew! Glad I wasn't there.

(murmur, laughter) All the animals – Bull shit, horse shit, cow shit, rat shit, bat shit. (laughter) First time I heard bat shit, I really came apart. A guy in Oklahoma, Boggs, said it, man. Aw! Bat shit. (laughter) Vera reminded me of that last night, ah (murmur). Snake shit, slicker than owl shit. (laughter) Get your shit together. Shit or get off the pot. (laughter) I got a shit-load full of them. (laughter) I got a shit-pot full, all right. Shit-head, shit-heel, shit in your heart, shit for brains, (laughter) shit-face, heh (laughter) I always try to think how that could have originated; the first guy that said that. Somebody got drunk and fell in some shit, you know. (laughter) Hey, I'm shit-face. (laughter) Shit-face, today. (laughter) Anyway, enough of that shit. (laughter) The big one, the word fuck that's the one that hangs them up the most. [']Cause in a lot of cases that's the very act that [438 US 726, 754] hangs them up the most. So, it's natural that the word would, uh, have the same effect. It's a great word, fuck, nice word, easy word, cute word, kind of. Easy word to say. One syllable, short u. (laughter) Fuck. (Murmur) You know, it's easy. Starts with a nice soft sound fuh ends with a kuh. Right? (laughter) A little something for everyone. Fuck (laughter) Good word. Kind of a proud word, too. Who are you? I am FUCK. (laughter) FUCK OF THE MOUNTAIN. (laughter) Tune in again next week to FUCK OF THE MOUNTAIN. (laughter) It's an interesting word too, [']cause it's got a double kind of a life – personality – dual, you know, whatever the right phrase is. It leads a double life, the word fuck. First of all, it means, sometimes, most of the time, fuck. What does it mean? It means to make love. Right? We're going to make love, yeh, we're going to fuck, yeh, we're going to fuck, yeh, we're going to make love. (laughter) we're really going to fuck, yeh, we're going to make love. Right? And it also means the beginning of life, it's the act that begins life, so there's the word hanging around with words like love, and life, and yet on the other hand, it's also a word that we really use to hurt each other with, man. It's a heavy. It's one that you have toward the end of the argument. (laughter) Right? (laughter) You finally can't make out. Oh, fuck you man. I said, fuck you. (laughter, murmur) Stupid fuck. (laughter) Fuck you and everybody that looks like you. (laughter) man. It would be nice to change the movies that we already have and substitute the word fuck for the word kill, wherever we could, and some of those movie cliches would change a little bit. Madfuckers still on the loose. Stop me before I fuck again. Fuck the ump, fuck the ump, fuck the ump, fuck the ump, fuck the ump. Easy on the clutch Bill, you'll fuck that engine again. (laughter) The other shit one was, I don't give a shit. Like it's worth something, you know? (laughter) I don't give a shit. Hey, well, I don't take no shit, (laughter) you know what I mean? You know why I don't take no shit? (laughter) [438 US 726, 755] [']Cause I don't give a shit. (laughter) If I give a shit, I would have to pack shit. (laughter) But I don't pack no shit cause I don't give a shit. (laughter) You wouldn't shit me, would you? (laughter) That's a joke when you're a kid with a worm looking out the bird's ass. You wouldn't shit me, would you? (laughter)

It's an eight-year-old joke but a good one. (laughter) The additions to the list. I found three more words that had to be put on the list of words you could never say on television, and they were fart, turd and twat, those three. (laughter) Fart, we talked about, it's harmless It's like tits, it's a cutie word, no problem. Turd, you can't say but who wants to, you know? (laughter) The subject never comes up on the panel so I'm not worried about that one. Now the word twat is an interesting word. Twat! Yeh, right in the twat. (laughter) Twat is an interesting word because it's the only one I know of, the only slang word applying to the, a part of the sexual anatomy that doesn't have another meaning to it. Like, ah, snatch, box and pussy all have other meanings, man. Even in a Walt Disney movie, you can say, We're going to snatch that pussy and put him in a box and bring him on the airplane. (murmur, laughter) Everybody loves it. The twat stands alone, man, as it should. And two-way words. Ah, ass is okay providing you're riding into town on a religious feast day. (laughter) You can't say, up your ass. (laughter) You can say, stuff it! (murmur) There are certain things you can say its weird but you can just come so close. Before I cut, I, uh, want to, ah, thank you for listening to my words, man, fellow, uh space travelers. Thank you man for tonight and thank you also. (clapping whistling)

Social and psychological research

The law cannot be viewed in a vacuum of case decisions. Instead, we must go beyond the black letter law to make linkages to current findings in social research. One connection between the laws of broadcast indecency and research is scientific attempts to link media content to antisocial effects on children or even adults. Despite the common assumption that regulation is needed to protect children, one exhaustive study by Donnerstein, Wilson, and Linz (1992) of all available empirical evidence failed to find a link between indecent broadcasts and any harmful effects. No studies on the scientific effects on exposure to indecent language were found, but the literature did suggest that younger children have lower comprehension than older ones. In fact, young children have no understanding of sexual matters, and those between the ages of five and fifteen tended also to be sexually illiterate. Into the teenage years, research suggested that sexually provocative music lyrics appeared to be not heard or understood.

Social science evidence produces a pattern that challenges the normative assumptions of interest groups that influence politicians, media, and the public. Disturbingly, courts have tended to defer to legislation and regulation – even in the absence of solid evidence. It is illogical to expect much effect on young children who lack knowledge, understanding, and interest in sexual content (Donnerstein et al., 1992). Presumably, as young people grow older, they are not exposed to sexual media content in a social vacuum. One could argue that the fear over negative media effects on children comes from a concern that such messages will compete favorably against opposing attempts to construct moral frameworks through families, churches, schools, and other social organizations. This fear is difficult to rationalize in light of the great differences in amount of time of exposure between positive and negative messages, so defined. Particularly with reference to fleeting uses of profanity, it is difficult to conclude that these would produce noticeable long-term effects. If they did, the psychological evidence should appear.

Linz, Donnerstein, Shafer, Land, McCall, and Graesser (1995), studying the broader issue of obscenity law, found that it "derives its content nearly exclusively from a consideration of community morals and values" (p. 127). When local prosecutors try obscenity cases and these get media attention, researchers have discovered that people come to assume that the community standard is one of intolerance:

> The greater the attention given law enforcement activities by the media in a community, the more the average observer may assume that citizens of the community are intolerant. However, when members of the community are individually questioned, they may express a much higher level of tolerance for sexually explicit materials.
>
> (ibid.: 134)

Thus, the misperception may also lead to obscenity law that is based upon an incorrect assumption: "The discrepancy between community tolerance and the obscenity code may exist because sexually explicit depictions of consensual behavior are no longer perceived as *harmful* [emphasis in the original text] by community members" (p. 160). The same may be true for broadcast indecency in the face of moral crusades by interests groups, a Congress intent on appearing responsive and an FCC faced with following policy. It could well be that the vast majority of Americans have no real problem with indecent broadcasts.

Instead, the parental fears may be driven by media accounts that frame indecency as a serious social problem. Under such circumstances, mass media research has consistently noted over the years what is called a "third-person effect" – people have been known to worry that weaker *others* are more susceptible than themselves to harm from the media. It is a mistake to make generic assumptions about broad-based effects on any general group, including children.

It is worth repeating what I concluded in my book on this topic a decade ago – the notion of what is or is not indecent is socially defined by a society. Children do not see indecency until it is *defined for them* by outside social forces. As George Carlin clearly observed in his ironic monologue, the word "fuck" may or may not be a "dirty" word because its meaning can be beautiful or ugly. In fact, the word has no meaning until our society assigns one or more meanings. The fear over broadcast indecency, then, is that broadcasters may have an unfair advantage by exposing children – especially unsupervised children – to content that their parents have defined as inappropriate in a social context. Legal constructions are placed within the social context that they emerge from and exist in – law and policy are seen as serving social functions.

Consider the concept of "public interest." It is central to the meaning of the Communications Act of 1934. The allocation of broadcast facilities is based on the FCC's interpretation of the statutory language, "if public convenience, interest, or necessity will be served." To the broadcast manager, however, "public interest" moves from being an abstract legal construction to an operationalized station behavioral objective. It becomes an economic imperative to serve those interests that attract and maintain audience size and steadily increase station revenues.

Particularly when speaking about government regulation of mass media content, media practitioners and the general public may be confused by legal tests and constructions. Broadcast indecency challenges our belief in a near-absolute First Amendment because media practitioners may see the content as not worth the trouble, and the public may see it as socially undesirable. While individual FCC commissioners and others in the bureaucracy may be sympathetic to the First Amendment and the industry stance, the congressional power of the budget forces regulation to happen consistent with the wishes of lawmakers and the president. The policy often seems quite isolated from social changes.

Social theory and computer-mediated communication

Broadcast indecency may also be studied from a social–cultural perspective. Social theory and postmodernism place media within a context of a consumer society: "Consumer society has effectively displaced moral categories such as those based upon deference and thrift and replaced them with the hedonistic search for satisfaction" (Stevenson, 1995: 149). Clearly, the market for sexual content exists. Thus, the market may erect "barriers of social exclusion" through goods as object "signs" that are interesting to consumers:

> The meaning of objects is established through the organisation of signs into codes. It is only through these codes that human beings come to realise their sense of self and their needs. The codes themselves are hierarchically ordered, being used to signify distinctions of status and prestige.
>
> (ibid.)

The capitalist beauty of such a sign-ordered system is that materialistic "needs" will never be fully met. Thus, media become the engine that drives consumption by displaying the latest fads. Popularization of entertainers, such as Howard Stern, happens across media platforms – radio, broadcast television, cable, and new media. The Internet feeds hedonism by allowing an individual to search and browse in personalized ways that feed psychographic tendencies.

The struggle for control of cyberspace has been joined by those who would commercialize it to the point of hedonism and those who insist it is more egalitarian than elitist:

> Cyberspace is both public and private, the communication is one-to-one, one-to-many, and many-to-many. And, because cyberspace is open-minded space, its users will develop it in new ways regardless of what restrictions commercial service providers attempt to impose on it . . . The collectivist ideology does not expect that freedom in cyberspace will be absolute . . . But the sense of common good that drives the collectivity of CMC users tolerates the boundaries drawn by the desire to maintain the *whole* in the face of potentially drastic restructuring amid regulatory constraints.
>
> (Fernback, in Jones, 1997: 50)

Some in the computer-mediated communication (CMC) movement are willing to justify limitations on free expression as a means to "squelch" that which is "clearly irrelevant or malicious" – flame wars and "nonsense" are treated as disruptive: "Nonetheless, the groups that would appear to be the harshest dissenters – hackers, neo-Nazi propagandists, anarchists – are the ones who tend to benefit most from the First Amendment guarantees in cyberspace" constraints (Fernback, in Jones, 1997: 50–1). When it comes to sexual content, computer media have been protected by the courts.

At the same time as courts have been involved in extensive litigation over broadcast and Internet indecency, the technological revolution that is the worldwide web has produced an entirely new field of study that has implications on our concerns in this book. CMC addresses how media *convergence* – the blending of print and all forms of electronic media – is changing the landscape with respect to the once assumed reality of spectrum scarcity, which is the basis for broadcast regulation. We now live in a world in which anyone with a relatively inexpensive personal computer and access to inexpensive service space and time, has an ability to *podcast* audio and video content. Unlike broadcasting, this new downloadable media world exists in an unregulated and unlicensed environment. Some of it carries an "explicit" label on such services as iTunes.

CMC also helps us understand some of the theoretical and underlying concerns of media messages – identity, interaction, community, power, culture, gender, and other issues. CMC explores media technology influences – creation of interaction, community formation, and identity definition (Barnes, 2003). The Internet has been related to social behavioral change within families (Surratt, 2001). Ferguson and Perse (2000) suggested that the Internet could replace television as a dominant medium. Use of media technologies (Pavlik, 1996) are said to potentially produce gratifications (Lin, 1993).

Online media usage may contribute to development of so-called cybercultures – alternative social realities (Jones, 1997; du Gay, Evans & Redman, 2000; Bell, 2001). In the face of ever increasing pressure to regulate broadcasting, economic pressure to move sexual content to premium pay channels and media consolidation, the Internet became the place to market indecent and even potentially obscene content.

Chapter summary

Theories of the First Amendment have argued that the marketplace of ideas works to advance society. Various models of free expression exist. The use of scrutiny places the government in a position of defending the need for regulation by identifying substantial interests. Further, such a legal framework limits government to narrowly tailored restrictions on speech. The Carlin monologue at issue in the *Pacifica* case exemplifies the point that there is no scientific evidence to support the view that profanity harms children. In an age of computer-mediated communication, the regulation of such broadcast speech is suspect. Broadcast regulation has driven some indecent content to the Internet.

Review questions

1 What do you think are the strengths and weakness of the marketplace of ideas?
2 What are the arguments for and against using strict scrutiny as a legal standard for courts reviewing broadcast indecency cases?
3 Do you believe that the Carlin monologue is appropriate content for the broadcast medium? Why or why not?
4 How might researchers go about studying the effects of indecency on children? What would be the challenges of such research?
5 Should lawmakers, the FCC, and the courts consider social changes in beliefs about sexual content if people do not see harm in it? Why or why not?

4

ADULT ENTERTAINMENT

Adult entertainment in general, and pornography specifically, were the first profitable Internet businesses. However, this is not purely a product of technological change. After all, prostitution has often been described as the "oldest profession." Sexuality, it seems, is of great public interest.

The pornography business

The porn business rests on the social reality that there is a market for explicitly sexual media. The development of photography, motion pictures, and videotape simplified the processes of producing sexually charged materials. In previous generations, the production, distribution, and sale of sexual content was challenging. First, cameras and video cameras began as expensive technologies that took a fair amount of skill to operate. Today, production equipment is inexpensive and relatively easy to use. Second, before the Internet, distribution required creation of a distribution network that evaded local authorities. Third, the sale of porn in pre-Internet years involved the operation of a local business, as well as perhaps the cloaking of the content behind wrappers and set off from more socially acceptable products. The Internet created a global distribution network that offers off-shore and out-of-state businesses the opportunity to skirt obscenity laws.

Box 4.1 *Girls Gone Wild* **video producer guilty of exploiting children**

Joe Francis is a Santa Monica, California, businessman who has made millions since 1998 selling soft-core college campus Spring Break pornography *Girls Gone Wild* videotapes and DVDs (Figure 4.1). In 2006, he pleaded guilty to a federal sexual exploitation of children Section 2257 charge and faced more than two million dollars in fines (Hoffman, 2006a).

Figure 4.1 Girls Gone Wild pornography issue. Source: GirlsGoneWild.com

Francis "failed to keep records of the ages and identities of the women who appeared in his films," according to a US Department of Justice complaint (p. 1). Francis admitted that, "footage of minors engaging in sexually explicit conduct appeared in at least two DVDs he released" (p. 1).

The videos, sold via cable channel advertising during late-night hours, bring in about $40 million per year. Mantra Films Inc. is owned by Francis, 33, who agreed to pay $1.6 million in fines and restitution to settle similar charges in Florida.

The agreements were designed to "ensure that 'Girls Gone Wild' will comply with an important law designed to prevent the sexual exploitation of minors and puts other producers on notice that they must be in compliance as well," Assistant Atty. Gen. Alice S. Fisher said in a statement.

Francis avoided jail time under the plea agreements, in which he admitted that during 2002 and 2003 his companies produced films in violation of record-keeping and labeling federal laws.

"We regret that this occurred and will make sure that no other minors are used in 'Girls Gone Wild' films," Francis told a court.

Francis, who faced a seventy-seven-count indictment in Panama City for sexual activity involving a sixteen-year-old and a seventeen-year-old, avoided the criminal charges because evidence was illegally obtained. However, he and his company continued to face a civil complaint of child abuse and sexual exploitation filed by parents.

Mantra Films also has paid more than one million dollars to the Federal trade Commission over questionable business practices involving the sale of the videos.

Hoffman (2006a)

⊛Department of Justice

FOR IMMEDIATE RELEASE

TUESDAY, SEPTEMBER 12, 2006

WWW.USDOJ.GOV

CRM

(202) 514-2007

TDD (202) 514-1888

"Girls Gone Wild" Pleads Guilty In Sexual Exploitation Case

Companies, Founder to Pay $2.1 Million in Fines and Restitution

WASHINGTON – A California company doing business under the name "Girls Gone Wild" has pleaded guilty to charges that it failed to create and maintain age and identity documents for performers in sexually explicit films that it produced and distributed, and that it failed to label its DVDs and videotapes as required by federal law, Assistant Attorney General Alice S. Fisher of the Criminal Division and US Attorney Gregory R. Miller of the Northern District of Florida announced today.

Santa Monica-based Mantra Films, Inc. entered its plea agreement today before US District Judge Richard Smoak at US District Court in Panama City, FL. A second related company, MRA Holdings, LLC, also entered into a deferred prosecution agreement.

Under the agreements, Joseph Francis, the founder of the two companies, agreed to plead guilty to offenses to be filed later in US District Court in Los Angeles, and the companies and Francis agreed to pay fines and restitution totaling $2.1 million.

The charges in this case are believed to be the first to be filed under a law – often referred to as Section 2257 – passed by Congress to prevent the sexual exploitation of children. The law protects against the use of minors in the production of sexually explicit material by requiring producers to create and maintain age and identity records for every performer in sexually explicit movies and other media. Producers and distributors must also label their products with the name of the custodian of the records and their location.

"This case sends an important message about the Justice Department's commitment to protecting children from all forms of sexual exploitation," said Assistant Attorney General Alice S. Fisher. "Today's agreements ensure that Girls Gone Wild will comply with an important law designed to prevent the sexual exploitation of minors and puts other producers on notice that they must be in compliance as well."

US Attorney Gregory R. Miller noted, "This prosecution makes clear that those who seek to enrich themselves at the expense of our children's innocence in violation of the laws intended to protect them will be held to answer in federal court."

In statements filed in court today, Girls Gone Wild admitted filming performers and producing and distributing sexually explicit video materials during all of 2002 and part of 2003 while violating the record-keeping and labeling laws.

Mantra Films, Inc. pleaded guilty to three counts of failing to keep the required records and seven labeling violations. Each count refers to a different film produced or distributed by Mantra. MRA Holdings, LLC, entered into a deferred prosecution agreement concerning the information filed in court charging the company with ten labeling violations. As part of that agreement, the government will dismiss the charges at the end of a three-year period if MRA Holdings abides by all of its obligations under the agreement. MRA Holdings' obligations include a public acknowledgment of criminal wrongdoing, cooperating with the government in future investigations, fully complying with the record keeping laws, and payment of fines and restitution.

MRA Holdings also agreed that during the three-year deferral period it would employ an independent, outside monitor selected by the government and provide the monitor complete access to the books and records, production facilities, and other locations required to ensure the company's compliance with federal law relating to the production of visual materials under the name Girls Gone Wild, or any other name.

Of the $2.1 million in fines and restitution, $1.6 million is to be paid by Mantra and MRA and $500,000 is to be paid by Francis.

In May 2006, Attorney General Alberto R. Gonzales – pursuant to "Project Safe Childhood" – asked the Federal Bureau of Investigation to begin conducting regular inspections of records kept by producers of sexually explicit materials pursuant to Title 18, United States Code, Section 2257. Producers are required to keep records on performers to include true name and date of birth and produce these records on demand. These regulations and resulting inspections are designed to prevent producers from hiring minors as performers, and carry criminal penalties for violations.

The cases are being prosecuted by Trial Attorney Sheila Phillips of the Obscenity Prosecution Task Force of the Department of Justice, US Attorney Gregory Miller, and Assistant US Attorney Dixie Morrow of the Northern District of Florida. The Justice Department's Obscenity Prosecution Task Force was formed to focus on the prosecution of adult obscenity nationwide. The Task Force is directed by Brent D. Ward.

Investigation of the cases was conducted by the Adult Obscenity Squad of the Federal Bureau of Investigation, which is based in Washington, DC.

Source
http://www.usdoj.gov/opa/pr/2006/September/06_crm_610.html

The production of adult films, which generate billions of dollars in California, is subject to the health issues related to sex, such as HIV–AIDS. Performer employees, or independent contractors, are theoretically protected under federal workplace health and safety laws (Jordan, 2005):

> Production companies hire performers to carry out specific sexual acts on film. The nature of the act itself is determined by the production company, . . . and is performed under the production company's direction . . . Scenes sometimes require several hours to film, and require prolonged sexual contact in order to obtain a well shot scene . . . Production companies have control over the sexual acts shot during film production, leaving the performer without any meaningful discretion in performing his or her duties that would enable a finding of independent contractor status . . . The performers are needed only to act out the specific sexual act, and the maneuvers required are inherent in the sexual act performed . . . Production companies' control over workers' performance in their films indicates that adult film performers are treated as employees as opposed to independent contractors.
>
> (ibid.: 436)

A "2004 HIV outbreak has presented the adult film industry with an unprecedented barrage of questions regarding its employment practices, worker safety, and the potential for state regulation to prevent further STD and HIV transmission" (ibid.: 444).

In the distant corners of the globe, governments and industry groups now grapple with how to apply laws to the distribution of adult media content. For example, in Jakarta, Indonesia, in late 2006, *TEMPO Interactive* reported that all members of the Indonesian Private Television Association challenged Decree No. 32/2002 on Broadcasting as criminal – the Indonesian Broadcasting Commission (KPI) has, to this point, stopped short of criminal sanctions for violations:

"There is no detailed definition of the content of the program to be categorized as a crime," said the association's executive secretary, Gilang Iskandar, when contacted by *Tempo* on Wednesday night (20/12). KPI took the Article 36 as the basis to give the report to the police.

The Article 26, Paragraph 5-2, says that a television station is forbidden to expose elements of violence, indecency, gambling and abuse of narcotics and illegal drugs. However, in what forms a program is regarded to contain those elements is not explained in detail.

(Damayanti, Ninin, 2006, para. 34)

The Indonesian Private Television Association in 2004 agreed to reduce violent and pornographic broadcasts. However, not all stations comply with the industry agreement, and some in the government want to criminalize offenses.

Media law on pornography

Pornography, or "porn," is a socially defined class of sexual communication, which may or may not be protected under national laws, which may or may not clearly define the term. The term may be distinguishable from legal definitions in the US and Europe of obscenity or indecency. Pornography is generally considered the depiction of graphic sexual behavior usually designed to promote sexual arousal. Pornographic material may be either legal erotica or illegal obscenity. Many have questioned the validity of the distinction between erotica and pornography, the latter being a pejorative and subjective term. The legal problem is twofold: (1) What constitutes graphic sexual depiction? (2) How does one judge whether or not the purpose of the sexual content is to arouse?

Child pornography has been the subject of law, as was the case in *New York* v. *Ferber* (1982), in which the US Supreme Court identified a compelling government interest in protecting minors from exploitation. However, in *Ashcroft* v. *Free Speech Coalition* (2002), the Supreme Court struck down unconstitutional regulation of speech in the Child Pornography Protection Act of 1996.

The European Union agreed to an anti-indecency television policy in a 1997 Directive to member states aimed at restricting pornographic programs that "might seriously impair the physical, mental or moral development of minors." Concern had been expressed about distribution of erotic satellite television services, but national laws and norms are varied across nations.

Historical references and international pornography laws

Pornography has been in existence for centuries. Some of the earliest cave paintings, sculpture, and pottery discovered by archeologists contain sexual references. Obviously, humans have been engaged in sexual behavior since the beginning, so a preoccupation with it in communication and the arts should not be surprising. Pornography is considered a general term that is distinct from its legal definitions addressed under a wide range of obscenity laws. "Pornography" is a word first found in the writing of the Greeks in relation to discussion about "porne" or prostitute. The ancient Romans produced erotic floor art and wall paintings, as well as having an interest in sexual and reproductive concerns. In about 1650, some of the first pornography appears to have been published using printing presses. Berl Kutchinski, a Danish criminologist, often is cited as has having identified in the 1970s pornography in translated works that addressed sodomy and other "bawdy" topics. Much debate and discussion on pornography have followed. Italian writer Pietro Aretino has been called the founding father of modern porn based upon a sixteenth-century work called the *School of Whoredom*.

Erotic art of the Antiquity was discovered in the ruins of Pompeii, and pornographic political images exist from France. In England, sex was first a legal issue in 1663 with the conviction in London of Sir Charles Sedley for breach of peace by becoming drunk, removing his clothes, uttering profane remarks, and pouring urine on a crowd below a tavern balcony. This indecency was not blasphemous, as was the case with previous convictions. Common law courts in England did not tend to be faced with pornography cases. Nevertheless, in 1708, James Read was indicted for publishing the book *The Fifteen Plagues of a Maidenhead*. In the dismissal of the indictment, Lord Justice Powell wrote,

> This is for printing bawdy stuff but reflects on no person, and a libel must be against some particular person or persons, or against the Government . . . There is no law to punish it, I wish there were, but we cannot make law; it indeed tends to the corruption of good manners, but that is not sufficient for us to punish.

Still, in 1727 Edmund Curll was convicted for corrupting public morals by publishing *Venus in the Cloister, or the Nun in Her Smock*. A few years later, John Cleland's *Fanny Hill, or Memoirs of a Woman of Pleasure* (1749) was also widely translated, yet later judged to be illegal in the USA. The Bishop of London condemned this comedy about the sexual exploits of a maiden who moves to the city as "an open insult upon religion and good manners." It managed to avoid all profanity in its text, and no legal action in London was taken against it. The actual term "pornography" was first used in England during the 1800s.

Technological development of photography and video expanded the distribution of pornography. Much of what we consider pornography today has its roots in Scandinavia and the USA, where there was a dramatic increase in production in the 1960s and 1970s. Movies such as *Last Tango in Paris* and *Deep Throat* brought pornographic images into the mainstream. In *Menefee* v. *City and County of Denver* (1976), a conviction for possession of the *Deep Throat* film was reversed, and the US federal appellate court found the Colorado statute was unconstitutionally vague. The US Supreme Court, in *Hicks* v. *Miranda* (422 US 322 (1974)) and *Butler* v. *Dexter* (1975), returned to lower courts convictions based upon the film. However, an obscenity conviction based upon possession of *Deep Throat* was upheld in *Young* v. *Abrams* (1983). It and another widely distributed movie, *Debbie Does Dallas*, were found not to be obscene, however, under contemporary community standards of New York (*United States* v. *Various Articles of Obscene Merchandise*, 1983).

During this period, child pornography surfaced from Europe, Africa, and Asia. Japanese pornography, which began to mingle sex with violence, has flourished using a variety of realistic and animated approaches. A 1986 US Attorney General's report on pornography found a link between porn and organized crime.

Twentieth-century magazines and adult books found a global market. When the worldwide web exploded on the scene in the mid-1990s, pornography could be easily distributed internationally and became the first profitable online industry.

In the absence of international pornography laws, national laws prevail that are designed to curb or prohibit the production, distribution, and sale of sexual materials. Current enforcement typically involves attempts to identify sexual predators in the online environment and to prosecute them. For example, the US Department of Justice in 2006 sought a judicial order against the search engine Google to turn over records on millions of users' searches as part a government effort to uphold online pornography law.

Christopher Manion, Obscenity Treaty Project Director of the National Obscenity Law Center, told the World Congress of Families III in 2004 that pornography is a uniquely international problem "thanks to instant digital technologies, it threatens every home, thanks to cable and satellite TV, and the internet." The Morality in Media organization has targeted criminal pornography, as well as softer content. For example, various efforts were launched over the years to clear the airwaves of broadcast indecency.

Pornography is sometimes related to prostitution. Depending upon perspective, legal scholars have treated the sale of sexual conduct as either a modern form of slavery or a legal right of work. An extension of prostitution is the depiction of sexual behavior in multimedia forms. These portrayals may or may not be distributed for sale. Clearly, such behavior raises international human rights issues.

While laws vary widely from nation to nation, a general international agreement exists on the need to prevent child pornography, although the age of sexual consent is also not standardized. End Child Prostitution, Child Pornography and Trafficking of Children for Sexual Purposes (ECPAT) has Special Consultative Status with the Economic and Social Council of the United Nations (ECOSOC) in order to prevent sexual exploitation of children around the globe. ECPAT has found a connection between Internet child pornography and sexual exploitation of minors and has sought national legislation in more than 100 countries. The Computer Crime Research Center has concluded that,

> Challenges to any study of international child pornography include: 1) the lack of any uniform definition of what child pornography entails; 2) lack of data regarding the production and distribution of child pornography in many parts of the world, particularly Africa and Latin America; and 3) shifting global patterns of production and consumption of child pornography.

The Advertisement Law of the People's Republic of China (1995) is one example of how, despite new consumer and market orientations, free expression may be limited in the area of pornography. Unprotected speech includes that which has "information suggesting pornography, superstition, terror, violence or hideousness."

In Japan, soliciting prostitution from a child (under age 18) is punishable under the Law for Punishing Acts Related to Child Prostitution and Child Pornography, and for Protecting Children. Prior to 2005, no law existed to prohibit sex trafficking.

Legal Definitions of Pornography

The typical legal concern involves sexual depictions of people under eighteen years of age, such as the case in the Canadian Penal Code. Nevertheless, this is not universal. This definition, however, is far from being universally adopted. The age of concern drops to 16 under Australian law, and 15 in some US states. However, US federal child pornography statutes that make illegal the creation and distribution of photographs or video limit such sexual behavior between an adult and a teenager. In Europe, "audiovisual material which uses children in a sexual context" is restricted under the Council of Europe definition. The International Criminal Police

Organization (Interpol) definition of child pornography goes beyond visual representation to include a "child's sexual behaviour or genitals." A study of child pornography laws in 184 Interpol member countries around the world in 2006 found that more than half of these countries (95) had no laws addressing child pornography. Interpol found that other countries had inadequate laws.

Obscenity under US law

As explained earlier but worth emphasizing, in the USA, *Miller* v. *California* (1973) utilized a three-part test to judge whether content was obscene and, thus, not protected speech under the First Amendment:

1 whether the average person, applying contemporary community standards, would find that the work, taken as a whole, appeals to prurient interests;
2 whether the work depicts or describes, in a patently offensive way, sexual conduct specifically defined by applicable state law;
3 whether the work, taken as a whole, lacks serious literary, artistic, political, or scientific value.

In the USA, a local jury might be asked to determine whether the pornographic material appeals to prurient interests based upon a judgment of local community standards. State law is applied to the question of patent offensiveness, if obscenity is not protected as a matter of state constitutional law. However, a large loophole is the third prong of the *Miller* test, which allows sexual material to be legal where serious value is found.

Print media: newspapers and magazines

As a general rule, print media have the most freedom to publish sexual material. This is because it is easiest to restrict access to children for example, by zoning adult bookstores and other businesses away from schools and other locations where children may be present.

Print media stake the largest claim to near-absolute First Amendment protection in the United States, as well as to historical common law protection in England and the former colonies.

Print media may be sold in select stores, covered in wrappers, restricted to sections and, thus, are easier controlled. Additionally, society has historically been less concerned with material that requires literacy skills in order to consume. Unlike broadcasting and electronic media, print media are not as widely accessible to minors.

Broadcasting

In the USA, the FCC has restricted indecent speech to a late evening hours "safe harbor" when children are not likely to be present in the audience. Broadcast indecency, which blurs the definition between indecent and obscene, is defined as material involving sexual or excretory activities or organs that panders or titillates without value. This is determined in context, and each situation is unique. Profanity, which generally is considered indecent, may not be so in certain serious contexts. The FCC applies a national contemporary community standard for the broadcast medium.

Cable

Generally, cable systems are either free from indecency regulation or have more freedom than their broadcast brethren. In countries where pornography is outlawed, this generally applies to all media forms. That being said, in the United States there is increasing pressure to regulate cable media because of its explicit sexual content.

One proposal has been to offer consumers à la carte channel choices. Another has been to group channels and create a "family tier" of offerings. Pricing is also an issue. However, cable media providers respond that they face increased competition from satellite competitors. Additionally, without grouping of current basic and advanced cable tiers, less popular cable channels would no longer be subsidized, and high-quality programs might disappear.

Internet law

European nations were some of the first to restrict Internet distribution. For example, Germany prosecuted and sentenced a manager of a subsidiary of CompuServe in 1998 for distribution of newsgroup online pornography. The decision was later reversed when a court found that a subordinate was not in a position to limit illegal content access. Under German law, pornography is grouped with racist, violent, and other speech that is considered harmful.

Sexual media depictions often are unsolicited. Therefore, concerns have been expressed about the proliferation of Internet spam. Unwanted emails often make offers of a sexual or pornographic nature, and attempts to use email filters have been frequently defeated by the marketers of porn.

Future issues

Pornography definitions frequently run into difficulty because the line between porn and art is not clear. Digital artists commonly depict sex, and multimedia materials may blur the age of actors. The use of home computers, digital cameras, and video recording equipment has created a new revolution in the production and distribution of pornography. Inexpensive and readily available equipment allows individuals to create their own erotic or pornographic materials. Enforcement of laws generally halts at one's front door, unless the sexual content involves illegal behavior or distribution.

Zoning and the law

McGinnis (2005: 625) found adult entertainment zoning to be a controversial matter in local politics:

> In recent years, many cities have engaged in well-publicized zoning action to regulate and even to eliminate the presence of adult-entertainment businesses within their borders. . . These efforts are largely a response to the adverse impacts adult businesses have on surrounding communities . . . A 1989 survey of studies done on the topic, for example, showed that the presence of adult-entertainment businesses in a neighborhood leads to decreases in property values, increases in property crimes and sex crimes, and general neighborhood deterioration . . . When several adult businesses are concentrated in a particular area, these effects are often worse.

Nevertheless, the First Amendment must be considered when addressing the legalities of zoning ordinances and their degree of restriction (*Renton* v. *Playtime Theatres, Inc.*, 1986). Zoning may be legal if it both serves a substantial governmental interest and also offers some alternatives for adult content to exist. By regulating the time, place, and manner of business locations, zoning laws are considered content neutral by the courts. This being said, such regulation does affect certain types of speech.

Pay cable channels

The ability to scramble or block premium channels creates the opportunity to offer adult content to paying adults while at the same time preventing viewing by most children. The use of a credit card to pay for such services, or the inclusion on a bill, allows parents wishing to protect minors to do so. Of course, this does not mean that enterprising young people, or those with parents who either are neglectful or see value in exposing children to the adult world, cannot gain access. Technology has not changed the "back-alley" interest by minors in sex.

In a sense, cable offers a zoning solution through the use of blocking technologies. No solution is 100 percent effective. In the end, cable has a distinct advantage in this regard over broadcasting, which goes out through the ether to a general public.

Satellite radio and television

Like cable, satellite offers the ability to screen audience members through a purchasing mechanism. No wonder that Howard Stern's adult-oriented content works so well in this environment – without the controversy attached to general broadcasts.

Still, satellite (like cable) seems to be an intermediate technology. Over time, broadband Internet technologies will become the more efficient way to distribute all forms of content to a wired and wireless audience.

X-rated movies

The rating system for motion pictures, which came in response to political pressures, offers the industry the opportunity to label its most sexually explicit content. While such adult-only films may target an adult audience that wants to see sex shown, the playing of a film in a local movie house requires that boundaries be understood. Any showing is subject to review by local prosecutors, who may bring charges against businesses in violation of local community standards under the *Miller* test.

In the same way, local video stores may have their content confiscated and their owners may be charged under obscenity laws.

Given these concerns and the availability of new media technologies, the tendency is to offer the most extreme content through the mail or Internet – using DVD, streaming, or compressed file formats. The mp4 file type plays video on computers, iPods, and other portable technologies. This makes it increasingly difficult for authorities to regulate the availability of adult content.

Chapter summary

Pornography and adult media content have been issues for hundreds of years. Some explicit content exploits young people. The most effective approaches by government have been to zone the content to places not available to minors. The broadcast indecency "safe harbor" is seen by some commentators as an effective time, place, and manner restriction. In this regard, pay cable services, satellite media, and the Internet offer technological solutions.

Review questions

1 How should the pornography business be regulated in this and other countries? How do local standards affect access to adult content?
2 Is the Girls Gone Wild business exploitive of young people, responding to the marketplace, or both? What should be done about it, if anything?
3 Pornography has apparently been around a long time. Why is there an interest? Can it be restricted?
4 Should obscenity be allowed if it can be strictly restricted from children? Why or why not?
5 Are pay services on cable, satellite media, and the Internet the best possible place for adult content? Do adults have any right to access such content on "free" services, such as broadcasting?

5

THE LEGACY OF *PACIFICA* AND THE *ACTION FOR CHILDREN'S TELEVISION* CASES

More than a quarter of a century has passed since the landmark *Pacifica* (1978) decision, which split the United States Supreme Court. However, the decision stands as the most significant in defining broadcast indecency law in the United States. The case was followed by a series of United States Court of Appeals, District of Columbia decisions that more narrowly addressed enforcement issues. In this chapter, we examine these cases.

A single complaint

One complaint prompted action by the FCC in the *Pacifica* case. A George Carlin monologue, "Filthy Words," from the *Occupation Foole* album, was broadcast on New York radio station WBAI-FM on October 30, 1973. The station responded to FCC inquiries by defending Carlin as a "social satirist" (Figure 5.1). In response, the FCC ordered a file note in its order. Essentially, the licensee was placed on notice and could face action for future complaints.

The FCC found that broadcasting was a unique medium because of traditional scarcity arguments. Not everyone who wants a broadcast license may have one. So, those who do have special responsibilities to serve the "public interest, convenience, and necessity." This presumption has been challenged by economic theorists, who have argued that all goods are scarce resources, including the paper it requires to publish a newspaper.

The FCC action against the 2 p.m. broadcast of the Carlin monologue was seen by the FCC and the Supreme Court not as enforcement of an outright ban, but rather as part of a "channeling" policy to move indecent programs to times of day when children were not likely to be in the audience.

George Carlin remembered the *Pacifica* case in his later comic routines: "The original seven words were, shit, piss, fuck, cunt, cocksucker, motherfucker, and tits. Those are the ones that will curve your spine, grow hair on your hands and (laughter) maybe, even bring us, God help us, peace without honor (laughter) um, and a bourbon. (laughter)."

Figure 5.1 Comic George Carlin had popular albums during the Vietnam War era. Source: www.GeorgeCarlin.com

Figure 5.2 George Carlin: "The original seven words were, shit, piss, fuck, cunt, cocksucker, mother-fucker, and tits. Those are the ones that will curve your spine, grow hair on your hands and (laughter) maybe, even bring us, God help us, peace without honor (laughter) um, and a bourbon. (laughter)."

It was not clear, however, how the channeling approach could be squared with 18 USC §1464, the criminal statute which seemed to ban broadcast indecency. In part, the conceptual tiptoeing emerged because §1464 was not consistent with a separate prohibition against "censorship" of broadcasting found in §326 of the Communications Act of 1934.

A divided US Supreme Court, led by Justice Stevens, in *Pacifica* found: "A requirement that indecent language be avoided will have its primary effect on form, rather than content, of serious communication," and that, "There are few, if any, thoughts that cannot be expressed by the use of less offensive language" (p. 743, fn. 18). A twenty-four-hour ban, as an absolute prohibition, could be reasoned to be "censorship" not narrowly crafted (*United States* v. *O'Brien*, 1968). A governmental restriction should be "no greater than essential" to further a substantial interest.

But a dissenting opinion noted that "taboo surrounding the words" in the Carlin monologue was not universal. Justice Brennan rejected the idea that alternative words are always useful: "it is doubtful that the steril-ized message will convey the emotion that is an essential part of so many communications" (see New Indecency Enforcement Standards, 1987). The Commission broadened its thinking, moving away from the Carlin words to a "generic" approach in the definition of broadcast indecency: "Language or material that depicts or describes, in terms patently offensive as measured by contemporary community standards for the broadcast medium, sexual or excretory activities or organs." The FCC also found reasonable risk that children would be in the audience after 10 p.m., the previously protected time (*Pacifica Foundation*, 1987; *Regents of the University of California*, 1987).

Political implications of an indecency ban

In late 1988, when the FCC shifted under congressional pressure and issued a twenty-four-hour ban on indecent broadcasts, it made it clear that the new §1464 enforcement rule came, "Pursuant to a recent Congressional directive," and that the enforcement was "required by the express language of this new legislation" (FCC 88-416, point 3). It has long been understood that communications policy operates within a political context.

The rule amounted to a reinterpretation of 18 USC §1464, which previously had been applied "to prohibit the broadcast of obscene programming during the entire day and indecent programming only when there was a reasonable risk that children might be in the audience."

FCC order and the Diaz Statement

On December 19, 1988, the FCC adopted an order to enforce 18 USC §1464 "on a 24 hours per day basis." Noting that the agency funding bill (Pub. L. No. 100-459), signed by then President Reagan on October 1, 1988, required the FCC to promulgate such an order, the agency fell into "compliance." An administrative law agency, such as the FCC, derives virtually all of its authority from the power delegated to it by congress. Therefore, the FCC must follow the direction of lawmakers, which also fund its entire operation.

The FCC was forced to ignore the precedent of prior rules that prohibited "obscene" broadcasts but allowed "indecent" material when the risk was minimal that children were in the audience. Commissioner Patricia Diaz Dennis, in a separate statement, raised the critical issue: "I have serious doubts whether our new rule will pass constitutional muster." She noted that the *Pacifica* ruling was narrow, emphasizing the time of day of a broadcast as a variable.

At the same time that the FCC was faced with the continuing precedent of *Pacifica*, it also dealt with the US Court of Appeals for the District of Columbia, which had ruled that the FCC had not justified even a 10 p.m. to 6 a.m. rule for "channeling" indecent speech. How then, Diaz wondered, could "an outright ban" be justified?

Dial-a-porn: Sable Communications

For the first time since the late 1970s, the US Supreme Court found a case that led it to comment further on indecency. However, the Supreme Court used the telephone case to distinguish broadcasting and hold its *Pacifica* ground. In the case of "dial-a-porn" telephone messages, the Supreme Court in 1989 ruled that indecent but not obscene messages are constitutionally protected. In striking down a congressional ban, the Supreme Court refused to define the difference between the two types of speech. Further, it balked at the opportunity to directly use the case as a vehicle to rethink the *Pacifica* ruling. But, at the same time, it constructed language that the lower court could use in order to strike down the 24-hour ban.

In *Sable Communications* v. *FCC* (1989), in an opinion delivered by Justice White, the Supreme Court treated telephone indecency and broadcast indecency as "distinguishable" because of "an emphatically narrow holding" in *Pacifica*: "Pacifica is readily distinguishable from this case, most obviously because it did not involve a total ban on broadcasting indecent material" (p. 116). The FCC rule was not "intended to place an absolute prohibition on the broadcast of this type of language, but rather sought to channel it to times of day when children most likely would not be exposed to it" (p. 127). In *Pacifica*, the issue of a total ban was not before the court. Still, the value of *Sable* was minimal in the distinct case of broadcast indecency because of the *Pacifica* finding that broadcasting has a "uniquely pervasive" ability to "intrude on the privacy of the home without warning as to program content" – content parents might want to keep out of reach of small children: Placing a telephone call is not the same as turning on a radio and being taken by surprise by an indecent message. At every opportunity since *Pacifica*, the US Supreme Court has consistently distinguished broadcasting as a unique medium because of spectrum scarcity.

Unlike an unexpected outburst on a radio broadcast, the message received by one who places a call to a dial-a-porn service is not so invasive or surprising that it prevents an unwilling listener from avoiding exposure to it. While the Supreme Court did not tamper with *Pacifica*, it surely did provide the lower court with a basis to strike down a twenty-four-hour ban by reiterating in the broadcast context that: "the government may not 'reduce the adult population . . . to . . . only what is fit for children'" (p. 127).

The Court, then, took a functional approach rather than a content-based approach by accepting the notion that government is free to regulate to "protect" just children: "For all we know from this record, the FCC's technological approach to restricting dial-a-porn messages to adults who seek them would be extremely effective, and only a few of the most enterprising and disobedient young people will manage to secure access to such messages" (p. 129). That would be acceptable, in the view of the *Sable* court, if it were not for the concurrent effect of limiting access to adults: "It is another case of 'burn[ing] up the house to roast the pig'" (p. 131). In a concurrence, Justice Scalia agreed with the view "that a wholesale prohibition upon adult access to indecent speech cannot be adopted merely because the FCC's alternate proposal would be circumvented by as few children as the evidence suggests" (p. 132). He went further in appearing to question the shaky legal distinction between indecency and obscenity:

> But where a reasonable person draws the line in this balancing process – that is, how few children render the risk unacceptable – depends in part upon what mere "indecency" (as opposed to "obscenity") includes. The more narrow the understanding of what is "obscene," and hence the more pornographic what is embraced within the residual category of "indecency," the more reasonable it becomes to insist upon greater assurance of insulation from minors.
>
> (p. 132)

The theory advanced requires a view of "indecency" as residual or "leftover" speech, protected only because it is not obscene. It is speech that fails to cross a regulatory line. The location is along an indecency–obscenity continuum. Such an approach artfully dodged the *elements* of prohibited speech – what the FCC would later address as context of the communication.

The concurrence in part, dissent in part, of Justice Brennan, joined by Justices Marshall and Stevens, spoke more to the issue of definitional problems. Citing his own words in *Paris Adult Theatre I*, Brennan repeated: "the concept of 'obscenity' cannot be defined with sufficient specificity and clarity to provide fair notice to persons who create and distribute sexually oriented materials, to prevent substantial erosion of protected speech as a by-product of the attempt to suppress unprotected speech, and to avoid very costly institutional harms" (p. 133). Here, the functional concern is with a chilling effect on producers of material irrespective of how specific audience members view it as "indecent" or "obscene." The court, having failed to specify a definition – perhaps because it is so problematic – retreated.

The "marketplace" would seem to dictate that all producers must face the whims of audience taste. Brennan's goal appeared to be to clear the way for the audience to exercise marketplace pressures without government regulation exercising a sifting role beforehand: "Hence, the Government cannot plausibly claim that its legitimate interest in protecting children warrants this draconian restriction on the First Amendment rights of adults who seek to hear the messages that Sable and others provide" (pp. 134–5).

Decision and reasoning

In order to understand the influence of the DC Circuit on broadcast indecency policy, the court's reaction to other political institutions in a series of cases beginning in the late 1980s must be examined.

Act I

The DC Circuit first attempted to sort out the post-*Pacifica* world of broadcast indecency in *Action for Children's Television* v. *FCC (Act I)* (1988). The *Act I* case held that the FCC had changed its enforcement standard in 1987, stating, "[w]e uphold the generic definition the FCC has determined to apply, case-by-case, in judging indecency complaints, but we conclude that the Commission has not adequately justified its new, more restrictive channeling approach, *i.e.*, its curtailment of the hours when non-obscene programs containing indecent speech may be broadcast" (p. 1334).

In an opinion filed by Circuit Judge Ruth Bader Ginsburg, the court seemed to remind the FCC that indecent speech is protected by the First Amendment, and the "avowed objective is not to establish itself as censor but to *assist parents* in controlling the material young children will hear" (p. 1337). Although the DC Circuit appeared constrained by the precedent of *Pacifica* with respect to vagueness challenges to the indecency policy, the court volleyed the issue back to the FCC by holding that there was insufficient evidence to support time channeling to late-night hours as an effective method to protect children. The petitioners in the case had argued that the new standard was "'inherently vague' and was installed without any evidence of a problem justifying a thickened regulatory response" (p. 1338). The court found that, while indecency has First Amendment protection, the FCC may regulate children's access to it. Specifically, the court, citing the *Red Lion* precedent, stated that "[b]roadcasting is a unique medium; it is not possible simply to segregate material inappropriate for children, as one may do, *e.g.* in an adults-only section of a bookstore. Therefore, channeling must be especially sensitive to the First Amendment interests of broadcasters, adults, and parents" (p. 1340).

The DC Circuit utilized the decision as a vehicle to tell the FCC it "would be acting with utmost fidelity to the First Amendment were it to reexamine, and invite comment on, its daytime, as well as evening, channeling prescriptions" (p. 1340). The court instructed the FCC that it needed evidence to support a rule for promoting parental, not government control: "A securely-grounded channeling rule would give effect to the government's interest in promoting parental supervision of children's listening, without intruding excessively upon the licensee's range of discretion or the fare available for mature audiences and even children whose parents do not wish them sheltered from indecent speech" (p. 1344). The *Act I* case, however, settled little and was only the beginning of the DC Circuit's attempt to influence the political process.

Act II

In *Action for Children's Television* v. *FCC (Act II)* (1991), the DC Circuit upheld its *Act I* decision in spite of an FCC twenty-four-hour ban ordered by Congress. The court said it had ordered the FCC to hold hearings and determine when stations could broadcast indecency, but "[b]efore the Commission could carry out this court's mandate, Congress intervened" (p. 1504). Two months after the *Act I* decision, the 1989 funding bill contained a "rider" requiring the FCC to enforce indecency regulation "*on a 24 hour per day basis*" (p. 1509). Faced with new orders, the FCC abandoned plans to follow the *Act I* orders. Then, in 1989, the US Supreme Court in *Sable Communications, Inc.* v. *FCC* rejected a "blanket ban on indecent commercial telephone message services" at the same time as distinguishing dial-a-porn services from broadcasting.

The *Act II* court restated its *Act I* admonishment, declaring "[b]roadcast material that is indecent but not obscene is protected by the first amendment; accordingly, the FCC may regulate such material only with due respect for the high value our Constitution places on freedom and choice in what the people say and hear" (p. 1508). The court additionally stated that "[w]hile 'we do not ignore' Congress' apparent belief that a total ban on broadcast indecency is constitutional, it is ultimately the judiciary's task, particularly in the First Amendment context, to decide whether Congress has violated the Constitution" (p. 1508).

The court rationalized that Congress's action came before the *Act I* decision, "thus, the relevant congressional debate occurred without the benefit of our constitutional holding in the case" (p. 1508). The court argued that the precedent of *Act I* and of *Sable Communications* guaranteed adult access to indecency, and limited regulation to that which would "restrict children's access." The court agreed with one FCC commissioner who had called the mandate unconstitutional. The court stated, "neither the Commission's action prohibiting the broadcast of indecent material, nor the congressional mandate that prompted it, can pass constitutional muster under the law of this circuit" (p. 1509). Then the court spoke directly to the political tangle the FCC found itself in over the blanket ban:

> We appreciate the Commission's constraints in responding to the appropriations rider. It would be unseemly for a regulatory agency to throw down the gauntlet, even a gauntlet grounded on the Constitution, to Congress. But just as the FCC may not ignore the dictates of the legislative branch, neither may the judiciary ignore its independent duty to check the constitutional excesses of Congress. We hold that Congress' action here cannot preclude the Commission from creating a safe harbor exception to its regulation of indecent broadcasts.
>
> (pp. 1509–10)

The court had flexed its political muscle and cloaked it in judicial responsibility. The DC Circuit clarified that, even though it was Congress which had original responsibility for regulating broadcasting as interstate commerce, and had delegated that authority to the FCC, it was the DC Circuit that was charged with protecting the First Amendment of the US Constitution. While the court was by no means staking out absolutist ground, it was bending over backwards to fashion a limited regulatory scheme – one that would still need to be supported by forthcoming data. In the end, the remand of the *Act II* case volleyed the political ball back into the court of the FCC and set the stage for *Act III*.

Act III

A three-judge panel of the DC Circuit once more reviewed broadcast indecency regulation in *Action for Children's Television* v. *FCC (Act III)* (1993). In *Act III*, a group of broadcasters, programmers, listeners, and viewers had challenged a provision in the Public Telecommunications Act of 1992 – the public broadcasting funding bill – which directed the FCC to ban indecent material between 6 a.m. and midnight.

In *Act III*, the court refused to accept the notion that much had changed since its previous decisions, stating, "[w]hile we break some new ground, our decision that the ban violates the First Amendment relies principally upon two prior decisions of this court in which we addressed similar challenges to FCC orders restricting the broadcasting of 'indecent' material, as defined by the FCC" (p. 177). In reviewing the FCC's 1993 implementation order, the DC Circuit agreed that children need to be protected from indecency and that parents might need help from the government in protecting their children from indecent broadcasts. However, the DC Circuit rejected the idea – restated from *Pacifica* – that children *and* adults need to be protected from "indecent material in the privacy of their homes." The court stated, "we accept as compelling the first two interests involving the welfare of children, but in our view, the FCC and Congress have failed to tailor their efforts to advance these interests in a sufficiently narrow way to meet constitutional standards" (p. 171). The DC Circuit then identified its curious political position as a buffer between FCC actions and Supreme Court interpretations: "While *Act I* acknowledges that *Pacifica* 'identified' an interest in 'protecting the adult listener from intrusion, in the form of offensive broadcast materials, into the privacy of the home,' it does not endorse its legitimacy" (p. 175).

The *Act III* court, rather than emphasizing the narrow First Amendment view of *Pacifica*, took a much broader position. The government has no general interest, the court wrote, in protecting *adults* "primarily because the official suppression of constitutionally protected speech runs counter to the fundamental principle of the First Amendment that debate on public issues should be uninhibited, robust, and wide-open" (p. 175). It is significant that the court, on this point, chose to select a print media case to interpret the First Amendment. The suggestion is made in the first three *Act* cases that a narrow regulatory slice has been carved – one that will be justified only when the governmental interest of protecting *children* is supported by hard data. The burden is on the government, and it is substantial. Even if the case can be made, the opinion accepts the notion of parental responsibility:

> Viewers and listeners retain the option of using program guides to select with care the programs they wish to view or hear. Occasional exposure to offensive material in scheduled programming is of roughly the same order that confronts the reader browsing in a bookstore. And as a last resort, unlike residential picketing or public transportation advertising "the radio [and television] can be turned off".
>
> (p. 175)

The DC Circuit struck a solid blow to the foundation of broadcast regulation in its view that broadcast speech has core First Amendment value. In challenging the notion of intrusion of broadcast signals into one's home, the court pointed out that listeners and viewers have controls that can be exercised without turning to the government.

Left with the government interest in protecting children from broadcast indecency, the DC Circuit restrained the FCC by applying a "least restrictive means" test (p. 177). Any ban would have to survive such a test, and, according to the court, "the government did not properly weigh viewers' and listeners' First Amendment rights when balancing the competing interests in determining the widest safe harbor period consistent with the protection of children" (p. 177). While some sort of safe harbor might survive judicial scrutiny, the court wrote: "we are at a loss to detect any reasoned analysis supporting the particular safe harbor mandated by Congress" (p. 178). As a matter of political power, the court of appeals effectively stopped Congress and its administrative agency in their regulatory tracks.

On the issue of parental supervision and the validity of a safe harbor, the court clearly rejected the FCC argument when it wrote: "one could intuitively assume that as the evening hours wear on, parents would be better situated to keep track of their children's viewing and listening habits" (p. 178). The FCC argument is grounded in the notion that parents cannot effectively supervise the television and/or radio habits of their children. The court's response is clear:

> [T]he government has not adduced any evidence suggesting that the effectiveness of parental supervision varies by time of day or

night, or that the particular safe harbor from midnight to 6 a.m. was crafted to assist parents at specific times when they especially require the government's help to supervise their children. The inevitable logic of the government's line of argument is that indecent material can never be broadcast, or, at most, can be broadcast during times when children are surely asleep; it could as well support a limited 3:00 a.m.-to-3:30 a.m. safe harbor as one from midnight to 6 a.m.

(p. 178)

The protection of children argument is further tempered by the conclusion that *Pacifica* addressed only the need to protect children under the age of 12. The FCC, instead, had attempted to treat "teens aged 12–17 to be the relevant age group for channeling purposes" in the *Act* cases" (p. 179). However, the DC Circuit noted: "[w]hen the government affirmatively acts to suppress constitutionally protected material in order to protect teenagers as well as younger children, it must remain sensitive to the expanding First Amendment interests of maturing minors" (p. 180).

Circuit Judge Harry Edwards, in a concurring opinion, toyed with the complicated issue of indecency regulation. Beyond not knowing what effects indecent content might have on which children, Edwards considered what would happen if "most parents would prefer to retain the right to decide" (p. 184). Judge Edwards argued that the government's interest "is tied directly to the magnitude of the harms sought to be prevented" (p. 185). Yet, the FCC failed to show "precisely what those harms are" (p. 185).

In short, the *Act III* opinion might have been a powerful weapon against *any* broadcast indecency regulation – had the panel's 1993 decision not been vacated in 1994. Instead, as we will see, a regulatory position re-emerged.

Interpretations of the opinion

The *Act III* decision raised significant issues about the vague definition for indecency, the appropriate time of day for a safe harbor, and the role of context in case-by-case decision-making. The three cases demonstrated quite clearly that the broadcast indecency issue would not be settled during the 1990s.

The tangled regulatory process of the FCC had indirectly protected the First Amendment rights of free speech for broadcasters. The regulation of broadcast indecency occurs not in local communities of interest, but in our nation's capital. Locked in the political milieu that is Washington, DC, an offending broadcaster may escape consequences for years. Even the large fines of the past few years were limited to a select few broadcasts. The vast majority of programs never face regulatory scrutiny.

We have known for years that large corporate broadcasters can withstand significant fines. When Infinity Broadcasting President and CEO Mel Karmazin agreed in late 1995 to pay $1.7 million to settle Howard Stern's indecency complaints – a move designed to clear the record for a new round of multimillion-dollar transactions – he told *Broadcasting & Cable* magazine: "we want to have a good relationship with the government without in any way, shape or form compromising what we believe to be our First Amendment rights" (September 11, 1995, p. 9).

Political generalizations

The authors of *The Politics of Broadcast Regulation* identified seven generalizations about regulatory policy-making (Krasnow *et al.*, 1982). These may help us to analyze recent developments and make predictions about future action. The case of "shock jock" Howard Stern is a recent example of the process.

1 *Participants seek conflicting goals from the process.* In the case of broadcast indecency regulation, not everybody can be a winner. The protection of children, if possible, would come at the expense of diminishing free speech rights for broadcasters and adult listeners. The various positions ranging from absolute free speech to a total ban suggest the political reality that compromise with the broadcast industry is likely. In 2006, the FCC's omnibus order dealt with a series of cases, as the Commission carefully outlined what was and was not indecent in context.

2 *Participants have limited resources insufficient to continually dominate the policy-making process.* Broadcasters interested in challenging FCC regulatory initiatives must make an economic decision about the value of their actions. Likewise, programmers must weigh their options. The sheer slow pace of regulatory change is in stark contrast to rapid media change. The networks, most recently, determined that it was worth the cost of lawyers to challenge to shifting standards for broadcast indecency.

3 *Participants have unequal strengths in the struggle for control or influence.* The court of appeals, largely because the Supreme Court has avoided further significant review of broadcast indecency, holds the position of "court of last resort." However, the court of appeals' authority ends with the publication of its decisions. During the current decades-long struggle, the FCC has refused the court's suggestion to collect and analyze hard data on damaging effects. Perhaps, had the FCC examined the social research, it would have been forced to make the case that there was no interest in protecting children from indecency, given the lack of evidence on negative effects.

4 *The component subgroups of participant groups do not automatically agree on policy options.* The absolutist First Amendment view of Howard Stern's broadcast group, as well as others representing shock jock deejays, is not shared by all broadcasters. In fact, there have been those who have argued that such blue radio is bad for the long-term health of the industry. Likewise, members of the court of appeals and the FCC have disagreed over the years about free speech rights. The *Pacifica* decision of the Supreme Court is perhaps the best example of division.

5 *The process tends toward policy progression by small or incremental steps rather than massive changes.* In a sense, the dispute over broadcast indecency arose because the FCC attempted something larger than incremental policy change in the late 1980s. The reaction from interest groups was swift. The judicial review slammed the brakes on any attempt at massive change in policy. The most recent cases in the Second Circuit and Third Circuit appeals courts guarantee that the broader issues will not be resolved for years to come.

6 *Legal and ideological symbols play a significant role in the process.* The symbol of children as being defenseless against indecent broadcast is perhaps the most potent one in this process. Freedom and autonomy are also important ideological symbols in the indecency debate. Precedent is perhaps the most significant legal symbol, and it surfaces when a court of appeals expresses being bound by it. Likewise, judicial review is an important legal symbol in the process. The FCC's enforcement functions essentially as a federal district court, so all of its decisions based upon particular sets of facts may be appealed into the federal appellate courts.

7 *The process is usually characterized by mutual accommodation among participants.* Early on, it was difficult to see much mutual accommodation on broadcast indecency. As a highly polarized issue, the middle ground for compromise seemed difficult to discover. As time went on, however, broadcasters sought safer ground by firing announcers, establishing policies, and writing employment contracts that place some responsibility for indecency violations on the people producing content. In a sense, the safe harbor time period is on example of mutual accommodation – broadcasters would rather have some periods when indecency is legal rather than a total ban. For sure, they would appreciate a safe harbor that included more time, especially times when audiences are larger, but some time is better than none. Development of a ratings system, the V-chip, and public information campaigns are all examples of mutual accommodation by both the government and broadcasters in the interest of avoiding government regulation. In this sense, both the FCC and the industry seek to preserve the First Amendment rights of broadcasters while also

appeasing and subduing the mob political pressures to crack down on indecency.

Developments

The FCC's rulings in 2006 and the subsequent appeal by the major networks of indecency fines set the stage for the possibility that the Supreme Court might again be faced with addressing broadcast indecency. By previously distinguishing telephone and Internet pornography, as well as by maintaining the historical division between broadcasting and cable television, the Supreme Court created a temporary legal solution. However, justices also left the door open to the possibility that technological change might breathe new life into broadcasters' long-stated arguments that the scarcity rationale does not justify treating them as second-class citizens with respect to the First Amendment. In one of its omnibus rulings, the FCC acknowledged:

> The Commission has regulated the broadcast of indecent programming for decades, and our authority in this area has long been upheld as constitutional by the US Supreme Court. During the last few years, however, we have witnessed increasing public unease with the nature of broadcast material. In particular, Americans have become more concerned about the content of television programming, with the number of complaints annually received by the Commission rising from fewer than 50 in 2000 to approximately 1.4 million in 2004. At the same time, broadcasters have sought guidance from the Commission about our rules, arguing that they lack certainty regarding the meaning of our indecency and profanity standards. The decisions we issue today respond to both of these concerns.
>
> (In the Matter of Complaints, 2006, March 15, p. 2).

The FCC's position with broadcasters was that it intends to carry out its responsibility to follow the law:

> . . . we apply these indecency and/or profanity standards to the complaints before us on a case-by-case basis. We begin with cases in which we have determined that the broadcast licensee apparently aired indecent and/or profane material and propose forfeitures against the licensee. The monetary forfeitures proposed demonstrate that the Commission will exercise its statutory authority to ensure that the broadcast of indecent and/or profane material will be appropriately sanctioned.
>
> (ibid.: 2–3)

The FCC's collective set of decisions, which included the Super Bowl case, were said to "enable broadcasters to better understand the boundaries of our indecency and profanity standards, while at the same time responding to the concerns expressed by hundreds of thousands of citizens in complaints filed with the Commission" (p. 3).

Political implications

Without significant action from the United States Supreme Court on broadcast indecency policy, it appears mired in posturing by interest groups, the FCC and the industry. Broadcast indecency regulation continues to be a popular target for conservative lawmakers who wish to demonstrate their support for "family values." Rarely have politicians contested this approach by articulating the nation's core belief in free expression.

The FCC is faced with a political decision. It must preserve its interests by following the statute law and congressional direction. While 2007 brought a shift in power from Republicans to Democrats, and this meant a change of all committee chairs, the law of indecency remains on the books. As the FCC reiterated in its omnibus order:

> Section 1464 of title 18, United States Code, prohibits the broadcast of obscene, indecent, or profane programming . . . The FCC rules implementing that statute, a subsequent statute establishing a "safe harbor" during certain hours, and the Communications Act of 1934, as amended (the "Act"), prohibit radio and television stations from broadcasting obscene material at any time and indecent material between 6 a.m. and 10 p.m . . . Broadcasters also may not air profane material during this time period.
>
> (p. 3)

At the same time, however, the FCC seeks to employ a balancing approach between the authority it has maintained via a string of Supreme Court decisions to regulate the unique media of broadcasting – *NBC, Red Lion* and *Pacifica* – and the statutory language that both empowers the commission, but also restrains it from censorship powers:

> Enforcement of the provisions restricting the broadcast of indecent, obscene, or profane material is an important component of the Commission's overall responsibility over broadcast radio and television operations. At the same time, however, the Commission must be mindful of the First Amendment to the United States Constitution and section 326 of the Act, which prohibit the Commission from censoring program material or interfering with

broadcasters' free speech rights. . . As such, in making indecency determinations, the Commission proceeds cautiously and with appropriate restraint.

(p. 4)

Despite the FCC's failure in the past to clarify for broadcasters how it judges specific content to be indecent or not, the Commission again relied upon the notion of "full context" as the crucial variable:

In our assessment of whether broadcast material is patently offensive, "the *full context* in which the material appeared is critically important.". . . Three principal factors are significant to this contextual analysis: (1) the explicitness or graphic nature of the description; (2) whether the material dwells on or repeats at length descriptions of sexual or excretory organs or activities; and (3) whether the material panders to, titillates, or shocks the audience . . . In examining these three factors, we must weigh and balance them on a case-by-case basis to determine whether the broadcast material is patently offensive because "[e]ach indecency case presents its own particular mix of these, and possibly, other factors.". . . In particular cases, one or two of the factors may outweigh the others, either rendering the broadcast material patently offensive and consequently indecent, . . . or, alternatively, removing the broadcast material from the realm of indecency.

(p. 5)

While the FCC continues to attempt to make objective these contextual factors, its own language defines an inherently subjective determination. The first judgment of whether or not content "describes or depicts sexual or excretory activities or organs" is somewhat problematic in that sex and excretion are indecent only in specific contexts. Nevertheless, an objective decision about the presence or absence of one or both of these elements is clearly possible. It is, however, the second prong of the FCC analysis that is entirely subjective. For the FCC must "determine whether, taken in context, the material is patently offensive as measured by contemporary community standards for the broadcast medium." Context requires a summative judgment about a broad set of facts that are *taken out of the context of a local community and its social and cultural meanings*. Patent offensiveness is judged, in the end, by five FCC commissioners who may or may not share our personal, moral, and social values. Finally, the attempt to establish a national contemporary community standards test is a bastardization of the local community standards test derived from *Miller*. Local prosecutors making an obscenity case before a local jury may reasonably ask them to judge the community standards of Wichita, Reno, or Pensacola. The same cannot be said for the FCC concluding that the *entire* country would find an agreed-upon standard that Janet Jackson's momentary breast flash was indecent in the context of the halftime show.

The FCC slips even further when it comes to profanity by concluding that "fuck" is always indecent and other words are judged in context:

> In the *Golden Globe Awards Order*, we concluded that the "F-Word" constituted "profane language" within the meaning of 18 USC §1464 because, in context, it involved vulgar and coarse language "so grossly offensive to members of the public who actually hear it as to amount to a nuisance.". . . We indicated in that decision that we would analyze other potentially profane words on a case-by-case basis.
>
> (p. 6)

Likewise, *The Oprah Winfrey Show* and its "discussion of teenage sexual practices" on March 18, 2004, which "included an examination by the host and her guests and audience of serious parental/supervisory issues" in context was found to be acceptable by the FCC:

Winfrey:	Yeah. So you say – let's talk about that secret language, Michelle.
Ms Burford:	Yes.
Winfrey:	I didn't know any of this.
Ms Burford:	I have – yeah, I have – I've gotten a whole new vocabulary, let me tell you.
Winfrey:	I did not know any of this. Does this – does this mean I am no longer hip?
Ms Burford:	Salad-tossing. I'm thinking cucumbers, lettuce, tomatoes. OK? I am definitely not hip.
Winfrey:	OK – so – OK, so what is a salad toss?
Ms Burford:	OK, a tossed salad is – get ready; hold on to your underwear for this one – oral anal sex. So oral sex to the anus is what tossed salad is. Hi, Mom. OK. A rainbow party is an oral sex party. It's a gathering where oral sex is performed. And a – rainbow comes from – all of the girls put on lipstick and each one puts her mouth around the penis of the gentleman or gentlemen who are there to receive favors and makes a mark in a different place on the penis, hence the term rainbow. So . . .
Winfrey:	OK. And so what does pre – so what does pretty boy mean? A pretty boy.
Ms Burford:	Pretty boy is a sexually active boy, someone who's been fairly promiscuous. So it isn't maybe what you would

	have thought pretty boy meant in your time.
Winfrey:	And dirty means what? Does dirty mean . . .
Ms Burford:	Dirty means a diseased – means a diseased girl. And along with that the term that some teens are using to mean HIV is High Five, 'high' and then the Roman numeral 'V.' High Five. So if you got High-Fived by Jack, you got diseased by Jack. You got – you got HIV.
Winfrey:	It means he gave you HIV.
Ms Burford:	He gave you HIV. Yeah.
Winfrey:	Yeah. OK. And boo – booty call is pretty common, right?
Ms Burford:	Yeah, that's – yeah, that's pretty pervasive. Yeah, that's an early morning or late-at-night call for sex that involves no real relationship. Maybe 2 a.m., guy calls girl, and says, "Meet me at so and so location, we have sex, we leave," booty call. You all got that?

(pp. 43–4)

The FCC found that the broadcast clearly was sexual and turned to its indecency analysis. While the discussion was "highly graphic" and it was extended in an entire segment titled "The Secret Language of Teens," the FCC concluded: "Given this particular context, though, our findings with regard to the first two factors of our analysis are outweighed by our conclusion under the third factor of our contextual analysis that the complained-of material, in context, is not pandering and is not used to titillate or shock" (p. 44):

> The program segment focuses on the "secret lives" of many teenagers. Through guests – parents, teenagers, and others – serious discussions take place about the disturbing, secret teenage behavior portrayed in the movie *Thirteen*. Guests speak of serious, potentially harmful behaviors of teens – such as drug use, drinking, self-mutilation, and sexual activity – how teenagers hide those behaviors from their parents, and how parents might recognize and address those behaviors with their teens. The material is not presented in a vulgar manner and is not used to pander to or titillate the audience. Rather, it is designed to inform viewers about an important topic. To the extent that the material is shocking, it is due to the existence of such practices among teenagers rather than the vulgarity or explicitness of the sexual depictions or descriptions. It would have been difficult to educate parents regarding teenagers' sexual activities without at least briefly describing those activities and alerting parents to the little-known terms (*i.e.,* "salad tossing," "rainbow party") that many teenagers use to refer

to them . . . For many of the same reasons, we have previously denied complaints about similar educational broadcasts.

(p. 44)

Thus, the FCC concluded that, "the manner and purpose of a presentation may well preclude an indecency determination even though other factors, such as explicitness, might weigh in favor of an indecency finding" (p. 45). Still the summary judgment on patent offensiveness rests on the mythical national standard.

Politics of broadcast regulation

The generalizations made in *The Politics of Broadcast Regulation* (Krasnow *et al.,* 1982) seem to apply well to the case of broadcast indecency policy-making in the 1990s. Still, one can argue that a systems model approach for understanding the process favors description over prediction. What is needed is more comprehensive theory-building in the area of normative media concerns. Any political model would need to build upon social theory which would help predict how regulation functions on an economic landscape.

Future research on broadcast indecency regulations should recognize previous generalizations and begin to link them to larger social theories of mass communication. Missing from most previous analyses is a grounding in social theory. The emphasis has been on summarizing and describing court decisions. These legal analyses fall short of providing an understanding of the law in a social context. Legal commentators would do well to look to law reviews and scholarly communication journals for analyses that link broadcast indecency regulation to what we know about governmental and social control of communication messages.

If reason is to be brought to bear on broadcast indecency policy, then "deregulation" must be distinguished from "policy-making" through a clear set of goals.

The future of deregulation and policy-making should be grounded in historical First Amendment free speech principles and theoretic predictions about the limitation of content regulation in a free society.

Chapter summary

The Carlin monologue and the *Pacifica* decision defined more than thirty years of broadcast regulation in the area of indecency. Three appellate court decisions in the late 1980s and early 1990s clarified but failed to resolve the fundamental issues. A singularly significant concern is the lack of establishment of a clear definition for indecency. Even if such rules could be adequately developed, the lack of evidence about negative effects undermines the need for a regulatory scheme designed to protect children. Broadcast indecency remains an excellent example of slow, political and incremental policy-making.

Review questions

1 What circumstances, if any, could you imagine to justify the criminalization of broadcast indecency?
2 Why shouldn't broadcasters always use "alternative words" in order to avoid a broadcast indecency case?
3 How might you argue that the imposition of a safe harbor missed the chance the FCC had to successfully defend a total ban on broadcast indecency? Had the FCC persisted with the total ban approach, what might have happened?
4 What are the conflicting goals that participants in the broadcast indecency policy-making system? Who participates?
5 In seeking to protect the First Amendment, what policy-making goals should be set for broadcast indecency by the FCC?

6

CABLE TELEVISION, NEW
TECHNOLOGIES, AND NEW
DEFINITIONS

New technologies have historically posed a challenge to the broadcast indecency regulation argument. As cable diffused into the national marketplace during the late 1970s and 1980s, the expansion in the number of channels offered diversity of media content and even public access channels for those wanting a media voice. Cable channels were not regulated in the same manner as broadcast channels, and this eventually led to a fundamental problem: indecency that would not be allowed by the FCC over the broadcast airwaves was acceptable on cable channels. Eventually, by the late 1990s, programs such as Howard Stern's edited television version of his radio show could be seen. Over time, viewers made less and less distinction between the broadcast channels and cable channels positioned on their local system. Additional new technologies, such as satellite broadcasting and Internet broadcasting, neither of which restricted indecency, raised additional questions about the need to treat terrestrial broadcasters differently.

First Amendment rights

Communication law and regulation are experiencing an ongoing revolution because of social challenges unleashed by a wide array of new technologies. As new media allow individuals to take on the role of publishers (such as through the use of weblogs and podcasts), there are new freedoms and responsibilities. On a broader scale, web sites offer a vast array of content. New media borrow in remediation from "old" media (Bolter & Grusin, 1999: 5), yet it is also argued that "we are dealing with a unique form of communication" in the online world (Pryor, 2003: 57). The diffusion of new technologies often involves the adoption of new ideas: "The newness means that some degree of uncertainty is involved in diffusion" (Rogers, 1995: 6). The diffusion of the worldwide web has been explosive since its introduction to the general public around 1994. By 2006, more than 77 percent or 172 million American adults were using the web – an increase of about 5 percent per year since 2002 (The Harris Poll, 2006). Neilsen/NetRatings estimated that there were more than 200 million users in the

United States. About 135 million of those were said to be active users, and there may be as many as 1 billion online across the world. As the number of users continues to rise, the convergence of printed text, photographs, audio and video presents challenges across the legal spectrum, from libel and privacy to obscenity and copyright issues.

Digital technology also unleashed stiff competition between potential providers of video services, and some of the regulatory battles were about which companies and media technologies would survive and prosper. Telecommunication deregulation allowed, for example, telephone companies to provide video services and cable companies to offer telephone services. This form of cross-media competition came at a time of mergers and corporate consolidation. "Telecommunications cartels" like Time Warner threatened to monopolize mass media, including the Internet: "Advertising and other corporate promotion on the Internet seem to grow exponentially, with 'the system' becoming more fully embedded in the cyber world each day" (Bagdikian, 2000: x).

On Capitol Hill, lawmakers in 2007 introduced legislation to guarantee net neutrality, which sought to limit Internet pricing tied to connection speeds and perhaps introduce further inequality among content providers on the web. High-speed Internet providers have the ability to strike deals with favored clients and position them to get more visitors to their sites, but this comes at a price. Cable and telephone Internet service providers (ISPs) offered to charge Google and Yahoo to send and receive data faster in a highly competitive environment. Regulators and courts have been asked to decide what constitutes fair competition.

The First Amendment and cyberspace

New communication technologies are explicit in understanding the First Amendment today, but lawmakers, regulators and the courts frequently address technology issues. Congress, the FCC, the Federal Trade Commission (FTC), other regulatory bodies applying administrative law, and the courts must choose either to:

1 regulate an emerging technology before it is well understood or widely used;
2 regulate during the uncertain developmental and evolutionary period;
3 attempt to formulate logical and consistent regulatory models after the new technology is in general use; or
4 avoid regulation altogether.

Specific cases rest on the constitutional standards of regulation, and frequently are debated by jurists and legal scholars. The developmental history of a new technology may affect the willingness of the courts to apply the First Amendment.

One example of confusing regulation is the FTC implementation of the Children's Online Privacy Protection Act, known as "COPPA," originally part of congressional attempts to protect children in cyberspace (Federal Trade Commission, 1999). Under this regulation web sites were required to post privacy policies, provide notice and obtain parental consent prior to collecting certain personal information from children. Internet operators could submit self-regulatory plans for dealing with children under the age of 13, and many web sites responded by simply restricting access. The FTC sought to protect identifiable information – names, addresses, email addresses, and telephone numbers. This led to about 147 individuals and corporations filing comments in opposition to the rules. Retailer Amazon. com complained that the rule was "likely to interfere with the overall customer experience and inherent benefits of the Internet" (COPPA, 1999). The FTC, nevertheless, continued to seek expansion of Internet consumer privacy responsibilities for regulation. The rapidly changing technological and legal landscape remained complex for those wishing to make sense out of the ever-changing rules.

Non-broadcast video options

Cable systems provide service to most non-broadcast video consumers, and cable is the way that most people view broadcast signals in the United States. Congress has been much more concerned with rising cable rates and lack of competition in the cable industry than they have about indecent content. In *US* v. *Playboy Entertainment* the Supreme Court tackled the issue of scrambled cable signals. Under the method of cloaking premium pay channels, viewers were left with squiggly lines that sometimes offered a glimpse of the video or portions of the audio. Congress enacted §505 of the Telecommunications Act of 1996 (47 USCS 561), and it required cable television operators to block sexually oriented channels by:

1 fully scrambling or blocking the channels; or
2 using "time channeling" to restrict programming to hours when children were unlikely to be in the audience, similar to the broadcast safe harbor approach.

Most cable operators responded by channeling the programs to late evening hours. A federal lawsuit claimed that the regulation violated the First Amendment and asked for an injunction against §505. At issue was whether or not nonobscene programming could be restricted on cable television, as it had in the broadcast context. A three-judge panel initially sided with the government in favor of the restriction. Later, however, the full District Court in Delaware found §505 to be a content-based restriction and suggested that a separate rule, §504, was less restrictive by allowing consumers to request that a channel be blocked from their home. The Supreme Court upheld the decision because the majority found that §505 violated the First Amendment free speech guarantee by being a content-based regulation. The rule singled out specific programmers, restricted access by adults and was not the least restrictive approach to address the problem.

While the Supreme Court recognized that many people would find the sexual programming offensive, it held that:

> The effect of the federal statute on the protected speech is now apparent. It is evident that the only reasonable way for a substantial number of cable operators to comply with the letter of §505 is to time channel, which silences the protected speech for two-thirds of the day in every home in a cable service area, regardless of the presence or likely presence of children or of the wishes of the viewers. According to the District Court, "30 to 50 percent of all adult programming is viewed by households prior to 10 p.m.," when the safe-harbor period begins . . . To prohibit this much speech is a significant restriction of communication between speakers and willing adult listeners, communication which enjoys First Amendment protection. It is of no moment that the statute does not impose a complete prohibition. The distinction between laws burdening and laws banning speech is but a matter of degree. The Government's content-based burdens must satisfy the same rigorous scrutiny as its content-based ban.
>
> (p. 812)

Thus, Justice Anthony Kennedy and the majority thoroughly distinguished the First Amendment issues they found in this cable case from those found in broadcasting under *Pacifica*. As such, the Supreme Court employed a strict scrutiny analysis and treated cable as it did dial-a-porn in the *Sable* case and the Internet in the *Reno* case about indecency:

> Since §505 is a content-based speech restriction, it can stand only if it satisfies strict scrutiny . . . If a statute regulates speech based on its content, it must be narrowly tailored to promote a compelling Government interest . . . If a less restrictive alternative would serve the Government's purpose, the legislature must use that alternative . . . ("[The CDA's Internet indecency provisions'] burden on adult speech is unacceptable if less restrictive alternatives would be at least as effective in achieving the legitimate purpose that the statute was enacted to serve"). ("The Government may . . . regulate the content of constitutionally protected speech in order to promote a compelling interest if it chooses the least restrictive

means to further the articulated interest"). To do otherwise would be to restrict speech without an adequate justification, a course the First Amendment does not permit.

(p. 813)

Still, the Court left open the right to restrict content in both broadcasting and cable because of their unique abilities to reach large audienes. So, the argument was nuanced to avoid striking down the precedent of the *Pacifica* decision:

> Where the designed benefit of a content-based speech restriction is to shield the sensibilities of listeners, the general rule is that the right of expression prevails, even where no less restrictive alternative exists. We are expected to protect our own sensibilities "simply by averting [our] eyes". . . Here, of course, we consider images transmitted to some homes where they are not wanted and where parents often are not present to give immediate guidance. Cable television, like broadcast media, presents unique problems, which inform our assessment of the interests at stake, and which may justify restrictions that would be unacceptable in other contexts. . . No one suggests the Government must be indifferent to unwanted, indecent speech that comes into the home without parental consent. The speech here, all agree, is protected speech; and the question is what standard the Government must meet in order to restrict it. As we consider a content-based regulation, the answer should be clear: The standard is strict scrutiny. This case involves speech alone; and even where speech is indecent and enters the home, the objective of shielding children does not suffice to support a blanket ban if the protection can be accomplished by a less restrictive alternative.

(pp. 813–14)

More directly, Justice Kennedy wrote that cable had more freedom than broadcasting because of the technological differences:

> There is, moreover, a key difference between cable television and the broadcasting media, which is the point on which this case turns: Cable systems have the capacity to block unwanted channels on a household-by-household basis. The option to block reduces the likelihood, so concerning to the Court in *Pacifica* . . . that traditional First Amendment scrutiny would deprive the Government of all authority to address this sort of problem. The corollary, of course, is that targeted blocking enables the Government to support parental authority without affecting the First Amendment interests of speakers and willing listeners – listeners for whom,

99

if the speech is unpopular or indecent, the privacy of their own homes may be the optimal place of receipt. Simply put, targeted blocking is less restrictive than banning, and the Government cannot ban speech if targeted blocking is a feasible and effective means of furthering its compelling interests. This is not to say that the absence of an effective blocking mechanism will in all cases suffice to support a law restricting the speech in question; but if a less restrictive means is available for the Government to achieve its goals, the Government must use it.

(p. 815)

The long-term significance of this approach is clear. Once broadcast radio and television convert from analog to digital, the ability to employ blocking will open the door to a possible end to the legal distinction that currently supports broadcast indecency regulation. For when it comes to content restrictions, the First Amendment requires consideration of all alternatives:

> In addition, market-based solutions such as programmable televisions, VCRs, and mapping systems (which display a blue screen when tuned to a scrambled signal) may eliminate signal bleed at the consumer end of the cable . . . Playboy made the point at trial that the Government's estimate failed to account for these factors . . . Without some sort of field survey, it is impossible to know how widespread the problem in fact is, and the only indicator in the record is a handful of complaints . . . If the number of children transfixed by even flickering pornographic television images in fact reached into the millions we, like the District Court, would have expected to be directed to more than a handful of complaints.

(p. 821)

Box 6.1 Appendix to the opinion of the court

Sections 505 and 640 of the Telecommunications Act of 1996, Pub. L. 104, 110 Stat. 136, 47 USC §561 (1994 ed., Supp. III), provides in relevant part:

Section 505. Scrambling of sexually explicit adult video service programming

(a) Requirement
In providing sexually explicit adult programming or other programming that is indecent on any channel of its service primarily dedicated to

sexually-oriented programming, a multichannel video programming distributor shall fully scramble or otherwise fully block the video and audio portion of such channel so that one not a subscriber to such channel or programming does not receive it.

(b) Implementation
Until a multichannel video programming distributor complies with the requirement set forth in subsection (a) of this section, the distributor shall limit the access of children to the programming referred to in that subsection by not providing such programming during the hours of the day (as determined by the Commission) when a significant number of children are likely to view it.

(c) "Scramble" defined
As used in this section, the term "scramble" means to rearrange the content of the signal of the programming so that the programming cannot be viewed or heard in an understandable manner.

Section 504 of the Telecommunications Act of 1996, Pub. L. 104, 110 Stat. 136, 47 USC §560 (1994 ed., Supp. III), provides in relevant part:

Section 640. Scrambling of cable channels for nonsubscribers

(a) Subscriber request
"Upon request by a cable service subscriber, a cable operator shall, without charge, fully scramble or otherwise fully block the audio and video programming of each channel carrying such programming so that one not a subscriber does not receive it."

(b) "Scramble" defined
As used in this section, the term "scramble" means to rearrange the content of the signal of the programming so that the programming cannot be viewed or heard in an understandable manner.

In a brief separate opinion by Justice John Paul Stevens, an implicit marketplace of ideas orientation emerged:

> The First Amendment assumes that, as a general matter, "information is not in itself harmful, that people will perceive their own best interests if only they are well enough informed, and that the best means to that end is to open the channels of communication rather than to close them". . . The very fact that the programs marketed by Playboy are offensive to many viewers provides a justification for protecting, not penalizing, truthful statements about their content.

(p. 821)

Justice Clarence Thomas, who also agreed with the opinion, observed that an alternative approach for those concerned about the Playboy content would be to treat it as obscenity and prosecute offenders under the *Miller* standard:

> It would seem to me that, with respect to at least some of the cable programming affected by §505 of the Telecommunications Act of 1996, the Government has ample constitutional and statutory authority to prohibit its broadcast entirely. A governmental restriction on the distribution of obscene materials receives no First Amendment scrutiny . . . Though perhaps not all of the programming at issue in the case is obscene as this Court defined the term in *Miller* . . . one could fairly conclude that, under the standards applicable in many communities, some of the programming meets the *Miller* test. If this is so, the Government is empowered by statute to sanction these broadcasts with criminal penalties . . . obscene or otherwise unprotected by the Constitution of the United States shall be fined under title 18 or imprisoned not more than 2 years, or both).
>
> (pp. 829–30)

Further, Justice Antonin Scalia dissented on the view that the sexual content offered in cable channels should enjoy First Amendment protection:

> We have recognized that commercial entities which engage in "the sordid business of pandering" by "deliberately emphasizing the sexually provocative aspects of [their nonobscene products], in order to catch the salaciously disposed," engage in constitutionally unprotected behavior . . . ("In my opinion, the use to which various materials are put – not just the words and pictures themselves – must be considered in determining whether or not the materials are obscene"). This is so whether or not the products in which the business traffics independently meet the high hurdle we have established for delineating the obscene, viz., that they contain no "serious literary, artistic, political, or scientific value". . . . We are more permissive of government regulation in these circumstances because it is clear from the context in which exchanges between such businesses and their customers occur that neither the merchant nor the buyer is interested in the work's literary, artistic, political, or scientific value. "The deliberate representation of petitioner's publications as erotically arousing . . . stimulates the reader to accept them as prurient; he looks for titillation, not for saving intellectual content". . . . Thus, a business that "(1) offers . . . hardcore sexual material, (2) as a constant and intentional

objective of [its] business, [and] (3) seeks to promote it as such" finds no sanctuary in the First Amendment.

(pp. 831–2)

Justice Stephen Breyer also wrote a dissenting opinion, finding that: "the statutory scheme reflects more than a congressional effort to control incomplete scrambling" (p. 836). Justice Breyer found that the majority missed the point that the channels in question were entirely programming sexual content, as well as the fact that the Congress was attempting a careful approach:

> The majority, in describing First Amendment jurisprudence, scarcely mentions the words "at least as effective" – a rather surprising omission since they happen to be what this case is all about. But the majority does refer to *Reno*'s understanding of less restrictive alternatives.. and it addresses the Government's effectiveness arguments . . . I therefore assume it continues to recognize their role as part of the test that it enunciates.

(p. 841)

His major disagreement was the opinion that allowing parents to request channel blocking would not be as effective as the requirements rejected by the Court:

> Unlike the majority, I believe the record makes clear that §504's opt-out is not a similarly effective alternative. Section 504 (opt-out) and §505 (opt-in) work differently in order to achieve very different legislative objectives. Section 504 . . . gives parents the power to tell cable operators to keep any channel out of their home. Section 505 does more. Unless parents explicitly consent, it inhibits the transmission of adult cable channels to children whose parents may be unaware of what they are watching, whose parents cannot easily supervise television viewing habits, whose parents do not know of their §504 "opt-out" rights, or whose parents are simply unavailable at critical times. In this respect, §505 serves the same interests as the laws that deny children access to adult cabarets or X-rated movies . . . These laws, and §505, all act in the absence of direct parental supervision.

(pp. 841–2)

Justice Breyer concluded that adults have rights to communicate, and the rules were a legal exercise of legislative powers. "It must be kept narrow lest the Government improperly interfere with the communication choices that adults have freely made," Justice Breyer wrote in rejecting the idea that

103

such speech could be regulated through obscenity law. "To rely primarily upon law that bans speech for adults is to overlook the special need to protect children" (p. 847).

Satellite issues

In 1934, when Congress passed the Communications Act, it did not envision satellites circling the earth and remaining in a fixed position relative to cities below. The Communications Act did not mention direct broadcast satellites (DBSs). The FCC licenses DBSs. The FCC uses flexible regulations. The FCC uses the term "direct-to-home" to address satellite issues.

Satellite operators operate under standards adopted by the International Telecommunications Union, the worldwide body overseeing spectrum use. US satellite operators need not strictly comply with ITU rules, but ultimately the ITU must approve the deviations from its standards, or the operators must come into compliance.

The 1992 Cable Act required the FCC to establish certain public interest obligations of satellite operators, such as rules regarding political communication, retransmission consent (but not the must-carry rules), and equal employment opportunities. In 1998, the FCC adopted rules requiring DBS providers to set aside 4 percent of their channel capacity for noncommercial educational or informational programming, as required by the public interest section of the law.

Digital television

"Digital television" (DTV) is rapidly replacing the 1941 transmission standard called "NTSC." DTV improves picture and sound quality, and it also opens the possibility of more sophisticated program blocking and filtering mechanisms by converting television to computer processes. Additionally, there has been some pressure on the FCC to impose certain public interest obligations on broadcasters in return for the new digital channels. During the 1990s, the government considered what those should be, with suggestions ranging from free air time for political candidates to not carrying hard liquor advertisements. The digital television revolution is likely to unleash a wide range of interactive, computer-like services that interface with television programming.

The Internet

The Internet is a part of the convergence of telephone, television, and computers, providing an extensive, international broadband network. Some analysts predict that a single broadband network could replace television, radio, telephones, mail, newspapers, and other forms of communication. The Internet presents legal problems and solutions in the area of indecency.

A portion of the Telecommunications Act of 1996, called the Communications Decency Act (CDA), made it illegal to knowingly send or make available to minors any indecent or obscene material. The CDA was one of four unsuccessful US government attempts (under two presidents and three sessions of Congress) to restrict or filter access by children to pornography, particularly on the Internet. The CDA of 1996, the Child Pornography Prevention Act of 1996 (CPPA), and the Child Online Protection Act of 1998 (COPA) have all failed various legal challenges. In 2003, however, the Supreme Court reversed a lower court and upheld the Children's Internet Protection Act of 2000 (CIPA).

In 1997, the Supreme Court found part of the CDA's indecency provisions unconstitutional. In *Reno* v. *ACLU,* the Supreme Court acknowledged Congress's concern with preventing children from being the targets of, or having access to, sexually explicit communications. However, it said that the CDA's ban on indecency was both vague and overbroad. The law did not define indecency in a way that conformed to previous Supreme Court decisions.

The Supreme Court distinguished between the Internet and broadcasting. The Internet does not use the limited public spectrum, and people are not as likely to be exposed inadvertently to sexually explicit material on the Internet as they might be on broadcast stations. Accordingly, adult Internet users should not suffer the reduced First Amendment protections that apply to radio and television station operators, the Supreme Court reasoned. However, the Supreme Court concluded that obscene material may be banned from the Internet because the First Amendment does not protect any obscene messages, regardless of medium. Most importantly, it treated web site operators as publishers: "Publishers may either make their material available to the entire pool of Internet users, or confine access to a selected group, such as those willing to pay for the privilege" (p. 853). The Supreme Court has consistently called for narrowly tailored restrictions on Internet speech and application of traditional obscenity law. From a legal perspective, the Internet was viewed as similar to print media with respect to the First Amendment.

The *Reno* decision reflected the Court's 1989 position in *Sable Communications* v. *FCC,* when it said that Congress may prohibit obscene telephone communications but may not impose a complete ban on indecent "dial-a-porn" messages available via telephone for a fee. Although the Supreme Court had ruled in 1978 in *FCC* v. *Pacifica Foundation* that the FCC could constitutionally restrict indecency on broadcast stations, it found in *Sable Communications* that telephones are markedly different from broadcasting. Broadcasting is ubiquitous, uniquely powerful and easily available to children, the Supreme Court held. In contrast, a person must consciously and actively choose to access a dial-a-porn telephone service providing indecent material. Likewise, people pay to subscribe to gain access to the Internet, and filtering software is available to assist parents in protecting their children from offensive messages. And pornography sites are often supported by additional user subscription fees. Congress later adopted a law requiring dial-a-porn businesses to make their services available only through a pre-subscription arrangement, credit card payment or other method that would make it difficult for children to gain access to the indecent messages. Attempts to enact similar restrictions for the Internet have been more problematic.

While courts use the *Miller* v. *California* definition of obscenity for print and visual media, questions existed about applying it to the Internet. For example, in 1996, the Sixth US Circuit Court of Appeals upheld the conviction on federal obscenity charges of two people who operated a computer bulletin board from their California home. The subscriber bulletin board service offered sexually explicit materials. The couple was charged in Memphis with transmitting obscene material. A postal official had subscribed to the bulletin board, obtained computer files and ordered six videotapes, all containing sexually explicit material. A jury found that the material violated the local, contemporary community standards of Memphis and convicted the couple of transporting obscene images across state lines via the Internet. The lower court rejected the argument that the ruling effectively established a national standard for obscenity, contrary to the Supreme Court's *Miller* test, or that upholding the conviction would mandate that all material sent over the Internet be no more explicit than permitted by the most restrictive community. The court said the defendants could, and should, have made certain when screening subscribers that their materials would not be received in restrictive communities.

Concerned by the high court's elimination of the CDA's online indecency ban, Congress enacted and President Bill Clinton signed the Child Online Protection Act (COPA) in October 1998 to prevent children from accessing material harmful to minors. Six months later, the US Department of Justice was in the US Court of Appeals for the Third Circuit to challenge a district court order that enjoined enforcement of the new law. In February 1999, a federal judge in Pennsylvania stopped application of Congress's second attempt to shield children from Internet pornography. COPA would have required commercial web sites to collect credit card numbers or some other proof of age before they allow Internet users to access targeted materials. The law called for a fine of $50,000 and up to six months in prison for any commercial provider who knowingly made harmful material available to minors under the age of 17.

In June 2000, an appeals court struck another blow to COPA by upholding the district court ruling. The Third US Circuit Court of Appeals held that the ACLU's attack on the constitutionality of the act would likely succeed. Then, in 2002, the Supreme Court held in *Ashcroft* v. *ACLU* that community standards may be used to identify material that is harmful to minors. Ruling on COPA, the Supreme Court found use of *Miller* v. *California* language distinguishable because all three prongs of the test must be used. While the earlier *Reno* decision failed because only the patently offensive standard was utilized, the COPA statute also employed *Miller's* "prurient interest" and "serious value" tests. Justice Clarence Thomas, writing for the 8–1 majority, reiterated the point that, unlike the first two prongs, the third allows a court to set aside community standards in favor of "whether a reasonable person would find . . . value in the material, taken as a whole" (p. 579). The decision remanded the case for further review by lower courts. Only Justice John Paul Stevens dissented, contending: "In the context of the Internet . . . community standards become a sword rather than a shield. If a prurient appeal is offensive in a puritan village, it may be a crime to post it on the World Wide Web" (p. 603).

In 2004, the Supreme Court sided 5–4 with a lower court decision to block COPA, but the case was remanded to update evidence on the effectiveness of Internet filters, as well as other existing laws and technologies. In an opinion written by Justice Anthony Kennedy, the Supreme Court held: "Content-based prohibitions, enforced by severe criminal penalties, have the constant potential to be a repressive force in the lives and thoughts of free people" (p. 664). It noted that Congress had since passed two other laws, one prohibiting misleading domain names, and another creating a "Dot Kids" domain. The decision to return the case to the district court relied upon the *Reno* decision and the idea that filtering software satisfies the least restrictive means test better than forcing commercial web sites to verify user age. The Supreme Court, however, refused to accept the appellate court conclusion that use of community standards was overbroad. The Supreme Court distinguished and clarified the differences between the district court opinion, which held that the statute must be narrowly tailored to serve a compelling government interest, and the appellate court's unconstitutional finding, which the Supreme Court's majority refused to accept without fresh evidence.

The Supreme Court's majority sought, by placing the burden on the government, to seek less restrictive alternatives: "The purpose of the test is to ensure that speech is restricted no further than necessary to achieve the goal, for it is important to assure that legitimate speech is not chilled or punished" (p. 667).

The Supreme Court affirmed its belief that filters are less restrictive and more effective in blocking all porn sites, not just those in the United States. Minors may be able to obtain credit cards and access a pornographic web site, and filters also are not entirely effective. However, filters go beyond web sites and may be used to block email. The Supreme Court concluded that parents and libraries may be encouraged to use filters.

Justices Stevens and Ruth Bader Ginsburg would have gone further. Their concurrence supported the appellate court reasoning that use of community standards warranted striking the law down as unconstitutional. However, Justice Antonin Scalia dissented, holding that restricting commercial pornography is consistent with existing law. Justice Stephen Breyer's dissent, meantime, found that COPA advanced a compelling interest and followed the *Miller* test. The Supreme Court was severely divided on the question of whether filters solve the problem, as well as how best to fit restrictions within the requirements of the First Amendment.

In 1999, the Supreme Court had let stand a lower court ruling upholding another part of the Communications Decency Act. The Court issued a one-sentence order that allowed the government to enforce a CDA ban on obscene and indecent email that is intended to harass or annoy the recipient. In *ApolloMedia Corp.* v. *Reno* (1998), a San Francisco company challenged a provision that made it a felony to initiate "the transmission of, any comment, request, suggestion, proposal, image, or other communication which is obscene, lewd, lascivious, filthy, or indecent, with intent to annoy, abuse, threaten, or harass another person." Annoy.com had allowed people to send anonymous and lewd electronic mail to public officials. San Francisco Attorney William Bennett Turner argued that the provision unconstitutionally punishes indecent material under the *Miller* test:

> There is no conceivable government interest that could justify §223's content prohibition of "indecent" speech . . . The government cannot even advance the interest in protecting children from exposure to "indecent" material – the interest that it unsuccessfully urged to support the other provisions of the Act held unconstitutional . . . The provisions at issue here apply regardless of the age of the recipient, govern communications among adults, and have no safe harbor defense.
>
> (1996 US Briefs 511, February 27, 1997)

Nevertheless, the Supreme Court refused to revisit its earlier decision. In another case dealing with children's access to sexually explicit materials online, a federal judge enjoined enforcement of a Virginia library's policy to block public access to such Internet sites. While recognizing a compelling government interest in reducing illegal access to pornography, the court suggested that the library had adopted an overbroad policy to address speculative concerns with no evidence of either illegal access or citizen complaints. At issue was whether a public library could use content categories to restrict Internet access. The lawsuit against the library board alleged that such a policy violated the First Amendment and was an unconstitutional prior restraint. An earlier ruling declared: "The First Amendment applies to, and limits, the discretion of a public library to place content-based restrictions on access to constitutionally protected materials within its collection" (*Mainstream Loudon*, 1998: 794-5). The court held that receiving Internet information was consistent with the type of public forum routinely offered by the library.

In another twist on the library issue, seven Minneapolis librarians claimed that the amount of pornography on Central Library computers created a "hostile, offensive, palpably unlawful working environment." Library patrons downloading pornographic images prompted at least two bills in Minnesota to require blocking or filtering software on all school and library computers. Ultimately, the library director apologized to the public and announced plans to require sign-ins at workstations, as well as limiting computer use to thirty minutes.

A three-judge panel in the Third Circuit (Philadelphia) at first rejected the Children's Internet Protection Act (CIPA), which requires filtering software on computers at all libraries supported by federal funds. The court unanimously ruled the law unconstitutional (*American Library Ass'n v. United States*, a. 2002). It found that filters tended to overblock educational content:

> While most libraries include in their physical collection copies of volumes such as *The Joy of Sex* and *The Joy of Gay Sex*, which contain quite explicit photographs and descriptions, filtering software blocks large quantities of other, comparable information about health and sexuality . . .. One teenager testified that the Internet access in a public library was the only venue in which she could obtain information important to her about her own sexuality. Another . . . witness described using the Internet to research breast cancer and reconstructive surgery for his mother . . . Even though some filtering programs contain exceptions for health and education, the exceptions do not solve the problem of overblocking constitutionally protected material . . . not only information relating to health and sexuality that might be mistaken for pornography or erotica, but also vast numbers of Web pages and sites that could not even arguably be construed as harmful.
>
> (p. 406)

The district court found that the four most popular filtering software programs blocked thousands of web sites that were not pornographic, and this raised First Amendment issues. The court rejected the government's argument that current technology is imperfect but effective in blocking most hard-core porn sites. The court accepted the plaintiff's argument against the government that libraries constitute a public forum subject to a strict scrutiny First Amendment analysis:

Because the filtering software mandated by CIPA will block access to substantial amounts of constitutionally protected speech whose suppression serves no legitimate government interest, we are persuaded that a public library's use of software filters is not narrowly tailored to further any of these interests. Moreover, less restrictive alternatives exist that further the government's legitimate interest in preventing the dissemination of obscenity, child pornography, and material harmful to minors, and in preventing patrons from being unwillingly exposed to patently offensive, sexually explicit content.

(p. 410)

The court noted that there are less restrictive options such as enforcement of library rules prohibiting access to pornography or making available unfiltered computers in restricted areas. Instead, the measure would have restricted federal funds to any library that failed to keep minors from visual depictions of content found to be obscene, pornographic, or generally harmful to minors. Citing *FCC* v. *League of Women Voters of California* (1984) and other cases, the district court concluded that the government has no right to restrict speech for content reasons: "By interfering with public libraries' discretion to make available to patrons as wide a range of constitutionally protected speech as possible, the federal government is arguably distorting the usual functioning of public libraries as places of freewheeling inquiry" (p. 490). CIPA, which would have been enforced through actions of the FCC and provisions of the Library Services Technology Act, was enjoined from going into effect while the Supreme Court considered an appeal. The Court was faced with a series of arguments outlined by the American Civil Liberties Union about the CIPA law. The ACLU contended the law violated the First Amendment.

Nevertheless, six justices agreed to reverse the lower court's decision and uphold the new law. Chief Justice Rehnquist, for a plurality, wrote that Internet pornography has been a serious problem for public libraries: "Some patrons also expose others to pornographic images by leaving them displayed on Internet terminals or printed at library printers" (*United States v. American Library Ass'n*, 2003, p. 200). The federal government provides two sources of funding to public libraries: (1) discounted rates for Internet access and (2) technology grants for equipment. The Court considered filtering "reasonably effective" (ibid.: 200). Further, the law allows libraries to disable filters "to enable access for bona fide research or other lawful purposes" (ibid.: 201). The plurality rejected the First Amendment issues that the lower court raised but noted library decision-making and the need for broad discretion.

The Chief Justice found instead that "the government has broad discretion to make content-based judgments in deciding what private speech to make available to the public" (ibid.: 204). Funding decisions typically use content-based criteria: "Public library staffs necessarily consider content in making collection decisions and enjoy broad discretion In making them" (ibid.: 205). In this view, a public library is not a public forum: "A public library does not acquire Internet terminals in order to create a public forum for Web publishers to express themselves, any more than it collects books in order to provide a public forum for the authors of books to speak" (ibid.: 206). Instead, the plurality said library resources exist "to facilitate research, learning, and recreational pursuits by furnishing materials of requisite and appropriate quality" (ibid.: 204). Because the Chief Justice found that a library is not a public forum, he refused to apply a strict scrutiny standard:

> A library's need to exercise judgment in making collection decisions depends on its traditional role in identifying suitable and worthwhile material; it is no less entitled to play that role when it collects material from the Internet than when it collects material from any other source. Most libraries already exclude pornography from their print collections because they deem it inappropriate for inclusion. We do not subject these decisions to heightened scrutiny; it would make little sense to treat libraries' judgments to block online pornography any differently, when these judgments are made for the same reason.
>
> (ibid.: 208)

The decision held that adults may ask a librarian to unblock a site or disable a filter because "the Constitution does not guarantee the right to acquire information at a public library without any risk of embarrassment" (ibid.: 209).

In a separate concurring opinion, Justice Stephen Breyer also rejected the strict scrutiny approach: "The statutory restriction in question is, in essence, a kind of 'selection' restriction (a kind of editing)" (ibid.: 216). CIPA "seeks to restrict access to obscenity, child pornography, and, in respect to access to minors, material that is comparably harmful" (ibid.: 218). This is especially true when there is a need to be "shielding" children from exposure (ibid.: 219).

But, in a dissenting opinion, Justice Stevens wrote that CIPA "operates as a blunt nationwide restraint on adult access to 'an enormous amount of valuable information' that individual librarians cannot possibly review" (ibid.: 220). He argued that government "may not suppress lawful speech" and reduce adult access to "only what is fit for children" (ibid.: 222). He wrote:

> Unless we assume that the statute is a mere symbolic gesture, we

must conclude that it will create a significant prior restraint on adult access to protected speech. A law that prohibits reading without official consent, like a law that prohibits speaking without consent, "constitutes a dramatic departure from our national heritage and constitutional tradition."

(ibid.: 225)

Justice Stevens saw local library discretion as similar to academic freedom at a university, and penalizing funding violates the First Amendment: "An abridgment of speech by means of a threatened denial of benefits can be just as pernicious as an abridgment by means of a threatened penalty" (ibid.: 227).

In a strident separate dissent, Justice David H. Souter, joined by Justice Ruth Bader Ginsburg, wrote that the CIPA statute "says only that a library 'may' unblock, not that it must" (ibid.: 233). Justice Souter criticized the statute:

> Children could be restricted to blocked terminals, leaving other unblocked terminals in areas restricted to adults and screened from casual glances. And of course the statute could simply have provided for unblocking at adult request, with no questions asked. The statute could, in other words, have protected children without blocking access for adults or subjecting adults to anything more than minimal inconvenience, just the way (the record shows) many librarians had been dealing with obscenity and indecency before the imposition of federal conditions.
>
> (ibid.: 234)

Justice Souter wrote that a local library could not, on its own, impose adult restrictions. He found CIPA to sanction censorship, not editing of materials – the Court's opinion ignored that when a library does not have a book, a patron may use interlibrary loan to get it:

> [T]he Internet blocking here defies comparison to the process of acquisition. Whereas traditional scarcity of money and space require a library to make choices about what to acquire, and the choice to be made is whether or not to spend the money to acquire something, blocking is the subject of a choice made after the money for Internet access has been spent or committed . . . Thus, deciding against buying a book means there is no book (unless a loan can be obtained) . . . The proper analogy therefore is not passing up a book that might have been bought; it is either to buying a book and then keeping it from adults lacking an accept-

112

able "purpose," or to buying an encyclopedia and then cutting out
pages with anything thought to be unsuitable for all adults.

(ibid.: 236–7)

Souter wrote that CIPA and the Supreme Court's support for it defied the
history of American libraries. He reminded the Court that by the time of
McCarthyism, the American Library Association had explicitly opposed
censorship in its own Bill of Rights. The American library tradition has
favored adult access to materials and adult inquiry. Souter concluded,
"There is no good reason, then, to treat blocking of adult enquiry as anything different from the censorship it presumptively is" (ibid.: 242).

The Supreme Court has become increasingly interested in visiting issues
addressed in Internet law, especially when there is concern about children
accessing obscene or pornographic content and when children are victim-
ized by the pornography industry.

The question of whether computer-animated "virtual child pornography" could be restricted came before the Supreme Court in 2001. An
appeals court held that the Child Pornography Prevention Act of 1996
(CPPA) was unconstitutional in prohibiting the use of computer images
that do not involve real children but simply appear to be minors (*Free Speech
Coalition* v. *Reno*, 1999). At issue was whether there was a government
interest beyond attempting to protect real victims of child pornography.
In a 6–3 decision, the Supreme Court ruled that CPPA violated the First
Amendment.

The Supreme Court held that, because the statute defined images as
"any visual depiction, including any photograph, film, video, picture, or
computer-generated image or picture" that "is, or appears to be, a minor
engaging in sexually explicit conduct," the language was "overbroad and
unconstitutional" (*Ashcroft* v. *Free Speech Coalition*, 2002: 241). The Court
explicitly cited *Sable* in rejecting government arguments that virtual child
pornography could be used by pedophiles to seduce children.

Justice Anthony Kennedy's opinion found the law went beyond law the
Supreme Court set forth in its child pornography case, *New York* v. *Ferber*
(1982): "As a general rule, pornography can be banned only if obscene,
but under *Ferber*, pornography showing minors can be proscribed whether
or not the images are obscene under the definition set forth in *Miller*"
(*Ashcroft* v. *Free Speech Coalition*, 2002: 240). However, the restriction
on images that are the product of computer morphing was found to be
too sweeping. By directly quoting the First Amendment, it was clear that
Justice Kennedy and the Court's majority found CPPA to be a disturbing
intrusion on First Amendment rights:

[A] law imposing criminal penalties on protected speech is a stark
example of speech suppression. The CPPA's penalties are indeed

113

severe. A first offender may be imprisoned for 15 years . . . A repeat offender faces a prison sentence of not less than 5 years and not more than 30 years . . . While minor punishments can chill speech, . . . this case provides a textbook example of why we permit facial challenges to statutes that burden expression. With these severe penalties in force, few legitimate movie producers or book publishers, or few speakers in any capacity, would risk distributing images in or near the uncertain reach of this law. The Constitution gives significant protection from overbroad laws that chill speech within the First Amendment's vast and privileged sphere. Under this principle, the CPPA is unconstitutional on its face if it prohibits a substantial amount of protected expression.

(ibid.: 244)

The articulation of a "vast and privileged sphere" of First Amendment protection is expansive in terms of the type of speech under the umbrella of safety. Outside the safe zone are "defamation, incitement, obscenity, and pornography produced with real children" (p. 246). By contrast, the Supreme Court was concerned that CPPA might render illegal Shakespeare's *Romeo and Juliet* or the popular movie *American Beauty*. CPPA, the Court found, failed to distinguish isolated sexual scenes from the *Miller* requirement to evaluate the "work as a whole." Interestingly, the Supreme Court rejected the argument that because virtual child pornography and real child pornography might soon be impossible to distinguish, prosecution would become difficult:

> The hypothesis is somewhat implausible. If virtual images were identical to illegal child pornography, the illegal images would be driven from the market by the indistinguishable substitutes. Few pornographers would risk prosecution by abusing real children if fictional, computer images would suffice.
>
> (ibid.: 254)

In his concurrence, Justice Thomas wrote the government failed to provide evidence of any case in which someone charged with production of illegal child pornography had raised reasonable doubt by contending the images were virtual and not of real children.

Justice O'Connor, writing for Chief Justice Rehnquist and Justice Antonin Scalia, offered a partial dissent. They disagreed that CPPA's virtual child pornography ban was overbroad: "Such images whet the appetites of child molesters, . . . given the rapid pace of advances in computer-graphics technology, the Government's concern is reasonable" (ibid.: 263–4). Chief Justice Rehnquist added in a separate dissent that the CPPA statute had clearly defined explicit content as sex that was "genital–genital," "oral–genital," "anal–genital or oral–anal," "bestiality," "masturbation," "sadistic or masochistic abuse," or "lascivious exhibition of the genitals or pubic area" (ibid.: 268). Chief Justice Rehnquist and Justice Scalia argued unsuccessfully that the definition relates only to hard-core child pornography and not to classic plays or movies.

Indecency, obscenity, and the new media world

As lawmakers and the courts continue to struggle with indecency and obscenity issues across a variety of media, it appears that there are few boundaries to the investigation of the problem. The ESPN cable network, which normally does not use a delay system in its coverage of live sports, was forced to do just that during the 2006 Little League World Series. This followed a player's use of the F-word that was captured by a field microphone. A second profanity also made it on the air after the cable sports network added a five-second delay. Spokesman Mark Mandell said natural sound is "poignant and interesting," but ESPN did not want to place kids "in a bad light" from what might slip out under pressure: "These two incidents are things we don't tolerate . . . We will do everything humanly and technically possible to make sure it never happens again" (Eggerton, 2006, August 28).

Meantime, the television industry, facing pressure from critics, lawmakers, and regulators, launched a $300 million campaign to educate parents through a web site, public service announcements, and brochures (Figure 6.1).

The expensive campaign was designed to tell parents they have both control of and responsibility for their children's television viewing. Some lawmakers would like to force cable operators to unbundle cable television

Figure 6.1 The industry urges parents to monitor viewing by their children. Source: http://www.controlyourtv.org/

packages that force viewers to pay for groups of channels, including some that parents do not want their kids to see.

McCann-Erickson Chief Creative Officer, Joyce Thomas, said: "We did not want to wag our fingers at parents. We did not want to suggest that the content they view is inappropriate. What we are saying is that not all content that you view is appropriate for children. We used popular TV genres – like murder mysteries and urban dramas with drug uses – as examples" (Eggerton, 2006, August 28: 10).

While the industry favors use of parental controls, the FCC points out that less than half – about 119 million of 280 million television sets in the country – have V-chip technology. Even when available, many critics contend that it tends to either block too many or too few shows.

Chapter summary

Cable and other new media have presented issues for lawmakers and the courts because of sexual content available to children. The Supreme Court, however, has ruled that the First Amendment restricts the government from forcing a channeling approach to adult content. Instead, it backed a rule that gives parents the right to ask for channels to be blocked. In the case of the Internet, the Supreme Court has treated web sites like publishers, but it did uphold a law requiring public libraries that accept federal funds to restrict access to computers and install filtering software for those PCs available to children. Media industries continue to promote information campaigns that tell parents how to use technology to keep their children from accessing adult content.

Review Questions

1 How does media convergence make it more difficult to treat broadcasting as a unique medium?
2 What is scrambling? What are its strengths and weaknesses as a technology?
3 What changes will digital television bring to the broadcast indecency issue?
4 Is it possible to keep children away from all adult content in a library? Why or why not should this be done?
5 Do parents need help in protecting children from indecency? Have industry efforts to assist them been adequate?

7

NEW MEDIA ISSUES

The Internet made available to anyone able to use a computer and media equipment the ability to distribute content to a global audience. While it is difficult to attract large audiences, there are examples of individuals being able to use web sites to attract immediate attention. Furthermore, the children targeted for protection by lawmakers and the FCC are some of the most likely to know how to use the latest technologies. Meantime, the availability of questionable content occurred at the same time as the global desire for edgy media increased.

Cultural concerns about indecency

The *Arizona Republic* newspaper opined that, in the United States, one could observe through a variety of social artifacts a "coarsening of our culture" (*Arizona Republic*, 2006). One of the newspaper's examples was the controversy over FCC rules:

> Ostensibly, this is the residual fallout over Janet Jackson's "wardrobe malfunction" nearly two years ago. That event, in which the singer's breast was exposed during a Super Bowl halftime show, created an "enough is enough" sentiment throughout the nation and prompted the FCC to get tougher about enforcing indecency standards.
>
> (ibid.: para. 3)

The newspaper added: "The pervasiveness of crude language and behavior in popular entertainment represents a coarsening of the culture that should be the topic of a lot of public discussion far beyond the courtroom" (ibid.: para. 6). The *Arizona Republic* went on to argue, however, against the government solution:

> Relying on government regulation to curb excesses will always be problematic because it requires fine-tuned artistic and literary decisions from bureaucrats. The current rules would make it

problematic to read the works of literary masters over the radio. These include Toni Morrison, John Steinbeck, Truman Capote, John Updike, Gabriel Garcia Marquez and others.

(ibid.: para. 7)

The exercise of restraint or social responsibility by creators, however, does not tend to be rewarded in the fragmented new media environment.

In the face of coarsening media, however, politicians, such as former vice presidential candidate Joe Lieberman, suggest that government must play a role. The Connecticut Democrat US Senator told *Broadcasting & Cable* (2006, p. 10) magazine:

> I got into this fight back when my youngest daughter was about 4, and she happened to be watching a particularly raunchy TV show with her older brother. . . I heard some of the crude jokes on the show and was amazed it was on in the 'family hour,' when a lot of small children like our youngest were watching . . . It's one thing for a parent to turn off the TV, like I did when my daughter was watching that raunchy show more than a decade ago, but today kids have access to a whole new world of entertainment through a wide variety of devices, many of them small enough to fit in a shirt pocket . . . Technology is changing more rapidly than our ability to protect our kids. I believe the time has come to fight back.

Legislation, of course, is only one means of fighting back. The marketplace solution is to fight the speech we might define as "bad" with that which is defined as "good." In the age of computer-mediated communication, the opportunities exist to challenge mainstream media messages.

Computer-mediated communication

Computer-mediated communication (CMC) explores influences of new media and offers a set of core concepts:

- interaction – the use of technology to promote ongoing and meaningful communication;
- online communities – the interest in developing alternative realities in cyberspace; and
- sense of identity – the ability we each have to create and recreate identities, including sexual identities, in the online world (Barnes, 2003).

In this sense, the Internet is an important way in which people address social and cultural change by traversing great distances (Surratt, 2001).

Much like radio and television for previous generations, young people have embraced the Internet as a way to establish their identities (Ferguson & Perse, 2000). Youth and teenagers have a need to understand and establish sexual identity, and use of the Internet and its potential gratifications include relationship building with the opposite gender (Lin, 1993; Pavlik, 1996).

The Internet historically lacked media richness because email lacks nonverbal cues (Kahai & Cooper, 2003). However, video cameras, multimedia telephones, and interactive cybercultural web sites offer a venue for exploration of sexual identity (Jones, 1997; Bell, 2001).

The virtual culture of the Internet is now more than a decade into its development, but pioneering scholar Steve Jones has noted the lack of research about sex:

> Part of the reason so little empirical evidence exists about queers on line may be the difficulty of studying matters of sex and sexuality on the internet. Quite often, when someone learns that I work with the Pew Internet and American Life Project, the first question asked is what we have learned about on-line porn. Sex and porn are almost unavoidable on line, and the public wants to know how prevalent it really is and what to do about it. In truth, in our research we have learned just about nothing about porn on line. Our primary research method is the telephone survey. Random digit dialing around the country and asking interviewees about their use of the internet for porn is not likely to yield many useful or trustworthy results. Even asking questions about sexuality would cause many, if not most, of our respondents to hang up on us.
>
> (Jones, 1997: para. 6)

Research into trust and identity is one starting point for beginning to understand the range of sexuality online:

> I am convinced of the need to think further about the connections he draws between performance and context, because, at least at present, I would argue that the internet is largely about performance and context. If one were to replace the word identity with the word performance in the numerous theoretical interventions into on-line life, the result would leave agency foregrounded in ways that, thus far, internet studies have overlooked.
>
> (ibid.: para. 9)

The interest that so many have in exploring sexuality in the perceived safety of the online world suggests that, as long as young people are allowed to use the web, it will be impossible to "protect" them from potentially harmful messages, as the government so wants to do. From email to chat rooms, the Internet is filled with sexually indecent content. It provides a venue for content kept off the broadcast airwaves.

Box 7.1 Mancow thrives in post-indecency complaint career

Fox News in 2006 aired a new show with host Erich "Mancow" Muller (Figures 7.1 and 7.2), a shock jock who has been the target of numerous complaints to the FCC over indecency. Mancow was fired in 2005 after incurring about $300,000 in fines. David E. Smith, head of the Illinois Family Institute, filed indecency complaints against the Mancow show. Muller later made headlines by filing a lawsuit against Smith, but it was later dropped.

Figure 7.1 Mancow Muller was a leader among a new generation of shock jocks.
Source: mancow.com

Figure 7.2 Mancow's webpage.

Cliff Kincaid, president of America's Survival and contributing editor of the AIM Report, wrote this about Mancow:

Years ago I was duped into appearing on Muller's radio show to talk about the United Nations. I didn't know who he was at the time. When the interview quickly degenerated into insults and interruptions, I hung up the phone. Muller gave out my home phone number over the air, generating dozens of harassing calls to me and my wife, who was pregnant at the time. I complained to Muller's employer and received a financial settlement without having to file suit.

(Kincaid, 2006, para. 7)

Sources
Kincaid, Cliff (December 25, 2006). "Sleazy jock gets Fox show," http://www.americandaily.com/article/16943
Mancow.com.

Other Internet issues: YouTube

The web site YouTube.com is on the front line of Internet issues. YouTube makes it easy for people to publish audio and video files. For example, according to the Reuters news service in Sao Paulo, Brazil, a court there ordered YouTube to remove a sexual video. Model and ex-wife of soccer star Ronaldo, Daniela Cicarelli, filed a lawsuit against YouTube after a video of her appearing to have sex in shallow water on a beach found its way onto

Figure 7.3 YouTube sexual videos are difficult to regulate.

the web. It became the most popular video in Brazil. Cicarelli and her current boyfriend demanded $116,000 per day in damages. However, as soon as some copies of the video were removed, others were posted. Meanwhile, Cicarelli became something of a phenomenon on YouTube (Figure 7.3).

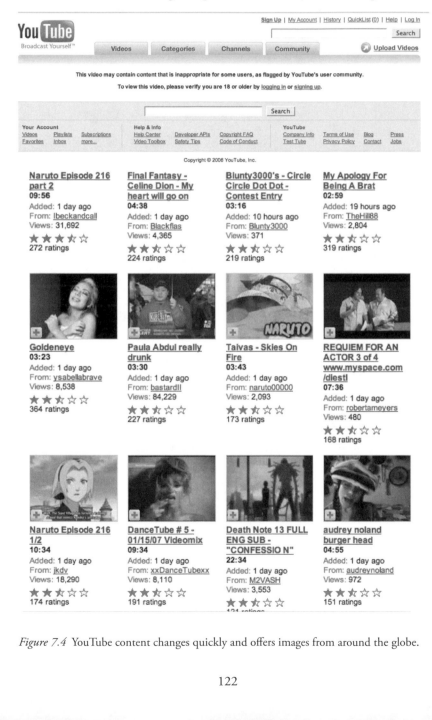

Figure 7.4 YouTube content changes quickly and offers images from around the globe.

YouTube reviews sexually provocative videos and employs a filtering system that requires site visitors to log in and prove their age before they can view adult-oriented content. It has become a popular site for people of all ages. Top-rated videos on any given day frequently deal with sexuality (Figure 7.4). YouTube's filtering screen appears to work to limit access to the most provocative of the videos.

While requiring viewers to log into YouTube may not prevent all minors from accessing adult videos, it does limit accidental access and will probably keep most children from easily seeing what may not be appropriate in the minds of their parents.

Box 7.2 Fox shows F-word during playoff game

During the January 13, 2007, National Football League playoff game between the Eagles and the Saints at the New Orleans Superdome, the Fox network showed a fan wearing a t-shirt that said "FUCK DA EAGLES." Fox spokesman Lou D'Ermilio told *Washington Post* blogger Frank Ahrens that the event happened at about 8:30 p.m. D'Ermilio told Ahrens that the image was recorded during a play and then appeared during a replay. "We regret it and apologize," D'Ermilio said. He claimed that the incident was "definitely unintentional." Various bloggers caught the image on their recorders and posted it across the web (Figure 7.6).

"One young woman (note I do not call her a "lady") was wearing a t-shirt reading 'F**K DA EAGLES.' Except her shirt had letters where the asterisks are," Ahrens wrote.

Fox was one of the networks challenging the FCC indecency policy on fleeting profanities during live broadcasts. Among the blog responses from readers, were these:

Figure 7.5 Fox Sports may have inadvertently used this crowd shot, which displayed the words "FUCK DA EAGLES." Source: http://awfulannouncing. blogspot.com/

Posted by: (missing) | January 13, 2007, 10:00 p.m.
I saw it, too. You sound positively Meese-esque about it, though. Or possibly Swaggart-like. Claiming that Fox deliberately aired the profanity is completely over the top. They were showing a replay right after the play, not playing it during the 11 o'clock news (where it will doubtless never air.) If the replay happened a significant period of time after the live feed, it would be different. In this case, it was immediately after the play happened. I seriously doubt there was any intention of flouting the (ridiculously overbearing) rules. If you can show a deliberate choice to knowingly air the profanity, then your point is valid. I doubt you'll reach that standard. This smacks of the celebrated Janet Jackson bare boob issue. It was on tv for a few seconds, just long enough for the guy (or gal) in charge to say "hey! Pan away!" There's no reason to believe it was a deliberate action.

Posted by: Mike | January 13, 2007, 10:30 p.m.
oh my God, I saw the 'F' word on TV! Quick, change the channel! Ahh, NBC, there's some decent all-American television, an episode of SVU about child-rape. Thanks god I'm not exposed to filth anymore!

Posted by: Bridgid | January 13, 2007, 10:40 p.m.
This is a colossal waste of time. The internet makes profanity on tv irrelevant. I had seen one playboy by the time I was 13; your average 10 year old today has seen German scat porn. But you go ahead and swat that ant Frank.

Posted by: Henry | January 13, 2007, 11:00 p.m.
We had better call the morality police and have that woman stoned to death. Oh wait, this is not taliban-era afghanistan . . .

Posted by: Eric | January 13, 2007, 11:45 p.m.
Seriously, Frank . . . this was clearly an error of obliviousness rather than judgment on Fox's part. They zeroed in on a buxom and excited young woman (following your decision not to call her "lady"– and let me respond, judge not lest ye be judged), and failed to notice that her well-worn shirt displayed an expletive. They were trying to show an excited and excitatory fan, not profanity; if they f***ed up, everyone makes mistakes sometimes (see above on "judge not . . ."). Lighten up, FCC –and you too, Frank, if this is an issue to you too.

Posted by: Ipanema | January 14, 2007, 12:34 a.m.
"It's equivalent to flipping a vulgar hand sign at the government."–Which is completely legal under the first amendment.

Posted by: Todd | January 14, 2007, 12:41 a.m.
There is absolutely no question but that the shirt said "f**k," and it is impossible that this somehow slipped through – the "woman" was in the front row, the camera operator and the directors had to know what her

shirt said before putting her on (I mean, they found her and focused on her), and they consciously chose to do it.

Now, is this the worst thing that has ever happened? No. But it is an example of astonishing arrogance – I was watching the game with my two seven-year old sons, both of whom can read quite well – and they both asked me what her shirt said. These people don't have the right to inject that into my living room and rub it in my kids' faces. They're just flexing their amorality.

As for those who call Ahrens names, merely for writing about this – you certainly impress. Very classy.

Posted by: Greg | January 14, 2007, 12:49 a.m.
Frank . . .Did you catch Reggie Bush mouthing M##her F##KER too? Did that offend you? No matter, no one plucking cares but you.

Posted by: JOHN G | January 14, 2007, 12:52 a.m.
This "indecency" stuff is over the top. I was 12–13 in 1962. Maybe my folks did not "ride herd" the way some of you imagine they ought to have, but I read the adult "sci-fi" of the day with their blessing and knew this work and others then. I was not scarred for life.

About the same time I went to Boy Scout Camp and my scoutmaster had us singing – for parent's visits – "Waiting on the Corner until the Pickup Comes" – and awarded a "Wind Breaker" merit badge to his assistant. THAT I thought was indecent. This was the same scoutmaster who made a point of confiscating copys [sic] of "Playboy" when we had paper drives.

This "indecency" campaign has reached the levels of total absurdity. In the third "Die Hard" movie, "Die Hard with a Vengence [sic]", Bruce Willis goes to Harlem and wears a sign that says "I hate N*****'s". It is central to the plot, as they say. I saw a recent version on broadcast TV where the sign was digitally altered to read, "I'm crazy". It's absurd!

"Indecency" is part of life, literature and art. Try a Shakespere [sic] play for example. I'm sick of being ruled by overly sensitive folk.

Posted by: webbedouin | January 14, 2007, 01:03 a.m.
The MF from Reggie Bush was unmistakable.

Posted by: farmasea | January 14, 2007, 01:05 a.m.
Perhaps the viewers who are watching this game with their children could take this opportunity to explain to said children that seeing or hearing a random 4 letter synonym for "intercourse" is hardly the end of the world.

Posted by: t_joe | January 14, 2007, 02:13 a.m.
Fox should not broadcast vile language and should be fined by the FCC. Let Fox and Rupert Murdoch pay off the national debt and I don't care if Fox pays off the national debt for the abhorrent televising.

I don't want to watch anything I would not want my mother or my sister to see.

Posted by: Demetrius Underwood | January 14, 2007, 08:55 a.m.
"T" YOU SHOULD CLOSE YOUR EYES THEN, IF YOU DONT WANT YOUR MOTHER AND SISTER TO SEE ANYTHING THAT YOU DONT WANT TO SEE, WAKE UP, THIS IS THE REAL WORLD

Posted by: tallyho | January 14, 2007, 09:18 a.m.
Frank,
Something very similar was shown during the Gator Bowl in 1 Jan 2007 between West Virginia and Georgia Tech on CBS.
    At one point, they scanned the crowd and prominently displayed a WVU fan wearing a sweatshirt that read:
    West F___kin Virginia
    Here's the picture:

    http://mountainlair.blogspot.com/2006/12/3ots-bad-case-of-shakes. html
Nice,
Hoover

Posted by: AParent | January 14, 2007, 09:26 a.m.
Profanity being yelled at the games is exactly why I no longer go. I hope the FCC and the team owners do us all a big favor and cleans up this sleeze.

Posted by: KEVIN SCHMIDT, STERLING VA | January 14, 2007, 06:11 p.m.
you people really make me fear the world that my children will be living in 10 years from now.

Posted by: right-wing idiot that forces my morality on everyone else (eyeroll) | January 14, 2007, 08:00 p.m.

Source
Ahrens, Frank (2007, January 14, 2007; 3:28 p.m. ET). "Fox responds;" Previous: "Fox Airs Profanity During Eagles-Saints Game." *Washington Post* Blog (http://blog.washingtonpost.com/posttech/2007/01/fox_airs_profanity_ during_eagl_1.html; and http://blog.washingtonpost.com/posttech/2007/01/ fox_responds_on_broadcast_of_p.html?nav=rss_blog)

Libel, privacy, and copyright

The posting of unapproved videos and images, including indecent ones, offers the possibility that some content will be deemed defamatory, an invasion of privacy, or improper violation of property rights. Nevertheless, some courts have offered ISPs insulation from possible lawsuit over libel (*Zeran* v. *America Online*, 1997). A federal district court protected America Online from a lawsuit by a former Clinton administration official seeking damages following a Drudge Report story (*Blumenthal* v. *Drudge and America Online*, 1998).

The Internet also challenges traditional norms of intellectual property rights for computer-originated and -transmitted material. Original material is protected by copyright upon its creation, and the creator has exclusive rights to reproduce and distribute the work, as well as the right to create other works derived from the original. Therefore, uploading a document, copying an Internet posting and retransmitting the posting without permission could all violate copyright law (*Playboy Enters., Inc.* v. *Frena*, 1993). Even browsing through material on a computer, which causes a copy of the digital information to be held in temporary memory, could possibly constitute illegal copying. Alternately, this might be interpreted as the digital form of reading a book in a library or a magazine at a newsstand, and not a copyright infringement (*Religious Technology Ctr.* v. *Netcom On-Line Communications Servs.*, 1995).

In 1995 and again in 1998, Congress updated copyright laws in part to deal with these issues. Congress enacted the Digital Millennium Copyright Act (DMCA) of 1998 to eliminate an apparent loophole in the Digital Performance Rights in Sound Recordings Act that had permitted webcasters to digitally transmit recordings without copyright licenses or fees. The new law grants webcasters a statutory license to transmit, with certain limitations, recordings at fees established voluntarily or by a Copyright Arbitration Royalty Panel. The established fees put an end to many webcasts as cost-prohibitive.

In the meantime, the Supreme Court upheld the Sonny Bono Copyright Term Extension Act of 1998 as a constitutional exercise of congressional powers (*Eldred* v. *Ashcroft*, 2003). The 7–2 decision dismissed concerns about free expression. However, Justices Stevens and Breyer wrote dissenting opinions, which raised concerns about the large proportion of unused content protected under the latest extension. Justice Breyer wrote: "The Copyright Clause and the First Amendment seek related objectives – the creation and dissemination of information" (ibid.: 244). In this view, the two should work together to promote free expression and dissemination of ideas. The law extended the existing copyights on, for example, Disney's Mickey Mouse for another twenty years to 2023. The extension kept many Twentieth Century icons, as well as lesser known media content, out of the public domain for general use.

A 1995 committee report of the US Patent and Trademark Office to consider copyright questions on the Internet failed to resolve these issues. While the committee suggested that computer transmissions should be considered "copies" similar to photocopies of a book page, it decided that existing copyright law was generally adequate to deal with the Internet. Conditions are changing so quickly on the Internet that one policy group suggested that Napster and similar file-sharing software should be outlawed. However, measures to protect intellectual property by gathering user data clash with those wishing to increase online privacy protection.

Privacy protection is difficult on the Internet. At work, employees who occasionally use the Internet for personal reasons could find that their employers have access to everything sent and received online. People using the Internet from home for such services as banking or shopping and for sending email messages could find they have less privacy protection than when engaging in such activities by mail or in person.

New technologies also have threatened to erode traditional common law views about the sanctity of privacy in one's home. Privacy becomes a question when law enforcement authorities want to tap into computer transmissions the way they do telephone calls. Web-based telephone services, such as Vonage, posed an interesting problem for regulators and the courts.

Another privacy issue involves web site content that is considered a threat. A federal jury in Portland, Oregon, ordered abortion protesters to pay $109 million in damages resulting from the Nuremberg Files site. The site was ordered to be closed down for resembling a hit list of abortion providers, some of whom were the victims of anti-abortion violence. Names and towns of doctors providing abortions were listed on the site, which featured dripping blood and fetus parts.

Former US Senate Democratic Leader Tom Daschle of South Dakota concluded that Congress had not kept pace with technological change: "Internet users are often promised basic privacy protection, only to have their expectations disappointed and their personal information put up for sale or disseminated in ways to which they never consented" (Report Card, 2000). The global nature of telecommunications will pose new challenges because indecent and obscene messages and media may be stored on servers anywhere on the planet.

Chapter summary

New media technologies have reduced entry barriers for those wishing to produce and disseminate media. Thus, the availability of indecent, profane, and obscene content is likely to increase on the Internet. Computer-mediated communication helps explain the desire of people to create identities, increase interaction, and build online communities.

Sexual identity is one example of how the web appears to reduce inhibitions. When performers are removed from the broadcast media, they are likely to reappear online. Further, previously unknown producers can use services such as YouTube to reach a vast audience. When broadcasters slip up online, bloggers can catch profanities and replay them online. Such content stimulates online discussion. The Internet environment, therefore, is one that is fertile for sprouting libel, privacy, and copyright litigation.

Review questions

1 Should the availability of online profanity keep the FCC from regulating broadcast indecency? Why or why not?
2 How might the Internet influence the development of sexual identity for young people?
3 Should YouTube be forced to remove all offensive videos? How could this be done on an ongoing basis?
4 Should Fox television have been fined for showing the "FUCK DA EAGLES" shirt?
5. How should lawmakers, regulators, and the courts address online libel, invasion of privacy, and copyright violations?

8

THE FIGHT OVER
INDECENT CONTENT

The FCC's indecency orders in 2006 focused on the role that context plays in making a judgment about whether or not a specific incident is found to be actionable. This chapter explores those decisions and examines the problems with contextual analyses.

Indecent content and the FCC

NBC Telemundo, KWHY-TV

The FCC's orders cover a wide range of broadcast content. Consider *Con El Corazón En La Mano*, broadcast on NBC Telemundo, KWHY-TV, Los Angeles, October 9, 2004. The Spanish-language movie featured a 15-minute scene airing at about 8:15 p.m. depicting a couple engaging in sexual intercourse while another man watched. The FCC, after viewing a videotape, said "the scene in question depicts a man raping a woman in a public restroom while another man stands nearby, acting as a look-out." NBC Telemundo responded that, "the complained-of material is not actionably indecent because it does not include depictions of nude sexual or excretory organs, offensive language or other material that the Commission previously has deemed indecent." However, the FCC found that the scene was patently offensive, explicit and graphic:

> The material depicts a woman being savagely attacked and raped in a public restroom. One man grabs the woman and forcibly kisses her as she struggles to free herself. He strikes her to the floor and, kneeling down, grabs one of her breasts as she screams. As they struggle together on the floor, the camera focuses on their hips, showing his hand pulling her underwear down her bare thigh as he maneuvers on top of her with his groin between her legs. She forces him off her by grabbing his testicles, but the other man blocks her escape from the room, and the first man again pulls her to the floor, re-mounts her and begins kissing her. She appears to cease resisting and returns his kisses. The camera again pans to

their hips, showing his hand fumbling at his zipper. They quite clearly appear to have sexual intercourse, with his groin thrusting into hers as she moans, until he finally stops and rolls off of her. The scene then continues for several minutes, depicting her reaction to the attack. The material by its very design is extraordinarily intense and extremely graphic.

The FCC found that the lack of nudity did not mitigate "the sexual nature of the scene." Further, the length of the scene was considered: "We have repeatedly held that a persistent focus on sexual material is a relevant factor in evaluating the potential offensiveness of broadcasts." The FCC also found the scene to be "shocking," and the maximum fine at that time of $32,500 was issued, despite a viewer warning that aired before the movie began: "Although inclusion of a warning might warrant a lower forfeiture under certain circumstances, we find that it does not here in light of all of the circumstances surrounding the apparent violation, including the shocking and gratuitous nature of the scene and the fact that it was prerecorded."

KCSM-TV

The Blues: Godfathers and Sons aired on KCSM, San Mateo, a noncommercial educational station, on March 11, 2004, between 8:42 and 9:32 p.m. A complaint followed focusing on profanities within the PBS documentary. The station responded that, "[t]he intent of the program is to provide a window into [the world of the individuals being interviewed] with their own words, all of which becomes an educational experience for the viewer." The FCC used its Golden Globe Awards Order to conclude that the words "fuck" and "shit" are indecent. The FCC considers "fuck" to be "one of the most vulgar, graphic, and explicit descriptions of sexual activity in the English language," and it justifies a finding that such content is patently offensive. Similarly, repeated use of the word "shit" crosses the line, as it is considered "to be one of the most vulgar, graphic and explicit words relating to excretory activity in the English language."

The complaint noted that the program included the following:

8:42 p.m.:	"See those, motherfucker? Gotta pay those motherfucking notes."
8:51 p.m.:	"What's my job? You stupid motherfucker, your job is to follow me."
9:00 p.m.:	"Shit it's good to be next to you."
9:04 p.m.:	"there's no white bullshit with [Paul] Butterfield."
9:13 p.m.:	"I'll buy some shit."
9:14 p.m.:	"This is the kind of shit I buy."

9:23 p.m.:   "Cocksucker Blues" (used as an on-screen Chyron
              to identify a song title).
9:32 p.m.:   "This poor fucker."

The repeated use of the two words was treated different from isolated profanities. Further, the time of the broadcast, when children were likely to be in the audience, led the FCC to find the content as "shocking."

> While San Mateo contends that the expletives in question were not removed from the program so that the viewpoints of those being interviewed would be accurately reflected, as discussed below we disagree that the use of such language was necessary to express any particular viewpoint in this case . . . We also note that many of the expletives in the broadcast are not used by blues performers. For example, based on our review of the DVD and transcript, Marshall Chess, a former label owner and record producer, states in discussing the relationship between Chess Records and its artists, "my dad had so many people at his funeral, my uncle said, 'You see all those motherfuckers? They're coming to make sure he's dead, so they don't have to pay back those motherfuckin' notes.'" In another scene, discussing his relationship with his father at Chess Records, Marshall Chess states, "[h]e said, 'What's your job? You stupid motherfucker! Your job is watching me!'" During a scene showing hip-hop artists Kyle Jason, Juice, and Chuck D. shopping in a record store with Chess, Kyle Jason states, "I'll buy some shit," and Juice states, "This looks crazy! See that? This is the kind of shit I buy! I mean, my man is wearing pink gear – that shit, that shit is crazy right there! I'm buyin' it!"

The FCC concluded that: "The 'F-Word' is a vulgar sexual term so grossly offensive to members of the public that it amounts to a nuisance and is presumptively profane." The FCC distinguished the case from the *Saving Private Ryan* film:

> Although in this case the profane language may have had some communicative purpose, we do not believe that San Mateo has demonstrated that it was essential to the nature of an artistic or educational work or essential to informing viewers on a matter of public importance, or that the substitution of other language would have materially altered the nature of the work . . . this case is unlike *Saving Private Ryan*, where we concluded that deleting offensive words "would have altered the nature of the artistic work and diminished the power, realism and immediacy of the film experience for viewers." While we recognize here that the

132

documentary had an educational purpose, we believe that purpose could have been fulfilled and all viewpoints expressed without the repeated broadcast of expletives.

The FCC proposed a $15,000 fine for the violation of its indecency rules:

> By broadcasting the program complete with these expletives, San Mateo effectively abdicated this aspect of its programming control to an outside entity, PBS . . . On the other hand, however, we do recognize that the expletives here were contained in a documentary, and while we conclude that the arguments made by the licensee are mistaken, we do find that the licensee may have been under the good faith belief that the use of these expletives served a legitimate informational purpose. Additionally, we recognize the fact that the licensee runs a small, community station that airs college level educational courses for most of the day.

Interestingly, the FCC proposed only a fine against the San Mateo station because only it had received a complaint. No other complaints were made against PBS or its affiliates across the country.

Fox Television

The 2003 Billboard Music Awards program on December 10 led to multiple complaints from the Parents Television Council (PTC) to the FCC. During the 8–10 p.m. broadcast, Nicole Richie uses profanity:

Paris Hilton: Now Nicole, remember, this is a live show, watch the bad language.
Nicole Richie: Okay, God.
Paris Hilton: It feels so good to be standing here tonight.
Nicole Richie: Yeah, instead of standing in mud and cow[blocked]. Why do they even call it *The Simple Life*? Have you ever tried to get cow shit out of a Prada purse? It's not so fucking simple.

Fox defended the broadcast because it did not "contain any description or depiction of sexual or excretory organs or activities in a patently offensive manner." The FCC's indecency analysis found:

> During her appearance on the *Billboard Music Awards*, Ms. Richie uttered the "F-Word" and the "S-Word." Fox does not dispute that the "S-Word" refers to excrement. Fox contends, however, that Ms. Richie used the "F-Word" as a mere vulgar expletive to

express emphasis, not to depict or describe sexual activities. We disagree. Given the core meaning of the "F-Word," any use of that word inherently has a sexual connotation and falls within the first prong of our indecency definition. We conclude that the material at issue clearly describes sexual and excretory activity.

In a footnote, the FCC added that ". . . even if Ms. Richie was not literally referring to cow excrement, her use of the 'S-Word' would still fall within the subject matter prong of our indecency definition . . . The 'S-Word' has an excretory connotation, however it may be used. Its use invariably invokes a coarse excretory image in any context." The FCC has found that, even when such words are not repeated, they may be indecent – especially when "shit" appears along with "fuck."

> . . . most important to our analysis in this context, Ms. Richie's use of the "F-Word" and the "S-Word" here, during a live broadcast of a music awards ceremony when children were expected to be in the audience, was shocking and gratuitous. Indeed, Fox admits that the tone of the material was vulgar.

The FCC found that in the live broadcast of awards shows, Fox should be aware that there might be profanities and prepare:

> According to Fox, the original script called for Ms. Richie to make excretory references to "pig crap" and "cow manure," and to substitute the euphemism "freaking" for the "F-Word." Under the circumstances, there was a palpable risk that Ms. Richie would use the "F-Word" and the "S-Word" instead of the euphemisms in the script.

The FCC told broadcasters to use delay systems to block profanities. Fox had been using a five-second delay and actually blocked the first use of "shit" by Richie: "Fox could have avoided the indecency violation here by delaying the broadcast for a period of time sufficient to ensure that all offending words were blocked." The FCC found the case was actionable, but concluded that no fine could be ordered: ". . . we recognize that our precedent at the time of the broadcast indicated that the Commission would not take indecency enforcement action against isolated use of expletives."

KMBC-TV, Kansas City

Hearst-Argyle ABC affiliate KMBC was the subject of several complaints following the January 14 and May 6, 2003, broadcasts of *NYPD Blue*.

The 9 p.m. broadcasts featured use of the words "dick," "dickhead," and "bullshit." The FCC documented the following examples:

1/14/03 episode (Detective Sipowitz in response to his partner's arrest by Internal Affairs): "Alright, this is bullshit!"

2/4/03 episode (Detective Sipowitz to street officer regarding that officer's partner framing Sipowitz's partner): "Over time – over what – bullshit, a beef!"

2/11/03 episode (Sipowitz speaking to a prisoner who had tried to trick Sipowitz into believing the prisoner was getting transferred to a different prison): "Game's been run dickhead. You ship out tomorrow. Wrong cop."

2/18/03 episode (stated by a suspect who bragged about, but now denies, killing his daughter): "I told people I killed Samia to try and get respect back. She had ashamed me and my community look at me as a fool."
Detective 1: "You took credit for killing your daughter?! Bullshit!"

4/15/03 episode (detective harassing suspect who had harassed prosecutor): "I'm hoping this bullshit about you trying to get under ADA Haywood's skin is a misunderstanding."

4/8/03 episode (Sipowitz, referring to a wheelchair-bound, uncooperative witness to a murder): "and that dickhead in the wheel chair . . . threaten him with perjury and he'll fold."

4/29/03 episode (detective questioning witness/suspect): "Maybe we should clarify Daly. We drop jail time for good information – not bullshit that wastes our time."

4/29/03 episode (Sipowitz, talking to a suspect who had recruited a youth (whom the suspect thought was a minor) to commit a crime): "He's 16 Dickhead! An adult! . . ."

5/6/03 episode (captain to detective who harassed suspect in 4/15 episode): "He said you nearly assaulted his client last night."
Detective: "Well, that's a bunch of bullshit."

The FCC found that "dick" and "dickhead" were "references to a sexual organ and therefore fall within the first prong of our indecency definition." The FCC also found that "bullshit" was "a vulgar reference to the product of excretory activity and therefore falls within the first prong of our indecency definition."

First, we find that the terms "dick" and "dickhead," in this context, while understandably offensive to some viewers, are not sufficiently vulgar, explicit, or graphic descriptions of sexual organs or activities to support a finding of patent offensiveness. Second, while not dispositive, it is relevant that none of the programs dwell on these terms. Third, we find that those words, in context, are not sufficiently shocking to support a finding that they are patently offensive. Although the words are undeniably coarse and vulgar, they do not have the same level of offensiveness as the "F-Word" or "S-Word."

The FCC did, however, initially find that "bullshit" was a patently offensive derivative of "shit" – "under the circumstances presented here, is vulgar, graphic, and explicit."

To the extent ABC claims that the word was necessary for dramatic effect, mere dramatic effect does not justify use of patently offensive expletives during time periods when numerous children are likely to be in the audience. Programs utilizing patently offensive expletives for dramatic effect can be aired after 10 p.m.

The FCC found the content was "explicit and shocking and gratuitous." Nevertheless, no sanction was proposed because precedent at the time of the airings was that "isolated use of expletives" were not subject to FCC action. The policy emerged in the midst of the cases before the FCC.

The FCC charted a course from the cases above that placed broadcasters on notice that profanities – particularly "shit," "fuck," and their variations – were considered indecent. At the same time, several network programs were cleared on lesser offenses.

WJLA-TV

The FCC received complaints against WJLA-TV in Washington, DC, for the 9–11 p.m. broadcast of *Alias* on January 5, 2005. During the broadcast, a rescue scene is followed by one in a bedroom:

The male and female characters hug and stare at each other. In the next scene, which is the subject of the complaints, the male and female characters are in bed kissing, caressing and rubbing against each other. The scene is accompanied by off-camera music. There are no depictions of sexual organs in the scene. Afterwards, the couple lay side-by-side and stare at each other.

The FCC's indecency analysis concluded that the bed scene was sexual: "In particular, although there are no depictions of sexual organs, the episode depicts a couple in bed passionately kissing, caressing and rubbing against each other, each of which is a sexual activity." The scene, however, did not "depict sexual or excretory organs . . . [or] sexual activities in a graphic or explicit way."

The scene involves no display of sexual organs and contains no sexually graphic language. While viewers see the characters kissing, caressing, and rubbing; it is not clear whether the characters are engaged in sexual intercourse.

The FCC's contextual finding was that, "the sexual activity is not presented in a pandering, titillating or shocking manner."

While the episode shows the male and female characters kissing, caressing, and rubbing in bed, the overall context, including the camera angle, the background music, and the immediately preceding scene, is not shocking in contrast to clear and graphic depictions of sexual intercourse.

So, although the scene was considered sexual, the FCC did not find it to be patently offensive and denied the complaints.

NBC Television

The November 11, 2004, NBC broadcast of *Will and Grace* featured an episode called "Saving Grace Again." The 8:30 p.m. broadcast in the Central time zone, was about Grace preparing for her first date after a divorce:

She is being assisted by her roommate, Will, and is concerned about her appearance. Before leaving, she asks Will if there is "anything else" she should know about dating. Will responds by instructing her to "lean forward" and, as Grace does so, he places his hands on her dress adjusting her breasts upward to enhance her appearance. As Grace is leaving the apartment, she is greeted at the elevator by her friend, Karen, who also knows of the date and places her hand on Grace's breasts and appears to also adjust her bosoms upward.

The scene includes this dialogue:

Karen: Hey, hey come here, one more thing come here.
Grace: Will already adjusted them.
Karen: I wasn't adjusting them.

The FCC's indecency analysis summarily rejected the complaints:

Although the episode contains some sexual innuendo, the characters in the scene in question appear to touch Grace's breast area primarily to enhance her appearance during her date rather than to elicit a sexual response. We need not decide, however, whether the scene depicts or describes sexual activities or organs because even assuming that the first prong of our indecency analysis is met, we conclude that the material is not indecent because it is not patently offensive as measured by contemporary community standards for the broadcast medium.

The FCC said that "the context is generally humorous and consists of light-hearted ridicule and indirect references to the size of Grace's breasts and the efforts made by her friends to enhance her sexual appeal for her date by making her breasts look larger." The program was cleared because there was no nudity or specific description of sex. The FCC concluded that the scenes did not "pander, titillate, or shock," because they were about the anxiety associated with dating: "Moreover, the touching of the breasts is not portrayed in a sexualized manner, and does not appear to elicit any sexual response from Grace." Thus, the FCC denied the complaint.

CBS Television

A February 21, 2005, episode of *Two and a Half Men* produced FCC complaints and review.

> *Two and a Half Men* had a scene in which a female doctor "was doing a hernia check" on a male character "with his scrotum in her hand" while he was trying to seduce her . . . the scene in question takes place in a doctor's office and involves a hernia examination, which requires the male character to remove his pants and cough with the female doctor's hand on his scrotum. No nudity or touching, however, is actually depicted, and the examination is not eroticized . . . he comments suggestively that her hands are warm and asks her out to dinner. She expresses disbelief that he does not remember her and states that they dated while she was in medical school until he broke it off without explanation and began seeing her roommate. The scene ends with him making comments and sounds indicating that she is painfully squeezing his scrotum.

The FCC said that there was also a general complaint about the program's "raunchy" episodes featuring "a lot of talk about 'humping'" on *Two and a Half Men*. However, the FCC refused to consider a general program complaint:

> In order for us to process an indecency complaint, the complaint must identify a specific broadcast containing allegedly indecent

material. We cannot prosecute complaints about programs in general. The First Amendment to the United States Constitution and section 326 of the Act prohibit the Commission from censoring program material and from interfering with broadcasters' freedom of expression . . . Moreover, we previously rejected complaints regarding an episode of the program *Will and Grace* that made similar allegations.

The FCC's indecency analysis on the doctor's office scene concluded that it was not indecent because it was not patently offensive:

> . . . the material is not graphic or explicit. Although the episode suggests that one character is touching another's sexual organs, the apparent touching takes place off-camera; there is never any nudity, depiction of a sexual organ, or description of sexual organs or activities. Rather, viewers are left to surmise what is happening by one character's reactions to another. . . we do not believe the material shocks, panders, and/or titillates the viewing audience. As noted, actual touching of the male character's sexual organs is not depicted or described. Although the male character makes some mildly suggestive remarks to the doctor during the examination, the exam is not eroticized or presented in a manner that shocks, panders to, or titillates the audience.

The FCC denied the complaint in one of the few examples in which it invoked the anti-censorship language of statute law. Clearly, the FCC will not consider general censorship of ongoing broadcast programs. Instead, its contextual case-by-case analyses attempt to apply indecency law to various circumstances.

The special case of the Super Bowl

The FCC's omnibus order fined numerous CBS stations for the 2004 broadcast of Janet Jackson's bare breast during the halftime show of the Super Bowl and the teen orgy scene during an episode of *Without a Trace*. FCC Chair Kevin Martin issued the following statement:

STATEMENT OF CHAIRMAN KEVIN J. MARTIN

Re: complaints against various television licensees concerning their February 1, 2004. broadcast of the Super Bowl XXXVIII halftime show; complaints regarding various television broadcasts between February 2, 2002, and March 8, 2005; complaints against various television licensees concerning their December 31, 2004, broadcast of the program Without A Trace.

Congress has long prohibited the broadcasting of indecent and profane material and the courts have upheld challenges to these standards. But the number of complaints received by the Commission has risen year after year. They have grown from hundreds, to hundreds of thousands. And the number of programs that trigger these complaints continues to increase as well. I share the concerns of the public – and of parents, in particular – that are voiced in these complaints.

I believe the Commission has a legal responsibility to respond to them and resolve them in a consistent and effective manner. So I am pleased that with the decisions released today the Commission is resolving hundreds of thousands of complaints against various broadcast licensees related to their televising of 49 different programs. These decisions, taken both individually and as a whole, demonstrate the Commission's continued commitment to enforcing the law prohibiting the airing of obscene, indecent and profane material.

Additionally, the Commission today affirms its initial finding that the broadcast of the Super Bowl XXXVIII Halftime Show was actionably indecent. We appropriately reject the argument that CBS continues to make that this material is not indecent. That argument runs counter to Commission precedent and common sense.

FCC Commissioner Michael Copps added that regulators need to go further in addressing the impact of media consolidation. At the same time, he wrote that the FCC should address media violence, as well. The FCC has never regulated violence despite the the evidence that violence is potentially more harmful to children than indecency.

In the case of the Super Bowl, complaints led the FCC's Enforcement Bureau to launch an investigation and request a tape from CBS. The FCC found that the halftime show had a sexual context. In the first song, there were sexual references:

All my girls at the party
Look at that body
Shakin' that thing
Like I never did see
Got a nice package alright
Guess I'm gonna have to ride it tonight.

The FCC found that, "These lyrics use slang terms to refer to a man's sexual organs and sexual intercourse and were repeated two more times during the song."

P. Diddy and Nelly then performed medley of songs that contained sexual references and included Nelly's "crotch-grabbing gestures."

> These sexual references include the lyrics "I was like good gracious ass bodacious . . . I'm waiting for the right time to shoot my steam (you know)" and "[i]t's gettin' hot in here (so hot), so take off all your clothes (I am gettin' so hot)" in the Nelly song "Hot in Herre."

The closing song was "Rock Your Body." During the performance by Janet Jackson and Justin Timberlake, Timberlake urged that Jackson "allow him to 'rock your body' and 'just let me rock you 'til the break of day' while following her around the stage and, on several occasions, grabbing and rubbing up against her in a manner simulating sexual activity." As the song ends with the lyrics, "gonna have you naked by the end of this song," according to the FCC, "Timberlake pulled off the right portion of Jackson's bustier, exposing her breast to the television audience."

CBS defended the broadcast by arguing that:

- The material broadcast was not actionably indecent.
- The broadcast of Jackson's breast was accidental, and therefore was not "willful."
- The Commission's indecency framework is unconstitutionally vague and overbroad, both on its face and as applied to the halftime show.

The FCC, however, found the Jackson breast to be patently offensive in the full context of the halftime show:

> As discussed above, in our assessment of whether broadcast material is patently offensive, "the *full context* in which the material appeared is critically important" . . . In cases involving televised nudity, the contextual analysis necessarily involves an assessment of the entire segment or program, and not just the particular scene in which the nudity occurs . . . Accordingly, in this case, our contextual analysis considers the entire halftime show, not just the final segment during which Jackson's breast is uncovered. We find that, in context and on balance, the complained-of material is patently offensive as measured by contemporary community standards for the broadcast medium.

The FCC found that the depiction was sexual and graphic:

> Contrary to CBS's contention, we do evaluate the nudity in context. The offensive segment in question did not merely show a fleeting glimpse of a woman's breast, as CBS presents it. Rather, it showed a man tearing off a portion of a woman's clothing to reveal her naked breast during a highly sexualized performance and while he sang "gonna have you naked by the end of this song." From the viewer's standpoint, this nudity hardly seems "accidental," nor was it . . . This broadcast thus presents a much different case than would, for example, a broadcast in which a woman's dress strap breaks, accidentally revealing her breast for a fraction of a second.

Thus, the FCC levied significant fines: ". . . we find that CBS's size and resources, without question, support an upward adjustment to the maximum statutory forfeiture of $550,000 because a lesser amount would not serve as a significant penalty or deterrent to a company of its size and resources."

Explicit podcasting

The regulation of indecent broadcasting through a series of record fines in 2006 came just a new media technologies were redefining the issues. The ability of content producers to compress video files and produce podcasts presented an interesting challenge (Figures 8.1 and 8.2). Podcasts, which

Figure 8.1 A search of "explicit" on iTunes reveals content labeled as such. Buying music on iTunes can be done with a pre-paid card.

Figure 8.2 An ABC News podcast featured an interview with an Air Force training instructor who posed for pictures in Playboy magazine (January 13, 2007).

are *published* on the Internet, fall under the rule of the *Reno* case, which means that they are not regulated for indecency. Networks, syndicators, and individuals alike may make podcasts available, and children are able to obtain them. Through direct downloads or subscription feeds, podcasts are delivered to a computer and may then be copied to a portable device. Given that the stated goal of FCC regulation is to protect children from indecency, the broadcast medium may become further isolated as the lone form of media subject to such content restrictions.

Chapter summary

The FCC in 2006 cleared a wide range of broadcast indecency cases, and these included some examples of content that was actionable, as well as content that was not. The FCC is concerned with sexual or excretory material that is patently offensive and shocking. Sexual scenes, language that includes "shit" or "fuck," and suggestive music lyrics and dancing may all get a broadcaster in trouble with the government. Such government regulation, however, may be difficult to sustain in an age of web sites, blogs, and podcasting.

Review questions

1 Should a rape scene always be considered by the FCC as indecent? Why or why not?
2 Is there ever a case to be made for the use of profanity in the broadcast of a serious documentary? How does the FCC distinguish appropriate from inappropriate usage?

3　Should the networks always be required to use a time delay system for live awards shows and sports programs? If profanity is part of the reality of an event, is anything lost by eliminating it?

4　What should the rules be about indecency with respect to situation comedies? Does the context matter?

5　Will podcasting eventually render ineffective the current broadcast indecency regulation system? How do you protect children from sexual content?

9

POLITICAL AND RELIGIOUS
ISSUES

The issue of decency in media appears to have been driven by individuals and groups with religious and moral orientations seeking to influence society through the political process. From historical campaigns to the present, we can see participants inside and outside the government pointing to various media forms as a source of corruption of children, youth, and even adults.

The politics of regulation

Broadcast regulation has been found to be the product of political influence. The authors of *The Politics of Broadcast Regulation* identified seven generalizations about regulatory policy-making that apply to the context of broadcast indecency:

1 *Participants seek conflicting goals from the process.* In the case of broadcast indecency regulation, not everybody can be a winner. The protection of children, if possible, would come at the expense of diminishing free speech rights for broadcasters and adult listeners. The various positions ranging from absolute free speech to a total ban suggest the political reality that compromise with the broadcast industry is likely.

2 *Participants have limited resources insufficient to continually dominate the policy-making process.* Broadcasters interested in challenging FCC regulatory initiatives must make an economic decision about the value of their actions. Likewise, programmers must weigh their options. The sheer slow pace of regulatory change is in stark contrast to rapid media change. The FCC Infinity settlment, for example, according to Karmazin, will lead to new business opporunities: "Now we feel there will be many, many more broadcasters interested in taking Howard's [Stern] show into many more markets than he has been in up to now."

3 *Participants have unequal strengths in the struggle for control or influence.* The court of appeals, largely because the Supreme Court has avoided

further significant review of broadcast indecency, holds the position of "court of last resort." However, the court of appeals' authority ends with the publication of its decisions. During the current decade-long struggle, the FCC has ignored the Supreme Court's suggestion to collect and analyze hard data on damaging effects. The FCC, to its credit, has recognized that the results of media effects research have been inconclusive. The round of decision-making in mid-1995, as we will see, appears to acknowledge that the FCC is the administrative agency which must, in the end, answer to Congress on broadcast indecency.

4 *The component subgroups of participant groups do not automatically agree on policy options.* The absolutist First Amendment view of Howard Stern's broadcast group, as well as others representing shock jock DJs, is not shared by all broadcasters. In fact, there have been those who have argued that such blue radio is bad for the long-term health of the industry. Likewise, members of the court of appeals and the FCC have disagreed over the years about free speech rights. The *Pacifica* decision of the Supreme Court is perhaps the best example of division. Infinity Broadcasting continues to hold the position in court that FCC indecency rules *are* unconstitutional.

5 *The process tends toward policy progression by small or incremental steps rather than massive changes.* In a sense, the dispute over broadcast indecency arose because the FCC attempted something larger than incremental policy change in the late 1980s. The reaction from interest groups was swift. The judicial review slammed the brakes on any attempt at massive change in policy. In one round of decision-making, the question on the table was simply whether a "safe harbor" should begin at 8 p.m., 10 p.m., or midnight.

6 *Legal and ideological symbols play a significant role in the process.* The symbol of children as being defenseless against indecent broadcast is perhaps the most potent one in this process. Freedom and autonomy are also important ideological symbols in the indecency debate. Precedent is perhaps the most significant legal symbol, and it surfaces when the court of appeals expresses being bound by it. Likewise, judicial review is an important legal symbol in the process.

7 *The process is usually characterized by mutual accommodation among participants.* Early on, it was difficult to see much mutual accommodation on broadcast indecency. As a highly polarized issue, the middle-ground for compromise seemed difficult to discover. But developments in 1995 did, as the political model predicts, lead participants toward accommodation. In the case of Howard Stern's broadcasts, Infinity won a clean, expunged record, and the FCC persuaded the public that it was protecting children by regulating the public airwaves.

146

Religious concerns

The influence of religious participants in the political process can be seen as the historical product of religious conflict and resolution. Cooper (1985) outlined the contribution of Protestant Christianity to a "political vision" that valued freedom:

> Although always a part of biblical anthropology, the idea of individual conscience and responsibility was a special concern of Protestant reformers. The freedom of the individual conscience before God and the notion of salvation as a voluntary, personal experience, laid the groundwork for modern conceptions of democratic self-government and civil liberty. If the individual possesses transcendent freedom over against the religious community, then similarly, every person has political rights that transcend the interests of the political community. Liberty thus emerged as an aspect of justice and as a treasure belonging not only to individuals for their own sake but also to the community itself for the sake of openness to fuller ethical development.
>
> (p. 11)

Cooper, comparing the work of Martain to Niehbuhr, suggested that "the historical experience of modern secular society" offered lessons to a pluralistic religious approach:

> The great achievement of modern society was pluralism. Given the great diversity of ideas, traditions, and loyalties that Christians have inherited from their past, it followed that society would either impose a unitary vision at the expense of one part of the Christian family of faiths or it would choose a pluralistic organizational model. The violent clash of religious groups eventually gave way to the open society of religious pluralism. A diversity of faiths was tolerated within an overall Western milieu. It thus became possible to speak of "Western culture," and, somewhat imprecisely, of a "Judeo-Christian" heritage. Alongside religious and cultural pluralism, there arose a diversity of political life – with representative democracy as its vehicle – and a diversity of economic life. Each group or individual was free to defend its interests and pursue its goals as long as its activity did not infringe upon the rights of others. The modern secular society, at its best, became not a valueless and godless regime but a political society based on a pluralism of moral and spiritual values.
>
> (ibid.: 10–11)

Little research exists examining the interplay between religious crusades and intolerance for freedom. Yet, the current political landscape affords anecdotal evidence that a politics of intolerance is behind the current broadcast indecency controversy.

Religion, Washington, and indecency

Broadcasting & Cable (2006, June 19) editorialized on the "chill" that could be felt on the day of the signing of a law raising fines for broadcast indecency to ten times what they had been. When President Bush signed the Broadcast Decency Enforcement Act into law, representatives of the Parents Television Council (PTC) and the American Family Association (AFA), as well as all five FCC commissioners, were in attendance. "The picture spoke a thousand words to us, most of them unprintable" (ibid., p. 42) *Broadcasting & Cable* magazine editors said. Complaints about a teen orgy scene in the episode of *Without a Trace* came not from those who had actually watched the program, but rather from those who had seen a clip that remained for months on the PTC web site: ". . . the FCC should require complainants to swear in an affidavit that they viewed the show they find offensive *when it aired* on a TV station. That would allow the FCC to decide cases on rules, not in reaction to Web-mob pressure" (ibid.) the editorial said in response to the ability people have to complain at the FCC web site. "We also believe it would expose the indecency crusade for the sham it truly is" (ibid.).

The *Without a Trace* teen orgy scene, had it happened under the new higher indecency fines, would have cost CBS stations more than $30 million (Eggerton, 2006, June 12). The Broadcast Decency Enforcement Act of 2005, which increased fines tenfold, passed the US House on a vote of 379–35. Fines were raised to $325,000 per indecency, with a maximum of $3 million per incident. "The bill was championed by Sen. Sam Brownback (R-Kan.), an intensely religious man who also has his eye on the White House" (ibid.: 4). The Senate Majority Leader, Bill Frist, a Republican from Tennessee, said: "This sends a clear signal to the networks . . . If you peddle trash to kids, you're going to pay the price" (ibid.). Michigan Republican Representative Fred Upton said that the genesis of the legislation was complaints about Opie & Anthony's "Sex in St. Patrick's Cathedral" radio shock stunt, an event that led to the firing of the shock jocks and $375,000 in proposed fines – part of a $3 million Viacom settlement in 2004 of all of its complaints. Senator Sam Brownback added: "It's time that broadcast-indecency fines represent a real economic penalty and not just a slap on the wrist" (Eggerton, May 22: 3). Brownback has focused on "media decency" as a prime issue, and this is reflected in his United States Senate web site, as well as his press releases. I have reproduced one example here.

Box 9.1 Kansas Republican Sam Brownback
sees media decency as a reform issue

Source: http://brownback.senate.gov/pressapp/record.
   cfm?id=255842&&days=365&

Brownback Applauds Broadcast Decency Bill Passage

Bill increases broadcast indecency fines from $32,500 to $325,000

Thursday, May 18, 2006

WASHINGTON – US Senator Sam Brownback today applauded Senate passage by unanimous consent of S.193, the Broadcast Decency Enforcement Act, which increases by a factor of ten fines for broadcasting indecent material. Brownback authored and introduced the bill last January.

   I am glad the Senate took action and increased fines for broadcasters who show indecent material," said Brownback. "Radio and television waves are public property, and the companies who profit from using the public airwaves should face meaningful fines for broadcasting indecent material.

   Current fines levied against broadcasters by the Federal Communications Commission are limited to $32,500 per violation, and the Broadcast Decency Enforcement Act increases those fines to $325,000 per violation. The bill only raises FCC fines, and does not address other issues such as the definition of indecent material or how the fines are assessed. The bill does not grant the FCC new powers to revoke licenses from broadcasters who play offensive content.

   Brownback continued, "I urge the House to take action on increasing indecency fines so we can send a bill to the White House. It's time that broadcast indecency fines represent a real economic penalty and not just a slap on the wrist."

   Brownback is a member of the Judiciary Committee and the Appropriations Committee.

149

The raising of indecency fines is seen as something of a moral crusade to *restore* American values. Such a proposition assumes that there is a single value set, as opposed to pluralistic approaches to beliefs. Congressman Fred Upton is another politician focusing on the issue, and he became a prime sponsor in the United States House of Representatives. One of his press releases is reprinted here.

Box 9.2 Congressman Fred Upton seeks to have broadcasters think twice

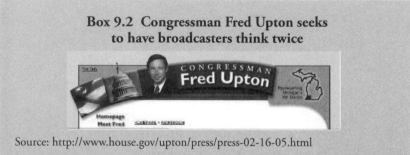

Source: http://www.house.gov/upton/press/press-02-16-05.html

PRESS RELEASE

FOR IMMEDIATE RELEASE.

CONTACT: Sean C. Bonyun

February 16, 2005, (202) 225-3761

US House Overwhelmingly Approves Upton Indecency Bill
Fines for Indecency Raised to $500,000

WASHINGTON, DC – The United States House of Representatives today overwhelmingly approved Congressman Fred Upton's (R-St. Joseph) legislation to clean up the public airwaves. Upton's legislation, H.R. 310, the Broadcast Indecency Act of 2005, would raise the amount the FCC can fine for indecency from $32,500 to $500,000 per violation. H.R. 310 passed the House by a vote of 389 to 38.

"Today, we are delivering something of real value to American families," said Upton. "There must be a level of expectation when a parent turns on the TV or radio between the family hours that the content will be suitable for children. A parent should not have to think twice about the content on the public airwaves. Unfortunately, that situation is far from reality. With passage of this legislation, I am confident that broadcasters will think twice about pushing the envelope. And our kids will be better off for it. I am pleased with the passage of this bill in the House today, not only as the bill's author, but more importantly as a parent."

In addition to raising the fines from $32,500 to $500,000 per violation, Upton's legislation also mandates a license revocation hearing (but does not dictate the outcome of the hearing) after the third offense by a broadcaster (the FCC currently has the authority to hold such a hearing after the first offense, but is not mandated to do so) and also imposes on the FCC a 180-day "shot clock" to act on indecency complaints filed by consumers. Additionally, the bill raises the amount the FCC can fine networks and entertainers who willfully or intentionally violate indecency standards from $11,000 to $500,000. The bill also includes protections for affiliates from fines in instances, such as the 2004 Super Bowl, where they did not know what was soon to be broadcast by the network.

"Using the public airwaves comes with the responsibility to follow the FCC decency standards that apply to programming that airs during the family hours of 6:00 a.m. to 10:00 p.m. – the likeliest times that children may be tuned in," said Upton during today's debate. "My bill does not alter current decency standards – the laws for indecency have been on the books for decades and they have been upheld in the courts."

Just over a year ago, Upton introduced similar legislation after all five FCC Commissioners, both Republican and Democrat, had lamented that the current level of fines was too low. The bill passed the House last March 11th by a vote of 391 to 22 and the Senate passed similar legislation by a vote of 99 to 1 on June 22nd.

Also, today the White House Office and Management and Budget released a statement in strong support of Upton's bill that said, "This legislation will make broadcast television and radio more suitable for family viewing by giving the Federal Communications Commission (FCC) the authority to impose stiffer penalties on broadcasters that air obscene or indecent material over the public airwaves. In particular, the Administration applauds the inclusion in the bill of its proposal to require that the FCC consider whether inappropriate material has been aired during children's television programming In determining the fine to be imposed for violations of the law."

Industry reaction to the legislative hammer of large fines has been swift. CBS pointed out that the *Without a Trace* episode dealing with "sex and substance abuse among unsupervised teens was fined while *Oprah Winfrey* was not fined for 'highly graphic and explicit' discussion of teen sexual practices" (Eggerton, 2006, December 11: 17). The network claimed in its filing that the contextual analysis performed by the FCC was discriminatory. PBS lawyers made a similar point in the FCC finding against the documentary *Godfathers and Sons*, while concluding that profanity in the film *Saving Private Ryan* was not actionable.

The ability of interest group moral crusaders to quickly gather large numbers of supporters online has clearly influenced the direction of public policy. The American Family Association (AFA) asked supporters to email the WB network – 27,290 of them did to complain about scenes in *The Bedford Diaries*. Without comment, the network decided to edit the show and play the cut scene on its web site. A day later, AFA Chair, Donald

Wildmon, emailed the supporters: "There is no question that your personal involvement resulted in the WB's announcing their decision to edit the most elicit scenes from the show" (Topcik, 2006: 7). AFA appeared to be energized by its success a month earlier.

Box 9.3 NBC show *Las Vegas* draws AFA complaints

In March of 2006, the FCC received 134,300 complaints about the NBC show *Las Vegas* (Figure 9.1) – more than twice as many complaints as it received about all shows combined in 2005. The Mississippi-based AFA "sent an alert to members asking them to complain about a February 6 *Las Vegas* episode that featured a scene in a strip club" (Eggerton & Grossman, 2006: 6). The clip was included in an email to members, and some complained. This led AFA to cover indecent portions of future videos. *Las Vegas* producer Gary Scott Thomson told *Broadcasting & Cable* magazine: "They complained about the scene, but they put the clip on their Web site where any kid can download it and see it . . . How is that consistent with their message? My kids found it online easily, thanks to the group, but I wouldn't let them watch my show because of its rating" (ibid.).

AFA uses a simple online form to activate members (Figure 9.2). The process begins with an email that sends people to the web site.

Figure 9.1 NBC network show *Las Vegas* raises eyebrows. http://www.nbc.com/Las_Vegas/

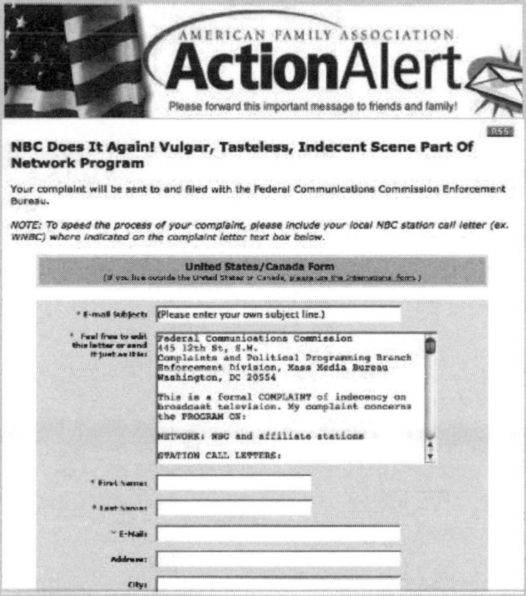

Figure 9.2 American Family Association urges computerized complaints. Source: https://secure.afa.net/afa/activism/takeaction.asp?id=185

The AFA's email described the *Las Vegas* strip club scene as "extremely graphic," and readers were linked to a viewing of it. NBC aired this scene during prime-time hours when they knew that millions of children would likely be watching," said AFA founder Don Wildmon. "But NBC didn't care if they exposed children to this kind of material. Please take action . . . and help us help our children." (WorldNetDaily, 2006: para. 3).

Impact of a crackdown

The $3.6 million fine against CBS for *Without a Trace* set a record, and the PTC challenged a Salt Lake City license. In another case, *The Surreal Life 2* (2004), the FCC concluded that "mere pixelation of sexual organs [which includes breasts . . .] is not necessarily determinative in our analysis" (Eggerton, 2006, March 20: 18). Writer and producer Tom Fontana told *Broadcasting & Cable* magazine: "It has always been a fight to do shows that are pushing the envelope . . . You're trying to find the balance between not being offensive and telling the whole story" (ibid.: 19).

A significant problem with the efforts to expunge media of indecency is that language remains a matter of subjectivity and interpretation. *Broadcasting & Cable* concluded: "Arguably, the word 'poop' is more strictly excretory. The FCC says that word is OK, just silly . . . Censorship, we remind the FCC, is not a family value. Nor an American one" (Editorial, 2006a: 42).

In the wake of the post-Janet Jackson wardrobe malfunction, the subsequent intense media attention of congressional hearings and the process of law-making, the following incidents were reported:

- The FCC received a complaint from the PTC over the ABC broadcast of *Live 8: A Worldwide Event,* on July 2, 2005. The Who's performance aired unedited with the question, "Who the fuck are you?" (*Broadcasting & Cable* (July 18, 2005, p. 4).
- WCBS-TV reporter Arthur Chi'en was fired after he used the F-word on hecklers during the 6 a.m. newscast. Following the Janet Jackson incident, CBS instituted a "zero-tolerance policy" (*Broadcasting & Cable,* May 23, 2005, p. 5).

Members of the industry, however, contend that the religious and political coalition behind the crackdown on broadcast indecency does not represent the vast mainstream of American society and culture. Instead, their view is that parents should be empowered to freely choose for their children rather than have the government mandate content standards.

TV Watch is a coalition formed by NBC, Fox, and CBS "to promote parental controls as preferable to a government crackdown on indecency" (Eggerton, 2005, May 9: 10). The American Conservative Union and the US Chamber of Commerce also signed on to the effort. A commissioned poll found:

- Ninety-one percent of Americans agree that "the sensitivities of a few should not dictate the choices for everyone else."
- Eighty-six percent of Americans favored increased "parental involvement."

Political activism, moral crusading, and draconian legislation, however, are only part of the mosaic that is the debate over decency. As 2007 began, two federal courts faced the question of how far the FCC could go – even with a congressional mandate – before it crossed the line of protection that is the First Amendment.

A market for religion

The portrayal of religion in secular mass media has presented interesting issues. One watchdog group concluded that while Hollywood continues to largely depict religion in negative terms, reality television programs frequently address issues of faith (Hoffman, 2006b). The PTC, which studied the question, concluded that the industry fails to serve Americans. The Media Research Center's critic, L. Brent Bozell, said: "The broadcast entertainment industry is completely disconnected from American public opinion' (ibid.: para. 3). Over half of positive portrayals of religion happened during reality television programs, but other types of programs tended to be negative:

> This year, the group pointed an angry finger at the Fox network, specifically such shows as *The Family Guy* and *House*, that it argues consistently mocked religion and people of faith. A Fox spokesman declined comment.
>
> (ibid.: para. 6)

There is a scholarly debate over whether or not such mentions of religion on television harm it or offer important attention.

Box 9.4 Faith in a Box study

The seventh Parents Teacher Council (PTC) study in 2005–06 on religion in prime-time television found that references to institutions ($n = 393$), faith ($n = 379$), and laity ($n = 303$) topped the list (Figure 9.3).

Figure 9.3 Faith in a Box study finds negative depictions.

Straightforward depictions of faith (particularly by contestants on reality programs) tended to be overwhelmingly positive, while in all other categories (especially on scripted dramas and comedy shows) negative depictions dominated. Such findings imply that while most Americans enthusiastically endorse religious belief, Hollywood tolerates an indistinct "spirituality" but is deeply negative towards openly religious individuals and organized religion.

(Gildemeister, 2005–06: para. 1)

The study of ABC, CBS, NBC, Fox, WB, and UPN found that:

- There were 1,425 depictions of religion – from a brief mention of God to extensive dialogue or entire scenes concerned with religion – an average of one mention per every 1.6 hours of television.
- Of all treatments of religion, 34 percent were positive while 35 percent were negative. Twenty-seven percent were either neutral or mixed in treatment. In 4 percent of cases the context was insufficient to make a determination.
- Fox had the highest percentage of anti-religious depictions, with one of every two depictions of religion – almost exactly half (49.7 percent) – being negative. NBC closely followed, with 39.3 percent of their depictions of religion being negative, while 35.4 percent of UPN depictions were negative. Thirty percent of ABC's portrayals were negative, followed by 29 percent of CBS's and 21 percent of WB's.
- Typical of the positive references to religion were:
  - Dunstin, who is suffering from cancer, says: "I just trust in the Lord to take care of my children and family. . .Sometimes you wonder, why me? But then . . . you give thanks to the Lord, pray, and move on" (ABC, *Extreme Makeover: Home Edition*, March 19, 2006); and
  - Danni leads her group in prayer to Jesus, giving thanks for their meal (CBS, *Survivor: Guatemala*, October 13, 2005).
- Typical of the negative references were:
  - At a church fundraiser, two men play a game called "Halo Toss," in which they must throw rings around the heads of statues of saints. One man states that "It's all a big scam." The second man asks, "The game?" The first man replies, "No, religion in general" (Fox, *The Simpsons*, March 19, 2006); and
  - House tells a religious patient that the patient is either psychotic or a scam artist for believing that God speaks to him (Fox, *House M.D.*, April 25, 2006).
- An example of a mixed references was:
  - Dr. Burke explains his personal beliefs to Cristina: "With all medical realities being equal, why does one patient live and another die? I believe there is a mind–body–spirit connection." Cristina responds: "Let me get this straight. You don't just celebrate Christmas, you actually believe in Santa Claus?" (ABC, *Grey's Anatomy*, December 11, 2006).

The PTC concluded:

> The vast majority of Americans hold religion to be of deep
> personal importance, and for many it is the center of their
> lives. Most Americans treat religious beliefs with respect and
> reverence and would like to see the entertainment media
> do so. In a November 2006 Zogby poll, a large majority
> (84 percent) of adults stated that they are not offended by
> references to God or the Bible on network television. Half
> (51 percent) of those responding expressed a wish for more
> network shows with positive messages, and even for specific
> references in programs to God, the Bible and religion. These
> sentiments are echoed by the overwhelming enthusiasm
> shown for religion on reality TV. On such programs, average
> Americans openly acknowledge the importance of religion
> and frequently demonstrate their belief in God by words,
> actions and prayer.
>
> (Gildemeister, 2005–06: para. 104)

PTC claimed that Hollywood has a "contempt for religion – and
for its own viewing audience – by deliberately portraying God as
subject of ridicule, and followers of organized religion as oppressive,
fanatical, hypocritical and hopelessly corrupt" (ibid.: para. 105).

The religious press in America reports on the concerns over media content. In general, the view expressed seems to be that groups such as the PTC
have had some success influencing the crackdown on broadcast indecency
and the raising of fines. However, there is skepticism about the prospects
of going further by tightening regulation of cable and new media. Clearly,
the First Amendment precedents make this unlikely. As premium channel
programs, such as HBO's *Sex in the City* and *The Sopranos*, make second
runs on cable channels (TBS, WGN, and A&E), Morality in Media's
Robert Peters suggested that the edited versions would be more and more
edgy.

In the face of these realities, a television industry guide, "Religious &
Faith-Based programming," published in *Broadcast & Cable* (2006) magazine reflects the move toward capturing a market form family-friendly
programs. For example, JCTV has this mission statement:

> JCTV is a family friendly digital network from TBN featuring
> faith-based cutting edge programs for the 13 to 29 age group.
> JCTV's format includes the latest in contemporary music

reinforcing positive lifestyles, original reality programs, youth-oriented game shows, relevant talk, comedy, extreme sports, and more.

(ibid.: 12A).

The network, which includes music videos aimed at young people, use the following slogan: "Oh, yeah, No FCC Indecency Fines. Guaranteed!"

TBN's main channel continues to the most watched faith channel in the United States. However, the market is expanding with channels such as iLifetv, The Church Channel and Daystar, which seeks "to reach souls with the good news of Jesus Christ" (p. 6A). As one industry expert, Frank Wright, told *Broadcasting & Cable*, "We have to bring to market programming that is more creative and more interesting to younger demos" (Winslow, 2006: 16).

Chapter summary

Political and religious issues commingle in the moral crusade that is the fight over broadcast indecency. On the one hand, interest groups such as the AFA influence key law-makers to impose a crackdown by arming the FCC with more restrictive laws and larger fines. On the other hand, the industry fights back with efforts to empower parents through an expensive public relations campaign. Additionally, they utilize the courts to pose First Amendment challenges to FCC actions that disregard the First Amendment rights of broadcasters to make content decisions. In the end, religion and morality can been seen as being misused by political activists to limit fundamental freedoms. Nevertheless, there is a growing counter-market for faith-based programming that seeks to offer family-friendly options. One might conclude that this is the ideal marketplace response to broadcast indecency.

Review questions

1 To what extent do you see the current fight over broadcast indecency as a campaign to legislate morality? Explain your reasons.
2 Why is broadcast indecency a useful example of incremental policy change, as described in the political model of broadcast regulation?
3 Do you believe that religious interest groups have activated a "mob" response to force legislators to raise fines? Why or why not?
4 Should a broadcaster be fired for one slip of the tongue on live air? Why or why not?
5 Does the broadcasting industry have a responsibility to protect children from messages that some people might find indecent or inappropriate? Why or why not?

10

TRENDS

FINES, ENFORCEMENT, LAWS, AND REGULATION

The combination of numerous judicial interpretations, anecdotal evidence on the rise of indecent media messages and their presumed effects, and a divided FCC produced a series of inconsistent rulings, vague definitions, and problematic public policy. Interestingly, the battle over morality in media messages has gone global.

Although the FCC began 2006 taking what at first appeared to be a new hard-line stance on broadcasters' use of indecency, by late in the year it had backtracked. In the midst of what many believed to be a losing federal case and changing political climate, the FCC reverted to its original view that news programs were exempt from indecency fines. However, the FCC held to its emerging view that even fleeting uses of profanity could be actionable under the law.

In November of 2006, despite its earlier ruling on the profanity of "shit," the FCC reversed its decision and re-established an exception for news programs. A *Survivor: Vanuatu* (Figure 10.1) contestant had used the word "bullshitter" on *The Early Show* on CBS in December of 2004.

A court had sent the case back to the FCC for further review on the question of whether or not the indecency happened during a "bona fide news interview" – *The Early Show* is produced by CBS's news division, and the program does some serious news reporting.

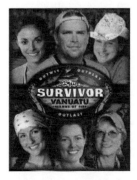

Figure 10.1 A *Survivor Vanuatu* contestant uttered the word "bullshitter" in an early morning news show interview.

The FCC decision related to a case more than a decade earlier: NPR's *All Things Considered* aired profanity in wiretaps played during the trial of mobster John Gotti. The profanity was exempted as being "an integral part" of the reporting. This appeared to create a First Amendment defense against indecency for news broadcasters, but there was confusion about this point during the crackdown of 2004–2006.

FCC Chair, Kevin Martin, told *USA Today* that, although the interview was "a close call," the decision was correct: "I believe the commission's exercise of caution with respect to news programming was appropriate in this instance" (Davidson, 2006: para. 6).

The FCC also dismissed indecency complaints against *NYPD Blue*, but it affirmed its rulings against Fox for the *Billboard Music Awards* shows in 2002 and 2003, which featured Cher and Nicole Richie using expletives. In the *NYPD Blue* case against a Kansas City station that is found earlier in this book, the FCC said a complaint by a Virginia viewer could not be considered.

Box 10.1 FCC tells the public about indecency regulation

The FCC created an extensive web site to inform the public about indecency regulation and explain the complaint process. The content of the site is reproduced here.

Regulation of obscenity, indecency, and profanity (http://www.fcc. gov/eb/oip/Welcome.html)

It is a violation of federal law to air obscene programming at any time. It is also a violation of federal law to broadcast indecent or profane programming during certain hours (see definitions). Congress has given the Federal Communications Commission (FCC) the responsibility for administratively enforcing the law that governs these types of broadcasts. The FCC has authority to issue civil monetary penalties, revoke a license, or deny a renewal application. In addition, violators of the law, if convicted in a federal district court, are subject to criminal fines and/or imprisonment for not more than two years.

The FCC vigorously enforces this law where we find violations. In 2004 alone, the FCC took action in twelve cases, involving hundreds of thousands of complaints, assessing penalties and voluntary payments totaling approximately $8,000,000. The Commission has also toughened its enforcement penalties by proposing monetary penalties based on each indecent utterance in a broadcast, rather than proposing a single monetary penalty for the entire broadcast.

At the same time, however, the Commission is careful of First Amendment protections and the prohibitions on censorship and interference with broadcasters' freedom of speech. The FCC has denied complaints in cases in which we determined the broadcast was not indecent based on the overall context of the programming. Regardless of the outcome, the FCC strives to address every complaint within nine months of its receipt.

Frequently asked questions (http://www.fcc.gov/eb/oip/FAQ. html#TheLaw)

Enforcement process

How do I file a complaint?
The FCC accepts complaints by letter, email, facsimile, or telephone. If possible, your complaint should include the call sign of the station, the community where the station is located (city, state), and the date and time of the broadcast. Although not required, including this information greatly assists the FCC in processing your complaint quickly and efficiently. Your complaint should also contain enough detail about the material broadcast that the FCC can understand the exact words and language used. It is very helpful if the complaint includes a partial tape or transcript of the aired material or a significant excerpt. Please see the link "How to file a Complaint" for more complete information, including information on FCC web and mailing addresses.

Do I need to provide a tape or transcript of the program?
No, a tape or transcript is not required. However, the FCC's determination as to whether material is indecent, profane, or potentially obscene rests upon its context. Your submission of a tape or transcript assists us in determining context, but an excerpt or description of the material may also be sufficient. FCC staff will usually send a letter of inquiry to the station if the complaint indicates that the program may be obscene, indecent or profane. At that stage of the investigation, the FCC usually requests a tape and transcript from the station.

What happens to my complaint once it is filed?
The "Complaint Process Flow Chart" link provides a general description of how the FCC processes complaints. Once a complaint is filed, FCC staff scan or otherwise record it in a database. The complaint is then forwarded to the staff responsible for initial review. A station licensee may receive a letter of inquiry from the FCC requesting the information necessary to complete the investigation. At any stage of the investigation, if the FCC concludes that we need more information to process your complaint, or that the material is not obscene, indecent or profane, we will notify you by letter. If the FCC determines that the material is indecent or profane, we will take further action, including possibly imposing monetary penalties. If the FCC determines that the material is arguably obscene, we will refer the matter to the Department of Justice. The Department of Justice has authority to bring criminal prosecutions

for the broadcast of obscene, indecent, or profane material. If convicted in a federal district court, violators may be subject to criminal fines and/or imprisonment.

How do I determine the status of my complaint?
You can ensure you remain apprised of the status of your complaint by sending a copy of your FCC complaint to the station that broadcast the material that you find offensive and by informing us you have done so. In doing this, you become a party to the investigation and all other parties to the investigation, including the FCC and the station licensee, must send you copies of all written communications between them, including any FCC letters of inquiry and licensee responses. You can also check on the status of your complaint by calling (202) 418-1420. You will be notified of the outcome of the FCC's investigation of your complaint via letter or by public order imposing a monetary sanction.

How long will it take for the FCC to act on my complaint?
The FCC has numerous staff persons in the Consumer & Governmental Affairs Bureau and the Enforcement Bureau processing, reviewing, and investigating allegations of obscenity, indecency and/or profanity. The FCC addresses these allegations as quickly as possible, striving to address every complaint within nine months of its receipt. However, because each case is different, we can't tell you how long it will take to resolve a particular complaint.

Will I be notified once the FCC has made a decision on my complaint?
You will be notified of the FCC's decision on your complaint, either by letter or email, or by public order. Because each case is different, it is hard to predict exactly how long it will take for the agency to reach a decision. We take all complaints seriously, and act on them as quickly as possible. We strive to address every complaint within nine months of its receipt.

The law

What are the statutes and rules regarding the broadcast of obscene, indecent, and profane programming?
Title 18 of the United States Code, Section 1464, prohibits the utterance of "any obscene, indecent or profane language by means of radio communication." Consistent with a subsequent statute and court case, the Commission's rules prohibit the broadcast of indecent material during the period of 6 a.m. and 10 p.m. FCC decisions also prohibit the broadcast of profane material between 6 a.m. and 10 p.m. Civil enforcement of these requirements rests with the FCC, and is an important part of the FCC's overall responsibilities. At the same time, the FCC must be mindful of the First Amendment to the United States Constitution and Section 326 of the Communications Act, which prohibit the FCC from censoring program material, or interfering with broadcasters' free speech rights.

What makes material "obscene?"

Obscene speech is not protected by the First Amendment and broadcasters are prohibited, by statute and regulation, from airing obscene programming at any time. According to the US Supreme Court, to be obscene, material must meet a three-prong test: (1) an average person, applying contemporary community standards, must find that the material, as a whole, appeals to the prurient interest (i.e., material having a tendency to excite lustful thoughts); (2) the material must depict or describe, in a patently offensive way, sexual conduct specifically defined by applicable law; and (3) the material, taken as a whole, must lack serious literary, artistic, political, or scientific value. The Supreme Court has indicated that this test is designed to cover hard-core pornography.

What makes material "indecent?"

Indecent material contains sexual or excretory material that does not rise to the level of obscenity. For this reason, the courts have held that indecent material is protected by the First Amendment and cannot be banned entirely. It may, however, be restricted to avoid its broadcast during times of the day when there is a reasonable risk that children may be in the audience. The FCC has determined, with the approval of the courts, that there is a reasonable risk that children will be in the audience from 6 a.m. to 10 p.m., local time. Therefore, the FCC prohibits station licensees from broadcasting indecent material during that period.

Material is indecent if, in context, it depicts or describes sexual or excretory organs or activities in terms patently offensive as measured by contemporary community standards for the broadcast medium. In each case, the FCC must determine whether the material describes or depicts sexual or excretory organs or activities and, if so, whether the material is "patently offensive."

In our assessment of whether material is "patently offensive," context is critical. The FCC looks at three primary factors when analyzing broadcast material: (1) whether the description or depiction is explicit or graphic; (2) whether the material dwells on or repeats at length descriptions or depictions of sexual or excretory organs; and (3) whether the material appears to pander or is used to titillate or shock. No single factor is determinative. The FCC weighs and balances these factors because each case presents its own mix of these, and possibly other, factors.

What makes material "profane?"

"Profane language" includes those words that are so highly offensive that their mere utterance in the context presented may, in legal terms, amount to a "nuisance." In its Golden Globe Awards Order the FCC warned broadcasters that, depending on the context, it would consider the "F-word" and those words (or variants thereof) that are as highly offensive as the "F-word" to be "profane language" that cannot be broadcast between 6 a.m. and 10 p.m.

What is the "safe harbor"?
The "safe harbor" refers to the time period between 10 p.m. and 6 a.m., local time. During this time period, a station may air indecent and/or profane material. In contrast, there is no "safe harbor" for the broadcast of obscene material. Obscene material is entitled to no First Amendment protection, and may not be broadcast at any time.

Are there certain words that are always unlawful?
No. Offensive words may be profane and/or indecent depending on the context. In the Golden Globe Awards Order, the FCC stated that it would address the legality of broadcast language on a case-by-case basis. Depending on the context presented, use of the "F-word" or other words as highly offensive as the "F-word" may be both indecent and profane, if aired between 6 a.m. and 10 p.m.

Does the FCC monitor particular radio or television programs?
The First Amendment to the U.S. Constitution and Section 326 of the Communications Act prohibit the FCC from censoring broadcasters. The FCC does not, therefore, monitor particular programs or particular performers, but rather enforces the prohibition on obscenity, indecency and profanity in response to complaints.

Does the FCC regulate violence on television?
The FCC does not currently regulate the broadcast of violent programming. On July 28, 2004, however, the FCC opened an inquiry into violent programming and its effect on children. The FCC has received public comments and opinions from many segments of the public. The FCC will publish and make available the report resolving the inquiry on the FCC web site.

Do the FCC's rules apply to cable and satellite programming?
In the past, the FCC has enforced the indecency and profanity prohibitions only against conventional broadcast services, not against subscription programming services such as cable and satellite. However, the prohibition against obscene programming applies to subscription programming services at all times.

FCC actions and statistics

What monetary sanctions has the FCC imposed for violation of its indecency, profanity, and obscenity restrictions?
The base monetary sanction for violation of the FCC's indecency, profanity, and/or obscenity restrictions is $7,000 per violation. The FCC may adjust this monetary sanction upwards, up to a current statutory maximum of $32,500 per violation, based on such factors as the nature, circumstances, extent and gravity of the violation, and, with respect to the violator, the degree of culpability, any history of prior offenses, ability to pay, and such other matters as justice may require.

During 2004, the FCC imposed monetary sanctions for indecency violations up to $1,183,000, for an aggregate annual total of $3,658,000. In addition, some entities chose to settle claims against them and made voluntary payments to the US Treasury, totaling $7,928,080 in 2004.

How many complaints has the FCC received about obscene, indecent, or profane programming?
The "Complaint And Enforcement Statistics" link to the left provides not only the previous month's count of the complaints received for the current year, but also lists the total number of complaints received by the FCC since 2000. The chart also identifies the number of programs cited by those complaints and categorizes those programs by service – broadcast television, broadcast radio, and cable/satellite. Finally, the chart provides information about the number and status of the forfeiture proceedings initiated by the Commission for each year since 1993.

What is a Notice of Apparent Liability for Forfeiture?
Any person or entity that the FCC determines has willfully or repeatedly violated the indecency, obscenity and/or profanity prohibitions is potentially liable for a forfeiture penalty, which is a monetary sanction paid to the United States Treasury. To impose such a penalty, the FCC must first issue a Notice of Apparent Liability for Forfeiture containing the FCC's preliminary findings and the amount of the proposed forfeiture. That decision contains the Commission's findings that, based on a preponderance of the evidence, the person or entity at issue has apparently violated the indecency, obscenity, and/or profanity prohibitions. The person or entity against which the penalty is proposed then may respond, in writing, and explain why no such forfeiture penalty should be imposed. The Commission will then issue a forfeiture order formally imposing the monetary sanction if it finds, by a preponderance of the evidence, that the person or entity has violated the indecency, obscenity or profanity prohibitions.

TV ratings and channel blocking

Can I block programming that offends me or my family?
Yes. FCC rules require all televisions 13 inches or larger to include the technology allowing you to block unwanted programming. Please see the "TV Ratings and Channel Blocking" link on the left for further information.

What is the "V-chip"?
The V-chip is a technology built into your television set that allows you to block television programming you don't want your children to watch. Most television shows now include a rating, as established by the broadcast or cable industry. The rating appears in the corner of your television screen during the first 15 seconds of a program and in TV programming

guides. This rating is encoded into the programs; the V-chip technology reads the encoded information and blocks shows accordingly. Using the remote control, parents can program the V-chip to block certain shows based on their ratings. If you lose your remote control/device or need help programming the V-chip, contact the manufacturer of your television set for a replacement or operating instructions.

The FCC requires all new television sets manufactured on or after January 1, 2000, that are 13 inches or larger to contain the V-chip technology. You can usually tell whether your television has a V-chip by looking at the packaging, including the owner's manual. If you no longer have these materials, the V-chip option usually appears as part of the television's menu if the set is equipped with this technology. If you want the V-chip function but your television set does not have it, you can get a set-top box, which works the same as a set with a built-in V-chip. Personal computers that include a television tuner and a monitor of 13 inches or greater are also required to include the V-chip technology. For complete information on the V-chip and other methods of preventing your children from viewing offensive material, see the "TV Ratings and Channel Blocking" link on the left.

What do the television ratings mean?
Ratings appear in the corner of your television screen during the first 15 seconds of each television program. The ratings are also included in many magazines that give TV ratings and in the television listings of many newspapers. All television programming is rated except news, sports, and unedited movies on premium cable channels. For more information on how you can control what your children view, please see the "TV Ratings and Channel Blocking" link on the left. Programs receive one of the following six possible ratings:

- TV-Y, (All Children) found only in children's shows, means that the show is appropriate for all children;

- TV-7, (Directed to Older Children) found only in children's shows, means that the show is most appropriate for children age 7 and up;

- TV-G (General Audience) means that the show is suitable for all ages but is not necessarily a children's show;

- TV-PG (Parental Guidance Suggested) means that parental guidance is suggested and that the show may be unsuitable for younger children (this rating may also include a V for violence, S for sexual situations, L for language, or D for suggestive dialog);

- TV-14 (Parents Strongly Cautioned) means that the show may be unsuitable for children under 14 (V, S, L, or D may accompany a rating of TV-14); and

- TV-MA (Mature Audience Only) means that the show is for mature audiences only and may be unsuitable for children under 17 (V, S, L, or D may accompany a rating of TV-MA).

While TV ratings are one attempt to label adult content, on the computer front Microsoft's operating system employs advanced parental controls and monitoring reports to track Internet usage.

How to file a complaint (http://www.fcc.gov/eb/oip/Compl.html)

Complaints may be filed via:

- Electronic Complaint Form FCC Form 475B (downloadable version)
- US mail sent to:
  FCC
  Enforcement Bureau, Investigations and Hearings Division
  445 12th Street, SW
  Washington, DC 20554
- Electronic mail at fccinfo@fcc.gov
- Toll Free: 1-888-CALL-FCC (1-888-225-5322)
- Fax: 1-866-418-0232

You can help us resolve your complaint more quickly by providing as much of the following information as possible: (1) the date and time the material was aired; (2) the call sign, channel, or frequency of the station; (3) the city and state where the program was viewed; and (4) as many details as possible about the content of the broadcast to help the FCC determine whether the material was obscene, profane, or indecent. You may support your allegations by a full or partial tape or transcript, or by providing a significant excerpt, but these are not required. The key is to provide enough information for staff to determine both the specific content of the complained-of material and the context in which it was broadcast. It is also helpful to include your address, e-mail address, phone number and time zone.

If you choose to submit a recording, you should send the recording to Federal Communications Commission, Investigations & Hearings Division/Enforcement Bureau, 9300 East Hampton Drive, Capital Heights, MD 20743. Any documentation of the programming becomes part of the Commission's records and cannot be returned.

Despite the FCC's attempts to explain and justify its elaborate regulatory scheme, the Commission had a difficult time defending its decisions in court. During a December 2006 hearing that was televised live on C-SPAN, an FCC lawyer struggled to answer probing questions from a three-judge panel at the United States Court of Appeals, Second Circuit, in New York. A lawyer representing Fox Television emphasized the vague definition of indecency – suggesting that the rules were even less understood at the end of the oral arguments.

Box 10.2 FCC lawyer challenged by Second Circuit Court of Appeals panel

A lawyer representing Fox Television and a United States Court of Appeals judge used profanity to make their points during December 2006 oral arguments in the *Fox Television* v. *FCC* case – one that questioned whether "fleeting expletives" can be considered indecent by the commission. Judge Pierre Leval and Fox attorney Carter G. Phillips of the law firm Sidley Austin Brown & Wood (Figure 10.2) both used profanity in arguments broadcast live on cable TV and one radio station to make their points. "Speech that is indecent must be more than a single use that is offensive,'" Phillips said.

Phillips said, "Do I think that you can regulate this kind of speech consistent with the First Amendment? I don't think so, but if the Court wishes to give the Commission an opportunity to undertake to make a kind of showing, if there's a bubble child out there and the child will be hugely disturbed by exposure to a single word, to me, that is utterly implausible."

Phillips challenged the validity of the FCC approach to broadcast indecency:

> Their argument is that you have to free children from any exposure to these particular words . . . and then they proceed in the same breath to recognize that exposure to these particular words is routinely permitted at particular times if it can be justified on particular grounds . . . all you're doing is creating a regime that says that this is better speech than this is. I can't imagine a regime that is more antithetical to First Amendment values.

The three-judge panel grilled government lawyer Eric Miller over what Fox called a radical new interpretation of rules dating back to the *Pacifica* (1978) case, which upheld the FCC right to regulate broadcast indecency in a narrow ruling (Figure 10.3).

Figure 10.2 FCC lawyer challenged by Second Circuit Court of Appeals panel.

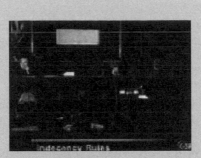

Figure 10.3 Oral arguments in the Second Circuit Court of Appeals.

A December 9, 2002, broadcast of the 2002 *Billboard Music Awards* show featured entertainer Cher responded to her critics by saying, "Fuck 'em," on live television (Figure 10.4).

In January 2003, a Golden Globes awards show on NBC, which was not part of the Fox case, featured U2 lead singer Bono using the phrase "fucking brilliant."

A year after the Cher incident, on the December 10, 2003, *Billboard Music Awards* show, Nicole Richie, who had starred in the reality TV show *The Simple Life*, quipped: "It was hardly all that simple – does anyone know how fucking hard it is to get cow shit out of a Prada purse?" No fines were levied against Fox in either case.

Figure 10.4 Cher uses the F-word on live television.

In March 2004, the FCC issued a clarifying ruling concluding that the "F-word, regardless of context, inherently has a sexual connotation." Prior to that order, the FCC had said that broadcast indecency was a matter of context.

FCC Attorney Miller, under intense questioning from the judicial panel, conceded that if a hypothetic news program decided to broadcast profanities used during the oral argument of the Fox case and added file footage of Cher and Richie to explain the case, there would be no liability under the broadcast indecency rules (Figure 10.5).

Judge Peter Hall asked, "So the bottom line of your argument here is that the FCC cannot regulate the fleeting expletive?"

"I think that's right," Phillips said, "although I don't have to sustain that argument. All I have to demonstrate is that they haven't done it to date."

Judge Hall then directly questioned FCC lawyer Miller on what role the regulation has played in placing broadcasters in a difficult position (Figure 10.6), and a transcript of this exchange is reproduced here.

Judge Hall: Taking your point of view, which I'm not sure I agree with, why isn't this a sort of sword of Damocles hanging over the heads of every broadcast station around?

Miller: Because the only thing that the Commission has decided in this case is that the . . .

Figure 10.5 Appeals Court Judge Peter Hall asks questions.

Figure 10.6 FCC Attorney Eric Miller is grilled by judges during oral arguments.

Judge Hall: That in those circumstances; the use of those words . . . recited for us several times is inappropriate and is subject to fine? Then let me give you a hypothetical, Mr. Miller. This is being fed out by cable here, and presumably the broadcast media can pick it up. Let's say they pick up a portion of Mr. Phillips' argument, and . . . the words "fuck" and "shit" are actually broadcast over 6 o'clock news tonight. Is that going to be the subject of FCC hand-slapping?

Miller: I think plainly not.

Judge Hall:	Because . . .?"
Miller:	For the reasons stated in this very order with respect to *The Early Show* case. The commission has emphasized that it will exercise great restraint when it comes to news programs.
Judge Hall:	Let me expand the hypothetical, to where Fox wanted to air, so its viewers are reminded of exactly what's at issue here – pulls up the clips from the *Billboard Music Awards* and shows those two instances of Cher and Nicole Richie as background or in conjunction with reporting on what's happening in this courtroom here today?
Miller:	To be indecent, the use of the language has to be patently offensive, which under the Commission's analysis requires that it be presented . . .
Judge Hall:	So how is a rebroadcast of the clip in the context of news any less offensive than it is in the *Billboard Awards?*
Miller:	Because in that context, as the Commission explained in *The Early Show* order, it's not being presented to pander or titillate or for shock value; it's being presented to inform viewers what the case is about.

Miller said that the FCC would not consider news programs, unlike other shows, in context as pandering, titillating, or airing profanities for shock value. Still, the discussion led judges, including Judge Pooler (Figure 10.7) and Judge Leval, to ask if broadcasters could protect themselves by putting a news label on various programs. *The Early Show*, however, is produced by the news division of CBS Television, and other entertainment programming does not have that cover.

Miller:	The Commission is not in the business of second-guessing the journalistic and editorial judgments of broadcasters.

Figure 10.7 Judge Rosemary Pooler.

Judge Pooler: So why can't they call everything news? You just said you can't slap "news" on just anything, and now you're saying you're not in the habit of second-guessing. Which is it?

Miller: The test that the Commission articulated in *The Early Show* order is that we said we would defer to CBS's plausible characterization as a "news show."

Judge Pooler: Did you mean to suggest by the use of the word "plausible" that it was a stretch?

Miller: Not necessarily. That word is just in there to emphasize that it is indeed a very broad exception, but questions of the breadth of the news exception are not implicated here, where there is concededly no journalistic theory on which . . .

Judge Leval: Are not important music awards somehow journalism?

Miller: One could perhaps argue that, but Fox does not make that argument; it didn't say that before the Commission; it hasn't said that in this court. At every stage of this case, it has made no effort to defend the language that was used by Ms. Richie or by Cher the year before.

Judge Leval: Are you suggesting, if they had, that it might be plausible?

Miller: It would depend on exactly what they said, but that would be something the Commission would have to take seriously. It's significant, I think, that the Commission has never found a broadcast to be indecent on the basis of an isolated expletive in the face of some claim that the use of that language is necessary for any journalistic or artistic purpose."

Judge Pooler: Are you suggesting now that this could save the FCC indecency policy? Are you telling the networks, who I think are all here today, to just make some kind of cockamamie claim and they'll survive?

Miller: It's not necessary for this court to decide exactly what sort of justification would be necessary and how that factors into the analysis of whether the use of the language is pandering or shocking or titillating."

Judge Pooler also targeted the rationale used by the FCC: "Is there a limit to what you can do to protect children in our society?" Miller said, "Indeed there is." Pooler responded that, "This seems to be a scheme that depends on what you think, instead of having an objective criteria broadcasters can use." Fox attorney Carter G. Phillips added that Miller's arguments further confused the law for broadcasters on what they may air or not: "I have no clue at this point what it is that's offensive." He added, "We have thirty years of unbroken precedent, where the commission recognizes that the use of its expletives is offensive to some, but has never declared that the use of these expletives is the basis for any kind of sanction."

C-SPAN and WCSP-TV aired the court proceedings live without a delay. Bruce Collins, C-SPAN vice president, seemed gratified and relieved at the discussion between lawyers and judges, telling reporters:

> Before today, everybody I talked to was telling me we were at risk of a complaint and a fine from the commission . . . I'm gratified to hear from the FCC that news coverage is not subject to liability. This is an area so convoluted, I don't know what to think.

Broadcasters won the Second Circuit appeal (Appendix G), and in late 2007 they awaited the Third Circuit Court of Appeals, which was considering other aspects of broadcast indecency regulation.

Sources

C-SPAN (December 20, 2006, 10 a.m).

Friedman, Wayne (December 22, 2006), Out of order: Fox slams FCC for indecency argument, The Media Daily Mail, (http://publications.mediapost.com/index. cfm?fuseaction=Articles.showArticleHomePage&art_aid=52937).

Kernes, Mark (December 21, 2006), Analysis: Fox Broadcasting's indecency case has close parallels to adult's obscenity problems (http://www.freespeechcoalition. com/FSCView.asp?coid=1018).

Neumeister, Larry (December 20, 2006). Appeals court panel grills government lawyer in indecency case, Associated Press (http://www.newsday.com/news/ local/wire/newyork/ny-bc-ny--broadcastindecenc1220dec20,0,2045553. story?coll=ny-region-apnewyork).

The FCC has been faced with defending its decisions in a series of controversial cases. The FCC's re-examination of cases involving news programs and its responsibility to enforce new fines passed by Congress and signed by the president mean that the commission must increase penalties to as much as ten times earlier maximum fines. LIN TV President and CEO Gary Chapman told *Broadcasting & Cable* magazine that the fines disproportionately threatened small market stations: "So the most profitable station in New York City would be treated the same as an AM station in Carbondale, Ill. Believe me, they don't have the same balance sheet" (Eggerton, 2006, June 19: 3). Prior to Republicans losing control of the US House and Senate, then House Telecommunication Chair Fred Upton, a Republican from Michigan, said the legislation produced greater industry responsibility. He said the decision to raise fines by ten times the previous amounts per incident grew from discussions he had in 2004 with then FCC Chair Michael Powell. Upton conceded that the FCC had a need to arrive at clearer definitions of indecency: "Broadcasters really do fear these penalties and want to make sure they operate within the confines of the law" (ibid.: 38). Upton said broadcasters have changed the language of personnel contracts, added delays to live events and have become more responsible. He said the *Playboy* decision affirmed the FCC standards on indecency, so legislators simply raised fines rather than altering the rules. While he supported the V-chip, he said too many parents do not use it, and too many old sets do not have it. He also urged the Federal Trade Commission (FTC) to increase fines for sexual content that appears in video games.

Table 10.1 Raising the broadcast fines: FCC's fines 2000–06

Year	No. of complaints received	No. of proposed fines	Amount of proposed fines
2000	111	7	$48,000
2001	346	7	$91,000
2002	13,922	7	$99,400
2003	166,683	3	$440,000
2004	1.4 million[a]	12	$7.9 million
2005	233,531	0	0
2006[b]	327,198	7	$4 million

Source: Paul Davidson, FCC changes rulings on indecency, *USA Today* (November 8, 2006) (http://www.usatoday.com/money/media/2006-11-07-indecency-usat_x.htm?csp=34.)

Note
a   More than 540,000 complaints related to the Super Bowl halftime show featuring Janet Jackson.
b   Federal Communications Commission (June, 2006).

Ownership issues and FCC enforcement

In the two decades since Ronald Reagan's FCC accelerated a push toward government deregulation, the broadcast indecency issue has unfolded just as owners have been allowed to license many more stations. At the time of *Pacifica*, a broadcast owner could possess only seven AM, seven FM, and seven television stations, and there were one-to-a-customer restrictions in a particular media market.

The earliest relaxation of ownership restrictions came with an increase from seven to twelve AM, FM, and TV stations. So, the numerical restrictions had give way to a formula emphasizing percentages of national audiences. By the time large corporate chains could cover one-third of the national audience with their broadcast signals, Clear Channel, which gained some notoriety through the "Bubba, the Love Sponge" cases, operated more than 1,200 stations across the nation with multiple stations in a single media market.

It had become fairly commonplace even in medium-sized media markets to find a single broadcast building that houses perhaps eight separate stations – a single-owner operation where there had been multiple owners in earlier years. Critics saw a connection between the changing ownership restriction and the tendency toward edgy programming. Mom and Pop radio stations, which were small twentieth-century businesses in local communities, had given way to the corporate boardroom in a distant city.

At the same time, the competitive pressures of satellite broadcasting, diverse and large numbers of cable channels, Internet broadcasting, podcasting, and portable music players that allowed listeners to store huge music libraries in their pockets meant that he industry would face inevitable change. Because broadcasters were the lone medium regulated for indecency restrictions, it seemed obvious that others would follow Howard Stern away from the conflict that is broadcast indecency. Stern told ABC's *Nightline* that satellite radio was liberating – allowing him to return to the freedom he had been afforded in the 1980s before the FCC began the crack down on broadcast indecency that continued into the new century.

Internet freedoms

The worldwide web and its ever-changing landscape continues to pose the toughest challenge to the regulation of broadcast indecency. Sites such as Google Video and YouTube offer endless possibilities for content producers and viewers alike. Money is now entering into the picture. San Jose's *The Mercury News* reported that sites such as Revver and Metcafe now pay artists $100 for every 20,000 views of their work (Ackerman & Marshall, 2007). Additionally, Dovetail.tv offered artists ten cents per download. The interest in attracting audiences should tend to drive content to the edge and raise new issues about indecency and even obscenity online. While most content will likely pass as clean, some artists will look to the web to produce content that has been rejected by large labels.

The global development of the Internet as a means to disseminate video has generated free speech issues as far away as Australia. Columnist Ross Fitzgerald (2007) reported that the Office of Film and Literature Classification uses a contextual analysis to determine if sexual references are educational or not – an educational context produces a R rating, while a titillating film is rated X and banned:

> It's a nonsense argument that seeks to stifle freedom of expression by claiming that speech in one situation is OK but identical speech in another situation causes brain damage to babies and makes adults want to rape and kill. It also says that speech or expression that educates or informs people is good but if the same speech makes them horny then it becomes bad. It's a patronising approach at best; at worst, it can serve as a justification for banning almost any dissident voice.
>
> (ibid.: para. 8)

Presumably, following the same logic, web video found to be not educational, but rather titillating, could be banned and blocked under the law.

Box 10.3 *Saturday Night Live* censored skit plays on YouTube

NBC's *Saturday Night Live* (SNL) in late 2006 decided to post an uncensored version of a skit on YouTube once network censors balked at it and cut the word "dick" from it in light of the ongoing struggle with the FCC over broadcast indecency.

Following the Saturday-night blanking of the word "dick" from the offensive phrase, "It's my dick in a box," (Figure 10.8) NBC used YouTube the next day to disseminate what was, in the words of one story about the incident, "deemed too racy for traditional television."

The skit was viewed more than five million times online in early December. The video clip then generated 7.5 million views in one week alone at the end of the month. It is not known how many children may have seen the uncensored skit online.

The YouTube video began with a disclaimer: "The following sketch contains explicit lyrics that were not contained in the original broadcast."

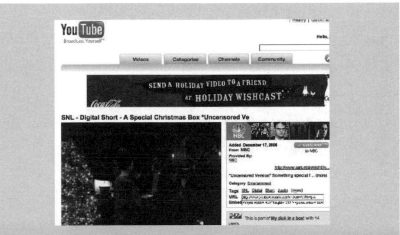

Figure 10.8 "It's my dick in a box." Justin Timberlake's "parody of two boy-band singers" featured the unusual Christmas present.

There also were more than 1,900 comments from viewers of the uncensored skit. Typical of the comments were these:

Shakur22 (17 minutes ago)
THE BEST video iv seen on youtube no doubt justin is the man after seein this vid props to who ever wrote this song

(Reply) (Mark as spam)

deetak (26 minutes ago)
is this a parody of an original song?

(Reply) (Mark as spam)

CoolJetta3 (55 minutes ago)
Justin Timberlake is always funny when they have him on SNL. This is the best yet

(Reply) (Mark as spam)

MsMadchatter (1 hour ago)
It really will be a holiday classic!

(Reply) (Mark as spam)

curvedhyperbole (1 hour ago) what was censored?
the word "dick?"

(Reply) (Mark as spam)

Susan95 (1 hour ago)
He's 17 mom. Believe me, he's very familiar with it all . . . he's been thinking about sex constantly for at least 4 years. And if he's not having sex, now that would be shocking. I think you need to come out of your cocoon.
Signed,
A 43 year old

(Reply) (Mark as spam)

hsl44det1 (1 hour ago)
I think I've watched this vid at least 15x.. Samberg, u da man

(Reply) (Mark as spam)

nanaduck (1 hour ago)
Did i mention your opinions anywhere? No. Just your poor spelling and grammar.

(Reply) (Mark as spam)

liannef (1 hour ago)
LMAO!! That's exactly what I thought when I saw this! Color Me Badd...LOL

(Reply) (Mark as spam)

Sources
Sullivan, Laurie (December 21, 2006). Uncensored SNL skit lands on net; NBC makes a bold move by uploading an uncensored Saturday Night Live clip onto YouTube (http://www.redherring.com/Article.aspx?a=20410&hed=Uncensored+SNL+Skit+Lands+on+Net&sector=Industries&subsector=EntertainmentAnd Media).
Teinowitz, Ira (January 1, 2007). "Skit's Web popularity: That's rich – SNL's 'Dick in a box,' clip blazes path to air naughtier content" (http://www.tvweek.com/article.cms?articleId=31201).
http://www.youtube.com/watch?v=1dmVU08zVpA

The Parents Television Council (PTC) has been one of the most active interest groups in challenging broadcasts such as the SNL skit. *Television Week* suggested to broadcasters that NBC's posting of the SNL skit offered a model for using the web to present sexual content not passing the FCC's tests:

Networks should, and probably will, brush aside these kinds of protests as they exploit the Internet as an outlet for material that's free of indecency strictures on what they can broadcast. To do otherwise would rob the broadcasters of an opportunity to evolve and produce a new wave of entertainment tailored to the Web that could draw viewers back to network television.

(Abrams, 2007: para. 5)

It would seem that the Supreme Court's decision in *Reno* that treated web producers as publishers offered the First Amendment protection to allow the shift away from the burdensome broadcast rules by using the Internet as a substitute platform.

Projections

The V-chip, previously offered as protection for edgy broadcasters, came to be considered a failure by the FCC (Eggerton, 2006, December 11). The FCC in 2006 conceded that the V-chip, once considered a technical solution to the broadcast indecency problem, "isn't much help in preventing kids from seeing programs that might have dicey content" (ibid.: 16). The FCC now contends that if parents will not assist in protecting their children, its role is to help parents do it. Despite industry arguments that FCC rulings on indecency are confusing, the Commission contends that broadcasters should understand the changing position of regulators:

> The FCC insisted that broadcasters have "only limited First Amendment protection" and that it gave the industry fair warning that it was changing policy on swear words . . . The FCC said that the "f-word," when used as an intensifier – for example, in Bono's remark (at the 2003 Golden Globe awards show on NBC) – is still covered by the indecency definition because its intensity "derives from its implicit sexual meaning."

(ibid.)

The FCC has consistently argued before various federal courts that it has narrowly tailored the regulation to promote the compelling interest that the government has to protect the nation's children. By creating a "safe harbor" in the hours 10 p.m. to 6 a.m., the FCC contends that broadcasters can avoid fines by channeling questionable content to late-night hours when children are not expected to be in the audience. Presumably, the need for broadcast regulation remains because, as the V-chip showed, parents tend not to be active in restricting viewing (Horowitz, 2006).

It could be that the desire to impose strict regulation swings like a pendulum. The system that is broadcast regulation policy-making seemed to show signs of retreat – both the FCC and broadcasters took a second look. PBS, for example, which previously had run scared, "changed its programmer guidelines from bleeping profane words" (Benson & Eggerton, 2006: 30).

At about the same time, *Broadcasting & Cable* magazine was amused by President George W. Bush's use of the word "shit" before television microphones at the G8 summit with world leaders. Bush had campaigned on family issues with the nation's moral political right. The magazine used the opportunity to editorialize about the concerns some broadcasters had of airing the language, and they instead bleeped it in news stories. The editorial said that while broadcasters did not fear specific FCC reprisal on this incident, the unwritten policy might be to show restraint when the president is cussing – "That's the scary reality the FCC's Language Police created by threatening whopping penalties . . ." (Editorial, 2006, July 24, p. 30).

Moral crusades in the United States have been with us throughout the more than 200 years of the nation's history. From the sentence of hard labor for "free love" editor Ezra Heywood in 1878 through the current struggle over indecency, "purity crusaders" have confronted "the tide of social change" (Cronin, 2006: 165, 202). At the same time, media outlets have historically been intertwined with the "consumer culture," including commercial speech advertising that often draws upon celebrity images of sexual and other wants "evocative of a primal drive" (Cashmore, 2006: 12–13).

In a crusading cultural context, social norms take hold that chill free expression for fear of government or other reprisals. The impact is noticeable. When Fox inadvertently showed a woman in a "Fuck da Eagles" t-shirt during a crowd shot of a football game, Fox Sports spokesman Dan Bell emphasized his apology: "It was unintentional, inadvertent, and we apologize." The apology was not enough for the Media Research Center's longtime critic Brent Bozell:

> This was not an incidental "oops" shot by Fox. Let us count the ways. 1) Out of 70,000 fans, this girl was targeted for coverage by the cameraman. 2) It wasn't a fleeting Janet Jackson moment: it stayed on screen for several seconds. 3) It wasn't even a live shot, where such mistakes can happen. That display of Saint fans' exultation was shot, then replayed after a replay of the successful action on the field. Thus 4) it had to be the director's decision deliberately to air this footage on national television.
>
> (Bozell, 2007: para. 5)

The network's explanation was that a time code covered the language when the shot was viewed in the production truck. However, Bozell said that the network should have apologized immediately rather than days later. At the same time, however, he acknowledged that profanity was now commonplace at sporting events. Therefore, one might also come to the conclusion that Fox and the other sports networks cannot entirely expunge profanity and still provide an accurate presentation of a game.

It would seem that the surest way to keep children from being exposed to profanity would be to create distance between them and the sources of it. This is fairly challenging in a culture that places some value on shocking language and displays. When the local grocery store parking lot is not always free of profane language, it is probably unrealistic to expect it on newscasts, sports broadcasts or event entertainment. The off button, while the surest method of protection through abstinence, does not address the lingering social and legal problem of the public interest standard and the special treatment of the public airwaves. From concerns about the increasing tolerance for crudeness in professional wrestling to the voice of a Tennessee state legislator who wants to fine broadcasters airing *Girls Gone Wild* "obscene" advertisements, there seems to be no end to the ongoing struggle to establish social-cultural norms of decency. In an international media environment, cultures clash and disagree about what is fit to air.

It is not yet clear whether or not the fight over broadcast indecency is coming to an end or merely getting ready to once again escalate. Meantime, the FCC has been studying media violence for two years – its report focuses on potential harms and the lack of regulatory teeth in this area of the law. *Broadcasting & Cable* magazine's John Eggerton (2007) speculated that violence may be about to become the new indecency. The major networks have profited from the ratings success of *CSI* and other crime dramas that have become more explicit in showing bodies and autopsy rooms in recent years. FCC Chair Kevin Martin seemed to draw the battle lines when he both praised and chastised broadcasters in the same breath: "I have said that, with hundreds of channels to choose from, consumers today have access to some of the best programming ever produced. But television today also contains some of the coarsest and most violent programming ever aired." Congressional leaders have promised to offer legislation that would arm the FCC with teeth to go after broadcasters daring to show excessive or explicit violence. The issue has been around for more than fifty years, fueled by psychological research that provides evidence for potential negative effects from violent media. As has been the case before, the industry will fire back with renewed efforts to self-police itself. The networks' preference remains to employ internal methods to restrict content rather than facing the heavy hand of the government.

Implications for defining free expression

In a previous examination of free expression theory, four propositions were developed for the study of the Internet that also hold some validity for understanding broadcast and Internet indecency (Lipschultz, 2000: 286–7). Applied in this context, we may conclude:

1 Free expression is not the product of an idealistic search for "truth" or objective reality, but rather it is subjective by its very nature. Individuals interpret (encode and decode) speech, which must be studied in a social context. Broadcast and Internet indecency, like the broader Internet, continues to be embedded within a social fabric, subjective to content providers and viewers. Thus, the definition of indecency is socially dependent upon individual values. The FCC's contextual analyses, for example, are problematic because their values may or may not match those of a consensus of Americans at any given time.

2 Free expression is not only understood in terms of presumed psychological value to individuals, but it is also a component in a social, political, and economic system. Clearly, broadcast and Internet indecency, as a social issue, has significant political and economic implications. The indecency crusade by the political right in recent years is paradoxical in light of the freedom orientation of "conservatives" with respect to their view of the role of government. A marketplace economic and social perspective requires one to have faith that positive values will emerge through the social process rather than the force of government power.

3 That which passes for "free expression" in no way resembles what might be at the fringes because all speech is limited by a variety of social constraints, both real and imagined. In the years since the Janet Jackson Super Bowl show, broadcast managers and their talent have often imposed self-restraint because of fears they had about morality campaigns against them, political posturing by members of Congress, the FCC's regulatory crackdown and the real threat of the loss of jobs from reactionary firings.

4 Popular concepts such as "social responsibility" and "marketplace of ideas" hold no utility in learning about free expression, except to the extent individuals adopt and use these notions as political tools of power. We might also add the phrase "family values" to the mix of language employed in order to culturally define political positions. While the number of voices continues to grow in the marketplace of ideas, the political response to sexual content often remains quite restrictive. Despite this approach, a wide range of sexual values remains in play for acceptance as social norms. Thus, the range of marketplaces voices often fails to produce much in the way of consensus or even valuable dialogue about area of conflict.

As this book was sent to press in late 2007, there remained many issues and unanswered questions. In the Third Circuit, oral arguments were held on CBS's appeal of the Super Bowl fine. This court refused a request by C-SPAN to air the arguments, as had been done in the Second Circuit. In Congress, a number of bills continued to propose stricter FCC rules on indecency. Perhaps this was a natural response to the belief that media continued to become more crude. One study even suggested that what was once labeled "family hour" – 7 p.m. – had yielded to adult-oriented television. Finally, on PBS, the Public Broadcasting Service offered its affiliates a "clean" version of a Ken Burns documentary on World War II. Those local stations fearing the FCC or questioning local community standards were free to play it safe by delaying or editing a few profanities.

In the absence of agreement, purveyors of sexual content routinely and cyclically test boundaries, politicians crusade for new boundaries, and the political system of interests moves rules rather slowly. Interestingly, this stalemate leaves room for substantial amounts of freedom to disseminate sexual content on broadcast airwaves and the web.

Chapter summary

The furor that was the post-Janet Jackson 2004 Super Bowl era had calmed by 2006. Even the FCC changed its mind and decided that, indeed, news broadcasts could legally use indecency in an interview context. In the courts, industry attorneys challenged the FCC and judges to justify what appeared to be an antiquated regulatory scheme. The *Without a Trace* CBS case led to a license challenge of KUTV, Salt Lake City – this means that the fines and the stakes are higher than ever before. CBS resisted pressure from the FCC to suspend employees for airing a teen orgy scene. Meantime, broadcast networks turned to the web to offer un-bleeped content, and millions responded by viewing. New media technology appeared to make it impossible to protect children by simply restricting broadcasters. Finally, as the indecency fights quieted, a new challenge to First Amendment rights emerged with the prospect of regulating media violence. This would be a more difficult fight for broadcasters because, unlike indecency, research on violence demonstrated potential negative effects. Broadcast and Internet indecency provide a useful paradigm for understanding how free expression is socially defined.

Review questions

1 Do you agree or disagree that the context of news broadcast should

have absolute First Amendment protection to air indecency? Why is news different from entertainment programming?

2 The FCC seems to have difficulty defending its position on the regulation of broadcast indecency: How could the courts provide cover for the FCC against congressional pressure to take a hard line?

3 Does the Internet guarantee that children are likely to be exposed to indecency? How do parents wishing to keep children from seeing adult content create effective restrictions?

4 How is media violence different from indecency? Do you support regulation of violence? Why or why not?

5 How would you assess the state of the First Amendment and free expression in the United States? What are the implications across the globe?

APPENDICES

Before the
Federal Communications Commission
Washington, D.C. 20554

In the Matter of	)
	)
Complaints Regarding Various Television Broadcasts	)
Between February 2, 2002 and	)
March 8, 2005	)

NOTICES OF APPARENT LIABILITY AND

MEMORANDUM OPINION AND ORDER

Adopted: February 21, 2006   **Released: March 15, 2006**

By the Commission: Chairman Martin, Commissioners Copps and Tate issuing separate statements; Commissioner Adelstein concurring, dissenting in part and issuing a statement.

TABLE OF CONTENTS

Heading   Paragraph #

I.   INTRODUCTION..1
II. BACKGROUND..8
III. DISCUSSION 22
     A. Notices of Apparent Liability for Forfeiture 22
         1. "The Surreal Life 2" (February 8, 2004)..22
         2. "Con El Corazón En La Mano" (October 9, 2004)...33
         3. "Fernando Hidalgo Show" (October 19, 2004) 43
         4. "Video Musicales" (February 2-March 8, 2002)..52
         5. "The Blues: Godfathers and Sons" (March 11, 2004)..72
         6. "The Pursuit of D.B. Cooper" (March 15, 2003)...87
     B. Indecent And/Or Profane Broadcasts But No Forfeiture Proposed...100
         1. "The 2002 Billboard Music Awards" (December 9, 2002)..101
         2. "The 2003 Billboard Music Awards" (December 10, 2003)..112
         3. "NYPD Blue" (various dates between January 14 and May 6, 2003) 125
         4. "The Early Show" (December 13, 2004) 137
     C. Broadcasts That Do Not Violate Indecency/Profanity/Obscenity Restrictions............................146
         1. "Alias" (January 5, 2005) 147
         2. "Will and Grace" (November 11, 2004) 153
         3. "Two and a Half Men" (February 21, 2005)..160
         4. "Committed" (March 8, 2005)..163
         5. "Golden Phoenix Hotel & Casino Commercial" (February 19, 2005) 166
         6. "The Oprah Winfrey Show" (March 18, 2004) 173
         7. Political Advertisement (October 14, 2004) 180
         8. "The Amazing Race 6" (December 21, 2004) 188
         9. Various Programs Containing Expletives (various dates between August 31, 2004 and
             February 28, 2005)..193
         10. "Family Guy" (January 16, 2005) 200
         11. "The Academy Awards" (February 27, 2005) 206
         12. "8 Simple Rules" (February 4, 2005)..210

13. "The Today Show" (January 11, 2005)..213
14. "The Simpsons" (September 9, 2004)..219
15. "America's Funniest Home Videos" (February 5, 2005)..224
16. "Green Bay Packers v. Minnesota Vikings" (January 9, 2005) 227
17. "Medium" (January 17, 2005)..230
IV. ORDERING CLAUSES 233

I.   INTRODUCTION

1.   The Commission has regulated the broadcast of indecent programming for decades, and our authority in this area has long been upheld as constitutional by the U.S. Supreme Court. During the last few years, however, we have witnessed increasing public unease with the nature of broadcast material. In particular, Americans have become more concerned about the content of television programming, with the number of complaints annually received by the Commission rising from fewer than 50 in 2000 to approximately 1.4 million in 2004. At the same time, broadcasters have sought guidance from the Commission about our rules, arguing that they lack certainty regarding the meaning of our indecency and profanity standards. The decisions we issue today respond to both of these concerns.

2.   In these decisions, we address hundreds of thousands of complaints alleging that various broadcast television programs aired between February 2002 and March 2005 are indecent, profane, and/or obscene. The cases we resolve today represent a broad range of factual patterns. Taken both individually and as a whole, we believe that they will provide substantial guidance to broadcasters and the public about the types of programming that are impermissible under our indecency standard. The cases also further refine our standard regarding the use of profane language in the broadcast medium and illustrate the types of language proscribed by that standard. Overall, the decisions demonstrate repeatedly that we must always look to the context in which words or images occur to determine whether they are indecent. In addition, while we find certain highly offensive language to be presumptively profane, we also take care to emphasize that such words may not be profane in specified contexts.

3.   Section II below is devoted to providing a full description of the Commission's standards for analyzing whether programming is indecent and/or profane and referencing the legal sources upon which these standards are based. In Section II, we also fully describe our methodology for calculating proposed forfeitures against broadcast licensees when there has been an apparent violation of our prohibitions against indecency and/or profanity.

4.   In Section III, we apply these indecency and/or profanity standards to the complaints before us on a case-by-case basis. We begin with cases in which we have determined that the broadcast licensee apparently aired indecent and/or profane material and propose forfeitures against the licensee. The monetary forfeitures proposed demonstrate that the Commission will exercise its statutory authority to ensure that the broadcast of indecent and/or profane material will be appropriately sanctioned.

5.   Section III next addresses cases in which we find the complained-of material indecent and/or profane but do not propose taking action against the licensee. In these cases, the licensee was not on notice at the time of the broadcast that we would deem the relevant material indecent or profane. For example, we hold that a single use of the word "shit" and its variants (the "S-Word") in the contexts presented is both indecent and profane. However, we do not propose adverse action in these cases because we have not previously announced this conclusion.

6.   Section III concludes with a discussion of a number of cases in which we determine that various words, phrases, or scenes that occur in a variety of programs, while undoubtedly upsetting to some viewers, do not warrant action against the broadcast station licensee. We reach these determinations either because the complained-of material is not within the scope of our indecency or profanity definitions or because, even if it is within the scope of our indecency definition, it is not, in the contexts before us, patently offensive as measured by contemporary community standards for the broadcast medium.

7.   Together, these decisions demonstrate the Commission's strong commitment to fulfilling the responsibility vested in us by Congress within the parameters of the United States Constitution. We believe that issuing these decisions as a single order will enable broadcasters to better understand the boundaries of our indecency and profanity standards, while at the same time responding to the concerns expressed by hundreds of

thousands of citizens in complaints filed with the Commission. In the end, our primary objective is to fulfill our statutory obligation to enforce the law in this area and to do so in a clear and consistent manner.

II.   BACKGROUND

8.   Section 1464 of title 18, United States Code, prohibits the broadcast of obscene, indecent, or profane programming.[1] The FCC rules implementing that statute, a subsequent statute establishing a "safe harbor" during certain hours, and the Communications Act of 1934, as amended (the "Act"), prohibit radio and television stations from broadcasting obscene material at any time and indecent material between 6 a.m. and 10 p.m.[2] Broadcasters also may not air profane material during this time period.[3]

9.   The federal prohibition against the broadcast of indecent and profane material is longstanding. In the Radio Act of 1927, Congress first provided that "[n]o person within the jurisdiction of the United States shall utter any obscene, indecent, or profane language by means of radio communication."[4] This prohibition was then reenacted as part of the Act and was moved subsequently to title 18 of the United States Code in 1948.

10.   *Indecency Analysis.* The federal courts have consistently upheld Congress's authority to regulate the broadcast of indecent material, as well as the Commission's interpretation and implementation of the governing statute. In 1978, the U.S. Supreme Court, in upholding the constitutionality of the prohibition against the broadcast of indecent material, concluded that "special treatment of indecent broadcasting" was appropriate. The Court noted that the Commission's authority to regulate indecent broadcast material is justified by two primary considerations, both of which are equally, if not more, applicable today. First, the broadcast media occupy "a uniquely pervasive presence in the lives of all Americans."[5] Indecent material "presented over the airwaves confronts the citizen, not only in public, but also in the privacy of their own home, where the individual's right to be left alone plainly outweighs the First Amendment rights of an intruder."[6] "Because the broadcast audience is constantly tuning in and out, prior warnings cannot completely protect the listener or viewer from unexpected program content."[7] Indeed, while the Supreme Court's observation regarding the pervasiveness of the broadcast media dates back to 1978, the ubiquity of television in the lives of Americans has only increased in the intervening 28 years. Second, the Supreme Court observed that "broadcasting is uniquely accessible to children, even those too

---

[1] 18 U.S.C. § 1464.

[2] *See* 47 C.F.R. § 73.3999; *see also* Public Telecommunications Act of 1992, Pub. L. No. 102-356, 106 Stat. 949 (1992) (setting the safe harbor of 10 p.m. to 6 a.m. for the broadcast of indecent material); *see also Action for Children's Television v. FCC,* 58 F. 3d 654 (D.C. Cir. 1995) *(en banc) ("ACT III"), cert. denied,* 516 U.S. 1072 (1996) (affirming restrictions prohibiting the broadcast of indecent material between the hours of 6 a.m. and 10 p.m.)

[3] *See Complaints Against Various Broadcast Licensees Regarding Their Airing of the "Golden Globe Awards" Program,* Memorandum Opinion and Order 18 FCC Rcd 19859 (Enf. Bur. 2004), *review granted,* 19 FCC Rcd 4975, 4981 ¶¶ 13 and 14 (2004) *("Golden Globe Awards Order"), petitions for stay and recon. pending.* The Commission established a "safe harbor" period from 10 p.m. to 6 a.m. during which profane speech may be legally broadcast as a narrowly tailored means of vindicating its compelling interests in assisting parents and protecting minors, consistent with the D.C. Circuit's decision that the same "safe harbor" period for indecent material is consistent with the Constitution. *See ACT III,* 58 F.3d at 667.

[4] 44 Stat. 1172.

[5] *FCC v. Pacifica Foundation,* 438 U.S. 726, 748 (1978) *("Pacifica").*

[6] *Id.*

[7] *Id.*

young to read."[8] This finding is even more relevant today given the increased accessibility of the broadcast media to children.[9]

    11.   Enforcement of the provisions restricting the broadcast of indecent, obscene, or profane material is an important component of the Commission's overall responsibility over broadcast radio and television operations. At the same time, however, the Commission must be mindful of the First Amendment to the United States Constitution and section 326 of the Act, which prohibit the Commission from censoring program material or interfering with broadcasters' free speech rights.[10] As such, in making indecency determinations, the Commission proceeds cautiously and with appropriate restraint.[11]

    12.   The Commission defines indecent speech as material that, in context, depicts or describes sexual or excretory activities or organs in terms patently offensive as measured by contemporary community standards for the broadcast medium.[12]

> Indecency findings involve at least two fundamental determinations. First, the material alleged to be indecent must fall within the subject matter scope of our indecency definition—that is, the material must describe or depict sexual or excretory organs or activities. . . . Second, the broadcast must be *patently offensive* as measured by contemporary community standards for the broadcast medium.[13]

---

[8] *Id.* at 749.

[9] *See* Donald F. Roberts, Ulla G. Foehr, and Victoria Rideout, *Generation M: Media in the Lives of 8-18 Year Olds* (March 2005) at 12-13 (finding that 99% of children 8-18 have a television set in their home and that 68% of children 8-18 have a television set in their bedroom).

[10] U.S. CONST., amend. I; 47 U.S.C. § 326. *See also United States v. Playboy Entertainment Group, Inc.,* 529 U.S. 803, 813-15 (2000).

[11] *See Action for Children's Television v. FCC,* 852 F.2d 1332, 1344, 1340 n. 14 (1988) (*"ACT I"*) (stating that "[b]roadcast material that is indecent but not obscene is protected by the First Amendment; the FCC may regulate such material only with due respect for the high value our Constitution places on freedom and choice in what people may say and hear," and that any "potential chilling effect of the FCC's generic definition of indecency will be tempered by the Commission's restrained enforcement policy.").

[12] *See Infinity Broadcasting Corporation of Pennsylvania,* Memorandum Opinion and Order, 2 FCC Rcd 2705 (1987) (subsequent history omitted) (citing *Pacifica Foundation,* Memorandum Opinion and Order, 56 FCC 2d 94, 98 (1975), *aff'd sub nom. Pacifica,* 438 U.S. 726).

[13] *Industry Guidance on the Commission's Case Law Interpreting 18 U.S.C. §1464 and Enforcement Policies Regarding Broadcast Indecency,* Policy Statement, 16 FCC Rcd 7999, 8002 ¶¶ 7-8 (2001) (*"Indecency Policy Statement"*) (emphasis in original). In applying the "community standards for the broadcast medium" criterion, the Commission has stated:

> The determination as to whether certain programming is patently offensive is not a local one and does not encompass any particular geographic area. Rather, the standard is that of an average broadcast viewer or listener and not the sensibilities of any individual complainant.

WPBN/WTOM License Subsidiary, Inc., Memorandum Opinion and Order, 15 FCC Rcd 1838, 1841 ¶ 10 (2000) (*"WPBN/WTOM MO&O"*). The Commission's interpretation of the term "contemporary community standards" flows from its analysis of the definition of that term set forth in the Supreme Court's decision in *Hamling v. United States,* 418 U.S. 87 (1974), *reh'g denied,* 419 U.S. 885 (1974). In *Infinity Broadcasting Corporation of Pennsylvania (WYSP(FM)),* Memorandum Opinion and Order, 3 FCC Rcd 930 (1987) (subsequent history omitted), the Commission observed that in *Hamling,* which involved obscenity, "the Court explained that the purpose of 'contemporary community standards' was to ensure that material is judged neither on the basis of a decisionmaker's personal opinion, nor by its effect on a particularly sensitive or insensitive person or group." *Id.* at 933 (citing 418 U.S. at 107). The Commission also relied on the fact that the Court in *Hamling* indicated that decisionmakers need not use any precise geographic area in evaluating material. *Id.* at 933 (citing 418 U.S. at 104-05). Consistent with

(continued....)

13. In our assessment of whether broadcast material is patently offensive, "the *full context* in which the material appeared is critically important."[14] Three principal factors are significant to this contextual analysis: (1) the explicitness or graphic nature of the description; (2) whether the material dwells on or repeats at length descriptions of sexual or excretory organs or activities; and (3) whether the material panders to, titillates, or shocks the audience.[15] In examining these three factors, we must weigh and balance them on a case-by-case basis to determine whether the broadcast material is patently offensive because "[e]ach indecency case presents its own particular mix of these, and possibly, other factors."[16] In particular cases, one or two of the factors may outweigh the others, either rendering the broadcast material patently offensive and consequently indecent,[17] or, alternatively, removing the broadcast material from the realm of indecency.

14. In each of the cases below in which the complaint alleges indecency, we apply the two-pronged indecency analysis described above. Specifically, we first determine whether the complained-of material is within the scope of our indecency definition; *i.e.*, whether it describes or depicts sexual or excretory activities or organs. If so, we then turn to the three principal factors of the second prong to determine whether, taken in context, the material is patently offensive as measured by contemporary community standards for the broadcast medium.

15. As evidenced below, our contextual analysis takes into account the manner and purpose of broadcast material.[18] For example, material that panders to, titillates, or shocks the audience is treated quite differently than material that is primarily used to educate or inform the audience. In particular, we recognize the need for caution with respect to complaints implicating the editorial judgment of broadcast licensees in presenting news and public affairs programming, as these matters are at the core of the First Amendment's free press guarantee.[19]

16. ***Profanity Analysis.*** In the *Golden Globe Awards Order*, we concluded that the "F-Word" constituted "profane language" within the meaning of 18 U.S.C. § 1464 because, in context, it involved vulgar and coarse language "so grossly offensive to members of the public who actually hear it as to amount to a nuisance."[20] We indicated in that decision that we would analyze other potentially profane words on a case-by-case basis.

17. Just as with indecent broadcasting, we are mindful that, in exercising our statutory authority over profane broadcast material, we must proceed with "due respect for the high value our Constitution places on freedom and choice in what the people say and hear."[21] In the *Golden Globe Awards Order*, we interpreted

---

(...continued from previous page)

Hamling, the Commission concluded that its evaluation of allegedly indecent material is "not one based on a local standard, but one based on a broader standard for broadcasting generally." *Id.* at 933.

[14] *Indecency Policy Statement*, 16 FCC Rcd at 8002 ¶ 9 (emphasis in original).

[15] *Id.* at 8002-15 ¶¶ 8-23.

[16] *Id.* at 8003 ¶ 10.

[17] *Id.* at 8009 ¶ 19 (*citing Tempe Radio, Inc (KUPD-FM)*, Notice of Apparent Liability for Forfeiture, 12 FCC Rcd 21828 (Mass Media Bur. 1997) (forfeiture paid), and *EZ New Orleans, Inc. (WEZB(FM))*, Notice of Apparent Liability for Forfeiture, 12 FCC Rcd 4147 (Mass Media Bur. 1997) (forfeiture paid) (finding that the extremely graphic or explicit nature of references to sex with children outweighed the fleeting nature of the references).

[18] *Indecency Policy Statement*, 16 FCC Rcd at 8010 ¶ 20 (noting that "the manner and purpose of a presentation may well preclude an indecency determination even though other factors, such as explicitness, might weigh in favor of an indecency finding").

[19] *See Syracuse Peace Council*, Memorandum Opinion and Order, 2 FCC Rcd 5043, 5050-51 ¶ 52 (1987) (subsequent history omitted) (eliminating the fairness doctrine, which placed an affirmative obligation on broadcasters to cover, and present contrasting viewpoints on, controversial issues of public importance).

[20] 19 FCC Rcd at 4981 ¶ 13.

[21] *ACT I*, 852 F.2d at 1344 (noting that "the potentially chilling effect of the FCC's generic definition will be tempered by the Commission's restrained enforcement policy.").

profanity, citing a decision by the U.S. Court of Appeals for the Seventh Circuit, as "denoting certain of those personally reviling epithets naturally tending to provoke violent resentment or denoting language so grossly offensive to members of the public who actually hear it as to amount to a nuisance."[22] In the context of broadcasting, however, it is not clear whether the "fighting words" portion of this definition applies. Given the nature of television and radio, it appears unlikely that broadcast material would provoke immediate violence between those uttering such words and the audience. Therefore, in the cases below, and as a general matter, we will analyze potentially profane language with respect to whether it is "so grossly offensive as to constitute a nuisance."

18.   Additionally, given the sensitive First Amendment implications in this area, we establish a presumption that our regulation of profane language will be limited to the universe of words that are sexual or excretory in nature or are derived from such terms. As our regulation of profane language is based on a nuisance rationale similar to that which forms the basis for indecency regulation, we believe that the same limitation on the scope of our regulation is appropriate and rests upon sound constitutional footing.[23] Although we recognize that additional words, such as language conveying racial or religious epithets, are considered offensive by most Americans, we intend to avoid extending the bounds of profanity to reach such language given constitutional considerations.[24]

19.   We conclude below that certain vulgar sexual or excretory terms are so grossly offensive to members of the public that they amount to a nuisance and are presumptively profane. We reserve that distinction for the most offensive words in the English language, the broadcast of which are likely to shock the viewer and disturb the peace and quiet of the home. We also note, however, that in rare cases, language that is presumptively profane will not be found to be profane where it is demonstrably essential to the nature of an artistic or educational work or essential to informing viewers on a matter of public importance.[25] As detailed below, we caution that we will find this exception to be applicable only in unusual circumstances.

20.   ***Forfeiture Calculations.*** The *Notices of Apparent Liability for Forfeiture* ("*NALs*") contained in this decision are issued pursuant to section 503(b)(1) of the Act. Under that provision, any person who is determined by the Commission to have willfully or repeatedly failed to comply with any provision of the Act or any rule, regulation, or order issued by the Commission or to have violated section 1464 of title 18, United States Code, shall be liable to the United States for a forfeiture penalty.[26] Section 312(f)(1) of the Act defines willful as "the conscious and deliberate commission or omission of [any] act, irrespective of any intent to violate" the law.[27] The legislative history to section 312(f)(1) of the Act clarifies that this definition of willful applies to both sections 312 and 503(b) of the Act,[28] and the Commission has so interpreted the term in the section 503(b) context.[29] The term "repeated" means that the action was committed or omitted more than once, or lasts more than one day.[30] We emphasize that every licensee is responsible for the decision to air particular programming and will be held accountable for violating federal restrictions on the willful or repeated broadcast of obscene, indecent, or profane material.

---

[22] 19 FCC Rcd at 1980 ¶ 12.

[23] *See Pacifica*, 438 U.S. at 748-751; *Golden Globe Awards Order*, 19 FCC Rcd at 4981-82 ¶¶ 13-16.

[24] *See, e.g., Raycom America, Inc.,* Memorandum Opinion and Order, 18 FCC Rcd 4186, 4187, ¶¶ 3-4 (2003); *Complaint of Julian Bond, Atlanta NAACP*, Letter, 69 FCC 2d 943 (Broadcast Bur. 1978).

[25] *See Complaints Against Various Television Licensees Regarding Their Broadcast on November 11, 2004 of the ABC Television Network's Presentation of the Film "Saving Private Ryan,"* Memorandum Opinion and Order, 20 FCC Rcd 4507, 4512-14 ¶¶ 13-18 (2005) ("*Saving Private Ryan*").

[26] 47 U.S.C. § 503(b)(1)(B) & D. *See also* 47 C.F.R. 1.80(a)(1).

[27] 47 U.S.C. § 312(f)(1).

[28] *See* H.R. Rep. No. 97-765, 97th Cong. 2d Sess. 51 (1982).

[29] *See Southern California Broadcasting Co.*, Memorandum Opinion and Order, 6 FCC Rcd 4387, 4388 (1991).

[30] *Callais Cablevision, Inc., Grand Isle, Louisiana*, Notice of Apparent Liability for Forfeiture, 16 FCC Rcd 1359, 1362 ¶ 9 (2001).

21.   The Commission's *Forfeiture Policy Statement* establishes a base forfeiture amount of $7,000 for the transmission of indecent or obscene materials.[31] The *Forfeiture Policy Statement* also specifies that the Commission shall adjust a forfeiture based upon consideration of the factors enumerated in section 503(b)(2)(D), such as "the nature, circumstances, extent and gravity of the violation, and, with respect to the violator, the degree of culpability, any history of prior offenses, ability to pay, and such other matters as justice may require."[32] For the cases in this decision, the statutory maximum forfeiture amount for each apparent violation occurring prior to September 7, 2004 was $27,500.[33] The statutory maximum forfeiture amount for violations discussed in this decision occurring on or after September 7, 2004 is $32,500.[34] Consistent with the *Forfeiture Policy Statement*, we calculate forfeiture amounts by: (1) determining whether to use the base statutory amount, the maximum statutory amount, or a different figure below the statutory maximum based upon consideration of the factors enumerated in section 503(b)(2)(D); and (2) multiplying that figure by the number of violations. Where repeated violations have occurred but the resulting total forfeiture amount would be excessive to achieve the appropriate level of punishment and deterrence, we also may adjust the total proposed forfeiture according to the stated statutory factors.

III.   DISCUSSION

A.   Notices of Apparent Liability for Forfeiture

1.   "The Surreal Life 2" (February 8, 2004)[35]

22.   *The Programming.* The Commission received a complaint alleging that WBDC Broadcasting, Inc. ("WBDC Broadcasting"), licensee of Station WBDC-TV, Washington, D.C.,[36] and other station affiliates of the WB Television Network (the "WB Network"), broadcast indecent material during the *Pool Party Episode* of the program "The Surreal Life 2" on February 8, 2004, at 9:00 p.m. Eastern Standard Time. On September 27, 2004, the Bureau sent a letter of inquiry to the WB Network concerning this and other episodes of "The Surreal Life 2."[37] In response to the letter of inquiry, the WB Network stated, *inter alia*, that Station WBDC-TV aired the complained-of episode on February 8, 2004 at 9:00 p.m. Eastern Standard Time.[38]

23.   "The Surreal Life 2" is a "reality-based" television program in which six cast members from diverse backgrounds share a luxurious house for 12 days. One of the six cast members, Ron Jeremy, is a veteran

---

[31] *See Commission's Forfeiture Policy Statement and Amendment of Section 1.80 of the Rules to Incorporate the Forfeiture Guidelines*, Report and Order, 12 FCC Rcd 17087, 17113 (1997), *recon. denied,* 15 FCC Rcd 303 (1999) ("*Forfeiture Policy Statement*"); *see also* 47 C.F.R. § 1.80(b).

[32] *Forfeiture Policy Statement*, 12 FCC Rcd at 17100-01 ¶ 27.

[33] Effective September 7, 2004, the Commission amended its rules to increase the maximum penalties to account for inflation since the last adjustment of the penalty rates. *See Amendment of Section 1.80 of the Commission's Rules*, Order, 19 FCC Rcd 10945, 10946 ¶ 6 (2004).

[34] *Id.*

[35] FCC File No. EB-04-IH-0166.

[36] *See* Letter from Lara Mahaney, Parents Television Council, to David H. Solomon, Chief, Enforcement Bureau, Federal Communications Commission (February 17, 2004). In its complaint, PTC incorrectly states that the call sign of the station is "KBDC-TV," but it appears that the complained-of station is Station WBDC-TV based on our review of the videotape of the program provided by PTC.

[37] *See* Letter from William H. Davenport, Chief, Investigations and Hearings Division, Enforcement Bureau, Federal Communications Commission, to John Maatta, Executive Vice-President and General Counsel, The WB Television Network (September 27, 2004).

[38] *See* Letter from Arthur H. Harding, Esquire, Fleischman and Walsh, L.L.P., counsel for The WB Television Network, to David Brown, Assistant Chief, Investigations and Hearings Division, Enforcement Bureau, Federal Communications Commission (October 6, 2004) ("October Response"); Letter from Arthur H. Harding, Esquire, Fleischmann and Walsh, L.L.P., counsel for the WB Television Network, to William H. Davenport, Chief, Investigations and Hearings Division, Enforcement Bureau, Federal Communications Commission (November 1, 2004).

actor in pornographic movies. In the *Pool Party Episode*, he gives a pool party for about twenty of his friends in the pornographic movie industry. During the ten-minute sequence depicting this party, the episode displays approximately 20 pixilated views of various female guests' nude breasts and, in one case, a female guest's entire nude body. In addition, there are numerous other examples of sexual images and innuendo, including two brief, pixilated scenes in which Mr. Jeremy touches or kisses a female guest's bare breast; a scene in which Andy Dick, another guest at the party, places his mouth on the top portion of a female cast member's breast and makes a comic sound, and the female cast member explains that they are just friends; another scene in which Andy Dick kisses a female guest's pixilated bare breast and spanks her buttocks, stating jestingly that she should go to her room and he'll join her there shortly; a scene where a female guest appears to sexually proposition a male cast member;[39] and a scene in which another female cast member suggests that the party attendees play a game of "strip truth or dare to get naked," saying to Ron Jeremy, "[c]ome on porn star, everyone knows about your big [bleep], though I haven't seen it."

24.   ***Indecency Analysis.*** We find that the material meets the first prong of the indecency test. As noted above, the episode contains several pixilated views of nude breasts and a nude body, as well as other sexual images and innuendo described above.[40] All of this material depicts or describes sexual activities and organs.

25.   Moving to the second prong of our indecency test, we also find that the material is, in the context presented here, patently offensive as measured by contemporary community standards for the broadcast medium. The first of the three principal factors in our contextual analysis weighs in favor of a finding of patent offensiveness because the material is explicit and graphic. In this regard, the mere pixilation of sexual organs is not necessarily determinative under our analysis because the material must be assessed in its full context.[41] Here, despite the obscured nature of the nudity, it is unmistakable that partygoers are exposing and discussing sexual organs as well as participating in sexual activities, such as when Mr. Jeremy touches or kisses an unclothed female breast. Indeed, a child watching this program could easily discern that nude or partially nude adults are attending a party and participating in, or soliciting participation in, sexual activities.[42] We, therefore, find that the complained-of material is explicit and graphic.

26.   With respect to the second prong of our contextual analysis, we find that the broadcast dwells on and repeats the sexual material. We have repeatedly held that repetition and persistent focus on sexual or excretory material is a relevant factor in evaluating the potential offensiveness of broadcasts.[43] In this case, the presentation of approximately 20 views of pixilated female nudity within a ten-minute segment, together with other depictions or descriptions of sexual organs or activities during the same episode, demonstrates that this episode dwells upon and repeats sexual material.

27.   Looking to the final prong of our test, we conclude that the broadcast material is presented in a manner that panders to, titillates, and shocks the audience. Among other things, the material depicts male cast members and party guests ogling, fondling, and kissing female party guests' bare breasts, a male party guest spanking a female guest's buttocks and placing his lips on a female cast member's breast, a female party guest

---

[39] In this scene, program participant Erik Estrada says that one of the female guests propositioned him with "an oral compliment." The camera then turns to a scene where the female guest in question says to Mr. Estrada: "Wanna come inside [bleep]." Mr. Estrada responds with a shocked facial expression. The camera then turns to a scene in which he says into the camera: "And I said 'ah you're very kind and generous, but you know what? I'm a married man.'"

[40] *See Complaints Against Various Licensees Regarding Their Broadcast of the Fox Television Network Program "Married By America" on April 7, 2003,* Notice of Apparent Liability for Forfeiture, 19 FCC Rcd 20191, 20194 ¶ 10 (2004) ("*Married By America NAL*") (program featuring bachelor and bachelorette parties with pixilated nudity of professional strippers met first prong of indecency standard).

[41] *Id.*

[42] *Id.* (finding that "although the nudity was pixilated, even a child would have known that the strippers were topless and that sexual activity was being shown.").

[43] *See Indecency Policy Statement,* 16 FCC Rcd at 8008 ¶ 17 (citing cases); *see also Married by America NAL,* 19 FCC Rcd at 20195 ¶ 11; ; *Entercom Seattle License, LLC,* Order on Review, 19 FCC Rcd 9069, 9073-74 ¶ 13 (2004) ("*Entercom Seattle Order on Review*"), *petition for recon. pending.*

sexually propositioning a male cast member, and a male and female cast member attempting to goad one another into disrobing, with the female cast member proposing a game of "strip truth or dare to get naked." The strong emphasis on the fact that some female party guests are pornographic film stars also panders to the audience.

28.   In reaching our determination, we disagree with WB Network's contention that "these isolated scenes contain no graphic depictions or profanity that might rise to the level of actionable indecency."[44] In support of its argument, WB Network cites the *KSAZ MO&O* and the *Buffy the Vampire Slayer MO&O* in which we denied indecency complaints. Both of these cases, however, are distinguishable from the *Pool Party Episode* of the "The Surreal Life 2." Each of those cases involved two fully clothed adults, and the individual scenes involved were less graphic, explicit, and sustained than the complained-of material here.

29.   In sum, because the material is explicit and graphic, is dwelled upon, and presented in a manner to titillate and shock viewers, we conclude that the broadcast of the material at issue here is patently offensive under contemporary community standards for the broadcast medium and thus apparently indecent. The complained-of material was broadcast within the 6 a.m. to 10 p.m. time frame relevant to an indecency determination under section 73.3999 of the Commission's rules.[45] Therefore, there is a reasonable risk that children may have been in the viewing audience and the broadcast is legally actionable.

30.   ***Forfeiture Calculation.*** In the instant case, WBDC Broadcasting consciously and deliberately broadcast this episode. Accordingly, we find that WBDC Broadcasting's broadcast in apparent violation of 18 U.S.C. § 1464 and 47 C.F.R. § 73.3999 was willful within the meaning of section 503(b)(1) of the Act, and subject to forfeiture.

31.   Based on the egregious nature of the broadcast material at issue, and the factors enumerated in section 503(b)(2)(D) of the Act, we further find that a forfeiture amount of $27,500, the statutory maximum in effect at the time of the broadcasts, is appropriate.[46] The gravity of the apparent violation is heightened by the degree to which the scene dwells on and repeats sexual material in a manner that titillates and shocks viewers. The scene lasts for over ten minutes, contains approximately twenty pixilated images of nude adults, including a fully nude body, and focuses almost entirely on men and women disrobing, ogling, fondling, kissing, and sexually propositioning one another during a pool party. Moreover, the *Pool Party Episode* of "The Surreal Life 2" is a taped program with an obvious sexual theme that could have been ascertained and preempted by the licensee or shown after 10 p.m.

32.   Although other stations also may have broadcast the *Pool Party Episode*, we propose a forfeiture only against WBDC Broadcasting, Inc. as the only licensee whose broadcast of the material was actually the subject of a viewer complaint to the Commission.[47] We recognize that this approach differs from that taken in previous Commission decisions involving the broadcast of apparently indecent programming.[48] Our commitment to an

---

[44] October Response at 2 (citing *KSAZ Licenses, Inc.*, Memorandum Opinion and Order, 19 FCC Rcd 15999 (2004) ("*KSAZ MO&O*") and *Complaints Against Various Broadcast Licensees Regarding Their Airing of the UPN Network Program "Buffy the Vampire Slayer" On November 20, 2001*, Memorandum Opinion and Order, 19 FCC Rcd 15995 (2004) ("*Buffy the Vampire Slayer MO&O*")).

[45] *See* 47 C.F.R. § 73.3999.

[46] The subject broadcast occurred prior to the September 7, 2004, effective date of the most recent adjustment of the statutory maximum forfeiture amount. Accordingly, the appropriate maximum statutory amount here is $27,500. *See supra* ¶ 21.

[47] The fact that WBDC may not have originated the programming in question is irrelevant to whether there is an indecency violation. *See Review of the Commission's Regulations Governing Programming Practices of Broadcast Television Networks and Affiliates*, Notice of Proposed Rulemaking, 10 FCC Rcd 11951,11961, ¶ 20 (1995) (internal quotation omitted) ("We conclude that a licensee is not fulfilling his obligations to operate in the public interest, and is not operating in accordance with the express requirements of the Communications Act, if he agrees to accept programs on any basis other than his own reasonable decision that the programs are satisfactory.").

[48] *See Married By America NAL*, 19 FCC Rcd at 20196 ¶ 16 (proposing forfeitures against all Fox Television Network affiliate stations that broadcast apparently indecent material). *See also Clear Channel Broadcasting Licenses, Inc. et al.*, Notice of Apparent Liability for Forfeiture, 19 FCC Rcd 6773, 6779 ¶ 16 (2004) (proposing forfeiture against all commonly owned and operated stations that broadcast the programming at issue, and directing

(continued....)

appropriately restrained enforcement policy, however, justifies this more limited approach towards the imposition of forfeiture penalties.[49] Accordingly, we propose a forfeiture of $27,500 against WBDC Broadcasting, Inc.

2.   "Con El Corazón En La Mano" (October 9, 2004)[50]

33.   *The Programming.* The Commission received a complaint alleging that NBC Telemundo License Co. ("NBC Telemundo"), licensee of Station KWHY-TV, Los Angeles, California, aired indecent material at approximately 8:15 p.m. on October 9, 2004, during a broadcast of the Spanish-language movie, "Con El Corazon En La Mano." The complaint alleged that the broadcast contains a scene depicting a man and woman engaged in sexual intercourse while another individual watches them.

34.   On April 8, 2005, the Bureau directed a letter of inquiry to NBC Telemundo concerning the broadcast.[51] NBC Telemundo responded by letters dated May 19 and June 24, 2005.[52] As confirmed by a videotape of the program provided by NBC Telemundo, the scene in question depicts a man raping a woman in a public restroom while another man stands nearby, acting as a lookout. NBC Telemundo acknowledges that it aired the movie over Station KWHY-TV, Los Angeles, California, beginning at 8:00 p.m. on October 9, 2004, and that the scene took place within the first 15 minutes of the broadcast.[53] NBC Telemundo maintains, however, that "the complained-of material is not actionably indecent because it does not include depictions of nude sexual or excretory organs, offensive language or other material that the Commission previously has deemed indecent."[54]

35.   *Indecency Analysis.* We find that the programming at issue is within the scope of our indecency definition because it clearly depicts sexual activity. NBC Telemundo does not deny that the material portrays a woman being raped.

36.   We also find that the complained-of material is, in the context presented, patently offensive as measured by contemporary community standards for the broadcast medium. Turning to the three principal factors that inform our contextual analysis, the scene is explicit and graphic. The material depicts a woman being savagely attacked and raped in a public restroom. One man grabs the woman and forcibly kisses her as she struggles to free herself. He strikes her to the floor and, kneeling down, grabs one of her breasts as she screams. As they struggle together on the floor, the camera focuses on their hips, showing his hand pulling her underwear down her bare thigh as he maneuvers on top of her with his groin between her legs. She forces him off her by grabbing his testicles, but the other man blocks her escape from the room, and the first man again pulls her to the floor, re-mounts her and begins kissing her. She appears to cease resisting and returns his kisses. The camera again pans to their hips, showing his hand fumbling at his zipper. They quite clearly appear to have sexual intercourse, with his groin thrusting into hers as she moans, until he finally stops and rolls off of her. The scene then continues for several minutes, depicting her reaction to the attack. The material by its very design is extraordinarily intense and extremely graphic. We reject NBC Telemundo's claim that the material is neither explicit nor graphic simply because it contained no actual nudity. For example, in the *Married By America NAL,* we found that scenes in which nudity is electronically obscured may be considered graphic and explicit if the sexual nature of the scene is

---

(...continued from previous page)
an investigation into stations owned by another licensee that broadcast the same program), *vacated per consent decree,* 19 FCC Rcd 10880 (2004).

[49] *See supra* ¶ 11 and note 11.

[50] FCC File No. EB-04-IH-0572.

[51] *See* Letter from William D. Freedman, Deputy Chief, Investigations and Hearings Division, Enforcement Bureau, to NBC Telemundo License Co. (April 8, 2005).

[52] *See* Letter from F. William LeBeau, Senior Regulatory Counsel and Assistant Secretary, NBC Telemundo License Co., to David Brown, Assistant Chief, Investigations and Hearings Division, Enforcement Bureau (May 19, 2005) ("Response"); Letter from F. William LeBeau, Senior Regulatory Counsel and Assistant Secretary, NBC Telemundo License Co., to David Brown, Assistant Chief, Investigations and Hearings Division, Enforcement Bureau (June 24, 2005).

[53] Response at 2-3.

[54] *Id* at 2.

unmistakable.[55] In this case, the sexual nature of the scene is unquestionable, and the material is undeniably graphic, notwithstanding the lack of nudity.

37.   Moving to the second factor in our contextual analysis, we conclude that the broadcast dwells on sexual material. We have repeatedly held that a persistent focus on sexual material is a relevant factor in evaluating the potential offensiveness of broadcasts.[56] The rape scene in question lasts several minutes and, contrary to NBC Telemundo's claim, is hardly ephemeral. As we stated in the *Indecency Policy Statement,* "[r]epetition and persistent focus on sexual or excretory material have been cited consistently as factors that exacerbate the potential offensiveness of broadcasts."[57]

38.   With respect to the third factor, we find the material to be shocking. In this regard, NBC Telemundo concedes that the rape scene was designed to portray the "intensity of [a] serious and unspeakable event . . . ."[58] We agree. Not only does the scene portray an "unspeakable" event of a profoundly disturbing sexual and violent nature, it depicts an incident that was unquestionably shocking and one to which children should not have been exposed. We reject NBC Telemundo's argument that the instant case is indistinguishable from *Saving Private Ryan,*[59] wherein we determined that graphic language throughout the movie was critical to portraying serious events realistically.[60] NBC Telemundo has not demonstrated here that the depiction of a woman being violently raped in such a sustained and graphic manner is essential. In any event, even if these aspects of the scene were essential to the movie, that finding would not alter our ultimate conclusion in this case because the other two factors weigh heavily in favor of a finding of patent offensiveness as measured by contemporary community standards for the broadcast medium. We also do not find that NBC Telemundo's parental advisory prior to its broadcast of "Con El Corazon En La Mano" insulates the licensee from liability.[61]

39.   In sum, because the material is explicit and graphic, is dwelled upon, and is shocking, we conclude that its broadcast was patently offensive under contemporary community standards for the broadcast medium and thus apparently indecent. The complained-of material was broadcast within the 6 a.m. to 10 p.m. time frame relevant to an indecency determination under section 73.3999 of the Commission's rules.[62] Therefore, there was a reasonable risk that children may have been in the viewing audience and the broadcast is legally actionable.

40.   ***Forfeiture Calculation.*** In the instant case, we find that NBC Telemundo consciously and deliberately broadcast the film in question. Accordingly, we find that NBC Telemundo's apparent violation of 18 U.S.C. § 1464 and section 73.3999 of our rules was willful within the meaning of section 503(b)(1) of the Act, and subject to forfeiture.

41.   We therefore turn to the proposed forfeiture amount, based on the factors enumerated in section 503(b)(2)(D) of the Act and the facts and circumstances of this case. We find that the statutory maximum,

[55] 19 FCC Rcd at 20194 ¶ 10. *See also Back Bay Broadcasting,* Notice of Apparent Liability for Forfeiture, 14 FCC Rcd 3997, 3998 (Mass Media Bur. 1999) ("*Back Bay NAL*") (forfeiture paid) (finding broadcast indecent despite attempt to obscure objectionable language because words remained clearly "recognizable, notwithstanding the editing").

[56] *See Indecency Policy Statement,* 16 FCC Rcd at 8008, ¶ 17 (citing cases); *see also "Married By America" NAL,* 19 FCC Rcd at 20195 ¶ 11; *Entercom Seattle Order on Review,* 19 FCC Rcd at 9073-74 ¶ 13.

[57] 16 FCC Rcd at 8008 ¶ 17.

[58] Response at 8.

[59] *Id.* at 7-8.

[60] *Saving Private Ryan,* 20 FCC Rcd at 4512-13, ¶ 14.

[61] *See Pacifica,* 438 U.S. at 748-49 (holding that warnings are not necessarily effective because the audience is constantly changing stations).

[62] *See* 47 C.F.R. § 73.3999.

$32,500,[63] is appropriate for several reasons. As discussed in detail above, the scene is extremely shocking, depicting a violent rape in a graphic and sustained manner. Also, the broadcast was prerecorded. NBC Telemundo knew that the film contained this material and should have taken efforts to edit the scene. Indeed, NBC Telemundo did include a warning of the upcoming scene. Although inclusion of a warning might warrant a lower forfeiture under certain circumstances, we find that it does not here in light of all of the circumstances surrounding the apparent violation, including the shocking and gratuitous nature of the scene and the fact that it was prerecorded. Therefore, we find that NBC Telemundo is apparently liable for a forfeiture of $32,500 for its October 9, 2004 broadcast of "Con El Corazon En La Mano."

42.   Although other stations may have broadcast the material at issue here between 6 a.m. and 10 p.m., we propose a forfeiture against only the licensee and station whose broadcast of the material was actually the subject of a viewer complaint to the Commission. We recognize that this approach differs from that taken in previous Commission decisions involving the broadcast of apparently indecent programming.[64] Our commitment to an appropriately restrained enforcement policy, however, justifies this more limited approach towards the imposition of forfeiture penalties.[65]

3.   "Fernando Hidalgo Show" (October 19, 2004)[66]

43.   *The Programming.* The Commission received a complaint alleging that Station WJAN-CA, Miami, Florida, aired indecent material during the October 19, 2004 broadcast of the program the "Fernando Hidalgo Show," a Spanish-language talk show. The complaint refers to a segment that involved partial female adult nudity. The segment was more than fifteen minutes in duration.

44.   On February 11, 2005, the Bureau sent a letter of inquiry to Sherjan Broadcasting Company, Inc., the licensee of Station WJAN-CA, concerning the material described above allegedly broadcast over the station.[67] Sherjan responded by letter dated March 14, 2005.[68] As confirmed by the videotape of the program provided by Sherjan, during the segment in question, the host introduces a female guest by stating, "before we present Juliana I want to tell the gentlemen to be careful because she is dressed in a way that can cause a heart attack."[69] The female guest then appears in an open-front dress, with her nipples covered, but her breasts otherwise fully exposed. As she makes her entrance, she pirouettes in front of the audience, then shakes her breasts towards the cameras. When she turns to face the host, he briefly stares at her breasts, then mugs for the camera. Sherjan acknowledges that the material in question was aired over Station WJAN-CA at 7:00 p.m. on October 19, 2004, and that the female guest appeared in an open-front dress.[70] However, Sherjan maintains that the complained-of material is not actionably indecent because it is "a comedy routine" and does not shock or titillate.[71]

---

[63] The subject broadcast occurred after the September 7, 2004, effective date of the most recent adjustment of the statutory maximum forfeiture amount. Accordingly, the appropriate maximum statutory amount here is $32,500. *See supra* ¶ 21.

[64] *See supra* note 48.

[65] *See supra* ¶ 11 and note 11.

[66] FCC File No. EB-04-IH-0625.

[67] *See* Letter from William D. Freedman, Deputy Chief, Investigations and Hearings Division, Enforcement Bureau, Federal Communications Commission, to Sherjan Broadcasting Company, Inc. (February 11, 2005) ("LOI").

[68] *See* Letter from Peter Tannenwald, Irwin, Campbell & Tannenwald, P.C., to David Brown, Assistant Chief, Investigations and Hearings Division, Enforcement Bureau, Federal Communications Commission (March 14, 2005).

[69] *Id.* at Attachment 2 (licensee's English-language translation of broadcast). Also according to the licensee's translation, immediately before the woman appears on stage, the host asks another guest, "Do you know Juliana?" The guest states that she knows "Juliana How Bad You Are," a popular Spanish-language song. The host replies, "Well this one is worse than that! And we're going to present her now!" *Id.*

[70] *Id.*

[71] *Id.* at 2.

45.   *Indecency Analysis.* We find that the programming at issue is within the scope of our indecency definition because it depicts sexual organs – specifically an adult woman's breasts. Sherjan argues that the complained-of material "did not include any description of sexual or excretory functions in either the video or audio portion, let alone graphic descriptions."[72] However, the indecency definition clearly encompasses depictions of sexual organs as well as sexual activities.[73] Moreover, the explicitness of the depiction is not relevant to the threshold issue of whether the material depicts or describes a sexual or excretory organ or activity, and is more appropriately considered in our analysis of whether the material is patently offensive.

46.   Turning to that issue, we find that, based on our contextual analysis, the material in question is patently offensive as measured by contemporary community standards for the broadcast medium. With respect to the first factor of our contextual analysis, we find that the material is explicit and graphic. The material clearly depicts a woman's naked breasts, which are sexual organs. In this respect, this case is similar to other cases in which we have held depictions of nudity to be graphic and explicit.[74] The fact that the guest's nipples are covered with jewelry does not render the depiction of her breasts, which were otherwise fully exposed, insufficiently graphic to weigh in favor of a finding of patent offensiveness.[75] Here, the audience had a sustained view of the guest's breasts from several different angles, and the dress only served to enhance the view.

47.   With respect to the second factor of our analysis, we find that the broadcast dwells on the sexual material. The guest's naked breasts are visible throughout much of the segment in question, which lasts more than fifteen minutes.[76] Furthermore, the camera focuses on the female guest's torso during much of that time. We have repeatedly held that repetition and persistent focus on sexual or excretory material is a relevant factor in evaluating the offensiveness of broadcasts.[77]

48.   With respect to the third factor, we find that the female guest's partial nudity shocked, pandered to, and titillated the audience. Indeed, the behavior of the guest and the host as she came on stage highlighted the titillating nature of the material. Finally, we reject the licensee's contention that the material broadcast is not indecent because it is "a comedy routine." Even if this segment was comedic, it is well settled that comedy formats do not insulate otherwise indecent material.[78]

49.   In sum, we find that the broadcast material referenced in the complaint contains an explicit and graphic depiction of sexual organs, and that the nudity is dwelled upon and shocked, pandered to, and titillated the audience. Therefore, we find that the material is patently offensive as measured by contemporary community standards for the broadcast medium and is apparently indecent. The complained-of material was broadcast within the 6 a.m. to 10 p.m. time frame relevant to an indecency determination under section 73.3999 of the Commission's

---

[72] *Id.* at 1-2.

[73] *See, e.g., Complaints Against Various Television Licensees Concerning Their February 1, 2004, Broadcast of the Super Bowl XXXVIII Halftime Show,* Notice of Apparent Liability for Forfeiture, 19 FCC Rcd 19230, 19235 ¶ 11 (2004) ("*Super Bowl NAL*") (finding that Super Bowl halftime show, which displayed a bare female breast, satisfied subject matter prong of indecency analysis) .

[74] *Id.,* 19 FCC Rcd at 19235 ¶ 13 (finding that a broadcast, which showed a performer's exposed breast, was graphic and explicit). *See also Young Broadcasting of San Francisco, Inc.,* Notice of Apparent Liability for Forfeiture, 19 FCC Rcd 1751, 1755 ¶ 11 (2004) ("*Young Broadcasting NAL*") (finding that a broadcast of performer's exposed penis was graphic and explicit).

[75] *See Super Bowl NAL,* 19 FCC Rcd at 19235-36, ¶ 13 (finding that a broadcast of performer's exposed breast was "clearly graphic," even though breast was partially covered).

[76] In this connection, we note that in the *Super Bowl NAL,* we found that the broadcast of an exposed breast was indecent, even though it lasted less than one second. *Id.*

[77] *See Indecency Policy Statement,* 16 FCC Rcd at 8008 ¶ 17 (citing cases); *see also Married By America NAL,* 19 FCC Rcd at 20195 ¶ 11; *Entercom Seattle Order on Review,* 19 FCC Rcd at 9073-74 ¶ 13.

[78] *See Pacifica,* 438 U.S. at 744 (upholding the Commission's finding that the broadcast of a comedy monologue featuring references to sexual activities and organs was patently offensive and violated the statutory prohibition on indecency).

rules.[79] Therefore, there is a reasonable risk that children may have been in the viewing audience at the time that the material at issue was broadcast, and the broadcast is legally actionable.

50.   ***Forfeiture Calculation.*** In the instant case, Sherjan consciously and deliberately aired the "Fernando Hidalgo Show." By airing the complained-of material, we find that Sherjan's apparent violation of section 73.3999 and 18 U.S.C. § 1464 was willful within the meaning of section 503(b)(1) of the Act, and subject to forfeiture.

51.   We therefore turn to the proposed forfeiture amount, based on the factors enumerated in section 503(b)(2)(D) of the Act and the facts and circumstances of this case. For the following reasons, we propose a forfeiture of $32,500, the statutory maximum, for this broadcast.[80] The scene is sustained, lasting 15 minutes, and contains no warning of the adult-oriented content. In addition, the gravity of the apparent violation is heightened because of its egregious nature. Thus we find Sherjan Broadcasting Company, Inc. is apparently liable for a forfeiture of $32,500 for its October 19, 2004 broadcast of the "Fernando Hidalgo Show."

4.   "Video Musicales" (February 2 -March 8, 2002)

52.   ***The Programming.*** The Commission received a series of written complaints from individuals associated with the group D'Vanguardia ("Complainants") alleging that Aerco Broadcasting Corp. ("Aerco"), licensee of Station WSJU-TV, San Juan, Puerto Rico, repeatedly broadcast indecent material between the hours of 6:00 a.m. and 10:00 p.m. during the "Video Musicales" program in early 2002.[81] After reviewing the complaints and videotapes provided by the Complainants, the Bureau directed a letter of inquiry to Aerco requesting further information about the music videos that Station WSJU-TV allegedly broadcast,[82] specifically including "DJ Joe, Fatal Fantasy 2 – Feat, Trebol, Clan,"[83] "DJ Joe, Fatal Fantasy 2-- Feat, Nejo, Speedy,"[84] "Operation Sandunga,"[85] and a promotional spot for a DVD entitled "Dangerous -- Fatal Fantasy 2."[86]

53.   Aerco responded to the Bureau's letter on March 23, 2004, providing a Spanish transcription and English translation of each of the music videos and other material.[87] Aerco states that it is not able to confirm whether it broadcast some of the material at the times and dates provided in the complaints and whether the music videos and other material on the videotape provided by the Complainants accurately reflect Station WSJU-TV's

---

[79] *See* 47 C.F.R. § 73.3999.

[80] The subject broadcast occurred after the September 7, 2004 effective date of the most recent adjustment of the statutory maximum forfeiture amount. Accordingly, the appropriate maximum statutory amount here is $32,500. *See supra* ¶ 21.

[81] *See* Letter from David Ramos and Gloria Cardona, D'Vanguardia, to David Solomon, Chief, Enforcement Bureau, Federal Communications Commission (March 12, 2002); Letter from David Ramos and Gloria Cardona, D'Vanguardia, to David Solomon, Chief, Enforcement Bureau, Federal Communications Commission (March 2, 2002); Letter from David Ramos and Gloria Cardona, D'Vanguardia, to David Solomon, Chief, Enforcement Bureau, Federal Communications Commission (February 26, 2002); Letter from David Ramos to David Solomon, Chief, Enforcement Bureau, Federal Communications Commission (February 26, 2002); Letter from Gloria Cardona and David Ramos, D'Vanguardia, to David Solomon, Chief, Enforcement Bureau, Federal Communications Commission (February 22, 2002).

[82] *See* Letter from Maureen F. Del Duca, Chief, Investigations and Hearings Division, Enforcement Bureau, to Aerco (December 24, 2003) ("LOI").

[83] FCC File Nos. EB-02-IH-0167, EB-02-IH-0198.

[84] FCC File Nos. EB-02-IH-0167, EB-02-IH-0199.

[85] FCC File Nos. EB-02-IH-0167, EB-02-IH-0199.

[86] FCC File No. EB-02-IH-0258.

[87] *See* Letter from John A. Borsari to Marlene H. Dortch, Secretary, Federal Communications Commission at Exhibits 1-A -- 6-B (March 23, 2004) ("Response").

APPENDIX A

broadcasts.[88] However, Aerco did not provide any documentation that challenged or raised questions about any of the complaints or videotapes made by the Complainants. Aerco also did not provide a complete record of its program logs for the dates alleged in the complaints.[89]

54.   Aerco asserts that it is not aware of any other complaints about the material in question and thus contends that each of the complaints represents only a single viewer who objects to the broadcast matter.[90] In addition, Aerco asserts that, in many instances, significant portions of the material are inaudible and thus an ordinary viewer would be not be able to understand the lyrics. Aerco explains that it hired an independent firm to prepare the transcript to respond to the Bureau's LOI, which isolated the music portion from the speaking portion to identify the lyrics.[91] Aerco asserts that the lyrics do not contain offensive or indecent language and that there were no nude scenes that would satisfy the Commission's standards for the definition of indecency.[92] Aerco concedes that some of the material is suggestive, but that any "sexual or excretory import to the innuendo or artistic license taken by the performers is subject to individual interpretation and to be categorized as indecent, and not merely poor taste, such innuendo must be unmistakable."[93]

55.   "DJ Joe, Fatal Fantasy 2 – Feat, Trebol, Clan." This song repeatedly mentions the singer's near-constant state of sexual arousal. There is a segment of the video in which a boy appears to masturbate in a bathroom stall. The lyrics accompanying the segment translate as follows:

> When I had been barely born, I instantly knew where I had come from. Since then until I grew up, I have always yearned to be inside a similar hole. In elementary school they called me Mr. Corner. In intermediate school they called me "little masturbator" because this is where my vice of rubbing myself incessantly began.[94]

---

[88] Id. at 1-5. Aerco states that several music videos, all entitled "Fatal Fantasy 2," were broadcast between January and March 2002. Thus, Aerco claims it cannot confirm the dates and times for the airing of the specific videos "DJ Joe, Fatal Fantasy 2 – Feat, Trebol, Clan" or "DJ Joe -- Fatal Fantasy 2." Id. at 2-3. In regard to "Operation Sandunga," Aerco states that it does not have any records of such a titled music video. Id. at 4. It asserts that Aerco broadcasts programs produced by independent producers after 10:00 p.m. and some of these broadcasts contain music videos that would not be reflected in Aerco's program logs. Id. at 4-5. Aerco further asserts that since these broadcasts are aired after 10:00 p.m., "Operation Sandunga" could not have been broadcast between 10:00 a.m. and 10:52 a.m., as alleged in the complaints. Id. at 5. Aerco confirms that it broadcast the promo for "Dangerous – Fatal Fantasy 2" on the four dates alleged in the Bureau LOI, but is unable to confirm the broadcast times. Id. at 4.

[89] Id. at Exhibit 7. In response to the Bureau LOI, Aerco provided a program log for only one of the nine days mentioned in the complaints. Aerco also provided program logs for multiple days not mentioned in the Bureau LOI. The program logs list dates and times of program material, but provide only partial titles of the music videos played. Thus, there are multiple entries for a program entitled "Fatal Fantasy," which could be any of three videos discussed in this Notice of Apparent Liability. Because of the confusing nature of Aerco's program logs and the fact that Aerco does not dispute the times and dates listed in the videotapes provided by the Complainants, we will rely only on the videotapes as the basis for the proposed forfeiture here.

[90] Id. at 8.

[91] Id. at 8-9.

[92] Id. at 9-10.

[93] Id. at 10.

[94] This translation is based upon our review of the material at issue. Aerco provides the following translation (the parenthetical is in Aerco's translation):

> Just barely a newborn, I soon knew where I'd come out from. Since then and until I grew up, in the same kind of hole I always like to be. In elementary school they called me "Mr. Hop." In junior high they called me "Punecinco" (invented word), because that's when I got into the habit of pleasing myself.

(continued....)

APPENDIX A

56. "DJ Joe, Fatal Fantasy 2 -- Feat. Nejo, Speedy." There are multiple segments in which women clad in bikini tops and thongs bend away from the camera – exposing their buttocks to the viewer -- and simulate sexual intercourse. The music video includes a specific scene of a woman bending away from the camera wearing a thong while one of the male singers slaps her on the buttocks. The lyrics accompanying the segment translate as follows:

> I pushed her from the front. I took her and had her. I took her bra off. I lowered her panties like old times. I will give it to you through the ass. I will give it to you through the ass.[95]

57. "Dangerous -- Fatal Fantasy 2." This promo for a DVD includes multiple scenes with scantily-clad women fondling themselves and each other in a sexual fashion. For example, there are scenes in which females caress their breasts, buttocks and/or genital area. The promo also includes several close-up camera shots of thong-clad buttocks, of scantily-clad breasts and crotches, and of a woman removing her top (with the shot changing just before her breasts are completely exposed). Some of these scenes also show a woman applying baby oil to another woman's buttocks and women caressing each other's breasts and buttocks.

58. "Operation Sandunga." This material contains scenes with scantily-clad women depicting lap dances and a scene simulating oral sex. In one scene, the male singer is seated on a sofa with his legs spread apart. In between his legs kneeling on the floor is a female with her back to the camera whose head bobs up and down over the male's genital area, simulating oral sex. In other scenes, the woman is also variously shown kneeling and gyrating between his legs or straddling one leg and gyrating with her chest in his face. According to Aerco, the lyrics for the scene in which oral sex is simulated translate to: "You have to lick, lick, lick, lick, lick … You have to lick, mami, really 'be' … 'tra', [sic] to feel my thing and lick, mami, really 'be' … 'tra', [sic] to feel my thing."[96]

59. *Indecency Analysis.* For the reasons discussed below, we find that each of the complained-of videos and promo is apparently indecent.

60. "DJ Joe, Fatal Fantasy 2 – Feat. Trebol, Clan." The material dwells on the singer's near-constant state of arousal, depicts a male child simulating masturbation, and the accompanying lyrics also refer to masturbation. We find, therefore, that the material meets the first prong of our indecency analysis.

61. Turning to the three principal factors that comprise our contextual analysis, as mentioned above, we also find that the material, in the context presented, is patently offensive under contemporary community standards for the broadcast medium. With respect to the first factor, the material explicitly depicts a male child simulating masturbation, and includes lyrics also graphically and explicitly describing masturbation, including characterization of the child as a "masturbator," and a description of "rubbing himself" incessantly. We find, with respect to the second factor, that the material repeatedly discusses the singer's sexual arousal. We also find that the simulated masturbation and lyrics that refer to masturbation by a male child are not only pandering and titillating, they are shocking.

62. "DJ Joe, Fatal Fantasy 2 -- Feat. Nejo, Speedy." We find that this material depicts simulated sexual activity between a woman in a thong and a male singer. The lyrics accompanying this depiction refer to

---

Response at Exhibit 1-B.

[95] This translation is based upon our review of the material at issue. Aerco provides the following translation:

> I used to push her with my front part and with my chest far away. I used to take her and screw her. The brassieres I used to take off, the panties I used to take down, like in the old days, I'm giving it to you, I'm giving it to you.

Response at Exhibit 3-B.

[96] *Id.* at Exhibit 6-B (punctuation included in the original).

sexual activity, including "I took her and had her," "I lowered her panties like old times," and "I will give it to you through the ass." This material also depicts and describes the buttocks, which are sexual and excretory organs.[97]

63.   We also find that the material, in the context presented, is patently offensive under contemporary community standards for the broadcast medium. The segment depicts simulated sexual intercourse and contains lyrics that graphically and explicitly describe sexual activities ("I will give it to you through the ass"). In this segment, women's buttocks are also clearly visible on screen. The segment dwells on and repeats the sexual material, the second factor in our analysis. We have repeatedly held that repetition and persistent focus on sexual material is a relevant factor in evaluating the potential offensiveness of broadcasts.[98] The camera angles throughout repeatedly dwell on shots that provide views of the female dancers' buttocks. The segment is focused entirely on the repetition of simulated sexual activity with accompanying lyrics that describe such activity. With respect to the third factor, we find that the simulated sexual activity, accompanied by explicit lyrics that reference sexual activity ("I will give it to you through the ass"), and the persistent visual focus on the female dancer's buttocks are presented in a manner that is obviously pandering and titillating.

64.   "Dangerous -- Fatal Fantasy 2." We find that this material meets the first prong of the Commission's indecency test. The material includes close-up shots of thong-clad buttocks, breasts and crotches, as well as females fondling their breasts, buttocks and genital areas while they dance, gyrate, and fondle one another in a sexually suggestive manner. These scenes clearly depict sexual organs and activities.

65.   We also find that this material, in the context presented, is patently offensive under contemporary community standards for the broadcast medium. The material contains close-up shots of thong-clad buttocks, a female fondling her genital area, and women caressing their own breasts and buttocks as well as those of others. Thus, we conclude that the material is graphic and explicit. Second, while not dispositive, it is relevant that these types of images appear numerous times throughout the promo and, therefore, that sexual images are sustained and repetitious. Finally, the close-up shots of thong-clad buttocks and women fondling their own breasts, buttocks and genital areas as well as the breasts and buttocks of other women in a sexually suggestive manner are presented in a pandering and titillating manner. Indeed, this material appears to have little other purpose. Therefore, because the complained-of material is explicit and graphic, repeated, and is pandering and titillating, we conclude that the promo is patently offensive and thus indecent.

66.   "Operation Sandunga." This material meets the first prong of the indecency test. As noted above, this material includes a scene and lyrics describing and depicting oral sex, a sexual activity. Accordingly, we find that the material describes and depicts a sexual activity. We also find that the material, in the context presented here, is patently offensive under contemporary community standards for the broadcast medium. With respect to the first principal factor that informs our contextual analysis, the scene and lyrics depict and describe a female performing oral sex in a manner that is graphic and explicit. With respect to the second factor, while not dispositive, it is relevant that sexual references are sustained and repeated. The scene depicting oral sex is coupled with numerous other scenes depicting the same woman gyrating suggestively as she kneels between the male singer's legs or straddles one of his legs with her chest thrust in his face, apparently simulating a "lap dance." Finally, the graphic depictions of oral sex, joined with the repeated and explicit lyrics in which men direct women to lick their genitals, panders to and titillates the audience. Therefore, because the complained-of material is explicit and graphic, repeated, and shocks, panders, and titillates, we conclude that the video is patently offensive and thus indecent.

67.   Aerco states that the music videos and other broadcast material at issue here may be suggestive, but are not indecent or obscene under prevailing standards.[99] Aerco cites the *Indecency Policy Statement* to support

---

[97] *See, e.g., City of Erie v. Pap's A.M.,* 529 U.S. 277 (2000) (Supreme Court did not disturb a city's indecency ordinance prohibiting public nudity, which listed the buttocks as among the body parts subject to the ordinance's ban on nudity); *Loce v. Time Warner Entertainment Advance/Newhouse Partnership,* 191 F.3d 256, 269 (2d. Cir. 1999) (upholding state district court's determination that Time Warner's decision to not transmit certain cable programming that it reasonably believed indecent (some of which included "close-up shots of unclothed breasts and buttocks") did not run afoul of the Constitution).

[98] *See Indecency Policy Statement,* 16 FCC Rcd at 8008 ¶ 17 (citing cases); *see also Married By America NAL,* 19 FCC Rcd at 20195 ¶ 11; *Entercom Seattle Order on Review,* 19 FCC Rcd at 9073-74 ¶ 13.

[99] *See* Response at 10.

its assertion.[100] We disagree with Aerco's analysis. These broadcasts combine sexually explicit language and innuendo with visual depictions that graphically depict the meaning of the lyrics.[101] We also do not agree with Aerco's argument that the lyrics are barely intelligible.

68.   According to the Complaints and videotapes, Aerco broadcast each of the music videos and the promo on multiple occasions. Aerco, in its *Response*, states that it is unable to determine whether it broadcast "DJ Joe, Fatal Fantasy 2 – Feat, Trebol, Clan" or "DJ Joe -- Fatal Fantasy 2-Feat, Nejo, Speedy" because its program logs list three music videos with similar titles.[102] Aerco confirms that the promo for the DVD titled "Dangerous – Fatal Fantasy 2" aired on the four dates alleged in the complaints, but states that it is unable to determine the broadcast times.[103] Aerco also asserts that it is unable to determine whether "Operation Sandunga" was aired on the date alleged in the complaint because it has no records of this music video.[104] Aerco states that it broadcast programs produced by independent producers after 10:00 p.m. and that it "could" have aired the independently produced "Operation Sandunga" music video during this time period.[105]

69.   Based on the complaints and the accompanying videotapes, and in the absence of any evidence to the contrary,[106] we find that Aerco broadcast each of the music videos and the promo in question multiple times – a total of at least 14 broadcasts - between the hours of 6 a.m. and 10 p.m., the time frame relevant to an indecency determination.[107] Because there is a reasonable risk that children may have been in the audience when the material in each was broadcast, the material broadcast is legally actionable. By broadcasting this material during these times over Station WSJU-TV, Aerco apparently violated the prohibitions in the Act and the Commission's rules against broadcast indecency.

70.   *Forfeiture Calculation.* Aerco consciously and deliberately broadcast the videos and the DVD promo. Accordingly, we find that the broadcasts in apparent violation of 18 U.S.C. § 1464 and 47 C.F.R. § 73.3999 were willful within the meaning of section 503(b)(1) of the Act. Additionally, Aerco aired this material a total of 14 times. Accordingly, we find that Aerco's apparent violation of 18 U.S.C. § 1464 and 47 C.F.R. § 73.3999 was also repeated.

71.   We therefore turn to the proposed forfeiture amount, based on the factors enumerated in section 503(b)(2)(D) of the Act and the facts and circumstances of this case. Based on consideration of the statutory factors,

---

[100] *Id.*

[101] To the extent that the music videos' and the promo's use of visual images in conjunction with lyrics to describe and depict sexual activity could be described as innuendo rather than direct references, they are nonetheless sufficiently graphic and explicit to render the material actionably indecent because the sexual import of those images in conjunction with those lyrics was "unmistakable." *See Married By America NAL,* 19 FCC Rcd at 20194 ¶ 10 (proposing forfeiture for airing nudity, finding that despite electronic blurring ("pixilation") "even a child would have known the strippers were topless and that sexual activity was being shown"). *See also Indecency Policy Statement,* 16 FCC Rcd at 8003-04 ¶ 12; *Telemundo of Puerto Rico License Corp. (WKAQ-TV),* Notice of Apparent Liability for Forfeiture, 16 FCC Rcd 7157, 7159, ¶ 8 (Enf. Bur. 2001) (forfeiture paid) (*"Telemundo NAL"*).

[102] *See* Response at 2-3.

[103] *Id.* at 4.

[104] *Id.* at 4.

[105] *Id.* at 4-5.

[106] *See Entercom Sacramento License, LLC,* Notice of Apparent Liability for Forfeiture, 19 FCC Rcd 20129 ¶ 5 (2004) (proposing a forfeiture in a case where the licensee could not deny the broadcast occurred).

[107] *See* 47 C.F.R. § 73.3999. Based on the videotape and data provided by the Complainants, we conclude that the station aired "DJ Joe, Fatal Fantasy 2- Feat, Trebol, Clan" between the hours of 6:00 a.m. and 10:00 p.m. on February 2 (12:00-12:43 p.m.), 22 (5:00-6:30 p.m.), 26 (3:00-3:30 p.m.) and 28, 2002 (2:05-2:50 p.m.); "DJ Joe, Fatal Fantasy 2-- Feat, Nejo, Speedy" on February 22 (5:30- 6:30 p.m.), 26 (6:00 -6:30 p.m.), March 6 (10:00-10:52 a.m.), and 27 (5:45-5:48 p.m.). We also find that the station aired "Dangerous -- Fatal Fantasy 2" on February 28 (2:05-2:50 p.m.), March 1 (1:13-1:53 p.m.), 4 (6:50 p.m.), 5 (9:40-10:17 a.m.) and 8, 2002 (11:51 a.m.- 12:55 p.m.). We also find that the station aired "Operation Sandunga" on March 6, 2002, between 10:00 and 10:52 a.m.

we find it is appropriate to use the statutory maximum amount of $27,500[108] to calculate the proposed forfeiture in this case. The gravity of the apparent violations is heightened in this case because, as discussed above, the music videos and the DVD promo at issue are extremely graphic and explicit, including close-up scenes of sexual fondling and simulated oral sex, which are repeated throughout the material. One broadcast segment explicitly depicts a child masturbating, and another repeatedly displays women's buttocks in a pandering and titillating manner. All of the material depict and describe sexual organs or activities in a highly shocking, vulgar, and gratuitous manner. In addition, this material could have been reviewed by Aerco prior to broadcast. Multiplying the statutory maximum amount of $27,500 by the 14 broadcasts at issue here results in a total forfeiture amount of $385,000. Under the specific circumstances of this case, however, we believe that such a forfeiture would be excessive to achieve the appropriate level of punishment and deterrence and that $220,000 is a more appropriate amount. We base this conclusion on several factors, including the fact that Aerco is the licensee of only San Juan, Puerto Rico, Stations WSJU-TV and WQBS(AM) and that it has no prior indecency violations. Therefore, for the reasons stated above, we propose a forfeiture of $220,000 against Aerco Broadcasting Corp. for its willful and repeated violations of 18 U.S.C. § 1464 and 47 C.F.R. § 73.3999.

5.   "The Blues: Godfathers and Sons" (March 11, 2004)[109]

72.   ***The Programming.*** The Commission received a complaint alleging that San Mateo County Community College District ("San Mateo"), licensee of noncommercial educational Station KCSM-TV, San Mateo, California, aired indecent material over the station during its broadcast of the program "The Blues: Godfathers and Sons" on March 11, 2004 between the hours of 8:42 and 9:32 p.m. Pacific Standard Time.[110] The complaint alleged that the broadcast, an episode of a prerecorded documentary series provided by the Public Broadcasting Service ("PBS"), contains numerous "obscenities," including the "F-Word," the "S-Word" and various derivatives of those words, in violation of the Commission's rules restricting the broadcast of indecent material.[111] The complainant therefore asked that the Commission investigate and take appropriate enforcement action.

73.   Thereafter, the Bureau sent a letter of inquiry to San Mateo, attaching a copy of the Complaint.[112] In its response, San Mateo acknowledges that it aired "The Blues: Godfathers and Sons," a documentary containing interviews of blues performers and a record producer, over Station KCSM-TV as alleged, between 8 and 10 p.m. on

---

[108] The subject broadcasts occurred prior to the September 7, 2004, effective date of the most recent adjustment of the statutory maximum forfeiture amount. Accordingly, the appropriate maximum statutory amount here is $27,500. *See supra* ¶ 21.

[109] FCC File No. EB-04-IH-0260.

[110] *See* Letter from complainant to the Investigations and Hearings Division, Enforcement Bureau, Federal Communications Commission March 18, 2004) ("Complaint").

[111] According to the Complaint, the program includes the following objectionable utterances broadcast between 8:42 and 9:32 p.m.:

> 8:42 p.m.: "See those, motherfucker? Gotta pay those motherfucking notes."
>
> 8:51 p.m.: "What's my job? You stupid motherfucker, your job is to follow me."
>
> 9:00 p.m.: "Shit it's good to be next to you."
>
> 9:04 p.m.: "there's no white bullshit with [Paul] Butterfield."
>
> 9:13 p.m.: "I'll buy some shit."
>
> 9:14 p.m.: "This is the kind of shit I buy."
>
> 9:23 p.m.: "Cocksucker Blues" (used as an on-screen Chyron to identify a song title).
>
> 9:32 p.m.: "This poor fucker."

[112] *See* Letter from William D. Freedman, Deputy Chief, Investigations and Hearings Division, Enforcement Bureau, to San Mateo (August 4, 2004) ("LOI ").

APPENDIX A

March 11, 2004, but not on any other dates between 6:00 a.m. and 10:00 p.m.[113] With its response, San Mateo provided a DVD and a written transcript of the program.[114] San Mateo does not dispute that it aired the material described in the complaint. It states, "[t]he intent of the program is to provide a window into [the world of the individuals being interviewed] with their own words, all of which becomes an educational experience for the viewer." Thus, San Mateo maintains that the language contained in the program was not "used in a prurient way, but rather as an infrequent conversational expression of the artist [being interviewed], and was not edited to remove their dialogue, which accurately reflected their viewpoints."[115] San Mateo represents that, subsequent to its station's airing of the program, PBS alerted its member stations that this and similar PBS-supplied programs contained material that might be deemed indecent in light of then-recent Commission rulings, and advised licensees that PBS had changed its procedures involving the editing of potentially indecent or offensive language in programming that it provides them and will now alert licensees to potential problems.[116]

74.   ***Indecency Analysis.*** The Commission determined in its *Golden Globe Awards Order* that the "F-Word" meets the first prong of the indecency test. We stated, "given the core meaning of the "F-Word," any use of that word or a variation, in any context, inherently has a sexual connotation, and therefore falls within the first prong of our indecency definition."[117] Similarly, we now find that the "S-Word," at issue here, has an inherently excretory connotation. In light of the core meanings of the "F-Word" and "S-Word," any use of those terms inherently has sexual or excretory connotations and falls within the first prong of our indecency definition.[118]

75.   We also find that the broadcast material is, in context, patently offensive as measured by contemporary community standards for the broadcast medium. First, as we stated in *Golden Globe Awards Order,* the "F-Word" is one of the most vulgar, graphic, and explicit descriptions of sexual activity in the English language. Its use invariably invokes a coarse sexual image."[119] Similarly, we find the "S-Word" to be one of the most vulgar, graphic and explicit words relating to excretory activity in the English language. Use of the "S-Word" invariably invokes a coarse excretory image. Consequently, we conclude that the broadcast by San Mateo of a program containing numerous uses of the "F-Word" and the "S-Word," under the circumstances presented here, is vulgar, graphic, and explicit.

76.   Second, the program repeats this language numerous times during the broadcast. We note that, while prior FCC staff actions had indicated as of the date this program aired that isolated broadcasts of certain expletives were not indecent or would not be acted upon, the program at issue here contains numerous repeated utterances of the "F-Word" and "S-Word," and their variants. Our precedent is clear that broadcasts containing numerous expletives may be actionably indecent.[120]

77.   Third, the gratuitous and repeated use of this language in a program that San Mateo aired at a time when children were expected to be in the audience is shocking. While San Mateo contends that the expletives in question were not removed from the program so that the viewpoints of those being interviewed would be accurately reflected, as discussed below we disagree that the use of such language was necessary to express any particular viewpoint in this case.[121] We also note that many of the expletives in the broadcast are not used by blues performers. For example, based on our review of the DVD and transcript, Marshall Chess, a former label owner and

---

[113] *See* Letter from Marilyn R. Lawrence, General Manager, KCSM-TV/(FM), to David Brown, Assistant Chief, Investigations and Hearings Division, Enforcement Bureau (August 27, 2004) ("Response") at 1.

[114] *Id.*

[115] Id.

[116] Id. San Mateo appears to refer to the *Golden Globe Awards Order.*

[117] *Golden Globe Awards Order,* 19 FCC Rcd at 4978 ¶ 8.

[118] *See Pacifica Foundation*, 56 FCC 2d at 99.

[119] *Golden Globe Awards Order,* 19 FCC Rcd at 4979 ¶ 9.

[120] *See Indecency Policy Statement,* 16 FCC Rcd at 8008 ¶ 16 (*citing Back Bay NAL,* 14 FCC Rcd at 3998, which found the broadcast of repeated uncensored uses of the "F-Word," among other expletives, to be indecent).

[121] *See infra* ¶ 82.

record producer, states in discussing the relationship between Chess Records and its artists, "my dad had so many people at his funeral, my uncle said, 'You see all those motherfuckers? They're coming to make sure he's dead, so they don't have to pay back those motherfuckin' notes.'" In another scene, discussing his relationship with his father at Chess Records, Marshall Chess states, "[h]e said, 'What's your job? You stupid motherfucker! Your job is watching me!'" During a scene showing hip-hop artists Kyle Jason, Juice, and Chuck D. shopping in a record store with Chess, Kyle Jason states, "I'll buy some shit," and Juice states, "This looks crazy! See that? This is the kind of shit I buy! I mean, my man is wearing pink gear—that shit, that shit is crazy right there! I'm buyin' it!"

78.   In sum, because the expletives in the program are vulgar, explicit, graphic, dwelled upon and shocking to the audience, we conclude that the broadcast of the material at issue here is patently offensive under contemporary community standards for the broadcast medium and thus apparently indecent. The complained-of material was broadcast within the 6 a.m. to 10 p.m. time frame relevant to an indecency determination under section 73.3999 of the Commission's rules.[122] Therefore, there is a reasonable risk that children may have been in the viewing audience and the broadcast is legally actionable.

79.   *Profanity Analysis.* In the *Golden Globe Awards Order,* the Commission concluded that the "F-Word" was profane within the meaning of 18 U.S.C. § 1464 because, in context, it constituted vulgar and coarse language "so grossly offensive to members of the public who actually hear it as to amount to a nuisance." We indicated in that decision that the Commission would analyze other potentially profane words on a case-by-case basis.

80.   The "F-Word" is a vulgar sexual term so grossly offensive to members of the public that it amounts to a nuisance and is presumptively profane. It is one of the most offensive words in the English language, the broadcast of which is likely to shock the viewer and disturb the peace and quiet of the home. Consistent with our decision in the *Golden Globe Awards Order,* we find here that the use of the "F-Word" in the program at issue violated 18 U.S.C. § 1464's prohibition of the broadcast of "profane" language.[123]

81.   In addition, we find that the "S-Word" is a vulgar excretory term so grossly offensive to members of the public that it amounts to a nuisance and is presumptively profane. Like the "F-Word," it is one of the most offensive words in the English language, the broadcast of which is likely to shock the viewer and disturb the peace and quiet of the home.

82.   As noted previously, in rare contexts, language that is presumptively profane will not be found to be profane where it is demonstrably essential to the nature of an artistic or educational work or essential to informing viewers on a matter of public importance.[124] However, we will find this to be the case only in unusual circumstances, and such circumstances are not present here. Although in this case the profane language may have had some communicative purpose, we do not believe that San Mateo has demonstrated that it was essential to the nature of an artistic or educational work or essential to informing viewers on a matter of public importance, or that the substitution of other language would have materially altered the nature of the work. In this respect, this case is unlike *Saving Private Ryan,* where we concluded that deleting offensive words "would have altered the nature of the artistic work and diminished the power, realism and immediacy of the film experience for viewers."[125] While we recognize here that the documentary had an educational purpose, we believe that purpose could have been fulfilled and all viewpoints expressed without the repeated broadcast of expletives.

83.   It is undisputed that the complained-of material, including the "F-Word" and the "S-Word," was broadcast within the 6 a.m. to 10 p.m. time frame relevant to a profanity determination under section 73.3999 of the Commission's rules. Because there was a reasonable risk that children may have been in the audience at the time the material at issue was broadcast on March 11, 2004, the material broadcast is legally actionable.[126]

84.   *Forfeiture Calculation.* San Mateo consciously and deliberately broadcast this episode.

---

[122] *See* 47 C.F.R. § 73.3999.

[123] *Id.* at 4981 ¶¶ 13-14.

[124] 20 FCC Rcd at 4512-14 ¶¶ 13-18.

[125] *Id.* at 4512-13 ¶¶ 13-14.

[126] *See ACT III,* 58 F.3d at 660-63.

Accordingly, we find that the broadcast in apparent violation of 18 U.S.C. § 1464 and 47 C.F.R. § 73.3999 was willful within the meaning of section 503(b)(1) of the Act, and subject to forfeiture.[127] Taking into account the statutory factors and the circumstances of this case, we conclude that the appropriate proposed forfeiture in this case is $15,000.

85.   The Commission's prohibition on the repeated use of expletives, including the "F-Word" and "S-Word," was well settled prior to March 2004.[128] The complained-of material contains numerous unedited expletives. The program in question was supplied to the licensee by PBS replete with two words that are among the most vulgar, graphic, and explicit descriptions of sexual and excretory activity in the English language, but whose propriety San Mateo nevertheless failed to question. By broadcasting the program complete with these expletives, San Mateo effectively abdicated this aspect of its programming control to an outside entity, PBS.[129] On the other hand, however, we do recognize that the expletives here were contained in a documentary, and while we conclude that the arguments made by the licensee are mistaken, we do find that the licensee may have been under the good faith belief that the use of these expletives served a legitimate informational purpose. Additionally, we recognize the fact that the licensee runs a small, community station that airs college level educational courses for most of the day. Under these circumstances, we believe that a proposed forfeiture in the amount of $15,000 is warranted here.[130]

86.   Although other stations may have also broadcast the subject episode of "The Blues: Godfathers and Sons," we propose a forfeiture only against San Mateo as the only licensee with a station whose broadcast of the material between 6 a.m. and 10 p.m. was the subject of a viewer complaint filed with the Commission.[131] We recognize that this approach differs from that taken in previous Commission decisions involving the broadcast of apparently indecent programming.[132] We find, in this case, however, that, in the absence of complaints concerning the program filed by viewers of other stations, it is appropriate that we sanction only the licensee of the station whose viewers complained about that program. Our commitment to an appropriately restrained enforcement policy, however, justifies this more limited approach towards the imposition of forfeiture penalties.[133] Accordingly, we propose a forfeiture of $15,000 against San Mateo.

---

[127] Because the broadcast in question was aired prior to the release of the *Golden Globe Awards Order*, our profanity finding will not factor in our determination of any sanction in this case.

[128] *See, e.g., Pacifica,* 438 U.S. at 744 (upholding the Commission's finding that the broadcast of the comedy monologue "Filthy Words" featuring, among other things, repeated uses of the F-Word and the S-Word was patently offensive and violated the statutory prohibition on indecency).

[129] San Mateo states that its arrangement with PBS required that it defer for several months from broadcasting the program, which aired over most PBS stations in October and November 2003. San Mateo represents that, because its scheduling is done three months in advance of the actual airdate, "the decision to air this series was made in November since the first episode of the series was aired in February." *Response* at 1. To the extent that San Mateo cites this circumstance to suggest that it did not have adequate notice that the expletives contained in the program were prohibited from broadcast prior to the Commission's issuance of the *Golden Globe Awards Order* on March 18, 2004, we reject this contention. To the contrary, San Mateo had months after the national airing of the episode at issue to ascertain the questionable content of the program and to take steps to ensure that it did not broadcast the repeated uses of objectionable words at issue.

[130] We exercise our prosecutorial discretion not to propose forfeitures based on the multiple utterances of expletives in this case because the use of individual expletives was not actionable under Commission precedent prior to the *Golden Globe Awards Order. See Golden Globe Awards Order,* 19 FCC Rcd at 4980 ¶ 12. While repetition of expletives in certain scenes might have qualified as actionable before the *Golden Globe Awards Order,* we decline to establish a method of identifying multiple utterances that applies only to pre-*Golden Globe Awards Order* programs.

[131] The fact that San Mateo may not have originated the programming in question is irrelevant to whether there is an indecency violation. *See supra* note 47.

[132] *See supra* note 48.

[133] *See supra* ¶ 11 and note 11.

6. "The Pursuit of D.B. Cooper" (March 15, 2003)[134]

87.   *The Programming.* A viewer filed a complaint with the Bureau alleging that Station KTVI(TV), St. Louis, Missouri, licensed to KTVI License, Inc ("KTVI"), repeatedly aired the "S-Word" on the afternoon of Saturday, March 15, 2003, during the broadcast of a movie featuring a fictional account of the fate of D.B. Cooper, the alias used by a person who disappeared after skyjacking an airplane and extorting money from an airline in 1971. The movie contains numerous scenes in which the "S-Word" is used: a scene in which D.B. Cooper refers to an aborted disguise ("shit"); a flashback scene between Cooper and his then-commanding officer ("horseshit"); a scene between the insurance investigator pursuing Cooper and the investigator's boss ("shit'); a café scene ("bullshit"); a scene between Cooper's father and ex-wife in which she describes Cooper as having a "shit-eating grin;" a scene after a fire ("bullshit" used twice); a scene during which Cooper escapes from his pursuers by boarding a river raft ("oh, shit!"); and a scene in which a former crony of Cooper buys a used car ("bullshit"). In a subsequent scene involving repairs to a car, an auto mechanic claims he will have the car running "slicker'n owl shit" and "smoother'n owl shit." When the car breaks down, Cooper refers back to the mechanic's words ("smoother'n owl shit" twice). At the end of the movie, in scenes in which Cooper is pursued by his former crony and the investigator, the "S-Word" is reiterated on several occasions: in a scene featuring the two pursuers ("shit"); a scene featuring a telephone call between the investigator and his boss ("shit"); a scene taking place aboard an airplane ("shit" and "oh, shit!"); a scene in which Cooper uses the airplane to chase a car driven by his former crony ("holy shit" and "shit"); and a scene after the airplane crashes ("bullshit").

88.   The Bureau sent the licensee a letter of inquiry and attached the complaint.[135] KTVI contends that the aired material is not actionably indecent. The licensee argues that the material at issue is not graphic or explicit, that it is not dwelled upon and that it is not titillating or presented for shock value.[136] KTVI does not claim to have provided any parental warnings prior to or during its broadcast of the film, which occurred from 2:00 to 4:00 p.m.[137]

89.   *Indecency Analysis.* KTVI acknowledges – and our review confirms – that the aired movie, "The Pursuit of D.B. Cooper," includes repeated uses of the words "shit," "bullshit," and "owl shit."[138] Each of those terms, of course, has a clear excretory connotation and describes an excretory activity. Thus, the complained-of material falls within the first prong of our indecency definition.

90.   Turning to the second step of our indecency analysis – whether the broadcast material is patently offensive – we conclude, looking at the three principal factors in our contextual evaluation, that the complained-of material is patently offensive under contemporary community standards for the broadcast medium.

91.   First, the material is quite graphic and explicit. The "S-Word" is a vulgar, graphic and explicit description of excrement. Its use invariably invokes a coarse excretory image. Consequently, we conclude that the broadcast of a program containing numerous uses of the "S-Word" and its variations, under the circumstances presented here, is vulgar, graphic and explicit.

92.   Second, the "S-Word," in various iterations, is used on a number of occasions. We note that, while prior Commission and staff actions had indicated as of the date this program aired that isolated broadcasts of certain expletives were not indecent or would not be acted upon,[139] the program at issue here contains repeated utterances of the "S-Word," and its variants. As noted above, the Commission has previously held that repeated use

---

[134] FCC File No. EB-03-IH-0136.

[135] *See* Letter from William H. Davenport, Chief, Investigations and Hearings Division, Enforcement Bureau, to KTVI License, Inc. (December 30, 2004).

[136] *See* Letter from John C. Quale, Counsel to KTVI License, Inc., to the Investigations and Hearings Division, Enforcement Bureau (January 31, 2005), and accompanying "Response of KTVI(TV), St. Louis, Missouri to FCC Letter of Inquiry" at 2.

[137] *Id.* at 1.

[138] These terms will be referred to collectively herein as the "S-Word."

[139] We note that in the *Golden Globe Awards Order,* which was issued after the conduct at issue in this case took place, the Commission overruled prior staff decisions finding that broadcasts containing a single expletive were not indecent. 19 FCC Rcd at 4980 ¶ 12.

of expletives may be actionably indecent.[140]

93.   Third, and most important to our analysis, multiple gratuitous iterations of the "S-Word" broadcast on a weekend afternoon at a time when children are likely to be in the audience, shock, pander to, and titillate the audience.[141] By failing to edit the movie, the licensee needlessly offended unsuspecting viewers in their homes on a weekend afternoon.[142]

94.   In sum, because the material is explicit and graphic, is dwelled upon, and shocks, panders, and titillates, we conclude that its broadcast here is patently offensive under contemporary community standards for the broadcast medium and thus apparently indecent. The complained-of material was broadcast within the 6 a.m. to 10 p.m. time frame relevant to an indecency determination under section 73.3999 of the Commission's rules.[143] Therefore, there is a reasonable risk that children may have been in the viewing audience and the broadcast is legally actionable.

95.   *Profanity Analysis.* In the *Golden Globe Awards Order*, the Commission concluded that the "F-Word" constituted "profane language" within the meaning of 18 U.S.C. § 1464 because, in context, it constituted vulgar and coarse language "so grossly offensive to members of the public who actually hear it as to amount to a nuisance."

96.   In this case, as in the related cases in this decision, we similarly find that the "S-Word" is a vulgar excretory term so grossly offensive to members of the public that it amounts to a nuisance and is presumptively profane. For the reasons stated above, use of the "S-Word" invariably invokes a coarse excretory image. Like the "F-Word," it is one of the most offensive words in the English language, the broadcast of which is likely to shock the viewer and disturb the peace and quiet of the home.

97.   In rare contexts, language that is presumptively profane will not be found to be profane where it is demonstrably essential to the nature of an artistic or educational work or essential to informing viewers on a matter of public importance.[144] We caution, however, that we will find this to be the case only in unusual circumstances, and such circumstances are clearly not present here. Although in this case, the profane language in this film may have had some communicative purpose, we do not believe that it was essential to the nature of an artistic or educational work or that editing the language would have materially altered the nature of the program. Based upon our review of the record in this case, we conclude that KTVI aired profane material between 6 a.m. and 10 p.m. in violation of 18 U.S.C. § 1464.

98.   *Forfeiture Calculation.* KTVI consciously and deliberately broadcast this film. Accordingly, we

---

[140] *See Indecency Policy Statement*, 16 FCC Rcd 7999, 8008 ¶ 16 (2001) (citing *Back Bay NAL* ,14 FCC Rcd at 3998, which found the broadcast of repeated uncensored references to the "F-Word," among other expletives, to be indecent).

[141] *Golden Globe Awards Order*, 19 FCC Rcd at 4979 ¶ 9. *See also Agape Broadcasting Foundation, Inc. (KNOM(FM))*, Notice of Apparent Liability for Forfeiture, 9 FCC Rcd 1679 (Mass Media Bur. 1999) (subsequent history omitted) (citing licensee's decision to run explicit material unedited, during a mid-afternoon broadcast when children were likely to be in the audience), *cited in Indecency Policy Statement*, 16 FCC Rcd at 8014, ¶ 21.

[142] In *Saving Private Ryan*, 20 FCC Rcd at 4513 ¶ 15, we found that that the network "did not intend the broadcast of a feature film as family entertainment, a fact clearly and explicitly stated in the introduction that precedes the film and is repeated in the aural and visual viewer advisory and voluntary parental code that follow each commercial break during the broadcast. Thus, parents had ample warning that this film contained material that might be unsuitable for children and could have exercised their own judgment about the suitability of the language for their children in the context of this film." Unlike *Saving Private Ryan*, we find that the vulgar material here could have been edited without materially altering the broadcast. Additionally, we disagree with the licensee's argument that all of the complained-of material was used as a means of expressing anger or frustration throughout the course of an intense car chase. As a factual matter, it is not correct that all of the material in question occurred during the scenes involving the car chase. Multiple iterations of the "S-Word" occurred in other scenes.

[143] *See* 47 C.F.R. § 73.3999.

[144] *See Saving Private Ryan*, 20 FCC Rcd at 4512-14 ¶¶ 13-18.

find that the broadcast in apparent violation of 18 U.S.C. § 1464 and 47 C.F.R. § 73.3999 was willful within the meaning of section 503(b)(1) of the Act, and subject to forfeiture.[145] We therefore turn to the proposed forfeiture amount, based on the factors enumerated in section 503(b)(2)(D) of the Act and the facts and circumstances of this case.

99.   We find that the statutory maximum of $27,500[146] is an appropriate proposed amount for the March 15, 2003 broadcast. The material was prerecorded, and KTVI could have edited the content prior to broadcast. In addition, as noted above, the gravity of the apparent violation is heightened here because of its shocking and gratuitous nature, involving as it does multiple gratuitous utterances of vulgar, graphic, and offensive expletives during a weekend afternoon broadcast. The Commission's prohibition of the broadcast of repeated uses of expletives such as the "S-Word" was well settled prior to its broadcast.[147] The program in question was replete with an expletive that is among the most vulgar, graphic, and explicit descriptions of excretory activity in the English language, but which KTVI nevertheless failed to edit out, suggesting indifference to our indecency regulations. Therefore, we find that KTVI License, Inc. is apparently liable for a proposed forfeiture of $27,500 for its March 15, 2003 broadcast of "The Pursuit of D.B. Cooper."[148]

B.   **Indecent And/Or Profane Broadcasts But No Forfeiture Proposed**

100.   In each of the following cases, we find that the broadcasts at issue are indecent and profane. Because of the specific circumstances associated with the broadcasts, however, we do not propose forfeitures. With one exception, these broadcasts preceded the Commission's decision in the *Golden Globe Awards* Order reversing precedent that had suggested that the isolated use of an offensive word like the "F-Word" is not indecent. In light of our decision not to impose a forfeiture based upon the facts of each case, we will not require the licensee of any of the stations that broadcast the material to report our finding here to us as part of their renewal applications and we will not consider the broadcast to impact adversely upon such licensees as part of the renewal process.

1.   **"The 2002 Billboard Music Awards" (December 9, 2002)**[149]

101.   *The Programming.* The Commission received a complaint concerning the December 9, 2002 broadcast of the "Billboard Music Awards" program over Fox Television Network ("Fox") stations, and specifically Station WTTG(TV), Washington, DC, between 8 and 10 p.m., Eastern Standard Time.[150] The complaint alleges that, during the broadcast, the performer Cher states, "People have been telling me I'm on the way out every year, right? So fuck 'em." The complaint alleges that the expletive was indecent and requests that the Commission levy

---

[145] Because the broadcast in question was aired prior to the release of the *Golden Globe Awards Order*, our profanity finding will not factor in our determination of any sanction in this case.

[146] The subject broadcasts occurred prior to the September 7, 2004, effective date of the most recent adjustment in the statutory maximum forfeiture amount. Accordingly, the appropriate maximum statutory amount here is $27,500. *See supra* ¶ 21.

[147] *See, e.g., Pacifica,* 438 U.S. at 744 (upholding the Commission's finding that the broadcast of the comedy monologue "Filthy Words" featuring, among other things, repeated uses of the S-Word was patently offensive and violated the statutory prohibition on indecency).

[148] We do not propose forfeitures based on each of the multiple utterances of expletives in this case because the broadcast took place before the Commission warned licensees that it might treat separate indecent utterances in the same program as separate violations. *See Infinity Broadcasting Operations, Inc. (WKRK-FM),* Notice of Apparent Liability for Forfeiture, 18 FCC Rcd 6915, 6918-19, ¶ 12 (April 3, 2003) ("*WKRK NAL*"), *vacated in non-relevant part, Viacom, Inc.*, Order and Consent Decree, 19 FCC Rcd 23100, 23107, ¶ 10 (2004) (vacating all indecency forfeitures against licensee's parent company but preserving the warnings in the *WKRK NAL* that the Commission might propose forfeitures for discrete violations in a single broadcast and might propose to revoke broadcast licenses for egregious or repeat violations).

[149] FCC File No. EB-03-IH-0460.

[150] *See* Letter from Lara Mahaney, Parents Television Council to David Solomon, Chief, Enforcement Bureau, Federal Communications Commission (August 22, 2003).

sanctions against each station licensee that aired the material. The Enforcement Bureau obtained a videotape of the offending broadcast that confirms the complaint's allegation.

102. ***Indecency Analysis.*** We held in the *Golden Globe Awards Order* that, given the core meaning of the "F-Word," any use of that word inherently has a sexual connotation and falls within the first prong of our indecency definition.[151] Cher's retort to her critics used language that we have found inherently describes sexual activity. The material, therefore, warrants further scrutiny to determine whether or not it was patently offensive as measured by contemporary standards for the broadcast medium. We conclude, looking at the three principal factors in our contextual analysis, that the material is patently offensive.

103. First, the complained-of material is quite graphic and explicit. As we indicated in the *Golden Globe Awards Order*, the "F-Word" is one of the most vulgar, graphic, and explicit words relating to sexual activity in the English language. Its use invariably invokes a coarse sexual image."[152] We conclude that the broadcast of the "F-Word," under the circumstances presented here, is vulgar, graphic and explicit.

104. Second, the fact that the material is not repeated or not dwelled upon at length, while relevant, is not dispositive. As the Commission indicated in the *Golden Globe Awards Order*: "[T]he mere fact that specific words or phrases are not sustained or repeated does not mandate a finding that material that is otherwise patently offensive to the broadcast medium is not indecent."[153]

105. Third, and most important to our analysis in this specific context, Cher's use of the "F-Word" here, at a live broadcast of an awards ceremony when children were expected to be in the audience, was shocking and gratuitous.[154] Cher chose to express her displeasure with her critics in a highly vulgar and coarse manner, and in doing so, needlessly offended unsuspecting viewers in the peace and quiet of their homes.

106. In sum, because the material is explicit and shocking and gratuitous, we conclude that the broadcast of the material at issue here is patently offensive under contemporary community standards for the broadcast medium and thus apparently indecent. Technological advances have made it possible to block the broadcast of offensive words without disproportionately disrupting a speaker's message.[155] Fox could have avoided the indecency violation here by delaying the broadcast for a period of time sufficient to ensure that all offending words were blocked.[156] It did not do so. As a result, the Fox affiliate WTTG(TV) broadcast highly offensive material within the 6 a.m. to 10 p.m. time frame relevant to an indecency determination under section 73.3999 of the Commission's rules. By broadcasting this material, the station apparently violated the prohibitions in 18 U.S.C. § 1464 and the Commission's rules against broadcast indecency.

107. ***Profanity Analysis.*** The "F-Word" is a vulgar sexual term so grossly offensive to members of the public that it amounts to a nuisance and is presumptively profane. The "F-Word" is one of the most offensive words in the English language, the broadcast of which is likely to shock the viewer and disturb the peace and quiet of the home. Consistent with our decision in the *Golden Globe Awards Order*, we find here that the use of the "F-Word" in the program at issue here apparently violated 18 U.S.C. § 1464's prohibition of the broadcast of "profane" language.[157]

108. In rare contexts, language that is presumptively profane will not be found to be profane where its use is demonstrably essential to the nature of an artistic or educational work or essential to informing viewers on a

---

[151] 19 FCC Rcd at 4978 ¶ 8.

[152] *Golden Globe Awards Order,* 19 FCC Rcd at 4979 ¶ 9.

[153] *Id.,* 19 FCC Rcd at 4980 ¶ 12.

[154] *Id.,* 19 FCC Rcd at 4979 ¶ 9.

[155] *See id.,* 19 FCC Rcd at 4980 ¶ 11.

[156] *See id.,* 19 FCC Rcd at 4980 ¶ 11. We note that Fox has pledged, whenever possible, to air future live entertainment programming with a five-minute delay. *See* Response at 9. While we applaud that change in Fox's practices, it does not excuse the apparent indecency violation in this case.

[157] *Id.,* 19 FCC Rcd at 4981 ¶¶ 13-14.

matter of public importance.[158] We caution, however, that we will find this to be the case only in unusual circumstances, and such circumstances are not present here. Although in this case, the profane language used by Cher may have had some communicative purpose, we do not believe that Fox has demonstrated that the use of such language was essential to informing viewers on a matter of public importance or that editing the language in question would have had a material impact on the network's function as a source of news and information. We note again that Fox or Station WTTG(TV) could have used a delaying technique to avoid the offending broadcast.

109.   It is undisputed that the complained-of material was broadcast within the 6 a.m. to 10 p.m. time frame relevant to a profanity determination under section 73.3999 of the Commission's rules. Because there was a reasonable risk that children may have been in the audience at the time the material at issue was broadcast, the material broadcast is legally actionable.[159]

110.   *No Sanction Proposed.* In the instant case, we find that the Fox Network affiliate Station WTTG(TV) consciously and deliberately broadcast the program in question. Accordingly, we find that the station's apparent violation of 18 U.S.C. § 1464 and section 73.3999 of our rules was willful. Thus, we conclude that the Fox affiliate Station WTTG(TV) aired indecent and profane material between 6 a.m. and 10 p.m. in apparent violation of 18 U.S.C. § 1464 and our rules.

111.   The gratuitous use of indecent and profane language on a national network broadcast ordinarily would warrant a forfeiture under the standards announced in the *Golden Globe Awards Order.* Nonetheless, we recognize that our precedent at the time of the broadcast indicated that the Commission would not take enforcement action against isolated use of expletives.[160] "But for the fact that existing precedent would have permitted this broadcast, it would be appropriate to initiate a forfeiture proceeding against [Fox] and other licensees that broadcast the program prior to 10 p.m."[161] Accordingly, we find that no forfeiture is warranted in this case.

2.   "The 2003 Billboard Music Awards" (December 10, 2003)[162]

112.   *The Programming.* The Commission received a number of complaints alleging that the Fox Television Network ("Fox" or "Fox Network") aired indecent material during the "Billboard Music Awards" program on December 10, 2003 between 8 and 10 p.m., Eastern Standard Time.[163] The complainants allege that, during the broadcast, Nicole Richie, an award presenter, uttered vulgar expletives in violation of the Commission's rules restricting the broadcast of indecent material.[164] The complainants request that the Commission levy sanctions against each station licensee that aired the remarks.

---

[158] *See Saving Private Ryan,* 20 FCC Rcd at 4512-14 ¶¶ 13-18.

[159] *See ACT III,* 58 F.3d at 660-63.

[160] *Golden Globe Awards Order,* 19 FCC Rcd at 4980 ¶ 12 (citing *Pacifica Foundation,* 2 FCC Rcd at 2699).

[161] *Golden Globe Awards Order,* 19 FCC Rcd at 4982 ¶ 15.

[162] FCC File Nos. EB-03-IH-0617, EB-04-IH-0295, EB-04-IH-0091.

[163] *See* Letter from Lara Mahaney, Parents Television Council to David Solomon, Chief, Enforcement Bureau, Federal Communications Commission (December 11, 2003). We also deny an additional complaint from PTC regarding another segment of that same broadcast. *See* Letter from Lara Mahaney, Parents Television Council, to David Solomon, Chief, Enforcement Bureau, Federal Communications Commission (January 22, 2004) (*"Second PTC Complaint"*). *See* note 195 *infra.*

[164] According to Fox, the Fox affiliate stations located within the Eastern and Central Time Zones broadcast the following exchange between Paris Hilton and Nicole Richie after they walked onstage to present an award:

Paris Hilton: Now Nicole, remember, this is a live show, watch the bad language.
Nicole Richie: Okay, God.
Paris Hilton: It feels so good to be standing here tonight.
Nicole Richie: Yeah, instead of standing in mud and cow[blocked]. Why do they even call it "The Simple Life"? Have you ever tried to get cow shit out of a Prada purse? It's not so fucking simple.

(continued....)

113.   The Bureau sent Fox a letter of inquiry and attached a transcript of the material in question.[165] Fox responded on January 30, 2004.[166] Fox contends that the aired material is not actionably indecent and does not contain any description or depiction of sexual or excretory organs or activities in a patently offensive manner.[167]

114.   ***Indecency Analysis.*** During her appearance on the "Billboard Music Awards," Ms. Richie uttered the "F-Word" and the "S-Word." Fox does not dispute that the "S-Word" refers to excrement.[168] Fox contends, however, that Ms. Richie used the "F-Word" as a mere vulgar expletive to express emphasis, not to depict or describe sexual activities.[169] We disagree. Given the core meaning of the "F-Word," any use of that word inherently has a sexual connotation and falls within the first prong of our indecency definition.[170] We conclude that the material at issue clearly describes sexual and excretory activity. The material, therefore, warrants further scrutiny to determine whether or not it is patently offensive as measured by contemporary community standards for the broadcast medium. We conclude, looking at the three principal factors in our contextual analysis, that it is.

115.   First, the complained-of material is quite graphic and explicit. The "F-Word" is one of the most vulgar, graphic, and explicit depictions of sexual activity in the English language. Its use invariably invokes a coarse sexual image.[171] Similarly, the "S-Word" is a vulgar, graphic, and explicit depiction of excretory activity. Its use invariably invokes a coarse excretory image. Consequently, we conclude that the broadcast of the "F-Word" and the "S-Word," under the circumstances presented here, is vulgar, graphic and explicit.

116.   Second, the fact that use of the words was not sustained or repeated, while relevant, is not dispositive. As the Commission indicated in the *Golden Globe Awards Order*: "[T]he mere fact that specific words or phrases are not sustained or repeated does not mandate a finding that material that is otherwise patently offensive to the broadcast medium is not indecent."[172]

117.   Third, and most important to our analysis in this context, Ms. Richie's use of the "F-Word" and the "S-Word" here, during a live broadcast of a music awards ceremony when children were expected to be in the audience, was shocking and gratuitous.[173] Indeed, Fox admits that the tone of the material was vulgar.[174]

118.   Like the broadcaster discussed the *Golden Globe Awards Order*, Fox was "on notice that an award presenter or recipient might use offensive language during the live broadcast, and it could have taken appropriate steps to ensure that it did not broadcast such language."[175] As the previous case involving Cher demonstrates, Fox had clear notice that celebrities at this program might utter offensive expletives, including the "F-Word" during the broadcast. Moreover, the record of this broadcast shows that Fox, as the producer of the program and the network

---

(...continued from previous page)
Fox advises that it edited the tape to remove the expletives before the program aired on tape delay over Fox Stations in the Mountain and Pacific time zones. *See* Letter from John C. Quale, Counsel to Fox Television Stations, Inc., to Investigations and Hearings Division, Enforcement Bureau (Jan. 30, 2004) ("Response") at 3-4, 8.

[165] *See* Letter from William D. Freedman, Deputy Chief, Investigations and Hearings Division, Enforcement Bureau, to Fox Television Stations, Inc. (January 7, 2004).

[166] *See supra* note 179.

[167] *See* Response at 12-13.

[168] *Id.* at 13. We note, however, that even if Ms. Richie was not literally referring to cow excrement, her use of the "S-Word" would still fall within the subject matter prong of our indecency definition. The "S-Word" has an excretory connotation, however it may be used. Its use invariably invokes a course excretory image in any context.

[169] Response at 13.

[170] *See Golden Globe Awards Order*, 19 FCC Rcd at 4978 ¶ 8; *see also Pacifica Foundation*, 56 FCC 2d at 99.

[171] *See Golden Globe Awards Order*, 19 FCC Rcd at 4979 ¶ 9.

[172] *Id.*, 19 FCC Rcd 4980 ¶ 12.

[173] *Id.* at 4979 ¶ 9.

[174] *See* Response at 13.

[175] 19 FCC Rcd at 4979 ¶ 10.

that carried it to affiliates throughout the country, deliberately sought to push the limits of decency. According to Fox, the original script called for Ms. Richie to make excretory references to "pig crap" and "cow manure," and to substitute the euphemism "freaking" for the "F-Word."[176] Under the circumstances, there was a palpable risk that Ms. Richie would use the "F-Word" and the "S-Word" instead of the euphemisms in the script.

119.   Technological advances have made it possible to block the broadcast of offensive words without disproportionately disrupting a speaker's message.[177] Indeed, Fox utilized a five-second delay during the broadcast in question and successfully blocked Ms. Richie's first use of the "S-Word."[178] Fox could have avoided the indecency violation here by delaying the broadcast for a period of time sufficient to ensure that all offending words were blocked.[179] It did not do so. As a result, it broadcast highly offensive material within the 6 a.m. to 10 p.m. time frame relevant to an indecency determination under section 73.3999 of the Commission's rules.

120.   In sum, because the material is explicit and shocking and gratuitous, we conclude that the broadcast of the material at issue here is patently offensive under contemporary community standards for the broadcast medium and thus apparently indecent. By broadcasting this material, the Fox affiliated stations whose broadcasts were the subject of viewer complaints to the Commission apparently violated the prohibitions in 18 U.S.C. § 1464 and the Commission's rules against broadcast indecency.[180]

121.   *Profanity Analysis.* In the *Golden Globe Awards Order*, the Commission concluded that the "F-Word" constituted "profane language" within the meaning of 18 U.S.C. § 1464 because, in context, it constituted vulgar and coarse language "so grossly offensive to members of the public who actually hear it as to amount to a nuisance." In this case, we similarly find that the "F-Word" is a vulgar sexual term and the "S-Word" is a vulgar excretory term, each of which is so grossly offensive to members of the public as to amount to a nuisance and that each word accordingly is presumptively profane. For the reasons stated above, use of the "F-Word" invariably invokes a coarse sexual image and use of the "S-Word" invariably invokes a coarse excretory image. Each of these words is among the most offensive words in the English language, the broadcast of which is likely to shock the viewer and disturb the peace and quiet of the home.

122.   In rare contexts, language that is presumptively profane will not be found to be profane where it is demonstrably essential to the nature of an artistic or educational work or essential to informing viewers on a matter of public importance.[181] We caution, however, that we will find this to be the case only in unusual circumstances,

---

[176] Response at 6.

[177] *See Golden Globe Awards Order,* 19 FCC Rcd at 4980 ¶ 11.

[178] *See* Response at 8.

[179] *See Golden Globe Awards Order,* 19 FCC Rcd at 4980 ¶ 11. We note that Fox has pledged, whenever possible, to air future live entertainment programming with a five-minute delay. *See* Response at 9. While we applaud that change in Fox's practices, it does not excuse the indecency violation in this case.

[180] PTC also filed a complaint concerning an exchange between musician David Grohl and "Triumph the Insult Comic Dog," a hand puppet, during the same program. *See Second PTC Complaint.* According to a partial transcript attached to the complaint, the exchange focused on whether the puppet would "poop" on various celebrities. The exchange also included the phrases "kick-ass lip-singer," "sex with a dog," "singers that suck," "a lot of crap," "my ass," and "you suck." The transcript supplied by PTC stated that the references to pooping on someone were "slang for insults." *Id.* Moreover, the word "poop" is more puerile than offensive. The other words and phrases in question are not generally considered to be as graphic, vulgar, and offensive as the "S-Word" or the "F-Word," and most are fairly commonly used in a non-sexual, non-excretory manner. Accordingly, although they may offend some people, we find that, viewed in the context in which they were used, "poop" and the other words and phrases in question were not patently offensive for the broadcast medium. *See, e.g., Complaints by Parents Television Council Against Various Broadcast Licensees Regarding Their Airing of Allegedly Indecent Material,* Memorandum Opinion and Order, 20 FCC Rcd 1931, 1938, ¶ 8 (2005) ("*PTC 2*") (in context, fleeting uses of words such as "penis," "dick," "testicle," "vaginal," "ass," "bastard," and "bitch" not indecent). We note, however, that in another context, such as a more graphic and explicit description of sexual or excretory organs or activities, the use of these words might contribute to a finding of indecency. We also conclude that these words were not profane in this context.

[181] *See Saving Private Ryan,* 20 FCC Rcd at 4512-14 ¶¶ 13-18.

and such circumstances are not present here. Although in this case, profane language may have had some communicative purpose, we do not believe that Fox has demonstrated that it was essential to informing viewers on a matter of public importance or that editing the language in question would have had a material impact on the network's function as a source of news and information.

123.   It is undisputed that the complained-of material was broadcast within the 6 a.m. to 10 p.m. time frame relevant to a profanity determination under section 73.3999 of the Commission's rules. Because there was a reasonable risk that children may have been in the audience at the time the material at issue was broadcast, the material broadcast is legally actionable.[182]

124.   *No Sanction Proposed.* Based upon our review of the record in this case, we conclude that the Fox Network affiliated stations in the Eastern and Central Time Zones whose broadcasts were the subject of viewer complaints to the Commission aired material in violation of 18 U.S.C. § 1464 and our rules. They each broadcast indecent and profane words in an awards show that aired between 6 a.m. and 10 p.m. and was watched by people of all ages. The licensees of these stations each consciously and deliberately broadcast the program in question. Accordingly, the apparent violation of 18 U.S.C. § 1464 and section 73.3999 of our rules was willful. The willful broadcast of indecent and profane material on a national network broadcast ordinarily would warrant a forfeiture under the standards announced in the *Golden Globe Awards Order*. Nonetheless, we recognize that our precedent at the time of the broadcast indicated that the Commission would not take indecency enforcement action against isolated use of expletives.[183] "But for the fact that existing precedent would have permitted this broadcast, it would be appropriate to initiate a forfeiture proceeding against [Fox] and other licensees that broadcast the program prior to 10 p.m."[184] Accordingly, we find that no forfeiture is warranted in this case.

3.   "NYPD Blue" (various dates between January 14 and May 6, 2003)[185]

125.   The Commission has received complaints alleging that KMBC Hearst-Argyle Television, Inc., licensee of Station KMBC-TV, Kansas City, Missouri, and other network stations affiliated with The ABC Television Network ("ABC") aired indecent material during several episodes of "NYPD Blue" broadcast between 9:00 and 10:00 p.m. Central Standard Time on various dates between January and May 2003.[186] The complaints allege that, in each of the identified episodes, one or more characters utter expletives in violation of the Commission's rules restricting the broadcast of indecent material. The complaints identify several expletives from the episodes at issue, specifically "dick," "dickhead" and "bullshit."[187]

---

[182] *See ACT III,* 58 F.3d at 660-63

[183] *See Golden Globe Awards Order* ,19 FCC Rcd at 4980 ¶ 12 (citing *Pacifica Foundation, Inc.,* Memorandum Opinion and Order, 2 FCC Rcd 2698, 2699 (1987)). The fact that the statement in question included two expletives is unlikely to have removed it from the former isolated use exception under Commission precedent. The only pre-*Golden Globe Awards Order* decision of which we are aware in which a forfeiture was proposed for a single phrase or statement involved the use of multiple expletives combined with a description of sexual activity. *See LBJS Broadcasting Company,* Notice of Apparent Liability for Forfeiture, 13 FCC Rcd 20956 (1998) (forfeiture paid) (finding broadcast apparently indecent for use of phrase "suck my dick you fucking cunt").

[184] *Golden Globe Awards Order,* 19 FCC Rcd at 4982 ¶ 15.

[185] FCC File No. EB-03-IH-0355.

[186] Collectively referred to as the "NYPD Blue Expletive Complaints."

[187] The following examples illustrate the typical use of these expletives in the episodes at issue:

1/14/03 episode (Det. Sipowitz in response to his partner's arrest by Internal Affairs): "Alright, this is Bullshit!"

2/4/03 episode (Det. Sipowitz to street officer regarding that officer's partner framing Sipowitz's partner): "Over time - over what – bullshit, a beef!"

2/11/03 episode (Sipowitz speaking to a prisoner who had tried to trick Sipowitz into believing the prisoner was getting transferred to a different prison): "Game's been run dickhead. You ship out tomorrow. Wrong cop."

2/18/03 episode (stated by a suspect who bragged about, but now denies, killing his daughter): "I told people I killed Samia to try and get respect back. She had ashamed me and my community look at me as a fool."

Det. 1: "You took credit for killing your daughter?! Bullshit!"

(continued....)

126.   The terms "dick" and "dickhead" are references to a sexual organ and therefore fall within the first prong of our indecency definition. Similarly, "bullshit," whether used literally or metaphorically, is a vulgar reference to the product of excretory activity and therefore falls within the first prong of our indecency definition. Accordingly, we must proceed to the three-part contextual analysis in our second prong to determine whether the material is patently offensive as measured by contemporary community standards for the broadcast medium. For the reasons stated below, we find "dick" and its derivative, "dickhead," not to be patently offensive in this context, whereas we find "bullshit" to be patently offensive in this context. Regarding the former term, we note that last year we found the same word and its variations not to be indecent in the context presented.[188]

127.   First, we find that the terms "dick" and "dickhead," in this context, while understandably offensive to some viewers, are not sufficiently vulgar, explicit, or graphic descriptions of sexual organs or activities to support a finding of patent offensiveness. Second, while not dispositive, it is relevant that none of the programs dwell on these terms. Third, we find that those words, in context, are not sufficiently shocking to support a finding that they are patently offensive. Although the words are undeniably coarse and vulgar, they do not have the same level of offensiveness as the "F-Word" or "S-Word." As we recently stated, "[a]lthough use of such words may, depending on the nature of the broadcast at issue, contribute to a finding of indecency, their use here was not patently offensive."[189] The broadcasts at issue here used these terms in a similar manner.[190] Therefore, under our three-part analysis and based on our precedent, we find the broadcasts of the terms "dick" and its derivative, "dickhead," as used in the "NYPD Blue" episodes at issue, are not patently offensive.

128.   However, we do conclude that the broadcasts of a derivative of the "S-Word" at issue here are patently offensive. First, consistent with our analysis of the "F-Word" in the *Golden Globe Awards Order*, we find the "S-Word" to be one of the most vulgar, graphic and explicit descriptions of excretory activity in the English language. Its use invariably invokes a coarse excretory image. We conclude that the broadcast of the "S-Word," under the circumstances presented here, is vulgar, graphic and explicit.

129.   Second, while the word is not dwelled upon, in the *Golden Globe Awards Order*, the Commission reversed precedent that had suggested that the isolated use of an offensive word like the "F-Word" is not indecent.[191] "[T]he mere fact that specific words or phrases are not sustained or repeated does not mandate a finding that

---

(...continued from previous page)

4/15/03 episode (Det. harassing suspect who had harassed prosecutor): "I'm hoping this bullshit about you trying to get under ADA Haywood's skin is a misunderstanding."

4/8/03 episode (Sipowicz, referring to a wheel-chair bound, uncooperative witness to a murder): "and that dickhead in the wheel chair . . . threaten him with perjury and he'll fold ."

4/29/03 episode (Det. questioning witness/suspect): "Maybe we should clarify Daly. We drop jail time for good information – not bullshit that wastes our time."

4/29/03 episode (Sipowicz, talking to a suspect who had recruited a youth (who the suspect thought was a minor) to commit a crime): "He's 16 Dickhead! An adult! . . ."

5/6/03 episode (Captain to Det. who harassed suspect in 4/15 episode): "He said you nearly assaulted his client last night."

Det: "Well, that's a bunch of bullshit."

[188] *See PTC 2*, 20 FCC Rcd at 1938, ¶ 8 (finding fleeting use of "dick" and its variations not indecent in context presented).

[189] *See Complaints Filed By Parents Television Council Against Various Broadcast Licensees Regarding Their Airing of Allegedly Indecent Material*, Memorandum Opinion and Order, 20 FCC Rcd 1920, 1926 ¶ 8 (2005) ("*PTC 1*"); *PTC 2*, 20 FCC Rcd at 1938 ¶ 8.

[190] *See PTC 1*, 20 FCC Rcd at 1926, ¶ 8 ("A number of complaints cite isolated uses of the word "dick" and variations thereof. In context and as used in the complained of broadcasts, these were epithets intended to denigrate or criticize their subjects. Their use in this context was not sufficiently explicit or graphic and/or sustained to be patently offensive.").

[191] 19 FCC Rcd at 4980 ¶ 12.

material that is otherwise patently offensive to the broadcast medium is not indecent."[192] Similarly, we find that the fact that these broadcasts did not dwell on the expletive, though relevant, is not dispositive under the circumstances presented here.

130.   Third, the intentional use of a derivative of the "S-Word" on a popular network program broadcast is shocking and gratuitous. In this regard, ABC does not claim that there was any political, scientific or other independent value to using the word here, or any other factor to mitigate its offensiveness. To the extent ABC claims that the word was necessary for dramatic effect, mere dramatic effect does not justify use of patently offensive expletives during time periods when numerous children are likely to be in the audience. Programs utilizing patently offensive expletives for dramatic effect can be aired after 10 p.m.

131.   In sum, because the material is explicit and shocking and gratuitous, we conclude that the broadcast of the material at issue here that contained derivatives of the "S-Word" is patently offensive under contemporary community standards for the broadcast medium and thus apparently indecent. The complained-of material was broadcast within the 6 a.m. to 10 p.m. time frame relevant to an indecency determination under section 73.3999 of the Commission's rules.[193] Therefore, there is a reasonable risk that children may have been in the audience and the broadcast is legally actionable.

132.   ***Profanity Analysis.*** In the *Golden Globe Awards Order*, the Commission concluded that the "F-Word" constituted "profane language" within the meaning of 18 U.S.C. § 1464 because, in context, it constituted vulgar and coarse language "so grossly offensive to members of the public who actually hear it as to amount to a nuisance." We indicated in that decision that the Commission would analyze other potentially profane words on a case-by-case basis.

133.   In this case, we find that the "S-Word" is a vulgar excretory term so grossly offensive to members of the public that it amounts to a nuisance and is presumptively profane. Like the "F-Word," it is one of the most offensive words in the English language, the broadcast of which is likely to shock the viewer and disturb the peace and quiet of the home.

134.   In rare contexts, language that is presumptively profane will not be found to be profane where it is demonstrably essential to the nature of an artistic or educational work or essential to informing viewers on a matter of public importance.[194] We caution, however, that we will find this to be the case only in unusual circumstances, and such circumstances are not present here. Although in this case, the profane language may have had some communicative purpose, we do not believe that ABC has demonstrated that it was essential to the nature of an artistic or educational work or essential to informing viewers on a matter of public importance. In this respect, this case is unlike *Saving Private Ryan*, where we concluded that deleting offensive words "would have altered the nature of the artistic work and diminished the power, realism and immediacy of the film experience for viewers." While we recognize that the expletives may have made some contribution to the authentic feel of the program, we believe that purpose could have been fulfilled and all viewpoints expressed without the broadcast of expletives.

135.   It is undisputed that the complained-of material was broadcast within the 6 a.m. to 10 p.m. time frame relevant to a profanity determination under section 73.3999 of the Commission's rules. Because there was a reasonable risk that children may have been in the audience at the time the material at issue was broadcast, the material broadcast is legally actionable.[195]

136.   ***No Sanction Proposed.*** In the instant case, we find that the ABC network affiliate Station KMBC-TV consciously and deliberately broadcast the material in question. Accordingly, we find that the apparent violations of 18 U.S.C. § 1464 and section 73.3999 of our rules were willful. The station aired indecent and profane material in violation of our rules because it broadcast indecent and profane words in a show that aired between 6 a.m. and 10 p.m. and was watched by people of all ages. The gratuitous use of indecent and profane language on a national network broadcast ordinarily would warrant a forfeiture under the standards announced in the *Golden Globe Awards Order*. Nonetheless, we recognize that our precedent at the time of the broadcast indicated that the

---

[192] *Id.*

[193] *See* 47 C.F.R. § 73.3999.

[194] *See Saving Private Ryan*, 20 FCC Rcd at 4512-14 ¶¶ 13-18.

[195] *See ACT III*, 58 F.3d at 660-63.

Commission would not take indecency enforcement action against the isolated use of expletives.[196] Thus, we will not impose any sanction in this case on the basis of our profanity finding. "But for the fact that existing precedent would have permitted this broadcast, it would be appropriate to initiate a forfeiture proceeding against [ABC] and other licensees that broadcast the program prior to 10 p.m."[197] Accordingly, we find that no forfeiture is warranted in this case.

4.   "The Early Show" (December 13, 2004)[198]

137.   *The Programming.* A viewer filed a complaint that CBS Television Network ("CBS") affiliate Station KDKA-TV, Pittsburgh, Pennsylvania, licensed to CBS Broadcasting, Inc., aired a variant of the "S-Word" during the program "The Early Show" on December 13, 2004, at approximately 8:10 a.m., Eastern Standard Time, during a live interview with cast member Twila Tanner of the CBS program "Survivor: Vanuatu." The Bureau requested a tape of the program from CBS, which CBS submitted. The tape shows, and CBS does not dispute, that Ms. Tanner described a fellow contestant of "Survivor: Vanuatu" as a "bullshitter."[199]

138.   *Indecency Analysis.* The Commission determined in the *Golden Globe Awards Order* that the "F-Word" meets the first prong of the indecency test. We stated, "given the core meaning of the "F-Word," any use of that word or a variation, in any context, inherently has a sexual connotation, and therefore falls within the first prong of our indecency definition."[200] Similarly, we now find that the "S-Word," including the variant of that word at issue here, is a vulgar, graphic, and explicit description of excretory material. Its use invariably invokes a coarse excretory image, even when its meaning is not the literal one. Accordingly, we must proceed to analyze whether the material, in context, is patently offensive as measured by contemporary community standards for the broadcast medium. Based on our examination of the three principal factors in our contextual analysis, we conclude that the material is patently offensive.

139.   First, the complained-of material is vulgar, graphic, and explicit. Consistent with our analysis of the "F-Word" in the *Golden Globe Awards Order*, we find the "S-Word" to be one of the most vulgar, graphic and explicit words describing excrement or excretory activity in the English language and, for the reasons stated above, its use inherently has an excretory connotation. We conclude that the broadcast of the "S-Word," under the circumstances presented here, is vulgar, graphic and explicit.

140.   Second, the fact that the material is not repeated or dwelled upon at length, while relevant, is not dispositive. As the Commission indicated in the *Golden Globe Awards Order:* "the mere fact that specific words or phrases are not sustained or repeated does not mandate a finding that material that is otherwise patently offensive to the broadcast medium is not indecent."[201] Consequently, non-repetitive broadcasts of the "S-Word" may be found indecent.

141.   Third, and most important to our analysis in this specific context, the use of the "S-Word," particularly during a morning news interview, is shocking and gratuitous.[202] Because the interview dealt with the outcome of one of the most popular prime-time shows on broadcast television among children, it is foreseeable that young children not only would be in the audience at that time of day, but also that they would be attentive listeners to the interview with Ms. Tanner. That CBS or the licensee of Station KDKA-TV failed to take measures to protect

---

[196] *See Golden Globe Awards Order*, 19 FCC Rcd at 4980 ¶ 12 (citing *Pacifica Foundation, Inc.*, 2 FCC Rcd at 2699).

[197] *Golden Globe Awards Order*, 19 FCC Rcd at 4982 ¶ 15.

[198] FCC File No. EB-05-IH-0007.

[199] In commenting on the strategy employed by the fellow contestant, Ms. Tanner stated: "I knew he was a bullshitter from Day One." The interviewer, Julie Chen, recognized the inappropriateness of the language, stating: "I hope we had the cue ready on that one . . . . We can't say that word . . . . There is a delay."

[200] *Golden Globe Awards Order*, 19 FCC Rcd at 4978 ¶ 8.

[201] *Id.*, 19 FCC Rcd at 4980 ¶12.

[202] *Id.*, 19 FCC Rcd at 4979 ¶ 9.

such viewers from vulgarity in a morning television interview is of particular concern and weighs heavily in our analysis.

142.   Viewing the evidence as a whole, while Ms. Tanner's vulgarity is not repeated, the patently offensive nature of the broadcast is clearly established under the first and third principal factors of our contextual analysis. The complained-of material was broadcast within the 6 a.m. to 10 p.m. time frame relevant to an indecency determination under section 73.3999 of the Commission's rules.[203] Therefore, there is a reasonable risk that children may have been in the audience and the broadcast is legally actionable.

143.   *Profanity Analysis.* In the *Golden Globe Awards Order,*, the Commission concluded that the "F-Word" constituted "profane language" within the meaning of 18 U.S.C. §1464 because, in context, it constituted vulgar and coarse language "so grossly offensive to members of the public who actually hear it as to amount to a nuisance." In this case, we similarly find that the "S-Word" is a vulgar excretory term so grossly offensive to members of the public that it amounts to a nuisance and is presumptively profane. For the reasons stated above, use of the "S-Word" invariably invokes a coarse excretory image. Like the "F-Word," it is one of the most offensive words in the English language, the broadcast of which is likely to shock the viewer and disturb the peace and quiet of the home.

144.   In rare contexts, language that is presumptively profane will not be found to be profane where it is demonstrably essential to the nature of an artistic or educational work or essential to informing viewers on a matter of public importance.[204] We caution, however, that we will find this to be the case only in unusual circumstances, and such circumstances are clearly not present here. Although in this case, Ms. Tanner's profane language may have had some communicative purpose, we do not believe that it was essential to informing viewers on a matter of public importance or that editing the language would have materially impacted the network's function as a source of news and information.

145.   *No Sanction Proposed.* We find that CBS Broadcasting, Inc., the licensee of CBS network affiliate Station KDKA-TV, consciously and deliberately broadcast the program in question. Accordingly, we find that the apparent violation of 18 U.S.C. § 1464 and section 73.3999 of our rules was willful. Thus based upon our review of the record in this case, we conclude that the licensee of this station aired material in violation of 18 U.S.C. § 1464 and our rules by broadcasting indecent and profane language between 6 a.m. and 10 p.m. during programming watched by a nationwide audience of all ages. The gratuitous use of indecent and profane language during a national broadcast ordinarily would warrant a forfeiture under the standards announced in *Golden Globe Awards Order.* However, we recognize that our precedent at the time of the broadcast did not clearly indicate that the Commission would take enforcement action against an isolated use of the "S-Word."[205] "But for the fact that existing precedent would have permitted this broadcast, it would be appropriate to initiate a forfeiture proceeding against [CBS] and other licensees that broadcast the program prior to 10 p.m."[206] Consequently, we find that no forfeiture is warranted in this case.

C.   **Broadcasts That Do Not Violate Indecency/Profanity/Obscenity Restrictions**

146.   In this section, we conclude that the complained-of programming does not warrant action against the licensee. Although some of this programming is undoubtedly upsetting to some viewers, we reach these determinations either because the programming is not within the scope of our indecency or profanity definitions or because it is not, in the contexts before us, patently offensive as measured by contemporary community standards for the broadcast medium.

---

[203] *See* 47 C.F.R. § 73.3999.

[204] *See Saving Private Ryan*, 20 FCC Rcd at 4512-14 ¶¶ 13-18.

[205] *See Golden Globe Awards Order*, 19 FCC Rcd at 4982 ¶ 15.

[206] *Id.*

1.   "Alias" (January 5, 2005)[207]

147.   ***The Programming.*** The Commission received complaints concerning the January 5, 2005 broadcast of the program "Alias" by Allbriton Communications, Inc., licensee of Station WJLA-TV, Washington, D.C., from 9:00 to 11:00 p.m. Eastern Standard Time.[208] The show depicts intelligence agents engaged in various covert operations. In this episode, a male and female character engage in a covert operation on a moving train. The female character having completed her portion of the operation is chased by an assailant. The chase leads to a cargo car and, after a fight with the assailant, the female character finds herself hanging out of the cargo car while the train crosses a high bridge. As the assailant attempts to force the female character off of the moving train, the male character, having been victorious in a separate fight with another assailant, rescues the female character from impending death. The male and female characters hug and stare at each other. In the next scene, which is the subject of the complaints, the male and female characters are in bed kissing, caressing and rubbing against each other. The scene is accompanied by off-camera music. There are no depictions of sexual organs in the scene. Afterwards, the couple lay side-by-side and stare at each other.

148.   ***Indecency Analysis.*** The episode's references to sexual activities place it within the subject matter scope of our indecency definition. In particular, although there are no depictions of sexual organs, the episode depicts a couple in bed passionately kissing, caressing and rubbing against each other, each of which is a sexual activity. Accordingly, we find that the material meets the first prong of our indecency standard. We now turn to the second prong of our indecency analysis, whether the material is patently offensive by contemporary community standards for the broadcast medium.

149.   Turning to the first of the three principal factors in our contextual analysis, the episode does not depict sexual or excretory organs and does not depict sexual activities in a graphic or explicit way. The scene involves no display of sexual organs and contains no sexually graphic language. While viewers see the characters kissing, caressing, and rubbing; it is not clear whether the characters are engaged in sexual intercourse.

150.   Regarding the second principal factor of our contextual analysis, while not dispositive, the sexual encounter between the male and female character is not fleeting.[209]

151.   With respect to the third principal component of our contextual analysis, we find that the sexual activity is not presented in a pandering, titillating or shocking manner. While the episode shows the male and female characters kissing, caressing, and rubbing in bed, the overall context, including the camera angle, the background music, and the immediately preceding scene, is not shocking in contrast to clear and graphic depictions of sexual intercourse.

152.   Accordingly, although the episode depicts sexual activities within the meaning of the Commission's indecency definition, taken as a whole, we conclude that it is not patently offensive as measured by contemporary community standards for the broadcast medium. While the sexual encounter between the two characters is not fleeting, the nature of the encounter is not sufficiently explicit or shocking to be patently offensive. Accordingly, the complaints are denied.

2.   "Will and Grace" (November 11, 2004)[210]

153.   ***The Programming.*** The Commission received a complaint concerning the November 11, 2004 broadcast of a "Will and Grace" episode titled "Saving Grace Again, Part 1." The episode was broadcast at 8:30 p.m. Central Standard Time over stations affiliated with the NBC Television Network. In the episode, the lead female character, Grace, is in her apartment preparing to go out on her first date after her recent divorce. She is being assisted by her roommate, Will, and is concerned about her appearance. Before leaving, she asks Will if there

---

[207] FCC File No. EB-05-IH-0351.

[208] The Commission received two complaints about this program. Neither complaint identified the specific broadcast station on which the program aired. However, we note that the program aired on the ABC Television Network and that both complaints were filed by individuals with addresses within the Washington, D.C. metropolitan area.

[209] Because this scene aired prior to 10 p.m., it falls within the scope of our indecency regulation.

[210] FCC File No. EB-05-IH-0049.

is "anything else" she should know about dating. Will responds by instructing her to "lean forward" and, as Grace does so, he places his hands on her dress adjusting her breasts upward to enhance her appearance. As Grace is leaving the apartment, she is greeted at the elevator by her friend, Karen, who also knows of the date and places her hand on Grace's breasts and appears to also adjust her bosoms upward.[211]

154.   *Indecency Analysis.* The first prong of our indecency analysis is whether the program depicts or describes sexual or excretory activities or organs and, therefore, is within the subject matter scope of the Commission's indecency definition. Although the episode contains some sexual innuendo, the characters in the scene in question appear to touch Grace's breast area primarily to enhance her appearance during her date rather than to elicit a sexual response. We need not decide, however, whether the scene depicts or describes sexual activities or organs because even assuming that the first prong of our indecency analysis is met, we conclude that the material is not indecent because it is not patently offensive as measured by contemporary community standards for the broadcast medium.

155.   In making this determination, we must look to the full context in which the material is presented. Here, the context is generally humorous and consists of light-hearted ridicule and indirect references to the size of Grace's breasts and the efforts made by her friends to enhance her sexual appeal for her date by making her breasts look larger.

156.   Regarding the first component of our contextual analysis, the touching of Grace's breasts is not presented in a graphic or explicit manner. The program contains no nudity and never explicitly shows or specifically describes sexual activities or organs. We find that the episode does not contain "graphic descriptions of sexual activities and organs or ... language that is so graphic as to qualify as indecent and profane."[212]

157.   With respect to the second component of our contextual analysis, while not dispositive, we find it relevant that the episode does not dwell upon or repeat references to sexual organs or activities.

158.   Finally, we do not find that the material at issue is used to pander, titillate, or shock - the third component of our contextual analysis. Rather, the episode addresses the anxiety associated with a first date and Grace's friends' efforts to lend assistance -- a topic that is not shocking, pandering, or titillating. Moreover, the touching of the breasts is not portrayed in a sexualized manner, and does not appear to elicit any sexual response from Grace.

159.   In sum, we find that, because of the absence of explicit portrayals of, or references to, sexual organs or activities; the brevity of the scene at issue; and the absence of shocking, pandering, and/or titillating effect, the episode, taken as a whole, is not patently offensive as measured by contemporary community standards for the broadcast medium, and therefore is not indecent. Accordingly, the complaint is denied.

3.   "Two and a Half Men" (February 21, 2005)[213]

160.   *The Programming.* The Commission received a complaint that the February 21, 2005 episode of the CBS Television Network program "Two and a Half Men" had a scene in which a female doctor "was doing a hernia check" on a male character "with his scrotum in her hand" while he was trying to seduce her.[214] The

---

[211] The following dialogue occurs:

Karen: "Hey, hey come here, one more thing come here."

Grace: "Will already adjusted them."

Karen: "I wasn't adjusting them."

[212] *NBC Telemundo License Co.,* Memorandum Opinion and Order, 19 FCC Rcd 23025, 23027 ¶ 7 (2004) ("*Coupling MO&O*") (denying complaints about sexual references during the program "Coupling").

[213] FCC File Nos. EB-05-IH-0515, EB-05-IH-0570.

[214] The complainant also generally alleges that "Two and a Half Men" episodes are "raunchy" with "a lot of talk about 'humping.'" In order for us to process an indecency complaint, the complaint must identify a specific broadcast containing allegedly indecent material. We cannot prosecute complaints about programs in general. The First Amendment to the United States Constitution and section 326 of the Act prohibit the Commission from censoring program material and from interfering with broadcasters' freedom of expression. *See* 47 U.S.C. § 326.

(continued....)

broadcast occurred between 9 and 10 p.m. Eastern Standard Time. Based on our review of a videotape provided by CBS, the scene in question takes place in a doctor's office and involves a hernia examination, which requires the male character to remove his pants and cough with the female doctor's hand on his scrotum. No nudity or touching, however, is actually depicted, and the examination is not eroticized. During the examination, to which the male character readily agrees because he apparently finds the doctor attractive, he comments suggestively that her hands are warm and asks her out to dinner. She expresses disbelief that he does not remember her and states that they dated while she was in medical school until he broke it off without explanation and began seeing her roommate. The scene ends with him making comments and sounds indicating that she is painfully squeezing his scrotum.

161.   *Indecency Analysis.* After reviewing a tape of the complained-of scene, we conclude that it is not indecent. Even assuming that the scene that the complainant describes falls within the scope of our indecency definition, it does not, in the context at issue here, satisfy the second prong of our indecency analysis – that is, it is not patently offensive under contemporary standards for the broadcast medium.

162.   Looking at the three principal factors that inform our contextual analysis, first, the material is not graphic or explicit. Although the episode suggests that one character is touching another's sexual organs, the apparent touching takes place off-camera; there is never any nudity, depiction of a sexual organ, or description of sexual organs or activities. Rather, viewers are left to surmise what is happening by one character's reactions to another. Turning to the second factor, while not dispositive, it is relevant that the scene at issue is not sustained or repeated. Finally, we do not believe the material shocks, panders, and/or titillates the viewing audience. As noted, actual touching of the male character's sexual organs is not depicted or described. Although the male character makes some mildly suggestive remarks to the doctor during the examination, the exam is not eroticized or presented in a manner that shocks, panders to, or titillates the audience. We conclude, based on our examination of these three factors, that the scene in question is not patently offensive under contemporary standards for the broadcast medium, and therefore is not indecent. Accordingly, we deny the complaint.

4.   "Committed" (March 8, 2005)[215]

163.   *The Programming.* The Commission received a complaint that the March 8, 2005 episode of the NBC Television Network program "Committed" had a scene "set in a gymnasium full of children" in which a woman is "grabbing the genitals of a man while he sang the national anthem." The broadcast occurred between 6 a.m. and 10 p.m. Eastern Standard Time. Our review of a videotape of the episode indicates that the episode does not show the woman touching the man's genitals – the touching is only suggested – and the suggested touching is not sexual in nature, but apparently intended by the female character to help the man hit the high notes of the national anthem.

164.   *Indecency Analysis.* Based on our review of the tape of this episode, we conclude that it is not indecent. Even assuming that the scene the complainant describes is within the scope of our indecency definition, we conclude that it does not satisfy the second prong of our indecency analysis – that is, it is not patently offensive under contemporary standards for the broadcast medium.

165.   Looking at the three principal factors that inform our contextual analysis, first, the material is not graphic or explicit. Although the episode suggests that one character is touching another's sexual organs, no touching is ever shown, and there is no nudity, depiction of a sexual organ, or description of sexual activity. Rather, viewers are left to surmise what is happening by one character's reactions to another. Turning to the second factor, while not dispositive, it is relevant that the scene at issue is not sustained or repeated. Finally, we do not believe the material shocks, panders, and/or titillates the viewing audience. Rather, it is not presented in a sexual manner. As noted, the touching is only suggested or implied, and neither the detail nor the tone of the scene makes it "shocking" or "titillating." We conclude, based on our examination of these three factors, that the program in question is not patently offensive under contemporary standards for the broadcast medium, and therefore is not indecent. Accordingly, we deny the complaint.

(...continued from previous page)
Moreover, we previously rejected complaints regarding an episode of the program "Will and Grace" that made similar allegations. *See KSAZ MO&O*, 19 FCC Rcd at 16001, ¶6.

[215] FCC File No. EB-05-IH-0257.

APPENDIX A

5.   "Golden Phoenix Hotel & Casino Commercial" (February 19, 2005)[216]

166.   **The Programming.** The Commission received a complaint concerning a commercial for the Golden Phoenix Hotel and Casino, located in Reno, Nevada, broadcast on February 19, 2005 by Sierra Broadcasting Company ("Sierra"), licensee of Station KRNV(TV), Reno, Nevada. The advertisement features a hotel show entitled "Perfect 10." It begins with ten women in casino show-style costumes suddenly jumping onto the bed of a fully clothed man who has been reading "Perfect 10" magazine, then features excerpts of singing and dancing from the show mixed with graphics, and ends with a brief view of the man alone on the bed with his partially bare upper torso and face covered by lipstick kisses. The voice-over describes the concept and content of the show and its male star (who is not the man in bed) and identifies the hotel. The complainant describes the bed scenes as "a mostly naked man laying in bed with . . . almost completely naked women exposing their breasts and other body parts [and] acting in a truly obscene and sexual manner." The complainant alleges that the commercial is obscene and briefly enumerates the criteria for that finding.

167.   **Obscenity Analysis.** We do not find the complained-of material obscene. Although the material does suggest sexual activity, the mere suggestion of such activity does not render material obscene. Obscene material, which is not protected by the First Amendment and may not be broadcast at any time, is defined by a three-prong test set forth by the Supreme Court in *Miller v. California*: (1) the average person, applying contemporary community standards, must find that the material, as a whole, appeals to the prurient interest; (2) the material must depict or describe, in a patently offensive way, sexual conduct specifically defined by applicable law; and (3) the material, taken as a whole, must lack serious literary, artistic, political or scientific value.[217] All three prongs of this test must be met before the material may be found to be obscene. This test is designed "to isolate 'hard core' pornography from expression protected by the First Amendment."[218] Based on our review, the advertisement at issue clearly does not constitute the type of "hard core pornography" covered by *Miller*.

168.   **Indecency Analysis.** The first prong of our indecency analysis is whether the program depicts or describes sexual or excretory activities or organs and, therefore, is within the subject matter scope of the Commission's indecency definition. Even assuming that the advertisement's suggestion of sexual activity meets the first prong of our indecency analysis, however, we conclude that it is not indecent because it is not patently offensive as measured by contemporary community standards for the broadcast medium.

169.   Turning to the first principal factor in our contextual analysis, we find that the material at issue is neither explicit nor graphic. In the first bed scene, the man is shown fully clothed on top of the bed, and the women's costumes, though sexually suggestive, do not actually display their sexual organs. Likewise, the women put their arms around the man in a manner that is suggestive rather than explicit or graphic. The second bed scene merely shows the man alone from the waist up, with his shirt unbuttoned and lipstick marks on his face, without depicting sexual activity or organs.

170.   Concerning the second principal factor of our contextual analysis, the material at issue is repeated or dwelled upon in the sense that there are two bed scenes, one at the beginning of the advertisement and one at the end. Note, however, that this factor is not dispositive. "No single factor generally provides the basis for an indecency finding."[219]

171.   Finally, with respect to the third factor of our contextual analysis, it does not appear that the bed scenes at issue shock, pander to, or titillate the viewing audience. No sexual acts or organs are shown. Among other things, no sexual acts or organs are shown, the voice-over is not explicitly sexual, and the camera angles do not present the material in a pandering manner.

172.   Viewing the advertisement as a whole, we conclude that it is not patently offensive. Although the bed scenes are repeated, this factor is outweighed, in this particular context, by the absence of any graphic or explicit portrayal of sexual activities or organs and our finding that it is not shocking, pandering to, or titillating. Therefore, we conclude that the advertisement is not indecent, and the complaint is denied.

---

[216] FCC File No. EB-05-IH-0314.

[217] 413 U.S. at 24.

[218] *Id.* at 29.

[219] *Indecency Policy Statement,* 16 FCC Rcd at at 8003 ¶ 10.

6. "The Oprah Winfrey Show" (March 18, 2004)[220]

173. ***The Programming***: The Commission received numerous complaints about the discussion of teenage sexual practices contained in the March 18, 2004 episode of the syndicated television program "The Oprah Winfrey Show." This particular episode included an examination by the host and her guests and audience of serious parental/supervisory issues including the complained-of discussion arising from the movie "Thirteen." The complaints cite the following discussion, which we verified from an official transcript of the program:

WINFREY: Yeah. So you say—let's talk about that secret language, Michelle.

Ms. BURFORD: Yes.

WINFREY: I didn't know any of this.

Ms. BURFORD: I have—yeah, I have—I've gotten a whole new vocabulary, let me tell you.

WINFREY: I did not know any of this. Does this—does this mean I am no longer hip?

Ms. BURFORD: Salad-tossing. I'm thinking cucumbers, lettuce, tomatoes. OK? I am definitely not hip.

WINFREY: OK—so—OK, so what is a salad toss?

Ms. BURFORD: OK, a tossed salad is—get ready; hold on to your underwear for this one—oral anal sex. So oral sex to the anus is what tossed salad is. Hi, Mom. OK. A rainbow party is an oral sex party. It's a gathering where oral sex is performed. And a –rainbow comes from—all of the girls put on lipstick and each one puts her mouth around the penis of the gentleman or gentlemen who are there to receive favors and makes a mark in a different place on the penis, hence the term rainbow. So…

WINFREY: OK. And so what does pre—so what does pretty boy mean? A pretty boy.

Ms. BURFORD: Pretty boy is a sexually active boy, someone who's been fairly promiscuous. So it isn't maybe what you would have thought pretty boy meant in your time.

WINFREY: And dirty means what? Does dirty mean…

Ms. BURFORD: Dirty means a diseased—means a diseased girl. And along with that the term that some teens are using to mean HIV is High Five, 'high' and then the Roman numeral 'V.' High Five. So if you got High-Fived by Jack, you got diseased by Jack. You got—you got HIV.

WINFREY: It means he gave you HIV.

Ms. BURFORD: He gave you HIV. Yeah.

WINREY: Yeah. OK. And boo—booty call is pretty common, right?

Ms. BURFORD: Yeah, that's—yeah, that's pretty pervasive. Yeah, that's an early morning or late-at-night call for sex that involves no real relationship. Maybe 2 AM, guy calls girl, and says, 'Meet me at so and so location, we have sex, we leave,' booty call. You all got that?

174. ***Indecency Analysis.*** There can be no question that the complained-of dialogue describes sexual activities, and therefore falls within the subject-matter scope of our indecency analysis. We thus turn to the second prong of our indecency analysis – a determination of whether the material at issue was patently offensive as measured by contemporary community standards for the broadcast medium.

175. Turning to the first factor in our contextual analysis, the broadcast here clearly describes sexual practices in very specific terms, and is highly graphic and explicit.

---

[220] FCC File No. EB-04-IH-0081.

APPENDIX A

176.   With respect to the second factor, the dialogue is not brief, but continues at length.[221] Indeed, the title of the segment is "The Secret Language of Teens," and the discussion of these terms for sexual activity is the subject of the entire segment.

177.   Given this particular context, though, our findings with regard to the first two factors of our analysis are outweighed by our conclusion under the third factor of our contextual analysis that the complained-of material, in context, is not pandering and is not used to titillate or shock.

178.   The program segment focuses on the "secret lives" of many teenagers. Through guests -- parents, teenagers, and others -- serious discussions take place about the disturbing, secret teenage behavior portrayed in the movie "Thirteen." Guests speak of serious, potentially harmful behaviors of teens– such as drug use, drinking, self-mutilation, and sexual activity, how teenagers hide those behaviors from their parents, and how parents might recognize and address those behaviors with their teens. The material is not presented in a vulgar manner and is not used to pander to or titillate the audience. Rather, it is designed to inform viewers about an important topic. To the extent that the material is shocking, it is due to the existence of such practices among teenagers rather than the vulgarity or explicitness of the sexual depictions or descriptions. It would have been difficult to educate parents regarding teenagers' sexual activities without at least briefly describing those activities and alerting parents to the little-known terms (*i.e.*, "salad tossing," "rainbow party") that many teenagers use to refer to them.[222] For many of the same reasons, we have previously denied complaints about similar educational broadcasts.[223]

179.   As we have previously stated, "the manner and purpose of a presentation may well preclude an indecency determination even though other factors, such as explicitness, might weigh in favor of an indecency finding."[224] Here, in light of the overall context of the broadcast, we find that the complained-of material is not patently offensive as measured by contemporary community standards for the broadcast medium, and, therefore, not indecent.

7.   Political Advertisement (October 14, 2004)[225]

180.   *The Programming.* The Commission received a complaint regarding a political advertisement that was aired by Multimedia KDSK, Inc., licensee of Stations KDSK-TV and KDNL-TV, St. Louis, Missouri, between 5:00 and 7:00 p.m. on October 14 and 15, 2004. The advertisement, sponsored by the Illinois Democratic Party and the Maag for Justice political campaign, was aired during the Illinois judicial election cycle. The complainant alleges -- and our review of photographic stills from the advertisement confirms -- that the spot included references to rape and sodomy in criticizing the competence of another candidate in the race for a seat on the Supreme Court of Illinois.[226] The complainant argues that this advertisement contains prurient speech, falls

---

[221] *Indecency Policy Statement,* 16 FCC Rcd at 8008, ¶ 17 (stating that "[r]epetition of and persistent focus on sexual or excretory material have been cited consistently as factors that exacerbate the potential offensiveness of broadcasts").

[222] *See Saving Private Ryan,* 20 FCC Rcd at 4513 ¶ 14 (noting that "[i]n short, the vulgar language here was not gratuitous and could not have been deleted without materially altering the broadcast").

[223] *See King Broadcasting Co.* (*KING-TV*), Memorandum Opinion and Order, 5 FCC Rcd 2971, ¶ 13 (1990) (finding that although a program dealt explicitly with teenage sexual issues and included very graphic sex organ models, "the material presented was clinical or instrumental in nature and not presented in a pandering, titillating or vulgar manner"); *see also Indecency Policy Statement,* 16 FCC Rcd at 8011-12 ¶ 21 (citing to staff decisions in which episodes of the "Oprah Winfrey Show" and "Geraldo Rivera Show" were found not indecent).

[224] *Id.,* 16 FCC Rcd at 8010 ¶ 20.

[225] FCC File No. EB-05-IH-0223.

[226] The photographic stills and text of the advertisement can be found at http://www.brennancenter.org/programs/downloads/buyingtime_2004/STSUPCT_IL_DPIL_KARMEIER_CHILDREN.pdf. The ad begins with a picture of a schoolyard through a chain-link fence, then shows a blurred image of a home, then superimposes a copy of the judicial decision over the home, then adds a picture of Judge Karmeier, and concludes with a picture of a jail cell, with Judge Karmeier's picture superimposed upon it. The narrator states:

(continued....)

outside the First Amendment protections of the Constitution of the United States, and should not have aired at a time when children were watching television.

181.   ***Obscenity Analysis.*** Although the complainant does not explicitly claim that the advertisement is obscene, we read his allegation that the spot contains prurient speech and is without First Amendment protection as an allegation that it is obscene. We find, however, that the complained-of material is not obscene. Although the material does refer to sexual activity, the mere mention of such activity does not render material obscene.[227] Obscene material, which is not protected by the First Amendment and may not be broadcast at any time, is defined by a three-prong test set forth by the Supreme Court in *Miller v. California*: (1) the average person, applying contemporary community standards, must find that the material, as a whole, appeals to the prurient interest; (2) the material must depict or describe, in a patently offensive way, sexual conduct specifically defined by applicable law; and (3) the material, taken as a whole, must lack serious literary, artistic, political or scientific value.[228] This test is designed "to isolate 'hard core' pornography from expression protected by the First Amendment."[229] All three prongs of this test must be met before the material may be found to be obscene.

182.   The material at issue here is not obscene because it does not meet the three-part definition articulated in *Miller v. California*. Although the advertisement discusses a criminal sexual assault, it is a political ad in a hotly contested judicial election and therefore, taken as a whole, it is not without serious political value. Because the material does not meet the third prong of the *Miller* definition, it is not obscene and it is not necessary to consider the other two prongs of the definition.[230]

183.   ***Indecency Analysis.*** Turning to our indecency analysis, we find that the complained-of material describes sexual activity by referencing rape and sodomy, thereby satisfying the first prong of our indecency analysis. We next turn to the second prong of our indecency analysis – a determination of whether the material at issue was patently offensive as measured by contemporary community standards for the broadcast medium.

184.   After reviewing the material, we find that the advertisement is not explicit or graphic, the first factor we must consider in our contextual analysis to determine whether material is patently offensive. The advertisement references rape and sodomy of children without supplying any detailed description or depiction. These references are significantly less graphic than other instances where political advertisements were considered "graphic" but not indecent.[231]

185.   Next, we examine the second factor in our contextual analysis: whether the material is repeated or dwelled upon. We find that rape and sodomy are each referenced only once in the advertisement, which therefore

---

(...continued from previous page)
He used candy to lure the children into the house. Once inside, the three children were sexually molested. A four-year old girl raped. Her brothers sodomized. A Belleville man was arrested and convicted for the crime after trying to develop pictures of the abuse. Despite prosecutor's objections, Judge Lloyd Karmeier gave him probation, saying "The court should grant leniency..." Another case where Karmeier let a violent criminal out into the community. Lloyd Karmeier -- the wrong choice for Supreme Court. Paid for by the Democratic Party of Illinois.

[227] *See WGBH Educational Foundation, Memorandum Opinion and Order,* 69 FCC 2d 1250, 1253-54 (1978) ("*WGBH MO&O*") (finding that offensive language, including expletives, does not fit within the established definition of obscenity).

[228] 413 U.S. at 24.

[229] *Id.* at 29.

[230] *Id.* at 23-24. *See Roth,* 354 U.S. 476; *but see Petition for Declaratory Ruling Concerning Section 312(A)(7) of the Communications Act,* Declaratory Ruling, 9 FCC Rcd. 7638 (1994), *reversed on other grounds sub nom Becker v. FCC,* 95 F.3d 75 (1996) (finding that campaign advertisements containing graphic abortion imagery were, in context, part of important political debate and thus were not indecent) ("*1994 Declaratory Ruling*").

[231] *Id.* at 7643 (depicting dead or aborted and bloodied fetuses in campaign advertisements was graphic, but not indecent).

does not repeat or dwell upon these subject areas. After citing these criminal acts, the advertisement moves on to discuss the sentence delivered to the perpetrator by one of the judicial candidates.

186.   Finally, we assess whether the material is used in a pandering, shocking or titillating manner. The advertisement calls attention primarily to the judgment of a judicial candidate, and mentions predatory sexual activities to call into question the candidate's judgment in sentencing a criminal. We do not consider such references pandering or titillating. While references to rape and sodomy are shocking, particularly when they involve children, we find that, on balance, the advertisement advocates against a particular judicial candidate rather than shocks, panders to, or titillates the audience.[232] In other words, to the extent that the material has "shock" value, it is not related to sexual or excretory activity but to the judge's allegedly "soft attitude" on crime.

187.   In this case, we find that all three of the principal factors in our contextual analysis weigh in favor of a finding that the complained-of material is not patently offensive as measured by contemporary community standards for the broadcast medium. While the references in this political advertisement to rape and sodomy were understandably upsetting to some viewers, subject matter alone does not render material indecent.[233] Therefore, we conclude that this advertisement is not indecent. Accordingly, we deny the complaint.[234]

8.   "The Amazing Race 6" (December 21, 2004)[235]

188.   ***The Programming.*** "The Amazing Race 6" is a CBS Television Network ("CBS") program in which two-person teams race around the world for a cash prize. The Commission received a complaint regarding the December 21, 2004 broadcast of the program by CBS affiliate Station KYW-TV, Philadelphia, Pennsylvania, licensed to CBS Broadcasting, Inc. According to the complaint, "[m]idway through that episode, my nine-year-old daughter asked me what was written on the side of a bus that the contestants were embarking upon. She stated that she thought that was a bad word that she was not supposed to say. Sure enough, the words 'FU** COPS' was [sic] visible on the side of the bus near the door where the contestants are getting on the bus."

189.   The Bureau obtained a videotape of the subject episode from CBS which confirms that, during a scene in which two of the contestants leave a train, the camera shot briefly includes some graffiti stating "Fuck Cops!" The graffiti is spray-painted in small white letters on the train's side.

190.   ***Indecency Analysis.*** We held in the *Golden Globe Awards Order* that, given the core meaning of the "F-Word," any use of that word inherently has a sexual connotation and falls within the first prong of our indecency definition.[236] The complained-of material here is language that we have found inherently describes sexual activity. The material, therefore, warrants further scrutiny to determine whether it was patently offensive as measured by contemporary community standards for the broadcast medium.

191.   Looking at the three principal factors that comprise our contextual analysis, we note first that, although the "F-Word" is depicted in the program, the image is not graphic or explicit. The graffiti is small, out of focus, and difficult to read. Unless one is looking directly at or for the words, the average viewer would not even notice the graffiti. Second, while not dispositive, it is relevant that the material is not repeated or dwelled upon. Indeed, the image is displayed only momentarily. Finally, the shot of the graffiti is not shocking, pandering, or titillating because it is barely visible. Indeed, the average viewer would not have noticed the graffiti. Since each of the three factors examined above weighs against a finding of patent offensiveness, we conclude that the material is not patently offensive and therefore not indecent.

192.   ***Profanity Analysis.*** In the *Golden Globe Awards Order*, we found that the "F-Word" constituted profane language within the meaning of 18 U.S.C. § 1464 because, in context, it constituted vulgar and

---

[232] *Id.*

[233] *See Indecency Policy Statement*, 16 FCC Rcd at 8011 ¶ 21.

[234] Because we find that the advertisement is not indecent, we need not decide whether the Commission may propose forfeitures against licensees that broadcast indecent political advertisements outside of the safe harbor. *See generally Becker v. FCC*, 95 F.3d 75 (D.C. Cir. 1996).

[235] FCC File No. EB-05-IH-0394.

[236] *See Golden Globe Awards Order*, 19 FCC Rcd at 4978 ¶ 8; *see also Pacifica Foundation*, 56 FCC 2d at 99.

coarse language "so grossly offensive to members of the public who actually hear it as to amount to a nuisance."[237] Based upon our review of the record in this case, however, we conclude that CBS did not air profane material in violation of 18 U.S.C. § 1464. As we have indicated elsewhere in this Order, we believe that the "F-Word" is presumptively profane because it is so grossly offensive as to constitute a nuisance.[238] This, however, is one of the rare instances in which this presumption is effectively rebutted. Unlike the broadcast spoken utterance of the "F-Word" at issue in the *Golden Globes Award Order*, the written version of the word during this broadcast, for the reasons mentioned above, would not have been noticed by the average viewer. As such, we find it impossible to conclude that its broadcast was "likely to shock the viewer and disturb the piece and quiet of the home"[239] and thus amount to a nuisance. For all of these reasons, we find that the broadcast is not profane, and the complaint is denied.

       9.   **Various Programs Containing Expletives (various dates between August 31, 2004 and February 28, 2005)**

       193.   *The Programming.* The Commission has before it twenty complaints concerning programming that contains the following allegedly obscene, indecent, or profane words and phrases: "hell," "damn," "bitch," "pissed off," "up yours," "ass," "for Christ's sake," "kiss my ass," "fire his ass," "ass is huge," and "wiping his ass." We conclude that, while these words and phrases are understandably upsetting to some viewers, in the contexts used here, they are neither obscene, indecent, nor profane. The complaints include:

       (a) an October 19, 2004, complaint against Viacom International, Inc., licensee of Station WTOG(TV), St. Petersburg, Florida, for its alleged October 18, 2004 broadcast of "The Simpsons" program, in which the phrases "up yours," and "hell" were allegedly aired between 7:00 and 7:30 p.m. The complainant believes that the material was "obscene."[240]

       (b) a November 4, 2004 complaint against TVT License, Inc., licensee of Station WTVT(TV), Tampa, Florida, for a November 4, 2004 broadcast of the "North Shore" program, in which the words "bitch" and "hell" were allegedly broadcast during an unspecified time period. The complainant believes that the material was "profane."[241]

       (c) a November 18, 2004 complaint against KTVI License, Inc., licensee of Station KTVI(TV), St. Louis, Missouri, for its alleged October 26, 2004 broadcast of the "Father of the Pride" program, in which the phrases "damn," "hell," and "my ass is huge," were allegedly aired at approximately 8:00 p.m.[242] The complainant believes that the material "lacks serious literary, artistic, political or scientific value and meets the standard of the prohibition issued by the FCC."

       (d) a September 22, 2004 complaint against Meredith Corporation, licensee of Station WSMV-TV, Nashville, Tennessee, for its alleged August 31, 2004 broadcast of the "Father of the Pride" program, in which the phrases "bitch" and "slutty sister" were used and "an animal trainer was accosted by a sexually aroused chimpanzee."[243] The complainant further alleges that a sexual double-entendre was made through the animated lion character's statement "'Big Daddy's ready for lovin' . . . it may be nine o'clock in New York, but right here it's mountin' time.'" The complainant alleges that the material is indecent.

---

[237] *Golden Globe Awards Order,* 19 FCC Rcd at 4981 ¶¶ 13-14.

[238] *Id.* at 19 FCC Rcd at 4980 ¶ 12 (citing *Tallman v. United States,* 465 F.2d 282, 285 (7th Cir. 1972)).

[239] *See supra* ¶ 19.

[240] FCC File No. EB-05-IH-0316.

[241] FCC File No. EB-05-IH-0317.

[242] FCC File No. EB-05-IH-0385.

[243] FCC File No. EB-04-IH-0459.

(e) an undated complaint against Viacom International, Inc., licensee of Station WTOG(TV), St. Petersburg, Florida, for its alleged October 25, 2004 broadcast of the "Girlfriends" program, in which the word "ass" was allegedly aired during the 9:00 to 9:30 p.m. time period.[244] The complainant believes that the material was "offensive."

(f) an undated complaint against an unspecified UPN affiliate for its alleged November 29, 2004 broadcast of the "Half and Half" program in which the word "damn" was allegedly aired during the 9:00 to 9:30 p.m. time period.[245] The complainant believes that the material was "profane."

(g) a December 20, 2004 complaint against an unspecified UPN affiliate for its alleged December 20, 2004 broadcast of the "Second Time Around" program in which the phrases "get your ass out here," "I gave you the damn keys," and "damn flashlight" were allegedly aired at approximately 9:50 p.m.[246] The complainant believes that the material was both "profane" and "obscene."

(h) an undated complaint against Viacom International, Inc., licensee of Station WTOG(TV), St. Petersburg, Florida, for its alleged December 1, 2004 broadcast of the "America's Next Top Model" program in which the words "ass" and "bitch" were allegedly aired during the 8:00 to 9:00 p.m. time period.[247] The complainant believes that the material was "profane."

(i) an undated complaint against Viacom International, Inc., licensee of Station WTOG(TV), St. Petersburg, Florida, for its alleged December 21, 2004 broadcast of the "Family Matters" program in which the word "hell" was allegedly aired during the 10:30 and 11:00 a.m. time period.[248] The complainant believes that the material was both "obscene" and "profane."

(j) an undated complaint against Viacom International, Inc., licensee of Station WTOG(TV), St. Petersburg, Florida, for its alleged broadcast of the "Cuts" program on February 28, 2005 during which the words "ass" and "damn" were allegedly aired during the 8:30 to 9:00 p.m. time period.[249] The complainant believes that the material was "inappropriate."

(k) an undated complaint against McGraw-Hill Broadcasting Company, Inc., licensee of Station KMGH-TV, Denver, Colorado, for its alleged broadcast of an unspecified program on January 25, 2005 during which the phrases "my Mom's been wiping his ass," "he said his parents would fire her ass," and "a pissed-off ex-employee" were allegedly aired during the 9:00 to 10:00 p.m. period.[250] The complainant believes that the material was "obscene," "indecent" and "profane."

(l) an April 23, 2005 complaint against TVT License, Inc., licensee of Station WTVT(TV), Tampa, Florida, for a December 9, 2004 broadcast of the "North Shore" program, in which the words "ass" and "hell" were allegedly broadcast between 9 and 10 p.m.. The complainant believes that the material was indecent.[251]

---

[244] FCC File No. EB-05-IH-0318.

[245] FCC File No. EB-05-IH-0421.

[246] FCC File No. EB-05-IH-0428.

[247] FCC File No. EB-05-IH-0420.

[248] FCC File No. EB-04-IH-0422.

[249] FCC File No. EB-05-IH-0423.

[250] FCC File No. EB-05-IH-0696.

[251] FCC File No. EB-05-IH-0417.

194.   ***Obscenity Analysis.*** We deny the complaints to the extent that they allege the foregoing broadcasts are obscene.[252] The three-part obscenity test set forth in *Miller v. California* requires that (1) an average person, applying contemporary community standards, would find that the material, as a whole, appeals to the prurient interest; (2) the material depicts or describes, in a patently offensive way, sexual conduct specifically defined by applicable law; and (3) the material, taken as a whole, lacks serious literary, artistic, political, or scientific value.[253] This test is designed "to isolate 'hard core' pornography from expression protected by the First Amendment."[254] Nothing in the record indicates that the foregoing broadcasts depict the kind of "hard core pornography" covered by *Miller*, or that, *as a whole*, they appeal to the prurient interest or lack serious literary, artistic, political, or scientific value.[255]

195.   ***Indecency Analysis.*** Although only three complaints explicitly allege that the cited material is indecent,[256] we will perform our indecency analysis on all the allegations about offensive language. Several of the complaints cite similar terms without providing any context. For example, complainants challenge uses of the words "up yours," "ass," "hell," "damn," and "bitch."[257] One complaint, about Station WSMV-TV's August 31, 2004 broadcast of an episode of "Father of the Pride," concerns references to an animated character's sister being "slutty," and to various sexual acts, including animal sex and bestiality.[258] Another complaint, against Station KMGH-TV, concerns the phrases "my Mom's been wiping his ass," and "he said his parents would fire her ass," and "either that or a pissed-off ex-employee."[259]

196.   The words "hell," "bitch," "slutty," and "damn" do not refer to sexual or excretory organs or activity and therefore fall outside the subject matter scope of our indecency rules. We will assume *arguendo* that the remaining allegations describe or depict sexual or excretory organs or activities and therefore fall within the subject matter scope of our indecency rules. Specifically, the word "ass," and the phrases "wiping his ass" and "fire her ass," in the context of the programs, refer to the buttocks, which are sexual and excretory organs.[260] Likewise, the term "pissed off" is a derivative of "piss," which refers to the act of urination. Moreover, the references to sexual acts, including animal sex and bestiality, describe sexual activity. Although the phrase "up yours" is more vague, the speaker arguably is referring to a sexual or excretory organ of the listener. Thus, we must proceed to determine whether these terms or references are patently offensive as measured by contemporary community standards for the broadcast medium under the second step of our indecency analysis.

197.   We find that, although the complained-of word "ass," and the phrases "up yours," "my ass is huge," "wiping his ass," "fire her ass," and "pissed off" are coarse expressions, in the context presented, they are not sufficiently vulgar, graphic, or explicit to support a finding of patent offensiveness. To the extent the complaints describe the context in which the word "ass" is used, it is used in a nonsexual sense to denigrate or insult the speaker or another character. The word "piss" is used as part of a slang expression that means "angry." The word "ass" and the phrase "pissed off" do not invariably invoke coarse sexual or excretory images, and in the context presented they do not rise to the level of offensiveness of the "F-Word" or "S-Word." Moreover, while not dispositive, none of these complaints suggest that the remarks are repeated or dwelled upon. Although the phrases may have a

---

[252] The allegations of obscenity concern, specifically, the phrases "up yours," "hell," "get your ass out here," "I gave you the damn keys," "I was holding the damn flashlight," "my Mom's been wiping his ass," "kiss my ass," "his parents would fire his ass," and "either that or a pissed-off ex-employee."

[253] 413 U.S. at 24.

[254] *Id.* at 29.

[255] *See WGBH MO&O*, 69 FCC 2d at 1253-54 (finding that offensive language, including expletives, does not fit within the established definition of obscenity).

[256] *See supra* ¶ 193(c), (e), and (j).

[257] *See supra* ¶ 193(a)-(c), (e)-(j), (l).

[258] *See supra* ¶ 193(d).

[259] *See supra* ¶ 193(k).

[260] *See supra* note 97.

marginally shocking effect, that impact is not so marked as to convince us that the overall context of the broadcast was indecent. Moreover, we note that last year we found that the fleeting use of some of these same terms was not indecent in the contexts presented.[261] The manner in which these terms are used in the complained-of broadcasts resembles that presented in our previous decisions. Therefore, based on our precedent, the complained-of broadcasts are not indecent.

198.   With regard to the remaining allegations in the complaint against the August 31, 2004 episode of "Father of the Pride," we find that the material is not indecent. First, the animated lion character's utterance of the phrase "it's mountin' time," although apparently used as a sexual reference, is not, in the context of the instant broadcast, sufficiently explicit or graphic to be deemed patently offensive. While the animated imagery accompanying the lion character's comment does portray him making a circular pelvic motion while uttering the phrase "mountin' time," it does not contain any depiction of sexual organs or explicit sexual acts. Moreover, the sexual reference is neither repeated nor dwelled upon, and is not shocking, pandering, or titillating. Similarly, we find no merit to the allegation that the material visually depicting "an animal trainer [being] accosted by a sexually aroused chimpanzee" is indecent. Contrary to the complainant's allegation of portrayed bestiality, the scene in question depicts the effect of a trainer's application of animal pheromones, apparently arousing a chimpanzee to attempt to caress and nuzzle him. It does not contain any depiction of sexual organs or sexually explicit acts and is not titillating or shocking. Consequently, we find that the foregoing material, while offensive to some viewers, is not patently offensive under our indecency standard.

199.   *Profanity Analysis.* Several of the complaints allege that the use of the words "bitch," "hell" or "damn," or phrases including their variants, are profane. These words are not sexual or excretory terms, and thus are presumed not to be profane.[262] On the other hand, the words "ass" and "piss" and their derivatives do describe sexual or excretory activities. As noted above, we discussed these terms in two decisions last year, finding that neither was not sufficiently graphic or explicit in context to be indecent,[263] and further holding that the term "pissed" was not profane in the context presented.[264] Similarly, we conclude that the use of these terms here in context is not so grossly offensive to members of the public as to amount to a nuisance and thus be deemed profane. Accordingly, we deny the complaints.

10.   "Family Guy" (January 16, 2005)[265]

200.   *The Programming.* The Commission received a complaint concerning the January 16, 2005 broadcast of "Family Guy" over Fox Television Network-affiliated stations, and specifically Station WTTG-TV, Washington, D.C., at 9:00 p.m. Eastern Standard Time. The episode in question, titled "And The Weiner Is ....," includes dialogue in which cartoon characters say "penis," along with euphemisms for the male sex organ, within the episode's subject: a father's concern that he is not as well-endowed as his son.

201.   *Indecency Analysis.* The episode's references to "penis" clearly places it within the subject matter scope of our indecency definition as the word "penis" refers to a sexual organ.[266] We thus turn to the second prong of our indecency analysis – whether the material at issue was patently offensive as measured by contemporary

---

[261] *See PTC 1,* 20 FCC Rcd at 1926, ¶ 8 (finding that, in context, fleeting uses of words including "bitch" and "ass" not sufficiently explicit or graphic to support a finding of patent offensiveness); *PTC 2,* 20 FCC Rcd at 1938 ¶ 8 (finding that, in context, words including "hell," "damn," "pissed," "bitch," not sufficiently explicit or graphic to support a finding of patent offensiveness). We note that, in contrast, in *Golden Globe Awards,* 19 FCC Rcd at 4979 ¶ 9, we found that a single use of the "F-Word" during the live broadcast of an awards ceremony was explicit and graphic because "its use invariably invokes a coarse sexual image."

[262] *See supra* ¶ 18.

[263] *See PTC 1,* 20 FCC Rcd at 1926, ¶ 8 (finding that use of the term "ass" was not indecent in context); *PTC 2,* 20 FCC Rcd 1938, ¶ 8 (finding that broadcast references to "hell," "damn," "bitch," and "pissed" were not indecent).

[264] *Id.* (finding that several words, including "pissed," were not profane in context).

[265] FCC File No. EB-05-IH-0084.

[266] *Young Broadcasting NAL,* 19 FCC Rcd at 1754 ¶ 9 (finding that broadcast material that showed a male performer's genitalia satisfied the subject matter prong of the indecency analysis).

community standards for the broadcast medium. In making this determination, we must look to the full context in which the material is presented, including the explicit or graphic nature of the description, whether it dwells on or repeats at length descriptions of sexual organs or activities, and whether it appears to pander or is used to titillate or shock. While the program's cartoon format may make it more attractive to younger viewers, the context is generally a humorous series of scenes of increasingly desperate behavior by the cartoon family father as he tries to compensate for his self-perceived inadequacies after learning that his son's penis is larger than his own.

202.   Regarding the first component of our contextual analysis, the program contains no nudity and never actually shows or graphically describes any sexual organ. The episode merely refers to the cartoon son's penis and shows the cartoon father's and mother's reactions upon learning of it. Moreover, the specific euphemisms that are employed, such as "wang" and "little banana," are relatively inoffensive. In a similar case, the Commission found that several episodes of the program "Coupling" were not sufficiently vulgar, explicit, or graphic to qualify as indecent, even though they repeatedly referred to sexual activities and organs.[267] The Commission concluded that although the episodes included "sustained and repeated use of sexual innuendo and double entendre . . . none of the episodes contain[ed] graphic descriptions of sexual activities and organs or use[d] language that is so graphic as to qualify as indecent and profane."[268]

203.   Regarding the second component of our contextual analysis, the episode does dwell upon and repeat various references to penises. As we have noted previously, however, no single factor in our indecency analysis is generally dispositive.[269]

204.   Finally, we do not find that the material is used to pander, titillate, or shock. Rather, the episode at issue addresses the father's feelings of inferiority, and the topic is presented in an indirect, humorous manner, without the use of graphic or explicit details.

205.   In sum, although the word "penis" and euphemisms for that word are repeated several times in the episode, we find that because of the absence of explicit or graphic descriptions or depictions of any sexual organ, along with the absence of shocking, pandering, and/or titillating effect, the episode, taken as a whole, is not patently offensive as measured by contemporary community standards for the broadcast medium and is therefore not indecent. Accordingly, the complaint is denied.

11.   "The Academy Awards" (February 27, 2005)[270]

206.   ***The Programming.*** The Commission received several complaints against the ABC Television Network's broadcast of "The Academy Awards" program, alleging that show host Chris Rock uttered vulgar and offensive comments including "sit their asses down," and the statement that the "Superman" film "sucked." One complainant further alleges that the program featured a video montage in which a male actor was "naked from the waist up, standing in the background, [while a female actor] was apparently eating a sausage or other item, but it appeared to be superimposed and gave the appearance of her performing oral sex on the man." The segments in question were all broadcast during the evening of February 27, 2005 before 10 p.m. Eastern Standard Time.

207.   ***Indecency Analysis.*** With respect to the first prong of the indecency analysis, we find that the broadcast falls within the scope of the indecency definition.[271] We will assume *arguendo* that, in certain contexts, the term "sucked" may refer to oral sex. The phrase "sit their asses down" refers to the buttocks, which are sexual and excretory organs. Similarly, the video clip described in the complaint uses video images to allude to oral sex, a sexual activity, and thus is within the scope of our indecency definition. We therefore evaluate whether the foregoing material is "patently offensive" as measured by the contemporary community standards for the broadcast medium under the second step of our indecency analysis.

---

[267] *See Coupling MO&O*, 19 FCC Rcd at 23027 ¶ 7.

[268] *Id.*

[269] *Indecency Policy Statement*, 16 FCC Rcd at 8003 ¶ 10.

[270] FCC File No. EB-05-IH-0277.

[271] *See supra* ¶ 12.

208.   We find that although the complained-of phrases "sit their asses down" and "sucked" may be coarse expressions, in the context presented, they are not sufficiently vulgar, explicit, or graphic to support a patent offensiveness finding.[272] First, in the context presented, the word "sucked" is not an explicit or graphic description of sexual or excretory organs or activities. Its use does not invariably invoke a coarse sexual image. The phrase "sit their asses down" includes a coarse expression for the buttocks, but involves a command to sit down, rather than referring to sexual or excretory activity. In addition, while not dispositive, neither remark is repeated or dwelled upon. Furthermore, while this terminology may have been upsetting to some viewers, it is not sufficiently graphic, explicit, or sustained to support the conclusion that it was shocking, pandering or titillates the audience. Although use of such phrases may, depending on the context involved, contribute to a finding of indecency, their use here was not patently offensive and therefore not indecent.

209.   Moreover, we find that the program's video montage, which allegedly "gave the appearance of" a depiction of oral sex, is not actionably indecent. In a recent case, the Commission denied substantially similar complaints directed against the broadcast of segments from the film "Austin Powers: The Spy Who Shagged Me."[273] Significantly, in this case, as in the "Austin Powers" film, the material cited in the complaint does not actually depict sexual organs or activities; it only uses superimposed images to allude to oral sex. Therefore, we find that the material does not explicitly or graphically depict sexual organs or activities. Furthermore, the image was extremely brief, lasting a mere fraction of a second. Finally, the visual allusion, in context, is not shocking or titillating, and in any event, is simply not explicit and graphic enough to be patently offensive as measured by contemporary community standards for the broadcast medium. Therefore, we find that it was not indecent. Accordingly, the complaints are denied.

12.   "8 Simple Rules" (February 4, 2005)[274]

210.   *The Programming.* The Commission received a complaint regarding the February 4, 2005 broadcast of the ABC Television Network program, "8 Simple Rules" between 6 a.m. and 10 p.m. Eastern Standard Time. According to the complaint, "[a]t the conclusion of the episode, I observed the mother and the oldest child as they stood near a hamster cage in the home. The older girl looked into a hamster cage and asked '… what is it doing?' … then the girl said '… hamsterbating.' This was a reference [that] the hamster was 'masturbating.'" The complaint urges the Commission to issue a public warning or fine against ABC and "to take a position not to allow this type of behavior and language on television."

211.   *Indecency Analysis.* As an initial matter, we will assume but not decide that the broadcast falls within the subject-matter prong of our analysis, as it references the sexual activity of masturbation. We conclude, however, that the program is not indecent because it is not patently offensive as measured by the contemporary community standards for the broadcast medium.

212.   Turning to the three principal factors that inform our contextual analysis, while the use of the term "hamsterbating" would be interpreted by many viewers as constituting a veiled reference to the sexual activity of masturbation, the term is neither graphic nor explicit, and the program never depicts any sexual activity or organ. Moreover, although not dispositive, it is also relevant to our analysis that the allusion to masturbation is not in any way sustained or dwelled upon. Finally, we conclude that while the use of the term "hamsterbating" may have disturbed some viewers of this program, which is aimed in part at a younger audience, the term's shock value is marginal at best, and in this context is outweighed by the non-explicit and non-repeated nature of the allegedly indecent material. For all of these reasons, we deny the complaint.

---

[272] *See PTC 2*, 20 FCC Rcd at 1938 ¶ 8 (in context, words "dick," "hell," damn," "orgasm," "penis," "testicles," "breast," "nipples," "can," "pissed," "crap," "bastard," and "bitch" were not sufficiently explicit or graphic to be patently offensive).

[273] *See PTC 1*, 20 FCC Rcd at 1926-27, ¶¶ 7-9.

[274] FCC File No. EB-05-IH-0465.

13.   "The Today Show" (January 11, 2005)[275]

213.   *The Programming.* The Commission received a complaint about the January 11, 2005 broadcast of "The Today Show" between 6 a.m. and 10 p.m. Eastern Standard Time. That program contained a segment showing scenes of the devastating floods and mudslides that had occurred in California and of various rescue efforts. In one scene, viewers see an attempt to pull a man wearing only a shirt from raging water onto the safety of a highway overpass. As the man is hauled from water level to the boat, his penis is briefly exposed. At the end of the scene, the rescuers lose their grip on the man, and he goes crashing back into the water, narrowly missing a pillar of the overpass as he falls.

214.   *Indecency Analysis.* In conducting our indecency analysis in this case, it is important to recognize and emphasize the context of the broadcast material. The complained-of segment contained contemporaneous coverage of an important news event. Therefore, we must exercise particular caution here as the complaint involves programming that implicates core First Amendment concerns. The first prong of our indecency analysis is whether the program depicts or describes sexual or excretory activities or organs and, therefore, is within the subject matter scope of the Commission's indecency definition. The broadcast clearly falls within the subject matter scope of our indecency definition because the scene includes a view of a man's penis, which is a sexual organ.[276] We thus turn to the second prong of our indecency analysis – a determination of whether the material at issue was patently offensive as measured by contemporary community standards for the broadcast medium.

215.   Regarding the first principal component of our contextual analysis, although the Commission previously has found exposure of adult sexual organs to be graphic and explicit in certain situations,[277] in this particular context, we find that the complained-of material is not graphic or explicit. The shot of the man's penis is not at close range, and the overall focus of the scene is on the rescue attempt, not on the man's sexual organ. Here, the distant image of a man's penis in footage displaying efforts to rescue him from mortal peril is not explicit or graphic.

216.   With respect to the second principal component of our contextual analysis, the segment does not dwell on or repeat the image of the victim's penis. To the contrary, the segment can be fairly described as providing only a brief glimpse of the penis that is incidental to the overall action portrayed – a human rescue effort.

217.   Turning to the final principal component of our analysis, and the most important in this particular context, we find that the material does not pander to, titillate, or shock the viewing audience. Rather, it contains coverage of a significant news event and shows the human experience behind that event. To the extent there is shock value to the footage, it derives from the overall action portrayed -- the effort to rescue a human life -- not from the footage's minimal sexual content.

218.   Since the material taken as a whole is not graphic or explicit, does not dwell on or repeat images of a sexual organ or activity, and does not appear to shock, pander, and/or titillate, it does not satisfy the second prong of our indecency analysis and, therefore, we deny the complaint. In doing so, we again recognize the need for particular caution with respect to complaints implicating the editorial judgment of broadcast licensees in presenting news and public affairs programming, as these matters are at the core of the First Amendment's free press guarantee.[278] We also emphasize the critical importance of context in determining whether a broadcast is patently offensive. In this regard, the contrast between this case and the *Young Broadcasting NAL* is instructive. Each involves the brief, accidental exposure of male frontal nudity during a news program. Unlike in this case, however,

---

[275] FCC File No. EB-05-IH-0365.

[276] See *Young Broadcasting NAL*, 19 FCC Rcd at 1754 (finding that a broadcast of performer's exposed penis satisfies subject matter prong of indecency analysis).

[277] *Id. See also Super Bowl NAL*, 19 FCC Rcd at 19235 (finding that a broadcast of performer's breast was graphic and explicit).

[278] See *Syracuse Peace Council*, 2 FCC Rcd at 5050-51 ¶ 52 (eliminating the fairness doctrine, which placed an affirmative obligation on broadcasters to cover, and present contrasting viewpoints on, controversial issues of public importance).

the performer's penis in the *Young Broadcasting NAL* was exposed at relatively close range.[279] More importantly, the display was not incidental to the coverage of a news event; rather, it occurred during an interview of performers who appear nude to manipulate their genitalia, and as the performer stood up to give an off-camera demonstration to the show's hosts.[280] Here, in contrast, the program's focus is a rescue effort, and the complained-of material is incidental and easily could evade the notice of a viewer focused on this effort.

14.   "The Simpsons" (September 9, 2004)[281]

219.   ***The Programming.*** The Commission received a complaint regarding the broadcast of an episode of "The Simpsons" over Station WTTG(TV), Washington, D.C., at 6:30 p.m. Eastern Daylight Time on September 9, 2004.[282] The complaint states that the program contains a graphic and explicit depiction of a scene in a strip club. The Bureau requested and received a videotape of the program in question from Fox Television Stations, Inc., the licensee of the station.

220.   "The Simpsons" is an animated comedy series featuring a number of regular characters, including the elderly Mr. Burns and his assistant Smithers. The complained-of episode, entitled "Hunka Hunka Burns In Love," deals with Mr. Burns's romantic ineptitude. The scene in question shows Mr. Burns leading Smithers into a club with a "Girls Girls Girls" sign and saying, "Maybe there are some girls in here." In the club, female cartoon characters dance around poles clothed in two-piece or one-piece lingerie or underwear. Mr. Burns reacts by saying, "Great Heavens! This is one of those nude female fire stations! Oh, I'd always be second place to some kitten stuck in a tree. Let's go, Smithers." Smithers is momentarily depicted as crouching and whimpering in embarrassment as he is cornered by two dancers. Although the complaint states that the scene depicts physical contact between Smithers and a female cartoon dancer's buttocks, we were unable to confirm this statement based on our viewing of the tape.

221.   ***Indecency Analysis.*** As an initial matter, for purposes of this analysis, we assume without deciding that the depiction of female cartoon characters dancing in lingerie falls within the subject-matter prong of our indecency standard. We conclude, however, that the program is not indecent because it is not patently offensive as measured by the contemporary community standards for the broadcast medium.

222.   Regarding the first principal component of our contextual analysis, we conclude that the complained-of material does not graphically or explicitly depict sexual organs or activities. Although the movements of the two female dancers shown with Smithers are somewhat sexually suggestive, and one of the dancers is shown from behind wearing a "thong," the scene is not graphic. No cartoon character is shown completely nude, and there are no clear depictions of physical contact involving the cartoon character's sexual organs in the scene. Moreover, although a cartoon might be patently offensive if it contained sufficiently graphic or explicit depictions of sexual or excretory organs or activities, in this context the animation weighs against a finding of patent offensiveness: the characters are linear representations, and to the extent they are depicted in sexually-suggestive clothing or situations, the animation makes those depictions inherently less graphic and explicit than, for example, those involved in the "Video Musicales" program discussed above in Section III.A.4.

223.   With respect to the second principal component of our contextual analysis, the scene is relatively brief and does not dwell on depictions of sexual organs or activities.[283] Turning to the final principal component of our analysis, we do not find that the material is panders to, titillates, or shocks the viewing audience within the context of the program at issue. Rather, the scene is a relatively brief vignette about the male characters' romantic

---

[279] 19 FCC Rcd at 1752.

[280] *Id.* at 1756-57. Noting the comments of off-camera employees urging the performers to conduct a nude demonstration, and the partially off-camera demonstration to the show's hosts, the Commission found that the display was pandering, titillating and shocking, notwithstanding the licensee's precautions to prevent such a display. *Id.* at 1757.

[281] FCC File No. EB-05-IH-0041.

[282] *See* Complaint dated September 8, 2004.

[283] *Compare Married By America,* 19 FCC Rcd at 20195, ¶ 12 (finding material to be sustained where scene at issue lasted approximately 6 minutes).

ineptitude. Since the material taken as a whole is not graphic, explicit, or sustained and does not appear to shock, pander, and/or titillate, we find that it is not patently offensive. Accordingly, we deny the complaint.

15.   "America's Funniest Home Videos" (February 5, 2005)[284]

224.   *Programming.* The Commission received a complaint regarding the February 5, 2005 episode of the ABC Television Network program "America's Funniest Videos" ("AFV") that was broadcast over Station WHAM (TV), Rochester, New York. The complaint alleged that this episode, which aired from 8:00 to 8:30 p.m. Eastern Standard Time, included a clip in which a "butt plug" was allegedly inserted into a naked, male infant. As part of the investigation in this matter, the Enforcement Bureau requested and received from the licensee a videotape of that AFV episode. This videotape reveals that the episode depicted a naked infant falling back onto his pacifier, which then becomes wedged between his buttocks.

225.   *Indecency Analysis.* The first prong of our indecency analysis is whether the program depicts or describes sexual or excretory activities or organs, and, therefore, is within the subject matter scope of the Commission's indecency definition. Because this videotape depicts a child's nude buttocks, we find that it depicts both excretory and sexual organs,[285] and the broadcast therefore falls within the subject matter scope of our indecency analysis. We must then turn to the next part of our analysis – whether the broadcast was "patently offensive" as measured by contemporary community standards for the broadcast medium.

226.   Turning to the first principal factor in our contextual analysis of whether material is patently offensive, the segment at issue shows a naked infant falling back onto his pacifier, which then becomes wedged between his buttocks and is therefore marginally explicit. With regard to the second factor, while not dispositive, the broadcast does not dwell on or repeat at length any description or depiction of sexual or excretory organs or activities.[286] Rather, the program shows the relevant segment once and then moves on to other videotapes. And finally, the footage does not appear to shock, pander, or titillate. The depiction, submitted by the infant's parents, is not sexualized in any manner whatsoever. In conclusion, based on our review of the full context of the broadcast, we find that the broadcast is not indecent. Although, as indicated above, the footage is somewhat explicit, its brevity and the absence of any shocking, pandering, or titillate effect on the audience outweigh that factor in our analysis. As we held in the *Indecency Policy Statement*, "no single factor generally provides the basis for an indecency finding."[287] Accordingly, the complaint is denied.

16.   "Green Bay Packers v. Minnesota Vikings" (January 9, 2005)[288]

227.   *The Programming.* The Commission received complaints regarding a broadcast over the Fox Television Network ("Fox" or "Fox Network") on the evening of January 9, 2005 prior to 10 p.m. Eastern Standard Time. The complaints allege that during the broadcast of the National Football League playoff game between the Green Bay Packers and the Minnesota Vikings, Fox broadcast the image of a player for the visiting Vikings team who, after scoring a touchdown, acted as if he were lowering his pants and exposing his buttocks to the crowd at Green Bay's Lambeau Field, although he remained fully clothed at all times. In other words, the player pretended to "moon" the crowd. The complaints seek an indecency finding and proposed monetary forfeitures against all Fox Network affiliate stations.

228.   *Indecency Analysis.* Assuming without deciding that the broadcast of a mimed "mooning" depicts a sexual or excretory organ and thus falls within the subject matter prong of our indecency analysis, we nevertheless conclude that the material is not patently offensive as measured by contemporary community standards for the broadcast medium and thus is not indecent.

---

[284] FCC File No. EB-05-IH-0212.

[285] *See supra* note 97.

[286] *See PTC 2*, 20 FCC Rcd at 1938 ¶ 9 (finding that a rudimentary depiction of a cartoon boy's buttocks was fleeting, and, in context, was not sufficiently graphic or explicit, or sustained, to rise to the level of being patently offensive).

[287] *Indecency Policy Statement*, 16 FCC Rcd at 8003 ¶ 10.

[288] FCC File No. EB-05-IH-0032.

229.   Each of the three principal factors that inform our contextual analysis weighs against a finding of patent offensiveness. First, the display involves only mimed actions by a fully-clothed player and thus is not graphic or explicit. Second, although not dispositive, it is also relevant that the images are not dwelled upon; the images appear for only a few seconds, and are not replayed during the broadcast. Finally, while we can understand why many viewers may have perceived the player's touchdown celebration as plainly inappropriate, we do not believe that his fully clothed display titillates or rises to the level of shocking behavior. Accordingly, we deny the complaints.

17.   "Medium" (January 17, 2005)[289]

230.   *The Programming.* The Commission received a complaint concerning the NBC Television Network ("NBC") broadcast of the program "Medium," at 9:00 p.m. Central Standard Time on January 17, 2005. The Enforcement Bureau requested and received a videotape of the program from NBC. A review of the tape discloses that the episode begins with a husband and wife being counseled by a therapist in an office setting. During the course of conversation with the couple, the therapist asks the husband to act out his selfish feelings by doing something with (or to) his wife, even if society might not approve of the act, and tells him that he should not be embarrassed because the therapist "has seen it all." In response, the husband stands up and faces this wife. He then pulls out a gun from his waist, and shoots his wife in the face.[290] The complainant objects to this portrayal of sex associated with violence against women broadcast at that hour of the evening.

231.   *Indecency Analysis.* As discussed above, our definition of indecent programming is limited to material that describes or depicts sexual or excretory organs or activities.[291] Violence *per se* is not currently within the defined subject matter scope of these limitations on broadcast programming. The complained-of portion of the episode arguably contains dialogue that suggests the possibility that the husband might wish to engage in some kind of sexual activity with his wife. However, no such activity is described or takes place, and thus the material is not within the scope of our indecency definition. Accordingly, we must deny the complaint.

232.   We wish to emphasize, however, that we understand the concerns of the complainant and others with the issue of violent programming on television, as well as the bizarre and shocking violence that is portrayed in the complained-of episode. Last year, at Congress's urging, we initiated a proceeding to examine violent television programming and its impact on children.[292] In doing so, we sought information about the nature and amount of violent television programming, its effects, what measures are available to control exposure to media violence, and the need for and the legal basis of our ability, if any, to regulate in this area. We have invited the public to submit comments for our consideration, and are currently reviewing those comments and determining our next steps.

IV.   ORDERING CLAUSES

233.   Accordingly, IT IS ORDERED, pursuant to section 503(b) of the Communications Act of 1934, as amended, and section 1.80 of the Commission's rules, that NBC Telemundo License Co., licensee of Station KWHY-TV, Los Angeles, California is hereby NOTIFIED of its APPARENT LIABILITY FOR FORFEITURE in the amount of $32,500 for willfully violating 18 U.S.C. § 1464 and section 73.3999 of the Commission's rules by its October 9, 2004, broadcast of the movie "Con El Corazon En La Mano."[293]

---

[289] FCC File No. EB-05-IH-0463.

[290] The complaint states that the husband "unzips his pants" before shooting his wife, but our review of the videotape shows that the husband appears to simply remove a handgun from the area of his waist. No unzipping of pants is shown or heard during the scene.

[291] *See Indecency Policy Statement,* 16 FCC Rcd at 8000 ¶ 4 (noting that "in addition, the [*Pacifica*] Court quoted the Commission's definition of indecency with apparent approval. The definition, "language or material that, in context depicts or describes, in terms patently offensive as measured by contemporary community standards for the broadcast medium, sexual or excretory organs," has remained substantially unchanged since the time of the *Pacifica* decision") (internal citations omitted).

[292] *See Violent Television Programming and Its Impact on Children,* Notice of Inquiry, 19 FCC Rcd 14394 (2004).

[293] NAL Account Number 200632080007, FRN No. 0014139422, Facility ID No. 26231.

234.   IT IS FURTHER ORDERED that a copy of this *NAL and MO&O* shall be sent by Certified Mail, Return Receipt Requested, to F. William LeBeau, Senior Regulatory Counsel & Assistant Secretary, NBC Universal, Inc., 1299 Pennsylvania Avenue, N.W., 11th Floor, Washington, D.C. 20004.

235.   IT IS FURTHER ORDERED, pursuant to section 503(b) of the Communications Act of 1934, as amended, and section 1.80 of the Commission's rules, that Sherjan Broadcasting Company, Inc., licensee of Station WJAN-CA, Miami, Florida, is hereby NOTIFIED of its APPARENT LIABILITY FOR FORFEITURE in the amount of $32,500 for willfully violating 18 U.S.C. § 1464 and section 73.3999 of the Commission's rules by its October 19, 2004, broadcast of the "Fernando Hidalgo Show."[294]

236.   IT IS FURTHER ORDERED that a copy of this *NAL and MO&O* shall be sent by Certified Mail, Return Receipt Requested, to Peter Tannenwald, counsel for Sherjan Broadcasting Company, Inc., Irwin Campbell & Tannenwald, PC, 1730 Rhode Island Avenue, N.W., Suite 200, Washington, D.C. 20036-3101.

237.   IT IS FURTHER ORDERED, pursuant to section 503(b) of the Communications Act of 1934, as amended, and section 1.80 of the Commission's rules, that Aerco Broadcasting Corp., licensee of Station WSJU-TV, San Juan, Puerto Rico, is hereby NOTIFIED of its APPARENT LIABILITY FOR FORFEITURE in the amount of $220,000 for willfully and repeatedly violating 18 U.S.C. § 1464 and section 73.3999 of the Commission's rules by its broadcast of various music videos, described above in the *NAL and MO&O*, during the "Video Musicales" program from January through March 2002.[295]

238.   IT IS FURTHER ORDERED that a copy of this *NAL and MO&O* shall be sent by Certified Mail, Return Receipt Requested, to John A. Borsari, counsel for Aerco Broadcasting Corp., John A. Borsari & Associates, PLLC, 2111 Wilson Blvd., P.O. Box 100009, Suite 700, Arlington, Virginia 22210; and David Ramos, D'Vanguardia, 497 Ave. E. Pol. Apartado 187, San Juan, Puerto Rico 00926-5636.

239.   IT IS FURTHER ORDERED, pursuant to section 503(b) of the Communications Act of 1934, as amended, and section 1.80 of the Commission's rules, that WBDC Broadcasting, Inc., licensee of Station WBDC-TV, Washington, D.C., is hereby NOTIFIED of its APPARENT LIABILITY FOR FORFEITURE in the amount of $27,500 for willfully violating 18 U.S.C. § 1464 and section 73.3999 of the Commission's rules by its February 8, 2004 broadcast of "The Surreal Life 2."[296]

240.   IT IS FURTHER ORDERED that a copy of this *NAL and MO&O* shall be sent by Certified Mail, Return Receipt Requested, to Arthur H. Harding, Fleischman and Walsh, LLP, counsel for the WB Television Network, 1919 Pennsylvania Avenue, N.W., Suite 600, Washington, D.C. 20006; R. Clark Wadlow and Thomas P. Van Wazer, Sidley Austin Brown & Wood LLP, counsel for WBDC Broadcasting, Inc., 1501 K Street, N.W., 10th Floor, Washington, D.C. 20005; and Dan Issett, Director of Corporate and Government Affairs, Parents Television Council, 325 S. Patrick Street, Alexandria, Virginia 22314.

241.   IT IS FURTHER ORDERED, pursuant to section 503(b) of the Communications Act of 1934, as amended, and section 1.80 of the Commission's rules, that San Mateo County Community College District, licensee of noncommercial educational Station KCSM-TV, San Mateo, California, is hereby NOTIFIED of its APPARENT LIABILITY FOR FORFEITURE in the amount of $15,000 for willfully violating 18 U.S.C. § 1464 and section 73.3999 of the Commission's rules by its broadcast of "The Blues: Godfathers and Sons" on March 11, 2004.[297]

242.   IT IS FURTHER ORDERED that a copy of this *NAL and MO&O* shall be sent by Certified Mail, Return Receipt Requested, to Marilyn R. Lawrence, General Manager, Station KCSM-TV, San Mateo County Community College District, 1700 West Hillsdale Blvd, San Mateo, California 94402.

243.   IT IS FURTHER ORDERED, pursuant to section 503(b) of the Communications Act of 1934, as amended, and section 1.80 of the Commission's rules, that KTVI License, Inc., licensee of Station KTVI(TV), St. Louis, Missouri, is hereby NOTIFIED of its APPARENT LIABILITY FOR FORFEITURE in the amount of

---

[294] NAL Account Number 200632080008, FRN No. 0003756897, Facility ID No. 60165.

[295] NAL Account Number 200632080010, FRN No. 0003732435, Facility ID No. 4077.

[296] NAL Account Number 200632080011, FRN No. 0002833267, Facility ID No. 30576.

[297] NAL Account Number 200632080012, FRN No. 0001545185, Facility ID No. 58912.

APPENDIX A

$27,500 for willfully violating 18 U.S.C. § 1464 and section 73.3999 of the Commission's rules by its broadcast of "The Pursuit of D.B. Cooper" on March 15, 2003.[298]

244.   IT IS FURTHER ORDERED that a copy of this *NAL and MO&O* shall be sent by Certified Mail, Return Receipt Requested, to John C. Quale, Counsel for KTVI License, Inc., Skadden Arps Meagher & Flom, LLP, 1440 New York Avenue, N.W., Washington, D.C. 20005-2111.

245.   IT IS FURTHER ORDERED, pursuant to section 1.80 of the Commission's rules, that within thirty (30) days of the release of these *NALs*, each licensee identified above SHALL PAY the full amount of its proposed forfeiture or SHALL FILE a written statement seeking reduction or cancellation of their proposed forfeiture.

246.   Payment of each forfeiture must be made by check or similar instrument, payable to the order of the Federal Communications Commission. Payments must include the relevant NAL/Acct. No. and FRN No. referenced above. Payment by check or money order may be mailed to Federal Communications Commission, P.O. Box 358340, Pittsburgh, Pennsylvania 15251-8340. Payment by overnight mail may be sent to Mellon Bank/LB 358340, 500 Ross Street, Room 1540670, Pittsburgh, Pennsylvania 15251. Payment by wire transfer may be made to ABA Number 043000261, receiving bank Mellon Bank, and account number 911-6106.

247.   The responses, if any, must be mailed to William H. Davenport, Chief, Investigations and Hearings Division, Enforcement Bureau, Federal Communications Commission, 445 12th Street, S.W., Room 4-C330, Washington D.C. 20554, and MUST INCLUDE the relevant NAL/Acct. No. referenced for each proposed forfeiture above.

248.   The Commission will not consider reducing or canceling a forfeiture in response to a claim of inability to pay unless the respondent submits: (1) federal tax returns for the most recent three-year period; (2) financial statements prepared according to generally accepted accounting practices ("GAAP"); or (3) some other reliable and objective documentation that accurately reflects the respondent's current financial status. Any claim of inability to pay must specifically identify the basis for the claim by reference to the financial documentation submitted.

249.   Requests for payment of the full amount of these *NALs* under an installment plan should be sent to: Associate Managing Director -- Financial Operations, 445 12th Street, S.W., Room 1-A625, Washington, D.C. 20554.[299]

250.   Accordingly, IT IS ORDERED that the complaints in the above-referenced *NAL* proceedings ARE GRANTED to the extent indicated herein, AND ARE OTHERWISE DENIED, and the complaint proceedings ARE HEREBY TERMINATED.

251.   IT IS FURTHER ORDERED that the complaints referenced in these *NALs and MO&O* are GRANTED to extent set forth herein and otherwise DENIED.[300]

FEDERAL COMMUNICATIONS COMMISSION

Marlene H. Dortch
Secretary

---

[298] NAL Account Number 200632080089, FRN No. 0003476009, Facility ID No. 35693.

[299] *See* 47 C.F.R. § 1.1914.

[300] Consistent with section 503(b) of the Act and consistent Commission practice, for the purposes of the forfeiture proceeding initiated by each *NAL* in this *Order*, the only party or parties to such proceeding will be the licensee or licensees specified above.

Federal Communications Commission

FCC 06-17

STATEMENT OF
CHAIRMAN KEVIN J. MARTIN

Re: *Complaints Against Various Television Licensees Concerning Their February 1, 2004 Broadcast of the*
Super Bowl XXXVIII Halftime Show; Complaints Regarding Various Television Broadcasts Between
February 2, 2002 and March 8, 2005; Complaints Against Various Television Licensees Concerning Their
December 31, 2004 Broadcast of the Program "Without A Trace"

Congress has long prohibited the broadcasting of indecent and profane material and the courts have upheld challenges to these standards. But the number of complaints received by the Commission has risen year after year. They have grown from hundreds, to hundreds of thousands. And the number of programs that trigger these complaints continues to increase as well. I share the concerns of the public - and of parents, in particular - that are voiced in these complaints.

I believe the Commission has a legal responsibility to respond to them and resolve them in a consistent and effective manner. So I am pleased that with the decisions released today the Commission is resolving hundreds of thousands of complaints against various broadcast licensees related to their televising of 49 different programs. These decisions, taken both individually and as a whole, demonstrate the Commission's continued commitment to enforcing the law prohibiting the airing of obscene, indecent and profane material.

Additionally, the Commission today affirms its initial finding that the broadcast of the Super Bowl XXXVIII Halftime Show was actionably indecent. We appropriately reject the argument that CBS continues to make that this material is not indecent. That argument runs counter to Commission precedent and common sense.

241

STATEMENT OF
COMMISSIONER MICHAEL J. COPPS

Re: *Complaints Regarding Various Television Broadcasts Between January 1, 2002 and March 12, 2005*

    Complaints Against Various Television Licensees Concerning Their December 31, 2004 Broadcast of the Program "Without A Trace," Notice of Apparent Liability for Forfeiture

    Complaints Against Various Television Licensees Concerning Their February 1, 2004, Broadcast of the Super Bowl XXXVIII Halftime Show, Forfeiture Order

    In the past, the Commission too often addressed indecency complaints with little discussion or analysis, relying instead on generalized pronouncements. Such an approach served neither aggrieved citizens nor the broadcast industry. Today, the Commission not only moves forward to address a number of pending complaints, but does so in a manner that better analyzes each broadcast and explains how the Commission determines whether a particular broadcast is indecent. Although it may never be possible to provide 100 percent certain guidance because we must always take into account specific and often-differing contexts, the approach in today's orders can help to develop such guidance and to establish precedents. This measured process, common in jurisprudence, may not satisfy those who clamor for immediate certainty in an uncertain world, but it may just be the best way to develop workable rules of the road.

    Today's Orders highlight two additional issues with which the Commission must come to terms. First, it is time for the Commission to look at indecency in the broader context of its decisions on media consolidation. In 2003 the FCC sought to weaken its remaining media concentration safeguards without even considering whether there is a link between increasing media consolidation and increasing indecency. Such links have been shown in studies and testified to by a variety of expert witnesses. The record clearly demonstrates that an overwhelming number of the Commission's indecency citations have gone to a few huge media conglomerates. One recent study showed that the four largest radio station groups which controlled just under half the radio audience were responsible for a whopping 96 percent of the indecency fines levied by the FCC from 2000 to 2003.

    One of the reasons for the huge volume of complaints about excessive sex and graphic violence in the programming we are fed may be that people feel increasingly divorced from their "local" media. They believe the media no longer respond to their local communities. As media conglomerates grow ever larger and station control moves farther away from the local community, community standards seem to count for less when programming decisions are made. Years ago we had independent programming created from a diversity of sources. Networks would then decide which programming to distribute. Then local affiliates would independently decide whether to air that programming. This provided some real checks and balances. Nowadays so many of these decisions are made by vertically-integrated conglomerates headquartered far away from the communities they are supposed to be serving—entities that all too often control both the distribution *and* the production content of the programming.

    If heightened media consolidation is indeed a source for the violence and indecency that upset so many parents, shouldn't the Commission be cranking that into its decisions on further loosening of the ownership rules? I hope the Commission, before voting again on loosening its media concentration protections, will finally take a serious look at this link and amass a credible body of evidence and not act again without the facts, as it did in 2003.

    Second, a number of these complaints concern graphic broadcast violence. The Commission states that it has taken comment on this issue in another docket. It is time for us to step up to the plate and tackle the issue of violence in the media. The U.S. Surgeon General, the American Academy of Pediatrics, the American Psychological Association, the American Medical Association, and countless other medical and scientific organizations that have studied this issue have reached the same conclusion: exposure to graphic and excessive media violence has harmful effects on the physical and mental health of our children. We need to complete this proceeding.

APPENDIX A

STATEMENT OF
COMMISSIONER JONATHAN S. ADELSTEIN
CONCURRING IN PART, DISSENTING IN PART

Re: *Complaints Regarding Various Television Broadcasts Between February 2, 2002 and March 8, 2005,* Notices of Apparent Liability and Memorandum Opinion and Order

I have sworn an oath to uphold the Constitution[301] and to carry out the laws adopted by Congress.[302] Trying to find a balance between these obligations has been challenging in many of the indecency cases that I have decided. I believe it is our duty to regulate the broadcast of indecent material to the fullest extent permissible by the Constitution because safeguarding the well-being of our children is a compelling national interest.[303] I therefore have supported efforts to step up our enforcement of indecency laws since I joined the Commission.

The Commission's authority to regulate indecency over the public airwaves was narrowly upheld by the Supreme Court with the admonition that we should exercise that authority with the utmost restraint, lest we inhibit constitutional rights and transgress constitutional limitations on government regulation of protected speech.[304] Given the Court's guidance in *Pacifica,* the Commission has repeatedly stated that we would judiciously walk a "tightrope" in exercising our regulatory authority.[305] Hence, within this legal context, a rational and principled "restrained enforcement policy" is not a matter of mere regulatory convenience. It is a constitutional requirement.[306]

Accordingly, I concur in part and dissent in part with today's decision because, while in some ways the decision does not go far enough, in other ways it goes too far. Significantly, it abruptly departs from our precedents by adopting a new, weaker enforcement mechanism that arbitrarily fails to assess fines against broadcasters who have aired indecent material. Additionally, while today's decision appropriately identifies violations of our indecency laws, not every instance determined to be indecent meets that standard.

We have previously sought to identify all broadcasters who have aired indecent material and hold them accountable. In this Order, however, the Commission inexplicably fines only the licensee whose broadcast of indecent material was the subject of a viewer's complaint, even though we know millions of other Americans were exposed to the offending broadcast. I cannot find anywhere in the law that Congress told us to apply indecency regulations only to those stations against which a complaint was specifically lodged. The law requires us to prohibit the broadcast of indecent material, period. This means that we must enforce the law anywhere we determine it has been violated. It is willful blindness to decide, with respect to network broadcasts we know aired nationwide, that we will only enforce the law against the local station that happens to be the target of viewer complaints. How can

---

[301] U.S. CONST., amend. I.

[302] Congress has specifically forbidden the broadcast of obscene, indecent or profane language. 18 U.S.C. § 1464. It has also forbidden censorship. 47 U.S.C. § 326.

[303] *See, e.g., N.Y. v. Ferber,* 458 U.S. 747, 756-57 (1982).

[304] *See FCC v. Pacifica Foundation,* 438 U.S. 726, 750 (1978) (emphasizing the "narrowness" of the Court's holding); *Action for Children's Television v. FCC,* 852 F.2d 1332, 1344 (D.C. Cir. 1988) (*"ACT I"*) ("Broadcast material that is indecent but not obscene is protected by the [F]irst [A]mendment.").

[305] *See* Brief for Petitioner, FCC, 1978 WL 206838 at *9.

[306] *ACT I, supra* note 4, at 1344 ("[T]he FCC may regulate [indecent] material only with due respect for the high value our Constitution places on freedom and choice in what the people say and hear."); *Id.* at 1340 n.14 ("[T]he potentially chilling effect of the FCC's generic definition of indecency will be tempered by the Commission's restrained enforcement policy."). *See also Complaints Regarding Various Television Broadcasts Between February 2, 2002 and March 8, 2005,* Notices of Apparent Liability and Memorandum Opinion and Order, FCC 06-17 at note 11 (rel. March 15, 2006).

we impose a fine solely on certain local broadcasters, despite having repeatedly said that the Commission applies a national indecency standard – not a local one?[307]

The failure to enforce the rules against some stations but not others is not what the courts had in mind when they counseled restraint. In fact, the Supreme Court's decision in *Pacifica* was based on the uniquely pervasive characteristics of broadcast media.[308] It is patently arbitrary to hold some stations but not others accountable for the same broadcast. We recognized this just two years ago in *Married By America*.[309] The Commission simply inquired who aired the indecent broadcast and fined all of those stations that did so.

In the *Super Bowl XXXVIII Halftime Show* decision, we held only those stations owned and operated by the CBS network responsible, under the theory that the affiliates did not expect the incident and it was primarily the network's fault.[310] I dissented in part to that case because I believed we needed to apply the same sanction to every station that aired the offending material. I raise similar concerns today, in the context of the instant Order.

The Commission is constitutionally obligated to decide broadcast indecency and profanity cases based on the "contemporary community standard," which is "that of the average broadcast viewer or listener." The Commission has explained the "contemporary community standard," as follows:

> We rely on our collective experience and knowledge, developed through constant interaction with lawmakers, courts, broadcasters, public interest groups and ordinary citizens, to keep abreast of contemporary community standards for the broadcast medium.[311]

I am concerned that today's Order overreaches with its expansion of the scope of indecency and profanity law, without first doing what is necessary to determine the appropriate contemporary community standard.

The Order builds on one of the most difficult cases we have ever decided, *Golden Globe Awards*,[312] and stretches it beyond the limits of our precedents and constitutional authority. The precedent set in that case has been contested by numerous broadcasters, constitutional scholars and public interest groups who have asked us to revisit and clarify our reasoning and decision. Rather than reexamining that case, the majority uses the decision as a springboard to add new words to the pantheon of those deemed to be inherently sexual or excretory, and consequently indecent and profane, irrespective of their common meaning or of a fleeting and isolated use. By failing to address the many serious concerns raised in the reconsideration petitions filed in the *Golden Globe Awards* case, before prohibiting the use of additional words, the Commission falls short of meeting the constitutional standard and walking the tightrope of a restrained enforcement policy.

---

[307] *See, e.g., In re Sagittarius Broadcasting Corporation,* Memorandum Opinion and Order, 7 FCC Rcd 6873, 6876 (1992) (subsequent history omitted).

[308] *See Pacifica Found.,* 438 U.S. at 748-49 (recognizing the "uniquely pervasive presence" of broadcast media "in the lives of all Americans"). In today's Order, paragraph 10, the Commission relies upon the same rationale.

[309] *See Complaints Against Various Licensees Regarding Their Broadcast of the Fox Television Network Program "Married by America" on April 7, 2003,* Notice of Apparent Liability for Forfeiture, 19 FCC Rcd 20191, 20196 (2004) (proposing a $7,000 forfeiture against each Fox Station and Fox Affiliate station); *reconsideration pending. See also Clear Channel Broad. Licenses, Inc.,* 19 FCC Rcd 6773, 6779 (2004) (proposing a $495,000 fine based on a "per utterance" calculation, and directing an investigation into stations owned by other licensees that broadcast the indecent program). In the instant Omnibus Order, however, the Commission inexplicably fines only the licensee whose broadcast of indecent material was actually the subject of a viewer's complaint to the Commission. *Id.* at ¶ 71.

[310] *See Complaints Against Various Television Licensees Concerning Their February 1, 2004, Broadcast of the Super Bowl XXXVIII Halftime Show,* Notice of Apparent Liability, 19 FCC Rcd 19230 (2004).

[311] *In re Infinity Radio License, Inc.,* Memorandum Opinion and Order, 19 FCC Rcd 5022, 5026 (2004).

[312] *In re Complaints Against Broadcast Licensees Regarding Their Airing of the "Golden Globe Awards" Program,* Memorandum Opinion and Order, 19 FCC Rcd 4975 (2004); *petitions for stay and reconsideration pending.*

This approach endangers the very authority we so delicately retain to enforce broadcast decency rules. If the Commission in its zeal oversteps and finds our authority circumscribed by the courts, we may forever lose the ability to protect children from the airing of indecent material, barring an unlikely constitutional amendment setting limitations on the First Amendment freedoms.

The perilous course taken today is evident in the approach to the acclaimed Martin Scorsese documentary, "The Blues: Godfathers and Sons." It is clear from a common sense viewing of the program that coarse language is a part of the culture of the individuals being portrayed. To accurately reflect their viewpoint and emotions about blues music requires airing of certain material that, if prohibited, would undercut the ability of the filmmaker to convey the reality of the subject of the documentary. This contextual reasoning is consistent with our decisions in *Saving Private Ryan*[313] and *Schindler's List*.[314]

The Commission has repeatedly reaffirmed, and the courts have consistently underscored, the importance of content *and* context. The majority's decision today dangerously departs from those precedents. It is certain to strike fear in the hearts of news and documentary makers, and broadcasters that air them, which could chill the future expression of constitutionally protected speech.

We should be mindful of Justice Harlan's observation in *Cohen v. California*.[315] Writing for the Court, he observed:

> [W]ords are often chosen as much for their emotive as their cognitive force. We cannot sanction the view that the Constitution, while solicitous of the cognitive content of individual speech, has little or no regard for that emotive function which, practically speaking, may often be the more important element of the overall message sought to be communicated.[316]

Given all of these considerations, I find that today's decision, while reaching some appropriate conclusions both in identifying indecent material and in dismissing complaints, is in some ways dangerously off the mark. I cannot agree that it offers a coherent, principled long-term framework that is rooted in common sense. In fact, it may put at risk the very authority to protect children that it exercises so vigorously.

---

[313] *In the Matter of Complaints Against Various Television Licensees Regarding Their Broadcast on November 11, 2004, of the ABC Television Network's Presentation of the Film, "Saving Private Ryan,"* Memorandum Opinion and Order, 20 FCC Rcd 4507, 4513 (2005) ("Deleting all [indecent] language or inserting milder language or bleeping sounds into the film would have altered the nature of the artistic work and diminished the power, realism and immediacy of the film experience for viewers"); *See also Peter Branton*, Letter by Direction of the Commission, 6 FCC Rcd 610 (1991) (concluding that repeated use of the f-word in a recorded news interview program not indecent in context).

[314] *In the Matter of WPBN/WTOM License Subsidiary, Inc.*, 15 FCC Rcd 1838 (2000).

[315] 403 U.S. 15 (1971).

[316] *Id*. at 26 ("We cannot indulge the facile assumption that one can forbid particular words without also running a substantial risk of suppressing ideas in the process").

STATEMENT OF
COMMISSIONER DEBORAH TAYLOR TATE

Re: Complaints Against Various Television Licensees Concerning Their February 1, 2004, Broadcast of the Super Bowl XXXVIII Halftime Show, Forfeiture Order; *Complaints Against Various Television Licensees Concerning Their December 31, 2004 Broadcast of the Program "Without A Trace,"* Notice of Apparent Liability; *Complaints Regarding Various Television Broadcasts Between February 2, 2002 and March 8, 2005,* Notices of Apparent Liability and Memorandum Opinion and Order

Today marks my first opportunity as a member of the Federal Communications Commission to uphold our responsibility to enforce the federal statute prohibiting the airing of obscene, indecent or profane language.[317] To be clear – I take this responsibility very seriously. Not only is this the law, but it also is the right thing to do.

One of the bedrock principles of the Communications Act of 1934, as amended, is that the airwaves belong to the public. Much like public spaces and national landmarks, these are scarce and finite resources that must be preserved for the benefit of all Americans. If numbers are any indication, many Americans are not happy about the way that their airwaves are being utilized. The number of complaints filed with the FCC reached over one million in 2004. Indeed, since taking office in January 2006, I have received hundreds of personal e-mails from people all over this country who are unhappy with the content to which they – and, in particular, their families – are subjected.

I have applauded those cable and DBS providers for the tools they have provided to help parents and other concerned citizens filter out objectionable content. Parental controls incorporated into cable and DBS set-top boxes, along with the V-Chip, make it possible to block programming based upon its content rating. However, these tools, even when used properly, are not a complete solution. One of the main reasons for that is because much of the content broadcast, including live sporting events and commercials, are not rated under the two systems currently in use.

I also believe that consumers have an important role to play as well. Caregivers – parents, in particular – need to take an active role in monitoring the content to which children are exposed. Even the most diligent parent, however, cannot be expected to protect their children from indecent material broadcast during live sporting events or in commercials that appear during what is marketed to be "appropriate" programming.

Today, we are making significant strides toward addressing the backlog of indecency complaints before this agency. The rules are simple – you break them and we will enforce the law, just as we are doing today. Both the public and the broadcasters deserve prompt and timely resolution of complaints as they are filed, and I am glad to see us act to resolve these complaints. At the same time, however, I would like to raise a few concerns regarding the complaints we address in these decisions.

First, I would like to discuss the complaint regarding the 6:30 p.m. Eastern Daylight Time airing of an episode of *The Simpsons*. The *Order* concludes that this segment is not indecent, in part because of the fact that *The Simpsons* is a cartoon. Generally speaking, cartoons appeal to children, though some may cater to both children and adults simultaneously. Nevertheless, the fact remains that children were extremely likely to have been in the viewing audience when this scene was broadcast. Indeed, the marketing is aimed at children. If the scene had involved real actors in living color, at 5:30 p.m. Central Standard Time, I wonder if our decision would have been different? One might argue that the cartoon medium may be a more insidious means of exposing young people to such content. By their very nature, cartoons do not accurately portray reality, and in this instance the use of animation may well serve to present that material in a more flattering light than it would if it were depicted through live video. I stop short of disagreeing with our decision in this case, but note that the animated nature of the broadcast, in my opinion, may be cause for taking an even closer look in the context of our indecency analysis.

Second, our conclusion regarding the 9:00 p.m. Central Standard Time airing of an episode of *Medium* in which a woman is shot at point-blank range in the face by her husband gives me pause. While I agree with the result

---

[317] *See* 18 U.S.C. § 1464.

in this case, I question our conclusion that the sequence constitutes violence *per se* and therefore falls outside the scope of the Commission's definition of indecency. Without question, this scene is violent, graphically so. Moreover, it is presented in a way that appears clearly designed to maximize its shock value. And therein lies my concern. One of the primary ways that this scene shocks is that it leads the viewer to believe that the action is headed in one direction – through dialogue and actions which suggest that interaction of a sexual nature is about to occur – and then abruptly erupts in another – the brutally violent shooting of a wife by her husband, in the head, at point-blank range. Even though the Commission's authority under Section 1464 is limited to indecent, obscene, and profane content, and thus does not extend to violent matter, the use of violence as the "punch line" of titillating sexual innuendo should not insulate broadcast licensees from our authority. To the contrary, the use of sexual innuendo may, depending on the specific case, subject a licensee to potential forfeiture, regardless of the overall violent nature of the sequence in which such sexual innuendo is used.

*   *   *

       Finally, I would like to express my hope and belief that the problem of indecent material is one that can be solved. Programmers, artists, writers, broadcasters, networks, advertisers, parents, public interest groups, and, yes, even Commissioners can protect two of our country's most valuable resources: the public airwaves and our children's minds. We must take a stand against programming that robs our children of their innocence and constitutes an unwarranted intrusion into our homes. By working together, we should promote the creation of programming that is not just entertaining, but also positive, educational, healthful, and, perhaps, even inspiring.

Before the
Federal Communications Commission
Washington, D.C. 20554

In the Matter of)
)
Complaints Against Various Television Licensees) File No. EB-05-IH-0035[1]
Concerning Their December 31, 2004 Broadcast)
of the Program "Without A Trace")

NOTICE OF APPARENT LIABILITY FOR FORFEITURE

Adopted: February 21, 2006   **Released: March 15, 2006**

By the Commission: Chairman Martin, Commissioners Copps and Tate issuing separate statements; Commissioner Adelstein concurring and issuing a statement.

I.   INTRODUCTION

1.   In this *Notice of Apparent Liability for Forfeiture ("NAL")*, issued pursuant to section 503(b) of the Communications Act of 1934, as amended (the "Act"), and section 1.80 of the Commission's rules,[2] we find that the CBS Television Network ("CBS") affiliated stations and CBS owned-and-operated stations listed in Attachment A aired material that apparently violates the federal restrictions regarding the broadcast of indecent material.[3] Specifically, during the *Our Sons and Daughters* episode of the CBS program "Without a Trace" on December 31, 2004, at 9:00 p.m. in the Central and Mountain Time Zones, these licensees each broadcast material graphically depicting teenage boys and girls participating in a sexual orgy. Based upon our review of the facts and circumstances of this case, we conclude that the licensees listed in Attachment A are apparently liable for a monetary forfeiture in the amount of $32,500 per station for broadcasting indecent material in apparent violation of 18 U.S.C. § 1464 and section 73.3999 of the Commission's rules.

II.   BACKGROUND

2.   Section 1464 of title 18, United States Code, prohibits the broadcast of obscene, indecent, or profane programming.[4] The FCC rules implementing that statute, a subsequent statute establishing a "safe harbor" during certain hours, and the Act prohibit radio and television stations from broadcasting obscene material at any time and indecent material between 6 a.m. and 10 p.m.

3.   ***Indecency Analysis.*** Enforcement of the provisions restricting the broadcast of indecent, obscene, or profane material is an important component of the Commission's overall responsibility over

---

[1] The NAL/Acct. Nos. and FRN numbers for each licensee subject to this Notice of Apparent Liability For Forfeiture are contained in Attachment A hereto.

[2] 47 U.S.C. § 503(b); 47 C.F.R. § 1.80.

[3] *See* 18 U.S.C. § 1464, 47 C.F.R. § 73.3999.

[4] 18 U.S.C. § 1464.

broadcast radio and television operations. At the same time, however, the Commission must be mindful of the First Amendment to the United States Constitution and section 326 of the Act, which prohibit the Commission from censoring program material or interfering with broadcasters' free speech rights.[5] As such, in making indecency determinations, the Commission proceeds cautiously and with appropriate restraint.[6]

4. The Commission defines indecent speech as material that, in context, depicts or describes sexual or excretory activities or organs in terms patently offensive as measured by contemporary community standards for the broadcast medium.[7]

> Indecency findings involve at least two fundamental determinations. First, the material alleged to be indecent must fall within the subject matter scope of our indecency definition—that is, the material must describe or depict sexual or excretory organs or activities. . . . Second, the broadcast must be *patently offensive* as measured by contemporary community standards for the broadcast medium.[8]

5. In our assessment of whether broadcast material is patently offensive, "the *full context* in which the material appeared is critically important."[9] Three principal factors are significant to this contextual analysis: (1) the explicitness or graphic nature of the description; (2) whether the material dwells on or repeats at length descriptions of sexual or excretory organs or activities; and (3) whether the

---

[5] U.S. CONST., amend. I; 47 U.S.C. § 326. *See also United States v. Playboy Entertainment Group, Inc.,* 529 U.S. 803, 813-15 (2000).

[6] *See Action for Children's Television v. FCC,* 852 F.2d 1332, 1344, 1340 n. 14 (1988) ("*ACT I*") (stating that "[b]roadcast material that is indecent but not obscene is protected by the First Amendment; the FCC may regulate such material only with due respect for the high value our Constitution places on freedom and choice in what people may say and hear," and that any "potential chilling effect of the FCC's generic definition of indecency will be tempered by the Commission's restrained enforcement policy.").

[7] *See Infinity Broadcasting Corporation of Pennsylvania,* Memorandum Opinion and Order, 2 FCC Rcd 2705 (1987) (subsequent history omitted) (citing *Pacifica Foundation,* Memorandum Opinion and Order, 56 FCC 2d 94, 98 (1975), *aff'd sub nom. Pacifica,* 438 U.S. 726).

[8] *Industry Guidance on the Commission's Case Law Interpreting 18 U.S.C. §1464 and Enforcement Policies Regarding Broadcast Indecency,* Policy Statement, 16 FCC Rcd 7999, 8002 ¶¶ 7-8 (2001) ("*Indecency Policy Statement*") (emphasis in original). In applying the "community standards for the broadcast medium" criterion, the Commission has stated:

> The determination as to whether certain programming is patently offensive is not a local one and does not encompass any particular geographic area. Rather, the standard is that of an average broadcast viewer or listener and not the sensibilities of any individual complainant.

WPBN/WTOM License Subsidiary, Inc., Memorandum Opinion and Order, 15 FCC Rcd 1838, 1841 ¶ 10 (2000) ("*WPBN/WTOM MO&O*"). The Commission's interpretation of the term "contemporary community standards" flows from its analysis of the definition of that term set forth in the Supreme Court's decision in *Hamling v. United States,* 418 U.S. 87 (1974), *reh'g denied,* 419 U.S. 885 (1974). In *Infinity Broadcasting Corporation of Pennsylvania (WYSP(FM)),* Memorandum Opinion and Order, 3 FCC Rcd 930 (1987) (subsequent history omitted), the Commission observed that in *Hamling,* which involved obscenity, "the Court explained that the purpose of 'contemporary community standards' was to ensure that material is judged neither on the basis of a decisionmaker's personal opinion, nor by its effect on a particularly sensitive or insensitive person or group." *Id.* at 933 (citing 418 U.S. at 107). The Commission also relied on the fact that the Court in *Hamling* indicated that decisionmakers need not use any precise geographic area in evaluating material. *Id.* at 933 (citing 418 U.S. at 104-05). Consistent with *Hamling,* the Commission concluded that its evaluation of allegedly indecent material is "not one based on a local standard, but one based on a broader standard for broadcasting generally." *Id.* at 933.

[9] *Indecency Policy Statement,* 16 FCC Rcd at 8002 ¶ 9 (emphasis in original).

material panders to, titillates, or shocks the audience.[10] In examining these three factors, we must weigh and balance them on a case-by-case basis to determine whether the broadcast material is patently offensive because "[e]ach indecency case presents its own particular mix of these, and possibly, other factors."[11] In particular cases, one or two of the factors may outweigh the others, either rendering the broadcast material patently offensive and consequently indecent,[12] or, alternatively, removing the broadcast material from the realm of indecency.

6.   In this *NAL*, we apply the two-pronged indecency analysis described above. Specifically, we first determine whether the complained-of material is within the scope of our indecency definition; *i.e.*, whether it describes or depicts sexual or excretory activities or organs. We then turn to the three principal factors of the second prong to determine whether, taken in context, the material is patently offensive as measured by contemporary community standards for the broadcast medium.

7.   Our contextual analysis takes into account the manner and purpose of broadcast material.[13] For example, material that panders to, titillates, or shocks the audience is treated quite differently than material that is primarily used to educate or inform the audience. In particular, we recognize the need for caution with respect to complaints implicating the editorial judgment of broadcast licensees in presenting news and public affairs programming, as these matters are at the core of the First Amendment's free press guarantee.[14]

8.   ***Forfeiture Calculations.*** This *NAL* is issued pursuant to section 503(b)(1) of the Act. Under that provision, any person who is determined by the Commission to have willfully or repeatedly failed to comply with any provision of the Act or any rule, regulation, or order issued by the Commission or to have violated section 1464 of title 18, United States Code, shall be liable to the United States for a forfeiture penalty.[15] Section 312(f)(1) of the Act defines willful as "the conscious and deliberate commission or omission of [any] act, irrespective of any intent to violate" the law.[16] The legislative history to section 312(f)(1) of the Act clarifies that this definition of willful applies to both sections 312 and 503(b) of the Act,[17] and the Commission has so interpreted the term in the section 503(b) context.[18] We emphasize that every licensee is responsible for the decision to air particular programming and will be held accountable for violating federal restrictions on the willful or repeated broadcast of obscene, indecent, or profane material.

---

[10] *Id.* at 8002-15 ¶¶ 8-23.

[11] *Id.* at 8003 ¶ 10.

[12] *Id.* at 8009 ¶ 19 (*citing Tempe Radio, Inc (KUPD-FM)*, Notice of Apparent Liability for Forfeiture, 12 FCC Rcd 21828 (Mass Media Bur. 1997) (forfeiture paid), and *EZ New Orleans, Inc. (WEZB(FM))*, Notice of Apparent Liability for Forfeiture, 12 FCC Rcd 4147 (Mass Media Bur. 1997) (forfeiture paid) (finding that the extremely graphic or explicit nature of references to sex with children outweighed the fleeting nature of the references).

[13] *Indecency Policy Statement*, 16 FCC Rcd at 8010 ¶ 20 (noting that "the manner and purpose of a presentation may well preclude an indecency determination even though other factors, such as explicitness, might weigh in favor of an indecency finding").

[14] *See Syracuse Peace Council*, Memorandum Opinion and Order, 2 FCC Rcd 5043, 5050-51 ¶ 52 (1987) (subsequent history omitted) (eliminating the fairness doctrine, which placed an affirmative obligation on broadcasters to cover, and present contrasting viewpoints on, controversial issues of public importance).

[15] 47 U.S.C. § 503(b)(1)(B) & D. *See also* 47 C.F.R. 1.80(a)(1).

[16] 47 U.S.C. § 312(f)(1).

[17] *See* H.R. Rep. No. 97-765, 97th Cong. 2d Sess. 51 (1982).

[18] *See Southern California Broadcasting Co.*, Memorandum Opinion and Order, 6 FCC Rcd 4387, 4388 (1991).

9. The Commission's *Forfeiture Policy Statement* establishes a base forfeiture amount of $7,000 for the transmission of indecent or obscene materials.[19] The *Forfeiture Policy Statement* also specifies that the Commission shall adjust a forfeiture based upon consideration of the factors enumerated in section 503(b)(2)(D), such as "the nature, circumstances, extent and gravity of the violation, and, with respect to the violator, the degree of culpability, any history of prior offenses, ability to pay, and such other matters as justice may require."[20] The statutory maximum forfeiture amount for violations occurring on or after September 7, 2004, is $32,500.[21]

III. DISCUSSION

10. ***The Programming.*** The Commission received numerous complaints alleging that certain affiliates of CBS and CBS owned-and-operated stations (listed in Attachment A) broadcast indecent material during the *Our Sons and Daughters* episode of the CBS program "Without a Trace" on December 31, 2004, at 9:00 p.m. in the Central and Mountain Time Zones.

11. The December 31, 2004 episode at issue concerns an FBI investigation into the disappearance and possible rape of a high school student. During an interrogation, a witness recalls a party held at the home of a teenager. As she recounts the details of the party, the program cuts to a "flashback" scene. The scene -- which forms the basis of the viewer complaints -- consists of a series of shots of a number of teenagers engaged in various sexual activities, including sex between couples and among members of a group. Although the scene contains no nudity, it does depict male and female teenagers in various stages of undress. The scene also includes at least three shots depicting intercourse, two between couples and one "group sex" shot. In the culminating shot of the scene, the witness exclaims to the others in the party that the victim is a "porn star." The action briefly returns to the present, as the witness pauses in her story, then the flashback resumes, as the victim is shown wearing bra and panties, straddled on top of one male character, while two other male characters kiss her breast near the bra strap. The lower portion of the panties is shaded, but she is shown moving up and down while the male teenager thrusts his hips into her crotch.

12. ***Indecency Analysis.*** We find that the material meets the first prong of the indecency test. While no nudity is shown, it is clear, as detailed above, that the scene depicts numerous sexual activities.

13. We also find that the material is, in the context presented here, patently offensive as measured by contemporary community standards for the broadcast medium. Turning to the first principal factor in our contextual analysis, the scene is explicit and graphic. The material contains numerous depictions of sexual conduct among teenagers that are portrayed in such a manner that a child watching the program could easily discern that the teenagers shown in the scene were engaging in sexual activities, including apparent intercourse.[22] The background sounds, which include moaning, add to the graphic and explicit sexual nature of the depictions. The scene is not shot as clinical or educational material, and the movements, sounds, and comments contained in the scene are highly sexually charged.

---

[19] *See Commission's Forfeiture Policy Statement and Amendment of Section 1.80 of the Rules to Incorporate the Forfeiture Guidelines*, Report and Order, 12 FCC Rcd 17087, 17113 (1997), *recon. denied*, 15 FCC Rcd 303 (1999) ("*Forfeiture Policy Statement*"); *see also* 47 C.F.R. § 1.80(b).

[20] *Forfeiture Policy Statement*, 12 FCC Rcd at 17100-01 ¶ 27.

[21] *See Amendment of Section 1.80 of the Commission's Rules*, Order, 19 FCC Rcd 10945, 10946 ¶ 6 (2004) (amending rules to increase maximum penalties due to inflation since last adjustment of penalty rates).

[22] *See Complaints Against Various Licensees Regarding Their Broadcast of the Fox Television Network Program "Married By America" on April 7, 2003*, Notice of Apparent Liability for Forfeiture, 19 FCC Rcd 20191, 20194 ¶ 10 (2004) (finding that "although the nudity was pixilated, even a child would have known that the strippers were topless and that sexual activity was being shown").

14.   Next, although not dispositive, we find it relevant that the broadcast dwells on and repeatedly depicts the sexual material, the second principal factor in our analysis. The scene in question contains several depictions of apparent sexual intercourse.

15.   As for the third factor, we find that the complained-of material is pandering, titillating, and shocking to the audience. The explicit and lengthy nature of the depictions of sexual activity, including apparent intercourse, goes well beyond what the story line could reasonably be said to require. Moreover, the scene is all the more shocking because it depicts minors engaged in sexual activities.[23]

16.   In sum, because the scene is explicit, dwells upon sexual material, and is shocking and titillating, we conclude that the broadcast of the material at issue here is patently offensive under contemporary community standards for the broadcast medium and thus apparently indecent. The complained-of material was broadcast within the 6 a.m. to 10 p.m. time frame relevant to an indecency determination under section 73.3999 of the Commission's rules.[24] Therefore, there is a reasonable risk that children may have been in the viewing audience and the broadcast is legally actionable.

17.   *Forfeiture Calculation.* We find that the CBS affiliates and CBS owned-and-operated stations listed in Attachment A consciously and deliberately broadcast the episode in question. Accordingly, we find that each broadcast in apparent violation of 18 U.S.C. § 1464 and 47 C.F.R. § 73.3999 was willful within the meaning of section 503(b)(1) of the Act, and subject to forfeiture.

18.   We therefore turn to the proposed forfeiture amount, based on the factors enumerated in section 503(b)(2)(D) of the Act and the facts and circumstances of this case. We find that the statutory maximum of $32,500 is an appropriate proposed forfeiture amount for each violation arising out of the December 31, 2004 broadcasts.[25] The gravity of the apparent violation is heightened in this case because, as discussed above, the material graphically depicts teenage boys and girls participating in a sexual orgy. While there is no nudity, the scene is highly sexually charged and explicit. Moreover, the material is particularly egregious because it focuses on sex among children. In addition, the program is prerecorded, and CBS and its affiliates could have edited or declined the content prior to broadcast.[26] Therefore, we find that each of the licensees listed in Attachment A is apparently liable for a proposed forfeiture of $32,500 for broadcast of the December 31, 2004 episode of "Without A Trace." prior to 10 p.m.[27]

19.   Although we are informed that other stations not mentioned in any complaint also broadcast the complained-of episode of "Without A Trace," we propose forfeitures only against those licensees whose broadcasts of the material between 6 a.m. and 10 p.m. were actually the subject of viewer complaints to the Commission. We recognize that this approach differs from that taken in previous Commission decisions involving the broadcast of apparently indecent programming. Our commitment to an appropriately restrained enforcement policy, however, justifies this more limited approach towards the imposition of forfeiture penalties. Accordingly, we propose forfeitures as set forth in Attachment A.

---

[23] In any event, even if the depictions had been more essential to the program, the other two factors weigh heavily in favor of a finding of patent offensiveness as measured by contemporary community standards for the broadcast medium, so we would not alter our ultimate conclusion in this case.

[24] *See* 47 C.F.R. § 73.3999.

[25] *See supra* ¶ 9.

[26] 19 FCC Rcd at 21096 ¶ 16.

[27] The fact that the stations in question may not have originated the programming in question is irrelevant to whether there is an indecency violation. *See Review of the Commission's Regulations Governing Programming Practices of Broadcast Television Networks and Affiliates,* Notice of Proposed Rulemaking, 10 FCC Rcd 11951,11961, ¶ 20 (1995) (internal quotation omitted) ("We conclude that a licensee is not fulfilling his obligations to operate in the public interest, and is not operating in accordance with the express requirements of the Communications Act, if he agrees to accept programs on any basis other than his own reasonable decision that the programs are satisfactory.").

IV. ORDERING CLAUSES

20.   Accordingly, IT IS ORDERED, pursuant to section 503(b) of the Communications Act of 1934, as amended, and section 1.80 of the Commission's rules, that the licensees of the stations that are affiliates of the CBS Television Network and of the stations owned and operated by CBS listed in Attachment A are hereby NOTIFIED of their APPARENT LIABILITY FOR FORFEITURE in the amount of $32,500 per station for willfully violating 18 U.S.C. § 1464 and section 73.3999 of the Commission's rules by their broadcast of the program "Without a Trace" on December 31, 2004.

21.   IT IS FURTHER ORDERED that a copies of this *NAL* shall be sent by Certified Mail, Return Receipt Requested, to Anne Lucey, Senior Vice President, Regulatory Affairs, CBS, 1501 M Street, N.W., Suite 1100, Washington, D.C. 20005, and to the licensees of the stations listed in Attachment A, at their respective addresses noted therein.

22.   IT IS FURTHER ORDERED, pursuant to section 1.80 of the Commission's rules, that within thirty (30) days of the release of this *NAL*, each licensee identified in Attachment A SHALL PAY the full amount of its proposed forfeiture or SHALL FILE a written statement seeking reduction or cancellation of their proposed forfeiture.

23.   Payment of the forfeitures must be made by check or similar instrument, payable to the order of the Federal Communications Commission. Payments must include the relevant NAL/Acct. No. and FRN No. referenced in Attachment A. Payment by check or money order may be mailed to Federal Communications Commission, P.O. Box 358340, Pittsburgh, Pennsylvania 15251-8340. Payment by overnight mail may be sent to Mellon Bank/LB 358340, 500 Ross Street, Room 1540670, Pittsburgh, Pennsylvania 15251. Payment by wire transfer may be made to ABA Number 043000261, receiving bank Mellon Bank, and account number 911-6106.

24.   The responses, if any, must be mailed to William H. Davenport, Chief, Investigations and Hearings Division, Enforcement Bureau, Federal Communications Commission, 445 12th Street, S.W., Room 4-C330, Washington D.C. 20554, and MUST INCLUDE the relevant NAL/Acct. No. referenced for each proposed forfeiture in Attachment A hereto.

25.   The Commission will not consider reducing or canceling a forfeiture in response to a claim of inability to pay unless the respondent submits: (1) federal tax returns for the most recent three-year period; (2) financial statements prepared according to generally accepted accounting practices ("GAAP"); or (3) some other reliable and objective documentation that accurately reflects the respondent's current financial status. Any claim of inability to pay must specifically identify the basis for the claim by reference to the financial documentation submitted.

26.   Requests for payment of the full amount of this *NAL* under an installment plan should be sent to: Associate Managing Director -- Financial Operations, 445 12th Street, S.W., Room 1-A625, Washington, D.C. 20554.[28]

---

[28] *See* 47 C.F.R. § 1.1914.

27.   Accordingly, IT IS ORDERED that the complaints in this *NAL* proceeding ARE GRANTED to the extent indicated herein, AND ARE OTHERWISE DENIED, and the complaint proceeding IS HEREBY TERMINATED.[29]

FEDERAL COMMUNICATIONS COMMISSION

Marlene H. Dortch
Secretary

---

[29] Consistent with section 503(b) of the Act and consistent Commission practice, for the purposes of the forfeiture proceeding initiated by this *NAL*, the only parties to such proceeding will be licensees specified in Attachment A hereto.

ATTACHMENT A
PROPOSED FORFEITURES FOR DECEMBER 31, 2004
BROADCASTS OF "WITHOUT A TRACE"

Licensee Name and Mailing Address	FRN No.	NAL Acct. No.	Station Call Signs and Communities of License	Facility ID Nos.	Proposed Forfeiture Amount
Alabama Broadcasting Partners 3020 Eastern Boulevard Montgomery, AL 36123	0003828738	200632080014	WAKA (TV) Selma, AL	701	$32,500
Alaska Broadcasting Company, Inc. 1007 W. 32nd Ave Anchorage, AK 99503	0006160915	200632080015	KTVA (TV) Anchorage, AK	49632	$32,500
Arkansas Television Company c/o Gannett Co., Inc. 7950 Jones Branco Dr. Mclean, VA 22107	0003756442	200632080016	KTHV (1V) Little Rock, AR	2787	$32,500
Barrington Broadcasting Quincy Corporation 2500 W. Higgins Road Ste 880 Hoffman Estates, IL 60195	0011063302	200632080017	KHQA-TV Hannibal, MO	4690	$32,500
Barrington Broadcasting Missouri Corp. 2500 W. Higgins Road Suite 880 Hoffman Estates, IL 60195	0012140109	200632080018	KRCG (TV) Jefferson City, MO	41110	$32,500
Catamount Bcstg of Fargo LLC 1350 21st Ave. South Fargo, ND 58103	0002474161	200632080019	KXJB-TV Valley City, ND	49134	$32,500

Licensee Name and Mailing Address	FRN No.	NAL Acct. No.	Station Call Signs and Communities of License	Facility ID Nos.	Proposed Forfeiture Amount
CBS Broadcasting, Inc. 2000 K Street, N.W. Suite 725 Washington, DC 20006	0003482189	200632080020	KCCO-TV Alexandria, MN	9632	$130,000
			WBBM-TV Chicago, IL	9617	
			WCCO-TV Minneapolis, MN	9629	
			WFRV-TV Green Bay, WI	9635	
CBS Stations Group of Texas, L.P. 2000 K Street, N.W. Ste. 725 Washington, DC 20006	0001767078	200632080021	KEYE-TV Austin, TX	33691	$65,000
			KTVT (TV) Fort Worth, TX	23422	
CBS Television Stations, Inc. 2000 K Street, N.W. Suite 725 Washington, DC 20006	0004425773	200632080022	KCNC-TV Denver, CO	47903	$32,500
Chelsey Broadcasting Company of Casper, LLC 2923 East Lincolnway Cheyenne, WY 82001	0008721292	200632080023	KGWC-TV Casper, WY	63177	$32,500
ComCorp of Indiana License Corp. P.O. Drawer 53708 Lafayette, LA 70505	0004328308	200632080024	WEVV (TV) Evansville, IN	72041	$32,500
Coronet Comm Co. 99 Pondfield Rd Bronxville, NY 10708	0003757457	200632080025	WHBF-TV Rock Island, IL	13950	$32,500

Licensee Name and Mailing Address	FRN No.	NAL Acct. No.	Station Call Signs and Communities of License	Facility ID Nos.	Proposed Forfeiture Amount
Des Moines Hearst-Argyle Television, Inc. c/o Brooks, Pierce, Et. Al. P.O. Box 1800 Raleigh, NC 27602	0002573277	200632080026	KCCI (TV) Des Moines, IA	33710	$32,500
Eagle Creek Broadcasting of Laredo, LLC 2111 University Park Drive, Ste. 650 Okemos, MI 48864	0007262348	200632080027	KVTV (TV) Laredo, TX	33078	$32,500
Eagle Creek Broadcasting of Corpus Christi, LLC 2111 University Park Dr Ste 650 Okemos, MI 48864	0007277445	200632080028	KZTV (TV) Corpus Christi, TX	33079	$32,500
Emmis Television License LLC 3500 W Olive Ave Ste. 1450 Burbank, CA 915051	0002884252	200632080029	KBIM-TV Roswell, NM	48556	$195,000
			KGMB (TV) Honolulu, HI	36917	
			KMTV (TV) Omaha, NE	35190	
			KREZ-TV Durango, CO	48589	
			KRQE (TV) Albuquerque, NM	48575	
			WTHI-TV Terre Haute, IN	70655	
Fisher Broadcasting Idaho TV, LLC 100 4th Ave N Ste 510 Seattle, WA 98101	0005848445	200632080030	KBCI-TV, Boise, ID	49760	$32,500
Fisher Broadcasting-SE Idaho TV LLC 100 4th Ave N Ste 510 Seattle, WA 9810	0005848619	200632080090	KIDK (TV) Idaho Falls, ID	56028	$32,500

Licensee Name and Mailing Address	FRN No.	NAL Acct. No.	Station Call Signs and Communities of License	Facility ID Nos.	Proposed Forfeiture Amount
Freedom Bcstg of TX Licensee LLC PO Box 7128 Beaumont, TX 77726	0010053064	200632080031	KFDM-TV Beaumont, TX	22589	$32,500
Glendive Bcstg Corp. 210 S Douglas St Glendive, MT 59330	0003749892	200632080032	KXGN-TV Glendive, MT	24287	$32,500
Gray Television Licensee, Inc. 4141 East 29th Street Bryan, TX 77801	0002746022	200632080033	KBTX-TV Bryan, TX	6669	$325,000
			KGIN (TV) Grand Island, NE	7894	
			KKTV (TV) Colorado Springs, CO	35037	
			KOLN (TV) Lincoln, NE	7890	
			KWTX-TV Waco, TX	35903	
			KXII (TV) Sherman, TX	35954	
			WIBW-TV Topeka, KS	63160	
			WIFR (TV) Freeport, IL	4689	
			WSAW-TV Wausau, WI	6867	
			WVLT-TV Knoxville, TN	35908	
Griffin Entities, LLC, 3993 Howard Hughes Parkway, Suite 250, Las Vegas, NV 89109	0002147155	200632080034	KWTV (TV) Oklahoma City, OK	25382	$32,500

Licensee Name and Mailing Address	FRN No.	NAL Acct. No.	Station Call Signs and Communities of License	Facility ID Nos.	Proposed Forfeiture Amount
Griffin Licensing, L.L.C. 3993 Howard Hughes Pkwy., Ste 250 Las Vegas, NV 89109	0004283339	200632080035	KOTV (TV) Tulsa, OK	35434	$32,500
Hoak Media of Colorado LLC 500 Crescent Court, Suite 220 Dallas, TX 75240	0009455809	200632080036	KREX-TV Grand Junction, CO	70596	$32,500
Hoak Media of Wichita Falls, L.P. 13355 Noel Road Dallas, TX 75240	0009510603	200632080037	KAUZ-TV Wichita Falls, TX	6864	$32,500
ICA Broadcasting I, LTD 700 N Grant St Odessa, TX 79761	0003758976	200632080038	KOSA-TV Odessa, TX	6865	$32,500
Indiana Broadcasting, LLC 4 Richmond Square Providence , RI 02906	0007641590	200632080039	WANE-TV Fort Wayne, ID WISH-TV Indianapolis, IN	39270 39269	$65,000
KCTZ Communications, Inc. 1128 East Main Bozeman, MT 59715	0001811827	200632080040	KBZK (TV) Bozeman, MT	33756	$32,500
KDBC License, LLC 500 South Chinowth Rd Visalia, CA 93277	0010811776	200632080041	KDBC-TV El Paso, TX	33764	$32,500
KENS-TV, Inc. 400 South Record St. Dallas, TX 75202	0008654188	200632080042	KENS-TV San Antonio, TX	26304	$32,500

Licensee Name and Mailing Address	FRN No.	NAL Acct. No.	Station Call Signs and Communities of License	Facility ID Nos.	Proposed Forfeiture Amount
Ketchikan TV, LLC P.O. Box 348 2539 North Highway 67 Sedalia, CO 80135	0005039896	200632080043	KTNL (TV) Sitka, AK	60519	$32,500
KGAN Licensee, LLC Shaw Pittman LLP. Attn: K. Schmeltzer 2300 N Street, N.W. Washington, DC 20037	0009405226	200632080044	KGAN (TV) Cedar Rapids, IA	25685	$32,500
KHOU-TV LP 1945 Allen Parkway Houston, TX 77019	0004542346	200632080045	KHOU-TV Houston, TX	34529	$32,500
KLFY, LP P.O. Box 1800 Raleigh, NC 27602	0005575733	200632080046	KLFY-TV Lafayette, LA	35059	$32,500
KMOV-TV, Inc. 1 Memorial Drive St. Louis, MO 63102	0001569110	200632080047	KMOV (TV) St. Louis, MO	70034	$32,500
KPAX Communications, Inc. P.O. Box 4827 Missoula, MT 59806	0001811827	200632080048	KPAX-TV Missoula, MT	35455	$32,500
KRTV Communications, Inc. Post Office Box 2989 Great Falls, MT 59403	0004523304	200632080049	KRTV (TV) Great Falls, MT	35567	$32,500
KSLA License Subsidiary, LLC RSA Tower 20th Fl 201 Monroe St Montgomery, AL 36104	0003733045	200632080050	KSLA-TV Shreveport, LA	70482	$32,500

Licensee Name and Mailing Address	FRN No.	NAL Acct. No.	Station Call Signs and Communities of License	Facility ID Nos.	Proposed Forfeiture Amount
KTVQ Communications, Inc. 3203 3rd Ave North Billings, MT 59101	0001628551	200632080051	KTVQ (TV) Billings, MT	35694	$32,500
KUTV Holdings, Inc. 2000 K Street, N.W. Suite 725 Washington, DC 20006	0009072380	200632080052	KUTV (TV) Salt Lake City, UT	35823	$32,500
KXLF Communications, Inc. 1003 Montana Street Butte, MT 59701	0001563956	200632080053	KXLF-TV Butte, MT	35959	$32,500
Libco, Inc. 2215 B Renaissance Drive, Ste 5 Las Vegas, NV 89119	0001881523	200632080054	KGBT-TV Harlingen, TX	34457	$32,500
Malara Broadcast Group of Duluth Licensee, LLC 5880 Midnight Pass Rd Apt 701 Siesta Key, FL 34242-2104	0002836237	200632080055	KDLH (TV) Duluth, MN	4691	$32,500
MMT License, LLC 900 Laskin Road Virgina Beach, VA 23451	0009745027	200632080056	KYTX (TV) Nacogdoches, TX	55644	$32,500
Media General Broadcasting of South Carolina Holdings, Inc. 333 East Franklin Street Richmond, VA 23219	0002207520	200632080057	KBSH-TV Hays, KS KIMT (TV) Mason City, IA WKRG-TV Mobile, AL	66415 66402 73187	$97,500

Licensee Name and Mailing Address	FRN No.	NAL Acct. No.	Station Call Signs and Communities of License	Facility ID Nos.	Proposed Forfeiture Amount
Media General Communications, Inc. 333 East Franklin Street Richmond, VA 23219	0002050185	200632080058	WDEF-TV Chattanooga, TN	54385	$162,500
			WHLT (TV) Hattiesburg, MS	48668	
			WIAT (TV) Birmingham, AL	5360	
			WJHL-TV Johnson City, TN	57826	
			WJTV (TV) Jackson, MS	48667	
Meredith Corp. 1716 Locust St Des Moines IA 50309-33203	0005810726	200632080059	KCTV (TV) Kansas City, MO	41230	$66,000
			KPHO-TV Phoenix, AZ	41223	
Mission Broadcasting, Inc. 544 Red Rock Dr Wadsworth, OH 44281	0003725389	200632080060	KOLR (TV) Springfield, MO	28496	$32,500
Neuhoff Family Partnership 11793 Lake House Court North Palm Beach, FL 33408	0005011648	200632080061	KMVT (TV) Twin Falls, ID	35200	$32,500
News Channel 5 Network, LP 474 James Robertson Pky. Nashville, TN 37219	0002054880	200632080062	WTVF (TV) Nashville, TN	36504	$32,500
New York Times Management Services Corporate Center 1, International Plaza 2202 N.W. Shore Blvd., Suite 370 Tampa, FL 33607	0003481587	200632080063	KFSM-TV Fort Smith, AK	66469	$97,500
			WHNT-TV Huntsville, AL	48693	
			WREG-TV Memphis, TN	66174	

Licensee Name and Mailing Address	FRN No.	NAL Acct. No.	Station Call Signs and Communities of License	Facility ID Nos.	Proposed Forfeiture Amount
Nexstar Broadcasting, Inc. 909 Lake Carolyn Parkway Ste 1450 Irving, TX 75039	0009961889	200632080064	KLBK-TV Lubbock, TX	3660	$187,500
			KLST (TV) San Angelo, TX	31114	
			KTAB-TV Abilene, TX	59988	
			WCIA (TV) Champaign, IL	42124	
			WMBD-TV Peoria, IL	42121	
Noe Corp. LLC 1400 Oliver Road Monroe, LA 71211	0008295198	200632080065	KNOE (TV) Monroe, LA	48975	$32,500
Panhandle Telecasting Company PO Box 10 Amarillo, TX 79105	0001662899	200632080066	KFDA-TV Amarillo, TX	51466	$32,500
Pappas Arizona License, LLC 500 South Chinowth Road Visalia, CA 93277	0004934683	200632080067	KSWT (TV) Yuma, AZ	33639	$32,500
Primeland Television, Inc. 4 Richmond Sq Ste 200 Providence, RI 02906	0007641590	200632080068	WLFI-TV Lafayette, IN	73204	$32,500
Queen B Television, LLC 141 S. 6th Street P.O. Box 1867 Lacrosse, WI 54601	0003769973	200632080069	WKBT (TV) La Crosse, WI	74424	$32,500
Raycom America License Subsidiary, LLC RSA Tower 20th FL 201 Monroe St Montgomery, AL 36104	0001835289	200632080070	KFVS-TV Cape Giradeau, MO	592	$65,000
			KOLD-TV Tucson, AZ	48663	

Licensee Name and Mailing Address	FRN No.	NAL Acct. No.	Station Call Signs and Communities of License	Facility ID Nos.	Proposed Forfeiture Amount
Reiten Television, Inc. 1625 West Villard Dickinson, ND 58701	0002476885	200632080071	KXMA-TV Dickinson, ND KXMB-TV Bismarck, ND KXMC-TV Minot, ND KXMD-TV Williston, ND	55684 55686 55685 55683	$130,000
Saga Broadcasting, LLC 73 Kercheval Ave Grosse Pointe Farms, MI 48236	0005237599	200632080072	WXVT (TV) Greenville, MS	25236	$32,500
Saga Quad States Communications, LLC 73 Kercheval Ave Grosse Pointe Farms, MI 48236	0003574084	200632080073	KOAM-TV Pittsburg, KS	58552	$32,500
Sagamore Hill Broadcasting of Wyoming/Northern Colorado, LLC Two Embarcadero Ctr. 23rd Floor San Francisco, CA 94111	0009676958	200632080074	KGWN-TV Cheyenne, WY KSTF (TV) Gering, NE	63166 63182	$65,000
Television Wisconsin, Inc. P.O. Box 44965 Madison, WI 53744	0002715563	200632080075	WISC-TV Madison, WI	65143	$32,500
United Communications Corp. 715 58th Street Kenosha, WI 53140	0002210383	200632080076	KEYC-TV Mankato, MN	68853	$32,500
WAFB License Subsidiary LLC RSA Tower 20th Fl 201 Monroe St Montgomery, AL 36104	0003733060	200632080077	WAFB (TV) Baton Rouge, LA	589	$32,500

Licensee Name and Mailing Address	FRN No.	NAL Acct. No.	Station Call Signs and Communities of License	Facility ID Nos.	Proposed Forfeiture Amount
Waitt Broadcasting, Inc. 1125 S 103rd St Ste 200 Omaha, NE 6812	0004957650	200632080078	KMEG (TV) Sioux City, IA	39665	$32,500
WCBI-TV, LLC 27 Abercorn Street Savannah, GA 31412	0005413471	200632080079	WCBI-TV Columbus, MS	12477	$32,500
WDJT-TV Limited Partnership 26 N Halsted St Chicago, IL 60661	0009562265	200632080080	WDJT-TV Milwaukee, WI	71427	$32,500
WMDN, Inc. P.O. Box 2424 Meridian, MS 39302	0001744838	200632080081	WMDN (TV)	73255	$32,500
WSBT, Inc. 300 W. Jefferson Blvd. South Bend, IN 46601	0008712937	200632080082	WSBT-TV South Bend, IN	73983	$32,500
WWL-TV, Inc. 1024 North Rampart St. New Orleans, LA 70116	0008654154	200632080083	WWL-TV New Orleans, LA	74192	$32,500
Young Broadcasting of Rapid City, Inc. P.O. Box 1800 Raleigh, NC 27602	0003475449	200632080084	KCLO-TV Rapid City, SD	41969	$32,500
Young Broadcasting of Sioux Falls, Inc. P.O. Box 1800 Raleigh, NC 27602	0003475464	200632080085	KELO-TV Sioux Falls, SD KPLO-TV Reliance, SD	41983 41964	$65,000

STATEMENT OF
CHAIRMAN KEVIN J. MARTIN

Re: *Complaints Against Various Television Licensees Concerning Their February 1, 2004 Broadcast of the Super Bowl XXXVIII Halftime Show; Complaints Regarding Various Television Broadcasts Between February 2, 2002 and March 8, 2005; Complaints Against Various Television Licensees Concerning Their December 31, 2004 Broadcast of the Program "Without A Trace"*

Congress has long prohibited the broadcasting of indecent and profane material and the courts have upheld challenges to these standards. But the number of complaints received by the Commission has risen year after year. They have grown from hundreds, to hundreds of thousands. And the number of programs that trigger these complaints continues to increase as well. I share the concerns of the public - and of parents, in particular - that are voiced in these complaints.

I believe the Commission has a legal responsibility to respond to them and resolve them in a consistent and effective manner. So I am pleased that with the decisions released today the Commission is resolving hundreds of thousands of complaints against various broadcast licensees related to their televising of 49 different programs. These decisions, taken both individually and as a whole, demonstrate the Commission's continued commitment to enforcing the law prohibiting the airing of obscene, indecent and profane material.

Additionally, the Commission today affirms its initial finding that the broadcast of the Super Bowl XXXVIII Halftime Show was actionably indecent. We appropriately reject the argument that CBS continues to make that this material is not indecent. That argument runs counter to Commission precedent and common sense.

STATEMENT OF
COMMISSIONER MICHAEL J. COPPS

Re: *Complaints Regarding Various Television Broadcasts Between January 1, 2002 and March 12, 2005, Notices of Apparent Liability and Memorandum Opinion and Order*

Complaints Against Various Television Licensees Concerning Their December 31, 2004 Broadcast of the Program "Without A Trace," Notice of Apparent Liability

Complaints Against Various Television Licensees Concerning Their February 1, 2004 Broadcast Of The Super Bowl XXXVII Halftime Show, Forfeiture Order

In the past, the Commission too often addressed indecency complaints with little discussion or analysis, relying instead on generalized pronouncements. Such an approach served neither aggrieved citizens nor the broadcast industry. Today, the Commission not only moves forward to address a number of pending complaints, but does so in a manner that better analyzes each broadcast and explains how the Commission determines whether a particular broadcast is indecent. Although it may never be possible to provide 100 percent certain guidance because we must always take into account specific and often-differing contexts, the approach in today's orders can help to develop such guidance and to establish precedents. This measured process, common in jurisprudence, may not satisfy those who clamor for immediate certainty in an uncertain world, but it may just be the best way to develop workable rules of the road.

Today's Orders highlight two additional issues with which the Commission must come to terms. First, it is time for the Commission to look at indecency in the broader context of its decisions on media consolidation. In 2003 the FCC sought to weaken its remaining media concentration safeguards without even considering whether there is a link between increasing media consolidation and increasing indecency. Such links have been shown in studies and testified to by a variety of expert witnesses. The record clearly demonstrates that an overwhelming number of the Commission's indecency citations have gone to a few huge media conglomerates. One recent study showed that the four largest radio station groups which controlled just under half the radio audience were responsible for a whopping 96 percent of the indecency fines levied by the FCC from 2000 to 2003.

One of the reasons for the huge volume of complaints about excessive sex and graphic violence in the programming we are fed may be that people feel increasingly divorced from their "local" media. They believe the media no longer respond to their local communities. As media conglomerates grow ever larger and station control moves farther away from the local community, community standards seem to count for less when programming decisions are made. Years ago we had independent programming created from a diversity of sources. Networks would then decide which programming to distribute. Then local affiliates would independently decide whether to air that programming. This provided some real checks and balances. Nowadays so many of these decisions are made by vertically-integrated conglomerates headquartered far away from the communities they are supposed to be serving—entities that all too often control both the distribution *and* the production content of the programming.

If heightened media consolidation is indeed a source for the violence and indecency that upset so many parents, shouldn't the Commission be cranking that into its decisions on further loosening of the ownership rules? I hope the Commission, before voting again on loosening its media concentration protections, will finally take a serious look at this link and amass a credible body of evidence and not act again without the facts, as it did in 2003.

Second, a number of these complaints concern graphic broadcast violence. The Commission states that it has taken comment on this issue in another docket. It is time for us to step up to the plate and tackle the issue of violence in the media. The U.S. Surgeon General, the American Academy of Pediatrics, the American Psychological Association, the American Medical Association, and countless other medical and scientific organizations that have studied this issue have reached the same conclusion: exposure to graphic and excessive media violence has harmful effects on the physical and mental health of our children. We need to complete this proceeding.

APPENDIX B

STATEMENT OF
COMMISSIONER JONATHAN S. ADELSTEIN
CONCURRING

Re: *Complaints Against Various Television Licensees Concerning Their December 31, 2004 Broadcast of the Program "Without A Trace,"* Notice of Apparent Liability for Forfeiture

I have sworn an oath to uphold the Constitution[30] and to carry out the laws adopted by Congress.[31] Trying to find a balance between these obligations has been challenging in many of the indecency cases that I have decided. I believe it is our duty to regulate the broadcast of indecent material to the fullest extent permissible by the Constitution because safeguarding the well-being of our children is a compelling national interest.[32] I therefore have supported efforts to step up our enforcement of indecency laws since I joined the Commission.

The Commission's authority to regulate indecency over the public airwaves was narrowly upheld by the Supreme Court with the admonition that we should exercise that authority with the utmost restraint, lest we inhibit constitutional rights and transgress constitutional limitations on government regulation of protected speech.[33] Given the Court's guidance in *Pacifica,* the Commission has repeatedly stated that we would judiciously walk a "tightrope" in exercising our regulatory authority.[34] Hence, within this legal context, a rational and principled "restrained enforcement policy" is not a matter of mere regulatory convenience. It is a constitutional requirement. [35]

Accordingly, I concur with the instant decision, but concur in part and dissent in part with the companion Omnibus Order[36] because, while in some ways the Omnibus decision does not go far enough, in other ways it goes too far. Significantly, it abruptly departs from our precedents by adopting a new, weaker enforcement mechanism that arbitrarily fails to assess fines against broadcasters who have aired indecent material. Additionally, while the Omnibus Order appropriately identifies violations of our indecency laws, not every instance determined to be indecent meets that standard.

We have previously sought to identify all broadcasters who have aired indecent material and hold them accountable. In the Omnibus Order, however, the Commission inexplicably fines only the licensee whose broadcast of indecent material was the subject of a viewer's complaint, even though we know

---

[30] U.S. CONST., amend. I.

[31] Congress has specifically forbidden the broadcast of obscene, indecent or profane language. 18 U.S.C. § 1464. It has also forbidden censorship. 47 U.S.C. § 326.

[32] *See, e.g., N.Y. v. Ferber,* 458 U.S. 747, 756-57 (1982).

[33] *See FCC v. Pacifica Foundation,* 438 U.S. 726, 750 (1978) (emphasizing the "narrowness" of the Court's holding); *Action for Children's Television v. FCC,* 852 F.2d 1332, 1344 (D.C. Cir. 1988) (*"ACT I"*) ("Broadcast material that is indecent but not obscene is protected by the [F]irst [A]mendment.").

[34] *See* Brief for Petitioner, FCC, 1978 WL 206838 at *9.

[35] *ACT I, supra* note 4, at 1344 ("the FCC may regulate [indecent] material only with due respect for the high value our Constitution places on freedom and choice in what the people say and hear."); *Id.* at 1340 n.14 ("[T]he potentially chilling effect of the FCC's generic definition of indecency will be tempered by the Commission's restrained enforcement policy.").

[36] *Complaints Regarding Various Television Broadcasts Between February 2, 2002 and March 8, 2005*, Notices of Apparent Liability and Memorandum Opinion and Order (decided March 15, 2006) (hereinafter "Omnibus Order").

millions of other Americans were exposed to the offending broadcast. I cannot find anywhere in the law that Congress told us to apply indecency regulations only to those stations against which a complaint was specifically lodged. The law requires us to prohibit the broadcast of indecent material, period. This means that we must enforce the law anywhere we determine it has been violated. It is willful blindness to decide, with respect to network broadcasts we know aired nationwide, that we will only enforce the law against the local station that happens to be the target of viewer complaints. How can we impose a fine solely on certain local broadcasters, despite having repeatedly said that the Commission applies a national indecency standard – not a local one?[37]

The failure to enforce the rules against some stations but not others is not what the courts had in mind when they counseled restraint. In fact, the Supreme Court's decision in *Pacifica* was based on the uniquely pervasive characteristics of broadcast media.[38] It is patently arbitrary to hold some stations but not others accountable for the same broadcast. We recognized this just two years ago in *Married By America*.[39] The Commission simply inquired who aired the indecent broadcast and fined all of those stations that did so.

In the *Super Bowl XXXVIII Halftime Show* decision, we held only those stations owned and operated by the CBS network responsible, under the theory that the affiliates did not expect the incident and it was primarily the network's fault.[40] I dissented in part to that case because I believed we needed to apply the same sanction to every station that aired the offending material. I raise similar concerns today, in the context of the Omnibus Order.

The Commission is constitutionally obligated to decide broadcast indecency and profanity cases based on the "contemporary community standard," which is "that of the average broadcast viewer or listener." The Commission has explained the "contemporary community standard," as follows:

> We rely on our collective experience and knowledge, developed through constant
> interaction with lawmakers, courts, broadcasters, public interest groups and ordinary
> citizens, to keep abreast of contemporary community standards for the broadcast
> medium.[41]

I am concerned that the Omnibus Order overreaches with its expansion of the scope of indecency and profanity law, without first doing what is necessary to determine the appropriate contemporary community standard.

---

[37] *See, e.g., In re Sagittarius Broadcasting Corporation,* Memorandum Opinion and Order, 7 FCC Rcd 6873, 6876 (1992) (subsequent history omitted).

[38] *See Pacifica Found.*, 438 U.S. at 748-49 (recognizing the "uniquely pervasive presence" of broadcast media "in the lives of all Americans"). In today's Order, paragraph 10, the Commission relies upon the same rationale.

[39] *See Complaints Against Various Licensees Regarding Their Broadcast of the Fox Television Network Program "Married by America" on April 7, 2003,* Notice of Apparent Liability for Forfeiture, 19 FCC Rcd 20191, 20196 (2004) (proposing a $7,000 forfeiture against each Fox Station and Fox Affiliate station); *reconsideration pending. See also Clear Channel Broadcast Licenses, Inc.,* 19 FCC Rcd 6773, 6779 (2004) (proposing a $495,000 fine based on a "per utterance" calculation, and directing an investigation into stations owned by other licensees that broadcast the indecent program). In the instant Omnibus Order, however, the Commission inexplicably fines only the licensee whose broadcast of indecent material was actually the subject of a viewer's complaint to the Commission. *Id.* at ¶ 71.

[40] *See Complaints Against Various Television Licensees Concerning Their February 1, 2004, Broadcast of the Super Bowl XXXVIII Halftime Show,* Notice of Apparent Liability, 19 FCC Rcd 19230 (2004).

[41] *In re Infinity Radio License, Inc.,* Memorandum Opinion and Order, 19 FCC Rcd 5022, 5026 (2004).

The Omnibus Order builds on one of the most difficult cases we have ever decided, *Golden Globe Awards*,[42] and stretches it beyond the limits of our precedents and constitutional authority. The precedent set in that case has been contested by numerous broadcasters, constitutional scholars and public interest groups who have asked us to revisit and clarify our reasoning and decision. Rather than reexamining that case, the majority uses the decision as a springboard to add new words to the pantheon of those deemed to be inherently sexual or excretory, and consequently indecent and profane, irrespective of their common meaning or of a fleeting and isolated use. By failing to address the many serious concerns raised in the reconsideration petitions filed in the *Golden Globe Awards* case, before prohibiting the use of additional words, the Commission falls short of meeting the constitutional standard and walking the tightrope of a restrained enforcement policy.

This approach endangers the very authority we so delicately retain to enforce broadcast decency rules. If the Commission in its zeal oversteps and finds our authority circumscribed by the courts, we may forever lose the ability to protect children from the airing of indecent material, barring an unlikely constitutional amendment setting limitations on the First Amendment freedoms.

The perilous course taken today is evident in the approach to the acclaimed Martin Scorsese documentary, "The Blues: Godfathers and Sons." It is clear from a common sense viewing of the program that coarse language is a part of the culture of the individuals being portrayed. To accurately reflect their viewpoint and emotions about blues music requires airing of certain material that, if prohibited, would undercut the ability of the filmmaker to convey the reality of the subject of the documentary. This contextual reasoning is consistent with our decisions in *Saving Private Ryan*[43] and *Schindler's List*.[44]

The Commission has repeatedly reaffirmed, and the courts have consistently underscored, the importance of content *and* context. The majority's decision today dangerously departs from those precedents. It is certain to strike fear in the hearts of news and documentary makers, and broadcasters that air them, which could chill the future expression of constitutionally protected speech.

We should be mindful of Justice Harlan's observation in *Cohen v. California*.[45] Writing for the Court, he observed:

> [W]ords are often chosen as much for their emotive as their cognitive force. We cannot sanction the view that the Constitution, while solicitous of the cognitive content of individual speech, has little or no regard for that emotive function which, practically speaking, may often be the more important element of the overall message sought to be communicated.[46]

---

[42] *In re Complaints Against Broadcast Licensees Regarding Their Airing of the "Golden Globe Awards" Program*, Memorandum Opinion and Order, 19 FCC Rcd 4975 (2004); *petitions for stay and reconsideration pending*.

[43] *In the Matter of Complaints Against Various Television Licensees Regarding Their Broadcast on November 11, 2004, of the ABC Television Network's Presentation of the Film, "Saving Private Ryan,"* Memorandum Opinion and Order, 20 FCC Rcd 4507, 4513 (2005) ("Deleting all [indecent] language or inserting milder language or bleeping sounds into the film would have altered the nature of the artistic work and diminished the power, realism and immediacy of the film experience for viewers."). *See also Peter Branton*, Letter by Direction of the Commission, 6 FCC Rcd 610 (1991) (concluding that repeated use of the f-word in a recorded news interview program not indecent in context).

[44] *In the Matter of WPBN/WTOM License Subsidiary, Inc.*, 15 FCC Rcd 1838 (2000).

[45] 403 U.S. 15 (1971).

[46] *Id.* at 26 ("We cannot indulge the facile assumption that one can forbid particular words without also running a

(continued....)

Given all of these considerations, I find that the Omnibus Order, while reaching some appropriate conclusions both in identifying indecent material and in dismissing complaints, is in some ways dangerously off the mark. I cannot agree that it offers a coherent, principled long-term framework that is rooted in common sense. In fact, it may put at risk the very authority to protect children that it exercises so vigorously.

(...continued from previous page)
substantial risk of suppressing ideas in the process.").

STATEMENT OF
COMMISSIONER DEBORAH TAYLOR TATE

Re: *Re: Complaints Against Various Television Licensees Concerning Their February 1, 2004, Broadcast of the Super Bowl XXXVIII Halftime Show,* Forfeiture Order; *Complaints Against Various Television Licensees Concerning Their December 31, 2004 Broadcast of the Program "Without A Trace,"* Notice of Apparent Liability for Forfeiture; *Complaints Regarding Various Television Broadcasts Between February 2, 2002 and March 8, 2005,* Notices of Apparent Liability and Memorandum Opinion and Order

Today marks my first opportunity as a member of the Federal Communications Commission to uphold our responsibility to enforce the federal statute prohibiting the airing of obscene, indecent or profane language.[47] To be clear – I take this responsibility very seriously. Not only is this the law, but it also is the right thing to do.

One of the bedrock principles of the Communications Act of 1934, as amended, is that the airwaves belong to the public. Much like public spaces and national landmarks, these are scarce and finite resources that must be preserved for the benefit of all Americans. If numbers are any indication, many Americans are not happy about the way that their airwaves are being utilized. The number of complaints filed with the FCC reached over one million in 2004. Indeed, since taking office in January 2006, I have received hundreds of personal e-mails from people all over this country who are unhappy with the content to which they – and, in particular, their families – are subjected.

I have applauded those cable and DBS providers for the tools they have provided to help parents and other concerned citizens filter out objectionable content. Parental controls incorporated into cable and DBS set-top boxes, along with the V-Chip, make it possible to block programming based upon its content rating. However, these tools, even when used properly, are not a complete solution. One of the main reasons for that is because much of the content broadcast, including live sporting events and commercials, are not rated under the two systems currently in use.

I also believe that consumers have an important role to play as well. Caregivers – parents, in particular – need to take an active role in monitoring the content to which children are exposed. Even the most diligent parent, however, cannot be expected to protect their children from indecent material broadcast during live sporting events or in commercials that appear during what is marketed to be "appropriate" programming.

Today, we are making significant strides toward addressing the backlog of indecency complaints before this agency. The rules are simple – you break them and we will enforce the law, just as we are doing today. Both the public and the broadcasters deserve prompt and timely resolution of complaints as they are filed, and I am glad to see us act to resolve these complaints. At the same time, however, I would like to raise a few concerns regarding the complaints we address in these decisions.

First, I would like to discuss the complaint regarding the 6:30 p.m. Eastern Daylight Time airing of an episode of *The Simpsons*. The *Order* concludes that this segment is not indecent, in part because of the fact that *The Simpsons* is a cartoon. Generally speaking, cartoons appeal to children, though some may cater to both children and adults simultaneously. Nevertheless, the fact remains that children were extremely likely to have been in the viewing audience when this scene was broadcast. Indeed, the marketing is aimed at children. If the scene had involved real actors in living color, at 5:30 p.m. Central

---

[47] *See* 18 U.S.C. § 1464.

APPENDIX B

Standard Time, I wonder if our decision would have been different? One might argue that the cartoon medium may be a more insidious means of exposing young people to such content. By their very nature, cartoons do not accurately portray reality, and in this instance the use of animation may well serve to present that material in a more flattering light than it would if it were depicted through live video. I stop short of disagreeing with our decision in this case, but note that the animated nature of the broadcast, in my opinion, may be cause for taking an even closer look in the context of our indecency analysis.

Second, our conclusion regarding the 9:00 p.m. Central Standard Time airing of an episode of *Medium* in which a woman is shot at point-blank range in the face by her husband gives me pause. While I agree with the result in this case, I question our conclusion that the sequence constitutes violence *per se* and therefore falls outside the scope of the Commission's definition of indecency. Without question, this scene is violent, graphically so. Moreover, it is presented in a way that appears clearly designed to maximize its shock value. And therein lies my concern. One of the primary ways that this scene shocks is that it leads the viewer to believe that the action is headed in one direction – through dialogue and actions which suggest that interaction of a sexual nature is about to occur – and then abruptly erupts in another – the brutally violent shooting of a wife by her husband, in the head, at point-blank range. Even though the Commission's authority under Section 1464 is limited to indecent, obscene, and profane content, and thus does not extend to violent matter, the use of violence as the "punch line" of titillating sexual innuendo should not insulate broadcast licensees from our authority. To the contrary, the use of sexual innuendo may, depending on the specific case, subject a licensee to potential forfeiture, regardless of the overall violent nature of the sequence in which such sexual innuendo is used.

* * *

Finally, I would like to express my hope and belief that the problem of indecent material is one that can be solved. Programmers, artists, writers, broadcasters, networks, advertisers, parents, public interest groups, and, yes, even Commissioners can protect two of our country's most valuable resources: the public airwaves and our children's minds. We must take a stand against programming that robs our children of their innocence and constitutes an unwarranted intrusion into our homes. By working together, we should promote the creation of programming that is not just entertaining, but also positive, educational, healthful, and, perhaps, even inspiring.

FCC 06-19

Before the
Federal Communications Commission
Washington, D.C. 20554

In the Matter of	)
	)
COMPLAINTS AGAINST VARIOUS	) File No. EB-04-IH-0011
TELEVISION LICENSEES	)
CONCERNING THEIR FEBRUARY	) NAL/Acct. No. 200432080212
1, 2004 BROADCAST OF THE SUPER	)
BOWL XXXVIII HALFTIME SHOW	)

FORFEITURE ORDER

Adopted: February 21, 2006   **Released: March 15, 2006**

By the Commission: Chairman Martin, Commissioners Copps and Tate issuing separate statements; Commissioner Adelstein concurring and issuing a statement.

I.   INTRODUCTION

1.   In this *Forfeiture Order* ("*Order*"), issued pursuant to section 503(b) of the Communications Act of 1934, as amended (the "Act"), and section 1.80 of the Commission's rules,[1] we impose a monetary forfeiture in the amount of $550,000 against CBS Corporation ("CBS"), as the licensee or the ultimate parent company of the licensees of the television stations listed in the Appendix ("CBS Stations").[2] We find that CBS violated 18 U.S.C. § 1464 and the Commission's rule regulating the broadcast of indecent material[3] in its broadcast of the halftime show of the National Football League's Super Bowl XXXVIII over the CBS Stations on February 1, 2004, at approximately 8:30 p.m. Eastern Standard Time.[4]

---

[1] 47 U.S.C. § 503(b); 47 C.F.R. § 1.80.

[2] The Appendix is an updated version of Appendix A from the Notice of Apparent Liability in this proceeding. *See Complaints Against Various Television Licensees Concerning Their February 1, 2004, Broadcast of the Super Bowl XXXVIII Halftime Show*, Notice of Apparent Liability, 19 FCC Rcd 19230 (2004) (the "*NAL*"). The *NAL* was directed to Viacom, Inc., which was the ultimate corporate parent company of the licensees in question at that time. As of December 31, 2005, Viacom, Inc. effected a corporate reorganization in which the name of the ultimate parent company of the licensees of the CBS Stations was changed to CBS Corporation. Accordingly, we generally refer to the company herein as CBS even for periods preceding the reorganization. As part of the reorganization, certain non-broadcast businesses, including MTV Networks, were transferred to a new company named Viacom Inc. At the time of the violations, however, the CBS Stations and MTV Networks were corporate affiliates under common control.

[3] 47 C.F.R. § 73.3999.

[4] We note that viewers in markets served by each of the CBS Stations filed complaints with the Commission concerning the February 1, 2004 broadcast of the Super Bowl XXXVIII halftime show.

II. BACKGROUND

2. The halftime show in question was a live broadcast of music and choreography produced by MTV Networks ("MTV"), which was then a Viacom, Inc. subsidiary. The halftime show lasted approximately fifteen minutes and aired over the CBS Stations and other television stations affiliated with the CBS Television Network. The show received considerable notoriety due to an incident at the end of its musical finale, in which Justin Timberlake pulled off part of Janet Jackson's bustier, exposing one of her breasts to the television audience.

3. Following the Super Bowl broadcast and the receipt of complaints, the Enforcement Bureau ("Bureau") issued a letter of inquiry ("LOI") to CBS, seeking information about the halftime show, followed by a letter requesting videotapes of the complete Super Bowl programming broadcast over the CBS Television Network stations on February 1, 2004, including the halftime show (collectively, the "Broadcast Videotape").[5] In response, CBS provided a videotape of the broadcast of the halftime show to the Bureau on February 3, 2004,[6] an "interim response" to the Bureau's inquiries on February 10, 2004,[7] the Broadcast Videotape on February 14, 2004,[8] and a complete response to the LOI on March 16, 2004.[9]

4. The script and Broadcast Videotape of the halftime show provided by CBS confirm that the show contained repeated sexual references, particularly in its opening and closing performances. The first song, "All For You," performed by Janet Jackson, began with the following lines, referring to a man at a party:

> All my girls at the party
> Look at that body
> Shakin' that thing
> Like I never did see
> Got a nice package alright

---

[5] *See* Letter from William D. Freedman, Deputy Chief, Investigations and Hearings Division, Enforcement Bureau, Federal Communications Commission, to Howard Jaeckel, Vice President and Associate General Counsel, CBS, dated February 2, 2004; Letter from William D. Freedman, Deputy Chief, Investigations and Hearings Division, Enforcement Bureau, Federal Communications Commission, to Robert Corn-Revere, Esquire, dated February 10, 2004.

[6] *See* Letter from Robert Corn-Revere, Esquire to William D. Freedman, Deputy Chief, Investigations and Hearings Division, Enforcement Bureau, Federal Communications Commission, dated February 3, 2004.

[7] Letter from Robert Corn-Revere, Esquire to William D. Freedman, Deputy Chief, Investigations and Hearings Division, Enforcement Bureau, Federal Communications Commission, dated February 10, 2004 (the "*CBS Interim Response*").

[8] Letter from James S. Blitz, Esquire to William D. Freedman, Deputy Chief, Investigations and Hearings Division, Enforcement Bureau, Federal Communications Commission, dated February 14, 2004.

[9] Letter from Susanna M. Lowy, Esquire to William D. Freedman, Deputy Chief, Investigations and Hearings Division, Enforcement Bureau, Federal Communications Commission, dated March 16, 2004 (the "*CBS Response*"). Although many of CBS's responses to the LOI's inquiries are contained in both the *CBS Interim Response* and the *CBS Response*, for purposes of simplicity, unless otherwise noted, references herein will be to the latter. CBS requested confidential treatment of the bulk of the materials attached to its Response, including electronic mail and other documents relevant to the planning of the halftime show. We do not rule on CBS's request at this time because it is unnecessary to do so for purposes of this Order. Consistent with the request, however, we limit ourselves to describing or characterizing the substance of the materials and providing record citations herein, rather than actually quoting the materials or otherwise incorporating them into the Order. The Confidential Appendix, however, contains quotations to various documents in the record.

APPENDIX C

Guess I'm gonna have to ride it tonight.[10]

These lyrics use slang terms to refer to a man's sexual organs and sexual intercourse and were repeated two more times during the song. Following that performance, P. Diddy and Nelly presented a medley of songs containing occasional references to sexual activities, emphasized by Nelly's crotch-grabbing gestures.[11] Then, after a medley by performer Kid Rock, Jackson reappeared for a performance of "Rhythm Nation" and then the closing song, "Rock Your Body," a duet in which she was joined by Justin Timberlake. During the finale, Timberlake urged her to allow him to "rock your body" and "just let me rock you 'til the break of day" while following her around the stage and, on several occasions, grabbing and rubbing up against her in a manner simulating sexual activity.[12] At the close of the song, while singing the lyrics, "gonna have you naked by the end of this song," Timberlake pulled off the right portion of Jackson's bustier, exposing her breast to the television audience.[13]

    5.   The Commission released its *NAL* on September 22, 2004, pursuant to section 503(b) of the Act and section 1.80 of the Commission's rules, finding that CBS apparently violated the federal restrictions regarding the broadcast of indecent material.[14] We noted that our indecency analysis involves two basic determinations. The first determination is whether the material in question depicts or describes sexual or excretory organs or activities.[15] We found that the broadcast material contained, *inter alia*, a performance by Jackson and Timberlake that culminated in the on-camera exposure of one of Jackson's breasts, thereby meeting the first standard.[16] The second determination is whether the material is patently offensive as measured by contemporary community standards for the broadcast medium.[17] We observed that, in our assessment of whether broadcast material is patently offensive, "the *full context* in which the material appeared is critically important."[18] Three principal factors are significant to this contextual analysis: (1) the explicitness or graphic nature of the description or depiction of sexual or excretory organs or activities; (2) whether the material dwells on or repeats at length descriptions or depictions of sexual or excretory organs or activities; and (3) whether the material appears to pander or is used to

---

[10] Broadcast Videotape. *See also CBS Response*, Ex. 9 at 7-10; www.azlyrics.com/lyrics/janetjackson/allforyou.html.

[11] These sexual references include the lyrics "I was like good gracious ass bodacious . . . I'm waiting for the right time to shoot my steam (you know)" and "[i]t's gettin' hot in here (so hot), so take off all your clothes (I am gettin' so hot)" in the Nelly song "Hot in Herre." Broadcast Videotape. *See also CBS Response*, Ex. 9 at 16, 18; www.lyricsstyle.com/n/nelly/hotinherre.html.

[12] Broadcast Videotape. *See also CBS Response*, Ex. 9 at 36-37; www.lyricsondemand.com/j/justintimberlakelyrics/rockyourbodylyrics.html.

[13] Broadcast Videotape.

[14] *See* 18 U.S.C. § 1464; 47 C.F.R. § 73.3999; and 47 U.S.C. § 503(b).

[15] *See Industry Guidance on the Commission's Case Law Interpreting 18 U.S.C. § 1464 and Enforcement Policies Regarding Broadcast Indecency,* Policy Statement, 16 FCC Rcd 7999, 8002, ¶ 7 (2001) *("Indecency Policy Statement").*

[16] *NAL*, 19 FCC Rcd at 19235, ¶ 11.

[17] The "contemporary standards for the broadcast medium" criterion is that of an average broadcast listener and does not encompass any particular geographic area. *Indecency Policy Statement*, 16 FCC Rcd at 8002, ¶ 8 and n. 15. CBS suggests that we should rely on third-party public opinion polls to determine whether the material is patently offensive as measured by contemporary community standards for the broadcast medium. *Opposition* at 33-34. In determining whether material is patently offensive, we do not rely on polls, but instead apply the three-pronged contextual analysis described in the text. CBS provides no legal support for a departure from that approach.

[18] *NAL,* 19 FCC Rcd at 19235, ¶ 12, *quoting Indecency Policy Statement*, 16 FCC Rcd at 8002, ¶ 9 (emphasis in original).

titillate or shock.[19] In examining these three factors, we stated that we must weigh and balance them on a case-by-case basis to determine whether the broadcast material is patently offensive because "[e]ach indecency case presents its own particular mix of these, and possibly, other factors."[20] We noted that, in particular cases, one or two factors may outweigh the others, either rendering the broadcast material patently offensive and consequently indecent[21] or, alternatively, removing the broadcast from the realm of indecency.[22]

      6.   The Commission examined all three factors in the NAL and determined that, in context and on balance, the halftime show is patently offensive as measured by contemporary community standards for the broadcast medium. The Commission determined that the broadcast of partial nudity in this instance was explicit and graphic and appeared to pander to, titillate and shock the viewing audience. Therefore, the Commission determined that the material was patently offensive as measured by contemporary community standards for the broadcast medium, even though the nudity was brief.[23]

      7.   The Commission concluded, based upon its review of the facts and circumstances of this case, that CBS was apparently liable for a monetary forfeiture in the amount of $550,000, calculated by applying the maximum forfeiture of $27,500 to each CBS Station, for broadcasting indecent material in apparent violation of 18 U.S.C. § 1464 and section 73.3999 of the Commission's rules.[24] In contrast, the Commission proposed no forfeiture against any licensee other than CBS. It did so based on its finding that no licensee of a non-CBS-owned CBS affiliate was involved in the selection, planning or approval of the material for the halftime show, nor could any such licensee reasonably have anticipated that Viacom's production of the show would contain indecent material.[25] On November 5, 2004, CBS submitted its *Opposition* to the *NAL*.[26]

---

[19] *Indecency Policy Statement,* 16 FCC Rcd at 8002-15, ¶¶ 8-23.

[20] *NAL,* 19 FCC Rcd at 19235, ¶ 12, *quoting Indecency Policy Statement,* 16 FCC Rcd at 8003, ¶ 10.

[21] *NAL,* 19 FCC Rcd at 19235, ¶ 12; *Indecency Policy Statement,* 16 FCC Rcd at 8009, ¶ 19 (citing *Tempe Radio, Inc. (KUPD-FM)*, 12 FCC Rcd 21828 (Mass Media Bur. 1997) (forfeiture paid), and *EZ New Orleans, Inc. (WEZB(FM))*, 12 FCC Rcd 4147 (Mass Media Bur. 1997) (forfeiture paid), which found that the extremely graphic or explicit nature of references to sex with children outweighed the fleeting nature of the references.

[22] *NAL,* 19 FCC Rcd at 19235, ¶ 12; *Indecency Policy Statement,* 16 FCC Rcd at 8010, ¶ 20 (noting that "the manner and purpose of a presentation may well preclude an indecency determination even though other factors, such as explicitness, might weigh in favor of an indecency finding.")

[23] *NAL,* 19 FCC Rcd at 19235-36, ¶¶ 12-14.

[24] *Id.* at 19236-40, ¶¶ 16-24. The Commission recently amended its rules to increase the maximum penalties to account for inflation since the last adjustment of the penalty rates. However, the new rates apply to violations that occur or continue after September 7, 2004, and therefore do not apply here. *See Amendment of Section 1.80(b) of the Commission's Rules, Adjustment of Forfeiture Maxima to Reflect Inflation,* Order, 19 FCC Rcd 10945, 10946, ¶ 6 (2004).

[25] *Id.,* 19 FCC Rcd at 19240-41, ¶ 25.

[26] "*Opposition to Notice of Apparent Liability for Forfeiture*" by CBS, dated November 5, 2004 ("*Opposition*"). In addition to CBS's Opposition, we also received filings from non-parties to this proceeding that we are treating as filings by amici curiae. One such filing is a "*Petition for Partial Reconsideration of Notice of Apparent Liability for Forfeiture*" submitted by Saga Quad States Communications, LLC, and Saga Broadcasting, LLC, which argues that the *NAL* improperly imposes a new requirement on network affiliate stations to employ delay technology to prescreen network feeds. The *NAL* urges such licensees to take reasonable precautions to prevent the broadcast of indecent programming over their stations, but this is not a new requirement. *See NAL,* 19 FCC Rcd at 19241, ¶ 25. *See also Complaints Against Various Licensees Regarding Their Broadcast of the Fox Network Program "Married by America"* on April 7, 2003, *Notice of Apparent Liability for Forfeiture,* 19 FCC Rcd 20191 (2004) ("*Married by*

(continued....)

III.   DISCUSSION

8.   CBS does not dispute that the halftime show included a segment in which Justin Timberlake pulls off a portion of Jackson's bustier to reveal her breast at the end of the performance of a song containing the lyrics quoted above.[27] CBS nonetheless argues that the material broadcast was not actionably indecent.[28] CBS also maintains that the broadcast of Jackson's breast was accidental, and therefore was not "willful" under section 503(b)(1)(B) of the Act.[29] CBS further argues that the Commission's indecency framework is unconstitutionally vague and overbroad, both on its face and as applied to the halftime show.[30] As discussed below, we reject CBS's arguments and find the broadcast indecent for the reasons set forth herein. We reject CBS's assertion that the material at issue is not indecent because it is not patently offensive. In addition, we reject CBS's interpretation of the term "willful" and also address specific circumstances indicating that: (1) CBS consciously omitted the actions necessary to ensure that actionably indecent material would not be aired; and (2) the performers' willful actions here were attributable to CBS under established principles of agency and respondeat superior. Finally, we reject CBS's constitutional arguments, as the courts have repeatedly upheld the constitutionality of the Commission's indecency framework and our analysis of the halftime show is consistent with that framework. We therefore conclude that the broadcast of this material by the Viacom Stations violated 18 U.S.C. § 1464 and our rule against indecent broadcasts between 6 a.m. and 10 p.m., and that the maximum statutory forfeiture is warranted.

9.   *Indecency Analysis.* The indecency analysis undertaken in the *NAL* followed the approach that the Commission has consistently applied. First, the material alleged to be indecent must fall within the subject matter scope of our indecency definition, *i.e.,* "the material must describe or depict sexual or excretory organs or activities."[31] The *NAL* properly concluded that the broadcast of an exposed female

---

(...continued from previous page)

America") (response pending); 47 C.F.R. § 73.658(e)(1) (prohibiting television stations from entering into arrangements with networks that restrict their right to reject programming that the stations reasonably believe to be unsatisfactory or unsuitable or contrary to the public interest). Another such filing by Litigation Recovery Trust ("LRT") is styled a "Petition for Reconsideration" but fails to meet the requirements of Section 1.106(b)(1) of our rules for petitions for reconsideration by non-parties. First, a petition for reconsideration of a Notice of Apparent Liability is not appropriate under Section 1.106(b)(1) because such action is only a notice, not a Commission decision that is subject to reconsideration. Furthermore, even if a petition for reconsideration were appropriate here, LRT does not make the showings required under that rule that a non-party "state with particularity the manner in which the person's interest are adversely affected by the action taken, and show good reason why it was not possible for him to participate in the earlier stages of the proceeding." 47 C.F.R. § 1.106(b)(1). In substance, LRT's filing is a supplement to a prior request for rulemaking on a matter that is outside the scope of, and is not affected by, this decision.

[27] *Opposition* at 11. CBS does take issue with the *NAL*'s statement that the nudity lasted for 19/32 of a second, stating that the actual time was 9/16 of a second. *Id.* at 11 n. 7. We accept CBS's determination as to the duration, but we find no practical difference here. We also note that the brevity of the image is considered in connection with just one of three contextual factors, and no single factor is dispositive. *See Indecency Policy Statement,* 16 FCC Rcd at 8003, ¶ 10 ("Each indecency case presents its own particular mix of these [three], and possibly other, factors, which must be balanced to ultimately determine whether the material is patently offensive and therefore indecent. No single factor generally provides the basis for an indecency finding.").

[28] *Opposition* at 13-34.

[29] *Id.* at 35-38.

[30] *Id.* at 44-77.

[31] *Indecency Policy Statement,* 16 FCC Rcd at 8002, ¶ 7.

breast met this definition.[32] The halftime show broadcast therefore warrants further scrutiny to determine whether or not it was patently offensive as measured by contemporary community standards for the broadcast medium.

10. As discussed above, in our assessment of whether broadcast material is patently offensive, "the *full context* in which the material appeared is critically important."[33] In cases involving televised nudity, the contextual analysis necessarily involves an assessment of the entire segment or program, and not just the particular scene in which the nudity occurs.[34] Accordingly, in this case, our contextual analysis considers the entire halftime show, not just the final segment during which Jackson's breast is uncovered. We find that, in context and on balance, the complained-of material is patently offensive as measured by contemporary community standards for the broadcast medium.

11. Turning to the first principal factor of our contextual analysis, we conclude that a video broadcast image of Timberlake pulling off part of Jackson's bustier and exposing her bare breast, where the image of the nude breast is clear and recognizable to the average viewer, is graphic and explicit.[35] CBS maintains that none of the cases cited in the *NAL* to support the conclusion that the partial nudity in the halftime show was explicit and graphic involved a televised broadcast of a woman's breast.[36] We reject CBS's argument that our conclusion regarding this factor is flawed. The *NAL* correctly relied on *Young Broadcasting,* which supports the proposition that a scene showing nude sexual organs is graphic and explicit if the nudity is readily discernible.[37] In this case, although the camera shot is not a close-up, the nudity is readily discernible. Furthermore, Jackson and Timberlake, as the headline performers, are in the center of the screen, and Timberlake's hand motion ripping off Jackson's bustier draws the viewer's attention to her exposed breast. CBS suggests that the fact that this nudity was not "planned and approved by [CBS]" is somehow relevant to whether it is explicit and graphic in nature.[38] However, CBS's suggestion that planning or premeditation should be a factor in deciding whether a televised image

---

[32] *NAL,* 19 FCC Rcd at 19235, ¶ 11.

[33] *Indecency Policy Statement,* 16 FCC Rcd at 8002, ¶ 9 (emphasis in original).

[34] *See, e.g., Young Broadcasting of San Francisco, Inc.*, Notice of Apparent Liability for Forfeiture, 19 FCC Rcd 1751, 1755-57 (2004) ("*Young Broadcasting*") (response pending) (Commission makes an assessment of the entire segment of a morning news program involving an interview of and demonstration by cast members from a "Puppetry of the Penis" stage production in which adult male nudity was aired for less than a second (¶¶ 11-13); and distinguishes an earlier case involving non-fleeting adult frontal nudity in a broadcast of *Schindler's List* based on "the full context of its presentation, including the subject matter of the film [World War II and wartime atrocities], the manner of presentation, and the warnings that accompanied the broadcast of the film" (¶ 14)).

[35] We note that, although Jackson wore a piece of jewelry on her nipple, it only partially covered her nipple and did not cover her breast.

[36] *Opposition* at 21.

[37] *NAL,* 19 FCC Rcd at 19235, ¶ 13 and n. 42. CBS attempts to distinguish *Young Broadcasting* from this case. *See Opposition* at 19-20. However, CBS's analysis focuses on the foreseeability of the nudity in that case as compared to this case. As discussed below, foreseeability and premeditation relate to whether the broadcast of indecent matter was willful, and not to whether the material is graphic and explicit.

[38] *See Opposition* at 25 n.35. *See also id.* at 22. We agree that the exposure of Jackson's breast was not in the official script submitted by CBS, but CBS has not shown that it was unplanned. Clearly, the "costume reveal" that led to the exposure of the breast was at least planned by the performers (Jackson and Timberlake) and their choreographer, Gil Duldulao, who were hired by CBS for the halftime show. Timberlake's Declaration disavows any knowledge on his part that the costume reveal would lead to exposure of Jackson's breast, but Jackson's statement does not address her knowledge or intentions, and Duldulao did not provide a statement. *See CBS Response,* Ex. 7 and Ex. 8.

is explicit or graphic lacks any basis in logic or law.[39] Rather, the first factor in our contextual analysis focuses on the explicitness of the broadcast from the viewer's or listener's standpoint. Notwithstanding CBS's claimed befuddlement at how the televised image of a man tearing off a woman's clothing to reveal her bare breast could be deemed explicit, we believe that conclusion is clearly warranted by the facts here and fully consistent with the case law.[40]

12. The second principal factor in our contextual analysis is whether the material dwells on or repeats at length descriptions or depictions of sexual or excretory organs or activities. The *NAL* appropriately recognizes that the image of Jackson's uncovered breast during the halftime show is fleeting.[41] However, "even relatively fleeting references may be found indecent where other factors contribute to a finding of patent offensiveness."[42] In this case, even though we find that the partial nudity was fleeting, the brevity of the partial nudity is outweighed by the first and third factors of our contextual analysis.

13. Under the third principal factor of our analysis – whether the material appears to pander or is titillating or shocking – we examine how the material is presented in context.[43] The *NAL* found that "the manner of presentation of the complained-of material over each [CBS Station], for which Viacom failed to take adequate precautions, was pandering, titillating and shocking."[44] The *NAL* noted that the exposure of Jackson's breast followed "performances, song lyrics and choreography [that] discussed or simulated sexual activities."[45] Jackson's opening song contained repeated references to a man's "nice package" that she was "gonna have to ride . . . tonight" – slang references to male sexual organs and sexual intercourse. The P. Diddy/Nelly performance also contained sexual references, emphasized by

---

[39] CBS compares this case to a decision that it claims involves programming that is "considerably more explicit and clearly premeditated," in which the Commission imposed a base forfeiture rather than the maximum forfeiture imposed in this case. *See Opposition* at 22-23, citing *Married by America*. The appropriate level of the forfeiture is best addressed in a subsequent section, but at this point we note that the case cited involved a program in which certain body parts were digitally obscured by pixilation to avoid a display of partial nudity such as that aired by CBS to a national audience in this case. Thus, that case is not a particularly useful precedent in determining whether the material at issue here is graphic and explicit.

[40] CBS argues that our recent dismissals of complaints about programming that we found not to be graphic or explicit requires a similar decision here. *Opposition* at 23-25, citing *KSAZ Licensee, Inc.*, Memorandum Opinion and Order, 19 FCC Rcd 15999 (2004), and *Complaints Against Various Broadcast Licensees Regarding Their Airing of the UPN Network Program "Buffy the Vampire Slayer" on November 20, 2001*, Memorandum Opinion and Order, 19 FCC Rcd 15995 (2004). Neither case is apposite here because neither program included nudity. The other cases cited by CBS are inapposite for the same reason. *See Opposition* at 23-24.

[41] *See NAL*, 19 FCC Rcd at 19236, ¶ 14.

[42] *Indecency Policy Statement*, 16 FCC Rcd at 8009, ¶ 19. *See also Young Broadcasting; Tempe Radio*, Notice of Apparent Liability, 12 FCC Rcd 21828 (Mass Media Bur. 1997) (paid); *LBJS Broadcasting*, Notice of Apparent Liability, 13 FCC Rcd. 20956 (Mass Media Bur. 1998) (paid).

[43] *Indecency Policy Statement*, 16 FCC Rcd at 8010, ¶20.

[44] *NAL*, 19 FCC Rcd at 19236 n. 44. The *NAL* stated that "the nudity here was designed to pander to, titillate and shock the viewing audience." *Id.* at ¶ 14. To the extent that the language in the *NAL* could be interpreted to suggest that the broadcaster's state of mind is a decisional factor, we wish to clarify that this is not the case. Our *Indecency Policy Statement* frames this factor as *"whether the material appears to pander or is used to titillate*, or *whether the material appears to have been presented for its shock value." Indecency Policy Statement*, 19 FCC Rcd at 8003, ¶ 10 (emphasis in original). In making this determination, we focus on the material that was broadcast and its manner of presentation, not on the state of mind of the broadcaster or performer. *See Young Broadcasting*, 19 FCC Rcd at 1755-57, ¶¶ 13-14.

[45] *NAL*, 19 FCC Rcd at 19236, ¶ 14.

Nelly's crotch-grabbing gestures. Likewise, the duet by Jackson and Timberlake of "Rock Your Body" contained repeated references to sexual activities[46] and choreography in which Timberlake grabbed Jackson, slapped her buttocks, and rubbed up against her in a manner simulating sexual activity. These sexually suggestive performances culminated in the spectacle of Timberlake ripping off a portion of Jackson's bustier and exposing her breast while he sang "gonna have you naked by the end of this song." Clearly, the nudity in this context was pandering, titillating and shocking to the viewing audience, particularly during a prime time broadcast of a sporting event that was marketed as family entertainment and contained no warning that it would include nudity.[47] Contrary to CBS's contention, we do evaluate the nudity in context. The offensive segment in question did not merely show a fleeting glimpse of a woman's breast, as CBS presents it. Rather, it showed a man tearing off a portion of a woman's clothing to reveal her naked breast during a highly sexualized performance and while he sang "gonna have you naked by the end of this song." From the viewer's standpoint, this nudity hardly seems "accidental," nor was it.[48] This broadcast thus presents a much different case than would, for example, a broadcast in which a woman's dress strap breaks, accidentally revealing her breast for a fraction of a second.

     14.   Accordingly, we conclude that the Super Bowl XXXVIII halftime show contained material that was graphic, explicit, pandering, titillating and shocking and, in context and on balance, was patently offensive under contemporary community standards for the broadcast medium and thus indecent. Although the patently offensive material was brief, its brevity is outweighed in this case by the first and third factors in our contextual analysis. The complained-of material was broadcast within the 6 a.m. to 10 p.m. time frame relevant to an indecency determination under Section 73.3999 of the Commission's rules,[49] and is therefore legally actionable.

     15.   *Whether Violation was "Willful."* CBS argues that, if it did air indecent programming, its violation was "accidental" rather than "willful" and therefore cannot be sanctioned under section 503(b)(1) of the Act. In support of this argument, CBS cites definitions of "willful" from criminal and copyright law cases.[50] These definitions, however, are inapposite. Rather than borrowing definitions from unrelated areas of law, the Commission appropriately applies the definition of "willful" that appears in the Communications Act. Section 312(f)(1) of the Act defines "willful" as "the conscious and deliberate commission or omission of [any] act, irrespective of any intent to violate" the law.[51] As

---

[46] Timberlake sang the lyrics: "I've been watching you, I like the way you move, so go 'head and girl just do that ass-shakin' thing you do . . . I wanna rock your body, let me rock your body." Broadcast Videotape. *See also CBS Response*, Ex. 9 at 36-37; http://www.lyricsondemand.com/j/justintimberlakelyrics/rockyourbodylyrics.html.

[47] Indeed, CBS appears to concede that it was shocking, but maintains that "the 'costume reveal' was as much a shock to Viacom as to everyone else." *Opposition* at iii.

[48] *See CBS Response* at Ex. 7 and Ex. 8. Whether this nudity was planned or foreseeable by CBS and the stations that broadcast it is a distinct issue that is addressed below in the discussion of the "willfulness" factor.

[49] 47 C.F.R. § 73.3999.

[50] *See Opposition* at 37-38.

[51] The Conference Report to the 1982 amendment to the Act that added this definition stated: "Willful means that the licensee knew he was doing the act in question, regardless of whether there was an intent to violate the law." H.R. Rep. No. 97-765, 97th Cong. 2d Sess. 51 (1982). The Conference Report also makes it clear that this definition applies to section 503(b) of the Act as well as section 312. *See Southern California Broadcasting Co.*, Memorandum Opinion and Order, 6 FCC Rcd 4387, 4388 (1991). CBS initially acknowledges that "the Commission has held that in order to satisfy the willfulness requirement, the purported offender need not intend to violate the Act or an FCC rule, or even be aware the action in question constitutes a violation." *Opposition* at 36. Yet on the next page of its Opposition it urges us to apply criminal cases in which the scienter requirement has been held to require "an act done with a bad purpose" or an "evil motive." *Id.* at 37. Clearly, those cases have no application in interpreting the willfulness requirement in a regulatory statute authorizing the imposition of

(continued....)

discussed in detail below, CBS acted willfully because it consciously and deliberately broadcast the halftime show, whether or not it intended to broadcast nudity, and because it consciously and deliberately failed to take reasonable precautions to ensure that no actionably indecent material was broadcast.[52] CBS also is vicariously liable for the willful actions of the performers under the doctrine of respondeat superior.

16.   The Commission's forfeiture authority was enacted "to impel broadcast licensees to become familiar with the terms of their licenses and the applicable Rules, and to adopt procedures, including periodic review of operations, which will insure that stations are operated in substantial compliance with their licenses and the Commission's Rules."[53] The obligation of licensees to adopt measures to ensure compliance with the Act and the Commission's rules has particular force when it comes to broadcasters' responsibility for the programming that they broadcast to the public. Under well-established principles of broadcast regulation, "[b]roadcast licensees must assume responsibility for all material which is broadcast through their facilities," and that "duty is personal to the licensee and may not be delegated."[54]

17.   CBS claims that it had no advance knowledge that Timberlake planned to tear off part of Jackson's clothing to reveal her breast. Even assuming that this claim is true, however, we do not believe that this relieves CBS from responsibility for the indecent material that it broadcast. Rather, the record

---

(...continued from previous page)
administrative sanctions. We disagree with CBS's contention that criminal law definitions of "willful" are apt because 18 U.S.C. § 1464 is a criminal statute. *Id.* In *Pacifica*, the Supreme Court declined to consider questions relating to possible application of section 1464 as a criminal statute in upholding a broadcast indecency forfeiture imposed by the Commission. *FCC v. Pacifica Foundation*, 438 U.S. 726, 739 n.13 (1978) ("the validity of the civil sanctions [authorized under the Act] is not linked to the validity of the criminal penalty."). Likewise, we reject CBS's suggestion that the First Amendment requires statutes imposing civil penalties on speech to be interpreted to include the same scienter requirement as those imposing criminal penalties. *Opposition* at 38, citing *United States v. X-Citement Video, Inc.,* 513 U.S. 64, 77-78 (1994), *Smith v. California,* 361 U.S. 147 (1959), and *United States v. Reilly,* 2002 WL 31307170 (S.D.N.Y. 2002).

[52] We note that application of this standard to CBS does not "impose a strict liability requirement on protected speech." *Opposition* at 38, *citing Gertz v. Robert Welch, Inc.,* 418 U.S. 323 (1974). The Supreme Court held in *Gertz* that "the States should retain substantial latitude in their efforts to enforce a legal remedy for defamatory falsehood injurious to the reputation of a private individual," so long as they do not impose liability without fault. *Id.* at 345-46. As discussed *infra*, CBS clearly is at fault for broadcasting actionably indecent material during the Super Bowl telecast. We also note that CBS's reliance on *Saxe v. State College,* 240 F.3d 200, 206 (3d Cir. 2001), as holding that willful indifference is a legally insufficient basis for punishing speech, is misplaced. *See Opposition* at 38. *Saxe* held that a school district policy prohibiting "harassing" speech was unconstitutionally overbroad because it was not limited to vulgar or lewd speech or school-sponsored speech, and was not necessary to prevent substantial disruption or interference with the rights of students or the conduct of the school. The court did not address the intent required to impose liability for expressive speech or conduct under the First Amendment.

[53] *Crowell-Collier Broadcasting Corp.*, Memorandum Opinion and Order, 44 FCC 2444, 2449 (1961) (violation due to erroneous advice from the station's competent engineering consultant warrants a forfeiture).

[54] *Report and Statement of Policy re: Commission en banc Programming Inquiry,* 44 FCC Rcd 2303, 2313 (1960). *See also Yale Broadcasting Co. v. FCC,* 478 F.2d 594 (D.C. Cir.), *cert. denied,* 414 U.S. 914 (1973) (affirmed action of Commission reminding broadcast licensees of their duty to have knowledge of the content of their programming and on the basis of this knowledge to evaluate the desirability of broadcasting music dealing with drug use); *Gaffney Broadcasting, Inc.,* 23 FCC 2d 912, 913 (1970) ("licensees are responsible for the selection and presentation of program material over their stations, including . . . acts or omissions of their employees"); *Alabama Educational Television Commission,* 50 FCC 2d 461, 464 (1975) (AETC lost its license in part because it failed to maintain exclusive authority over all of its programming decisions); *WCHS-AM-TV Corp.,* 8 FCC 2d 608, 609 (1967) (maintenance of control over programming is a most fundamental obligation of the licensee).

reveals that CBS was acutely aware of the risk of unscripted indecent material in this production, but failed to take adequate precautions that were available to it to prevent that risk from materializing.

18.   It is disingenuous for CBS to argue that "the 'costume reveal' was as much a shock to Viacom as to everyone else."[55] CBS clearly recognized that the live broadcast of the Super Bowl halftime show posed a significant risk that indecent material would be aired. The extensive planning and preparation for the show highlighted this risk. CBS knew that MTV, the corporate affiliate that was producing the show, was seeking to push the envelope by, among other things, including sexually provocative performers and material.[56] In fact, the NFL expressed concerns about whether the planned halftime show might be heading in too risqué a direction and rebuffed MTV's desire to feature one performer because of a prior incident in which the performer unexpectedly removed her clothes during a national telecast of an NFL event.[57] MTV sought to overcome the NFL's objections to another performer by offering assurances that it would exercise control over her wardrobe and actions, despite its own doubts about its ability to do so.[58]

19.   CBS maintains that it selected Jackson and Timberlake "to minimize the possibility of the unexpected,"[59] but CBS was well aware that their selection did not obviate this risk. The NFL specifically expressed concerns to CBS about the costume that Jackson would wear during the halftime show.[60] Moreover, the NFL raised concerns about Timberlake's scripted line "gonna have you naked by the end of this song" that anticipated the stunt resulting in the broadcast nudity.[61] There were other warning signs as well. In a January 28, 2004 news item posted on MTV's website, Jackson's choreographer predicted that Jackson's performance would include "some shocking moments" and said "I don't think the Super Bowl has ever seen a performance like this . . . ."[62] Shortly before the game, one halftime show performer asked about the length of the audio delay, a question that MTV employees evidently recognized implied an intention to depart from the script.[63] Further, MTV learned the morning of the Super Bowl telecast of plans to use tearaway cheerleading outfits for dancers in another halftime performance in connection with a scripted line ("I wanna take my clothes off") that is quite similar to Timberlake's line ("gonna have you naked by the end of this song").[64] The record reflects CBS's awareness that there is always a risk that performers will ad-lib remarks or take unscripted actions, and

---

[55] *Opposition* at iii.

[56] *See, e.g.*, *CBS Response*, App. B-C at Bates stamped pgs. 18, 176, 219, 314, 1175, 1229, 1456. *See also Super Bowl NAL*, 19 FCC Rcd at 19238-39 ¶ 19 (discussing MTV's promotion of the sexually-provocative nature of the halftime show by, *inter alia*, posting on its website a news item entitled "Janet Jackson's Super Bowl Show Promises 'Shocking Moments,'" which quoted her choreographer Gil Dulduleo's prediction that her performance would include "some shocking moments."). Confidential Appendix 1.

[57] *See CBS Response*, App. B at Bates stamped pgs. 72, 96, 195, 218-19. Confidential Appendix 2.

[58] *See CBS Response*, App. B at Bates stamped pgs. 123, 355, 447. Confidential Appendix 3.

[59] *Opposition* at 18. *See CBS Response* at 9 (stating that Jackson and Timberlake were "proven, experienced talent").

[60] *See CBS Response*, App. B at Bates stamped p. 72. Confidential Appendix 4.

[61] *See CBS Response*, App. B at Bates stamped pgs. 39, 452-54. Confidential Appendix 5. *Cf. CBS Radio License, Inc. (WLLD(FM))*, Notice of Apparent Liability for Monetary Forfeiture, 15 FCC Rcd 23881, 23883, ¶ 8 (Enf. Bur. 2000) (given licensee's awareness of the actual language used in performers' recordings, it should have taken precautions to avoid airing actionably indecent material during a live, unscripted broadcast).

[62] *See Super Bowl NAL*, 19 FCC Rcd at 19238-39, ¶ 19; *CBS Response*, App. D at Bates stamped pgs. 2659.

[63] *See CBS Response*, App. B at Bates stamped p. 462. Confidential Appendix 6.

[64] *See CBS Response*, App. B at Bates stamped p. 458. Confidential Appendix 7.

that the risk level varies according to the nature of the performance.[65] In sum, there was a significant and foreseeable risk in a halftime show seeking to push the envelope and replete with sexual content that performers might depart from script and staging, and this is particularly true of Jackson and Timberlake given the sexually-provocative nature of their performance, the fact that it was promoted as "shocking," and the fact that it culminated with the scripted line "gonna have you naked by the end of this song."[66] Based on examination of the record, we conclude that CBS recognized the high risk that this broadcast raised of airing indecent material.[67]

20. Examination of the record also reveals that CBS failed to take adequate precautions to prevent the airing of unscripted indecent material. Aware of the risk of visual and spoken deviations from the script and staging -- that something spontaneous might occur or be said -- CBS made a calculated decision. It chose to rely on a five-second audio delay that would enable it to bleep offensive language but would not enable it to block unscripted visual moments. Thus, it could not cut off Jackson's "costume reveal" when it occurred – and it had no expectation that it would be able to block any indecent images.[68] Only *after* the Super Bowl halftime show – for the broadcast of the 2004 Grammy Awards – did CBS institute an audio *and* video delay "to ensure that no unexpected or unplanned video images would be broadcast."[69] CBS asserts that the delay used for the 2004 Grammy Awards was "unprecedented."[70] But CBS does not argue that use of a delay mechanism capable of editing video images during the Super Bowl halftime show would not have been feasible. The fact that use of such a delay mechanism would have been "far more technically complex and involved more broadcast standards staff to implement" than the delay that CBS actually used hardly excuses its omission under these circumstances.[71] Furthermore, CBS also failed to adopt other precautions available to it. For example, MTV's agreements with the performers did not require them to conform to the script or to CBS's broadcast standards and practices, notwithstanding the fact that MTV's agreement with the NFL contained provisions to this effect.[72] In addition, the record contains no evidence that MTV or CBS

---

[65] *See CBS Response*, App. B at Bates stamped pgs. 503-04, 511, 527. Confidential Appendix 5, 8. *See also supra*, ¶ 4. The risk of departures from the script was heightened here not only by the suggestive lyrics, but also by the fact that the line which occasioned Jackson's nudity was the culminating one in the script; the record reflects both the performers' and the producers' desire for a high-impact grand finale to the show. Confidential Appendix 9.

[66] *See Super Bowl NAL*, 19 FCC Rcd at 19237, ¶ 17 n.54, *citing Complaints Against Various Broadcast Licensees Regarding Their Airing of the "Golden Globe Awards" Program*, 19 FCC Rcd 4975, 4979 (2004) (network could have anticipated that a recipient at a live award ceremony might use profanity because similar mishaps had occurred in the past). CBS points out that the *Golden Globe Awards Order* was released after the Super Bowl telecast, *Opposition* at 19, but the issue here is whether CBS could have anticipated an unscripted costume reveal, not whether it had notice of the *Golden Globe Awards Order*.

[67] *See, e.g., supra*, ¶¶ 2, 4 and n. 4.

[68] *See Opposition* at 5 ("Historically, a five-second delay has been adequate to preclude the broadcast of any spontaneous or unplanned audio material. With such an arrangement, an individual from the broadcast standards department monitors the transmission of a live event and manually 'hits the button' to delete any objectionable material before it is broadcast. Although both the audio and visual transmission is delayed, five seconds does not provide sufficient time to edit video images. Accordingly, the precaution of a five-second delay could not prevent the broadcast of the unexpected images at the end of the halftime show.") (emphasis added). As indicated above, CBS also had reason to believe that its five-second audio delay might be inadequate to edit unscripted audio material during the halftime show. *See note 63 supra* and accompanying text.

[69] *CBS Response* at 5.

[70] *Id.* at 5, n.13.

[71] *CBS Response* at 5, n.13.

[72] *CBS Response*, App. B-C at Bates stamped pgs. 168-72, 431-34, 2152-2332, 2336-42, 2469. Confidential Appendix 10. CBS did not provide an executed agreement for either Jackson or Timberlake in response to the LOI,

(continued....)

communicated CBS's broadcast standards and practices to Jackson, Timberlake, or Jackson's choreographer before the show, despite the highly sexualized nature of the performances and the fact that MTV's contract with the NFL required MTV to communicate those standards and practices to all performers.[73]

21.   CBS also overstates the level of care it exercised in overseeing the halftime production. Critically, it failed to investigate Jackson's choreographer's "shocking moments" prediction, which was posted on MTV's website, despite CBS's concern about unscripted remarks or actions.[74] In addition, contrary to its contention,[75] each aspect of the halftime show was not reviewed in advance by CBS's Program Practices Department. As stated above, MTV learned for the first time on the morning of the Super Bowl telecast of plans for dancers to use tearaway cheerleading outfits to act out the line "I wanna take my clothes off."[76] It does not appear that these plans were reviewed by CBS's Program Practices Department because the rehearsals that CBS, MTV and NFL representatives reviewed occurred several days before the Super Bowl telecast, and the dancers were not in costume during the scene in question.[77]

22.   Under these circumstances, we believe that CBS can and should be held responsible for the patently offensive material that it broadcast to a nationwide audience. A contrary result would permit

---

(...continued from previous page)
but none of the contract drafts provided by CBS refers to a script or to broadcast standards and practices. The executed agreement for Jackson's choreographer likewise contains no such references.

[73] See Confidential Appendix 10. Because CBS's failure to take reasonable precautions to prevent the broadcast of actionably indecent material was conscious and deliberate, its reliance on *Mega Communications of New Britain Licensee, L.L.C.*, 19 FCC Rcd 11373 (Enf. Bur. 2004), is misplaced. *See Opposition* at 36, n.57 ("The same result should apply here, where Viacom took all reasonable precautions based on past experience—*including inspecting Ms. Jackson's costume*—but an unforeseeable violation nevertheless occurred."). The Bureau held in *Mega* that a licensee did not commit a willful violation of the Commission's antenna structure fencing requirements because it conducted regular inspections in compliance with those requirements and "the problem occurred shortly after an inspection by Mega." As the above discussion indicates, however, CBS consciously failed to prevent the airing of indecent material. Moreover, the *Mega* case is distinguishable because it involved actions by a third party, not the licensee. *Vernon Broadcasting, Inc.*, Memorandum Opinion and Order, 60 RR 2d 1275 (1986), illustrates this distinction. In *Vernon*, the Commission rescinded a forfeiture liability for a tower fencing violation as not willful, while affirming a liability for an unintentional violation of the public file rule. The distinction between the two situations was that the damage to the fence was caused by vandals, despite the station's regular process of inspections and repairs, whereas the public file violation arose from the station's own actions.

[74] *See* note 62 *supra* and accompanying text. CBS maintains that it interpreted the "shocking moments" quote innocently, stating that it believed the quote referred to Timberlake's surprise guest appearance, and that it "did not stand out because such hyperbolic language is not uncommon in the music world." *Opposition* at 7-8. As the Commission has indicated, CBS's explanation lacks credibility. *See NAL*, 19 FCC Rcd at 19239, n.64 ("at the start of the halftime segment, MTV included an onscreen credit for Timberlake, hardly a disclosure that would be made ten minutes before his appearance, had his participation in the program been the 'shocking moments' that it had publicized for days on its Internet site."). CBS's explanation also is dubious in light of the fact that the quote referred to "moments" in the plural, whereas it would have been expected to refer to a "moment" if it only concerned Timberlake's appearance. CBS has never provided a statement from Jackson's choreographer to explain what he meant by the quote. But even accepting CBS's argument that the choreographer's comment may have been innocent hyperbole, it should at least have caused CBS to look into the matter, given the level of concern at CBS and the NFL about the edgy lyrics and the possibility of inappropriate script departures. CBS gives no indication that it did so.

[75] *Opposition* at 4. *See CBS Response* at 9-10.

[76] *See CBS Response*, App. B at Bates stamped p. 458.

[77] *See CBS Response* at 9, App. B at Videotapes 6, 8 (Jackson/Timberlake Dress Rehearsal).

a broadcast licensee to stage a show that "pushes the envelope," send that show out over the air waves, knowingly taking the risk that performers will engage in offensive unscripted acts or use offensive unscripted language, and then disavow responsibility – leaving no one legally responsible for the result. We believe that these are fully appropriate circumstances for application of the "conscious and deliberate . . . omission" basis for finding "willfulness" incorporated by Congress into Section 503(b) of the Act.[78] Indeed, given the nondelegable nature of broadcast licensees' responsibility for programming and the means available to but declined by CBS to reduce the risk of the broadcast of indecent programming, it is difficult to conceive of a more appropriate context in which to apply that standard.

23.   Further, CBS is legally responsible here for another reason; it is fully responsible for the actions of Jackson, Timberlake, and Jackson's choreographer under the doctrine of respondeat superior. "It is well established that traditional vicarious liability rules ordinarily make principals or employers vicariously liable for acts of their agents or employees in the scope of their authority or employment."[79] The Commission has long held licensees responsible for the unauthorized acts of their agents under this doctrine.[80] Respondeat superior subjects a principal to vicarious liability when its agent-employee commits a tort while acting within the scope of employment.[81] Whether an agent is an employee for purposes of respondeat superior depends on whether the agent is subject to the principal's control or right to control the performance of the work.[82] An agent-employee acts within the scope of employment when performing work assigned by the employer or engaging in a course of conduct subject to the employer's control.[83]

24.   It is appropriate to impose vicarious responsibility on CBS for the willful actions of Jackson, Timberlake, and Jackson's choreographer under the doctrine of respondeat superior. Even assuming arguendo that the corporate officers and other corporate employees of CBS and MTV did not act willfully within the meaning of section 503(b)(1), there is no question that the performers did. Timberlake's declaration acknowledges a premeditated plan for him to tear off part of Jackson's clothing during the performance.[84] Jackson, Timberlake, and Jackson's choreographer were CBS agents for the halftime show performance; Jackson and Timberlake entered into agreements with MTV (MTV and CBS at the time were both Viacom subsidiaries) to perform during the halftime show, and Gil Duldulao contractually agreed to choreograph the dance.[85] Based on examination of the record, we also believe that

---

[78] 47 U.S.C. § 503(b)(1); 47 U.S.C. § 312(f).

[79] *Meyer v. Holley*, 537 U.S. 280, 285 (2003) (citations omitted).

[80] *See Dial-a-Page, Inc.*, 8 FCC Rcd 2767 (1993), *recon. den.*, 10 FCC Rcd 8825 (1995) (rule violation resulting from employee error was fully attributable to licensee under doctrine of respondeat superior and "willful" within the meaning of § 503(b)(1)); *Wagenvoord Broadcasting Co.*, 35 FCC 2d 361 (1972); *Eure Family Ltd. Partnership*, 17 FCC Rcd 7042, 7044 ¶ 7 (Enf. Bur. 2002) ("it is a basic tenet of agency law that the actions of an employee or contractor are imputed to the employer and 'the Commission has consistently refused to excuse licensees from forfeiture penalties where actions of employees or independent contractors have resulted in violations.'").

[81] *Restatement (Second) of Agency* § 219(1) (1957) (2nd Restatement). *See also Restatement (Third) of Agency* § 7.07 (T.D. No. 5 2004) (3rd Restatement).

[82] 2nd Restatement § 220. *See also* 3rd Restatement § 7.07.

[83] 2nd Restatement § 228.

[84] *CBS Response* at Att. 8 ("At the end of the song, I attempted to perform a 'costume reveal' by removing a portion of Ms. Jackson's costume and revealing the undergarment beneath. I had neither the intention nor the knowledge that the reveal could expose her right breast. The decision to add the 'costume reveal' to the finale was made by Ms. Jackson and her choreographer after final rehearsals for the Halftime Show. They informed me just before the performance began.").

[85] *See CBS Response*, App. B-C at Bates stamped pgs. 168-72, 431-34, 2152-2332, 2336-42; 2nd Restatement § 1 ("Agency is a legal concept which depends upon the existence of required factual elements: the manifestation by the

(continued....)

the three were CBS employees for purposes of applying the principle of respondeat superior. CBS had the right to control, and in fact exercised considerable control over, the halftime show:

> Each aspect of the halftime show was scripted in advance and a script of the halftime show was reviewed by the CBS Program Practices Department. In addition, employees of CBS, MTV, and the NFL attended two full run-throughs of the halftime show on Thursday, January 29 to review the production. The run-throughs were videotaped, and reviewed by representatives of CBS and the NFL. MTV producers then used the tape to individually review the rehearsal performances with the talent to instruct them on changes to be made in the actual performance on Super Bowl Sunday. Based on these procedures, certain changes were made to the show. For example, the costume worn by one of the dancers during the run-throughs was considered to be too revealing, and she was instructed to change it before the final show. There was also concern about some of the language, and changes were suggested. . . . Because Ms. Jackson was not in costume during the run-throughs, an executive producer subsequently checked to make sure that Ms. Jackson's wardrobe would conform to broadcast standards during the actual performance.[86]

25.   Thus, CBS exercised control over all aspects of the performers' conduct in the performance of the halftime show, including the script, staging and wardrobe used during the Jackson-Timberlake performance. Other factual indicia of control are present as well. CBS (through MTV) provided the set and set elements for the performance and dictated its time and place, as well as the time and place of production and press-related activities.[87] Many courts have held entertainers to be employees for respondeat superior and other purposes under similar circumstances.[88] Finally, the

---

(...continued from previous page)
principal that the agent shall act for him, the agent's acceptance of the undertaking and the understanding of the parties that the principal is to be in control of the undertaking."), *cited in Meyer v. Holley*, 537 U.S. at 286.

[86] *CBS Response* at 9-10. Although CBS had the right to exercise control over the halftime show, and in fact exercised considerable control, there were, as discussed above, significant lapses in the level of care that it exercised in overseeing the halftime production. *See* para. 17-22. Those lapses in supervision do not, however, negate the fact that the performances were subject to CBS's control and that CBS was thus vicariously responsible for the performers' actions within the scope of their employment under the doctrine of respondeat superior. *See* note 87 *infra*.

[87] *Id.* at Bates-stamped pgs. 168-72, 431-34, 2336-42. *See* 2nd Restatement § 220; 3rd Restatement § 7.07 (relevant factual indicia of control include "whether the agent or the principal supplies the tools and other instrumentalities required for the work and the place in which to perform it").

[88] *See P.T. Barnum's Nightclub v. Duhamell*, 766 N.E.2d 729 (Ind.App. 2002) (referring to 2nd Restatement factors in affirming denial of summary judgment as to whether male exotic dancer was an employee for respondeat superior purposes where "the Club exercised some degree of control over Ajishegiri's work, particularly with regard to work hours, conditions, and regulations, and was in the business of displaying adult entertainers (primarily female), but did not dictate the stylistic aspects of Ajishegiri's performance"); *White v. Frenkel*, 615 So.2d 535, 538-40 (La. App. 3 Cir. 1993) (professional wrestler was employee for respondeat superior purposes where, *inter alia*, promoter controlled who would win and who would lose wrestler's matches and had total control over who, where, and when wrestler wrestled); *Jeffcoat v. State Dept. of Labor*, 732 P.2d 1073, 1075-78 (Alaska 1987) (dancer was employee for purposes of state labor statute where, *inter alia*, club exercised some control over costumes and dances and total control over music and dancers' working hours); *Jack Hammer Assoc. v. Delmy Productions, Inc.*, 499 N.Y.S.2d 418, 419-20 (1st Dept. 1986) (actor was employee for purposes of determining availability of workers' compensation benefits where actor entered into a written contract for a stipulated sum for a term certain, time and place for his work was determined by production company, actor had to perform in a certain number of shows at specified times, and he had to follow a script and was subject to supervision of play's director). New York state courts have consistently held entertainers to be employees of the producers who engage them. *See Jack Hammer Assoc.*, 499 N.Y.S.2d at 419-20; *Challis v. Nat'l Producing Co.*, 88 N.Y.S.2d 731 (3d Dept. 1949) (circus clown); *Berman v.*

(continued....)

performers' actions were clearly within the scope of their employment. In this regard, the determining factor is not whether their actions were authorized by CBS but whether the performance was subject to CBS's control.[89] Put differently, their conduct was incident to the performance rather than "an independent course of conduct intended to serve no purpose of the employer."[90] Accordingly, the performers' willful actions are fully attributable to CBS under the doctrine of respondeat superior irrespective of whether the performers' actions were authorized by CBS.

26.   *Amount of Forfeiture.* CBS offers a variety of arguments that the forfeiture proposed in the *NAL* is excessive or unfair. First, it contends that it is unfair to impose a forfeiture on it, when no forfeiture was imposed on those affiliates of the CBS Television Network that are not owned by CBS.[91] Second, CBS argues that the *NAL* improperly cites "the history of recent indecent broadcasts by CBS owned radio stations" with a footnote to cases that are not completely adjudicated.[92] Third, CBS maintains that the forfeiture is excessive in relation to the duration of the nude scene and in light of CBS's precautionary measures.[93] Fourth, CBS argues that it had no prior notice that a brief scene of partial nudity constituted actionable indecency and thus should not be subject to any forfeiture.[94]

27.   We conclude that CBS's arguments do not justify a reduction in the amount of the proposed forfeiture. The *NAL* proposed no forfeiture against CBS Television Network affiliate stations that are not owned by Viacom because there is no evidence that the licensees of any of those stations played any role in the selection, planning or approval of the halftime show or that they could have reasonably anticipated that CBS's production of the halftime show would include partial nudity. CBS has not provided any contrary evidence. In contrast, CBS admits that it was closely involved in the production of the halftime show, and that its MTV affiliate produced it.

28.   With respect to the *NAL*'s reference to the history of indecent broadcasts by CBS's radio stations, we note that those cases have been resolved by a Consent Decree in which CBS admitted to certain violations, and the Commission agreed not to use that admission against CBS in any other

---

(...continued from previous page)
Burone, 88 N.Y.S.2d 327, 328 (3d Dept. 1949) (ballet dancer and variety artist). *See also In re Sims*, 602 N.Y.S.2d 225 (3d Dept. 1993) (finding a sufficient degree of direction and control by a conductor who hired musicians for imposition of respondeat superior liability although supervision was not direct). Here, the performers' agreements contain choice-of-law provisions specifying New York law. *CBS Response* at Bates-stamped pgs. 168-72, 431-34, 2336-42.

[89] 2nd Restatement § 228.

[90] 3rd Restatement § 7.07 ("an employee's conduct is outside the scope of employment when it occurs within an independent course of conduct intended to serve no purpose of the employer."). *See also id.* ("Alternative formulations avoid the use of motive or intention to determine whether an employee's tortious conduct falls within the scope of employment. These tests vary somewhat in how they articulate the requisite tie between the tortfeasor's employment and the tort. In general, such a tie is present only when the tort is a generally foreseeable consequence of the enterprise undertaken by the employer or is incident to it.").

[91] *Opposition* at 14.

[92] *Id.* at 39-40. CBS relies on section 504(c) of the Act, which provides that the Commission may not use the issuance of a notice of apparent liability in any other proceeding involving that person unless the forfeiture has been paid or there is a final court order for the payment of the forfeiture. CBS argues that the Commission not only must ignore cases in which there has been no final adjudication, but that it must consider CBS's long record of compliance with broadcast standards. *Id.* at 42.

[93] *Id.* at 41-43.

[94] *Id.* at 43.

proceeding, including this one.[95] Accordingly, we no longer rely on that history of indecent broadcasts in reaching our determination here. Nevertheless, we remain convinced that the upward adjustment to the statutory maximum is appropriate in light of all of the factors enumerated in section 503(b)(2)(D) of the Act, particularly the circumstances involving the preparation, execution and promotion of the halftime show by CBS, the gravity of the violation in light of the nationwide audience for the indecent broadcast, and CBS's ability to pay.[96] The crux of CBS's defense is that the blame lies with the performers who planned and carried out the costume reveal that resulted in the exposure of Jackson's breast. However, CBS's attempt to place blame on the performers in question is unavailing; as discussed above, the performers were acting as CBS's agents and CBS is responsible for their actions within the scope of their employment. In addition, CBS planned almost every element of the halftime show. In the course of doing so, it brushed off warning signs of the potential for actionably indecent behavior and failed to take adequate precautions to prevent the airing of indecent material. As a result of its decisions, an enormous nationwide audience,[97] including numerous children, was subjected without warning to the offensive spectacle of a man tearing off a woman's clothing on stage in the midst of a sexually charged performance. Finally, regarding the element of ability to pay and financial disincentives to violate the Act and rules,[98] we find that CBS's size and resources, without question, support an upward adjustment to the maximum statutory forfeiture of $550,000 because a lesser amount would not serve as a significant penalty or deterrent to a company of its size and resources.[99]

29. We also reject CBS's claim that it lacked prior notice that a brief scene of partial nudity might result in a forfeiture. Our rule against the broadcast of indecent material outside of the safe harbor hours has been in effect since 1993,[100] and our criteria for determining whether material is indecent were clearly spelled out in the *Policy Statement* issued in 2001. Furthermore, the *Young Broadcasting* decision, holding that a brief display of male frontal nudity was an apparent violation of that rule, was released shortly before the subject Super Bowl broadcast.[101] Thus, CBS was on notice that the broadcast of partial nudity could violate the indecency rule and statute. CBS tries to liken its situation to that of

---

[95] *See Viacom Inc.*, Order, 19 FCC Rcd 23100 (2004), *petition for recon. pending.* In light of that Consent Decree, entered into after the *NAL*, we conclude that CBS's history of past offenses is not relevant to our analysis. We note, however, that we disagree with, and have previously rejected, CBS's interpretation of section 504(c). We have made it clear that the Commission may rely on the underlying facts that provide the basis for a notice of apparent liability in a separate case. *See Forfeiture Policy Statement and Amendment of Section 1.80 of the Rules to Incorporate the Forfeiture Guidelines*, Report and Order, 15 FCC Rcd 303, 304-05, ¶¶ 3-5 (1999) ("*Forfeiture Policy Statement*"), *recon. denied*, 17 FCC Rcd 303 (1999).

[96] *See* 47 U.S.C. § 503(b)(2)(D) (the Commission "shall take into account the nature, circumstances, extent, and gravity of the violation and, with respect to the violator, the degree of culpability, any history of prior offenses, ability to pay, and such other matters as justice may require"); *NAL*, 19 FCC Rcd at 19237, ¶ 17.

[97] *See* http://www.usatoday.com/sports/football/super/2004-02-02-ratings_x.htm (stating that Super Bowl XXXVIII was "most-watched Super Bowl in history" with estimated 143.6 million viewers and 41.3 national rating).

[98] *See* 47 C.F.R. § 1.80, Note to Paragraph (b)(4), Section II, Upward Adjustment Criterion No. 2.

[99] *See* "Viacom Takes Big Write-Down, Creating a Loss," New York Times, Feb. 25, 2005, at C1 (reporting that Viacom, Inc. took a non-cash charge for 2004 to write down the value of its assets by 27%, to $49 billion, and that the company's revenue for the final quarter of 2004 was $6.3 billion); "While Shares Fell, Viacom Paid Three $160 Million," New York Times, April 16, 2005, at C1 (reporting that the company's top three executives received a total of $160 million in compensation for 2004).

[100] *See Enforcement of Prohibitions Against Broadcast Indecency*, Report and Order, 8 FCC Rcd 704 (1993), *modified*, 10 FCC Rcd 10558 (1995). CBS, Inc. and Infinity Broadcasting Corporation, both of which became Viacom, Inc. subsidiaries, submitted comments in that rulemaking proceeding. *Id.*, 8 FCC Rcd at 712.

[101] *Young Broadcasting*, 19 FCC Rcd at 1751 (release date of January 27, 2004).

NBC in the *Golden Globe Order*, where we declined to impose a forfeiture because we overruled precedent that had specifically held that isolated expletives were not actionably indecent.[102] We have never held, however, that fleeting nudity is not actionably indecent. On the contrary, as discussed above, we held that fleeting nudity was indecent in *Young Broadcasting* before the Super Bowl broadcast at issue here. The fact that this case is not identical to *Young Broadcasting* (or, indeed, any other case) certainly does not preclude us from imposing a forfeiture. The facts of most indecency cases are not identical to any that precede them. For example, the Commission has not been confronted before this case with a broadcast where a male performer ripped off the clothing of a female performer to reveal her breast in the midst of a song containing repeated sexual references and a dance containing simulated sexual activities. But any argument that CBS lacked adequate notice that such a performance would run afoul of the Commission's indecency regulations is groundless. The Commission is applying an established standard to the facts of a new case and is not overruling precedent. Thus, it is entirely lawful and appropriate to impose a forfeiture when we determine that the licensee has violated that standard.[103]

      30.   *Constitutional Issues.* CBS offers a number of arguments attacking the constitutional underpinnings of the Commission's indecency framework. We find no merit in those arguments.

      31.   We reject CBS's arguments that the Commission's indecency standard is vague, overbroad, and vests the Commission with excessive discretion.[104] Courts have upheld the indecency standard applied in the *NAL* and in this *Order* against facial vagueness and overbreadth challenges.[105] The D.C. Circuit also has rejected the argument that the Commission's indecency standard is overbroad because it may encompass material with serious merit.[106] We do not believe that requiring broadcasters to exercise care to prevent a televised depiction of naked sexual organs prior to 10 p.m. unduly "chills" exercise of their First Amendment rights. As the D.C. Circuit observed, "some degree of self-censorship is inevitable and not necessarily undesirable so long as proper standards are available."[107]

      32.   We also disagree with CBS that the *NAL* is inconsistent with the Supreme Court's *Pacifica* decision.[108] *Pacifica* stressed the importance of contextual analysis such as that reflected in this

---

[102] *Opposition* at 19, 27-28.

[103] As we find CBS legally responsible for the indecent broadcast based on both its own willful omission and its vicarious liability for the willful acts of its agents under the principle of respondeat superior, we need not address whether it could also be held responsible under Section 503(b)(1)(D) without a showing of willfulness.

[104] *Opposition* at 65-77.

[105] *See ACT III*, 58 F.3d at 659 (upholding the Commission's indecency definition against facial vagueness and overbreadth challenges). CBS's arguments about the Commission's discretion focus on the Commission's investigatory practices in cases where a complaint is based on a description of allegedly offensive programming, and not supported by a tape or a transcript. *Opposition* at 74-76. However, those arguments have nothing to do with this case, in which there was no dispute about what was broadcast and in which CBS issued a public apology to viewers for the violation of its broadcast standards. Similarly, CBS's contention about delay in the Commission's enforcement process (*Opposition* at 76-77) is irrelevant to this case. We also note that the D.C. Circuit has previously rejected this argument. *Action for Children's Television v. FCC*, 59 F.3d 1249, 1261-62 (D.C. Cir. 1995) ("*ACT IV*"), *cert. denied*, 516 U.S. 1072 (1996).

[106] *Action for Children's Television v. FCC*, 852 F.2d 1332, 1339 (D.C. Cir. 1988) ("*ACT I*") ("'serious merit' need not, in every instance, immunize material from FCC channeling authority").

[107] *ACT IV*, 59 F.3d at 1261; *see ACT III*, 58 F.3d at 666 ("Whatever chilling effect may be said to inhere in the regulation of indecent speech, these have existed ever since the Supreme Court first upheld the FCC's enforcement of section 1464 of the Radio Act.").

[108] *Opposition* at 44-53. In making this argument, CBS generally ignores the specific context of this case, preferring instead to opine about live television coverage of political and other events and even to lament "the end of live
(continued....)

Order.[109] Accordingly, we do not read *Pacifica* as precluding an indecency finding based on a brief depiction of partial nudity. The Supreme Court specifically stated that it had not decided whether an occasional expletive in a different setting (*e.g.*, a two-way radio conversation between a cab driver and a dispatcher, or a telecast of an Elizabethan comedy) would justify any sanction.[110] The Court's emphasis on the narrowness of its holding was meant to highlight the "all-important" role of context, not to deprive the Commission of power to regulate broadcast indecency except in situations involving extended or repetitious expletives or depictions of sexual or excretory organs or activities.[111]

33.   CBS also claims that the constitutional validity of our indecency enforcement practice has been undermined by a changed legal and technological landscape, citing the Supreme Court's decisions in *United States v. Playboy Entertainment Group, Inc.*,[112] *Reno v. ACLU*,[113] and *Denver Area Educational Telecommunications Consortium v. FCC*,[114] and pointing to the pervasiveness of cable and satellite television, and the development of online media and media recording technology (*e.g.*, videocassette recorders, DVD recorders and personal video recorders featuring time-shifting technology) and the V-chip.[115] Again, we disagree. In striking down as unconstitutional an Internet indecency standard, the Supreme Court expressly recognized in *Reno* the "special justifications for regulation of the broadcast media," citing *Red Lion* and *Pacifica*.[116] Moreover, in *Denver Area*, the Court addressed the constitutionality of a Commission order implementing provisions of the 1992 Cable Television Consumer Protection and Competition Act that concerned indecent and obscene cable programming, not over-the-air broadcasting. We find nothing in that opinion that undermines the constitutionality of our framework for enforcing our rule against the broadcast of indecent material outside the safe harbor hours.

34.   Furthermore, CBS's arguments about new technologies have no apparent application to this case. The V-chip technology cannot be utilized to block sporting events such as the Super Bowl because sporting events are not rated.[117] Nevertheless, even if the V-chip could be used to block sporting events,

---

(...continued from previous page)
broadcasting as we know it." *Id.* at 48. We reiterate that our decision is limited to the specific context of this case, which involves a Super Bowl halftime entertainment show that was produced by CBS, using performers selected and paid by CBS. For the reasons stated in the *NAL* and in this *Order*, there is ample support for our conclusion that CBS failed to take reasonable precautions to ensure that no actionably indecent material was broadcast in this context.

[109] *Pacifica*, 438 U.S. at 742 ("indecency is largely a function of context – it cannot be adequately judged in the abstract").

[110] *Id.*, 438 at 750; *see id.* at 760-61 (Powell, J., concurring).

[111] *Id.* at 750. The D.C. Circuit upheld the Commission's interpretation of *Pacifica* as not imposing such limits. *See ACT I*, 852 F.2d at 1338 (upholding the Commission's decision to depart from its prior policy of acting only in cases involving "the repeated use, for shock value, of words similar to those satirized in the Carlin 'Filthy Words' monologue. . . . The FCC rationally determined that its former policy could yield anomalous, even arbitrary, results.").

[112] 529 U.S. 803 (2000).

[113] 521 U.S. 844 (1997).

[114] 518 U.S. 717 (1996).

[115] *Opposition* at 53-61.

[116] Similarly, in *Playboy*, the Court distinguished broadcast services from cable due to differences in the nature of those media. *See United States v. Playboy Entertainment Group, Inc.*, 529 U.S. at 815.

[117] *See Implementation of Section 551 of the Telecommunications Act of 1996*, Report and Order, 13 FCC Rcd 8232, 8242-43, ¶ 21 (1998) (news programming, sports programming and advertisements are not included in the V-chip ratings system). Outside of the context of exempt programming such as sports programming, we agree that the V-

(continued....)

based on CBS's representations it appears that CBS would not have rated the Super Bowl halftime show as inappropriate for children.

35.   Finally, we address CBS's dire warnings that imposing sanctions in this case will have a chilling effect on live coverage of public events, such as national political conventions and presidential scandals, and "violates the Commission's own pledge" to "take no action which would inhibit broadcast journalism."[118] While we are sensitive to the impact of our decisions on speech and, in particular, on live news coverage, we do not believe that CBS's fears about the chilling effect of our decision here are well-founded. As discussed in detail above, this case involves a staged show planned by CBS and its affiliates, under circumstances where they had the means to exercise control and good reasons to take precautionary measures. These circumstances are obviously completely different from live coverage of breaking news events, which are not controlled by broadcasters, and this decision in no way suggests that we are imposing strict liability for such coverage or, indeed, any other programming.

36.   *Conclusion.* Under section 503(b)(1)(B) of the Act, any person who is determined by the Commission to have willfully failed to comply with any provision of the Act or any rule, regulation, or order issued by the Commission shall be liable to the United States for a monetary forfeiture penalty.[119] In order to impose such a forfeiture penalty, the Commission must issue a notice of apparent liability, the notice must be received, and the person against whom the notice has been issued must have an opportunity to show, in writing, why no such forfeiture penalty should be imposed.[120] The Commission will then issue a forfeiture if it finds by a preponderance of the evidence that the person has violated the Act or a Commission rule. For the reasons set forth above, we conclude under this standard that CBS is liable for a forfeiture for its willful violation of 18 U.S.C. § 1464 and section 73.3999 of the Commission's rules.

37.   The Commission's *Forfeiture Policy Statement* sets a base forfeiture amount of $7,000 for transmission of indecent materials.[121] The *Forfeiture Policy Statement* also specifies that the Commission shall adjust a forfeiture based upon consideration of the factors enumerated in section 503(b)(2)(D) of the Act, 47 U.S.C. § 503(b)(2)(D), such as "the nature, circumstances, extent and gravity of the violation, and, with respect to the violator, the degree of culpability, any history of prior offenses, ability to pay, and such other matters as justice may require."[122] In this case, taking all of these factors into consideration, for the reasons set forth above, we find that the *NAL* properly proposed the statutory maximum forfeiture of $550,000 against CBS.

(...continued from previous page)

chip is an important protection, but it does not eliminate the need for enforcing our indecency rule or undermine the constitutionality of that rule. We note that last year, CBS and the other major networks announced their participation with the Advertising Council in an educational campaign designed to improve awareness of the V-chip. The announcement stated that less than 10 percent of all parents are using the V-chip and 80 percent of all parents who currently own a television set with a V-chip are not aware that they have it. *See* News Release, "The Advertising Council and Four Major Television Networks Announce Unprecedented Partnership to Educate Parents About the V-Chip," http://www.adcouncil.org/about/news_033004 (March 30, 2004). In addition, numerous television sets in U.S. households lack V-chips.

[118] *Opposition* at 53, *quoting Pacifica Reconsideration Order*, 59 FCC 2d at 893. *See also Opposition* at ix, x, 46, 48-53.

[119] 47 U.S.C. § 503(b)(1)(B); 47 C.F.R. § 1.80(a)(1).

[120] 47 U.S.C. § 503(b); 47 C.F.R. § 1.80(f).

[121] *Forfeiture Policy Statement*, 12 FCC Rcd at 17113.

[122] *Id.*, 12 FCC Rcd at 17100-01, ¶ 27.

IV. ORDERING CLAUSES

38.   Accordingly, IT IS ORDERED THAT, pursuant to section 503(b) of the Act[123], and sections 0.311 and 1.80(f)(4) of the Commission's Rules[124], CBS Corporation IS LIABLE FOR A MONETARY FORFEITURE in the amount of $550,000 for willfully violating 18 U.S.C. § 1464 and section 73.3999 of the Commission's rules.

39.   Payment of the forfeiture shall be made in the manner provided for in section 1.80 of the Commission's rules within 30 days of the release of this *Order*. If the forfeiture is not paid within the period specified, the case may be referred to the Department of Justice for collection pursuant to section 504(a) of the Act.[125] Payment of the forfeiture must be made by check or similar instrument, payable to the order of the Federal Communications Commission. The payment must include the NAL/Acct. No. referenced above and the FRN(s) referenced in the Appendix. Payment by check or money order may be mailed to Federal Communications Commission, P.O. Box 358340, Pittsburgh, PA 15251-8340. Payment by overnight mail may be sent to Mellon Bank/LB 358340, 500 Ross Street, Room 1540670, Pittsburgh, PA 15251. Payment by wire transfer may be made to ABA Number 043000261, receiving bank Mellon Bank, and account number 911-6106.

40.   Requests for payment under an installment plan should be sent to: Associate Managing Director - Financial Operations, 445 12th Street, S.W., Room 1-A625, Washington, D.C. 20554.[126]

41.   IT IS FURTHER ORDERED THAT a copy of this FORFEITURE ORDER shall be sent by Certified Mail, Return Receipt Requested to CBS Corporation, 2000 K Street, N.W., Suite 725, Washington, DC 20006, and to its counsel, Robert Corn-Revere, Esquire, Davis Wright Tremaine LLP, 1500 K Street, N.W., Washington, DC 20005.

FEDERAL COMMUNICATIONS COMMISSION

Marlene H. Dortch
Secretary

---

[123] 47 U.S.C. § 503(b).

[124] 47 C.F.R. §§ 0.311, 1.80(f)(4).

[125] 47 U.S.C. § 504(a).

[126] *See* 47 C.F.R. § 1.1914.

APPENDIX

CBS-OWNED
CBS TELEVISION NETWORK AFFILIATES

Licensee	FCC Registration Number	Call Sign	Community of License	Facility ID No.
CBS Stations Group of Texas L.P.	0001767078	KEYE-TV	Austin, TX	33691
Viacom Inc.	0003612447	WJZ-TV	Baltimore, MD	25455
Viacom Inc.	0003612447	WBZ-TV	Boston, MA	25456
CBS Broadcasting Inc.	0003482189	WBBM-TV	Chicago, IL	9617
CBS Stations Group of Texas L.P.	0001767078	KTVT	Ft. Worth, TX	23422
CBS Television Stations Inc.	0003482189	KCNC-TV	Denver, CO	47903
CBS Broadcasting Inc.	0003482189	WFRV-TV	Green Bay, WI	9635
CBS Broadcasting Inc.	0003482189	WJMN-TV	Escanaba, MI	9630
CBS Broadcasting Inc.	0003482189	WWJ-TV	Detroit, MI	72123
CBS Broadcasting Inc.	0003482189	KCBS-TV	Los Angeles, CA	9628
CBS Television Stations Inc.	0003482189	WFOR-TV	Miami, FL	47902
CBS Broadcasting Inc.	0003482189	WCCO-TV	Minneapolis, MN	9629
CBS Broadcasting Inc.	0003482189	KCCO-TV	Alexandria, MN	9632
CBS Broadcasting Inc.	0003482189	KCCW-TV	Walker, MN	9640
CBS Broadcasting Inc.	0003482189	KDKA-TV	Pittsburgh, PA	25454
CBS Broadcasting Inc.	0003482189	KYW-TV	Philadelphia, PA	25453
CBS Broadcasting Inc.	0003482189	WCBS-TV	New York, NY	9610
KUTV Holdings, Inc.	0004499273	KUTV	Salt Lake City, UT	35823
KUTV Holdings, Inc.	0004499273	KUSG	St. George, UT	35822
CBS Broadcasting Inc.	0003482189	KPIX-TV	San Francisco, CA	25452

STATEMENT OF
CHAIRMAN KEVIN J. MARTIN

Re: *Complaints Against Various Television Licensees Concerning Their February 1, 2004 Broadcast of the Super Bowl XXXVIII Halftime Show; Complaints Regarding Various Television Broadcasts Between February 2, 2002 and March 8, 2005; Complaints Against Various Television Licensees Concerning Their December 31, 2004 Broadcast of the Program "Without A Trace"*

Congress has long prohibited the broadcasting of indecent and profane material and the courts have upheld challenges to these standards. But the number of complaints received by the Commission has risen year after year. They have grown from hundreds, to hundreds of thousands. And the number of programs that trigger these complaints continues to increase as well. I share the concerns of the public - and of parents, in particular - that are voiced in these complaints.

I believe the Commission has a legal responsibility to respond to them and resolve them in a consistent and effective manner. So I am pleased that with the decisions released today the Commission is resolving hundreds of thousands of complaints against various broadcast licensees related to their televising of 49 different programs. These decisions, taken both individually and as a whole, demonstrate the Commission's continued commitment to enforcing the law prohibiting the airing of obscene, indecent and profane material.

Additionally, the Commission today affirms its initial finding that the broadcast of the Super Bowl XXXVIII Halftime Show was actionably indecent. We appropriately reject the argument that CBS continues to make that this material is not indecent. That argument runs counter to Commission precedent and common sense.

STATEMENT OF
COMMISSIONER MICHAEL J. COPPS

Re: *Complaints Regarding Various Television Broadcasts Between January 1, 2002 and March 12, 2005,* Notices of Apparent Liability and Memorandum Opinion and Order

   Complaints Against Various Television Licensees Concerning Their December 31, 2004 Broadcast of the Program "Without A Trace", Notice of Apparent Liability

   Complaints Against Various Television Licensees Concerning Their February 1, 2004 Broadcast Of The Super Bowl XXXVII Halftime Show, Forfeiture Order

In the past, the Commission too often addressed indecency complaints with little discussion or analysis, relying instead on generalized pronouncements. Such an approach served neither aggrieved citizens nor the broadcast industry. Today, the Commission not only moves forward to address a number of pending complaints, but does so in a manner that better analyzes each broadcast and explains how the Commission determines whether a particular broadcast is indecent. Although it may never be possible to provide 100 percent certain guidance because we must always take into account specific and often-differing contexts, the approach in today's orders can help to develop such guidance and to establish precedents. This measured process, common in jurisprudence, may not satisfy those who clamor for immediate certainty in an uncertain world, but it may just be the best way to develop workable rules of the road.

Today's Orders highlight two additional issues with which the Commission must come to terms. First, it is time for the Commission to look at indecency in the broader context of its decisions on media consolidation. In 2003 the FCC sought to weaken its remaining media concentration safeguards without even considering whether there is a link between increasing media consolidation and increasing indecency. Such links have been shown in studies and testified to by a variety of expert witnesses. The record clearly demonstrates that an overwhelming number of the Commission's indecency citations have gone to a few huge media conglomerates. One recent study showed that the four largest radio station groups which controlled just under half the radio audience were responsible for a whopping 96 percent of the indecency fines levied by the FCC from 2000 to 2003.

One of the reasons for the huge volume of complaints about excessive sex and graphic violence in the programming we are fed may be that people feel increasingly divorced from their "local" media. They believe the media no longer respond to their local communities. As media conglomerates grow ever larger and station control moves farther away from the local community, community standards seem to count for less when programming decisions are made. Years ago we had independent programming created from a diversity of sources. Networks would then decide which programming to distribute. Then local affiliates would independently decide whether to air that programming. This provided some real checks and balances. Nowadays so many of these decisions are made by vertically-integrated conglomerates headquartered far away from the communities they are supposed to be serving—entities that all too often control both the distribution *and* the production content of the programming.

If heightened media consolidation is indeed a source for the violence and indecency that upset so many parents, shouldn't the Commission be cranking that into its decisions on further loosening of the ownership rules? I hope the Commission, before voting again on loosening its media concentration protections, will finally take a serious look at this link and amass a credible body of evidence and not act again without the facts, as it did in 2003.

Second, a number of these complaints concern graphic broadcast violence. The Commission states that it has taken comment on this issue in another docket. It is time for us to step up to the plate and tackle the issue of violence in the media. The U.S. Surgeon General, the American Academy of Pediatrics, the American Psychological Association, the American Medical Association, and countless other medical and scientific organizations that have studied this issue have reached the same conclusion: exposure to graphic and excessive media violence has harmful effects on the physical and mental health of our children. We need to complete this proceeding.

STATEMENT OF
COMMISSIONER JONATHAN S. ADELSTEIN
CONCURRING

Re: Complaints Against Various Television Licensees Concerning Their February 1,   2004 Broadcast
        of the Super Bowl XXXVIII Halftime Show, Forfeiture Order

I have sworn an oath to uphold the Constitution[1] and to carry out the laws adopted by Congress.[2] Trying to find a balance between these obligations has been challenging in many of the indecency cases that I have decided. I believe it is our duty to regulate the broadcast of indecent material to the fullest extent permissible by the Constitution because safeguarding the well-being of our children is a compelling national interest.[3] I therefore have supported efforts to step up our enforcement of indecency laws since I joined the Commission.

The Commission's authority to regulate indecency over the public airwaves was narrowly upheld by the Supreme Court with the admonition that we should exercise that authority with the utmost restraint, lest we inhibit constitutional rights and transgress constitutional limitations on government regulation of protected speech.[4] Given the Court's guidance in Pacifica, the Commission has repeatedly stated that we would judiciously walk a "tightrope" in exercising our regulatory authority.[5] Hence, within this legal context, a rational and principled "restrained enforcement policy" is not a matter of mere regulatory convenience. It is a constitutional requirement.[6]

Accordingly, I concur with today's Super Bowl Order, but concur in part and dissent in part with the companion Omnibus Order[7] because, while in some ways today's Omnibus decision goes too far, in other ways it does not go far enough. Significantly, it abruptly departs from our precedents by adopting a new, weaker enforcement mechanism that arbitrarily fails to assess fines against broadcasters who have aired indecent material. Additionally, while today's Omnibus decision appropriately identifies violations of our indecency laws, not every instance determined to be indecent meets that standard.

We have previously sought to identify all broadcasters who have aired indecent material, and hold them accountable. In the Omnibus Order, however, the Commission inexplicably fines only the licensee whose broadcast of indecent material was the subject of a viewer's complaint, even though we

---

[1] U.S. CONST., amend. I.

[2] Congress has specifically forbidden the broadcast of obscene, indecent or profane language. 18 U.S.C. § 1464. It has also forbidden censorship. 47 U.S.C. § 326.

[3] See, e.g., N.Y. v. Ferber, 458 U.S. 747, 756-57 (1982).

[4] See FCC v. Pacifica Foundation, 438 U.S. 726, 750 (1978) (emphasizing the "narrowness" of the Court's holding); Action for Children's Television v. FCC, 852 F.2d 1332, 1344 (D.C. Cir. 1988) ("ACT I") ("Broadcast material that is indecent but not obscene is protected by the [F]irst [A]mendment.").

[5] See Brief for Petitioner, FCC, 1978 WL 206838 at *9.

[6] ACT I, supra note 4, at 1344 ("the FCC may regulate [indecent] material only with due respect for the high value our Constitution places on freedom and choice in what the people say and hear."); Id. at 1340 n.14 ("[T]he potentially chilling effect of the FCC's generic definition of indecency will be tempered by the Commission's restrained enforcement policy.").

[7] Complaints Regarding Various Television Broadcasts Between February 2, 2002 and March 8, 2005, Notices of Apparent Liability and Memorandum Opinion and Order (decided March 15, 2006) (hereinafter "Omnibus Order").

know millions of other Americans were exposed to the offending broadcast. I cannot find anywhere in the law that Congress told us to apply indecency regulations only to those stations against which a complaint was specifically lodged. The law requires us to prohibit the broadcast of indecent material, period. This means that we must enforce the law anywhere we determine it has been violated. It is willful blindness to decide, with respect to network broadcasts we know aired nationwide, that we will only enforce the law against the local station that happens to be the target of viewer complaints. How can we impose a fine solely on certain local broadcasters, despite having repeatedly said that the Commission applies a national indecency standard – not a local one?[8]

The failure to enforce the rules against some stations but not others is not what the courts had in mind when they counseled restraint. In fact, the Supreme Court's decision in *Pacifica* was based on the uniquely pervasive characteristics of broadcast media.[9] It is patently arbitrary to hold some stations but not others accountable for the same broadcast. We recognized this just two years ago in *Married By America*.[10] The Commission simply inquired who aired the indecent broadcast and fined all of those stations that did so.

In the *Super Bowl XXXVIII Halftime Show* decision, we held only those stations owned and operated by the CBS network responsible, under the theory that the affiliates did not expect the incident and it was primarily the network's fault.[11] I dissented in part to that case because I believed we needed to apply the same sanction to every station that aired the offending material. I raise similar concerns today, in the context of the Omnibus Order.

The Commission is constitutionally obligated to decide broadcast indecency and profanity cases based on the "contemporary community standard," which is "that of the average broadcast viewer or listener." The Commission has explained the "contemporary community standard," as follows:

> We rely on our collective experience and knowledge, developed through constant interaction with lawmakers, courts, broadcasters, public interest groups and ordinary citizens, to keep abreast of contemporary community standards for the broadcast medium.[12]

I am concerned that the Omnibus Order overreaches with its expansion of the scope of indecency and profanity law, without first doing what is necessary to determine the appropriate contemporary community standard.

---

[8] *See, e.g., In re Sagittarius Broadcasting Corporation,* Memorandum Opinion and Order, 7 FCC Rcd 6873, 6876 (1992) (subsequent history omitted).

[9] *See Pacifica Found.,* 438 U.S. at 748-49 (recognizing the "uniquely pervasive presence" of broadcast media "in the lives of all Americans"). In today's Order, paragraph 10, the Commission relies upon the same rationale.

[10] *See Complaints Against Various Licensees Regarding Their Broadcast of the Fox Television Network Program "Married by America" on April 7, 2003,* Notice of Apparent Liability for Forfeiture,19 FCC Rcd 20191, 20196 (2004) (proposing a $7,000 forfeiture against each Fox Station and Fox Affiliate station); *reconsideration pending. See also Clear Channel Broadcast Licenses, Inc.,* 19 FCC Rcd 6773, 6779 (2004) (proposing a $495,000 fine based on a "per utterance" calculation, and directing an investigation into stations owned by other licensees that broadcast the indecent program). In the instant Omnibus Order, however, the Commission inexplicably fines only the licensee whose broadcast of indecent material was actually the subject of a viewer's complaint to the Commission. *Id.* at ¶ 71.

[11] *See Complaints Against Various Television Licensees Concerning Their February 1, 2004, Broadcast of the Super Bowl XXXVIII Halftime Show,* Notice of Apparent Liability, 19 FCC Rcd 19230 (2004).

[12] *In re Infinity Radio License, Inc.,* Memorandum Opinion and Order, 19 FCC Rcd 5022, 5026 (2004).

The Omnibus Order builds on one of the most difficult cases we have ever decided, the *Golden Globe Awards* case, [13] and stretches it beyond the limits of our precedents and constitutional authority. The precedent set in that case has been contested by numerous broadcasters, constitutional scholars and public interest groups who have asked us to revisit and clarify our reasoning and decision. Rather than reexamining that case, the majority uses the decision as a springboard to add new words to the pantheon of those deemed to be inherently sexual or excretory, and consequently indecent and profane, irrespective of their common meaning or of a fleeting and isolated use. By failing to address the many serious concerns raised in the reconsideration petitions filed in the *Golden Globe Awards* proceeding, before prohibiting the use of additional words, the Commission falls short of meeting the constitutional standard and walking the tightrope of a restrained enforcement policy.

This approach endangers the very authority we so delicately retain to enforce broadcast decency rules. If the Commission in its zeal oversteps and finds our authority circumscribed by the courts, we may forever lose the ability to protect children from the airing of indecent material, barring an unlikely constitutional amendment setting limitations on the First Amendment freedoms.

The perilous course taken today is evident in the approach to the acclaimed Martin Scorsese documentary, "The Blues: Godfathers and Sons." It is clear from a common sense viewing of the program that coarse language is a part of the culture of the individuals being portrayed. To accurately reflect their viewpoint and emotions about blues music requires airing of certain material that, if prohibited, would undercut the ability of the filmmaker to convey the reality of the subject of the documentary. This contextual reasoning is consistent with our decisions in *Saving Private Ryan*[14] and *Schindler's List*.[15]

The Commission has repeatedly reaffirmed, and the courts have consistently underscored, the importance of content *and* context. The majority's decision today dangerously departs from those precedents. It is certain to strike fear in the hearts of news and documentary makers, and broadcasters that air them, which could chill the future expression of constitutionally protected speech.

We should be mindful of Justice Harlan's observation in *Cohen v. California*.[16] Writing for the Court, he observed:

> [W]ords are often chosen as much for their emotive as their cognitive force. We cannot sanction the view that the Constitution, while solicitous of the cognitive content of individual speech, has little or no regard for that emotive function which, practically

---

[13] *In re Complaints Against Broadcast Licensees Regarding Their Airing of the "Golden Globe Awards" Program*, Memorandum Opinion and Order, 19 FCC Rcd 4975 (2004); *petitions for stay and reconsideration pending.*

[14] *In the Matter of Complaints Against Various Television Licensees Regarding Their Broad. on November 11, 2004, of the ABC Television Network's Presentation of the Film, "Saving Private Ryan,"* Memorandum Opinion and Order, 20 FCC Rcd 4507, 4513 (2005) ("Deleting all [indecent] language or inserting milder language or bleeping sounds into the film would have altered the nature of the artistic work and diminished the power, realism and immediacy of the film experience for viewers."). *See also Peter Branton*, Letter by Direction of the Commission, 6 FCC Rcd 610 (1991) (concluding that repeated use of the f-word in a recorded news interview program not indecent in context).

[15] *In the Matter of WPBN/WTOM License Subsidiary, Inc.*, 15 FCC Rcd 1838 (2000).

[16] 403 U.S. 15 (1971).

speaking, may often be the more important element of the overall message sought to be communicated.[17]

Given all of these considerations, I find that the Omnibus Order, while reaching some appropriate conclusions both in identifying indecent material and in dismissing complaints, is in some ways dangerously off the mark. I cannot agree that it offers a coherent, principled long-term framework that is rooted in common sense. In fact, it may put at risk the very authority to protect children that it exercises so vigorously.

---

[17] *Id.* at 26 ("We cannot indulge the facile assumption that one can forbid particular words without also running a substantial risk of suppressing ideas in the process.").

STATEMENT OF
COMMISSIONER DEBORAH TAYLOR TATE

Re: Complaints Against Various Television Licensees Concerning Their February 1, 2004 Broadcast of the Super Bowl XXXVIII Halftime Show, Forfeiture Order; *Complaints Regarding Various Television Broadcasts Between February 2, 2002 and March 8, 2005*, Notices of Apparent Liability and Memorandum Opinion and Order; *Complaints Against Various Television Licensees Concerning Their December 31, 2004 Broadcast of the Program "Without A Trace"*, Notice of Apparent Liability for Forfeiture

Today marks my first opportunity as a member of the Federal Communications Commission to uphold our responsibility to enforce the federal statute prohibiting the airing of obscene, indecent or profane language.[1] To be clear – I take this responsibility very seriously. Not only is this the law, but it also is the right thing to do.

One of the bedrock principles of the Communications Act of 1934, as amended, is that the airwaves belong to the public. Much like public spaces and national landmarks, these are scarce and finite resources that must be preserved for the benefit of all Americans. If numbers are any indication, many Americans are not happy about the way that their airwaves are being utilized. The number of complaints filed with the FCC reached over one million in 2004. Indeed, since taking office in January 2006, I have received hundreds of personal e-mails from people all over this country who are unhappy with the content to which they – and, in particular, their families – are subjected.

I have applauded those cable and DBS providers for the tools they have provided to help parents and other concerned citizens filter out objectionable content. Parental controls incorporated into cable and DBS set-top boxes, along with the V-Chip, make it possible to block programming based upon its content rating. However, these tools, even when used properly, are not a complete solution. One of the main reasons for that is because much of the content broadcast, including live sporting events and commercials, are not rated under the two systems currently in use.

I also believe that consumers have an important role to play as well. Caregivers – parents, in particular – need to take an active role in monitoring the content to which children are exposed. Even the most diligent parent, however, cannot be expected to protect their children from indecent material broadcast during live sporting events or in commercials that appear during what is marketed to be "appropriate" programming.

Today, we are making significant strides toward addressing the backlog of indecency complaints before this agency. The rules are simple – you break them and we will enforce the law, just as we are doing today. Both the public and the broadcasters deserve prompt and timely resolution of complaints as they are filed, and I am glad to see us act to resolve these complaints. At the same time, however, I would like to raise a few concerns regarding the complaints we address in these decisions.

First, I would like to discuss the complaint regarding the 6:30 p.m. Eastern Daylight Time airing of an episode of *The Simpsons*. The *Order* concludes that this segment is not indecent, in part because of the fact that *The Simpsons* is a cartoon. Generally speaking, cartoons appeal to children, though some may cater to both children and adults simultaneously. Nevertheless, the fact remains that children were extremely likely to have been in the viewing audience when this scene was broadcast. Indeed, the

---

[1] *See* 18 U.S.C. § 1464.

marketing is aimed at children. If the scene had involved real actors in living color, at 5:30 p.m. Central Standard Time, I wonder if our decision would have been different? One might argue that the cartoon medium may be a more insidious means of exposing young people to such content. By their very nature, cartoons do not accurately portray reality, and in this instance the use of animation may well serve to present that material in a more flattering light than it would if it were depicted through live video. I stop short of disagreeing with our decision in this case, but note that the animated nature of the broadcast, in my opinion, may be cause for taking an even closer look in the context of our indecency analysis.

Second, our conclusion regarding the 9:00 p.m. Central Standard Time airing of an episode of *Medium* in which a woman is shot at point-blank range in the face by her husband gives me pause. While I agree with the result in this case, I question our conclusion that the sequence constitutes violence *per se* and therefore falls outside the scope of the Commission's definition of indecency. Without question, this scene is violent, graphically so. Moreover, it is presented in a way that appears clearly designed to maximize its shock value. And therein lies my concern. One of the primary ways that this scene shocks is that it leads the viewer to believe that the action is headed in one direction – through dialogue and actions which suggest that interaction of a sexual nature is about to occur – and then abruptly erupts in another – the brutally violent shooting of a wife by her husband, in the head, at point-blank range. Even though the Commission's authority under Section 1464 is limited to indecent, obscene, and profane content, and thus does not extend to violent matter, the use of violence as the "punch line" of titillating sexual innuendo should not insulate broadcast licensees from our authority. To the contrary, the use of sexual innuendo may, depending on the specific case, subject a licensee to potential forfeiture, regardless of the overall violent nature of the sequence in which such sexual innuendo is used.

*   *   *

Finally, I would like to express my hope and belief that the problem of indecent material is one that can be solved. Programmers, artists, writers, broadcasters, networks, advertisers, parents, public interest groups, and, yes, even Commissioners can protect two of our country's most valuable resources: the public airwaves and our children's minds. We must take a stand against programming that robs our children of their innocence and constitutes an unwarranted intrusion into our homes. By working together, we should promote the creation of programming that is not just entertaining, but also positive, educational, healthful, and, perhaps, even inspiring.

INDECENCY COMPLAINTS and NALs: 1993 – 2006

Period Covered	# of Complaints Received[1]	# of Programs By Service	# of NALs[2]	# of NALs By Service	$ Amount of NALs[3]	Status
Jan.-June 2006	327,198 (1191 programs)	Radio: 389 TV: 512 Cable: 290	7	Radio: 0 TV: 7	$3,962,500	7 pending
2005	233,531 (1550 programs)	Radio: 488 TV: 707 Cable: 355	0	0	0	N/A
2004	1,405,419 (314 programs)	Radio: 145 TV: 140 Cable: 29	12	Radio: 9 TV: 3	$7,928,080[4]	4 paid, 1 agreed to be paid, 6 pending, 1 cancelled
2003	166,683 (375 programs)	Radio: 122 TV: 217 Cable: 36	3	Radio: 3	$440,000	1 paid, 2 agreed to be paid
2002	13,922 (389 programs)	Radio: 185 TV: 166 Cable: 38	7	Radio: 7	$99,400	2 paid, 3 agreed to be paid, 1 pending, 1 cancelled
2001	346 (152 programs)	Radio: 113 TV: 33 Cable: 6	7	Radio: 6 TV: 1	$91,000	5 paid, 2 cancelled
2000	111 (111 programs)	Radio: 85 TV: 25 Cable: 1	7	Radio: 7	$48,000	5 paid, 2 agreed to be paid
1999	N/A	N/A	3	Radio: 3	$49,000	3 paid
1998	N/A	N/A	6	Radio: 6	$40,000	5 paid, 1 forfeiture collection not pursued by DOJ
1997	N/A	N/A	7	Radio: 6 TV: 1	$35,500	5 paid, 2 cancelled
1996	N/A	N/A	3	Radio: 3	$25,500	1 paid, 2 cancelled
1995	N/A	N/A	1	Radio : 1	$4,000	1 paid
1994	N/A	N/A	7	Radio: 7	$674,500	4 paid, 3 cancelled
1993	N/A	N/A	5	Radio: 5	$665,000	4 paid, 1 cancelled

[1] The reported counts reflect complaints received by the Consumer and Governmental Affairs Bureau, complaints received separately by the Enforcement Bureau, and complaints e-mailed directly to the offices of the FCC Chairman and the respective offices of the Commissioners. The reported counts may also include duplicate complaints or contacts that subsequently are determined insufficient to constitute actionable complaints.

[2] An NAL may relate to a complaint for a prior year.

[3] These figures represent the amount of the original proposed forfeiture. See also note 4. In some instances, the forfeiture was ultimately reduced or rescinded.

[4] In addition to the amount of NALs issued for 2004, this figure includes amounts in the 6/9/04 Clear Channel consent decree ($952,500), the 8/12/04 Emmis consent decree ($258,000), and the 11/23/04 Viacom consent decree ($3,059,580).

Appendix E

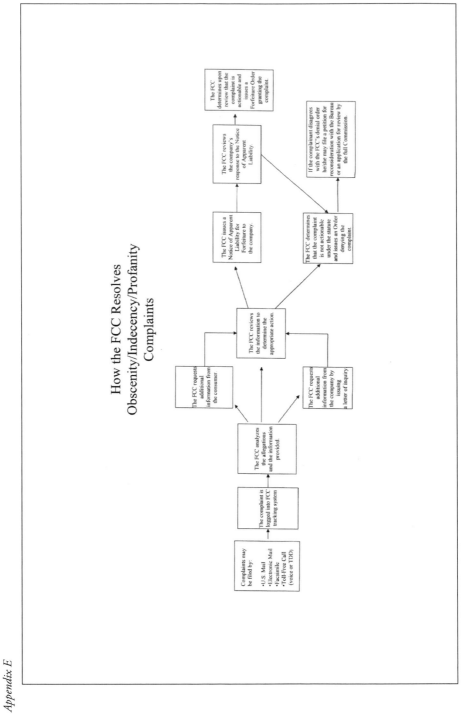

How the FCC Resolves
Obscenity/Indecency/Profanity
Complaints

Complaints may be filed by:
- U.S. Mail
- Electronic Mail
- Facsimile
- Toll-Free Call (voice or TDD)

The complaint is logged into FCC tracking system

The FCC analyzes the allegations and the information provided.

The FCC requests additional information from the consumer

The FCC requests additional information from the company by issuing a letter of inquiry.

The FCC reviews the information to determine the appropriate action.

The FCC issues a Notice of Apparent Liability for the company.

The FCC determines that the complaint is not actionable under the statute and issues an Order denying the complaint.

The FCC reviews the company's response to the Notice of Apparent Liability.

If the complainant disagrees with the FCC's denial order he/she may file a petition for reconsideration with the Bureau or an application for review by the full Commission.

The FCC determines upon review that the complaint is actionable and issues a Forfeiture Order granting the complaint.

APPENDIX F

Before the
Federal Communications Commission
Washington, D.C. 20554

In the Matter of)	
)	
Industry Guidance On the Commission's)	File No. EB-00-IH-0089
Case Law Interpreting 18 U.S.C. § 1464)	
and Enforcement Policies Regarding)	
Broadcast Indecency)	
)	

POLICY STATEMENT

Adopted: March 14, 2001   **Released:** April 6, 2001

By the Commission: Commissioners Ness and Furchtgott-Roth issuing separate statements; Commissioner Tristani dissenting and issuing a statement.

I.   INTRODUCTION

1.   The Commission issues this Policy Statement to provide guidance to the broadcast industry regarding our case law interpreting 18 U.S.C. § 1464 and our enforcement policies with respect to broadcast indecency. This document is divided into five parts. Section I gives an overview of this document. Section II provides the statutory basis for indecency regulation and discusses the judicial history of such regulation. Section III describes the analytical approach the Commission uses in making indecency determinations. This section also presents a comparison of selected rulings intended to illustrate the various factors that have proved significant in resolving indecency complaints. The cited material refers only to broadcast indecency actions and does not include any discussion of case law concerning indecency enforcement actions in other services regulated by this agency such as cable, telephone, or amateur radio. Section IV describes the Commission's broadcast indecency enforcement process. Section V is the conclusion.

II.   STATUTORY BASIS/JUDICIAL HISTORY

2.   It is a violation of federal law to broadcast obscene or indecent programming. Specifically, Title 18 of the United States Code, Section 1464 (18 U.S.C. § 1464), prohibits the utterance of "any obscene, indecent, or profane language by means of radio communication."[1] Congress has given the Federal Communications Commission the responsibility for administratively enforcing 18 U.S.C. § 1464. In doing so, the Commission may revoke a station license, impose a monetary forfeiture, or issue a warning for the broadcast of indecent material.[2] See 47 U.S.C. Sections 312(a)(6) and 503(b)(1)(D).

---

[1] Obscene and profane language and depictions are not within the scope of this Policy Statement.

[2] Although Section 1464 is a criminal statutue, the Commission has authority to impose civil penalties for the broadcast of indecent material without regard to the criminal nature of the statute. *FCC v. Pacifica Foundation*, 438 U.S. 726, 739, n. 13 (1978); *see also Action for Children's Television v. FCC*, 852 F.2d 1332, 1335 (continued....)

307

3.   The FCC's enforcement policy under Section 1464 has been shaped by a number of judicial and legislative decisions. In particular, because the Supreme Court has determined that obscene speech is not entitled to First Amendment protection, obscene speech cannot be broadcast at any time. [3] In contrast, indecent speech is protected by the First Amendment, and thus, the government must both identify a compelling interest for any regulation it may impose on indecent speech and choose the least restrictive means to further that interest. [4] Even under this restrictive standard, the courts have consistently upheld the Commission's authority to regulate indecent speech, albeit with certain limitations.

4.   *FCC v. Pacifica Foundation,* 438 U.S. 726 (1978), provides the judicial foundation for FCC indecency enforcement. In that case, the Supreme Court held that the government could constitutionally regulate indecent broadcasts.[5] In addition, the Court quoted the Commission's definition of indecency with apparent approval.[6] The definition, "language or material that, in context, depicts or describes, in terms patently offensive as measured by contemporary community standards for the broadcast medium, sexual or excretory activities or organs," has remained substantially unchanged since the time of the *Pacifica* decision.[7] Moreover, the definition has been specifically upheld against constitutional challenges in the *Action for Children's Television (ACT)* cases in the D.C. Circuit Court of Appeals.[8] Further, in *Reno v. ACLU,* 521 U.S. 844 (1997), the U.S. Supreme Court struck down an indecency standard for the Internet but did not question the constitutionality of our broadcast indecency standard. Rather, the Court recognized the "special

---

(Continued from previous page) ————————————
(D.C.Cir. 1988) (see n. 8 for full case history) (Commission has authority to sanction licensees for broadcast of indecent material). The Department of Justice is responsible for prosecution of criminal violations of the statute.

[3] *See Miller v. California,* 413 U.S. 15 (1973), *reh'g. denied,* 414 U.S. 881 (1973); *Sable Communications of California, Inc. v. FCC,* 492 U.S. 115 (1989); 47 C.F.R. § 73. 3999(a). Obscene speech is defined by a three-part test: (1) an average person, applying contemporary community standards, must find that the material, as a whole, appeals to the prurient interest; (2) the material must depict or describe, in a patently offensive way, sexual conduct specifically defined by applicable law; and (3) the material, taken as a whole, must lack serious literary, artistic, political, or scientific value. *Miller v. California,* 413 U.S. at 24.

[4] *Sable v. FCC,* 492 U.S. at 126.

[5] *Id.* at 748-50 (upholding Commission declaratory order that afternoon broadcast of a recording of a 12 minute monologue entitled "Filthy Words" was indecent as broadcast); *see also* 742-47 (Stevens, J.) and 757-61 (Powell, J.).

[6] *Id.* at 732.

[7] *Enforcement of Prohibitions Against Broadcast Indecency in 18 U.S.C. § 1464, 8 FCC Rcd 704, n. 10 (1993). See also Action for Children's Television v. FCC,* 852 F.2d 1332, 1338 (D.C.Cir. 1988) and *Action for Children's Television v. FCC ,* 58 F.3d 654, 657 (D.C. Cir. 1995) (see n. 8 for full case history).

[8] *Action for Children's Television v. FCC,* 852 F.2d 1332, 1339 (D.C.Cir. 1988) (*"ACT I"*); *Action for Children's Television v. FCC,* 932 F.2d 1504, 1508 (D.C. Cir. 1991*), cert. denied,* 112 S. Ct. 1282 (1992) (*"ACT II"*); *Action for Children's Television v. FCC ,* 58 F.3d 654, 657 (D.C. Cir. 1995*), cert. denied,* 116 S. Ct. 701 (1996) (*"ACT III"*).

justifications for regulation of the broadcast media that are not applicable to other speakers." *Reno v. ACLU*, 521 U.S. at 868.[9]

5.   Although the D.C. Circuit approved the FCC's definition of indecency in the *ACT* cases, it also established several restrictive parameters on FCC enforcement. The court's decisions made clear that the FCC had to identify the compelling government interests that warranted regulation and also explain how the regulations were narrowly tailored to further those interests. In *ACT I*, the court rejected as inadequately supported the Commission's determination that it could reach and regulate indecent material aired as late as 11:00 p.m., and remanded the cases involved to the Commission for proceedings to ascertain the proper scope of the "safe harbor" period, that is, the time during which indecent speech may be legally broadcast. Before the Commission could comply with the court's remand order, however, Congress intervened and instructed the Commission to adopt rules that enforced the provisions of 18 U.S.C. § 1464 on a "24 hour per day basis."[10] The rule adopted to implement this legislative mandate was stayed and was ultimately vacated by the court in *ACT II* as unconstitutional. In 1992, responding to the decision in *ACT II*, Congress directed the Commission to adopt a new "safe harbor" – generally 12 midnight to 6:00 a.m., but 10:00 p.m. to 6:00 a.m. for certain noncommercial stations. The Commission implemented this statutory scheme in January 1993.[11] Before this rule could become effective, however, the court stayed it pending judicial review. In 1995, the D.C. Circuit, *en banc*, held in *ACT III* that there was not a sufficient justification in the record to support a preferential "safe harbor" period for noncommercial stations and that the more restrictive midnight to 6:00 a.m. "safe harbor" for commercial stations was therefore unconstitutional. The court concluded, however, that the less restrictive 10:00 p.m. to 6:00 a.m. "safe harbor" had been justified as a properly tailored means of vindicating the government's compelling interest in the welfare of children and remanded the case to the Commission "with instructions to limit its ban on the broadcasting of indecent programs to the period from 6:00 a.m. to 10:00 p.m." *ACT III*, 58 F.3d at 669-70. The Commission implemented the court's instructions by appropriately conforming Section 73.3999 of its rules.[12] These changes became effective on August 28, 1995.[13]

6.   Thus, outside the 10:00 p.m. to 6:00 a.m. safe harbor, the courts have approved regulation of broadcast indecency to further the compelling government interests in supporting parental supervision of children and more generally its concern for children's well being. *Act III*, 58

---

[9] These special justifications included the history of extensive government regulation of the broadcast medium, the scarcity of available frequencies at its inception, and broadcast's "invasive" nature. *Id. See also Commission's Forfeiture Policy Statement and Amendment of Section 1.80 of the Rules to Incorporate the Forfeiture Guidelines*, 15 FCC Rcd 303, 305-06 (1999) ("courts have repeatedly upheld the Commission's indecency standard").

[10] *Making Appropriations for the Departments of Commerce, Justice, and State, the Judiciary and Related Agencies for the Fiscal Year Ending September 30, 1989, and for Other Purposes*, Pub. L. No. 100-459, Section 608, 102 Stat. 2186, 2228 (1988).

[11] *Public Telecommunications Act of 1992*, Pub. L. No. 102-356, § 16(a), 106 Stat. 949, 954 (1992); *Enforcement of Prohibitions Against Broadcast Indecency in 18 U.S.C. § 1464, Report and Order*, 8 FCC Rcd 704 (1993).

[12] *Enforcement of Prohibitions Against Broadcast Indecency in 18 U.S.C. § 1464, Memorandum Opinion and Order*, 10 FCC Rcd 10558 (1995).

[13] 60 FR 44439 (August 28, 1995).

F.3d at 661 (and cases cited therein).[14] The principles of enforcement articulated below are intended to further these interests.

III.   INDECENCY DETERMINATIONS

A.   <u>Analytical Approach</u>

7.   Indecency findings involve at least two fundamental determinations. First, the material alleged to be indecent must fall within the subject matter scope of our indecency definition – that is, the material must describe or depict sexual or excretory organs or activities. *WPBN/WTOM License Subsidiary, Inc. (WPBN-TV and WTOM-TV)*, 15 FCC Rcd 1838, 1840-41 (2000).

8.   Second, the broadcast must be *patently offensive* as measured by contemporary community standards for the broadcast medium. In applying the "community standards for the broadcast medium" criterion, the Commission has stated:

> The determination as to whether certain programming is patently offensive is not a local one and does not encompass any particular geographic area. Rather, the standard is that of an average broadcast viewer or listener and not the sensibilities of any individual complainant.

WPBN/WTOM License Subsidiary, Inc., 15 FCC Rcd at 1841.[15]

9.   In determining whether material is patently offensive, the *full context* in which the material appeared is critically important.[16] It is not sufficient, for example, to know that explicit

---

[14] The Commission has also identified "protection of the home against intrusion by offensive broadcasts" as a compelling government interest. The court did not address the validity of that interest. *ACT III*, 58 F.3d at 660-61. The Supreme Court has noted, however, that the "uniquely pervasive presence" of the broadcast media, with the audience continually tuning in and out, so as to make content warnings less effectual, is a reason for affording broadcast media more limited First Amendment protections as compared to other forms of communications. *FCC v. Pacifica Foundation*, 438 U.S. at 748-49.

[15] The Commission's interpretation of the term "contemporary community standards" flows from its analysis of the definition of that term set forth in the Supreme Court's decision in *Hamling v. United States*, 418 U.S. 87 (1974), *reh'g denied*, 419 U.S. 885 (1974). In *Infinity Broadcasting Corporation of Pennsylvania (WYSP(FM))*, 3 FCC Rcd 930 (1987) (subsequent history omitted), the commission observed that in *Hamling*, which involved obscenity, "the Court explained that the purpose of 'contemporary community standards' was to ensure that material is judged neither on the basis of a decisionmaker's personal opinion, nor by its effect on a particularly sensitive or insensitive person or group." 3 FCC Rcd at 933, *citing* 418 U.S. at 107. The Commission also relied on the fact that the Court in *Hamling* indicated that decisionmakers need not use any precise geographic area in evaluating material. 3 FCC Rcd at 933, *citing* 418 U.S. at 104-05. Consistent with *Hamling*, the Commission concluded that its evaluation of allegedly indecent material is "not one based on a local standard, but one based on a broader standard for broadcasting generally." 3 FCC Rcd at 933.

[16] *WPBN/WTOM License Subsidiary, Inc.*, 15 FCC Rcd at 1841; *Infinity Broadcasting Corp.*, 3 FCC Rcd 930, 931-32 (1987), *aff'd in part, vacated in part, remanded sub nom. Act I*, 852 F.2d 1332 (D.C. Cir. 1988) (subsequent history omitted).

sexual terms or descriptions were used, just as it is not sufficient to know only that no such terms or descriptions were used. Explicit language in the context of a *bona fide* newscast might not be patently offensive,[17] while sexual innuendo that persists and is sufficiently clear to make the sexual meaning inescapable might be.[18] Moreover, contextual determinations are necessarily highly fact-specific, making it difficult to catalog comprehensively all of the possible contextual factors that might exacerbate or mitigate the patent offensiveness of particular material.[19] An analysis of Commission case law reveals that various factors have been consistently considered relevant in indecency determinations. By comparing cases with analogous analytical structures, but different outcomes, we hope to highlight how these factors are applied in varying circumstances and the impact of these variables on a finding of patent offensiveness.

B.   Case Comparisons

10.   The principal factors that have proved significant in our decisions to date are: (1) the *explicitness or graphic nature* of the description or depiction of sexual or excretory organs or activities; (2) whether the material *dwells on or repeats at length* descriptions of sexual or excretory organs or activities; (3) *whether the material appears to pander or is used to titillate*, or *whether the material appears to have been presented for its shock value*. In assessing all of the factors, and particularly the third factor, the overall context of the broadcast in which the disputed material appeared is critical. Each indecency case presents its own particular mix of these, and possibly other, factors, which must be balanced to ultimately determine whether the material is patently offensive and therefore indecent. No single factor generally provides the basis for an indecency finding. To illustrate the noted factors, however, and to provide a sense of the weight these considerations have carried in specific factual contexts, a comparison of cases has been organized to provide examples of decisions in which each of these factors has played a particularly significant role, whether exacerbating or mitigating, in the indecency determination made.

11.   It should be noted that the brief descriptions and excerpts from broadcasts that are reproduced in this document are intended only as a research tool and should not be taken as a meaningful selection of words and phrases to be evaluated for indecency purposes without the fuller context that the tapes or transcripts provide. The excerpts from broadcasts used in this section have often been shortened or compressed. In order to make the excerpts more readable, however, we have frequently omitted any indication of these ellipses from the text. Moreover, in cases where material was included in a complaint but not specifically cited in the decision based on the complaint, we caution against relying on the omission as if it were of decisional significance. For example, if portions of a voluminous transcript are the object of an enforcement action, those portions not

---

[17] *Peter Branton*, 6 FCC Rcd 610 (1991), *aff'd sub nom. Branton v. FCC*, 993 F.2d 906 (D.C. Cir. 1993), *cert. denied 511 U.S. 1052* (1994).

[18] *See Great American Television and Radio Company, Inc. (WFBQ(FM))*, 6 FCC Rcd 3692 (MMB 1990) ("Candy Wrapper").

[19] *See e.g., Infinity Broadcasting Corp.*, 3 FCC Rcd 930, 931-32 (1987), *aff'd in part, vacated in part on other grounds, remanded sub nom. Act I*, 852 F.2d 1332 (D.C. Cir. 1988) (subsequent history omitted*)*.

included are not necessarily deemed not indecent. The omissions may be the result of an editing process that attempted to highlight the most significant material within its context. No inference should be drawn regarding the material deleted.

1.   Explicitness/Graphic Description Versus Indirectness/Implication

12.   The more explicit or graphic the description or depiction, the greater the likelihood that the material will be considered patently offensive. Merely because the material consists of double entendre or innuendo, however, does not preclude an indecency finding if the sexual or excretory import is unmistakable.

13.   Following are examples of decisions where the explicit/graphic nature of the description of sexual or excretory organs or activities played a central role in the determination that the broadcast was indecent.

WYSP(FM), Philadelphia, PA   **"Howard Stern Show"**

God, my testicles are like down to the floor . . . you could really have a party with these . . . Use them like Bocci balls.

(As part of a discussion of lesbians) I mean to go around porking other girls with vibrating rubber products . . .

Have you ever had sex with an animal? Well, don't knock it. I was sodomized by Lambchop.

Indecent – Warning Issued. *Infinity Broadcasting Corporation of Pennsylvania (WYSP(FM)),* 2 FCC Rcd 2705 (1987), *aff'd* 3 FCC Rcd 930 (1987), *aff'd in part, vacated in part on other grounds, remanded sub nom. Act I,* 852 F.2d 1332 (D.C. Cir. 1988) (subsequent history omitted). Excerpted material (only some of which is cited above) consisted of "vulgar and lewd references to the male genitals and to masturbation and sodomy broadcast in the context of . . . 'explicit references to masturbation, ejaculation, breast size, penis size, sexual intercourse, nudity, urination, oral-genital contact, erections, sodomy, bestiality, menstruation and testicles.'" 3 FCC Rcd at 932.

WSUC-FM, Cortland, NY   **"I'm Not Your Puppet" Rap Song**

The only thing that was on my mind, was just shoving my dick up this bitch's behind. I looked at the girl and said, babe, your ass ain't nothing but a base hit. I'm going to have to get rid of your ass, yeah, 'cause you're on my dick, dick, ding-a-ling. Popped my dick in her mouth, and we rocked it back and forth. Now that she sucked my dick and Tony fuck you in the ass. I pulled out my dick, popped it in her mouth, and she sucked it.

Indecent – NAL Issued. *State University of New York (WSUC-FM),* 8 FCC Rcd 456 (1993), *forfeiture reduced* 13 FCC Rcd 23810 (1998) (forfeiture paid). The Commission concluded that the language used in this broadcast "describes sexual activities in patently offensive terms and is therefore indecent." 8 FCC Rcd at 456.

Federal Communications Commission   **FCC 01-90**

WQAM(AM), Miami, FL   **"Uterus Guy" Song**

I don't want to grow up, I'm a uterus guy. I want to spend a week or so right here between your thighs. Inhale your clam, with my head jammed by your quivering, crushing gams. No, I don't want to get up or get a towel to dry, cause I wouldn't be a uterus guy. I don't want to get up, I'm a uterus guy and I know where to lick and chew exactly where you like. You'll have more fun when I make you come, with my nose between your thighs.

Indecent – NAL Issued. *WQAM License Limited Partnership (WQAM(AM))*, 15 FCC Rcd 1475 (1999), *aff'd* 15 FCC Rcd 2518 (2000), *recon. denied* FCC 00-266, released July 26, 2000. The Commission held that the "song's sexual import is lewd, inescapable and understandable." 15 FCC Rcd at 2520.

KROQ(FM), Los Angeles, CA   **"You Suck" Song**

I know you're really proud cause you think you're well hung but I think its time you learn how to use your tongue. You say you want things to be even and you want things to be fair but you're afraid to get your teeth caught in my pubic hair. If you're lying there expecting me to suck your dick, you're going to have to give me more than just a token lick. . . . Go down baby, you suck, lick it hard and move your tongue around. If you're worried about babies, you can lower your risk, by giving me that special cunnilingus kiss. . . . you can jiggle your tongue on my clit. Don't worry about making me have an orgasm. . . . You asshole, you shit. I know it's a real drag, to suck my cunt when I'm on the rag. You tell me it's gross to suck my yeast infection. How do you think I feel when I gag on your erection.

Indecent – NAL Issued. *Infinity Broadcasting Corporation of Los Angeles (KROQ(FM))*, 13 FCC Rcd 25349 (MMB 1998), *aff'd* 15 FCC Rcd 10667 (EB 2000), *petition for reconsideration pending* (graphically and explicitly describes sexual and excretory organs or activities).

WXTB(FM), Clearwater, FL   **"Bubba, The Love Sponge"**

Most women don't like swallowing, but I do. The trick is you need to swallow at the right time. Do it when you're deep throating. . . . I like pleasure giving, I like a pleasure giving woman who really, really likes to enjoy giving oral. . . . She does more than just go up and down, she's creative by licking, nibbling and using overall different techniques. . . . The sexy turn on for me is when I . . . expel into my partner's mouth. . . . I don't mind giving BJs . . . if a man doesn't get off, that means he wasn't quite excited by my techniques.

Indecent – NAL Issued. *Citicasters Co. (WXTB(FM))*, 13 FCC Rcd 22004 (1998), *aff'd* FCC 00-230, released June 27, 2000 (forfeiture paid).

14. Less explicit material and material that relies principally on innuendo to convey a sexual or excretory meaning have also been cited by the Commission as actionably indecent where the sexual or excretory meaning was unmistakable.

KLOL(FM), Houston, TX   **"Stevens and Pruett Show"**

The doctor was talking about size. The man complained earlier that he was so large that it was ruining his marriages. Big is good if the guy knows how to use it. She is so big she could handle anything. Some of these guys, a very few of them, a hand full are like . . . two hands full. Twelve inches, about the size of a beer can in diameter. So, now could you handle something like that? It's actually ruined marriages. A big organ for a big cathedral. Somebody big is just going to have to find somebody that's big.

Indecent – NAL Issued. *The Rusk Corporation (KLOL(FM))*, 8 FCC Rcd 3228 (1993) (forfeiture paid). As to the use of innuendo in the cited passages, the Commission said: "[W]hile [the licensee] may have substituted innuendo and double entendre for more directly explicit sexual references and descriptions in some instances, unmistakable sexual references remain that render the sexual meaning of the innuendo inescapable." 8 FCC Rcd at 3228.

KGB-FM, San Diego, CA   **"Candy Wrapper" Song**

I whipped out my Whopper and whispered, Hey, Sweettart, how'd you like to Crunch on my Big Hunk for a Million Dollar Bar? Well, she immediately went down on my Tootsie Roll and you know, it was like pure Almond Joy. I couldn't help but grab her delicious Mounds, ... this little Twix had the Red Hots. ... as my Butterfinger went up her tight little Kit Kat, and she started to scream Oh, Henry! Oh, Henry! Soon she was fondling my Peter Paul, and Zagnuts and I knew it wouldn't be long before I blew my Milk Duds clear to Mars and gave her a taste of the old Milky Way. ... I said, Look ... why don't you just take my Whatchamacallit and slip it up your Bit-O-Honey. Oh, what a piece of Juicy Fruit she was too. She screamed Oh, Crackerjack. You're better than the Three Musketeers! as I rammed my Ding Dong up her Rocky Road and into her Peanut Butter Cup. Well, I was giving it to her Good 'n Plenty, and all of a sudden, my Starburst. ... she started to grow a bit Chunky and ... Sure enough, nine months later, out popped a Baby Ruth.

Indecent – NAL Issued. *KGB, Inc. (KGB-FM)*, 7 FCC Rcd 3207 (1992), *forfeiture reduced* 13 FCC Rcd 16396 (1998) (forfeiture paid). *See also Great American Television and Radio Company, Inc. (WFBQ(FM)/WNDE(AM))*, 6 FCC Rcd 3692, 3693 (MMB 1990) (forfeiture paid) ("While the passages arguably consist of double entendre and indirect references, the language used in each passage was understandable and clearly capable of a specific sexual meaning and, because of the context, the sexual import was inescapable."); and *WIOD, Inc. (WIOD(AM))*, 6 FCC Rcd 3704 (MMB 1989) (forfeiture paid) ("notwithstanding the use of candy bar names to symbolize sexual activities, the titillating and pandering nature of the song makes any thought of candy bars peripheral at best").

KSJO(FM), San Jose, CA   **Song to Tune of "Beverly**
Hillbillies"

Come a listen to a story about a man named Boas, a poor politician that barely kept his winky fed, then one day he's poking a chick and up from his pants came a bubbling crude. Winky oil. Honey pot. Jail Bait. . . . So, he loaded up his winky and he did it with Beverly. Big Breasts. Only 15 years old.

Indecent – NAL Issued. *Narragansett Broadcasting Company of California, Inc. (KSJO(FM))*, 5 FCC Rcd 3821 (1990) (forfeiture paid). "Even in the cases of double entendre, not only was the language understandable and clearly capable of a specific sexual or excretory meaning but, because of the context, the sexual and excretory import was inescapable." 5 FCC Rcd at 3821.

**KMEL(FM), San Francisco, CA   "Rick Chase Show"; "Blow Me"
Song**

Blow me, you hardly even know me, just set yourself below me and blow me, tonight. Hey, a handy would certainly be dandy, but it's not enough to slow (unintelligible) me, hey, you gotta blow me all night. Hey, when you pat your lips that way, I want you night and day, when you squeeze my balls so tight. I want to blow my love, hey, with all my might.

Indecent – NAL Issued. *San Francisco Century Broadcasting, L.P. (KMEL(FM))*, 7 FCC Rcd 4857 (1992), *aff'd* 8 FCC Rcd 498 (1993) (forfeiture paid). Commission found that the language dwelled on descriptions of sexual organs and activities, "was understandable and clearly capable of a specific sexual meaning and, because of the context, the sexual import was inescapable." 8 FCC Rcd at 498.

15.   Compare the following case in which the material aired was deemed not to be actionably indecent.

**WFBQ(FM)/WNDE(AM), Indianapolis, IN   "Elvis" and "Power, Power,
Power"**

As you know, you gotta stop the King, but you can't kill him . . . So you talk to Dick Nixon, man you get him on the phone and Dick suggests maybe getting like a mega-Dick to help out, but you know, you remember the time the King ate mega-Dick under the table at a 095 picnic . . . you think about getting mega-Hodgie, but that's no good because you know, the King was a karate dude . . .

Power! Power! Power! Thrust! Thrust! Thrust! First it was Big Foot, the monster car crunching 4x4 pickup truck. Well, move over, Big Foot! Here comes the most massive power-packed monster ever! It's Big Peter! (Laughter) Big Peter with 40,000 Peterbilt horsepower under the hood. It's massive! Big Peter! Formerly the Big Dick's Dog Wiener Mobile. Big Peter features a 75-foot jacked up monster body. See Big Peter crush and enter a Volvo. (Laughter) . . . strapped himself in the cockpit and put Big Peter through its paces. So look out Big Foot! Big Peter is coming! Oh my God! It's coming! Big Peter! (Laughter)

Not Indecent. *Great American Television and Radio Company, Inc. (WFBQ(FM)/WNDE(AM))*, 6 FCC Rcd 3692 (MMB 1990). The licensee provided a fuller transcript of the cited "Elvis" excerpt and explained the context in which it was aired, arguing that no sexual meaning was intended and that no such meaning would be reasonably understood from the material taken as a whole. The licensee also explained the regional humor of the Power, Power, Power excerpt and the context in which it was broadcast. The Mass Media Bureau held that the material was not indecent because the "surrounding contexts do not appear to provide a background against which a sexual import is inescapable." 6 FCC Rcd at 3693.

16.   In assessing explicitness, the Commission also looks to the audibility of the material as aired. If the material is difficult or impossible to understand, it may not be actionably indecent. However, difficulty in understanding part of the material or an attempt to obscure objectionable material will not preclude a finding of indecency where at least some of the material is recognizable or understandable.

KGB-FM, San Diego, CA   **"Sit on My Face" Song**

Sit on my face and tell me that you love me. I'll sit on your face and tell you I love you, too. I love to hear you moralize when I'm between your thighs. You blow me away. Sit on my face and let me embrace you. I'll sit on your face and then I'll love you (?) truly. Life can be fine, if we both sixty-nine. If we sit on faces (?) the ultimate place to play (?). We'll be blown away.

Indecent – NAL Issued. *KGB, Inc. (KGB-FM)*, 7 FCC Rcd 3207 (MMB 1992), *forfeiture reduced* 13 FCC Rcd 16396 (1998) (forfeiture paid). The song was found to be actionably indecent despite English accent and "ambient noise" because the lyrics were sufficiently understandable. 7 FCC Rcd at 3207.

WWKX(FM), Woonsocket, RI   **"Real Deal Mike Neil Show"**

Douche bag, hey what's up, fu(Bleep)ck head? . . . You his fuck (Bleep) ho or what? You his fuck (Bleep) bitch man, where you suck his dick every night? . . . Suck some di(Bleep)ck make some money for Howard and pay your pimp okay?

Indecent – NAL Issued. *Back Bay Broadcasting (WWKX(FM))*, 14 FCC Rcd 3997, 3998 (MMB 1999) (forfeiture paid). Material was found to be actionably indecent despite attempt to obscure objectionable language because "editing was ineffective and merely resulted in a "bleep" in the middle of clearly recognizable words (or in some cases a "bleep" after the word)." The Mass Media Bureau held that "[b]ecause the words were recognizable, notwithstanding the editing," they were indecent within the context used in this broadcast.

2.   Dwelling/Repetition versus Fleeting Reference

17.   Repetition of and persistent focus on sexual or excretory material have been cited consistently as factors that exacerbate the potential offensiveness of broadcasts. In contrast, where sexual or excretory references have been made once or have been passing or fleeting in nature, this characteristic has tended to weigh against a finding of indecency.

WXTB(FM), Clearwater, FL   **"Bubba, The Love Sponge"**

Could you take the phone and rub it on you Chia Pet? Oh, let me make sure nobody is around. Okay, hang on a second (Rubbing noise). Okay I did it. . . . Now that really your little beaver? That was mine. Your what? That was my little beaver? Oh I love when a girl says beaver. Will you say it again for me honey please? It was my little beaver. . . . Will you say, Bubba come get my beaver? Bubba, would come get my little beaver? . . . tell me that doesn't do something for you. That is pretty sexy. . . . bring the beaver. It will be with me. We got beaver chow. I can't wait, will you say it for me one more time? Say what? My little beaver or Bubba come get my little beaver? Okay, Bubba come get my beaver. Will you say, Bubba come hit my beaver? Will you say it? Bubba, come hit my beaver. That is pretty sexy, absolutely. Oh, my God, beaver.

Indecent – NAL Issued. *Citicasters Co. (WXTB(FM))*, 13 FCC Rcd 15381 (MMB 1998) (forfeiture paid).

WXTB(FM), Clearwater, FL   **"Bubba, The Love Sponge"**

Well, it was nice big fart. I'm feeling very gaseous at this point but there, so far has been no enema reaction, as far as. There's been no, there's been no expelling? No expelling. But I feel mucus rising. . . . Can't go like. (Grunting sound) Pushing, all I keep doing is putting out little baby farts. . . . on the toilet ready to go. . . . Push it, strain it. It looks normal. Just average, average. Little rabbit one. Little rabbit pellets. I imagine maybe, we'll break loose. Push hard Cowhead. I'm pushing, I got veins popping out of my forehead. Go ahead, those moles might pop right off. You can tell he's pushing. I'm out of breath. One more, last one. One big push.

Indecent – NAL Issued. *Citicasters Co. (WXTB(FM))*, 13 FCC Rcd 22004 (1998), *aff'd* FCC 00-230, released June 27, 2000 (forfeiture paid). The cited material dwells on excretory activities and the Commission found it to be patently offensive.

18.   Compare the following cases where material was found not indecent because it was fleeting and isolated.

WYBB(FM), Folly Beach, SC   **"The Morning Show"**

The hell I did, I drove mother-fucker, oh. Oh.

Not Indecent. *L.M. Communications of South Carolina, Inc. (WYBB(FM))*, 7 FCC Rcd 1595 (MMB 1992). The "broadcast contained only a fleeting and isolated utterance which, within the context of live and spontaneous programming, does not warrant a Commission sanction." 7 FCC Rcd at 1595.

KPRL(AM)/KDDB(FM), Paso Robles, CA   **News Announcer Comment**

Oops, fucked that one up.

Not Indecent. *Lincoln Dellar, Renewal of License for Stations KPRL(AM) and KDDB(FM)*, 8 FCC Rcd 2582, 2585 (ASD, MMB 1993). The "news announcer's use of single expletive" does not "warrant further Commission consideration in light of the isolated and accidental nature of the broadcast."

19.   In contrast, even relatively fleeting references may be found indecent where other factors contribute to a finding of patent offensiveness. Examples of such factors illustrated by the following cases include broadcasting references to sexual activities with children and airing material that, although fleeting, is graphic or explicit.

KUPD-FM, Tempe, AZ   **Announcer Joke**

What is the best part of screwing an eight-year-old?   Hearing the pelvis crack.

Indecent – NAL Issued. *Tempe Radio, Inc. (KUPD-FM)*, 12 FCC Rcd 21828 (MMB 1997) (forfeiture paid). Although fleeting, the language clearly refers to sexual activity with a child and was found to be patently offensive.

WEZB-FM, New Orleans, LA   **Announcer Joke**

What's the worst part of having sex with your brother? . . . You got to fix the crib after it breaks and then you got to clean the blood off the diaper.

Indecent – NAL Issued. *EZ New Orleans, Inc. (WEZB(FM))*, 12 FCC Rcd 4147 (MMB 1997) (forfeiture paid).

KLBJ(FM), Austin, TX   **DJ Comments**

Suck my dick you fucking cunt.

Indecent – NAL Issued. *LBJS Broadcasting Company, L.P. (KLBJ(FM))*, 13 FCC Rcd 20956 (MMB 1998) (forfeiture paid). Although fleeting, the material is explicit and was found to be indecent.

3.   Presented in a Pandering or Titillating Manner or for Shock Value

20.   The apparent purpose for which material is presented can substantially affect whether it is deemed to be patently offensive as aired. In adverse indecency findings, the Commission has often cited the pandering or titillating character of the material broadcast as an exacerbating factor. Presentation for the shock value of the language used has also been cited. As Justice Powell stated in his opinion in the Supreme Court's decision affirming the Commission's determination that the broadcast of a comedy routine was indecent, "[T]he language employed is, to most people, vulgar and offensive. It was chosen specifically for this quality, and it was repeated over and over as a sort of verbal shock treatment." *FCC v. Pacifica Foundation*, 438 U.S. 726, 757 (1978) (Powell, J., concurring in part and concurring in the judgment). On the other hand, the manner and purpose of a presentation may well preclude an indecency determination even though other factors, such as explicitness, might weigh in favor of an indecency finding. In the following cases, the decisions looked to the manner of presentation as a factor supporting a finding of indecency.

KLOL(FM), Houston, TX   **"Stevens & Pruett Show"**

Sex survey lines are open. Today's question, it's a strange question and we hope we have a lot of strange answers. What makes your hiney parts tingle? When my husband gets down there and goes (lips noise). ... I love oral sex. ... Well, my boyfriend tried to put Hershey kisses inside of me and tried to lick it out and it took forever for him to do it.

Indecent – NAL Issued. *Rusk Corporation (KLOL(FM))*, 5 FCC Rcd 6332 (MMB 1990) (forfeiture paid). Explicit description in a program that focused on sexual activities in a lewd, vulgar, pandering and titillating manner.

APPENDIX F

WEBN(FM), Cincinnati, OH   **"Bubba, The Love Sponge"**

All I can say is, if you were listening to the program last night you heard Amy and Stacy . . . come in here, little lesbians that they are. Little University of Cincinnati ho's and basically that we could come over and watch them. We got over to the house. . . . They start making out a little bit. They go to bed. They get, they start, they're starting like a mutual 69 on the bed. Guido all of a sudden whips it out. . . . Rather than take care of each other . . . Guido is like knee deep with the butch bitch and all of a sudden here is the fem bitch looking at me. Hot. I get crazy. I hook up a little bit. Then Guido says, hey, I done got mine, how about we switching? So I went into the private bedroom with the butch bitch and then got another one.

Indecent – NAL Issued. *Jacor Broadcasting Corporation (WEBN(FM))*, 13 FCC Rcd 4152 (MMB 1997), *aff'd* 13 FCC Rcd 5825 (MMB 1997) (forfeiture paid). **WXTB(FM), Clearwater, FL**   **"Bubba, The Love Sponge"**

Take the phone and I want you to rub it on it hard. I want to hear the telephone, okay? Okay honey. (Rubbing noises) You hear that? A little bit longer though please. I'm on the edge right now. A little bit faster. (Rubbing noises) You get that? That's nice. Could you do it again and then scream my name out, please? Like you're having an orgasm? Yeah. Go ahead. Okay. (Rubbing noises) Mm mm. That's it? It's got to be longer than that Ginny, come on work with me. Be a naughty girl. Be a little slutty bitch that you are. One more time. Okay. (Rubbing Noises).

Indecent – NAL Issued. *Citicasters Co. (WXTB(FM))*, 13 FCC Rcd 15381 (MMB 1998) (forfeiture paid).

21.   In determining whether broadcasts are presented in a pandering or titillating manner, the context of the broadcast is particularly critical. Thus, even where language is explicit, the matter is graphic, or where there is intense repetition of vulgar terms, the presentation may not be pandering or titillating, and the broadcast may not be found actionably indecent.

KING-TV, Seattle, WA   **"Teen Sex: What About the Kids?"**

Broadcast of portions of a sex education class in a local high school that included the use of very realistic sex organ models and simulated demonstrations of various methods of birth control as well as frank discussions of sexual topics.

Not Indecent. *King Broadcasting Co. (KING-TV)*, 5 FCC Rcd 2971 (1990). The Commission held that although the program dealt explicitly with sexual issues and included the use of very graphic sex organ models, "the material presented was clinical or instructional in nature and not presented in a pandering, titillating or vulgar manner." 5 FCC Rcd at 2971.

WABC-TV, New York, NY   **"Oprah Winfrey Show"**
                                         (How to Make Romantic Relations with

Your Mate Better)

Okay, for all you viewers out there with children watching, we're doing a show today on how to make romantic relations with your mate better. Otherwise known as s-e-x. ... I'm very aware there are a number of children who are watching and so, we're going to do our best to keep this show rated "G" but just in case, you may want to send your kids to a different room. And we'll pause for a moment while you do that. ... According to experts and recent sex surveys the biggest complaints married women have about sex are ... their lovemaking is boring ... American wives all across the country have confessed to using erotic aids to spice up their sex life and ... thousands of women say they fantasize while having sex with their husbands. ... And most women say they are faking it in the bedroom.
[Quiz:] I like the way my partner looks in clothing. ... I like the way my partner looks naked. ... I like the way my partner's skin feels. ... I like the way my partner tastes. ...

[Psychologist and panelists:] Do you know that you can experience orgasm, have you experienced that by yourself? No, I have not ... Okay, one of the things that, well, you all know what I'm talking about. ... You need to at least know how to make your body get satisfied by yourself. Because if you don't know how to do it, how is he going to figure it out? He doesn't have your body parts, he doesn't know.

Not Indecent. Letter from Chief, Complaints and Investigations Branch, Enforcement Division, Mass Media Bureau to Chris Giglio (July 20, 1994). Subject matter alone does not render material indecent. Thus, while material may be offensive to some people, in context, it might not be actionably indecent.

KTVI-TV, St. Louis, MO   **"Geraldo Rivera Show"**
                                             (Unlocking the Great Mysteries of Sex)

We have seen such a slew of sex books ..."Your G-spot," "How to Have Triple Orgasms." One of the biggest myths ... either we go all the way or we do nothing. ... He just missed an opportunity to make love, not all the way ... but to share a moment of passion and a moment of closeness. ... It's important that a man learn to use the penis the way an artist uses a paintbrush ... and if a woman is also willing to learn how to move her vagina. ... With good control of PC muscles, a man can separate orgasm from ejaculation and have more than one orgasm. ... Really great sex is always based on feeling safe enough with your partner to open up. Passion is just the expression of a tremendous sense of connection you feel. If you think sex is pleasurable, try making love and having sex at the same time for turning pleasure into ecstasy.

Not Indecent.   Letter from Chief, Complaints and Investigations Branch, Enforcement Division, Mass Media Bureau, to Gerald P. McAtee (October 26, 1989). While offensive to some, the material was not found to be indecent.

WSMC-FM, Collegedale, TN   **"All Things Considered"**
[National Public Radio]

Mike Schuster has a report and a warning. The following story contains some very rough language. [Excerpt from wiretap of telephone conversation in which organized crime figure John Gotti uses "fuck" or "fucking" 10 times in 7 sentences (110 words).]

Not Indecent. *Peter Branton*, 6 FCC Rcd 610 (1991) (subsequent history omitted). Explicit language was integral part of a bona fide news story concerning organized crime; the material aired was part of a wiretap recording used as evidence in Gotti's widely reported trial. The Commission explained that it did "not find the use of such [coarse] words in a legitimate news report to have been gratuitous, pandering, titillating or otherwise "patently offensive" as that term is used in our indecency definition." 6 FCC Rcd at 610.

WPBN-TV, Traverse City, MI   **"Schindler's List" Film**
WTOM-TV, Cheboygan, MI

"Schindler's List" is a film that depicted a historical view of World War II and wartime atrocities. The movie contained depictions of adult frontal nudity.

Not Indecent. *WPBN/WTOM License Subsidiary, Inc. (WPBN-TV and WTOM-TV)*, 15 FCC Rcd 1838 (2000). The Commission ruled that full frontal nudity is not *per se* indecent. Rather, the "full context" of the nudity is controlling. Looking at "the subject matter of the film, the manner of its presentation, and the warnings that accompanied the broadcast," the Commission held that the nudity in "Schindler's List" was not actionably indecent.

WFLA(AM), Tampa, FL   **Announcer Comments**

Announcers allegedly referred to complainant, Chuck Harder, as "Suck Harder," "Suck," and "Suckie" throughout the broadcast and called the complainant a "useless piece of crap." Also referred to complainant's network, the Sun Radio Network as "Suck Harder Radio Network."

Not Indecent. *Jacor Broadcasting of Tampa Bay, Inc., Renewal of License of Station WFLA(AM)*, 7 FCC Rcd 1826 (ASD, MMB 1992). Cited language was used in the context of a discussion of a radio network that provided programming to a station competitor and was found, in context, not actionably indecent.

22.   Compare the following cases where licensees unsuccessfully claimed that, because of the context of the broadcasts (*i.e.*, alleged news stories), the broadcasts were not pandering.

KSD-FM, St. Louis, MO   **"The Breakfast Club"**

I've got this Jessica Hahn interview here in Playboy. I just want to read one little segment . . . the good part.

"[Jim Bakker] has managed to completely undress me and he's sitting on my chest. He's really pushing himself, I mean the guy was forcing himself. He put his penis in my mouth . . . I'm crying, tears are coming, and he is letting go. The guy came in my mouth. My neck hurts, my throat hurts, my head feels like it's going to explode, but he's frustrated and determined, determined enough that within minutes he's inside me and he's on top and he's

holding my arms. He's just into this, he's inside me now. Saying, when you help the shepherd, you're helping the sheep."

(followed by air personality making sheep sounds) This was rape. Yeah, don't you ever come around here Jim Bakker or we're going to cut that thing off.

<u>Indecent – NAL Issued</u>. *Pacific and Southern Company, Inc. (KSD-FM)*, 6 FCC Rcd 3689 (MMB 1990) (forfeiture paid). The broadcast contained excerpts from a *Playboy* magazine account of the alleged rape of Jessica Hahn by the Rev. Jim Bakker. The licensee explained the broadcast was newsworthy "banter by two on-air personalities reflecting public concern, criticism, and curiosity about a public figure whose reputedly notorious behavior was a widespread media issue at the time." Responding to the licensee's argument, the Mass Media Bureau stated that "although the program . . . arguably concerned an incident that was at the time 'in the news,' the particular material broadcast was not only exceptionally explicit and vulgar, it was . . . presented in a pandering manner. In short, the rendition of the details of the alleged rape was, in context, patently offensive." 6 FCC Rcd at 3689.

KNON(FM), Dallas, TX   **"I Want to Be a Homosexual"**
Song

But if you really want to give me a blowjob, I guess I'll let you as long as you respect me in the morning. Suck it baby. Oh yeah, suck it real good. . . . Are you sure this is your first rim job?. . . Stick it up your punk rock ass. You rub your little thing, when you see phony dikes in Penthouse magazine. . . . Call me a faggot, call me a butt-loving fudge-packing queer. . . You rub your puny thing, when you see something (?) pass you on the street.

<u>Indecent – NAL Issued</u>. *Agape Broadcasting Foundation, Inc. (KNON(FM))*, 9 FCC Rcd 1679 (MMB 1994), *forfeiture reduced* 13 FCC Rcd 9262 (MMB 1998) (forfeiture paid). Licensee claimed that "'the words and the song constitute political speech' aired in a good faith attempt to present meaningful public affairs programming . . . to challenge those who would use such language to stigmatize . . . members of the gay community." 13 FCC Rcd at 9263. The Mass Media Bureau responded that the licensee has "considerable discretion as to the times of the day . . . when it may broadcast indecent material. ... Consequently, we find unavailing Agape's argument that, in essence, its duty to air public affairs programming required a mid-afternoon presentation of lyrics containing repeated, explicit, and vulgar descriptions of sexual activities and organs." *Id.*

KSJO(FM), San Jose, California   **Lamont & Tonelli Show**

"...she should go up and down the shaft about five times, licking and sucking and on the fifth swirl her tongue around the head before going back down...."

"Show us how its done" (evidently the guest had some sort of a prop).

*"Well, if this was a real penis, it would have a ****ridge, I would like (sic) around the ridge like this..."*

[laughter, comments such as 'oh yeah, baby'].

Indecent – NAL Issued. *Citicasters Co., licensee of Station KSJO(FM), San Jose, California*, 15 FCC Rcd 19095 (EB 2000) (forfeiture paid). The licensee claimed that the program was a clinical discussion of oral sex. The Enforcement Bureau rejected this argument on the grounds that the disc jockeys' comments on her material showed that the material was offered in a pandering and titillating manner. "The disc jockeys' invitation to have Dr. Terry use a prop on a radio program, and their laughter and statements (such as "oh yeah, baby") while she conducted that demonstration shown that the material was intended to be pandering and titillating as opposed to a clinical discussion of sex."

23.   The absence of a pandering or titillating nature, however, will not necessarily prevent an indecency determination, as illustrated by the following case.

WIOD(AM), Miami, FL   **"Penis Envy" Song**

If I had a penis, ... I'd stretch it and stroke it and shove it at smarties ... I'd stuff it in turkeys on Thanksgiving day. ... If I had a penis, I'd run to my mother, Comb out the hair and compare it to brother. I'd lance her, I'd knight her, my hands would indulge. Pants would seem tighter and buckle and bulge. (Refrain) A penis to plunder, a penis to push, 'Cause one in the hand is worth one in the bush. A penis to love me, a penis to share, To pick up and play with when nobody's there. ... If I had a penis, ... I'd force it on females, I'd pee like a fountain. If I had a penis, I'd still be a girl, but I'd make much more money and conquer the world.

Indecent – NAL Issued. *WIOD, Inc. (WIOD(AM))*, 6 FCC Rcd 3704 (MMB 1989) (forfeiture paid). The Mass Media Bureau found the material to be patently offensive. In response to the licensee's assertion that this song was not pandering or titillating and therefore should not be considered indecent, the Bureau stated: "We believe . . . that it is not necessary to find that the material is pandering or titillating in order to find that its references to sexual activities and organs are patently offensive. (Citations omitted.) Moreover, humor is no more an absolute defense to indecency . . . than is music or any other one component of communication." 6 FCC Rcd at 3704.

IV.   ENFORCEMENT PROCESS

24.   The Commission does not independently monitor broadcasts for indecent material. Its enforcement actions are based on documented complaints of indecent broadcasting received from the public. Given the sensitive nature of these cases and the critical role of context in an indecency determination, it is important that the Commission be afforded as full a record as possible to evaluate allegations of indecent programming. In order for a complaint to be considered, our practice is that it must generally include: (1) a full or partial tape or transcript or significant excerpts of the program;[20] (2) the date and time of the broadcast; and (3) the call sign of the station involved. Any tapes or other documentation of the programming supplied by the complainant, of necessity, become

---

[20] *See Citicasters Co., licensee of Station KSJO(FM), San Jose, California*, 15 FCC Rcd 19095 (EB 2000) (forfeiture paid) ("While the complainant did not provide us with an exact transcript of the broadcast, we find that she has provided us with sufficient context to make the determination that the broadcast was indecent.").

part of the Commission's records and cannot be returned. Documented complaints should be directed to the FCC, Investigations and Hearings Division, Enforcement Bureau, 445 Twelfth Street, S.W., Washington, D.C. 20554.

25. If a complaint does not contain the supporting material described above, or if it indicates that a broadcast occurred during "safe harbor" hours or the material cited does not fall within the subject matter scope of our indecency definition, it is usually dismissed by a letter to the complainant advising of the deficiency. In many of these cases, the station may not be aware that a complaint has been filed.

26. If, however, the staff determines that a documented complaint meets the subject matter requirements of the indecency definition and the material complained of was aired outside "safe harbor" hours, then the broadcast at issue is evaluated for patent offensiveness. Where the staff determines that the broadcast is not patently offensive, the complaint will be denied. If, however, the staff determines that further enforcement action might be warranted,[21] the Enforcement Bureau, in conjunction with other Commission offices, examines the material and decides upon an appropriate disposition, which might include any of the following: (1) denial of the complaint by staff letter based upon a finding that the material, in context, is not patently offensive and therefore not indecent; (2) issuance of a Letter of Inquiry (LOI) to the licensee seeking further information concerning or an explanation of the circumstances surrounding the broadcast; (3) issuance of a Notice of Apparent Liability (NAL) for monetary forfeiture; and (4) formal referral of the case to the full Commission for its consideration and action.[22] Generally, the last of these alternatives is taken in cases where issues beyond straightforward indecency violations may be involved or where the potential sanction for the indecent programming exceeds the Bureau's delegated forfeiture authority of $25,000 (47 C.F.R. § 0.311).

27. Where an LOI is issued, the licensee's comments are generally sought concerning the allegedly indecent broadcast to assist in determining whether the material is actionable and whether a sanction is warranted. If it is determined that no further action is warranted, the licensee and the complainant will be so advised. Where a *preliminary* determination is made that the material was aired and was indecent, an NAL is issued. If the Commission previously determined that the broadcast of the same material was indecent, the subsequent broadcast constitutes egregious misconduct and a higher forfeiture amount is warranted. *KGB, Inc. (KGB-FM)*, 13 FCC Rcd 16396 (1998) ("higher degree of culpability for the subsequent broadcast of material previously determined by the Commission to be indecent").

28. The licensee is afforded an opportunity to respond to the NAL, a step which is required by statute. 47 U.S.C. § 503(b). Once the Commission or its staff has considered any response by the licensee, it may order payment of a monetary penalty by issuing a Forfeiture Order. Alternatively, if the preliminary finding of violation in the NAL is successfully rebutted by the

---

[21] In *Act IV*, the court rejected a facial challenge to the Commission's procedures for imposing forfeitures for the broadcast of indecent materials. *Action for Children's Television v. FCC*, 59 F.3d 1249 (D.C. Cir. 1995), *cert. denied*, 116 S. Ct. 773 (1996) ("*Act IV*").

[22] This section discusses the typical process. The Commission also has authority to send forfeiture cases to a hearing, in which case the procedures discussed here differ. *See* 47 U.S.C. § 503(b)(3). *See also* 47 U.S.C. § 312(b) (revocation hearing for violation of 18 U.S.C. § 1464).

licensee, the NAL may be rescinded. If a Forfeiture Order is issued, the monetary penalty assessed may either be the same as specified in the NAL or it may be a lesser amount if the licensee has demonstrated that mitigating factors warrant a reduction in forfeiture.

29.   A Forfeiture Order may be appealed by the licensee through the administrative process under several different provisions of the Commission's rules. The licensee also has the legal right to refuse to pay the fine. In such a case, the Commission may refer the matter to the U.S. Department of Justice, which can initiate a trial *de novo* in a U.S. District Court. The trial court may start anew to evaluate the allegations of indecency.

V.   CONCLUSION

30.   The Commission issues this Policy Statement to provide guidance to broadcast licensees regarding compliance with the Commission's indecency regulations.[23] By summarizing the regulations and explaining the Commission's analytical approach to reviewing allegedly indecent material, the Commission provides a framework by which broadcast licensees can assess the legality of airing potentially indecent material. Numerous examples are provided in this document in an effort to assist broadcast licensees. However, this document is not intended to be an all-inclusive summary of every indecency finding issued by the Commission and it should not be relied upon as such. There are many additional cases that could have been cited. Further, as discussed above, the excerpts from broadcasts quoted in this document are intended only as a research tool. A complete understanding of the material, and the Commission's analysis thereof, requires review of the tapes or transcripts and the Commission's rulings thereon.

---

[23] This Policy Statement addresses the February 22, 1994, Agreement for Settlement and Dismissal with Prejudice between the United States of America, by and through the Department of Justice and Federal Communications Commission, and Evergreen Media Corporation of Chicago, AM, Licensee of Radio Station WLUP(AM) Specifically, in paragraph 2(b) of the settlement agreement, the Commission agreed to "publish industry guidance relating to its caselaw interpreting 18 U.S.C. § 1464 and the FCC's enforcement policies with respect to broadcast indecency." *United States v. Evergreen Media Corp.*, Civ. No. 92 C 5600 (N.D. Ill., E. Div. 1994). The settlement agreement also provides that the forfeiture order imposed in *Evergreen Media Corporation of Chicago AM WLUP(AM))*, 6 FCC Rcd 502 (MMB 1991), is null and void and expunged from the record. It further specifies that the Notice of Apparent Liability issued to WLUP on February 25, 1993, *Evergreen Media Corporation of Chicago AM (WLUP(AM))*, 8 FCC Rcd 1266 (1993), became null and void and expunged from the record six months from the date of the agreement. Accordingly, those decisions are officially vacated.

VI.   ORDERING CLAUSE

31.   Accordingly, it is ORDERED that this Policy Statement is ADOPTED.

FEDERAL COMMUNICATIONS COMMISSION

Magalie Roman Salas
Secretary

Separate Statement of Commissioner Susan Ness

In Re: Industry Guidance on the Commission's Case Law Interpreting 18 U.S.C. 1464 and Enforcement Policies Regarding Broadcast Indecency

Our enforcement of the broadcast indecency statute compels the FCC to reconcile two competing fundamental obligations: (1) to ensure that the airwaves are free of indecent programming material during prescribed hours when children are most likely to be in the audience; and (2) to respect the First Amendment rights of broadcasters regarding program content.

Understandably, the public is outraged by the increasingly coarse content aired on radio and television at all hours of the day, including times when children are likely to be listening or watching. The flood of letters and e-mails we receive reflect a high degree of anger. As a parent, I share the public's frustration. Many parents feel that they cannot enjoy watching daytime or primetime television with their children for fear that their youngsters will be exposed to indecent material – content that just a few years ago would have been unimaginable on broadcast television.

Despite an onslaught of on-air smut, the Commission necessarily walks a delicate line when addressing content issues, and must be careful not to tread on the First Amendment -- the constitutional bulwark of our free society. Even words that might be construed as indecent are subject to some constitutional protection against government regulation.[1]

That said, the Supreme Court has seen fit, despite declining broadcast audience shares, to reaffirm the FCC's broadcast indecency enforcement role, given the "pervasive" and "invasive" characteristics of the free over the air broadcast medium.[2] Our Policy Statement on indecency reconciles our statutory mandate and constitutional obligation by providing helpful guidance to broadcasters and the public alike. The guidance we offer – a restatement of existing statutory, regulatory, and judicial law – establishes a measure of clarity in an inherently subjective area.

Recommended Procedural Improvements

We should strive to make our complaint procedures as user-friendly as possible.[3] I believe that our complaint process could be improved if, prior to acting on an indecency complaint, the Commission routinely forwarded the complaint to the licensee in question. The Policy Statement concedes that in "many [indecency] cases, the station may not be aware that a complaint has been filed."[4]

---

[1] *FCC v. Pacifica Foundation*, 438 U.S. 726, 746 (1978) (while offensive words might "ordinarily lack literary, political, or scientific value, they are not entirely outside the protection of the First Amendment), *cf. id.* at 745 ("obscenity may be wholly prohibited").

[2] See, *Reno v. ACLU*, 521 U.S. 844, 868 (1997).

[3] The Policy Statement is careful to point out that complaints need not be letter perfect, *see, e.g.,* n. 20 (citing Bureau decision that an inexact transcript may be sufficient to meet procedural requirements).

[4] Policy Statement at para. 24.

Moreover, many consumers feel that the Commission mechanically dismisses their complaints. I do not believe that broadcasters' First Amendment rights would be threatened if we were to send broadcasters a courtesy copy of complaints filed with the FCC. Indeed, most broadcasters *want* to be made aware of audience complaints. And consumers would be reassured that their views were being treated seriously.

Broadcasters Are Part of a National Community

Release of this Policy Statement alone will not solve the festering problem of indecency on the airwaves. However, it is entirely within the power of broadcasters to address it -- and to do so *without government intrusion*. It is not a violation of the First Amendment for broadcasters on their own to take responsibility for the programming they air, and to exercise that power in a manner that celebrates rather than debases humankind.

It is time for broadcasters to consider reinstating a voluntary code of conduct. I encourage broadcasters, the Bush Administration, and Congress swiftly to resolve any antitrust impediments to such action and move ahead.

We all are part of a National Community. As stewards of the airwaves, broadcasters play a vital leadership role in setting the cultural tone of our society. They can choose to raise the standard or to lower it. I hope that broadcasters will rise to the occasion by reaffirming the unique role of broadcasting as a family friendly medium. The public deserves no less.

Separate Statement of Commissioner Harold W. Furchtgott-Roth

In the Matter of Guidance on the Commission's Case Law Interpreting 18 U.S.C. Section 1464 and Enforcement Policies Regarding Broadcast Indecency

The Commission is obliged, under a settlement agreement, to issue guidance on its broadcast indecency policies. As the courts have noted, there is a certain "vagueness inherent in [this] subject matter."[1] I find that the policy statement establishes necessary boundaries for this elusive and highly subjective area of the law.

I must note, however, that Commission action to enforce the indecency guidelines would set the stage for a new constitutional challenge regarding our authority to regulate content. To be sure, *Red Lion v. FCC*[2] and its progeny, *FCC v. Pacifica*,[3] have not yet been overruled. Nevertheless, their continuing validity is highly doubtful from both an empirical and jurisprudential point of view.[4]

content providers.[5] A competitive radio marketplace is evolving as well, with dynamic new outlets for speech on the horizon.[6] Because of these market transformations, the ability of the broadcast industry to corral content and control information flow has greatly diminished.[7] In my judgment, as

---

[1]*Action for Children's Television v. FCC*, 852 F.2d 1332, 1338 (1998) (internal quotation and citation omitted).

[2]395 U.S. 367 (1969).

[3]438 U.S. 726 (1978).

[4]Since *Pacifica*, the Courts have repeatedly struck down indecency regulations and other content-based restrictions. *See, e.g., United States v. Playboy Entertainment Group, Inc.*, 120 S.Ct. 1878 (2000) (striking down statutory adult cable channel scrambling requirements); *Greater New Orleans Broadcasting Ass'n v. U.S.*, 527 U.S. 173 (1999) (striking down the statutory and regulatory bans on casino advertising for broadcast stations); *Reno v. ACLU*, 117 S.Ct. 2329 (1997) (striking down statutory internet indecency requirements); *Denver Area Educ. Telecomms. Consortium, Inc. v. FCC*, 518 U.S. 727 (1996) (striking down certain statutory indecency requirements for commercial leased access and public access channels on cable television systems); and *Sable Communications v. FCC*, 492 U.S. 115 (1989) (striking down a ban on indecent telephone messages). *See also, Time Warner Entertainment Co. v. FCC*, __ F.3d. __ (D.C. Cir. 2001) (striking down FCC cable ownership cap and channel occupancy limits); and *Charter Communications v. County of Santa Cruz*, __ F.Supp. __ (N.D. Cal. 2001) (striking down local cable franchise transfer requirements).

[5]Cable operators, cable overbuilders, OVS operators, internet service providers, wireless video systems, SMATV, common carriers, and satellite carriers are just some of the possible outlets for distributing video content. The promise of multiplexed digital television signals, available to everyone over-the-air, adds even more video programming choices for the American public.

[6]Satellite radio will debut soon and digital audio broadcasting holds out much promise for the future of terrestrial radio transmission. Both types of services will offer listeners more channels of programming at higher quality levels than is available today. Moreover, hundreds of radio stations are currently streaming content over the internet, with thousands of more to follow.

[7]*See* Joint Statement of Commissioners Powell and Furchtgott-Roth, *In re Personal Attack and Political Editorial Rules*, FCC Gen. Docket No. 83-484, at 5 and n. 15 (citing statistics on boom in communications outlets).

If rules regulating broadcast content were ever a justifiable infringement of speech, it was because of the relative dominance of that medium in the communications marketplace of the past.[8] As the Commission has long recognized, the facts underlying this justification are no longer true.[9] Today, the video marketplace is rife with an abundance of programming,[10] distributed by several types of alternative sources of programming and distribution increase, broadcast content restrictions must be eliminated.

For these reasons, I believe that the lenient constitutional standard for reviewing broadcast speech,

---

[8]*See, e.g., FCC v. Pottsville Broadcasting Co.*, 309 U.S. 134, 137 (1940) (ownership rules justified by "a widespread fear that in the absence of governmental control the public interest might be subordinated to monopolistic domination"); *see also Red Lion Broadcasting Co. v. FCC*, 395 U.S. 367 (1969) (justifying, at that point in history, a "less rigorous standard of First Amendment scrutiny" on the basis of "spectrum scarcity").

[9]*See 1985 Fairness Report*, 102 FCC 2d 145, 198-221 (1985); *Syracuse Peace Council*, 2 FCC Rcd 5043, 5053 (1985).

[10]There are well over two hundred channels of video programming developed by the cable and broadcast industries. In addition, hyper-localized programming, produced by public, educational and governmental entities, is now available on cable systems throughout the United States. Also, dozens of pay-per-view programming options exist for cable and satellite subscribers. Finally, internet users have access to tens of thousands of audio programming sources and streaming video technology will soon advance to the point that broadcast quality television will be available to anyone connected to the world wide web.

formally announced in *Red Lion*, rests on a shaky empirical foundation.[11]   Technology, especially digital communications, has advanced to the point where broadcast deregulation is not only warranted, but long overdue. In my view, the bases for challenging broadcast indecency has been well laid, and the issue is ripe for court review.[12]

I must note my amazement that it has taken over seven years for the Commission to fulfill its obligation to issue this item. While broadcast indecency is a delicate issue to discuss, it has not benefited the industry or the Commission to ignore the matter. I commend the Chairman for taking the initiative to move this item. Norm Goldstein and others staff members deserve special credit for crafting a document that makes the best of a difficult situation for the Commission.
With these observations in mind, I vote to adopt this policy statement.

---

[11]It is ironic that streaming video or audio content from a television or radio station would likely receive more constitutional protection, *see Reno*, than would the same exact content broadcast over-the-air. A more interesting First Amendment question will soon arise when digital television stations begin offering subscription services over-the-air. Will intermediate scrutiny apply because the pay service is akin to cable television or will a lesser standard apply because it is available over-the-air? The same inquiries attach to radio signals delivered to listeners on a subscription basis via satellite.

[12]Dissenting Statement of Commissioner Harold W. Furchtgott-Roth, *In the Matter of 1998 Biennial Regulatory Review: Review of the Commission's Broadcast Ownership Rules and Other Rules Adopted Pursuant to Section 202 of the Communications Act* (rel. June 20, 2000)

APPENDIX F

Federal Communications Commission	FCC 01-90

Dissenting Statement of Commissioner Gloria Tristani

In the Matter of Industry Guidance on the Commission's Case Law Interpreting 18 U.S.C. §1464 and Enforcement Policies Regarding Broadcast Indecency, EB File No. 00-IH-0089

I dissent from the issuance of this "Policy Statement" (hereinafter "Statement") for three reasons. First, the Statement creates a false impression that it satisfies an obligation assumed by the Commission in 1994. Second, the Statement perpetuates the myth that broadcast indecency standards are too vague and compliance so difficult that a Policy Statement is necessary to provide further guidance. Most importantly, this Statement diverts this Agency's attention and resources away from the ongoing problem of lax enforcement, which is a pressing concern of America's citizens.

The Statement notes that on February 22, 1994 the Commission entered into a Settlement Agreement with Evergreen Media Corporation (hereinafter "Agreement").[1] At fn 23 the Statement cites the terms of the Agreement as the source of our obligation to produce this Statement:

> Specifically, in paragraph 2(b) of the settlement agreement, the Commission agreed to "publish industry guidance relating to its caselaw interpreting 18 U.S.C. § 1464 and the FCCs enforcement policies with respect to broadcast indecency."[2]

The Agreement actually imposed a significantly more restricted obligation.

> *Within nine months of the date of this Agreement*, the FCC shall publish industry guidance relating to its caselaw interpreting 18 U.S.C. § 1464 and the FCCs enforcement policies with respect to broadcast indecency.[3]

Six and one half years later, it is clear the FCC did not observe the terms of the Agreement. While I cannot support the FCC's failure to comply with the timeline set forth in the original Agreement, the record does not disclose a single effort by Evergreen to seek specific performance under the Agreement. It is well settled that "equity aids the vigilant, not those who slumber on their rights," and doctrines such as laches are designed to promote diligence and prevent enforcement of stale claims.[4] The public interest is not served by permitting Evergreen to sit silently on the sidelines while Commission after Commission failed to act. Even if the FCC shirked its duty under the Agreement, as long as Evergreen

---

[1] *See United States v. Evergreen Media Corp.*, Civ. No. 92 C 5600 (N.D. Ill., E. Div. 1994).

[2] *See Policy Statement* at p. 17-18, n.23.

[3] *See Settlement Agreement* at p. 3.

[4] *See e.g. Powell v. Zuckert*, 366 F.2d 634, 636 (D.C.Cir.1966).

retained the benefit of dismissal of indecency cases against it as set out in the Agreement, a strong case exists that Evergreen ratified this agency's inaction for almost 7 years.[5]   If Evergreen Media Corporation had an enforceable interest in the Agreement, it has long since been waived.

Moreover, the obligation to issue the Statement was subject to several conditions precedent that bound Evergreen Media.[6] The Statement itself does not disclose whether Evergreen complied with its obligations, and with the exception of noting payment of $10,000 forfeiture, the record on file at the Commission is silent on the same point. FCC Mass Media Bureau records disclose that Evergreen Media no longer owns the license to which the Agreement's terms attached.   Finally, the Agreement does not bind the Commission to provide to Evergreen's assigns the relief set forth in the Agreement.[7] In the absence of the party executing the Agreement, and no successor to accede to those interests, it appears there is no extant legal duty or enforceable right upon which the issuance of the Statement can be based.

I turn next to the underpinnings of the need for this statement. The Statement provides:

> The Commission issues this Policy Statement to provide guidance to the broadcast industry regarding our case law interpreting 18 U.S.C. § 1464 and our enforcement policies with respect to broadcast indecency.[8]

First, settlement of a case involving a single licensee should not compel the FCC to adopt our most significant industry-wide Policy Statement on this subject, particularly when doing so does not serve the public interest. Second, there is nothing in the record demonstrating that Evergreen Media failed to understand the FCC's, or the U.S. Supreme Court's, cases on broadcast indecency. In fact Evergreen agreed to issue to its employees a "policy statement" that was to be based upon "the FCC's definition of broadcast indecency."[9] It his difficult to understand how Evergreen could both issue a policy statement containing the FCC's definition of indecency to its employees *and* simultaneously be unable to understand the FCC's definition. But leaving that quirk aside, there is simply no proof that broadcast licensees are in need of this Policy Statement. No factual basis exists for concluding that confusion about the standards or overreaching enforcement by the FCC requires this Statement.

---

[5] *See e.g., Buffum v. Peter Barceloux Co.*, 289 U.S. 227, 234 (1933).

[6] The Agreement provides the parties exchanged "consideration and mutual promises hereinafter stated."   *See Settlement Agreement* at p. 2 The Agreement describes, at Para. 3, several actions to be undertaken by Evergreen. The Agreement is a form of an executory contract the terms of which require timely satisfaction to constitute compliance. Failure by either party to perform would make the Agreement voidable or unenforceable.

[7] *See Settlement Agreement* at p. 4.

[8] *See Statement* at p.1.

[9] *See Settlement Agreement,* at p. 3.

Moreover, I am aware of no rush of inquiries by broadcast licensees seeking to learn whether their programs comply with our indecency caselaw. In the absence of such requests, this Policy Statement will likely become instead a "how-to" manual for those licensees who wish to tread the line drawn by our cases. It likely may lead to responses to future enforcement actions that cite the Statement as establishing false safe harbors. In the absence of proof that the Statement addresses concerns supported by the FCC's history of enforcement, or the record of the Evergreen case, the Statement is nothing more than a remedy in search of a problem. It would better serve the public if the FCC got serious about enforcing the broadcast indecency standards. For these reasons, I dissent.

06-1760
Fox v. FCC

UNITED STATES COURT OF APPEALS

FOR THE SECOND CIRCUIT

August Term, 2006

(Argued: December 20, 2006   Decided: June 4, 2007)

Docket Nos. 06-1760-ag (L), 06-2750-ag (CON), 06-5358-ag (CON)

FOX TELEVISION STATIONS, INC., CBS BROADCASTING, INC.,
WLS TELEVISION, INC., KTRK TELEVISION, INC., KMBC HEARST-
ARGYLE TELEVISION, INC., ABC, INC.,

        Petitioners,

              v.

FEDERAL COMMUNICATIONS COMMISSION, UNITED STATES
OF AMERICA,

        Respondents,

NBC UNIVERSAL, INC., NBC TELEMUNDO LICENSE CO., NBC
TELEVISION AFFILIATES, FBC TELEVISION AFFILIATES
ASSOCIATION, CBS TELEVISION NETWORK AFFILIATES, CENTER
FOR THE CREATIVE COMMUNITY, INC., doing business as CENTER
FOR CREATIVE VOICES IN MEDIA, INC., ABC TELEVISION AFFILIATES
ASSOCIATION,

        Intervenors.

Before: LEVAL, POOLER, and HALL, Circuit Judges.

       Fox Television Stations, Inc. ("Fox") petitions for review of the November 6, 2006, order

of the Federal Communications Commission ("FCC") issuing notices of apparent liability against two Fox broadcasts for violating the FCC's indecency regime. We find that the FCC's new

policy sanctioning "fleeting expletives" is arbitrary and capricious under the Administrative

Procedure Act for failing to articulate a reasoned basis for its change in policy. Accordingly, the

petition for review is GRANTED, the order of the FCC is VACATED, and the matter is

REMANDED to the agency for further proceedings consistent with this opinion.

Judge Leval dissents in a separate opinion.

CARTER G. PHILLIPS, Sidley Austin LLP, Washington D.C. (R. Clark Wadlow, James P. Young, Jennifer Tatel, David S. Petron, Sidley Austin LLP, Washington D.C. on the brief) *for Petitioner Fox Television Stations, Inc. and Intervenor FBC Television Affiliates Association.*

ERIC D. MILLER, Deputy General Counsel, for Samuel L. Feder, General Counsel, Federal Communications Commission, Washington D.C. (Matthew B. Berry, Daniel Armstrong, Jacob M. Lewis, Joseph R. Palmore, Federal Communications Commission and Jeffrey S. Bucholtz, Acting Assistant Attorney General, Thomas M. Bondy, Department of Justice, Washington D.C. on the brief) *for Respondents.*

Ellen S. Agress, Maureen A. O'Connell, Fox Television Stations, New York, NY *for Petitioner Fox Television Stations, Inc.*

Robert Corn-Revere, Ronald G. London, Amber L. Husbands, David M. Shapiro, Davis Wright Tremaine LLP, and Lee Levine, Levine Sullivan Koch & Schulz L.L.P., Washington D.C. *for Petitioner/Intervenor[1] CBS Broadcasting Inc.*

Miguel A. Estrada, Andrew S. Tulumello, Matthew D. McGill, Travis D. Lenkner, Gibson, Dunn, and Crutcher LLP, Washington D.C.; Richard Cotton, Susan Weiner, NBC Universal, Inc., New York, NY; and F. William LeBeau, NBC Universal, Inc. and NBC Telemundo License Co., Washington D.C. *for Intervenors NBC Universal, Inc. and NBC Telemundo License Co.*

Andrew J. Schwartzman, Parul P. Desai, Media Access Project, Washington D.C. *for Intervenor Center for Creative Voices in Media.*

Marjorie Heins, Brennan Center for Justice, Free Expression Policy Project, New

---

[1]CBS is a petitioner in Docket No. 06-1760 and an intervenor in Docket No. 06-5358.

York, NY *for Amici Curiae Brennan Center for Justice, American Civil Liberties Union, New York Civil Liberties Union, National Coalition Against Censorship, First Amendment Project, PEN American Center, American Booksellers Foundation for Free Expression, Writers Guild of America West, Directors Guild of America, Screen Actors Guild, American Federation of Television and Radio Artists, Writers Guild of America East, Minnesota Public Radio/American Public Media, National Federation of Community Broadcasters, Film Arts Foundation, Re:New Media, National Alliance for Media Arts and Culture, International Documentary Association, Working Films, and the Creative Coalition in support of Petitioners.*

John B. Morris, Jr., Sophia Cope, Center for Democracy & Technology and Adam D. Thierer, The Progress & Freedom Foundation, Washington D.C. *for Amici Curiae Center for Democracy & Technology and Adam Thierer, Senior Fellow with The Progress & Freedom Foundation ("PFF") and the Director of PFF's Center for Digital Media Freedom in support of Petitioners.*

Henry Geller, Washington D.C. and Glen O. Robinson, University of Virginia School of Law, Charlottesville, VA *for Amici Curiae Former FCC Officials in support of Petitioners.*

Robert R. Sparks, Jr., Sparks & Craig, LLP, McLean Virginia *for Amicus Curiae Parents Television Council in support of Respondents.*

Robert W. Peters, Robin S. Whitehead, Morality in Media, Inc., New York, NY *for Amicus Curiae Morality in Media, Inc. in support of Respondents.*

Thomas B. North, St. Ignace, MI *for Amicus Curiae Thomas B. North, Judge of Probate, Sixth Probate Court of Michigan, in support of Respondents.*

POOLER, Circuit Judge:

Fox Television Stations, Inc., along with its affiliates FBC Television Affiliates Association (collectively "Fox"), petition for review of the November 6, 2006, order of the Federal Communications Commission ("FCC") issuing notices of apparent liability against two Fox broadcasts for violating the FCC's indecency and profanity prohibitions.[2] Fox, along with

---

[2] The petitions for review filed by Fox and CBS in Docket No. 06-1760 and ABC in Docket No. 06-2750 pertain to portions of a prior order by the FCC that has since been vacated.

other broadcast networks and numerous amici, raise administrative, statutory, and constitutional challenges to the FCC's indecency regime. The FCC, also supported by several amici, dispute each of these challenges. We find that the FCC's new policy regarding "fleeting expletives" represents a significant departure from positions previously taken by the agency and relied on by the broadcast industry. We further find that the FCC has failed to articulate a reasoned basis for this change in policy. Accordingly, we hold that the FCC's new policy regarding "fleeting expletives" is arbitrary and capricious under the Administrative Procedure Act. The petition for review is therefore granted, the order of the FCC is vacated, and the matter is remanded to the Commission for further proceedings consistent with this opinion. Because we vacate the FCC's order on this ground, we do not reach the other challenges to the FCC's indecency regime raised by petitioners, intervenors, and amici.

BACKGROUND

The FCC's policing of "indecent" speech stems from 18 U.S.C. § 1464, which provides that "[w]hoever utters any obscene, indecent, or profane language by means of radio communication shall be fined under this title or imprisoned not more than two years, or both." The FCC's authority to regulate the broadcast medium is expressly limited by Section 326 of the Communications Act, which prohibits the FCC from engaging in censorship. See 47 U.S.C. § 326. In 1960, Congress authorized the FCC to impose forfeiture penalties for violations of Section 1464. See 47 U.S.C. § 503(b)(1)(D). The FCC first exercised its statutory authority to sanction indecent (but non-obscene) speech in 1975, when it found Pacifica Foundation's radio

---

Accordingly, those petitions for review are denied as moot. The remainder of this opinion addresses the petition for review filed by Fox in Docket No. 06-5358.

broadcast of comedian George Carlin's "Filthy Words" monologue indecent and subject to

forfeiture. See Citizen's Complaint Against Pacifica Found. Station WBAI(FM), N.Y, N.Y., 56

F.C.C.2d 94 (1975). True to its title, the "Filthy Words" monologue contained numerous

expletives in the course of a 12-minute monologue broadcast on the radio at 2:00 in the

afternoon. In ruling on this complaint, the FCC articulated the following description of

"indecent" content:

> [T]he concept of 'indecent' is intimately connected with the exposure of children
> to language that describes, in terms patently offensive as measured by
> contemporary community standards for the broadcast medium, sexual or excretory
> activities and organs, at times of the day when there is a reasonable risk that
> children may be in the audience. Obnoxious, gutter language describing these
> matters has the effect of debasing and brutalizing human beings by reducing them
> to their mere bodily functions, and we believe that such words are indecent within
> the meaning of the statute and have no place on radio when children are in the
> audience.

Id. at ¶ 11 (internal footnote omitted).

Pacifica appealed the FCC's order to the Court of Appeals for the D.C. Circuit. While

that appeal was pending, the FCC issued a "clarification" order in which it specifically noted that

its prior order was intended to address only the particular facts of the Carlin monologue as

broadcast, and acknowledged the concern that "in some cases, public events likely to produce

offensive speech are covered live, and there is no opportunity for journalistic editing." 'Petition

for Clarification or Reconsideration' of a Citizen's Complaint against Pacifica Foundation,

Station WBAI(FM), N.Y., N.Y., 59 F.C.C. 2d 892, at ¶ 4 n.1 (1976) ("Pacifica Clarification

Order"). The FCC stated that in such a situation, "we believe that it would be inequitable for us

to hold a licensee responsible for indecent language." Id.

Although acknowledging the FCC's additional clarification, the D.C. Circuit nevertheless concluded that the FCC's indecency regime was invalid. See Pacifica Found. v. FCC, 556 F.2d 9 (D.C. Cir. 1977). Labeling the Commission's actions censorship, the court found the FCC's order both vague and overbroad, noting that it would prohibit "the uncensored broadcast of many of the great works of literature including Shakespearian plays and contemporary plays which have won critical acclaim, the works of renowned classical and contemporary poets and writers, and passages from the *Bible*." Id. at 14.

The Commission appealed this decision to the Supreme Court, which reversed in a plurality opinion. In its brief to the Supreme Court, the FCC stressed that its ruling was a narrow one applying only to the specific facts of the Carlin monologue. See Br. of FCC at 41-49, FCC v. Pacifica Found., No. 77-528 (U.S. Mar. 3, 1978), available at 1978 WL 206838. The Court took the Commission at its word and confined its review to the specific question of whether the Commission could find indecent the Carlin monologue as broadcast. See FCC v. Pacifica Found., 438 U.S. 726, 732-35 (1978). The Court first rejected Pacifica's statutory argument that "indecent" in Section 1464 could not be read to cover speech that admittedly did not qualify as obscenity. Id. at 739. Finding that obscene, indecent, and profane have distinct meanings in the statute, the Court held that the FCC is permitted to sanction speech without showing that it satisfied the elements of obscenity. Id. at 739-41. The Court then rejected Pacifica's constitutional challenges. The Court stated that "of all forms of communication, it is broadcasting that has received the most limited First Amendment protection" because the broadcast medium is a "uniquely pervasive presence in the lives of all Americans" that extends into the privacy of the home and is "uniquely accessible to children, even those too young to read." Id. at 748-749. The Court therefore found that the FCC could, consistent with the First

Amendment, regulate indecent material like the Carlin monologue. The Court then once again

"emphasize[d] the narrowness of our holding . . . We simply hold that when the Commission

finds that a pig has entered the parlor, the exercise of its regulatory power does not depend on

proof that the pig is obscene." Id. at 750-51.

Justices Powell and Blackmun, who concurred in the judgment and supplied two of the

votes necessary for the 5-4 majority,[3] also emphasized in their concurring opinion that the

Court's holding was a narrow one limited to the facts of the Carlin monologue as broadcast. Id.

at 755-56 (Powell J., concurring). Foreshadowing the question now before us, they explicitly

noted that "[t]he Commission's holding, and certainly the Court's holding today, does not speak

to cases involving the isolated use of a potentially offensive word in the course of a radio

broadcast, as distinguished from the verbal shock treatment administered by respondent here."

Id. at 760-61 (Powell J., concurring). Furthermore, citing the FCC's brief to the Court, Justice

Powell stated that he did not foresee an undue chilling effect on broadcasters by the FCC's

decision because "the Commission may be expected to proceed cautiously, as it has in the past."

Id. at 761 n.4 (Powell J., concurring).

The FCC took the Pacifica Court's admonitions seriously in its subsequent decisions.[4]

Shortly after the Pacifica ruling, the FCC stated the following in an opinion rejecting a challenge

to a broadcaster's license renewal on the basis that the broadcaster had aired indecent

---

[3]The four dissenting justices would have held invalid any attempt by the FCC to prohibit indecent (non-obscene) speech. See Pacifica, 438 U.S. at 762-80.

[4]At the time, the Commission interpreted Pacifica as involving a situation "about as likely to occur again as Halley's Comet." Br. of Amici Curiae Former FCC Officials at 6 (quoting FCC Chairman Charles D. Ferris, Speech to New England Broad. Assoc., Boston, Mass. (July 21, 1978)).

programming:

> With regard to 'indecent' or 'profane' utterances, the First Amendment and the 'no censorship' provision of Section 326 of the Communications Act severely limit any role by the Commission and the courts in enforcing the proscription contained in Section 1464. The Supreme Court's decision in *FCC v. Pacifica Foundation*, 46 U.S.L.W. 5018 (1978), No. 77-528, decided July 3, 1978, affords this Commission no general prerogative to intervene in any case where words similar or identical to those in Pacifica are broadcast over a licensed radio or television station. <u>We intend strictly to observe the narrowness of the Pacifica holding.</u> In this regard, the Commission's opinion, as approved by the Court, relied in part on the repetitive occurrence of the 'indecent' words in question. The opinion of the Court specifically stated that it was not ruling that 'an occasional expletive . . . would justify any sanction . . .' Further, Justice Powell's concurring opinion emphasized the fact that the language there in issue had been 'repeated over and over as a sort of verbal shock treatment.' He specifically distinguished 'the verbal shock treatment [in Pacifica]' from 'the isolated use of a potentially offensive word in the course of a radio broadcast.'

<u>Application of WGBH Educ. Found.</u>, 69 F.C.C.2d 1250, at ¶ 10 (1978) (emphasis added)

(ellipses in original; internal footnotes and citations omitted). The FCC also specifically held

that the single use of an expletive in a program that aired at 5:30pm "should not call for us to act

under the holding of <u>Pacifica</u>." <u>Id.</u> at ¶ 10 n.6. A few years later, the Commission again rejected

a challenge to a license renewal that complained the broadcaster had aired indecent programming

in violation of Section 1464. The FCC acknowledged the complaint that the broadcaster on three

separate occasions had aired programming during the morning hours containing language such as

"motherfucker," "fuck," and "shit," but nevertheless concluded that "it is clear that the petitioner

has failed to make a *prima facie* case that [the broadcaster] has violated 18 U.S.C. 1464" since

the language did not amount to "verbal shock treatment" and the complainant had failed to show

this was more than "isolated use." <u>Application of Pacifica Found.</u>, 95 F.C.C.2d 750, at ¶¶ 16, 18

(1983).

It was not until 1987 that the FCC would find another broadcast "indecent" under Section 1464. See Infinity Broad. Corp., et al., 3 F.C.C.R. 930 (1987) ("Infinity Order"). The Commission explained:

> In cases decided subsequent to the Supreme Court's ruling [in Pacifica], the Commission took a very limited approach to enforcing the prohibition against indecent broadcasts. Unstated, but widely assumed, and implemented for the most part through staff rulings, was the belief that only material that closely resembled the George Carlin monologue would satisfy the indecency test articulated by the FCC in 1975. Thus, no action was taken unless material involved the repeated use, for shock value, of words similar or identical to those satirized in the Carlin "Filthy Words" monologue . . . As a result, the Commission, since the time of its ruling in 1975, has taken no action against any broadcast licensee for violating the prohibition against indecent broadcasts.

Id. at ¶ 4 (internal footnotes omitted). The Infinity Order affirmed on reconsideration three decisions issued simultaneously by the FCC in April 1987 that found certain programs indecent. See Pacifica Found., Inc., 2 F.C.C.R. 2698 (1987); The Regents of the Univ. of Cal., 2 F.C.C.R. 2703 (1987); Infinity Broad. Corp., 2 F.C.C.R. 2705 (1987). The FCC explained in the Infinity Order that it would no longer take the narrow view that a finding of indecency required the use of one of the seven "dirty words" used in Carlin's monologue. See Infinity Order, at ¶ 5. The FCC instead would use the generic definition of indecency it had articulated in connection with its prior decision in Pacifica. Id. Under the Commission's definition, "indecent speech is language that describes, in terms patently offensive as measured by contemporary community standards for the broadcast medium, sexual or excretory activities and organs. Such indecent speech is actionable when broadcast at times of the day when there is a reasonable risk that children may be in the audience." Regents of the Univ. of Cal., 2 F.C.C.R. 2703, at ¶ 3 (internal footnote omitted). The FCC also reaffirmed, however, the prevailing view that a fleeting expletive would not be actionable. See id. ("Speech that is indecent must involve more than an isolated use of an offensive word."); Pacifica Found., Inc., 2 F.C.C.R. 2698, at ¶ 13 ("If a complaint focuses solely on the use of expletives, we believe that under the legal standards set forth in Pacifica, deliberate and repetitive use in a patently offensive manner is a requisite to a finding of indecency."). Notably, in Pacifica Foundation, the Commission declined to make a finding of indecency against a radio broadcast of the program "Shocktime America," which had contained words and phrases such as "eat shit," "mother-fucker" and "fuck the U.S.A," in part because, without a transcript or tape of the program, the FCC was unable to determine "whether the use of patently offensive speech was isolated." Id. at ¶¶ 3, 17.

Broadcasters appealed the Infinity Order to the D.C. Circuit, challenging the FCC's definition of indecency as unconstitutionally vague. See Action for Children's Television v. FCC, 852 F.2d 1332 (D.C. Cir. 1988) ("ACT I"), superseded in part by Action for Children's Television v. FCC, 58 F.3d 654 (D.C. Cir. 1995) (in banc). The D.C. Circuit rejected this argument on the basis that the definition at issue was "virtually the same definition the Commission articulated in the order reviewed by the Supreme Court in the *Pacifica* case." Id. at 1338. The court concluded that Pacifica implicitly rejected any vagueness challenge to the FCC's definition of "indecent," which therefore foreclosed its ability to revisit any such argument. Id. at 1339. The court then invited correction from "Higher Authority" if its reading of Pacifica was incorrect. Id. Before leaving the First Amendment issue, however, the court explicitly noted that the "FCC has assured this court, at oral argument, that it will continue to give weight to reasonable licensee judgments when deciding whether to impose sanctions in a particular case. Thus, the potential chilling effect of the FCC's generic definition of indecency will be tempered by the Commission's restrained enforcement policy." Id. at 1340 n.14 (citing

Pacifica, 438 U.S. at 761 (Powell J., concurring)).

This restrained enforcement policy would continue. In 2001, pursuant to a settlement

agreement by which the FCC agreed to clarify its indecency standards, the Commission issued a

policy statement to "provide guidance to the broadcast industry regarding our case law

interpreting 18 U.S.C. § 1464 and our enforcement policies with respect to broadcast indecency."

Industry Guidance on the Commission's Case Law Interpreting 18 U.S.C. § 1464, 16 F.C.C.R.

7999, at ¶ 1 & ¶ 30 n.23 (2001) ("Industry Guidance"). The FCC first noted that "indecent

speech is protected by the First Amendment, and thus, the government must both identify a

compelling interest for any regulation it may impose on indecent speech and choose the least

restrictive means to further that interest." Id. at ¶ 3.

The FCC then explained that an indecency finding involves the following two

determinations: (1) whether the material falls within the "subject matter scope of [the] indecency

definition – that is, the material must describe or depict sexual or excretory organs or activities";

and (2) whether the broadcast is *patently offensive* as measured by contemporary community

standards for the broadcast medium." Id. at ¶¶ 7-8. The FCC considers the following three

factors in determining whether the material is patently offensive: "(1) the *explicitness or graphic

nature* of the description or depiction of sexual or excretory organs or activities; (2) whether the

materials *dwells on or repeats at length* descriptions of sexual or excretory organs or activities;

(3) *whether the material appears to pander or is used to titillate*, or *whether the material

appears to have been presented for its shock value.*" Id. at ¶ 10. The policy statement contained

numerous examples of prior FCC decisions evaluating whether certain material was indecent in an attempt to provide guidance to broadcasters. In discussing the second factor in the "patently offensive" analysis, the FCC cited examples distinguishing between material that "dwells" on the offensive content (indecent) and material that was "fleeting and isolated" (not indecent). Id. at ¶¶ 17-18.

This restrained enforcement policy would soon change. During NBC's January 19, 2003, live broadcast of the Golden Globe Awards, musician Bono stated in his acceptance speech "this is really, really, fucking brilliant. Really, really, great." Complaints Against Various Broadcast Licensees Regarding Their Airing of the "Golden Globe Awards" Program, 19 F.C.C.R. 4975, at ¶ 3 n.4 (2004) ("Golden Globes"). Individuals associated with the Parents Television Council filed complaints that the material was obscene and indecent under FCC regulations. Id. at ¶ 3. The FCC's Enforcement Bureau, however, denied the complaints on the basis that the expletive as used in context did not describe sexual or excretory organs or activities and that the utterance was fleeting and isolated. See Complaints Against Various Broadcast Licensees Regarding Their Airing of the "Golden Globe Awards" Program, 18 F.C.C.R. 19859, at ¶¶ 5-6 (Enforcement Bureau 2003) ("Golden Globes (Bureau Decision)"). The Bureau accordingly found that the speech "does not fall within the scope of the Commission's indecency prohibition," and reaffirmed FCC policy that "fleeting and isolated remarks of this nature do not warrant Commission action." Id. at ¶ 6.

Five months later, the full Commission reversed the Bureau's decision. First, the FCC held that any use of any variant of "the F-Word" inherently has sexual connotation and therefore falls within the scope of the indecency definition. Golden Globes, at ¶ 8. The FCC then held that "the 'F-Word' is one of the most vulgar, graphic, and explicit descriptions of sexual activity in the English language" and therefore the use of that word was patently offensive under contemporary community standards. Id. at ¶ 9. The Commission found the fleeting and isolated use of the word irrelevant and overruled all prior decisions in which fleeting use of an expletive was held not indecent. Id. at ¶ 12 ("While prior Commission and staff action have indicated that isolated or fleeting broadcasts of the 'F-Word' such as that here are not indecent or would not be acted upon, consistent with our decision today we conclude that any such interpretation is no longer good law.").

The FCC then held that the material in question was also "profane" under Section 1464. Id. at ¶ 13. The Commission acknowledged that prior decisions interpreting "profane" had defined that term as blasphemy, but found that nothing in its prior decisions limited the definition of profane in such a manner. Id. at ¶ 14. The Commission, however, declined to impose a forfeiture because "existing precedent would have permitted this broadcast" and therefore NBC and its affiliates "necessarily did not have the requisite notice to justify a penalty." Id. at ¶ 15. The Commission emphasized, though, that licensees were now on notice that any broadcast of the "F-Word" could subject them to monetary penalties and suggested that implementing delay technology would ensure future compliance with its policy. Id. at ¶ 17.

NBC, along with several other parties including Fox, filed petitions for reconsideration of the Golden Globes order, raising statutory and constitutional challenges to the new policy. NBC, Fox, and Viacom Inc. also filed a joint petition to stay the effect of the Golden Globes order. These petitions have been pending for more than two years without any action by the FCC. Nevertheless, the FCC has applied the policy announced in Golden Globes in subsequent cases.

On February 21, 2006, the FCC issued an order resolving various complaints against several television broadcasts. See Complaints Regarding Various Television Broadcasts Between February 2, 2002 and March 8, 2005, 21 F.C.C.R. 2664 (2006) ("Omnibus Order"). Through this order, the FCC intended to "provide substantial guidance to broadcasters and the public about the types of programming that are impermissible under our indecency standard." Id. at ¶ 2. In Section III.B of the Omnibus Order, the Commission found four programs—Fox's broadcast of the 2002 Billboard Music Awards, Fox's broadcast of the 2003 Billboard Music Awards, various episodes of ABC's NYPD Blue, and CBS's The Early Show—indecent and profane under the policy announced in Golden Globes. The factual situations at issue are as follows:

- **2002 Billboard Music Awards**: In her acceptance speech, Cher stated: "People have been telling me I'm on the way out every year, right? So fuck 'em."

- **2003 Billboard Music Awards**: Nicole Richie, a presenter on the show, stated: "Have you ever tried to get cow shit out of a Prada purse? It's not so fucking simple."

- **NYPD Blue**: In various episodes, Detective Andy Sipowitz and other characters used certain expletives including "bullshit," "dick," and "dickhead."

- **The Early Show**: During a live interview of a contestant on CBS's reality show Survivor: Vanuatu, the interviewee referred to a fellow contestant as a "bullshitter."

Id. at ¶¶ 101, 112 n. 64, 125, 137. In finding these programs indecent and profane, the FCC reaffirmed its decision in Golden Globes that any use of the word "fuck" is presumptively indecent and profane. Id. at ¶¶ 102, 107. The Commission then concluded that any use of the word "shit" was also presumptively indecent and profane. Id. at ¶¶ 138, 143. Turning to the second part of its indecency test, the FCC found that each of the programs were "patently offensive" because the material was explicit, shocking, and gratuitous. Id. at ¶¶ 106, 120, 131, 141. Citing Golden Globes, the Commission dismissed the fact that the expletives were fleeting and isolated and held that repeated use is not necessary for a finding of indecency. Id. at ¶¶ 104, 116, 129, 140. The FCC, however, declined to issue a forfeiture in each case for the express reason that the broadcasts in question occurred before the decision in Golden Globes, and thus "existing precedent would have permitted this broadcast." Id. at ¶¶ 111, 124, 136, 145.

Fox and CBS filed a petition for review of the Omnibus Order in this court. ABC filed a petition for review in the D.C. Circuit, which was then transferred to this court and consolidated with the petition for review filed by Fox and CBS. Before any briefing took place, however, the FCC moved for a voluntary remand in order to give the Commission the first opportunity to address petitioners' arguments and "ensure that all licensees are afforded a full opportunity to be heard before the Commission issues a final decision." See FCC Mot. for Voluntary Remand at 2, No. 06-1760 (July 6, 2006). On September 7, 2006, this court granted the FCC's request for remand and stayed enforcement of the Omnibus Order. The Commission was given sixty days to issue a final or appealable order, at which time the pending appeal would be automatically reinstated.

The FCC promptly issued a public notice soliciting comments on its decision in the Omnibus Order. Numerous parties, including those who have participated in the briefing in this appeal, submitted comments raising various statutory and constitutional arguments against the FCC's indecency regime. The FCC then issued a new order on November 6, 2006. See Complaints Regarding Various Television Broadcasts Between February 2, 2002 and March 8, 2005, FCC 06-166 (Nov. 6, 2006) ("Remand Order"). The Remand Order vacated Section III.B of the Omnibus Order in its entirety and replaced it with the Remand Order. Id. at ¶ 11. In the

Remand Order, the FCC reaffirmed its finding that the 2002 and 2003 Billboard Music Award

programs were indecent and profane, but reversed its finding against The Early Show. It also

dismissed on procedural grounds the complaint against NYPD Blue.[5]

With regard to the 2003 Billboard Music Awards, the Commission found that it would

have been actionably indecent even prior to the decision in Golden Globes because the

potentially offensive material was "repeated," since Nicole Richie used "two extremely graphic

and offensive words," and was "deliberately uttered" because of "Ms. Richie's confident and

fluid delivery of the lines." Id. at ¶ 22. With regard to the 2002 Billboard Music Awards, the

Commission "acknowledge[d] that it was not apparent that Fox could be penalized for Cher's

comment at the time it was broadcast." Id. at ¶ 60. In both cases, the FCC rejected Fox's

argument that fleeting expletives were not actionable, now characterizing its prior decisions on

that issue as "staff letters and dicta." Id. at ¶ 20. The Commission, however, declined to impose

a forfeiture for either broadcast. Id. at ¶¶ 53, 66.

Turning to The Early Show, the FCC reversed its finding that the expletive used was

indecent or profane because it occurred in the context of a "*bona fide* news interview." Id. at ¶

68. The Commission stated that in light of First Amendment concerns, "it is imperative that we

---

[5]The Commission dismissed the complaint against NYPD Blue because the only person who complained of the material resided in the Eastern time zone, where NYPD Blue aired during the "safe harbor" period after 10pm. Remand Order, at ¶ 75; see also 47 C.F.R. § 73.3999(b) (providing that broadcasting of indecent material is prohibited only between the hours of 6am and 10pm); Action for Children's Television v. FCC, 932 F.2d 1504 (D.C. Cir. 1991) ("ACT II") ("safe harbor" period is constitutionally required), superseded in part by Action for Children's Television v. FCC, 58 F.3d 654 (D.C. Cir. 1995) (in banc). In light of the FCC's revised decision regarding NYPD Blue, ABC is no longer participating in this appeal.

proceed with the utmost restraint when it comes to news programming," and found it "appropriate . . . to defer to CBS's plausible characterization of its own programming" as a news interview. Id. at ¶ 71-72. Given this context, the FCC declined to find the comment indecent or profane. Id. at ¶ 73.

In accordance with our September 6th order, this appeal was automatically reinstated on November 8, 2006. Fox then filed a petition for review of the Remand Order and moved to consolidate that appeal with the one already pending before this court. We granted the motion for consolidation as well as motions to intervene by CBS Broadcasting Inc. ("CBS") and NBC Universal Inc. and NBC Telemundo License Co. (collectively, "NBC"). We have also received several briefs from various amici.

DISCUSSION

Fox, CBS, and NBC (collectively, "the Networks"), supported by several amici, raise a variety of arguments against the validity of the Remand Order, including: (1) the Remand Order is arbitrary and capricious because the Commission's regulation of "fleeting expletives" represents a dramatic change in agency policy without adequate explanation; (2) the FCC's "community standards" analysis is arbitrary and meaningless; (3) the FCC's indecency findings are invalid because the Commission made no finding of scienter; (4) the FCC's definition of "profane" is contrary to law; (5) the FCC's indecency regime is unconstitutionally vague; (6) the FCC's indecency test permits the Commission to make subjective determinations about the quality of speech in violation of the First Amendment; and (7) the FCC's indecency regime is an impermissible content-based regulation of speech that violates the First Amendment. The FCC, also supported by several amici, dispute each of these contentions. We agree with the first argument advanced by the Networks, and therefore do not reach any other potential problems with the FCC's decision.

I.   Scope of Review

Before turning to the merits of the Networks' arguments, we first note that we reject the FCC's contention that our review here is narrowly confined to the specific question of whether the two Fox broadcasts of the Billboard Music Awards were indecent and/or profane. The Remand Order applies the policy announced in Golden Globes. If that policy is invalid, then we cannot sustain the indecency findings against Fox. Thus, as the Commission conceded during oral argument, the validity of the new "fleeting expletive" policy announced in Golden Globes and applied in the Remand Order is a question properly before us on this petition for review. As the D.C. Circuit explained in rejecting this precise argument in another proceeding, "the agency may not resort to adjudication as a means of insulating a generic standard from judicial review." ACT I, 852 F.2d at 1337.

II.   Administrative Procedure Act

Courts will set aside agency decisions found to be "arbitrary, capricious, an abuse of discretion, or otherwise not in accordance with law." 5 U.S.C. § 706(2)(A). As the Supreme Court has explained: "The scope of review under the 'arbitrary and capricious' standard is narrow and a court is not to substitute its judgment for that of the agency. Nevertheless, the agency must examine the relevant data and articulate a satisfactory explanation for its action including a 'rational connection between the facts found and the choice made.'" Motor Vehicle Mfrs. Ass'n of U.S., Inc. v. State Farm Mut. Auto. Ins. Co., 463 U.S. 29, 43 (1983). Agency action is arbitrary and capricious "if the agency has relied on factors which Congress has not intended it to consider, entirely failed to consider an important aspect of the problem, offered an explanation for its decision that runs counter to the evidence before the agency, or is so implausible that it could not be ascribed to a difference in view or the product of agency expertise." Id. Reviewing courts "may not supply a reasoned basis for the agency's action that the agency itself has not given." Id. (quoting SEC v. Chenery Corp., 332 U.S. 194, 196 (1947)). The Networks contend that the Remand Order is arbitrary and capricious because the FCC has made a 180-degree turn regarding its treatment of "fleeting expletives" without providing a reasoned explanation justifying the about-face. We agree.

First, there is no question that the FCC has changed its policy. As outlined in detail above, prior to the Golden Globes decision the FCC had consistently taken the view that isolated, non-literal, fleeting expletives did not run afoul of its indecency regime. See, e.g., Pacifica Clarification Order, 59 F.C.C. 2d 892, at ¶ 4 n.1 (advising broadcasters that "it would be inequitable for us to hold a licensee responsible for indecent language" that occurred during a live broadcast without an opportunity for journalistic editing); Application of WGBH Educ. Found., 69 F.C.C.2d 1250, at ¶ 10 & n.6 (distinguishing between the "verbal shock treatment" of the George Carlin monologue and "the isolated use of a potentially offensive word" and finding that the single use of an expletive in a program "should not call for us to act under the holding of Pacifica"); Pacifica Foundation, Inc., 2 F.C.C.R. 2698, at ¶ 13 ("If a complaint focuses solely on the use of expletives, we believe that under the legal standards set forth in Pacifica, deliberate and repetitive use in a patently offensive manner is a requisite to a finding of indecency." (emphasis added)); Industry Guidance, 16 F.C.C.R. 7999, at ¶¶ 17-18 (distinguishing between material that is repeated or dwelled on and material that is "fleeting and isolated") (citing L.M.

Communications of S.C., Inc., 7 F.C.C.R. 1595 (Mass Media Bureau 1992) (finding the single

utterance of "mother-fucker" not indecent because it was a "fleeting and isolated utterance

which, within the context of live and spontaneous programming, does not warrant a Commission

sanction"); Lincoln Dellar, For Renewal of the Licenses of Stations KPRL(AM) and

KDDB(FM), 8 F.C.C.R. 2582 (Audio Serv. Div. 1993) (news announcer's remark that he

"fucked that one up" not indecent because the "use of a single expletive" did not warrant further

review "in light of the isolated and accidental nature of the broadcast")). This consistent

enforcement policy changed with the issuance of Golden Globes:

> While prior Commission and staff action have indicated that isolated or fleeting
> broadcasts of the "F-Word" such as that here are not indecent or would not be
> acted upon, consistent with our decision today we conclude that any such
> interpretation is no longer good law . . . . The staff has since found that the
> isolated or fleeting use of the "F-Word" is not indecent in situations arguably
> similar to that here. We now depart from this portion of the Commission's 1987
> *Pacifica* decision as well as all of the cases cited in notes 31 and 32 and any
> similar cases holding that isolated or fleeting use of the "F-Word" or a variant
> thereof in situations such as this is not indecent and conclude that such cases are
> not good law to that extent.

Golden Globes, 19 F.C.C.R. 4975, at ¶ 12 (internal footnote omitted); see also id. at ¶ 14

(providing new definition of "profane" speech). The Commission declined to issue a forfeiture

in Golden Globes precisely because its decision represented a departure from its prior rulings.

See id. at ¶ 15 ("Given, however, that Commission and staff precedent prior to our decision today

permitted the broadcast at issue, and that we take a new approach to profanity, NBC and its

affiliates necessarily did not have the requisite notice to justify a penalty." (emphasis added)).

The Omnibus Order similarly declined to issue a forfeiture because "existing precedent would

have permitted this broadcast." Omnibus Order, 21 F.C.C.R. 2664, at ¶¶ 111, 124, 136, 145.

Although the Remand Order backpedals somewhat on this clear recognition that the

Commission was departing from prior precedent,[6] in its brief to this court, the FCC now

concedes that Golden Globes changed the landscape with regard to the treatment of fleeting

expletives. See Br. of Respondent FCC at 33 ("In the *Golden Globe Order*, the Commission

made clear that it was changing course with respect to the treatment of isolated expletives."); see

also Br. of Amici Curiae Former FCC Officials at 9 (noting that the "extraordinary and

unprecedented" decision in Golden Globes represented a radical change in policy that "greatly

expanded the scope of what constituted indecency").

Agencies are of course free to revise their rules and policies. See Chevron, U.S.A., Inc. v.

Natural Res. Def. Council, Inc., 467 U.S. 837, 863 (1984) ("An initial agency interpretation is

not instantly carved in stone."). Such a change, however, must provide a reasoned analysis for

departing from prior precedent. As this court has explained:

> [W]hen an agency reverses its course, a court must satisfy itself that the agency
> knows it is changing course, has given sound reasons for the change, and has
> shown that the rule is consistent with the law that gives the agency its authority to
> act. In addition, the agency must consider reasonably obvious alternatives and, if
> it rejects those alternatives, it must give reasons for the rejection, sufficient to
> allow for meaningful judicial review. Although there is not a "heightened
> standard of scrutiny . . . *the agency must explain why the original reasons for
> adopting the rule or policy are no longer dispositive.*" Even in the absence of
> cumulative experience, changed circumstances or judicial criticism, an agency is

---

[6]In the Remand Order, the FCC "reject[s] Fox's suggestion that Nicole Richie's
comments would not have been actionably indecent prior to our *Golden Globe* decision," and
would only concede that it was "not apparent" that Cher's comment at the 2002 Billboard Music
Awards would have been actionably indecent at the time it was broadcast. Remand Order, at ¶¶
22, 60. Decisions expressly overruled in Golden Globes were now dismissed as "staff letters and
dicta," and the Commission even implied that the issue of fleeting expletives was one of first
impression for the FCC in Golden Globes. Id. at ¶ 21 ("[I]n 2004, the Commission itself
considered for the first time in an enforcement action whether a single use of an expletive could
be indecent.").

> free to change course after reweighing the competing statutory policies. But such
> a flip-flop must be accompanied by a reasoned explanation of why the new rule
> effectuates the statute <u>as well as or better than the old rule</u>.

N.Y. Council, Ass'n of Civilian Technicians v. Fed. Labor Relations Auth., 757 F.2d 502, 508

(2d Cir. 1985) (second emphasis added; internal citations omitted); <u>see also</u> <u>State Farm</u>, 463 U.S.

at 41-42 ("A settled course of behavior embodies the agency's informed judgment that, by

pursuing that course, it will carry out the policies committed to it by Congress. There is, then, at

least a presumption that those policies will be carried out best if the settled rule is adhered to."

(internal quotation marks omitted)); <u>Huntington Hosp. v. Thompson</u>, 319 F.3d 74, 79 (2d Cir.

2002) ("While an agency is not locked into the first interpretation of a statute it embraces, it

cannot simply adopt inconsistent positions without presenting 'some reasoned analysis.'"); <u>Mr.</u>

<u>Sprout, Inc. v. United States</u>, 8 F.3d 118, 129 (2d Cir. 1993) ("When the Commission departs

from its own settled precedent, as here, it must present a 'reasoned analysis' that justifies its

change of interpretation so as to permit judicial review of its new policies."). An agency's

"failure to come to grips with conflicting precedent constitutes an inexcusable departure from the

essential requirement of reasoned decision making." <u>Ramaprakash v. FAA.</u>, 346 F.3d 1121,

1125 (D.C. Cir. 2003) (internal quotation marks omitted). Accordingly, agency action will be set

aside as arbitrary and capricious if the agency fails to provide a reasoned explanation for its

decision. <u>See</u>, <u>e.g.</u>, <u>Massachusetts v. EPA</u>, 127 S. Ct. 1438, 1463 (2007) ("EPA has offered no

reasoned explanation for its refusal to decide whether greenhouse gases cause or contribute to

climate change. Its action was therefore arbitrary, capricious, ... or otherwise not in accordance

with law.") (ellipses in original; internal quotation marks omitted); <u>State Farm</u>, 463 U.S. at 34

(agency's rescinding of rule requiring passive restraints in automobiles was arbitrary and capricious for failure to provide a reasoned explanation justifying revocation); see also Yale-New Haven Hosp. v. Leavitt, 470 F.3d 71, 72 (2d Cir. 2006) (agency action based on new rule governing Medicare reimbursement was arbitrary and capricious "because the Secretary did not satisfactorily explain his reasons" for changing historical practice); ANR Pipeline Co. v. Fed. Energy Regulatory Comm'n, 71 F.3d 897, 901 (D.C. Cir. 1995) ("[W]here an agency departs from established precedent without a reasoned explanation, its decision will be vacated as arbitrary and capricious.").

Our evaluation of the agency's reasons for its change in policy is confined to the reasons articulated by the agency itself. See State Farm, 463 U.S. at 50 ("[C]ourts may not accept appellate counsel's *post hoc* rationalizations for agency action. It is well-established that an agency's action must be upheld, if at all, on the basis articulated by the agency itself." (internal citation omitted)); Yale-New Haven Hosp., 470 F.3d at 81 ("Generally speaking, after-the-fact rationalization for agency action is disfavored."). The primary reason for the crackdown on fleeting expletives advanced by the FCC is the so-called "first blow" theory described in the Supreme Court's Pacifica decision. In Pacifica, the Supreme Court justified the FCC's regulation of the broadcast media in part on the basis that indecent material on the airwaves enters into the privacy of the home uninvited and without warning. 438 U.S. at 748. The Court rejected the argument that the audience could simply tune-out: "To say that one may avoid further offense by turning off the radio when he hears indecent language is like saying that the remedy for an assault is to run away after the first blow." Id. at 748-49. Relying on this statement in Pacifica, the Commission attempts to justify its stance on fleeting expletives on the basis that "granting an automatic exemption for 'isolated or fleeting' expletives unfairly forces viewers (including children) to take 'the first blow.'" <u>Remand Order</u>, at ¶ 25.

We cannot accept this argument as a reasoned basis justifying the Commission's new rule. First, the Commission provides no reasonable explanation for why it has changed its perception that a fleeting expletive was not a harmful "first blow" for the nearly thirty years between <u>Pacifica</u> and <u>Golden Globes</u>. More problematic, however, is that the "first blow" theory bears no rational connection to the Commission's actual policy regarding fleeting expletives. As the FCC itself stressed during oral argument in this case, the Commission does not take the position that *any* occurrence of an expletive is indecent or profane under its rules.[7] For example, although "there is no outright news exemption from our indecency rules," <u>Remand Order</u>, at ¶ 71, the Commission will apparently excuse an expletive when it occurs during a "*bona fide* news interview," <u>id.</u> at ¶ 72-73 (deferring to CBS's "plausible characterization" of a segment of The Early Show interviewing a contestant on its reality show Survivor: Vanuatu as news programming and finding expletive uttered during that part of the show not indecent or profane). Certainly viewers (including children) watching the live broadcast of The Early Show were "force[d]...to take the 'first blow'" of the expletive uttered by the Survivor: Vanuatu contestant. Yet the Commission emphasized during oral argument that its news exception is a broad one and "the Commission has never found a broadcast to be indecent on the basis of an isolated expletive in the face of some claim that the use of that language was necessary for any journalistic or artistic purpose." The Commission further explained to this court that a broadcast of oral

---

[7]Such a per se ban would likely raise constitutional questions above and beyond the concerns raised by the current policy. <u>See</u> <u>Pacifica</u>, 438 U.S. at 746 (plurality opinion) ("Although these words ordinarily lack literary, political, or scientific value, they are not entirely outside the protection of the First Amendment. Some uses of even the most offensive words are unquestionably protected.").

argument in this case, in which the same language used in the Fox broadcasts was repeated multiple times in the courtroom, would "plainly not" be indecent or profane under its standards because of the context in which it occurred. The Commission even conceded that a re-broadcast of precisely the same offending clips from the two Billboard Music Award programs for the purpose of providing background information on this case would not result in any action by the FCC, even though in those circumstances viewers would be subjected to the same "first blow" that resulted from the original airing of this material. Furthermore, the Commission has also held that even repeated and deliberate use of numerous expletives is not indecent or profane under the FCC's policy if the expletives are "integral" to the work. See Complaints Against Various Television Licensees Regarding Their Broadcast on November 11, 2004, of the ABC Televison Network's Presentation of the Film "Saving Private Ryan", 20 F.C.C.R. 4507, at ¶ 14 (2005) ("Saving Private Ryan") (finding numerous expletives uttered during film Saving Private Ryan not indecent or profane because deleting the expletives "would have altered the nature of the artistic work and diminished the power, realism and immediacy of the film experience for viewers"). In all of these scenarios, viewers, including children who may have no understanding of whether expletives are "integral" to a program or whether the interview of a contestant on a reality show is a "*bona fide* news interview," will have to accept the alleged "first blow" caused by use of these expletives. Thus, the record simply does not support the position that the Commission's new policy was based on its concern with the public's mere exposure to this language on the airwaves.[8] The "first blow" theory, therefore, fails to provide the reasoned

---

[8]Thus, our rejection of the agency's proffered rationale as the required "reasoned explanation" is not that the "Commission's change of standard is irrational because it is inconsistent" as the dissent suggests, dissent op. at [47], but that the Commission's proffered

explanation necessary to justify the FCC's departure from established precedent.[9]

The Remand Order makes passing reference to other reasons that purportedly support its change in policy, none of which we find sufficient. For instance, the Commission states that even non-literal uses of expletives fall within its indecency definition because it is "difficult (if not impossible) to distinguish whether a word is being used as an expletive or as a literal description of sexual or excretory functions." Remand Order, at ¶ 23. This defies any common-sense understanding of these words, which, as the general public well knows, are often used in everyday conversation without any "sexual or excretory" meaning. Bono's exclamation that his victory at the Golden Globe Awards was "really, really fucking brilliant" is a prime example of a non-literal use of the "F-Word" that has no sexual connotation. See Golden Globes (Bureau Decision), 18 F.C.C.R. 19859, at ¶ 5 ("As a threshold matter, the material aired during the 'Golden Globe Awards' program does not describe or depict sexual and excretory activities and

_____

rationale is disconnected from the actual policy implemented by the Commission. See State Farm, 463 U.S. at 43 (Agency action is arbitrary and capricious if the agency fails to "articulate a satisfactory explanation for its action including a 'rational connection between the facts found and the choice made.'") (emphasis added).

[9]The dissent takes the position that the "reasoned analysis" underlying the FCC's change in policy is its statement in Golden Globes that "given the core meaning of the 'F-Word,' any use of that word or a variation, in any context, inherently has a sexual connotation. . . . The 'F-Word' is one of the most vulgar, graphic and explicit descriptions of sexual activity in the English language. Its use invariably invokes a coarse sexual image." Dissent Op. at [43-44] (quoting Golden Globes, at ¶¶ 8-9). Much like the "first-blow" theory, however, this cannot provide the requisite "reasoned analysis" because it is not consistent with the Commission's actual policy. The FCC's change in policy cannot be based on a categorical view that "any use of that word or a variation, in any context, inherently has a sexual connotation," Golden Globes, at ¶ 8 (emphasis added), because, as discussed above, the Commission permits even numerous and deliberate uses of that word in certain contexts. Notably, the FCC did not rely on this statement from Golden Globes in arguing that it provided a reasoned explanation for its decision. See Br. of Respondent FCC, at 36-37.

organs .... Rather, the performer used the word 'fucking' as an adjective or expletive to
emphasize an exclamation."), rev'd by Golden Globes, 19 F.C.C.R. 4975 (2004). Similarly, as
NBC illustrates in its brief, in recent times even the top leaders of our government have used
variants of these expletives in a manner that no reasonable person would believe referenced
"sexual or excretory organs or activities." See Br. of Intervenor NBC at 31-32 & n.3 (citing
President Bush's remark to British Prime Minister Tony Blair that the United Nations needed to
"get Syria to get Hezbollah to stop doing this shit" and Vice President Cheney's widely-reported
"Fuck yourself" comment to Senator Patrick Leahy on the floor of the U.S. Senate).[10]

Similarly, the Commission's warning that a per se exemption for fleeting expletives
would "permit broadcasters to air expletives at all hours of the day so long as they did so one at a
time," Remand Order, at ¶ 25, is equally divorced from reality because the Commission itself
recognizes that broadcasters have never barraged the airwaves with expletives even prior to
Golden Globes, see Remand Order, at ¶ 29.[11] Finally, the Commission's claim that

---

[10]Contrary to the dissent's view, our rejection of this proffered rationale is not merely a
"difference of opinion" with the agency. Dissent op. at [52]. We reject this reason not because
we disagree with it, but because it is both unsupported by any record evidence as well as
contradicted by evidence submitted by the Networks. Thus, we need not consider whether the
FCC's statement that "any use of [the F-Word] or a variation, in any context, inherently has a
sexual connotation," in actuality means, "even when the speaker does not intend a sexual
meaning, a substantial part of the community, and of the television audience, will understand the
word as freighted with an offensive sexual connotation," as the dissent suggests. Id. at [51-52]
Even if we accept the dissent's reading, the FCC still has failed to set forth the required reasoned
explanation because its proffered rationale remains unsupported by any record evidence and
contradicted by the evidence submitted by the Networks. See Bowen v. Am. Hosp. Ass'n, 476
U.S. 610, 626 (1986) ("Agency deference has not come so far that we will uphold regulations
whenever it is possible to 'conceive a basis' for administrative action.") (plurality op).

[11]We agree with the dissent that this proffered rationale "is at most a small part of the
agency's justification for its action," dissent op. at [50], but because it is one of the reasons
advanced by the agency, we address it here. We disagree with the dissent, however, that our

"categorically requiring repeated use...is inconsistent with our general approach to indecency enforcement, which stresses the critical nature of context," Remand Order, at ¶ 23, also does not provide sufficient justification for its departure from prior precedent. First, the Commission's own policy of treating all variants of certain expletives as presumptively indecent and profane, whether used in a literal or non-literal sense, also fails to comport with this "general approach" that "stresses the critical nature of context." See, e.g., Golden Globes, 19 F.C.C.R. 4975, at ¶ 8 (declaring that "any use of [the F-Word] or a variation, in any context, inherently has a sexual connotation, and therefore falls within the first prong of our indecency definition") (emphasis added). In addition, the Commission's indecency test itself remains unchanged, but the Commission fails to provide a reasoned explanation for why a single, isolated expletive now should fit within the articulation of that test set forth in Golden Globes, see Pacifica Found., Inc., 2 F.C.C.R. 2698, at ¶ 13 ("If a complaint focuses solely on the use of expletives, we believe that under the legal standards set forth in Pacifica, deliberate and repetitive use in a patently offensive manner is a requisite to a finding of indecency.").

For decades broadcasters relied on the FCC's restrained approach to indecency regulation

---

rejection of this proffered rationale is a mere difference of opinion with the agency in predicting the future. The FCC's obligation to provide a "reasoned analysis" for its change in policy is not satisfied when the proffered rationale—that without its new policy the airwaves will be overtaken by fleeting expletives—is both unsupported by any evidence and directly contradicted by prior experience. We further note while the dissent attempts to provide support for the agency's prediction, including broadcasters' need to compete with cable "which increasingly make liberal use of their freedom to fill programming with such expletives," dissent op. at **[50]**, no evidence supporting this proposition is contained in the record that was considered by the FCC when rendering its decision. See, e.g., State Farm, 463 U.S. at 43 ("The reviewing court should not attempt itself to make up for [the agency's] deficiencies: 'We may not supply a reasoned basis for the agency's action that the agency itself has not given.'") (quoting SEC v. Chenery Corp., 332 U.S. 194, 196 (1947)).

and its consistent rejection of arguments that isolated expletives were indecent. The agency

asserts the same interest in protecting children as it asserted thirty years ago, but until the <u>Golden</u>

<u>Globes</u> decision, it had never banned fleeting expletives. While the FCC is free to change its

previously settled view on this issue, it must provide a reasoned basis for that change. <u>Cf.</u> <u>State</u>

<u>Farm</u>, 463 U.S. at 42 ("[A]n agency changing its course by rescinding a rule is obligated to

supply a reasoned analysis for the change <u>beyond that which may be required</u> when an agency

does not act in the first instance.") (emphasis added). The FCC's decision, however, is devoid of

any evidence that suggests a fleeting expletive is harmful, let alone establishes that this harm is

serious enough to warrant government regulation. Such evidence would seem to be particularly

relevant today when children likely hear this language far more often from other sources than

they did in the 1970s when the Commission first began sanctioning indecent speech. Yet the

Remand Order provides no reasoned analysis of the purported "problem" it is seeking to address

with its new indecency policy from which this court can conclude that such regulation of speech

is reasonable. <u>See, e.g.</u>, <u>United States v. Playboy Enter. Group, Inc.</u>, 529 U.S. 803, 822-23

(2000) (rejecting indecency regulation of cable television in part because "[t]he question is

whether an actual problem has been proved in this case. We agree that the Government has

failed to establish a pervasive, nationwide problem justifying its nationwide daytime speech

ban."); <u>Turner Broad. Sys. v. FCC</u>, 512 U.S. 622, 664 (1994) (remanding for additional fact

finding to determine whether speech regulation justified because government had failed to

demonstrate "that the recited harms are real, not merely conjectural, and that the regulation will

in fact alleviate these harms in a direct and material way"); <u>Quincy Cable TV, Inc. v. FCC</u>, 768

F.2d 1434, 1463 (D.C. Cir. 1985) (invalidating FCC regulation because "the Commission has failed entirely to determine whether the evil the rules seek to correct 'is a real or merely a fanciful threat'"); Home Box Office, Inc. v. FCC, 567 F.2d 9, 36 (D.C. Cir. 1977) ("[A] regulation perfectly reasonable and appropriate in the face of a given problem may be highly capricious if that problem does not exist." (internal quotation marks omitted)). The Commission has similarly failed to explain how its current policy would remedy the purported "problem" or to point to supporting evidence.

The Commission's new approach to profanity is supported by even less analysis, reasoned or not. The Commission sets forth no independent reasons that would justify its newly-expanded definition of "profane" speech, aside from merely stating that its prior precedent does not prevent it from setting forth a new definition, see Golden Globes, 19 F.C.C.R. 4975, at ¶ 14. To the extent the Commission believes its arguments for expanding its indecency enforcement support its new policy regarding profanity, those arguments are rejected for the reasons stated above. Furthermore, the Commission fails to provide any explanation for why this separate ban on profanity is even necessary. Prior to 2004, the Commission never attempted to regulate "profane" speech. In fact, the Commission took the view that a separate ban on profane speech was unconstitutional. See 122 Cong. Rec. 33359, 33359, 33364-65 (1976) (recommending Congress delete "profane" from Section 1464 "[b]ecause of the serious constitutional problems involved"); FCC, The Public and Broadcasting, 1999 WL 391297 (June 1999) ("Profanity that does not fall under one of the above two categories [indecent or obscene] is fully protected by the First Amendment and cannot be regulated."). The Commission again has not provided this court with a reasoned analysis of why it has undertaken this separate regulation of speech. Finally, the Commission provides no explanation of what harm this separate enforcement against profane speech addresses that is not already addressed by the FCC's indecency and obscenity enforcement. Particularly considering that the scope of the FCC's new profanity definition appears to be largely (if not completely) redundant with its indecency prohibition, see infra Part IV.A, this would seem to be an important question for the Commission to consider. The Remand Order, however, provides no indication that the Commission has engaged in any such analysis.

Accordingly, we find that the FCC's new policy regarding "fleeting expletives" fails to provide a reasoned analysis justifying its departure from the agency's established practice. For this reason, Fox's petition for review is granted, the Remand Order is vacated, and the matter is remanded to the FCC for further proceedings consistent with this opinion. Because we have found that the FCC's new indecency regime, announced in Golden Globes and applied in the Remand Order, is invalid under the Administrative Procedure Act, the stay of enforcement previously granted by this court in our September 6th order is vacated as moot.[12]

III.   Constitutional Challenges

"A fundamental and longstanding principle of judicial restraint requires that courts avoid reaching constitutional questions in advance of the necessity of deciding them." Lyng v. N.W. Indian Cemetery Protective Ass'n, 485 U.S. 439, 445 (1988). Thus, we refrain from deciding the various constitutional challenges to the Remand Order raised by the Networks. We note, however, that in reviewing these numerous constitutional challenges, which were fully briefed to

---

[12]We recognize that what follows is dicta, but we note that "dicta often serve extremely valuable purposes. They can help clarify a complicated subject. They can assist future courts to reach sensible, well-reasoned results. They can help lawyers and society to predict the future course of the court's rulings. They can guide future courts to adopt fair and efficient procedures. What is problematic is not the utterance of dicta, but the failure to distinguish between holding and dictum." The Honorable Pierre N. Leval, Judging Under the Constitution: Dicta About Dicta, 81 N.Y.U. L. Rev. 1249, 1253 (2006).

this court and discussed at length during oral argument, we are skeptical that the Commission can

provide a reasoned explanation for its "fleeting expletive" regime that would pass constitutional

muster. Because we doubt that the Networks will refrain from further litigation on these precise

issues if, on remand, the Commission merely provides further explanation with no other changes

to its policy, in the interest of judicial economy we make the following observations.

As an initial matter, we note that *all* speech covered by the FCC's indecency policy is

fully protected by the First Amendment. See Sable Commc'ns v. FCC, 492 U.S. 115, 126 (1989)

(noting that speech "which is indecent but not obscene is protected by the First Amendment");

Industry Guidance, 16 F.C.C.R. 7999, at ¶ 3 ("[I]ndecent speech is protected by the First

Amendment, and thus, the government must both identify a compelling interest for any

regulation it may impose on indecent speech and choose the least restrictive means to further that

interest."). With that backdrop in mind, we question whether the FCC's indecency test can

survive First Amendment scrutiny. For instance, we are sympathetic to the Networks' contention

that the FCC's indecency test is undefined, indiscernible, inconsistent, and consequently,

unconstitutionally vague. Although the Commission has declared that all variants of "fuck" and

"shit" are presumptively indecent and profane, repeated use of those words in "Saving Private

Ryan," for example, was neither indecent nor profane. And while multiple occurrences of

expletives in "Saving Private Ryan" was not gratuitous, Saving Private Ryan, 20 F.C.C.R. 4507,

at ¶ 14, a single occurrence of "fucking" in the Golden Globe Awards was "shocking and

gratuitous," Golden Globes, 19 F.C.C.R. 4975, at ¶ 9. Parental ratings and advisories were

important in finding "Saving Private Ryan" not patently offensive under contemporary

community standards, Saving Private Ryan, 20 F.C.C.R. 4507, at ¶ 15, but irrelevant in evaluating a rape scene in another fictional movie, see Omnibus Order, 21 F.C.C.R. 2664, at ¶ 38

(issuing maximum forfeiture penalty against NBC Telemundo for movie "Con el Corazón en la

Mano"). The use of numerous expletives was "integral" to a fictional movie about war, Saving

Private Ryan, 20 F.C.C.R. 4507, at ¶ 14, but occasional expletives spoken by real musicians were

indecent and profane because the educational purpose of the documentary "could have been

fulfilled and all viewpoints expressed without the repeated broadcast of expletives," Omnibus

Order, 21 F.C.C.R. 2664, at ¶ 82 (finding Martin Scorsese's PBS documentary "The Blues:

Godfathers and Sons" indecent). The "S-Word" on The Early Show was not indecent because it

was in the context of a "*bona fide* news interview," but "there is no outright news exemption

from our indecency rules," Remand Order, at ¶¶ 68, 71-73. We can understand why the

Networks argue that FCC's "patently offensive as measured by contemporary community

standards" indecency test coupled with its "artistic necessity" exception fails to provide the

clarity required by the Constitution, creates an undue chilling effect on free speech, and requires

broadcasters to "steer far wider of the unlawful zone," Speiser v. Randall, 357 U.S. 513, 526

(1958).

The Networks' position is further buttressed by the Supreme Court's decision in Reno v.

ACLU, 521 U.S. 844 (1997), which struck down as unconstitutionally vague a similarly-worded

indecency regulation of the Internet.[13] The Court found that the statute's use of the "general,

undefined terms 'indecent' and 'patently offensive' cover large amounts of nonpornographic

material with serious educational or other value. Moreover, the 'community standards' criterion

---

[13] Section 223(d) of the of the Communications Decency Act prohibited material that "in
context, depicts or describes, in terms patently offensive as measured by contemporary
community standards, sexual or excretory activities or organs." Reno, 521 U.S. at 860.

as applied to the Internet means that any communication available to a nation wide audience will be judged by the standards of the community most likely to be offended by the message." Id. at 877-78. Because of the "vague contours" of the regulation, the Court held that "it unquestionably silences some speakers whose messages would be entitled to constitutional protection," and thus violated the First Amendment. Id. at 874. Because Reno holds that a regulation that covers speech that "in context, depicts or describes, in terms patently offensive as measured by contemporary community standards, sexual or excretory activities or organs" is unconstitutionally vague, we are skeptical that the FCC's identically-worded indecency test could nevertheless provide the requisite clarity to withstand constitutional scrutiny. Indeed, we are hard pressed to imagine a regime that is more vague than one that relies entirely on consideration of the otherwise unspecified "context" of a broadcast indecency.

We also note that the FCC's indecency test raises the separate constitutional question of whether it permits the FCC to sanction speech based on its subjective view of the merit of that speech. It appears that under the FCC's current indecency regime, any and all uses of an expletive is presumptively indecent and profane with the broadcaster then having to demonstrate to the satisfaction of the Commission, under an unidentified burden of proof, that the expletives were "integral" to the work. In the licensing context, the Supreme Court has cautioned against speech regulations that give too much discretion to government officials. See, e.g., Forsyth County, Ga. v. Nationalist Movement, 505 U.S. 123, 130 (1992) ("A government regulation that allows arbitrary application is inherently inconsistent with a valid time, place, and manner regulation because such discretion has the potential for becoming a means of suppressing a particular point of view."); City of Lakewood v. Plain Dealer Publ'g Co., 486 U.S. 750, 758

(1988) (finding a permit scheme facially unconstitutional because "*post hoc* rationalizations by the licensing official and the use of shifting or illegitimate criteria are far too easy, making it difficult for courts to determine in any particular case whether the licensor is permitting favorable, and suppressing unfavorable, expression"). In succeeding on this challenge, the Networks need not prove that the FCC "has exercised [its] discretion in a content-based manner, but whether there is anything in [its policy] preventing [it] from doing so." Forsythe, 505 U.S. at 133 n.10 ("It is not merely the sporadic abuse of power by the censor but the pervasive threat inherent in its very existence that constitutes the danger to freedom of discussion.").

Finally, we recognize there is some tension in the law regarding the appropriate level of First Amendment scrutiny. In general, restrictions on First Amendment liberties prompt courts to apply strict scrutiny. FCC v. League of Women Voters, 468 U.S. 364, 376 (1984). Outside the broadcasting context, the Supreme Court has consistently applied strict scrutiny to indecency regulations. See, e.g., Playboy, 529 U.S. at 811-813 (holding that regulation proscribing indecent content on cable television was content-based restriction of speech subject to strict scrutiny); Sable, 492 U.S. at 126 (holding that indecency regulation of telephone messages was content-based restriction subject to strict scrutiny); Reno, 521 U.S. at 868 (holding that indecency regulation of Internet was a content-based restriction subject to strict scrutiny). At the same time, however, the Supreme Court has also considered broadcast media exceptional. "[B]ecause broadcast regulation involves unique considerations, our cases . . . have never gone so far as to demand that such regulations serve 'compelling' governmental interests." League of Women Voters, 468 U.S. at 376. Restrictions on broadcast "speech" have been upheld "when we [are] satisfied that the restriction is narrowly tailored to further a substantial governmental interest."

Id. at 380.

The Networks contend that the bases for treating broadcast media "different[ly]" have "eroded over time," particularly because 86 percent of American households now subscribe to cable or satellite services, Remand Order, at ¶ 49. As the Networks argue, this and other realities have "eviscerated" the notion that broadcast content is, as it was termed in Pacifica, 438 U.S. at 748-49, "uniquely pervasive" and "uniquely accessible to children." Whatever merit these arguments may have, they cannot sway us in light of Supreme Court precedent. See, e.g., Reno, 521 U.S. at 867 (noting that "as a matter of history" broadcast television has enjoyed less First Amendment protection than other media, including the internet); Pacifica, 438 U.S. at 748-50.

Nevertheless, we would be remiss not to observe that it is increasingly difficult to describe the broadcast media as uniquely pervasive and uniquely accessible to children, and at some point in the future, strict scrutiny may properly apply in the context of regulating broadcast television. In light of this possibility, the Networks rightly rest their constitutional argument in part on the holding of Playboy, which involved a challenge to a statute requiring cable operators who provide channels primarily dedicated to sexually explicit or otherwise indecent programming to either fully scramble these channels or limit their transmission to the 10pm to 6am safe harbor period. 529 U.S. at 806. The Supreme Court, applying strict scrutiny, invalidated the statute because a less restrictive alternative to the prohibition existed: "One plausible, less restrictive alternative could be found in another section of the [Telecommunications] Act [of 1996]: § 504, which requires a cable operator, 'upon request by a cable service subscriber . . . without charge, [to] fully scramble or otherwise fully block' any channel the subscriber does not wish to receive." Id. at 809-10. The Court held: This "targeted blocking is less restrictive than banning, and the Government cannot ban speech if targeted

blocking is a feasible and effective means of furthering its compelling interests." Id. at 815. In

so holding, the Court suggested its decision might go beyond the mechanistic application of strict

scrutiny, and rely in part on a notional pillar of free speech—namely, choice:

> When a student first encounters our free speech jurisprudence, he or she might think
> it is influenced by the philosophy that one idea is as good as any other, and that in art
> and literature objective standards of style, taste, decorum, beauty, and esthetics are
> deemed by the Constitution to be inappropriate, indeed unattainable. Quite the
> opposite is true. The Constitution no more enforces a relativistic philosophy or moral
> nihilism than it does any other point of view. The Constitution exists precisely so that
> opinions and judgments, including esthetic and moral judgments about art and
> literature, can be formed, tested, and expressed. What the Constitution says is that
> these judgments are for the individual to make, not for the Government to decree,
> even with the mandate or approval of a majority. Technology expands the capacity
> to choose; and it denies the potential of this revolution if we assume the Government
> is best positioned to make these choices for us.

Id. at 818. The Court specifically rejected the arguments that parents' ignorance of this option,

its underutilization, or its inability to be 100% effective rendered targeted blocking an ineffective

alternative: "It is no response that voluntary blocking requires a consumer to take action, or may

be inconvenient, or may not go perfectly every time. A court should not assume a plausible, less

restrictive alternative would be ineffective; and a court should not presume parents, given full

information, will fail to act." Id. at 824.

The Networks argue that the advent of the V-chip and parental ratings system[14] similarly

---

[14]In 1996, Congress mandated that every television, 13 inches or larger, sold in the United
States, come equipped with blocking technology commonly known as the V-chip. See 47 U.S.C.
§ 303(x) (stating that in the case of an "apparatus" designed to receive television signals, "such
apparatus [shall] be equipped with a feature designed to enable viewers to block display of all
programs with a common rating"). To implement V-chip technology, Congress also required a
television ratings system. The industry developed the "TV Parental Guidelines" rating system,
which was approved by the FCC. See In the Matter of Implementation of Section 551 of the
Telecommunications Act of 1996, 13 F.C.C.R. 8232, at ¶ 2.

provide a less restrictive alternative to the FCC's indecency ban. The FCC counters that the V-chip is an ineffective alternative because, in its view, few televisions feature a V-chip, most parents do not know how to use it, programs are often inaccurately rated, and fleeting expletives, such as those witnessed at the programs at issue here, could elude V-chip blocking even if the show during which they occurred was otherwise accurately labeled. See Remand Order, at ¶ 51 & n. 162. The FCC's arguments are not without merit, but they must be evaluated in the context of today's realities. The proliferation of satellite and cable television channels—not to mention internet-based video outlets—has begun to erode the "uniqueness" of broadcast media, while at the same time, blocking technologies such as the V-chip have empowered viewers to make their own choices about what they do, and do not, want to see on television. Playboy distinguished Pacifica on the grounds that "[c]able systems have the capacity to block unwanted channels on a household-by-household basis" and thus "[t]he option to block reduces the likelihood, so concerning to the Court in Pacifica, that traditional First Amendment scrutiny would deprive the Government of all authority to address this sort of problem." 529 U.S. at 815 (internal citation omitted). The FCC is free to regulate indecency, but its regulatory powers are bounded by the Constitution. If the Playboy decision is any guide, technological advances may obviate the constitutional legitimacy of the FCC's robust oversight.

IV. The FCC's Construction of Profane

The Networks also argue that the FCC employed an improper definition of "profane" under Section 1464. Although we need not reach this argument to dispose of this appeal, on remand, the FCC may desire to explain its gloss on the definition of "profane." In the Remand Order, the FCC applied its new definition of "profane" as set forth in Golden Globes. The FCC now defines "profane" as "those personally reviling epithets naturally tending to provoke violent resentment or denoting language which under contemporary community standards is so grossly offensive to members of the public who actually hear it as to amount to a nuisance." Golden Globes, 19 F.C.C.R. 4975, at ¶ 13 (quoting *Tallman v. United States*, 465 F.2d 282, 286 (7th Cir. 1972)). The FCC, noting that "shit" and "fuck" fall within this definition, ruled that Cher's and Nicole Richie's fleeting expletives were "profane," as well as indecent. Most dictionaries interpret the term "profane" to denote something that pertains to the irreligious, and since 1927, courts—as well as the FCC itself—have assumed that "profane" in the broadcast context refers to sacrilege, and nothing more. See, e.g. Duncan v. United States, 48 F.2d 128, 134 (9th Cir. 1931) (collecting cases and holding defendant "was properly convicted of using profane language" where he "referred to an individual as 'damned,' . . . used the expression 'By God' irreverently, and . . . announced his intention to call down the curse of God"); Gagliardo v. United States, 366 F.2d 720, 725 (9th Cir. 1966) ("the only words attributed to appellants which could even remotely be considered as being 'profane' . . . were 'God damn it'"); In re Complaint by Warren B. Appleton, Brockton, Mass., 28 F.C.C.2d 36 (1971) (analyzing the word "damn" as a matter of profanity). As the FCC notes, the Seventh Circuit's 1972 Tallman decision, 465 F.2d at 286, suggested an alternate definition for this term, but we do not believe the FCC can find refuge in this case. Tallman concerned a prosecution for obscenity, not profanity, and thus the Tallman court had no occasion to determine conclusively how profane should be interpreted. See id. ("The trial judge did not undertake to define the terms 'indecent' and 'profane,' but he had no occasion to do so because he determined that petitioner's utterances were properly classifiable as 'obscene.'"). The Tallman court's brief reference to "profane" served only to demonstrate that there may be a construction of "profane" that could pass constitutional scrutiny.

But the FCC's definition of "profane" here, would substantially overlap with the statutory term "indecent." This overlap would be so extensive as to render the statutory term "indecent" superfluous. Because our canons of statutory construction do not permit such an interpretation, see TRW Inc. v. Andrews, 534 U.S. 19, 31 (2001), we do not believe the FCC has proffered a reasonable construction of the term "profane." While we may owe Chevron deference to the FCC's construction, the FCC must still demonstrate that its construction is reasonable, particularly in light of Congressional intent, the canons of statutory construction, and the historical view of the plain meaning of this term.

CONCLUSION

As the foregoing indicates, we are doubtful that by merely proffering a reasoned analysis for its new approach to indecency and profanity, the Commission can adequately respond to the constitutional and statutory challenges raised by the Networks. Nevertheless, because we can decide this case on this narrow ground, we vacate and remand so that the Commission can set forth that analysis. While we fully expect the Networks to raise the same arguments they have raised to this court if the Commission does nothing more on remand than provide additional explanation for its departure from prior precedent, we can go no further in this opinion. Accordingly, we grant the petition for review, vacate the order of the FCC, and remand the case for further proceedings consistent with this opinion. The stay previously granted by this court is vacated as moot.

Leval, *J., dissenting*:

I respectfully dissent from my colleagues' ruling because I believe the Federal

Communications Commission ("FCC" or "Commission") gave a reasoned explanation for its

change of standard and thus complied with the requirement of the Administrative Procedures

Act, 5 U.S.C. § 706(2)(A).

A television broadcaster, Fox Television Stations, Inc., challenges the lawfulness of a

small change made by the FCC in its standards for adjudicating complaints of indecency over the

airwaves. The Commission exercises the responsibility of determining, upon receipt of public

complaints, whether a licensed broadcaster has violated 18 U.S.C. § 1464 by disseminating

indecent material over the airwaves. Beginning with its adjudication of complaints arising from

the broadcast of the Golden Globe Awards in 2002, the Commission instituted a change in its

manner of dealing with "fleeting," i.e. unrepeated, expletives. During this broadcast, rock-

musician Bono expressed delight over his receipt of an award by saying, "[T]his is really, really,

fucking brilliant." In a lengthy tradition of previous FCC rulings, absence of repetition of an

expletive had been virtually conclusive against finding an indecency violation. The staff

therefore recommended in Bono's case, largely because the expletive was unrepeated, that no

violation be found. *See Complaints Against Various Broadcast Licensees Regarding Their*

Airing of the "Golden Globe Awards" Program, 18 F.C.C.R. 19859, at ¶ 6 (Enforcement Bureau

2003). The Commission reversed the recommendation of its staff. Adopting a new altered

standard, which diminished the significance of the fact that the potentially offensive expletive

was not repeated, the Commission concluded that the broadcast of Bono's expletive constituted indecency in violation of § 1464. *See Complaints Against Various Broadcast Licensees Regarding Their Airing of the "Golden Globe Awards" Program*, 19 F.C.C.R. 4975, at ¶¶ 12, 17 (2004) ("*Golden Globes*").

The occurrences under review in this case followed soon after the Bono incident, during live broadcasts by Fox of Billboard Music Awards shows in 2002 and 2003. In the 2002 Billboard Music Awards, the actress and singer Cher, expressing triumphant delight upon her receipt of an award, said, "People have been telling me I'm on the way out every year, right? So fuck 'em." The incident during the 2003 Billboard Music Awards involved Nicole Richie and Paris Hilton, the co-stars of a serialized televised comedy show entitled, "The Simple Life," as presenters of awards. In "The Simple Life," Richie and Hilton play themselves as two spoiled, rich young women from Beverly Hills who cope with life on a farm. In joking reference to their own show, Richie said, "Why do they even call it 'The Simple Life?' Have you ever tried to get cow shit out of a Prada purse? It's not so fucking simple." The Commission received complaints about each incident. Referring to its newly changed policy developed in response to the Bono incident in *Golden Globes*, the Commission found that the two Billboard Music incidents were violations. *See Complaints Regarding Various Television Broadcasts Between February 2, 2002 and March 8, 2005*, 21 F.C.C.R. 13299 (2006) ("*Remand Order*"). Fox brought this action seeking to invalidate the Commission's rulings.

In adjudicating indecency complaints the Commission generally employs a context-based evaluation to determine whether the particular utterance is "*patently offensive* as measured by contemporary community standards." *Industry Guidance on the Commission's Case Law*

Interpreting 18 U.S.C. § 1464, 16 F.C.C.R. 7999, at ¶ 8 (2001) ("*Industry Guidance*") (emphasis in original). Factors weighing in favor of a finding of indecency are: "(1) the *explicitness or graphic nature* of the description or depiction of sexual or excretory organs or activities; (2) whether the material *dwells on or repeats at length* descriptions of sexual or excretory organs or activities; (3) *whether the material appears to pander or is used to titillate,* or *whether the material appears to have been presented for its shock value.*" *Industry Guidance*, at ¶ 10 (emphasis in original). Especially in relation to the "pandering" factor, a finding of violation is less likely if the broadcast of the utterance involved a genuine news report, or if censorship of the expletive would harm or distort artistic integrity. Prior to the Bono incident, the Commission attached great importance to the second factor, which focuses on whether an expletive was repeated. Under the pre-*Golden Globes* rulings, the fact that an utterance was fleeting was virtually conclusive in assuring it would not be deemed a violation (unless it breached special barriers, such as by referring to sexual activities with children). With its *Golden Globes* adjudication, however, the Commission adopted a less permissive stance. It announced that henceforth fleeting expletives would be judged according to a standard more closely aligned with repeated utterances of expletives. Thus, the Commission has declared that it remains unlikely to find a violation in an expletive that is broadcast in the context of a genuine news report, or where censorship by bleeping out the expletive would compromise artistic integrity, but it will no longer give a nearly automatic pass merely because the expletive was not repeated. *See Remand Order*, at ¶ 23.

The Commission explained succinctly why lack of repetition of the F-Word would no

longer result in a virtual free pass. "[W]e believe that, given the core-meaning of the 'F-Word,'
any use of that word or a variation, in any context, inherently has a sexual connotation . . . . The
'F-Word' is one of the most vulgar, graphic and explicit descriptions of sexual activity in the
English language. Its use invariably invokes a coarse sexual image." *Golden Globes,* at ¶¶ 8-9.
"[A]ny use of that word has a sexual connotation even if the word is not used literally." *Remand
Order*, at ¶ 16.

My colleagues find that in so altering its standards the Commission has acted illegally.
They rule that the Commission failed to give a reasoned analysis explaining the change of rule.
They accordingly find that the change of standard was arbitrary and capricious and therefore
violated the Administrative Procedure Act. I disagree. In explanation of this relatively modest
change of standard, the Commission gave a sensible, although not necessarily compelling,
reason. In relation to the word "fuck," the Commission's central explanation for the change was
essentially its perception that the "F-Word" is not only of extreme and graphic vulgarity, but also
conveys an inescapably sexual connotation. The Commission thus concluded that the use of the
F-Word – even in a single fleeting instance without repetition – is likely to constitute an offense
to the decency standards of § 1464.

The standards for judicial review of administrative actions are discussed in a few leading
Supreme Court opinions from which the majority quotes. Agencies operate with broad
discretionary power to establish rules and standards, and courts are required to give deference to
agency decisions. *See Chevron U.S.A., Inc. v. Natural Res. Def. Council, Inc.*, 467 U.S. 837, 844
(1984). A court must not "substitute its judgment for that of the agency." *Motor Vehicle Mfrs.*

Ass'n of U.S., Inc. v. State Farm Mut. Auto. Ins. Co., 463 U.S. 29, 43 (1983); *see also Vermont Yankee Nuclear Power Corp. v. Natural Res. Def. Council, Inc.*, 435 U.S. 519, 558 (1978) ("Administrative decisions should [not] be set aside . . . because the court is unhappy with the result reached."). In general, an agency's determination will be upheld by a court unless found to be "arbitrary and capricious." *See* 5 U.S.C. 706(2)(A).

An agency is free furthermore to change its standards. *See Chevron*, 467 U.S. at 863 ("An initial agency interpretation is not instantly carved in stone."); *Huntington Hosp. v. Thompson*, 319 F.3d 74, 79 (2d Cir. 2002) ("[A]n agency is not locked into the first interpretation of a statute it embraces."); *Ramaprakash*, 346 F.3d at 1125 ("Agencies are free to change course as their expertise and experience may suggest or require."). The Supreme Court has made clear that when an agency changes its standard or rule, it is "obligated to supply a reasoned analysis for the change." *State Farm*, 463 U.S. at 42. If an agency without explanation were to make an adjudication which is not consistent with the agency's previously established standards, the troubling question would arise whether the agency has lawfully changed its standard, or whether it has arbitrarily failed to adhere to its standard, which it may not lawfully do.[15] Accordingly our court has ruled that "an agency . . . cannot simply adopt inconsistent positions without presenting

---

[15] Judge Friendly noted:

> What gives concern is the manner, alas not atypical of the agencies, in which [a] change was made – slipped into an opinion in such a way that only careful readers would know what had happened, without articulation of reasons, and with prior authorities not overruled, so that the opinion writers remain free to pull them out of the drawer whenever the agency wishes to reach a result supportable by the old rule but not the new.

Henry J. Friendly, The Federal Administrative Agencies 63 (1962).

'some reasoned analysis.'" *Huntington Hosp.,* 319 F.3d at 79. Such explanation, we have said, is necessary so that the reviewing court may "be able to understand the basis of the agency's action so that it may judge the consistency of that action with the agency's mandate." *Mr. Sprout, Inc. v. United States*, 8 F.3d 118, 129 (2d Cir. 1993). The District of Columbia Circuit has similarly reasoned that an agency's "failure to come to grips with conflicting precedent constitutes an inexcusable departure from the essential requirement of reasoned decision making." *Ramaprakash*, 346 F.3d at 1125 (quotation marks omitted). In changing course, an agency must "provide a reasoned analysis indicating that prior policies and standards are being deliberately changed, not casually ignored." *Id.* at 1124 (quotation marks omitted).

In my view, in changing its position on the repetition of an expletive, the Commission complied with these requirements. It made clear acknowledgment that its *Golden Globes* and *Remand Order* rulings were not consistent with its prior standard regarding lack of repetition. It announced the adoption of a new standard. And it furnished a reasoned explanation for the change. Although one can reasonably disagree with the Commission's new position, its explanation – at least with respect to the F-Word – is not irrational, arbitrary, or capricious. The Commission thus satisfied the standards of the Administrative Procedures Act.

The Commission explained that the F-Word is "one of the most vulgar, graphic and explicit descriptions of sexual activity in the English language [whose] use invariably invokes a coarse sexual image." *Golden Globes*, at ¶ 9. In other words, the Commission found, contrary to its earlier policy, that the word is of such graphic explicitness in inevitable reference to sexual activity that absence of repetition does not save it from violating the standard of decency.

My colleagues offer several arguments in support of their conclusion that the Commission's explanation was not reasonable and therefore arbitrary and capricious. They argue (i) the Commission's position is irrational because of inconsistency resulting from the Commission's willingness to allow viewers to be subjected to a "first blow" if it comes in the context of a genuine news broadcast; (ii) the Commission's prediction that allowance of fleeting expletives will result in a great increase in their incidence is irrational because prior experience was to the contrary; and (iii) the Commission is "divorced from reality" believing that the F-Word invariably invokes a sexual connotation. I respectfully disagree.

The majority argues that the Commission's change of standard is irrational because it is inconsistent. The opinion goes on to explain:

> [T]he Commission does not take the position that *any* occurrence of an expletive is indecent . . . . [T]he Commission will apparently excuse an expletive when it occurs during a "*bona fide* news interview". . . . The Commission even conceded that a re-broadcast of precisely the same offending clips of the two Billboard Music Award programs for the purpose of providing background information on this case would not result in any action by the FCC . . . . [E]ven repeated and deliberate use of numerous expletives is not indecent . . . if the expletives are "integral" to the work [as in the case of the film "Saving Private Ryan"].

Majority op. at pages 24-25. The majority is of course correct that the Commission does not follow an all-or-nothing policy. Its standards do attempt to draw context-based distinctions, with the result that no violation will be found in circumstances where usage is considered sufficiently justified that it does not constitute indecency.

This, however, is in no way a consequence of the Commission's change of standard for fleeting expletives. It applies across the board to all circumstances. Regardless of whether the expletive was repeated or fleeting, the Commission will apply context-based standards to

381

determine whether the incident constituted indecency. A bona fide news context and recognition of artistic integrity favor a finding of no violation. The majority's criticism of inconsistency is not properly directed against the change of standard here in question, which has done nothing to increase the inconsistency. If anything, the change of standard has made the Commission more consistent rather than less, because under the new rule, the same context-based factors will apply to all circumstances. If there is merit in the majority's argument that the Commission's actions are arbitrary and capricious because of irrationality in its standards for determining when expletives are permitted and when forbidden, that argument must be directed against the entire censorship structure. It does not demonstrate that the Commission's change of standard for the fleeting expletive was irrational.

Furthermore, while the Commission will indeed allow the broadcast of the same material in some circumstances but not in others, I do not see why this differentiation should be considered irrational. It rather seeks to reconcile conflicting values. On the one hand, it recognizes, as stressed by the Supreme Court in *Pacifica*, the potential for harm to children resulting from exposure to indecency. On the other hand, the Commission has historically recognized that categorical prohibition of the broadcast of all instances of usage of a word generally considered indecent would suppress material of value, which should not be deemed indecent upon consideration of the context. This is not irrationality.[16] It is an attempt on the part

---

[16] Spectators in the courtroom observing the argument of this case would have heard the judges and the lawyers saying "fuck" in open court. Had the case been on another subject, such usage would surely have seemed inappropriate. Because of the issues in this case, the word was central to the issues being discussed. It is not irrational to take context into account to determine whether use of the word is indecent.

of the Commission over the years to reconcile conflicting values through standards which take account of context.

The majority then argues that the Commission reasoned irrationally when in its *Remand Order*, as a part of its explanation for its change of position, the Commission observed:

> [G]ranting an automatic exemption for "isolated or fleeting" expletives . . . would as a matter of logic permit broadcasters to air expletives at all hours of a day so long as they did so one at a time. For example, broadcasters would be able to air . . . offensive . . . words, regardless of context, with impunity . . . provided that they did not air more than one expletive in any program segment.

Remand Order, at ¶ 25. The majority asserts that this concern was "divorced from reality." Majority op. at page 27. On the majority's view, because broadcasters did not "barrage[] the airwaves with expletives" during the period prior to *Golden Globes* when fleeting expletives received a free pass, they would not do so in the future.

The agency has one prediction of what would likely occur in the future under the pre-*Golden Globes* policy. The majority has another. The majority may be right in speculating that the Commission's concern is exaggerated. Who knows? As a matter of law, it makes no difference. The court is obligated to give deference to agency judgment and may not substitute its judgment for that of the agency, or set aside an agency action merely because the court believes the agency is wrong. *See State Farm*, 463 U.S. at 43 (court must not "substitute its judgment for that of the agency"); *Vermont Yankee*, 45 U.S. at 558 ("Administrative decisions should [not] be set aside . . . because the court is unhappy with the result."). Only if the agency's action is "arbitrary and capricious" may the court nullify it. 5 U.S.C. § 706(2)(A).

Furthermore, if obligated to choose, I would bet my money on the agency's prediction.

The majority's view presupposes that the future would repeat the past. It argues that because the networks were not flooded with discrete, fleeting expletives when fleeting expletives had a free pass, they would not be flooded in the future. This fails to take account of two facts. First, the words proscribed by the Commission's decency standards are much more common in daily discourse today than they were thirty years ago. Second, the regulated networks compete for audience with the unregulated cable channels, which increasingly make liberal use of their freedom to fill programming with such expletives. The media press regularly reports how difficult it is for networks to compete with cable for that reason.[17] It seems to me the agency has good reason to expect that a marked increase would occur if the old policy were continued.

In any event, even if the majority could reasonably label *this aspect* of the Commission's reasoning "arbitrary and capricious," it still would not matter. The agency's action in changing the standard for fleeting expletives did not depend on the defensibility of this prediction. It is at most a small part of the agency's justification for its action.

Finally the majority disagrees with the Commission's view that the word "fuck"

---

[17] *See, e.g.*, Gail Pennington, *Kingpin There Are More Things in Heaven and Earth Than "Sopranos," NBC Insists*, St. Louis Post-Dispatch, Feb. 2, 2003, at F1 ("Although they tried at first to feign indifference, broadcasters have seethed for years over the critical acclaim and abundant awards handed to cable series like "The Sopranos." The complaint: that the playing field isn't level. Broadcasters are strained by FCC rules about content – nudity and sex, violence and language – that don't apply to cable."); Jim Rutenberg, *Few Viewers Object as Unbleeped Bleep Words Spread on Network TV*, N.Y. Times, Jan. 25, 2003, at B7 ("Broadcast television, under intensifying attack by saltier cable competitors, is pushing the limits of decorum further by the year, and hardly anyone is pushing back."); Jim Rutenberg, *Hurt by Cable, Networks Spout Expletives*, N.Y. Times, Sept. 2, 2001, at 11 ("Broadcast television is under siege by smaller cable competitors that are winning audiences while pushing adult content. In that climate, broadcast is fighting the perception that its tastes are lagging behind those of a media-saturated culture whose mores have grown more permissive.").

communicates an "inherently . . . sexual connotation [and] invariably invokes a coarse sexual image." *Golden Globes*, at ¶¶ 8-9. The majority notes that the F-Word is often used in everyday conversation without any sexual meaning. Majority op. at page 26. I agree with the majority that the word is often used without a necessary *intention on the part of the speaker* to refer to sex. A student who gets a disappointing grade on a test, a cook who burns the roast, or a driver who returns to his parked car to find a parking ticket on the windshield, might holler out the F-Word to express anger or disappointment. The word is also sometimes used to express delight, as with Bono's exhilarated utterance on his receipt of his award. Some use it more as a declaration of uncompromising toughness, or of alignment on the side of vulgarity against prissy manners, without necessarily intending to evoke any sexual meaning. Some use it to intensify whatever it is they may be saying, and some sprinkle the word indiscriminately throughout their conversation with no apparent meaning whatsoever.

The majority, however, misunderstands the Commission's reasoning, or in any event interprets it in the manner least favorable to the Commission. In observing that *fuck* "invariably invokes a coarse sexual image," *Golden Globes*, at ¶ 9, that this is so "even if the word is not used literally," *Remand Order*, at ¶ 16, and that its power to offend "derives from its sexual . . . meaning," *id.* at ¶ 23, the Commission did not mean that every speaker who utters the word invariably intends to communicate an offensive sexual meaning. The Commission explicitly recognized that the word can be used in a manner that does not intend a sexual meaning. A fairer reading of the Commission's meaning is that, even when the speaker does not intend a sexual meaning, a substantial part of the community, and of the television audience, will understand the word as freighted with an offensive sexual connotation. It is surely not irrational for the Commission to conclude that, according to the understanding of a substantial segment of the community, the F-Word is never completely free of an offensive, sexual connotation. It is no accident that in many languages, the equivalent of the F-Word finds usage, as in English, to express anger, disgust, insult, and confrontation.

What we have is at most a difference of opinion between a court and an agency. Because of the deference courts must give to the reasoning of a duly authorized administrative agency in matters within the agency's competence, a court's disagreement with the Commission on this question is of no consequence. The Commission's position is not irrational; it is not arbitrary and capricious.

I believe that in changing its standard, the Commission furnished a reasoned explanation, and thus satisfied the requirements of the Administrative Procedures Act.[18] I therefore respectfully dissent.[19]

---

[18] As each of the instances under review in this case involved the use of the F-Word, and because I find that the Commission has given a rational justification for its rule as applied to use of the F-Word, I do not consider the Commission's standard which makes it a decency violation to use the word "shit." In *Pacifica*, in upholding the constitutionality of censorship under § 1464, the Supreme Court stressed the accessibility of broadcasting to children. *See Pacifica*, 438 U.S. at 749; *Remand Order*, at ¶ 51. The potential for harm to children resulting from indecent broadcasting was clearly a major concern justifying the censorship scheme. In this regard, it seems to me there is an enormous difference between censorship of references to sex and censorship of references to excrement. For children, excrement is a main preoccupation of their early years. There is surely no thought that children are harmed by hearing references to excrement.

Nicole Richie's script called for her to say it was not easy to get "pig crap" out of a Prada purse. In delivering the line, Richie changed "pig crap" to "cow shit." Had she stuck with "pig crap," that reference would not have been a violation, but her change to "cow shit" could have resulted in forfeitures and perhaps even the loss of Fox's license to broadcast. In another instance, the Commission found a violation (which was later vacated on other grounds) because someone was described as a "bullshitter." *See Complaints Regarding Various Television Broadcasts Between February 2, 2002 and March 8, 2005*, 21 F.C.C.R. 2664 (2006); *Remand Order*, at ¶ 73. The justification is surely not that children will be harmed by hearing "shit" but not by hearing "crap." It appears that at least some of the Commission's prohibitions are not justified at all by the risk of harm to children but only by concern for good manners. When the censorship is exercised only to protect polite manners and not by reason of risk of harm, I question whether it can survive scrutiny. Because each instance of censorship at stake in this case involved the F-Word, which in the Commission's view inherently retains a sexual reference, the question does not arise in this case.

[19] I express neither agreement nor disagreement with my colleagues' added discussion of Fox's other challenges to the Commission's actions because, as the majority opinion recognizes, it is dictum and therefore not an authoritative precedent in our Circuit's law. In subsequent adjudications, the respect accorded to dictum depends on its persuasive force and not on the fact that it appears in a court opinion.

BIBLIOGRAPHY

Abrams, Marc (2007) "Nets should exploit Web for racier fare," *Television Week*, January 1 (http://www.tvweek.com/article.cms?articleId=31212).

Abrams v. *United States*, 250 US 616 (1919).

Ackerman, Elise, and Matt Marshall (2007) "Artists get payments from some video sites," *The Mercury News*, January 14 (http://www.mercurynews.com/mld/mercurynews/business/technology/16462257.htm).

Action for Children's Television v. *FCC (ACT I)*, 271 US App. DC 365, 852 F.2d 1332, 1340 (DC 1988).

Action for Children's Television v. *FCC (ACT II)*, 932 F.2d 1504 (DC Circuit 1991).

Action for Children's Television v. *FCC (ACT III)*, 11 F.3d 170 (DC Circuit 1993).

Albarran, Alan B. (1996) *Media Economics, Understanding Markets, Industries and Concepts*. Ames, IA: Iowa State University Press.

Amendment I, United States Constitution (1791).

American Library Ass'n v. *United States*, 201 F. Supp. 2d 401 (E.D. Pa. 2002).

Apollomedia Corp. v. *Reno*, 1998 W.L. 665108 N.D. Calif. 1998.

Arizona Republic (2006) "A coarsening of our culture," December 11 (http://www.azcentral.com/arizonarepublic/opinions/articles/1211mon2-11.html).

Ashcroft v. *ACLU*, 535 US 564 (2002).

Ashcroft v. *Free Speech Coalition*, 535 US 234 (2002).

Bagdikian, Ben H. (2000) *The Media Monopoly*, 6th edn. Boston, MA: Beacon Press.

Baran, Stanley J. (1999) *Introduction to Mass Communication, Media Literacy and Culture*. Mountain View, CA: Mayfield.

Barbatis, Gretchen S., Wong, Martin R., and Herek, Gregory M. (1983) "A struggle for dominance: Relational communication patterns in television drama," *Communication Quarterly* 31(2): 148, 155.

Barnes, Susan B. (2003) *Computer-mediated Communication, Human-to-Human Communication across the Internet*. Boston, MA: Allyn and Bacon.

Barnes v. *Glen Theatre*, 501 US 560 (1991).

Barrett, Neil (1997) *The State of the Cybernation*. London: Kogan Page.

Bartee, Wayne C., and Alice Fleetwood Bartee (1992) *Litigating Morality, American Legal Thought and its English Roots*. New York: Praeger.

Bell, David (2001) *An Introduction to Cybercultures*. London: Routledge.

Benjamin, Louise M. (1990) "The precedent that almost was: A 1926 court effort to regulate radio," *Journalism Quarterly* 67: 578–85.

Bennett, W. Lance (1996) *The Politics of Illusion*, 3rd edn. White Plains, NY: Longman.

Benson, Jim, and Eggerton, John (2006) "PBS revisits profanity policy," *Broadcasting & Cable*, July 31, p. 30.

Berger, Peter L., and Luckmann, Thomas (1967) *The Social Construction of Reality, a Treatise in The sociology of Knowledge*. New York: Anchor, Doubleday.

Berman, Ronald (1981) *Advertising and Social Change*. Beverly Hills: Sage.

Bhagwat, Ashutosh (2003) "What if I want my kids to watch pornography?: Protecting children from 'indecent' speech," *William & Mary Bill of Rights Journal* 11 (February): 671–725.

Bittner, John R. (1994) *Law and Regulation of Electronic Media*, 2nd edn. Englewood Cliffs, NJ: Prentice Hall.

Blanchard, Margaret A. (1992) "The American urge to censor: freedom of expression versus the desire to sanitize society – from Anthony Comstock to 2 Live Crew," *William & Mary Law Review* 33 (spring): 741–851.

Blanchard, Margaret A., and Semonche, John E. (2006) "Anthony Comstock and his adversaries: The mixed legacy of this battle for free speech," *Communication Law and Policy* 11: 317–66.

Block, Peter Alan (1990) "Modern-day sirens: Rock lyrics and the First Amendment," *Southern California Law Review* 63: 777–832.

Blumenthal v. *Drudge and America Online*, 992 F. Supp. 44 (DDC 1998).

Blumer, Herbert (1990) *Industrialization as an Agent of Social Change, a Critical Analysis*. New York: Aldine de Gruyter.

Blumler, Jay G., McLeod, Jack M., and Rosengren, Karl Erik (eds) (1992) *Comparatively Speaking: Communication and Culture Across Space and Time*. Newbury Park: Sage.

Bolter, Jay David, and Grusin, Richard (1999) *Remediation: Understanding New Media*. Cambridge, MA: MIT Press.

Booth-Butterfield, Steven, and Booth-Butterfield, Melanie (1991) "Individual differences in the communication of humorous messages," *The Southern Communication Journal* 56: 205–18.

Bourdieu, Pierre, and Coleman, James S. (1991) *Social Theory for a Changing Society*. Boulder, CO: Westview Press.

Bozell, L. Brent (2007) "Saints and swearing," Media Research Center, January 19 (http://www.mrc.org/BozellColumns/entertainmentcolumn/2007/col20070119.asp).

Branscomb, Anne Wells (1995) "Emerging media technology and the First Amendment – Anonymity, autonomy, and accountability: Challenges to the First Amendment in cyberspaces," *Yale Law Journal* 10:, 1639–79.

Branton v. *FCC*, 993 F.2d 906 (DC Circuit 1993), *cert. den.*

Broadcast indecency, in *18 USC, Section 1464*, 8 FCCR 704 (1993).

Broadcasting & Cable (2005, July 18) Fast Track. "ABC lets slip F-word slip," p. 4.

Broadcasting & Cable (2005, May 23) Fast Track. "CBS fires reporter for on-air f-word," p. 5.

Broadcasting & Cable (2006) "A TV industry guide: Religious & faith-based programming" (advertising supplement), August.

Brown, Keith, and Candeub, Adam (2005) "The law and economics of wardrobe malfunction," *Brigham Young University Law Review* 2005: 1463–513.

Bucy, Erik P. (2002) *Living in the Information Age, A New Media Reader*. Belmont, CA: Wadsworth.

Butler v. *Dexter*, 425 US 262 (1975).

Bungard, B. Chad (2006) "Indecent exposure: An economic approach to removing the boob from the tube," *UCLA Entertainment Law Review* 13: 195–239.

Calhoun, Craig (1991) "Indirect relationships and imagined communities: Large-scale social integration and the transformation of everyday life," in *Social theory for a Changing Society*, Pierre Boudieu and James S. Coleman (eds). Boulder, CO: Westview Press.

Calvert, Clay (1998) "The First Amendment and the third person: Perceptual biases of media harms & cries for government censorship," *CommLaw Conspectus* 6 (summer): 165–71.

Calvert, Clay (2004) "Bono, the culture wars, and a profane decision: The FCC's reversal of course on indecency determinations and its new path on profanity," *Seattle University Law Review* 28 (fall): 61–95.

Calvert, Clay (2005) "The First Amendment, the media and the Culture Wars: Eight important lessons from 2004 about speech, censorship, science and public policy," *California Western Law Review* 41: 325–60.

Cantor, Joanne R. (1976) "What is funny to whom? The role of gender," *Journal of Communication* 26: 164–72.

Carey, James W. (1992) *Communication as Culture, Essays on Media and Society*. New York: Routledge.

Caristi, Dom (1992). *Expanding Free Expression in the Marketplace, Broadcasting and the Public Forum*. New York: Quorum Books.

Carlin, John C. (1976) "The rise and fall of topless radio," *Journal of Communication* 26(1): 31–7.

Carter, T. Barton, Franklin, Marc A., and Wright, Jay B. (1989) *The First Amendment and the Fifth Estate, Regulation of Electronic Mass Media*, 2nd edn. Westbury, NY: The Foundation Press.

Carter, T. Barton, Franklin, Marc A., and Wright, Jay B. (1993) *The First Amendment and the Fifth Estate, Regulation of Electronic Mass Media*, 3rd edn. Westbury, NY: The Foundation Press.

Cashmore, Ellis (2006) *Celebrity/Culture*. New York: Routledge.

Center for Creative Voices in Media (2006, March 31) "Survey: Americans don't want government to censor TV," (http://www.creativevoices.us/phpbin/news/showArticle. php?id=154).

Ceruzzi, Paul E. (2003) *A History of Modern Computing*. Cambridge, MA: MIT Press.

Chafee, Jr., Zechariah (1941) *Free Speech in the United States*. Cambridge, MA: Harvard University Press.

Chapman, Anthony J., and Gadfield, Nicholas J. (1976) "Is sexual humor sexist?" *Journal of Communication* 26: 141–53.

Cohen, Akiba A., Adoni, Hanna, and Bantz, Charles R. (1990) *Social Conflict and Television news*. Sage Library of Social Research 183. Newbury Park: Sage.

Cohen, Jeremy (1989) *Congress Shall Make no Law, Oliver Wendell Holmes, the First Amendment, and Judicial Decision-making*. Ames, IA: Iowa State University Press.

Cohen, Jeremy, and Gleason. Timothy (1990) *Social Research in Communication and Law*. The Sage CommText Series, Vol. 23. Newbury Park: Sage.

Cohen v. California, 403 US 15 (1971).

Comstock, George (1989) *The Evolution of American Television*. Newbury Park: Sage, 1989.

Cooper, John W. (1985) *The Theology of Freedom, the Legacy of JACQUES MARIRAIN*. Macon, GA: Mercer University Press.

COPPA (1999) *Children's Online Privacy Protection Rule, Public Comments Received,* June 11 (available at http://www.ftc.gov/privacy/comments/amazoncom.htm).

Counch, Carl J. (1996) *Information Technologies and Social Orders.* New York, NY: Aldine De Gruyter.

Creech, Kenneth C. (1993) *Electronic Media Law and Regulation.* Boston, MA: Focal Press.

Cronin, Mary M. (2006) "The liberty to argue freely," *Journalism & Communication Monographs* 8: 163–219.

Crowley, David, and Heyer, Paul (1999) *Communication in History, Technology, Culture Society,* 3rd edn. New York: Addison Wesley Longman.

C-SPAN (2006, December 20, 10 a.m.) Broadcast of oral arguments, United States Court of Appeals, Second Circuit.

Curran, James and Gurevitch, Michael (eds) (1991) *Mass Media and Society,* New York: Routledge, Chapman & Hall.

Damayanti, Ninin (2006, December 22) "Television association rejects program criminalization," *TEMPO Interactive,* 2006 (http://www.tempointeractive.com/hg/ekbis/2006/12/22/brk,20061222-89946,uk.html).

Dancy, Jonathan (1993) *Moral reasons.* Oxford: Blackwell.

Davidson, Paul (2006, November 8) "FCC changes rulings on indecency," *USA Today* (http://www.usatoday.com/money/media/2006-11-07-indecency-usat_x.htm).

Denniston, Lyle (1998, June) "From George Carlin to Matt Drudge: The constitutional implications of bringing the paparazzi to America," *American University Law Review* 47, 1255–71.

Dominick, Joseph, Sherman, Barry L., and Copeland, Gary (1990) *Broadcasting/Cable and Beyond, an Introduction to Modern ElectroNIC media.* New York: McGraw-Hill.

Dominick, Joseph R., and Fletcher, James E. (1985) *Broadcasting Research Methods.* Newton, MA: Allyn and Bacon.

Donnerstein, Edward, Barbara Wilson, and Daniel Linz (1992, Winter). "Standpoint: On the regulation of broadcast indecency to protect children," *Journal of Broadcasting & Electronic Media* 36(1), 111–117.

Driscoll, Paul D. (1989, August) "The federal communications commission and broadcast indecency," Law Division, Association for Education in Journalism and Mass Communication.

du Gay, Paul, Evans, Jessica, and Redman, Peter (eds) (2000) *Identity: a Reader.* London: Sage.

Editorial (2006, March 20) "Clear as mud," *Broadcasting & Cable,* p. 42.

Editorial (2006, June 19) "The big chill becomes law," *Broadcasting & Cable,* p. 42.

Editorial (2006, July 24) "The president's bad word," *Broadcasting & Cable,* p. 30.

Eggerton, John (2005, May 9) Washington Watch, *Broadcasting & Cable,* p. 10.

Eggerton, John (2007, January 22) "Violence: The new indecency?" *Broadcasting & Cable* (http://www.broadcastingcable.com/article/CA6408809.html).

Eggerton, John (2006, March 20) "The FCC's full frontal assault on TV; The government cracks down, Hollywood feels the chill, *Broadcasting & Cable,* pp. 1, 18–19.

Eggerton, John (2006, May 15) "Washington Watch: Recent FCC fines confuse; Two challenges point up inconsistencies in the war on indecency," *Broadcasting & Cable,* p. 17.

Eggerton, John (2006, May 22) "Washington Watch: Brownback," *Broadcasting & Cable,* p. 3.

Eggerton, John (2006, June 12) "Indecency fines jump," *Broadcasting & Cable,* pp. 4, 14.

Eggerton, John (2006, June 19) "Washington Watch," *Broadcasting & Cable*, p. 3.

Eggerton, John (2006, July 10) "Indecency double take, FCC seeks another look at recent fines," *Broadcasting & Cable*, p. 34

Eggerton, John (2006, July 31) "Parental control, TV's new campaign is big but doesn't quiet calls for a la carte," *Broadcasting & Cable*, p. 10.

Eggerton, John (2006, July 31) "CBS pays fine to get its day in court," *Broadcasting & Cable*, p. 30.

Eggerton, John (2006, August 28) "Watch your @#$ percenting language! Little leaguers, Janet and serious documentarians all share a common problem," *Broadcasting & Cable*, p. 12.

Eggerton, John (2006, September 11) " 'Fleeting' profanities: OK for now? Court says decision pending review; FCC warns against saying too much," *Broadcasting & Cable*, p. 30.

Eggerton, John (2006, October 23) "Lieberman targets online content, And media ownership spurs 160,000+ FCC comments," *Broadcasting & Cable*, p. 10.

Eggerton, John (2006, November 27) "Indecency court challenges begin, Networks fire opening shot at FCC profanity rulings." *Broadcasting & Cable*, pp. 3, 10.

Eggerton, John (2006, December 11) "FCC hacks away at V-chip, Commission argues it's obligated to protect kids from profanity," *Broadcasting & Cable*, p. 16.

Eggerton, John, and Grossman, Ben (2006, March 13) "'Las Vegas' blasted at FCC," p. 6.

Eldred v. Ashcroft, 537 US 186, 223 (2003), *reh'g denied*, 538 US 916 (2003).

Emerson, Thomas I. (1966) *Toward a General Theory of the First Amendment*. New York, NY: Random House.

Emerson, Thomas I. (1970) *The System of Freedom of Expression*. New York, NY: Random House.

FCC v. League of Women Voters, 468 US 364 (1984).

FCC (2001) "In the Matter of Industry Guidance On the Commission's Case Law Interpreting 18 USC §1464 and Enforcement Policies Regarding Broadcast Indecency," File No. EB-00-IH-0089, Policy Statement, Adopted: March 14, 2001; Released: April 6, 2001.

Federal Communications Commission v. Pacifica Foundation, 438 US 726 (1978).

Federal Trade Commission (1999). Children's Online Privacy Protection Rule, 15 USC §6501.

Ferguson, Douglas A., and Perse, Elizabeth M. (2000) The World Wide Web as a functional Alternative to television. *Journal of Broadcasting & Electronic Media* 44(2), 155-174.

Fitzgerald, Ross (2007, January 15) "Battle for free speech rights in the courts," *The Australian* (http://www.theaustralian.news.com.au/story/0,20867,21058459-7583,00.html).

Flint, Joe (1992, January 13) "Evergreen to fight indecency charge, Since it has no avenue of appeal for FCC fine, it will refuse to pay; matter then gets handed over to Justice Department," *Broadcasting & Cable*, p. 91.

Flint, Joe (1992, October 26) "Hounding Howard: FCC's $ 100K fine, Radio personality Howard Stern," *Broadcasting & Cable*, p. 8.

Flint, Joe (1993, March 1) "Indecency rules under fire in courts, at FCC," *Broadcasting & Cable*, pp. 44–5.

Fowler, Mark S., and Brenner, Daniel L. (1982) "A marketplace approach to broadcast regulation," *Texas Law Review* 60(2), 207–58.

Fraleigh, Douglas M., and Joseph S. Tuman (1997) *Freedom of speech in the marketplace of ideas*. New York, NY: St. Martin's Press.

Free Speech Coalition v. *Reno*, 198 F.3d 1083 (9th Cir. 1999).

Freedom of Information Act, 5 USC Section 552.

Gey, Steven G. (2005) "The ninth annual Frankel Lecture, Address: Free will, religious liberty, and a partial defense of the French approach to religious expression in public schools," *Houston Law Review* 42: 1–79.

Gildemeister, Christopher (2005–06) "Faith in a Box," Parents Television Council (http://www.parentstv.org/PTC/publications/reports/religionstudy06/main.asp).

Gillmor, Donald M., Barron, Jerome A., Simon, Todd F., and Terry, Herbert A. (1990) *Mass Communication Law, Cases and Comment*, 5th edn. St. Paul, MN: West Publishing.

Ginsburg, Douglas H., Botein, Michael H., and Director, Mark D. (1991) *Regulation of the Electronic Mass Media, Law and Policy for Radio, Television, caBle and the New Video Technologies*, 2nd edn. St. Paul, MN: West Publishing.

Glasser, Theodore L. (1982, November) "The press, privacy, and community mores," Mass Communication Division, Speech Communication Association, Louisville, KY.

Godwin, Mike (1998) *Cyber rights: Defending Free Speech in the Digital Age*. New York: Times Books.

Goffman, Erving (1987) "Presentation of self in everyday life," in *Introducing Sociology, a Collection of Readings*, Richard T. Schaefer and Robert P. Lamm (eds). New York: McGraw-Hill.

Goldstein, Jeffrey H. (1976, Summer) "Theoretical notes on humor," *Journal of Communication* 26(3): 104–12.

Gordon, Joshua B. (2006, September) "Note, *Pacifica* is dead. Long live *Pacifica*: Formulating a new argument structure to preserve government regulation of indecent broadcasts," *Southern California Law Review* 79, 1451–98.

Graber, Doris A. (1989) *Mass Media and American politics*, 3rd edn, Washington, DC: Congressional Quarterly.

Gray, Cavender (1984) "'Scared Straight': Ideology and the media," in Ray Surette, ed., *Justice and the Media, Issues and Research*. Springfield, IL: Charles C. Thomas.

Greenwalt, Kent (1992) *Law and Objectivity*. New York: Oxford University Press.

Groce, Stephen B., and Cooper, Margaret (1990) "Just me and the boys? Women in local-level rock and roll," *Gender & Society* 4(2): 220–9.

Halevi, Charles Chi (1988, March 25) "Anti-Semitic jokes on radio, TV aren't one bit funny," Commentary, *Chicago Sun-Times*, p. 44.

Hartman, Mitchell (1990, October). "Attempts to limit 'indecent' speech worry broadcasters," *The Quill*, p. 32.

Hicks v. *Miranda*, 422 US 322 (1974).

Hilliard, Robert L. (1991) *The Federal Communications Commission, a Primer*. Boston, MA: Focal Press.

Hilliard, Robert L., and Keith, Michael C. (2003) *Dirty Discourse, Sex and indecency in American Radio*. Ames, IA: Iowa State Press.

Hindmarsh, Mike (1990) "How is pornographic?' (Not 'What is Pornography?')," Unpublished paper prepared for presentation to the Communication Theory and Methodology Division, Association for Education in Journalism and Mass Communication, Minneapolis MN.

Hoffman, Claire (2006a, September 13) "Maker of 'Girls Gone Wild' runs afoul of law on minors," *Los Angeles Times*, p. A-1.

Hoffman, Claire (2006b, December 23) "Watchdog group says TV negatively depicts religion," *Los Angeles Times*, Living Section (http://www.kentucky.com/mld/kentucky/living/religion/16287557.htm).

Holland, Bill (1993, April) "Infinity license in danger of revocation over Stern?" *Billboard*, p. 69.

Holsti, Ole R. (1969) *Content analysis for the social sciences and humanities*. Reading, MA: Addison-Wesley.

Horowitz, Norman (2006, December 4) "Indecency a matter for parents, not creators," *Television Week*, p. 10.

Horton, Donald, and R. Richard Wohl (1986) "Mass communication and para-social interaction: Observation on intimacy at a distance," in *InterMedia, Interpersonal Communication in a Media World*, 3rd edn, Gary Gumpert, and Robert Cathcart (eds), New York: Oxford University Press.

Huber, Peter W. (1997) *Law and Disorder in Cyberspace, Abolish the FCC and Let Common Law Rule the Telecosm*. Oxford: Oxford University Press.

Illinois Citizens Committee for Broadcasting v. *FCC*, 515 F. 2d 397 (DC Cir. 1974).

In Re Apparent Liability, WGLD-FM, 41 FCC 2d 919 (1973).

In Re Infinity Broadcasting Corp. of Pa., 3 FCCR 930 (1987).

In Re WUHY-FM Eastern Educational Radio, 24 FCC 2d 408 (1970).

In the Matter of Complaints Regarding Various Television Broadcasts Between February 2, 2002 and March 8, 2005 (March 15, 2006).

In the Matter of Complaints Against Various Television Licensees Concerning Their December 31, 2004 Broadcast of the Program "Without A Trace" (March 15, 2006).

In the Matter of Complaints Against Various Television Licensees Concerning Their February 1, 2004 Broadcast Of The Super Bowl XXXVIII Halftime Show (March 15, 2006).

In the Matter of Industry Guidance On the Commission's Case Law Interpreting 18 USC § 1464 and Enforcement Policies Regarding Broadcast Indecency (April 6, 2001).

In the Matter of Liability of Sagittarius Broadcasting Corporation, 1992 FCC LEXIS 6042 (October 23, 1992).

In the Matter of Enforcement of Prohibitions Against Broadcast Obscenity and Indecency in 18 USC Sec. 1464, Order, FCC 88-416 (Dec. 19, 1988).

In the Matter of Rob Warden, 70 F.C.C. 2d 1735 (1978).

Infinity Broadcasting Corp. of Pa., 2 FCC Rcd 2705, 3 FCC Rcd 930 (1987).

Jassem, Harvey, and Glasser, Theodore L. (1983) "Children, indecency, and the perils of broadcasting: The 'Scared Straight' case," *Journalism Quarterly* 60(3): 509–12.

Jensen, Robert (1998) "First Amendment potluck," *Communication Law and Policy* 3(4): 563–88.

Johnson, Thomas J., and Kaye, Barbara K. (1998) "Cruising is believing? Comparing Internet and traditional sources on media credibility measures," *Journalism & Mass Communication Quarterly* 75(2): 325–40.

Jones, Steven G. (1998) *Cybersociety 2.0, Revisiting Computer-mediated Communication and Community*. Thousand Oaks, CA: Sage.

Jones, Steve (1991, Winter) "Ban(ned) in the USA: Popular music and censorship," *Journal of Communication Inquiry* 15(1): 73–87.

Jones, Steve (2004) "Queers in Cyberspace: Introductory Comments,"Colloquium, University of Illinois-Chicago (http://tigger.uic.edu/~kgbcomm/mqms/HTML/401Jones.htm).

Jones, Steven G. (1997) *Virtual Culture, Identity & Communication in Cybersociety*. London: Sage.

Jordan, Christina (2005) "Note: The xxx-files: cal/OSHA's regulatory response to HIV in the adult film industry," *Cardozo Journal of Law & Gender* 12: 421–44.

Kahai, Surinder S., & Cooper, Randolph B. (2003) Exploring the core concepts of media richness theory: The impact of cue multiplicity and feedback immediacy on decision quality. *Journal of Management Information Systems, 20*(1): 263–99.

Kay, Jason (1995) "Note: Sexuality, live without a net: regulating obscenity and indecency on the global network," *Southern California Interdisciplinary Law Journal* 4: 355–89.

Kening, Dan (1993, April 21) "Stern's shock-talk show not playing in Chicago," *Chicago Tribune*, (zone n), p. 1.

Kim, Haeryon (1990, August) "The politics of broadcast deregulation: Beyond Krasnow, Longley, and Terry's 'Broadcast policy-making system'," Unpublished paper prepared for presentation to the Association for Education in Journalism and Mass Communication, Minneapolis, MN.

KING-TV, FCC 90-104, 1990 FCC LEXIS 2414, May 10, 1990.

Kipnis, Kenneth (1977) *Philosophical Issues in Law: Cases and Materials*. Englewood Cliffs, NJ: Prentice-Hall.

Kleiman, Howard M. (1986) "Indecent programming on cable television: legal and social dimensions," *Journal of Broadcasting & Electronic Media* 30(3): 275–94.

Kohut. Andrew (1994) *The Role of Technology in American Life*. The Times Mirror Center For The People & The Press.

Kontas, Gretta (1990) "Gender, disparaging humor and aggression, have we come far enough to laugh, baby?" Unpublished paper prepared for presentation to the Speech Communication Association.

Krasnow, Erwin G., Longley, Lawrence D., and Terry, Herbert A. (1982) *The Politics of Broadcast Regulation*, 3rd edn. New York: St. Martin's Press.

Kuhl, Craig (2006, October 30) "Parental control, Campaigns, tools seek 'sanity, not censorship,'" Special Report of Multichannel News and B&C, *Broadcasting & Cable*, pp. 1–4B.

Lambaise, Jacqueline J. (2003) "Sex – Online and in Internet advertising, in Tom Reichert and Jacqueline Lambiase (eds), *Sex in Advertising, Perspectives on the Erotic Appeal*. Mahwah, NJ: Lawrence Erlbaum Associates, pp. 247–69.

Lane, Frederick S. III (2000) *Obscene Profits, The Entrepreneurs of Pornography in the Cyber age*. New York: Routledge.

Levy, Leonard W. (1985) *Emergence of a Free Press*. New York: Oxford University Press.

Lewis, Anthony (1991) *Make No Law, The Sullivan Case and the First Amendment*. New York: Random House.

Lin, Carolyn A. (1993) Adolescent viewing and gratifications in a new media environment. *Mass Communication Review* 20(1–2): 39–50.

Lindgren, James (1994) "Defining pornography," *University of Pennsylvania Law Review* 141: 1153–275.

Linz, Daniel, Donnerstein, Edward, Shafer, Bradley J., Land, Kenneth C., McCall, Patricia L. and Graesser, Arthur C. (1995) "Discrepancies between the legal code and community standards for sex and violence: An empirical challenge to traditional assumptions in obscenity law," *Law & Society Review* 29(1): 127–68.

Lipschultz, Jeremy Harris (1989) " 'Political propaganda': the Supreme Court decision in *Meese v. Keene*," *Communications and the Law* 11(4): 25–44.

Lipschultz, Jeremy Harris (1991, September) "A content analysis of broadcast indecency non-actionable material," poster session paper, Broadcast Education Association, Radio '91, San Francisco, California.

Lipschultz, Jeremy Harris (1992) "Conceptual problems of broadcast indecency policy and application," *Communications and the Law* 14(2): 3–29.

Lipschultz, Jeremy Harris (1993) "The function of audience and community feedback in broadcast indecency complaints and station management responses: A comparative case study of WLUP-AM and KSJO-FM," *Communications and the Law* 15(2): 17–42.

Lipschultz, Jeremy Harris (1997) *Broadcast Indecency: FCC Regulation and the First Amendment*. Boston, MA: Focal Press.

Lipschultz, Jeremy Harris (2000) *Free Expression in the Age of the Internet: Social and Legal Boundaries*. Boulder, CO: Westview Press

Lister, Martin, Dovey, Giddings, Jon, Seth Grant, Iain, and Kelly, Kieren (2003) *New Media: A Critical Introduction*. New York: Routledge.

Lowery, Shearon A. Lowery, and DeFluer Melvin, L. (1988) *Milestones in Mass Communication*, 2nd edn. New York: Longman.

Mainstream Loudon v. *Bd. of Trustees of the Loudon County Library*, 2 F. Supp. 2d 783, 794-95 (ED Va. 1998).

McChesney, Robert W. (1999) *Rich Media, Poor Democracy; Communication Politics in Dubious Times*. Urbana, IL: University of Illinois Press.

McCormick, Jim (1993, Spring) "Protecting children from music lyrics: Sound recordings and 'harmful to minors' statutes," *Golden Gate University Law Review* 23: 679–99.

McGinnis, Matthew L. (2005, May) "Note: Sex, but not the city: Adult-entertainment zoning, the first amendment, and residential and rural municipalities," *Boston College Law Review* 46: 625–59.

McKay, Laura J. (1996) "The Communications Decency Act: Protecting children from on-line indecency," *Seton Hall Legislative Journal* 20: 463–502.

McLeod, Jack M., Sitrovic, M., Voakes, Paul S., Guo, Z. and Huang, K. (1998) "A model of public support for First Amendment rights," *Communication Law and Policy* 3(4): 479–514.

McLuhan, Marshall, and Bruce R. Powers (1989) *The Global Village, Transformations in World Life and Media in the 21ˢᵗ Century*. New York: Oxford University Press.

McQuail, Denis (1994). *Mass Communication Theory, an Introduction*, 3rd edn. London: Sage.

Martin, Shannon E. (1995) *Bits, Bytes, and Big Brother, Federal Information Control in the Technological Age*. Westport, CT: Praeger.

Media Access Project, 41 FCC 2d 179 (1973).

Messaris, Paul, and Kerr, Dennis (1984). "TV-related mother–child interaction and children's perceptions of TV characters," *Journalism Quarterly* 61(3): 662–6.

Middleton, Kent R., and Bill F. Chamberlin (1994) *The Law of Public Communication*, 3rd edn. New York: Longman.

Miller v. *California*, 413 US 15 (1973).

Mosco, Vincent (1996). *The Political Economy of Communication*. London: Sage.

Muller, Gale D. (1989, December) "WXRX radio special listenership study," Princeton, NJ: The Gallup Organization.

National Association of Broadcasters (1990, March 19) "FCC's Quello, Duggan talk about AM radio, indecency," *Radio Week*, p. 3.

National Broadcasting Company v. *United States*, 319 US 190 (1943).

Negroponte, Nicholas (1995) *Being Digital*. New York, NY: Alfred A. Knopf.

New Indecency Enforcement Standards, 2 FCC Rcd. 2726 (1987).

Office of Communication of United Church of Christ v. *FCC*, 359 F.2d 994, 1005-06 (DC Cir. 1966).

Order on reconsideration, Infinity Broadcasting Corp., 3 FCC Rcd 930 (1987).

Pacifica Foundation, 36 FCC 147 (1964).

Pacifica Foundation, 2 FCC Rcd. 2698 (1987).

Packard, Ashley (1998, December) "Infringement or impingement: Carving out an actual knowledge defense for sysops facing strict liability," *Journalism & Mass Communication Monographs*, No. 168.

Passler, Richard G. (1990, November) "Comment: regulation of indecent radio broadcasts: George Carlin revisited – what does the future hold for the seven 'dirty' words?" *Tulane Law Review* 65: 131–67.

Pavlik, John V. (1996). *New Media Technology, Cultural and Commercial Perspectives*. Boston, MA: Allyn and Bacon.

Pelofsky, Jeremy (2006, December 23) "Jackson's breast flash fine defended," Reuters (http://www.news.com.au/sundaymail/story/0,,20968184-23109,00.html).

Pember, Don R. (1993) *Mass Media Law*, 6th edn. Dubuque, IA: Brown & Benchmark.

Perritt, Jr., Henry H. (1996) *Law and the Information Superhighway*. New York, NY: John Wiley & Sons.

Phillips, Gregory B. (2005–06) "Note & comment, Indecent content on satellite radio: Should the FCC step in?" *Loyola of Los Angeles Entertainment Law Review* 26: 237-285.

Playboy Enters., Inc. v. Frena, 839 F. Supp. 1552 (M.D. Fla., 1993).

Pool, Ithiel De Sola (1983) *Technologies of Freedom*. Cambridge, MA: Harvard University Press.

Pool, Ithiel De Sola (1990) *Technologies Without Boundaries*, Eli M. Noam (ed.). Cambridge, MA: Harvard University Press.

Powell, Jon T. and Gair, Wally (eds) (1988) *Public Interest and the Business of Broadcasting, the Broadcast Industry Looks at Itself*. New York: Quorum Books.

Pryor, Larry (2003) Symposium: Learning Reconsidered. Education in the Digital Age: "Online Journalism and the Threat of Two Cultures," *Journalism & Mass Communication Educator* 57(4): 302.

Puig, Claudia (1992, October 8) "Howard Stern: The next generation of talk radio; industry insiders predict that the nationwide popularity of the renegade morning man will spawn a host of imitators," *Los Angeles Times*, p. f-1.

R. v. Hicklin, L.R. 3 Q.B. 360 (1868).

Radio-Television News Directors Association (1989, January 19). "RTNDA joins appeal for review of indecency rule," *Intercom* 6(2), 2.

Ray, William B. (1990) *FCC, The Ups and dOwns of Radio–TV Regulation*. Ames, IA: Iowa State University Press.

Red Lion Broadcasting Company v. FCC, 395 US 367 (1969).

Regents of the University of California, 2 FCC Rcd. 2703 (1987).

Reichert, Tom (2003) *The Erotic History of Advertising*. Amherst, NY: Prometheus Books.

Reichert, Tom, and Lambiase, Jacqueline (2006) "Peddling desire: Sex and the marketing of media and consumer goods," in T. Reichert and J. Lambaise (eds), *Sex in Consumer Culture, The Erotic Content of Media and Marketing*. Mahwah, NJ: Lawrence Erlbaum Associates, pp. 1–10.

Religious Technology Ctr. v. Netcom On-Line Communications Servs., 907 F. Supp. 1361 (ND Cal. 1995).

Reno v. ACLU, 521 US 844 (1997).

Report Card of the 106th Congress on Privacy (2000) United States Senate, December 14, 2000, at http://www.thomas.loc.gov.

Rivera-Sanchez, Milagros (1995) The Origins of the Ban on "Obscene, indecent, or profane" Language of the Radio Act of 1927, *Journalism Monographs,* No. 149.

Rogers, Everett M. (1995) *Diffusion of innovations,* 4th edn. New York, NY: Free Press.

Romano, Allison, and John Eggerton (2006, May 22) "Senate approves new indecency legislation, Fines could skyrocket," *Broadcasting & Cable*, pp. 3, 27.

Rooder, Brian J. (2005, November) "Broadcast indecency regulation in the era of the 'wardrobe malfunction': Has the FCC grown too big for its britches?" *Fordham Law Review 74*, 871–907.

Roth v. *United States*, 354 US 476 (1957).

Russell Research (2006) *TV Watch Study*, available at: Center for Creative Voices in Media (2006, March 31) "Survey: Americans don't want government to censor T," (http://www.creativevoices.us/php-bin/news/showArticle.php?id=154).

Sable Communications Inc. v. *FCC*, 492 US 115 (1989).

Schlessel, Jason S. (2002) "The deep pocket dilemma: Setting the parameters of talk show liability," *Cardozo Arts & Entertainment Law Journal* 20: 461–90.

Schulz, Muriel R. (1975) "The semantic derogation of woman," in *Language and Sex, Difference and dominance*, Barrie Thorne and Nancy Henley (eds). Rowley, MA: Newbury House.

Severin, Werner J., and Tankard, Jr., James W. (1992) *Communication Theories: Origins, Methods, and Uses in the Mass Media*, 3rd edn. New York: Longman.

Sheftel-Gomes, Nasoan (2006) "Article, Your revolution: The Federal Communications Commission, obscenity and the chilling of artistic expression on radio airwaves," *Cardozo Arts & Entertainment Law Journal* 24: 191–227.

Sherman, Aliza (1998) *Cybergrrl! A Woman's Guide to the World Wide Web*. New York: Ballantine Books.

Sherman, Barry L. (1987) *Telecommunications Management, The Broadcast & Cable Industries*. New York: McGraw-Hill.

Shields, Steven O. (1990, August) "Creativity and control in the work of American music radio announcers," Unpublished paper prepared for presentation to the Mass Communication and Society Division, Association for Education in Journalism and Mass Communication, Minneapolis, MA.

Siebert, Fred S., Peterson, Theodore and Schramm, Wilbur (1963) *Four Theories of the Press, the Authoritarian, Libertarian, Social Responsibility amd Soviet Communist Concepts of What the Press Should Be and Do*. Urbana, IL: University of Illinois Press.

Skafish, Bradley A. (2002, March) "NOTE, Smut on the small screen: The future of cable-based adult entertainment following *United States v. Playboy Entertainment Group*," *Federal Communications Law Journal* 54: 319–37.

Smethers, J. Steven (1998). "Cyberspace in the curricula: New legal and ethical issues," *Journalism & Mass Communication Educator* 52(4): 15–23.

Smiley, Marion (1992). *Moral Responsibility and the Boundaries of Community, Power and Accountability from a Pragmatic Point of View*. Chicago, IL: The University of Chicago Press.

Smith, Elizabeth Nau (1998) "Note: Children's exposure to indecent material on cable: *Denver Area Educational Telecommunications Consortium, Inc. v. FCC*, An interpretation of the Cable Television Consumer Protection and Competition Act of 1992," *DePaul Law Review* 47: 1041–86.

Smith, Tom W. (1990) "The polls – A report, The sexual revolution?" *Public Opinion Quarterly* 54: 415–35.

Smolla, Rodney A. (1992) *Free speech in an open society*. New York, NY: Alfred A. Knopf.

Sonderling, 41 FCC 2d 777 (1973).

Spitzer, Matthew L. (1997) "Article, An introduction to the law and economics of the V-chip," *Cardozo Arts & Entertainment Law Journal* 15: 429–501.

Spitzer, Matthew L. (1986) *Seven Dirty Words and Six Other Stories, Controlling the Content of Print and Broadcast*. New Haven, CT: Yale University Press.

Stark, Werner (1991) *The Sociology of Knowledge, Toward a Deeper Understanding of the History of Ideas*. New Brunswick, NJ: Transaction Publishers.

Starr, Michael, and Atkin, David (1989, August) "The Department of Communications: A plan for the abolition of the Federal Communications Commission," Radio-Television Journalism Division, Association for Education in Journalism and Mass Communication, national conference, Washington, DC.

Sterling, Christopher H. and Kittross, John M. (1990). *Stay tuned, A concise history of American broadcasting*, 2nd edn. Belmont, CA: Wadsworth.

Stevenson, Nick (1995). *Understanding Media Cultures, Social Theory and Mass Communication*. London: Sage.

Stewart, Lea P., Stewart, Alan D., Friendly, Sheryl A., and Cooper, Pamela J. (1990) *Communication Between the Sexes, Sex Differences and Sex-role Stereotypes*, 2nd edn. Scottsdale, AZ: Gorsuch Scarisbrick.

Sunstein, Cass R. (1993). *Democracy and the Problem of Free Speech*. New York: The Free Press.

Sunstein, Cass R. (1995, May). "Emerging media technology and the First Amendment: The First Amendment in cyberspace," *Yale Law Journal* 104: 1757–804.

Surratt, Carla G. (2001). *The Internet and Social Change*. Jefferson, NC: McFarland & Co.

Telecommunications Research and Action Center v. FCC, 800 F. 2d 1181 (DC Cir. 1986).

Terlip, Laura A. (1990, November). "Tough, tender & too good to be true?: Student attributions of sex roles to successful females in situation comedies," Unpublished paper prepared for presentation to the Women's Caucus, Speech Communication Association.

The Harris Poll (2006, May 24). http://www.harrisinteractive.com/harris_poll/printer-friend/index.asp?PID=668; Cf. The Media Audit, April 25, 2002, (http://www.themediaaudit.com/ growth.htm).

Thompson, Jr., Edward H., and Pleck, Joseph H. (1987) "The structure of male role norms," in *Changing Men, New Directions in Research on Men and Masculinity*, Michael S. Kimmel (ed.). Newbury Park: Sage.

Topcik, Joel (2006, April 3) "Victory for decency crusaders? Not so fast," *Broadcasting & Cable*, p. 7.

Turow, Joseph (1974) "Talk show radio as interpersonal Communication," *Journal of Broadcasting* 18(2): 171–9.

United States v. American Library Ass'n, 539 US 194 (2003).

United States v. O'Brien, 391 US 367 (1968).

White, Cindy L. (1988) "Liberating laughter: An inquiry into the nature, content and functions of feminist humor," in *Women Communicating: Studies of Women's Talk*, Barbara Bate, and Anita Taylor (eds). Norwood, NJ: Ablex.

Winer, Laurence H. (1997). "Article, The *Red Lion* of cable, and beyond? –*Turner Broadcasting v. FCC*," *Cardozo Arts & Entertainment Law Journal* 15: 1–68.

United States, et al. v. Playboy Entertainment Group, Inc., 529 US 803 (2000).

United States v. *Thomas*, 74 F.3d 701 (6th Cir. 1996).

United States v. Various Articles of Obscene Merchandise, 709 F.2d 132 (2d Cir. 1983).

US v. Playboy Entertainment (529 US 803, 2000).

Winick, Charles (1976) "The social contexts of humor," *Journal of Communication* 26(3): 124–8.

Winslow, George (2006, February 13) "Mega-church, Mega-TV," *Broadcasting & Cable*, pp. 16–18.

WorldNetDaily (2006, February 9) "Strip scene on NBC protested; Prime-time segment from 'Las Vegas' has family group steaming," accessed December 1, 2006, from, http://worldnetdaily.com/news/article.asp?ARTICLE_ID=48742.

Wright, Charles R. (1986). *Mass Communication, A Sociological Perspective*, 3rd edn. New York: Random House.

Wright, R. George (1990). *The Future of Free Speech Law*. New York: Quorum Books.

Yale Broadcasting v. *FCC*, 478 F.2d 594 (DC Cir. 1973).

Young v. Abrams, 698 F.2d 131(2d Cir. 1983).

Yorke, Jeffrey (1992, August 18) "Locking on the shock jocks," *Washington Post*, p. d-7.

Yorke, Jeffrey (1992, October 27) "Stern talk results in fine," *Washington Post*, p. c7.

Zemach, Temera, and Akiba A. Cohen (1986, Fall) "Perception of gender equality on television and in social reality," *Journal of Broadcasting & Electronic Media* 30(4): 427–44.

Zeran v. *America Online*, 129 F.3d 327 (4th Cir. 1997).

47 United States Code, Section 326.

47 USC, Sections 312 and 503.

INDEX

ABC 154, 156, 175
A&E 157
Abrams v. *United States* 48–9
academic freedom 112
Ackerman, E. 175
ACLU (American Civil Liberties Union)
    105, 107, 110
Action for Children's Television v. *FCC* 81–6
administrative law 52
Advertisement Law of the People's
    Republic of China 70
AFA (American Family Association) 148,
    151–3
All Things Considered 160
ALA (American Library Association) 110,
    113
Annoy.com 108
ApolloMedia Corp. v. *Reno* 108
Areopagitica 48
Arizona Republic 117
Ashcroft v. *Free Speech Coalition* 67, 107,
    113
average viewer 9

bad tendency 50
Bagdikian, B. 96
balancing 7, 50, 89
Barnes, S. 61, 118
barriers to entry 51
Bell, D. 61, 119
Benjamin, L. M. 17
Billboard Music Awards 169
Blackstone, W. 52
Blanchard, M. A. 1, 15
Blumenthal v. *Drudge and America Online*
    127
Bolter, J. D. 95

Bowdler, T. 1
Bozell, L. B. 155, 180
Brenner, D. L. 32
Breyer, S. 103–4, 111
Broadcast Decency Enforcement Act
    148–9
Broadcast Indecency Policy Statement 8
Brownback, S. 148–9
Bubba the Love Sponge 53, 175
Bush, G.W. 180
Butler v. *Dexter* 69, 95–101

cable television 72, 74
Carlin, G. 53–8, 76–7, 93
CBS 14–15, 20, 138–42, 148, 153–4, 156
censorship 112
Center for Creative Voices in Media 12–14
Chapman, G. 174
channeling 76–7, 81, 85, 97
Cher 169
China 70
CIPA (Children's Internet Protection Act
    of 2000) 105, 109–13
clear and present danger 50
Clear Channel Communications 3, 175
Clinton, B. 106
codes 59
common law 52, 71
Communications Act of 1934 21, 23, 59,
    77, 104; *see also* Section 326; Section
    1464
Communications Decency Act 105
community 61
compelling government interest 107
computer-mediated communication
    59–61, 118
Comstock, A. 1, 15

contemporary community standards 7, 90–1, 106–7
contextual analysis 3, 7, 90, 92, 130, 151
convergence 60, 105
Cooper, R. B. 119, 147
COPA (Child Online Protection Act of 1998) 105–7
COPPA (Children's Online Privacy Protection Act) 97
copyright 96, 127–8
CPPA (Child Pornography Protection Act of 1996) 67, 105, 113–15
C-SPAN (Cable-Satellite Public Affairs Network) 167, 173, 183
culture 61
cyberspace 60, 96, 118

DBS (Direct Broadcast Satellite) 104
Debbie Does Dallas 69
Deep Throat 69
Dennis, P. D. 78
Dennis v. US 49
Department of Justice 63–6, 69
dial-a-porn 78–9, 82, 98, 106; *see also Sable Communications v. FCC*
diffusion 95
digital television 104
DMCA (Digital Millennium Copyright Act) 127
Donnerstein, E. 57–8
dot kids 107
Douglas, W. O. 49–50
du Gay, P. 61

Edwards, H. 85
Eggerton, J. 15, 115–16, 148, 151–4, 174, 179, 181
Eldred v. Ashcroft 127
Emerson, T. 3, 52
ESPN (Entertainment Sports Programming Network) 115
European Union 67
Evans, J. 61

fairness doctrine 26, 31
Family Shakespeare 1
family values 89, 182
Fanny Hill, or Memoirs of a Woman of Pleasure 68
FCC v. League of Women Voters of California 110
FCC v. Pacifica Foundation 8–9, 27, 53, 106

Federal Communications Commission 1–3, 8–9, 11–14, 18, 27–31, 33, 52, 58,72, 76–94, 96, 104, 117, 145–6, 149–51, 159–67
Federal Radio Commission 18
Federal Trade Commission 96–7, 174
Ferguson, D. A. 61, 119
fiduciary responsibility 27
First Amendment 1, 6–8, 24, 32, 49–50, 52, 59, 61, 71, 73, 80–4, 86, 88, 93, 97–103, 112, 127, 146, 154, 157, 160, 168, 183
Fitzgerald, R. 176
Fontana, T. 153
Fowler, M. S. 32
Fox TV 154–6, 167–70
Fowler, M. 31
Francis, J. 62, 64
free expression 1–2, 4, 16, 48, 60, 89
Free Speech Coalition v. Reno 113
fuck 54, 56, 59, 76, 91, 123, 133, 136, 154, 180; *see also* F-word 2, 15, 115, 123–4, 126, 131–4, 136, 154, 163, 169, 171, 179
full context 9

Gattuso, J. 10
Geraldo Rivera Show 42–3
Germany 71
Ginsburg, R. B. 81, 112
Girls Gone Wild 62–6
Godfathers and Sons 151; *see also The Blues: Godfathers and Sons*
Golden Globe Awards Order 91, 131, 179
Google 69, 96, 175
Gotti, J. 160
Graesser, A. C. 58
Grossman, B. 152
Grusin, R. 95

Hall, P. 170
Harris Poll 95
HBO 157
Heritage Foundation 10
Hicks v. Miranda 69
HIV 66, 92
Holliday, M. 45
Hoover, H. 17
Hoffman, C. 62, 64, 155
Horowitz, N. 179

identity 61, 118–19

In the Matter of Complaints 88
In the Matter of Industry Guidance On the
    Commission's Case Law Interpreting
18 USC §1464 and Enforcement Policies
    Regarding Broadcast Indecency 33
Indonesia 66
Infinity Broadcasting 3, 86, 145–6
ISP (Internet Service Provider) 96
interaction 61
Interpol 71
ITU (International Telecommunications
    Union) 104
iTunes 60

Jackson, Janet 1, 11, 14, 91, 117, 139,
    154, 180, 182
Japan: Law for Punishing Acts Related
    to Child Prostitution and Child
    Pornography 69
JCTV 157–8
Jones, S. G. 60–1, 119
Jordan, C. 66

Kahai, S. S. 119
Karmazin, M. 145
KCSM-TV 131
Kennedy, A. 98, 107, 113
KGB-FM 38
Kincaid, C. 120–1
KING-TV 41
KTVI-TV 42–3
KLBJ-FM 40
KLOL-FM 36
KMBC-TV 134–6
KNON-FM 43–4
KPRL-AM 39
Krasnow, E. G. 17–18, 86, 93
Kuhl, C. 45
KUPD-FM 39
Kutchinski, B. 68
KWHY-TV 130

Land, K.C. 58
Las Vegas 152
Last Tango in Paris 69
least restrictive means 84, 98, 103, 107
Leval, P. 168
libel 96, 127–8
Library 109, 111–12
Lieberman, J. 118
Lin, C.A. 61, 119
Linz, D. 57–8

Lipschultz, J. H. 4, 182
Little League World Series 115
Live 8: A Worldwide Event 154
local television news 12
Longley, L. D. 17–18

McCall, D. L. 58
McGinnis, M. L. 73
Mainstream Loudin 109
marketplace of ideas 5, 61, 80, 182
Marshall, M. 175
Martin, K. 160
Media Research Center 155, 180
Menefee v. *City and County of Denver* 69
Miller v. *California* 6 7, 11, 53, 71, 74,
    91, 102, 106–7, 114
Miller, E. 168
Milton, J. 48
minors 108, 110, 113, 122
Minow, N. 13, 27–31
morals 16, 58–9, 145, 180, 182
Muller, E. "Mancow" 120–1
music lyrics 35

narrowly tailored restrictions 50, 107; least
    restrictive means 18–26, 51, 89
National Broadcasting Company v. *United*
    States 18–26, 51, 89
National Public Radio 43, 60
NBC 13–14, 20, 124, 130, 137–8, 152–4,
    176, 179
Neilsen/Netratings 95–6
Ness, S. 9
Net neutrality 96
New Indecency Enforcement Standards 77
newscast 34
New York v. *Ferber* 67, 113
NYPD Blue 160

obscenity 6–8, 11, 58, 61, 80, 96, 102,
    112, 163
O'Connor, S. D. 114
Opie & Anthony 148
oral anal sex 91

Pacifica: *Pacifica Foundation* 8–9, 14, 17,
    51, 53–7, 61, 76–83, 93, 98–9, 106,
    146, 168, 175
parents 79
Parents Television Council 14, 148,
    154–5, 157, 178
Paris Adult Theatre I 80
patently offensive 7, 9, 34, 39, 90, 130,

171
Patrick, D. 32
Pavlik, J. V. 61, 119
PBS 1
Pelofsky, J. 14
Perse, E. M. 14, 61, 119
Phillips, C. 168
Playboy 102, 174
Playboy v. *Frena* 127
podcasts 15, 60, 95, 106, 142
Pooler, R. 171
poop 154
pornography 15, 62, 67–73, 110–11, 113,
    119; child pornography 70; *see also*
    adult entertainment
Postcards from Buster 5–6, 16
Powell, M. 174
power 61
prior restraint 112
privacy 79, 96, 127–8
profanity 33, 53, 88, 159
prurient interest 7
Pryor, L. 95
public access 95
public forum 110–11
public interest, convenience and necessity
    21, 59, 76, 181
public opinion 4, 48
Public Telecommunications Act of 1992
    83

Radio Act of 1927 17, 24
ratings 52
Reagan, R. 78, 175
reality television 155, 159
Red Lion Broadcasting Company v. *FCC*
    26–7,51, 81, 89
Redman, P. 61
Regents of the University of California 78
Rehnquist, W. 110, 114
Religious Technology Ctr. v. *Netcom On-Line*
    127
remediation 95
Reno v. *ACLU* 98, 103, 105, 107 142, 179
Renton v. *Playtime Theatres* 73
Richie, N. 15, 169
Rintels, J. 12
Rivera-Sanchez, M. 17
Rogers, Everett M. 95
Russell Research 45–6

Sable Communications v. *FCC* 78–80, 82,
    98, 106, 113

safe harbor 9, 11–12, 51, 72, 82, 85, 87,
    89, 97–8, 164; *see also* channeling
satellite 1, 11, 67, 72, 74, 95, 104; Serius
    3–4; erotic 67
Saturday Night Live 176–8
Saving Private Ryan 2–3, 11, 132, 151
Scalia, A. 79, 102, 114
scarcity 46, 51, 60, 76, 79, 88, 112; *see also*
    spectrum
School of Whoredom 68
scrambling 97, 100–1
Section 326 77, 90, 162
Section 1464 8, 33–4, 77–8, 89, 91, 162;
    see also Communications Act of 1934
self-censorship 6
Semonche, J. E. 1, 15
Sex in the City 157
Shafer, B.J. 58
shit: s-word 15, 76
shock jocks 1–3, 86, 120
signs 59–60
social norms 1, 4
social responsibility 5, 118, 182
social theory 59–61, 93
Souter, D. H. 112–13
spectrum 46, 79, 96, 104
Spellings, M. 5
status quo 53
statute law 89
Stern, H. 2–3, 51, 53, 60, 74, 86, 95,
    145–6, 175
Stevens, J. P. 101, 107
Stevenson, N. 59
strict scrutiny 50–2, 98–9, 111
Super Bowl 1, 89, 117
Supreme Court 7–8, 18–27, 76, 88–9,
    97–8, 107–8, 113, 145–6, 179, 182
Surratt, C. G. 61, 118
Survivor: Vanuatu 159

TBS 157
Telecommunications Act of 1996 32, 97,
    100–2, 105
Telemundo 130
Terry, H. A. 17–18
The Bedford Diaries 151–2
The Blues: Godfathers and Sons 13, 151
The Fifteen Plagues of a Maidenhead 68
The Joy of Gay Sex 109
The Joy of Sex 109
The Sopranos 157
The Surreal Life 2 153

third person effect 58
Timberlake, Justin 1, 14, 177
Thomas, C. 102, 114
Thomas, J. 115–16
time, place and manner restrictions 73, 93
Topcik, J. 152
TV Watch 45–6, 154

United States v. *O'Brien* 51, 77
United States v. *Various Articles of Obscene Merchandise* 69
UPN 156
Upton, F. 148, 150–1, 174
US v. *Playboy Entertainment* 97

values 58
vast and privileged sphere 114
vast wasteland 12
V-chip 2, 45, 87, 116, 165–6, 174, 179
Venus in the Cloister, or the Nun in Her Smock 68
Viacom 148
Vietnam 51
violence 51

WABC-TV 42
WB 151, 156
WCSP-TV 173

WEBN-FM 41
WEZB-FM 40
WFBQ-FM 37
WGN 17, 157
Wildmon, D. 151–3
Wilson B. 57
Winfrey, O. 42, 91, 151
Winslow, G. 158
WIOD-AM 44–5
Without a Trace 2, 15, 139, 148, 151, 153
WJLA-TV 136–7
Wright, F. 158
WSMC-FM 43
WSUC-FM 35
WXTB-FM 36, 38
WYBB-FM 39
WYSP-FM 35

X-rated movies 74, 103

Yahoo 96
YouTube 121–6, 175
Young v. Abrams 69

Zeran v. America Online 127
Zogby Poll 157
zoning 73